WORK, STUDY, TRAVEL ABROAD

WORK, STUDY, TRAVEL ABROAD

THE WHOLE WORLD HANDBOOK

TENTH EDITION
1990–1991

EDITED BY DEL FRANZ

Council on International
Educational Exchange

ST. MARTIN'S PRESS
NEW YORK

WORK, STUDY, TRAVEL ABROAD. Copyright © 1990 by the Council on International Educational Exchange. All rights reserved. Printed in the United States of America. No part of this book may be used or reproduced in any manner whatsoever without written permission except in the case of brief quotations embodied in critical articles or reviews. For information, address St. Martin's Press, 175 Fifth Avenue, New York, N.Y. 10010.

Design by Robert Bull Design.

LC card number: 84-646778

First edition

10 9 8 7 6 5 4 3 2 1

CONTENTS

COUNCIL TRAVEL OFFICES ix
PREFACE xiii
ABOUT THE COUNCIL xv
ACKNOWLEDGMENTS xxi

CHAPTER ONE GOING ABROAD 1

CHAPTER TWO THE ESSENTIALS 5

CHAPTER THREE WORKING ABROAD 15

CHAPTER FOUR STUDYING ABROAD 30

CHAPTER FIVE MAKING YOUR TRAVEL PLANS 42

CHAPTER SIX WESTERN EUROPE 55

Austria 70
Belgium 77
Denmark 81
Finland 85
France 89
Germany 106
Greece 119
Iceland 122
Ireland 124
Italy 130
Luxembourg 140
Malta 141
The Netherlands 143
Norway 147
Portugal 151
Spain 153
Sweden 163
Switzerland 167
United Kingdom of Great Britain and Northern Ireland 172

CHAPTER SEVEN EASTERN EUROPE 195

Czechoslovakia 200
Germany (Democratic Republic) 203
Hungary 206
Poland 209
The U.S.S.R. 213
Yugoslavia 220

CONTENTS

CHAPTER EIGHT   THE MIDDLE EAST AND NORTH AFRICA   223

- Cyprus   228
- Egypt   230
- Israel   234
- Morocco   241
- Tunisia   244
- Turkey   247

CHAPTER NINE   AFRICA SOUTH OF THE SAHARA   251

- Cameroon   257
- Ghana   259
- Ivory Coast   261
- Kenya   263
- Liberia   267
- Malawi   268
- Nigeria   270
- Senegal   273
- Sierra Leone   275
- South Africa   277
- Tanzania   279
- Togo   281
- Zambia   283
- Zimbabwe   284

CHAPTER TEN   SOUTH ASIA   287

- India   291
- Nepal   297

CHAPTER ELEVEN   EAST ASIA   301

- China   305
- Hong Kong   316
- Japan   319
- Korea (South)   332
- Taiwan (Republic of China)   335

CHAPTER TWELVE   SOUTHEAST ASIA   339

- Indonesia   342
- Malaysia   347
- The Philippines   349
- Singapore   353
- Thailand   355

CHAPTER THIRTEEN   AUSTRALIA AND THE SOUTH PACIFIC   359

- Australia   362
- Fiji   370
- New Zealand   371

CHAPTER FOURTEEN   CANADA   377

CHAPTER FIFTEEN   THE CARIBBEAN   387

Bahamas   390
Dominican Republic   392
Jamaica   394

CHAPTER SIXTEEN   MEXICO AND CENTRAL AMERICA   398

Costa Rica   403
Honduras   406
Mexico   408

CHAPTER SEVENTEEN   SOUTH AMERICA   419

Argentina   423
Bolivia   427
Brazil   429
Chile   436
Colombia   439
Ecuador   443
Peru   446
Uruguay   449
Venezuela   451

APPENDIX I   MEMBERS OF THE COUNCIL ON INTERNATIONAL EDUCATIONAL EXCHANGE   453

APPENDIX II   HIGH SCHOOL PROGRAMS   465

INDEX   468

COUNCIL TRAVEL OFFICES

CALIFORNIA

Berkeley
2511 Channing Way
Berkeley, CA 94704
(415) 848-8604

La Jolla
UCSD Price Center, Q-076
La Jolla, CA 92093
(619) 452-0630

Long Beach
1818 Palo Verde Avenue, Suite E
Long Beach, CA 90815
(213) 598-3338
(714) 527-7950

Los Angeles
1093 Broxton Avenue, Suite 220
Los Angeles, CA 90024
(213) 208-3551

San Diego
4429 Cass Street
San Diego, CA 92109
(619) 270-6401

San Francisco
312 Sutter Street, Suite 407
San Francisco, CA 94108
(415) 421-3473

919 Irving Street, Suite 102
San Francisco, CA 94122
(415) 566-6222

Sherman Oaks
14515 Ventura Blvd., Suite 250
Sherman Oaks, CA 91403
(818) 905-5777

CONNECTICUT

New Haven
Yale Co-op East
77 Broadway
New Haven, CT 06520
(203) 562-5335

DISTRICT of COLUMBIA

Washington, D.C.
1210 Potomac Street NW
Washington, DC 20007
(202) 337-6464

GEORGIA

Atlanta
12 Park Place South
Atlanta, GA 30303
(404) 577-1678

ILLINOIS

Chicago
1153 North Dearborn Street
Chicago, IL 60616
(312) 951-0585

Evanston
831 Foster Street
Evanston, IL 60201
(708) 475-5070

LOUISIANA

New Orleans
8141 Maple Street
New Orleans, LA 70118
(504) 866-1767

MASSACHUSETTS

Amherst
79 South Pleasant Street (2nd fl., rear)
Amherst, MA 01002
(413) 256-1261

Boston
729 Boylston Street, Suite 201
Boston, MA 02116
(617) 266-1926

Cambridge
1384 Massachusetts Avenue,
Suite 206
Cambridge, MA 02138
(617) 497-1497

Stratton Student Center
MIT W20-024
84 Massachusetts Avenue
Cambridge, MA 02139
(617) 225-2555

MINNESOTA

Minneapolis
1501 University Avenue, SE,
Room 300
Minneapolis, MN 55414
(612) 379-2323

COUNCIL TRAVEL OFFICES

NEW YORK

New York

205 East 42nd Street
New York, NY 10017
(212) 661-1450

New York Student Center
356 West 34th Street
New York, NY 10001
(212) 564-0142

35 West 8th Street
New York, NY 10011
(212) 254-2525

NORTH CAROLINA

Durham

703 Ninth Street, Suite B2
Durham, NC 27705
(919) 286-4664

OREGON

Portland

715 SW Morrison, Suite 600
Portland, OR 97205
(503) 228-1900

RHODE ISLAND

Providence

171 Angell Street, Suite 212
Providence, RI 02906
(401) 331-5810

TEXAS

Austin

1904 Guadalupe Street, Suite 6
Austin, TX 78705
(512) 472-4931

Dallas

Executive Tower Office Center
3300 West Mockingbird Lane,
Suite 101
Dallas, TX 75235
(214) 350-6166

WASHINGTON

Seattle

1314 Northeast 43rd Street, Suite 210
Seattle, WA 98105
(206) 632-2448

WISCONSIN

Milwaukee

2615 North Hackett Avenue
Milwaukee, WI 53211
(414) 332-4740

FRANCE

Aix-en-Provence

12, rue Victor Leydet
13100 Aix-en-Provence
(42) 38-58-82

Nice

37bis, rue d'Angleterre
06000 Nice
(93) 82-32-83

Paris

31, rue St. Augustin
75002 Paris
(1) 42-66-20-87

51, rue Dauphine
75006 Paris
(1) 43-25-09-86

16, rue de Vaugirard
75006 Paris
(1) 46-34-02-90

49, rue Pierre Charron
75008 Paris
(1) 43-59-23-69

GERMANY

Düsseldorf

Graf-Adolf-Strasse 18
4000 Düsseldorf 1
(211) 32-90-88

JAPAN

Tokyo

Sanno Grand Building, Room 102
2-14-2 Nagata-cho
Chiyoda-ku, Tokyo 100
(03) 581-7581

UNITED KINGDOM

London

28A Poland Street
London W1V 3DB

CIEE ADMINISTRATIVE CENTERS

USA
CIEE International
Administrative Center
205 East 42nd Street
New York, NY 10017
(212) 661-1414

France
CIEE European Administrative Center
49, rue Pierre Charron
75008 Paris
(1) 43-59-23-69

CIEE
Centre Franco-Americain Odéon
1, Place de l'Odéon
75006 Paris
(1) 46-34-16-10

Germany
CIEE
Thomas-Mann-Strasse 33
5300 Bonn 1
(228) 659746

Hong Kong
CIEE Southeast Asia Office
Arts Centre
2 Harbour Road
12/F Wanchai
(5) 283251

Italy
CIEE
c/o John Cabot International College
Via Massaua 7
00162 Rome
(6) 831-07-27

Japan
CIEE Japan Administrative Center
Sanno Grand Building, Room 205
2-14-2 Nagata-cho
Chiyoda-ku, Tokyo 100
(03) 581-5517

CIEE Western Japan Regional
Liaison Office
c/o Kyoto YMCA Youth Center
Karasuma Imadegawa Sagaru
Kamigyo-ku, Kyoto 602
(075) 432-6855

Spain
CIEE
Domenico Scarlatti, 9
28003 Madrid
(1) 243-60-87

United Kingdom
CIEE
33 Seymour Place
London W1H 6AT
(1) 706-3008

PREFACE

The 1990–91 edition of *Work, Study, Travel Abroad: The Whole World Handbook* marks the tenth edition of the book. The Council on International Educational Exchange has been updating and revising this book every other year since the first edition was prepared in 1972. New in this edition are maps of different regions of the world, country introductions by people who know those countries well, and recommendations of books to read and movies to see before going to specific countries. You'll also find brief descriptions of over 1,000 work, study, and travel programs abroad—hundreds more than appeared in the 1988–89 edition.

Throughout this book we've inserted the comments of persons who've just come back from a work, study, or travel experience abroad. These quotes have been gathered from interviews, letters, and evaluation forms, as well as from questionnaires distributed at colleges and universities across the country. Where we have permission, we've included the name of the person who made the comments; in other cases, we've simply used the quote anonymously.

Two years of effort have gone into writing the tenth edition of this book. Hundreds of people—including professors and advisers on various college campuses, students recently returned from abroad, and Council personnel from Hong Kong to Bonn—have been involved in the project. We've researched the latest international travel information, updated program offerings, reviewed books and movies, created maps, put together fact sheets, and collected useful suggestions from people who've recently been overseas. We hope you'll be able to use some of the information we've gathered to make your trip more rewarding. We also hope that when you return from your trip abroad, you too will be part of the effort to revise and update the 1992–93 edition.

Important Note

All information cited in this book, including prices, is subject to change. To the best of its ability, the Council had verified the accuracy of the information as *Work, Study, Travel Abroad* went to press. However, international air fares for peak summer travel in 1990 had not yet been announced. Therefore, most of the fares listed throughout this book are those that were in effect for the summer of 1989. For information on all of the above services, get a free copy of the latest edition of the Council's *Student Travel Catalog* or check with any Council Travel office (see pages ix–x).

ABOUT THE COUNCIL

The Council on International Educational Exchange (CIEE) is a private, nonprofit membership organization with offices in the U.S., Europe, and Asia. In its 43 years of service to the educational community, CIEE has emerged as one of the foremost organizations promoting international education and student travel.

The Council was founded in 1947 to help reestablish student exchanges after the Second World War. In its early years, the Council chartered ocean liners for transatlantic student sailings, arranged group air travel, and organized orientation programs to prepare students and teachers for educational experiences abroad. Over the years, the Council's mandate has broadened dramatically as the interests of its ever-increasing membership have spread beyond Europe to Africa, Asia, and Latin America. Today, the Council assumes a number of important responsibilities that include developing and administering programs of international educational exchange throughout the world, coordinating work-abroad programs as well as international workcamps, and facilitating inexpensive international travel for students, teachers, and other budget travelers.

This section will give you an idea of what the Council does and how it can help you. For more information on any of the following services, contact the appropriate department at CIEE, 205 East 42nd Street, New York, NY 10017. Please be as specific as possible about your request.

Study Abroad

In cooperation with a number of North American colleges and universities, the Council's Academic Programs Department administers study programs for college and university students in Brazil, China, Costa Rica, the Dominican Republic, France, Hungary, Indonesia, Japan, Poland, Spain, and the U.S.S.R. Designed for undergraduates and graduates alike, the programs are open to qualified students at U.S. and Canadian institutions of higher education. Program options include the following:

- an advanced Russian language program at Leningrad State University
- an intermediate Russian language and Soviet area studies program at Kalinin State University
- an intermediate Russian language program for science students at Novosibirsk State University
- East European studies programs at Karl Marx University in Budapest and the Central School of Planning and Statistics in Warsaw
- a French language, culture, and civilization program at the University of Haute Bretagne in Brittany
- a critical studies program in literature, film, and related contemporary theory at the University of Paris III
- an internship and study program in Paris
- a language and area studies program at the University of Alicante in Spain
- liberal arts and language and society programs at the University of Seville
- a Spanish language and Caribbean area studies program at the Universidad Católica Madre y Maestra in the Dominican Republic

- Chinese language and area studies programs at Peking, Nanjing, and Fudan Universities
- business and society programs at the University of International Business and Economics (Beijing), Obirin University (Tokyo), and the University of Seville (Seville)
- an Indonesian language, performing arts, and area studies program at the Institut Keguruan Dan Ilmu Pendidikan in Malang, Indonesia
- a summer program in tropical biology at the Monteverde Institute in Costa Rica
- an academic year program at the University of São Paulo in Brazil

Work Abroad

The Council's Work Abroad Department operates a series of work-exchange programs that allow U.S. students to obtain temporary employment in Britain, Ireland, France, Germany, New Zealand, Costa Rica, and Jamaica. These programs enable students to avoid the red tape and bureaucratic difficulties that usually accompany the process of getting permission to work in a foreign country. Along with the necessary employment authorization, Work Abroad participants receive general information on the country, tips on employment, a list of possible employers to contact, and helpful hints on housing and travel. In each country the program is offered in cooperation with a national student organization or CIEE office that provides an orientation, advice on job-seeking and accommodations, and serves as a sponsor during the participant's stay.

International Voluntary Service

The Council's International Voluntary Service Department operates an international workcamp program for young people interested in short-term voluntary service overseas. Volunteers are placed with organizations conducting projects in Belgium, Canada, Czechoslovakia, Denmark, France, Hungary, Ireland, the Netherlands, Poland, Portugal, Spain, Turkey, the U.S.S.R., the United Kingdom, West Germany, or Yugoslavia. Examples of the types of projects available are: taking part in a nature conservation project; restoring a historical site; working with children or the elderly; and constructing low-income housing. Workcamps bring young people from many countries together and get them involved in a local community. The Council also operates workcamps at various locations around the U.S.

High School Programs

The Council administers School Partners Abroad, which matches junior and senior high schools in the U.S. with counterpart schools in Europe, Asia, and Latin America. The program involves participating schools in an array of year-round curriculum-related activities, the centerpiece of which is an annual exchange of students and teachers. During the short-term exchange, visiting students and teachers participate fully in the life of the host school, attending regular classes, joining in extracurricular activities, and living with local families.

Also available to U.S. high school students is Youth in China, a unique summer study program in Xi'an, China. The program combines travel with a period of residence and language study at a Chinese secondary school. American participants live with Chinese roommates and participate in a full academic program.

Adult/Professional Programs

Continuing education is another area in which the Council is very active. The Professional and Secondary Education Programs Department designs and administers a wide variety of short-term seminars and in-service training programs for groups of both American and foreign professionals, including secondary school teachers and administrators, university faculty, business managers, and other "adult learners." As an additional service, the Council is able to custom-design international education programs on behalf of CIEE-member or cooperating institutions.

Student Services

Through its Information and Student Services Department, the Council sponsors the International Student Identity Card (ISIC) in the United States. Over 120,000 cards are issued each year by the Council's New York headquarters, its 29 Council Travel offices, and more than 400 issuing offices at colleges and universities across the country. Cardholders receive travel-related discounts, basic accident/medical insurance coverage while traveling abroad, and access to a 24-hour toll-free emergency hotline. Also sponsored by the Council are the International Youth Card for those under 26, and the International Teacher Identity Card for full-time faculty—both of which provide discounts and benefits similar to the ISIC.

The department also administers the International Student Identity Card Scholarship Fund. Supported in part by the sale of the ISIC in the U.S., the fund offers travel grants to U.S. high school and undergraduate students planning study or service projects in the Third World countries of Africa, Asia, and Latin America.

In its role as the "information clearinghouse" of the Council, the Information and Student Services Department answers more than a quarter of a million inquiries on work, study, and travel abroad each year. To keep campus advisers and others in the field of international education informed, the Council publishes a free monthly newsletter called *Campus Update*.

Publications

Probably the most widely circulated publication in the student travel field is the Council's *Student Travel Catalog*—a free 64-page brochure that is read by hundreds of thousands of people each year. The *Catalog* contains all kinds of useful information for anyone considering a trip abroad, as well as forms that can be used to order Council publications and apply for Council programs.

In addition to *Work, Study, Travel Abroad: The Whole World Handbook*, the Council publishes:

- *The Teenager's Guide to Study, Travel, and Adventure Abroad*, written by Marjorie Cohen for CIEE and published by St. Martin's Press, an award-winning compendium of short- and long-term overseas opportunities for youths 12 to 18 years of age
- *Where to Stay USA*, a state-by-state listing of more than 1,700 places to

spend the night for under $30, with special city sections and general travel advice for anyone touring the United States; updated every other year by CIEE and published by Prentice Hall
- *Volunteer! The Comprehensive Guide to Voluntary Service in the U.S. and Abroad,* published jointly by CIEE and the Commission on Voluntary Service and Action (CVSA), a guide to hundreds of long- and short-term opportunities for voluntary service in every corner of the world.

Educators, administrators, and researchers in the field of study abroad can request a free publications catalog describing all the many books, pamphlets, studies, reports, and occasional papers produced by the Council.

Travel Services

Council Travel operates a network of 29 retail travel offices across the country that provide travel assistance to students, teachers, and other budget travelers planning individual or group trips to any part of the world. What follows is a listing of other services they offer:

- low-cost flights between the U.S. and Europe, Asia, the South Pacific, Africa, the Middle East, Latin America, and the Caribbean on scheduled and charter carriers; many of these fares are available only to students or young people and are offered only through Council Travel offices
- rail passes, including Eurail, BritRail, and French Rail passes
- a range of tours designed especially for young people interested in visiting the Soviet Union, bicycling through southern China, trekking in Nepal, and other unusual opportunities
- issues the International Student Identity Card, the International Youth Card, and the International Teacher Identity Card
- car-rental plans in Europe
- language courses in seventeen European cities
- travel insurance, guidebooks, and travel gear

In addition to its services for individuals, Council Travel provides educational institutions with a complete range of travel services designed to simplify travel planning for groups. The Group Services Department can arrange anything from transportation and accommodations to lectures, study programs, special events, sightseeing, and meals.

Charter Flights

Council Charter, a subsidiary of CIEE, offers flights to students and nonstudents alike that connect U.S. cities with a number of European cities. Cities served vary slightly from year to year; in 1989 flights were available to Amsterdam, Brussels, Geneva, London, Madrid, Malaga, Nice, Paris, Rome, and Zurich. Council Charter flights can be linked with land arrangements at any of these destinations.

CIEE Membership

At present, over 200 educational institutions and organizations in the United States and abroad are members of the Council. As members, they may take advantage of the Council's information and publication services; become involved in the Council's advocacy, evaluation, and consultation activities; and participate in conferences and services organized by the Council. Membership allows educational institutions and organizations to play a central role in the operation and development of exchanges at a national and international level. See Appendix I for a listing of the Council's member institutions and organizations.

ACKNOWLEDGMENTS

So many people in so many countries have been involved in the two-year effort to rewrite and update this edition that any attempt to name all the individuals who contributed would be futile. There are, however, a few names that deserve special recognition.

This book would not have been possible without the help of CIEE representatives at the universities and other organizations that are members of CIEE. These people provided information about programs abroad, suggested books to read and films to see, and helped establish contact with students across the U.S. who recently returned from work, study, and travel experiences abroad. A collective thank you to all of them.

Equally helpful has been the assistance of CIEE staff around the world. Adrienne Downey, who served as assistant editor on this project, deserves special recognition; her editorial skills and thorough research were of enormous value. Thanks also to staff members Guetty Felin and Ching-Ching Ni who assisted with various phases of this project and to Larry Feldman and Mindy Naiman who reviewed the manuscript and offered advice. Finally, the constructive suggestions and general support offered by Joseph Hickey have been greatly appreciated throughout this process.

The literature and film sections owe their usefulness to the information provided by a variety of persons familiar with certain countries or regions. Special thanks to Neil Sobania, Kurt Gamerschlag, Michael Woolf, Rick LeVert, Mary Leonard, Sonja Stollman, Alvin Realuyo, and Juliette Shapland; their expertise was a valuable asset.

Finally, I would like to thank all the readers who have sent in comments and information. Receiving reactions and contributions from users of the book is especially helpful and encouraging. I hope that readers will continue to provide the feedback necessary for a useful book serving the needs of young people going abroad for a study, work, or travel experience.

WE WANT TO HEAR FROM YOU

Can you tell us anything you found out during your travels that will help make the next edition of *Work, Study, Travel Abroad: The Whole World Handbook* more informative? Do you want to write a country introduction, recommend reading material, or offer suggestions that we can quote in the next edition? Persons we quote will receive a free copy of the next edition of this book. Please send correspondence to the Editor, *Work, Study, Travel Abroad*, CIEE, 205 East 42nd Street, New York, NY 10017.

CHAPTER ONE
GOING ABROAD

> *"Going abroad is a voyage of discovery. You discover the world beyond your own country. But you also discover your own country, because, for the first time, you can see it from another perspective and compare it to another way of life."*
> —Michelle Corbin, Brockton, Massachusetts

This book is *not* a traditional travel guide. In it you won't find the best discos in Helsinki, what to see in Thailand, or where to stay in Nairobi. Most bookstores are packed with travel guides that provide this kind of information for virtually any country or region you may want to visit.

This book is something different. It's for the international traveler who wants to be more than just a tourist seeing the sights; it's for those who really want to get to know and understand another country and culture. In this book you'll find information that will help you to experience other countries as an insider, either as a student or a worker. Want to know about voluntary service, international workcamps, summer jobs, or internships in other countries? What about study-abroad programs, study-travel tours, or summer language programs? All of these are included, in addition to information about cheap flights, rail passes, passports and visas, student identity cards, and so on.

Most readers of this book will be college students who want to consider all the options open to them before making a decision. But *Work, Study, Travel Abroad* is for everyone thinking about international travel, whether they're going abroad for the first time or simply want their next trip abroad to be the greatest experience possible.

Why Travel Abroad?

The Council's worldwide staff represents a vast spectrum of political and personal beliefs, but we all agree on one thing—the need to encourage all types of international educational exchange. Americans must learn more about the rest of the world—not simply to compete rigorously in ever more internationalized markets or to maintain our role as a world leader, but also in order to understand global issues and help battle global problems. Whether you're concerned with human rights, the environment, hunger and misery caused by poverty in the Third World, or questions of war and peace in a nuclear age, you need to understand the world beyond our national borders. Even issues that used to be considered as only of local or national importance—the unemployment rate, the price of gasoline, or the use of chlorofluorocarbons in refrigerators, to name a few—are today issues that require understanding of the transnational systems of which our own are only one part. Firsthand experience is probably the best way to increase one's knowledge of the world we share with so many other nations and peoples.

But experiencing life in another country and culture will not only broaden your understanding of the world around you; it will also give you a new perspective on the things most familiar to you. A professor once asked his students what their concept of color would be if they had spent their whole lives in a room where everything was red. The students quickly realized that they would have no concept of green or blue. But only after giving it some thought did they realize they would also have no idea of what red was, never having had the opportunity to experience what not-red might be. Most people who experience a foreign culture find that at least as important as the knowledge they gain about a different part of the world is the chance to see their own country and culture from a new, broader perspective.

Fortunately, we need not spend a lot of time extolling the benefits of going abroad, since most people find that it's not only an enriching educational experience but also great fun. On the other hand, don't expect everything to be wonderful all the time. If you really try to get the most out of your experience abroad, you'll undoubtedly find that coping with a new culture and (sometimes) language is not always easy. To keep problems to a minimum, as well as to get the most out of your time abroad, you'll have to do some careful planning. And that's exactly why we've written this book.

Where to Go and What to Do

Everyone thinking of going abroad faces two basic questions: Where to go and what to do? Should you go to Europe or be more adventuresome and explore some part of Asia, Africa, or Latin America? Should you work, study, travel, or do a little of all three? This book will help you explore the possibilities. And once you've made up your mind, it will help you with the necessary preparations.

Before you decide where to go, be sure to consider all your options. While most Americans going abroad still travel to Europe, an increasing number are opting for study, work, voluntary service, or educational travel experiences in the Third World countries of Africa, Asia, and Latin America. Why not seriously consider helping to build an irrigation system in Latin America or studying Japanese business and society in Tokyo? What about traveling the Nile by felucca or seeing for yourself the effects of deforestation in the Brazilian rain forest? Because the Third World provides such vivid social, economic, and cultural contrasts with our own way of life, you'll discover a radically different perspective from which to examine your beliefs, values, and assumptions. And, with over three-quarters of the world's population living in Third World countries, an understanding of some of their aspirations as well as some of their problems will prove to be invaluable preparation for living and working in an increasingly interdependent world. Consider what two students told us about their experiences:

> *"My four months in Africa proved intellectually, physically, and emotionally challenging. I discovered the intricacies of a very foreign culture, learned the commonalities that exist between African and American lifestyles, and marveled at uniquely African tradition, culture, morals, and beliefs. I gained a sense of my priorities in life and set new goals for my career path. It is important to realize, however, that much of what I gained from my African experience came from frustration, loneliness, and a whole lot of soul searching. It wasn't all positive. But it was perhaps the greatest learning experience I could ever have imagined."*

> *"Most significantly, my studies in Mexico made me a more sensitive person. As an architecture student, I was humanized and humbled to think of design in more universal terms—the simple Mayan hut is an enduring form that*

will persist long after the demise of the suburban shopping mall. And Mexican cities, no matter how congested, are much more civilized and humane than our sleek, modern ones. There, public squares every few blocks are a fact of life and not something you have to persuade planning boards and cities to implement.''

Wherever you decide to go or whatever you decide to do, we have a couple of suggestions before you plunge in. Be open and flexible, but be realistic about yourself and your trip. Consider all the options, talking to family, friends, foreign students, academic advisers, or anyone you know who's been abroad. In the end, however, the decision is yours.

To help you decide what to do abroad, you'll find general information about working, studying, and traveling in Chapters 3, 4, and 5. But don't leave the country without looking at Chapter 2, which provides the practical information you'll need to know about passports and visas, student identity cards and discounts, insurance, et cetera. Each of the remaining chapters focuses on a specific region of the world—twelve in all. These chapters will give you information on specific countries and the work, study, and travel opportunities offered in each by the various member organizations and institutions of the Council on International Educational Exchange.

We hope the information we've compiled in this book is useful to you. Now it's up to you!

For Further Reading

Here are some books and periodicals that can help prepare you for the cultural transition and adjustments of foreign travel.

Intercultural Communication: A Reader, edited by Larry A. Samovar and Richard E. Porter, includes articles and studies about verbal and nonverbal cross-cultural communication by Edward T. Hall and other experts in the field (fifth edition published by Wadsworth Press in 1988). It's in many libraries, but if you can't find it, you can order it from Intercultural Press, P.O. Box 768, Yarmouth, ME 04096 for $18.95, plus $1.50 for postage.

On Being Foreign: Culture Shock in Short Fiction, edited by Tom J. Lewis and Robert E. Jungman, is an anthology of short selections from well-known writers around the world, including Hermann Hesse, Jorge Luís Borges, Paul Theroux, and Albert Camus. Selections focus on different aspects of adapting to life in a foreign culture. The book is available in paperback for $14.95, plus $1.50 for postage, from Intercultural Press (see address above).

Survival Kit for Overseas Living, by L. Robert Kohls, discusses the many things to consider, including culture shock, once you've made the decision to live abroad. Available from Intercultural Press (see address above) for $7.95, plus $1.50 postage.

Transitions Abroad is a bimonthly magazine geared to economy travel, overseas study programs, work opportunities, and educational travel. Each issue focuses on a specific subject area or country. The summer issue is the annual educational travel directory, providing information sources on study, work, educational travel, and living abroad. Ordered separately, this special issue costs $6.95. Sample copies of regular issues are $4.50. Subscriptions cost $15 per year and are available from the publisher, Clayton A. Hubbs, Box 344, 18 Hulst Road, Amherst, MA 01004.

The Teenager's Guide to Study, Travel, and Adventure Abroad, written with high school students specifically in mind, contains sections to help students find out if they're ready for travel abroad, make the necessary preparations, and then get the most from the experience. From cycling in China to mosaic-making in Italy, nearly 200 programs are described, including language programs, summer camps, homestays, study-tour programs, and workcamps. Also included are interviews with teenagers who have participated in some of the programs listed. Prepared by CIEE and published by St. Martin's Press, the 1989–90 edition (286 pages) costs $9.95 and is available at many bookstores or from CIEE's publications department (add $1.00 for book-rate postage or $2.50 for first-class postage).

CHAPTER TWO
THE ESSENTIALS

"Would you go out on a date without getting ready? Would a school team go to a game without practicing? The same is true for going abroad—you've got to make some preparations. Looking back, I should have even done more—especially reading."
—Heather Davies, Los Altos, California

Before you leave, no matter where you're heading, there are certain official documents to be obtained and arrangements to be made. As soon as the decision to go abroad has been made, you should start getting the formalities out of the way.

Passports

You need a passport to enter into or return from just about every country in the world.

Passports for U.S. citizens 18 years or over are valid for 10 years and cost $35, plus a $7 execution fee (see below for details). For anyone under 18, they are valid for 5 years and cost $20, plus the $7 fee. The demand for passports is usually heavy, but between March and August it's at its heaviest. Apply several months before departure, and if you're going to need visas, allow yourself even more time.

If it's your first passport application, you must apply in person at: (1) a U.S. post office authorized to accept passport applications; (2) a federal or state court; or (3) one of the passport agencies located in Boston, Chicago, Honolulu, Houston, Los Angeles, Miami, New Orleans, New York, Philadelphia, San Francisco, Seattle, Stamford, or Washington, D.C.

To apply, you'll need to bring: (1) proof of U.S. citizenship—this can be a copy of a birth certificate, naturalization certificate, or consular report of birth abroad; (2) two recent, identical photographs two inches square; (3) proof of identity, such as a valid driver's license; and (4) the completed form DSP-11, "Passport Application."

You may apply by mail and avoid the $7 execution fee if (1) you have had a passport within eleven years of the new application; (2) you are able to submit your most recent passport with the application; and (3) your previous passport was not issued before your eighteenth birthday. In addition to sending your previous passport and two new passport-size photographs, you must complete form DSP-82, "Application for Passport by Mail." It generally takes four to six weeks to process a passport, and even longer during the peak travel season.

Your passport should be kept with you at all times while traveling. One good way to assure this is to put it into a pouch that is tied at the neck or worn around the waist like a belt. This pouch can hold travelers checks as well, and should always be kept inside your clothing. Passport holders and pouches are sold at all Council Travel offices (see pages ix–xi).

Loss, theft, or destruction of a valid passport is a serious matter and should be reported immediately to local police and the nearest U.S. embassy or consulate. (If the loss occurs in the U.S., notify Passport Services, Department of State, Washington, DC 20520.) If you lose your passport while abroad, you will need to get a replacement at a U.S. embassy or consulate—an experience that will be much less frustrating if you have with you two extra passport photos and a photocopy of your original passport showing the number and date as well as the place of issuance. In case your passport is stolen or lost, you also should have with you—but in a separate place from your passport—both proof of citizenship (an expired passport or copy of your birth certificate) and proof of identity (a driver's license or other photo ID).

"Keep your passport with you always—even when you take a bath!"

Visas

A visa is an endorsement or stamp placed in your passport by a foreign government permitting you to visit that country for a specified purpose and a limited time, e.g., a three-month tourist visa. To study in a particular country, you may need a special student visa. In most cases, you'll have to obtain visas before you leave the United States. Apply directly to the embassies or nearest consulates of the countries you plan to visit or check with a travel agent. The Passport Services of the Department of State *cannot* help you get a visa.

Since the visa is usually stamped directly onto one of the blank pages in your passport, you'll need to fill in a form and give your passport to an official of each foreign embassy or consulate. You may need one or more photos. (Have extras made when you're having passport pictures taken.) You may also have to pay for some visas. The whole process can take several weeks, so if you have more than one to get, apply well in advance of your trip. Double-check visa requirements right before you leave.

Some countries (Mexico and Canada, for example) allow U.S. citizens to enter and stay without a passport or visa but require a tourist card. If a country you plan to visit requires a tourist card, you can get one from any embassy, consulate, or airline that serves that country, or at your port of entry. Some tourist cards require a fee.

A publication entitled *Foreign Visa Requirements* lists the entry requirements for U.S. citizens traveling to most foreign countries, as well as where and how to apply for visas. Single copies are available for 50¢ from the Consumer Information Center, Pueblo, CO 81009. Although this publication is updated annually, changes sometimes do occur after the publication has gone to press.

Customs

When you come back to the U.S., you'll have to go through customs. The U.S. government prohibits Americans from bringing back certain articles and imposes import fees or duties on other items. Everything you'll need to know about customs regulations for your return to the U.S. can be found in *Know Before You Go*, a pamphlet available from U.S. Customs Services, Box 7407, Washington, DC 20044.

Travel to "Trouble Spots"

If you're planning a trip to a country where a political problem has existed for a while or has just flared up, a reliable source of information is the Citizens Emergency Center (CEC), operated by the State Department in Washington,

DC. The center will inform travelers of any State Department advisories warning of potential danger or recommending special precautions, or, in more extreme cases, even suggesting postponing travel to certain countries or regions. Recorded travel advisories can be obtained anytime from a push-button phone by calling (202) 647-5225. If you're using a dial phone, call between 8:00 A.M. and 10:00 P.M., Monday through Friday, or between 9 A.M. to 3 P.M. on Saturday.

Health

Rather than go into specifics here about something as important as your health, we'll refer you to experts and a few good books on the subject. But before we do, we want to emphasize that the two greatest threats to travelers' health today are diseases against which you *cannot* be inoculated. One is diarrhea, which is often contracted from drinking unsafe water. The other is malaria; most types of malaria can be prevented, but medications must begin *before* you arrive in the infected area and must continue after you've left.

One organization that has been working energetically to alert travelers about the risks of malaria and other health problems worldwide is the International Association of Medical Assistance to Travellers (IAMAT). IAMAT is a nonprofit organization with centers in 450 cities in 120 different countries. Members receive a pocket-size directory listing IAMAT centers abroad, a world immunization chart (which we particularly recommend), and various publications and maps that alert travelers to existing health problems throughout the world. You can contact IAMAT at 417 Center Street, Lewiston, NY 14092.

The following books are recommended reading. You won't need to consult all of them, but do try to look through at least one. Getting sick while you travel is miserable.

- *How to Stay Well While Traveling in the Tropics*, by Douglas T. Keshishian (Dennis-Landman Publishers, 1150 18th Street, Santa Monica, CA 90403). This 36-page book concentrates on health problems in the tropical areas of Asia, Africa, and South America. The information is compiled from medical texts, specialists on tropical medicine, and the personal experiences of the author. It costs $2.95, plus 65¢ for postage and handling.
- *The Pocket Doctor* is a pocket-sized publication written specifically for travelers. You can order it from Mountaineers Books, 306 2nd Avenue W, Seattle, WA 98119 for $2.95, including postage.
- *Health Information for International Travel* is published by the Centers for Disease Control and is available from the Superintendent of Documents, U.S. Government Printing Office, Washington, DC 20402 for $4.75 (ask for stock #017–023–00183–3).
- *Staying Healthy in Asia, Africa, and Latin America*, by Dirk Schroeder, is basic enough for the short-term traveler yet complete enough for someone living or traveling off the beaten path. Order it from Volunteers in Asia, Box 4543, Stanford, CA 94309 for $7.95, plus $1.50 postage.

Some general advice: Make sure you're in good general health before setting out. Go to the dentist before you leave on your trip, have an extra pair of eyeglasses or contact lenses made up (or at least have your doctor write out your prescription), and if you take along any prescription drugs, pack them in clearly marked bottles and have the prescription with you in case a customs officer asks for it.

Insurance

Check to see whether your medical and accident insurance policies are valid when you are traveling outside the United States. You should never underestimate the importance of being insured when traveling abroad. If you purchase an International Student Identity Card (see the following section of this chapter), you will automatically receive basic accident/sickness insurance for travel outside the continental U.S., valid from the time of purchase until the ID's expiration date. Also included is a toll-free emergency hotline number for travelers needing legal, financial, or medical assistance.

You should also investigate the various plans for baggage and flight insurance. Baggage or personal-effects insurance covers damage to or loss of your personal belongings while traveling. Flight insurance covers the cost of your fare if you are unable to take a flight you have already paid for. One insurance package, Trip-Safe Insurance, provides a variety of options that may be purchased in any combination for any period of time from a month to a year. Details can be found in the *Student Travel Catalog* or by contacting a Council Travel office.

International Student Identity Card (ISIC)

More than a million students worldwide purchase the International Student Identity Card each year. If you are a junior high, senior high, college, university, or vocational student planning to travel outside the U.S., you should investigate the benefits this card provides. (From here on, we will refer to it as the ISIC.)

The ISIC entitles its holders to discounts on transportation and accommodations, as well as to reduced admission to museums, theaters, cultural events, and historic sites. Best known of the ISIC discounts are student/youth fares on international flights connecting cities in the United States, Africa, Asia, Europe, Latin America, and the South Pacific. Cardholders can save up to 50 percent of commercial fares on many of these routes. Information on worldwide student and youth fares is available from any Council Travel office (see pages ix–xi). A listing of specific ISIC discounts in 64 countries is contained in a booklet distributed to all purchasers of the ISIC. Even in countries that do not have a national student travel bureau, the card is often recognized as proof of student status and can be helpful in securing whatever student discounts are around. The best thing to do, no matter where you are, is to show your card first and ask if there are any discounts available, whether it's for subway fare, admission to a museum, or a room in a hotel.

Besides the student discounts, the ISIC provides automatic health insurance. Every student who buys the ISIC in the U.S. receives accident and sickness coverage while they're abroad for as long as their card is valid. Also available to ISIC holders is a toll-free hotline for travelers needing emergency assistance. (For more information on insurance benefits, see the preceding section of this chapter.)

The ISIC is the creation of the International Student Travel Confederation (ISTC), an organization of 64 national student travel bureaus. In the past it was necessary to obtain a second card, called the International Union of Students Card, in order to qualify for student discounts in Eastern Europe. As the result of growing international cooperation and *glasnost* in the field of educational exchange, however, the ISIC now has worldwide support.

If imitation is the sincerest form of flattery, the ISIC has had more than its share. Forgeries and imitations of the card have appeared and will probably continue to appear from time to time, both in the U.S. and abroad. The ISIC trademark, which is registered by the International Student Travel Confederation, distinguishes the authentic card from forgeries or imitations.

To obtain the ISIC, you must submit a passport-size photo and proof that you are a student enrolled in junior or senior high school, college, a university, or a vocational program leading to a degree or diploma. College students can prove student status with a letter from the registrar or dean stamped with a school seal, a clear photocopy of a transcript or grade report for the most recent term, or a bursar's receipt indicating payment for the present, or a future, term. High school students can prove student status with a photocopy of a report card or a letter from a principal or guidance counselor on school stationery. There is no maximum age limit, but you must be at least 12 years of age. (Age restrictions may apply on some discounts.) The card's 16-month validity period begins on September 1 and continues through December 31 of the following year.

In the United States the ISIC is sponsored by the Council on International Educational Exchange, the U.S. member of the ISTC. Available in 1990 for $10, it may be obtained from CIEE, any Council Travel office, or any one of 400 authorized issuing offices at colleges and universities across the country. The *Student Travel Catalog*, available free from CIEE or a Council Travel office, contains a form that also can be used to apply for the card by mail.

For details on the ISIC Scholarship Fund, which provides financial aid to students studying or doing voluntary service in Third World Countries, see page 37.

International Teacher Identity Card

In the last several years the ISTC, sponsor of the International Student Identity Card, has worked to open its low-cost educational travel network to elementary, secondary, vocational, and college faculty. The International Teacher Identity Card provides teachers with benefits similar to those that students holding the ISIC enjoy. Although the development of a teacher's identity card is still in its beginning stages, it is now possible for holders to save up to 40 percent on flights between the U.S. and Europe, the South Pacific, or Asia. Holders of the card also receive automatic medical insurance while traveling abroad and can take advantage of a 10-percent discount on teacher refresher courses at any Eurocentre location (see page 41). The card, which has the sponsorship of the International Association of Universities, costs $10 in 1990. To obtain one, contact CIEE or any Council Travel office.

International Youth Card

Anyone up to age 26 is eligible for the International Youth Card, formerly known as the Youth International Educational Exchange (YIEE) Card. This document, sponsored by the Federation of International Youth Travel Organizations (FIYTO), entitles holders to youth discounts in 40 countries. The youth card also carries flight discount benefits and the same insurance and travel assistance benefits as the student and teacher cards described above. For more information on the International Youth Card, contact CIEE or any Council Travel office.

"I didn't think I was eligible for discounts because I was no longer a student. Being able to use my youth ID was a nice surprise."

Mail

If you want to receive mail while you are abroad but do not have a mailing address, you can have mail sent to you in care of *Poste Restante* (General Delivery) at the central post office in the cities you'll be visiting. You simply go to the post office and pick up any mail that has arrived for you, usually paying a small charge for each item received.

If you buy American Express traveler's checks or have an American Express card, you can have your letters (but not packages) sent to an American Express office. For a list of foreign offices abroad, write to American Express, 65 Broadway, New York, NY 10006. American Express offices return mail to the sender if not claimed within 30 days.

Important Note: Many organizations abroad request that you enclose international postal-reply coupons when writing for information. International postal-reply coupons cost 95¢ each and can be purchased at any U.S. post office. The organization receiving the coupon can exchange it for stamps from their own national post office when responding to your request by mail. For most countries, you'll need to enclose two international postal-reply coupons to ensure an airmail response.

Money

Without a doubt, the best way to carry your money abroad is in traveler's checks. The most common traveler's checks are American Express, Citicorp, Thomas Cook, and Visa. Most traveler's checks cost one percent of the total dollar amount you're buying (for example, $5 for $500 in traveler's checks).

In deciding what kind of traveler's checks to buy, try to determine how widely the check is recognized as well as the number of offices the issuing agency has abroad (in case your checks are lost or stolen). Remember that you won't have to go to an overseas office of the issuing agency if you just want to convert your checks to local currency. Most banks will cash them readily; in fact, in most European countries you'll get a better exchange rate with traveler's checks than with cash. Try to avoid changing your money in hotels or restaurants, where the rate of exchange is usually less favorable.

In many countries, especially those of the Third World, currency is often available in exchange shops (*bureaux de change* or *cambios*), where the rate of exchange is much better than that offered by banks. Be sure to investigate all options for the best rate of exchange, especially if you're going to be changing large amounts of money. But beware of currency exchange with money changers on the street; in most countries this type of transaction is illegal.

Conversion tables listing rates of exchange for dollars in different currencies are found in most guidebooks. Daily currency rates also are quoted in many newspapers, including *The New York Times* and *The Wall Street Journal*. Two further sources of information are *Values and Measures of the World* and *Travel Tips and Currency Guide*, both available from the Swiss Bank Corporation, Advertising and Public Relations, 4 World Trade Center, New York, NY 10048.

You'll be able to buy foreign currency in air, ship, or train terminals once you arrive, but rates are often better in town. It's a good idea, however, to have some local currency with you when you first arrive in a country, especially if it's late at night.

If you run short of money, traveler's checks or cash can be cabled to you from the U.S. in care of a bank or agency such as American Express or Thomas Cook. If your bank has a foreign branch, you can have money transferred to you there as well. It's best to do this in major cities, however, and to make arrangements as far in advance of imminent destitution as possible. You can get more information on wiring money abroad from the agencies that issue your traveler's checks or from your local Western Union office.

Your own credit card or ATM (Automatic Teller Machine) card may allow you access to ATMs overseas. Check with the financial institution that issues the card to find out if it participates in an ATM network with overseas members.

A Word of Warning: Many countries restrict the entry of persons who can't demonstrate that they have a return plane ticket and/or a certain amount of money for each day they plan to spend in the country. These regulations are designed to keep out people whose lack of money may make them wards of the state. Usually, however, these regulations are enforced (or not enforced) quite erratically, based most often on the person's age and appearance. Check with the consulate of the country you plan to visit to see what kind of proof of solvency you will be expected to show.

> "A quick and inexpensive solution to financial crises is to have an American Express money order sent by mail. Transit time is less than the turnover time for a check from a personal account; it can be cashed immediately. It is also guaranteed to the same extent as traveler's checks and is much less expensive than wiring money."

> "It's a good idea not to get too much of any unstable currency because it can't be exchanged at a rate anywhere near the original exchange. And if you take it out of the country to a place that's not on good diplomatic terms with the first country, it won't even be worth a good laugh."

Becoming Informed

In order to get the most out of your experience abroad, you'll need to do some reading up on the countries you'll be visiting. Guidebooks, novels, histories, and social, economic, and political studies are some of the things that you might want to take a look at before going. Investigate what your library has, ask teachers or professors what they recommend, and visit your local bookstore to see what it has in stock. We especially recommend that you look at books and movies from the country you're going to. For many of the countries covered in this book, you'll find we've suggested movies and works of literature that provide insight into that particular country's culture. In addition, described below are some reading suggestions appropriate for persons going anywhere —from Canada to Madagascar.

No matter where you go, you'll be asked questions about U.S. foreign policy, especially matters that directly affect the countries you visit. The best thing to do is prepare yourself in advance by reading newspapers such as *The New York Times* and the *Christian Science Monitor*, which are known for their coverage of international affairs. Especially valuable are the publications of the Foreign Policy Association, a nonprofit, nonpartisan organization dedicated to informing Americans about the complexities of foreign-policy issues. One of the best ways to quickly inform yourself about foreign-policy topics is to read *Great Decisions*, which describes the pros and cons of alternative courses of action on eight different foreign-policy issues each year. *Great Decisions* (the 1989 edition cost $9.00, plus $1.75 for postage and handling) and other publications on foreign-policy topics are available from the Foreign Policy Association, 729 Seventh Avenue, New York, NY 10019.

For a quick and easy introduction to the culture of the country you're going to, we recommend "Culturgrams." These are country-by-country profiles of the customs, manners, and lifestyles you'll encounter in 96 countries. (The four-page briefings also discuss typical greetings and attitudes, religion, politics, et cetera.) Published by Brigham Young University's David M. Kennedy Center of International Studies, the guides are available for 50¢ each, or $25 for the entire set. You can order them from the Center's Publication Services, 280 HRCB, Brigham Young University, Provo, UT 84602.

Also useful for learning about the country you're going to is the *Transcultural Study Guide*, prepared by Volunteers in Asia, an organization that emphasizes increased understanding between cultures. Believing that the questions asked to a large extent determine the answers and conclusions that follow, the guide suggests questions for looking at another culture from a humanitarian perspective. To order, write to Volunteers in Asia, Box 4543, Stanford, CA 94309 ($4.95 plus $1.50 postage).

> *"Read, read, read! Read as many books, pamphlets, guides, et cetera as you can before going on your trip. It is so much easier to understand places that you visit if you know some kind of background about them. Plus, it helps to alleviate any fears you may have about your trip and helps you form realistic expectations."*
> —Kathy A. Flotz, Calumet City, Illinois

Packing

On their first trip abroad, everybody seems to take more than they need. There's a simple rule you can follow in packing for that first international trip, however: Get out everything you think you'll need, pack half of that, and leave the rest at home. Travel veterans make an art out of getting around efficiently; they pack lightly (some take no more than what they're allowed to carry on board the plane), leave their bags in city train stations or airports, and fetch them only after finding suitable lodging.

Be sure to take clothes that are easy to care for. Plan to dress comfortably, but be sensitive to local customs. For example, in many countries shorts should only be worn when involved in sports, and you should always be properly covered when visiting places of worship. Remember, too, that without a converter and adapter plug, your U.S. appliances will be worthless in most other countries. For suggestions on what to pack, check guidebooks for the country or region you are going to, or talk to someone who has been there.

> *"All the equipment you plan on bringing should be packed and then go for a long hike with it. This will help you make choices on what to bring and what to leave at home, but at least bring rain gear."*
> —Don Groeneveld, Muskegon Heights, Michigan

Drugs

In one recent year, over 3,000 Americans were arrested in 59 foreign countries for drug offenses; 1,500 ended up in jail. Many young people think that drug laws and their enforcement are more lenient in other countries than at home. This is simply not true. While there may be a few countries that seem to have a more liberal attitude toward drugs, in most countries prosecution of offenders for both the possession and sale of drugs and narcotics is more severe than it is in the United States.

You should be aware of the serious consequences that can result from the possession or sale of drugs, including marijuana, in many parts of the world. In some countries, the law makes no distinction between soft and hard drugs in the arrest, detention, trying, and sentencing of Americans. You've probably even heard some of the horror stories of young people jailed in foreign countries. Americans have been jailed abroad for possessing as little as a tenth of an ounce (three grams) of marijuana. In some cases, penalties for drug violations have included pretrial detention for months or even years and lengthy prison sentences without parole. Many countries do not permit bail in drug-trafficking cases.

Remember that when traveling abroad you are no longer protected by U.S. law but are subject to the laws of the country in which you are traveling. Should you get into some legal difficulty, the U.S. consulate can provide you with a list of local attorneys and contact your family at home for you—but it can't get you out of trouble or pay your legal fees.

If you are required, for medical reasons, to take any drug that may be subject to abuse statutes, be sure that you have your prescription bottle and a copy of your prescription along with you. Remember, too, that the U.S. Bureau of Customs will inspect your baggage upon your return to the United States, and that it is tightening its enforcement procedures.

For people who want more information, the brochure entitled *Travel Warning on Drugs Abroad* (available free from the Bureau of Consular Affairs, Room 6811, Department of State, Washington, DC 20520) has all the cold, hard facts.

For Persons With Disabilities

In the last decade there has been growing participation in the world of international travel and exchange by persons with disabilities. This is partly the result of laws passed by the federal government that reflect a national commitment to end discrimination on the basis of handicaps as well as to bring persons with disabilities into the mainstream of American life. But it is also the result of a growing awareness on the part of these people that they, too, are entitled to face the challenges and enjoy the benefits of international travel and exchange.

An organization that is active in the advocacy of the disabled traveler is Mobility International USA (MIUSA). The organization, with its main office in London, was founded in 1973; the U.S. branch was opened in 1981. Working both with persons with disabilities as well as with the organizers and administrators of international educational exchange programs, MIUSA has helped persons with disabilities participate more fully in the world community. Besides publishing a quarterly newsletter called *Over the Rainbow*, MIUSA has put together two booklets, edited by Susan Sygall, that are highly recommended.

The first, *A World of Options: A Guide to International Educational Exchange, Community Service and Travel for Persons with Disabilities* ($12 for members, $14 for nonmembers), lists more than 75 programs for volunteer, study, and host-family living geared especially for persons with disabilities. It also contains useful information on travel, accommodations, and publications. Participants provide firsthand accounts of what they have learned from international exchange. The second publication, *A Manual for Integrating Persons with Disabilities into International Educational Exchange Programs*, is targeted at the staffs and volunteers of service and exchange organizations. It costs $14 for MIUSA members, $16 for nonmembers. MIUSA has also produced two videocassettes about its work: *Mi Casa Es Su Casa* (in Spanish or English) describes a Costa Rica exchange, and *Looking Back, Looking Forward* features interviews with participants in various MIUSA exchanges.

In addition, MIUSA sponsors month-long international exchanges for disabled and nondisabled persons, most recently in Germany, the People's Republic of China, Costa Rica, and England. Upcoming exchanges are planned for the Soviet Union, Africa, and Denmark. For more information on this organization, write to Mobility International-USA, P.O. Box 3551, Eugene, OR 97403 or call (503) 343-1284 (voice or TDD).

Another useful source of information is the Information Center for Individuals with Disabilities, which publishes a fact sheet listing tour operators, travel agents, and travel resources for the disabled. The center is located at Fort Point Place, 27-43 Wormwood Street, Boston, MA 02210-1606.

Itinerary: The Magazine for Travelers with Physical Disabilities ($10 for six issues) is another publication of interest to those who want to travel in the U.S. or abroad. To subscribe, contact Whole Person Tours, P.O. Box 2012, Bayonne, NJ 07002; (201) 858-3400.

"The Germans were very cordial and so ready to learn and exchange ideas on how to improve the life of disabled people. They wanted to know all about our independent living movement, transportation systems, civil rights laws, and about the integration of disabled people into social activities. . . . Our social events and sightseeing tours not only bonded Germans and Americans in a deep friendship but served as an example to the German citizens we came in contact with that the world is made up of disabled and able-bodied people alike, and we are all here for one basic reason—to live and enjoy life to its fullest."

For Further Reading

The U.S. Department of State has several pamphlets that can help you make the necessary travel preparations. A good source of basic information, including such subjects as how to judge a travel program, information on charter flights, and where to get help when you are in trouble abroad, is *Your Trip Abroad* (stock #044-000-02203-6). Another Department of State pamphlet, *A Safe Trip Abroad* (stock #044-000-02140-4), reminds travelers of a number of common-sense precautions and also gives tips on protecting against the possibility of a terrorist act. Finally, there's *Tips for Americans Residing Abroad* (stock #044-000-02024-6), which introduces the reader to topics such as tax considerations and voting procedures while abroad. These pamphlets can be ordered for $1 each from the U.S. Government Printing Office, Washington, DC 20402.

CHAPTER THREE
WORKING ABROAD

"Working there I really learned a lot about the culture, the people, and the language . . . but, more than anything else, I learned a lot about me."
—Jeff Peters, Seattle, Washington

Have you ever considered picking grapes in southern France? A business or marketing internship in Japan? What about volunteering to work in a clinic in Kenya or teaching school in Bolivia? Each year, CIEE receives about 50,000 inquiries on the subject of working overseas. Getting a job abroad can help you finance your travels, provide valuable job experience, and allow you to really get to know a country and its people.

Finding a job abroad is not easy, but it is most certainly possible. To deal with the wide range of options available, we've divided this chapter into three general sections: Short-Term Jobs, Voluntary Service, and Long-Term Employment.

SHORT-TERM JOBS

Summer Jobs

"I wanted to live in Europe for an extended period and couldn't afford it otherwise. When given the option of waitressing in London or Lansing, Michigan, the choice was obvious."
—Jenny Dailey, DeWitt, Michigan

The choice, unfortunately, is seldom this simple. If you're thinking of working abroad for a short time, you probably will have to limit your choice of country to those that make special provisions for students seeking a working vacation or other short-term work.

Unemployment is an ailment afflicting many economies of the world. Even Australia, which once upon a time encouraged people to come and job-hunt, is suffering from record unemployment. And in the countries of Western Europe that belong to the European Economic Community, jobs that were once available to foreigners are now restricted to citizens of other Community countries.

For most countries, you will be required to have a work permit before you can obtain work. Some countries will not grant a permit until you have a promise of a job from an employer, and some employers say they cannot hire you without a work permit. Many students can never get beyond this frustrating catch-22 situation.

For over 20 years, the Council has been operating a work program that eliminates the red tape and enables students to get work permits in France, Germany, Britain, Ireland, New Zealand, Costa Rica, and Jamaica. In 1988, about 6,000 American students took advantage of the program. As a participant in the CIEE Work Abroad Program, you receive the necessary authorization to work in the country you have chosen to visit, along with a program handbook containing general information on the country, tips on employment, a list of possible employers to contact, and helpful hints on housing and travel. In each country, the program is offered in cooperation with an overseas national student organization whose staff is available to advise you on hunting for a job as well as a place to live, and will provide you with an informal orientation upon arrival. For most countries in this program, work authorization is for summer jobs only. But in France, Ireland, and the United Kingdom, work authorization for short-term employment can be arranged at any time of the year. For details on the program, write the Work Exchanges Department at CIEE, 205 East 42nd Street, New York, NY 10017.

Working a short-term unskilled job in another country probably will earn you enough to cover your food, lodging, and day-to-day living expenses. You should not expect to earn enough to pay for your air transportation, but if you are lucky you may save enough to cover some of your travel costs after you leave your job. Whatever job you find probably will not be glamorous, although two students participating in the program found themselves serving the Queen during Prince Andrew's royal wedding reception in 1986. Remember that in the final analysis employers only want someone who will do the job well and are not interested in romantic notions you may have about working in a foreign country.

"Working abroad in Germany made me feel like a 'real' German for a while. Travel doesn't give you the flavor of living inside the society, experiencing its daily routine, social habits, and etiquette. It was satisfying to improve my language abilities and feel I really lived there—to know where to shop, where to go, and be stopped and asked for directions. But only working can also become dreary; if possible, do some traveling!"
—Indra Reinbergs, Attleboro, Massachusetts

"The whole experience of working in Wales really helped me to learn not only about other people and their ideas, feelings, and way they live, but also about myself. Not that everything was always wonderful and without problems. Far from it. But my overall feeling is that I wouldn't have given up the experience for anything. In many ways it was just as much, if not more, of an education, than the one I received at school."
—Russell Lehrer, Suffern, New York

The Council's Work Abroad Program is open only to U.S. students. Canadians who wish to go on a working holiday abroad should contact Travel CUTS/Canadian Federation of Students (187 College Street, Toronto, Ontario M5T 1P7). This member organization of the Council operates SWAP (Student Work Abroad Programme), which sends students to a number of overseas destinations.

Another possibility for summer employment abroad is working with one of a number of U.S. organizations that offer international programs:

- American Youth Hostels seeks group leaders for hiking, bicycling, train, and bus tours abroad. Contact AYH, P.O. Box 37613, Washington, DC 20013-7613. Candidates must successfully complete an AYH leadership training course, which is offered at five locations in the U.S.
- The Experiment in International Living, an organization that sends small groups of U.S. high school and college students abroad, has summer leader and semester academic director positions available around the world. You must be at least 24 years of age and have experience in cross-cultural living and working with American teenagers or college students; language capability is required for some countries.

- The YMCA hires American students for summer camp counselor positions in 24 countries around the world: Australia, Austria, Colombia, France, Germany, Greece, Hong Kong, Hungary, Israel, Italy, Japan, Jordan, Mexico, Nepal, New Zealand, Nigeria, Peru, Spain, Sweden, Switzerland, Trinidad and Tobago, Tunisia, the United Kingdom, and the U.S.S.R. Experience working with children is a must. Application forms should be completed by January 1 (October 1 for camps in the southern hemisphere). Write the International Camp Counselor Program/Abroad, 356 West 34th Street, 3rd Floor, New York, NY 10001.

One of the best sources for information is the *Directory of Overseas Summer Jobs*, which lists 50,000 jobs worldwide, from Australia to Yugoslavia. Each listing tells you whom to contact, length of employment, number of openings, rates of pay, how and when to apply, duties, and qualifications sought. Revised annually, the directory is available from Writer's Digest Books, 1507 Dana Avenue, Cincinnati, OH 45207 and costs $9.95, plus $2.50 postage.

Another useful publication is *Work Your Way Around the World*, which contains good advice for anyone planning a long working trip. Although at times the advice verges on the bizarre, overall it's very practical and comprehensive. The book, written by Susan Griffith, is published by Vacation Work in England, but is available in the U.S. through Writer's Digest Books for $12.95, plus $2.50 postage (see address above).

You'll also want to check *Working Holidays*. Updated annually, it contains approximately 350 pages of information on paid and voluntary work opportunities in over 100 nations. Published in the United Kingdom, it's available in the U.S. for $18.95 from the Institute of International Education, 809 United Nations Plaza, New York, NY 10017.

If you're interested in work taking care of children, an excellent resource is *The Au Pair and Nanny's Guide to Working Abroad* by Susan Griffith and Sharon Legg. The book discusses the pros and cons of working as a nanny or au pair and provides suggestions on preparing for and coping with the experience. Also included is a discussion of working regulations in different countries and a listing of agencies that provide placement services. Published by Vacation Work in England, it is available in the U.S. through Writer's Digest Books (1507 Dana Avenue, Cincinnati, OH 45207) for $10.95, plus $2.50 postage.

Internships and Trainee Programs

Although finding internships or trainee programs abroad may require some research, they have become quite popular. Interns not only get the opportunity to learn the skills required for a specific profession but also get the chance to develop the cross-cultural communication skills that have become vital in the global environment in which many professionals and business executives now function.

Internships may be paid or unpaid positions—more often the latter—in a company, an organization, or an educational institution. The motivating factor is the applicant's overall desire to train, update, or strengthen a particular skill or field of study. Some assignments may include tedious or clerical tasks in addition to meaningful project work. Remember, too, that an overseas internship will no doubt require some economic initiative on your part, since few positions are salaried; most likely you will have to spend some money to get there.

Begin planning your internship experience abroad as far in advance as possible. You'll find internship/traineeship opportunities described under the "Work" heading of the individual country sections later in this book. Also check under the "Study" heading for internship options that may be part of the study-abroad programs offered by U.S. colleges and universities. You should also be aware of two international organizations that arrange traineeships around the world for students possessing certain skills:

- AIESEC—U.S. The International Association of Students in Economics and Commerce (known by its French initials, AIESEC) offers a reciprocal internship exchange program for college students in the fields of accounting, business, computer sciences, economics, finance, and marketing. Opportunities, available in 69 countries worldwide, allow participants to apply theoretical training to practical situations. Internships last from six weeks to 18 months and offer remuneration sufficient to cover living expenses; housing arrangements are handled by AIESEC. The program is restricted to sophomores, juniors, and seniors at the 77 U.S. colleges and universities that are AIESEC members. To find out if your institution is a member, check with the career-placement or study-abroad office on your campus. For more information, contact AIESEC—U.S., 841 Broadway, Suite 608, New York, NY 10003; (212) 979-7400.
- IAESTE Trainee Program. The International Association for the Exchange of Students for Technical Experience (IAESTE) provides on-the-job training for students in engineering, architecture, mathematics, computer sciences, and the natural and physical sciences in 50 countries around the world. Juniors, seniors, and graduate students enrolled in an accredited college or university are eligible to apply. Each trainee is paid a maintenance allowance to cover living expenses while training. Fluency in the language is required for some countries. The application deadline for summer placements is December 10; for long-term placements of 3 to 12 months, a minimum of four months processing time is required. For more information, contact IAESTE Trainee Program, c/o Association for International Practical Training, 320 Park View Building, 10480 Little Patuxtent Parkway, Columbia, MD 21044-3502.

Before taking off, be certain to plan your project fully with a study-abroad or academic adviser. Talk to someone who has completed an internship abroad—if possible, one in your field of study. And keep an open mind even if the feedback you get is not all positive—some individuals require a more structured program.

The most helpful resource book on internships is the *Directory of International Internships*, which is put together by various offices at Michigan State University. Listed are approximately 500 international internships offered by educational institutions, government agencies, and private organizations. It costs $12.50, and can be ordered from the Office of Overseas Study, Room 108 International Center, Michigan State University, East Lansing, MI 48823; (517) 353-8920.

Another helpful book, *1989 Internships*, is revised annually and focuses mostly on internships available within the U.S. but also includes a chapter on positions overseas. You can check your library or career-placement office for a copy or order it for $21.95, plus $2.50 postage, from Writer's Digest Books (see address on p. 17).

Now somewhat out of date, *The International Directory for Youth Intern-*

ships lists more than 400 intern positions within the United Nations system in addition to other nongovernmental organizations sponsoring internship programs. The most recent edition was published in 1984 and is available for $4.75, plus $2.50 postage and handling, from Learning Resources in International Studies, 777 United Nations Plaza, New York, NY 10017.

VOLUNTARY SERVICE

Workcamps

If you want to do something a bit unusual but very rewarding, you might consider joining a workcamp. Workcamps bring together groups of people from various parts of the world to work (usually manual labor) on projects as varied as building a school in Africa to restoring a castle in France. The focus is on projects that meet community needs such as health care, education, environmental conservation, construction of low-cost housing, or restoration of historical sites.

There are hundreds of workcamps all over the world open to Americans. For a directory of organizations conducting such camps, consult the book *Volunteer!* (see page 24). Usually there are no special requirements for participants other than a willingness to work. Most participants are young, and often time is set aside for cultural activities, group discussions, and field trips.

CIEE recruits several hundred volunteers for placement each year with workcamp organizations in Belgium, Britain, Canada, Czechoslovakia, Denmark, France, Germany, Hungary, Ireland, the Netherlands, Poland, Portugal, Spain, Turkey, the U.S.S.R., and Yugoslavia, as well as in its own workcamps in the United States. The camps are located in a variety of settings, from small villages to big cities, from national parks and forests to archaeological digs, and from farmhouses to historic monuments and castles; they usually last two, three, or four weeks. No salary is paid, but room and board are provided. CIEE is currently in the process of establishing exchanges with workcamp organizations in several African countries and may have limited placement opportunities in 1990. Write CIEE's International Voluntary Service Department for further information on current workcamps. Canadians can apply for similar opportunities through the Canadian Bureau of International Education (see below).

Another organization involved in international workcamps is Volunteers for Peace (VFP), a nonprofit membership organization that has been coordinating workcamp in more than 36 countries in North America, Western and Eastern Europe, Africa, and the Caribbean since 1981. Most volunteers participate for two to three weeks during the summer; those who register by May have the best selection. Volunteers must be at least 18 years old and pay a fee of $60 to $80. An additional membership fee of $10 entitles you to a copy of the annual *International Workcamp Directory*. For more information, write Volunteers for Peace, 43 Tiffany Road, Belmont, VT 05730; (802) 259-2759.

The World Council of Churches sponsors short-term workcamp projects during the summer in several countries of Africa, Asia, and the Middle East. Locations vary from year to year. Some workcamps require a knowledge of French; for others, English is sufficient. Most involve the construction of schools or other community buildings or rural development work. Local people often work alongside the volunteers on the project. Volunteers must be 18 to 30 years old, pay their own travel expenses, and contribute $3 per day toward their living expenses. For further information on what workcamps are planned in a particular year, write to Ecumenical Youth Action, World Council of Churches, 150 route de Ferney, 1211 Geneva 20, Switzerland.

The Canadian Bureau for International Education (CBIE) offers a program of international workcamps in most European countries, including Czechoslovakia, Hungary, and Poland. The camps involve manual labor or social work; a few combine both. Projects generally last three to four weeks and take place from June to October. Participants must be 18, except in France or West Germany, where anyone 16 or over may apply. There's no maximum age, and persons with disabilities may participate in all but the most strenuous manual-labor camps. Participants pay their own transportation costs (food and lodging are provided by the host community), and there's a $115 registration fee. Canadians should contact CBIE, 85 Albert Street, Suite 1400, Ottawa, Ontario K1P 6A4, Canada. U.S. citizens may apply for similar opportunities through CIEE or Volunteers for Peace (see above).

Also be sure to check the work sections in the country-by-country descriptions later in this book. The workcamp programs of CIEE member organizations and institutions are described under the countries in which they are located.

"We did masonry and carpentry work inside an old barn to make a community room. We had no plumbing or electricity and slept in a barn, but I think that made us better as a group because we really had to work together and help each other. . . . I have a thousand wonderful anecdotes about the camp, but I wouldn't know where to begin. It was a wonderful experience, unique to a group of people from all over the world who worked together toward a common goal."

"The work provides a loose structure and a continuity which holds people to a place and to one another long enough for bonds to form. You spend enough time with people to see through the differences to underlying similarities, and through the similarities to underlying differences. The greatest works of a culture are its people."
—Don Hudson, Auburn, Alabama

Field-Research Projects

Volunteering to participate in a field-research project is similar to a workcamp experience. Participation in such a project offers the fun and excitement of working with a group of volunteers in an exotic setting as well as the chance to increase your knowledge of history, archaeology, geology, ecology and biology. Possibilities include helping to excavate a Bronze Age city in Israel, conducting a wildlife census in the rain forest of Liberia, studying sea lions off the coast of Mexico, or scuba diving to explore a long-submerged French settlement in the Caribbean. Participation in a field-research project, however, can be expensive; see page 36 for a discussion of scholarships and grants for which you might qualify.

Participation in an archaeological dig can be especially rewarding. Some excavations accept inexperienced volunteers, while others insist on volunteers who have some training or experience. The best source of information on archaeological field work is the Archaeological Institute of America (AIA). Each February, AIA publishes *Archaeological Fieldwork Opportunities Bulletin*, which includes listings of opportunities for volunteers at excavations, field schools, and educational programs in several countries, including the

U.S. Please note, however: Good health is always required for participants in archaeological field work, as well as adaptability to unusual foods and local conditions. The *Bulletin* costs $6 for AIA members and $8 for nonmembers. The Institute is also the publisher of *Archaeology* magazine, which twice yearly presents the "Travel Guide," a special feature listing excavations in progress as well as archaeological sites that welcome visitors as observers or active members of the field crew. Contact the Archaeological Institute of America, 675 Commonwealth Avenue, Boston, MA 02215.

Another nonprofit organization, Earthwatch, recruits volunteers age 16 and over for field-research expeditions in 43 countries and 25 states. Projects include working with Australian scientists studying the kangaroo, helping with archaeological excavations in France and England, and gathering data on volcanoes in Iceland and Costa Rica. Expeditions are directed by university professors, and volunteers participate for two to three weeks. Membership in Earthwatch costs $25 per year, which includes six issues of *Earthwatch Magazine*. To participate, volunteers must be members of Earthwatch and pay a tax-deductible fee to cover the cost of room and board, equipment, and ground transportation; the fee ranges from $790 to $1,650, depending on the project. For further information, contact Earthwatch, 680 Mount Auburn, Box 403N, Watertown, MA 02272; (612) 926-8200.

The Foundation for Field Research is another nonprofit organization that supports scientific projects by recruiting volunteers willing to donate their labor and pay a fee to participate in a field-research project. Projects in the disciplines of archaeology, botany, geology, mammology, ornithology, paleontology, and primatology are conducted all over the world, and vary in length from two days to one month; the contribution can range from $125 to $1,900. The Foundation also publishes *Explorer News*, a free newspaper describing the projects volunteers can join. Contact the Foundation for Field Research, P.O. Box 2010, Alpine, CA 92001; (619) 445-9264.

Short-Term Voluntary Service

In addition to workcamps and field research projects, a variety of other short-term voluntary service opportunities are available abroad. Programs last anywhere from a few weeks to a few months. Some of those most popular with young people in the United States are listed below:

- The American Friends Service Committee offers a variety of short-term voluntary service opportunities in Mexico and several other Latin American countries. Projects last about seven weeks and involve working in construction, recreation, education, etc. Volunteers must be at least 18 years of age and able to speak Spanish. Contact the American Friends Service Committee, 1501 Cherry Street, Philadelphia, PA 19102.
- Amigos de las Americas conducts summer programs that provide community health services in a variety of Latin American countries. Volunteers need no experience in health care but must be proficient in Spanish; the minimum age is 16. Programs last from four to six weeks. For further information, contact Amigos de las Americas, 5618 Star Lane, Houston, TX 77057.
- Operation Crossroads Africa operates community self-help projects in several African and Caribbean countries. Groups of eight to twelve American volunteers work with community members for six to eight weeks. The focus is on cross-cultural understanding through close community involvement.

Contact Operation Crossroads Africa, 150 Fifth Avenue, New York, NY 10011.

Long-Term Voluntary Service

Many people prefer a longer term of voluntary service abroad than that available through a workcamp or field-research project. Fortunately, the options in the field of voluntary service are unlimited, with programs all over the world involving individuals in all sorts of voluntary service opportunities lasting anywhere from a few weeks to several years. And all share the same underlying goal—to involve participants in cooperative projects that respond to human needs and enrich people's lives. Volunteers in such programs are motivated by a sense of commitment, as well as by the rewards of personal and professional growth they derive from this type of work.

The space available in this book permits us to list only a sampling of the organizations that place Americans in long-term voluntary service positions overseas. For a more complete listing of such organizations consult the book *Volunteer!* (see page 24).

- Brethren Volunteer Service is a Christian service program dedicated to advocating justice and peace, as well as serving basic human needs in the U.S. and 18 countries overseas. Volunteers, who must be at least 18 years old, provide a variety of community services, including education, health care, office work, construction, et cetera. Contact Brethren Volunteer Service, 1451 Dundee Avenue, Elgin, IL 60120 for further information.
- The Episcopal Church's Volunteers for Mission acts as a clearinghouse, matching volunteers with projects in the U.S. and abroad. Assignments last from one to two years and include teaching, social work, technology, agriculture, et cetera. For further information, contact Volunteers for Mission, Episcopal Church Center, 815 Second Avenue, New York, NY 10017.
- International Christian Youth Exchange (ICYE) offers persons ages 18–24 voluntary service opportunities in the fields of health care, education, the environment, construction, et cetera. The one-year program has homestay and academic-credit options; scholarships are also available. Service opportunities are offered in Australia, Austria, Belgium, Brazil, Bolivia, China, Colombia, Costa Rica, Denmark, Finland, France, West Germany, Ghana, Honduras, Iceland, Italy, Japan, Kenya, South Korea, Liberia, Mexico, New Zealand, Nigeria, Norway, Poland, Sierra Leone, Spain, Sweden, Switzerland, and the United Kingdom. For more information, contact International Christian Youth Exchange, 134 West 26th Street, New York, NY 10001.
- The International Liaison of Lay Volunteers in Mission is the official center for the U.S. Catholic Church's promotion, referral, and recruitment of lay mission volunteers. While it does not have its own voluntary service programs, it does serve as a clearinghouse for others. *Response*, its free publication, provides information on 144 organizations with openings for volunteers in the U.S. and abroad. Contact the International Liaison of Lay Volunteers in Mission, 4121 Harewood Road NE, Washington, DC 20017; (800) 543-5046 for further information.
- International Voluntary Services is an independent, nonprofit organization that provides skilled and experienced volunteer technicians for projects serving the needs of low-income people in the Third World. The organi-

zation recruits internationally for technicians to work with locally based groups in agriculture, health care, business cooperatives, community development, and water resources. IVS volunteers serve a minimum of two years and receive a cost-of-living allowance, housing, medical benefits, travel costs, and a monthly stipend. Contact International Voluntary Services, 1424 16th Street NW, #204, Washington, DC 20036.
- The Mennonite Central Committee (MCC) offers an overseas program that enables volunteers with skills in agriculture, rural development, public health education, and water development to serve in about 50 countries in Asia, Africa, and Latin America. The minimum age for overseas placement is 22, and in most cases a college degree is essential. Contact MCC, 21 South 12th Street, Akron, PA 17501.
- The Presbyterian Church's Mission Volunteers/International program offers overseas voluntary service opportunities for periods ranging from one month to two years. For most of the overseas projects it is necessary to be a communicant member of the church, however. The *Voluntary Service Bulletin*, published each December, is the main source of information about positions available. For further information, contact Mission Volunteers/International, Presbyterian Church (USA), 100 Witherspoon Street, Louisville, KY 40202-1396.
- The YMCA World Service Worker program enlists participants for two-year internship positions working with YMCAs in Africa, Asia, and Latin America. Typical assignments include community development, youth programs, physical education, recreation, camping, and teaching English as a foreign language. Transportation, stipend, health and life insurance, and room and board are provided. Applicants must be college graduates with relevant experience and skills, and must be sponsored by a local U.S. YMCA. For more information, contact Overseas Personnel Programs, YMCA of the USA, 101 N. Wacker Drive, Chicago, IL 60606. The Y's Intern Abroad Program offers similar opportunities to persons, including college students, interested in a shorter term of service. Interns pay their own costs, which can range from $500 to $2,500. Contact the YMCA of Metropolitan Washington, Intern Abroad Program, 1625 Massachusetts Avenue NW, Suite 700, Washington, DC 20036.

Service-Learning

You may also want to consider an interesting, relatively new opportunity that combines the concept of voluntary service with academic credit. In the words of Howard Berry, founder of an organization called the Partnership for Service-Learning, "Service-learning is a powerful union of two traditional goals, academic study and service to the world. Through service-learning programs for a semester, a summer, or a year, students may continue formal learning and, at the same time, have the experience of working with others to address human needs."

The Partnership offers programs in England, Ecuador, Jamaica, the Philippines, France, and Liberia (other programs are being developed in China and Mexico). Projects usually have to do with the fields of health care, education, or community development, and are available during the academic year, the January interim, and the summer. Students spend 15 to 20 hours per week in a service capacity while taking a full academic load. There is also an administrative fee that covers academic instruction, service placement and supervision, orientation, room, basic board, and field trips; air fare is extra. For more information, contact the Partnership for Service-Learning, 815 Second Avenue, Suite 315, New York, NY 10017; (212) 986-0989. Most colleges and universities grant academic credit for participation in the programs of the Partnership, but you'll want to check with your own institution before applying.

Publications on Voluntary Service Abroad

CIEE publishes a guide to voluntary service programs and workcamps entitled *Volunteer! The Comprehensive Guide to Voluntary Service in the U.S. and Abroad*. Copublished with the Commission on Voluntary Service and Action (CVSA), the book lists over 170 organizations that place participants in voluntary service assignments. Opportunities may last a week, a month, six months, or up to a year or two, and range from positions for highly skilled professionals to assignments for people with no special skills other than a sincere desire to help. *Volunteer!* costs $6.95 (plus $2.50 for first-class or $1 for book-rate postage) and can be ordered directly from CIEE, 205 East 42nd Street, New York, NY 10017.

The Coordinating Committee for International Voluntary Service is the most widely known source of information on nongovernmental voluntary service programs thoughout the world. A nonprofit organization representing 124 member organizations, CCIVS was created in 1948 under the aegis of UNESCO as a permanent committee to facilitate international voluntary service exchanges and to assist UNESCO in the implementation of its programs relating to youth and international development. A list of its publications can be obtained by writing directly to CCIVS; every two years the Committee publishes *Workcamp Organizers*, which lists addresses of short-term programs in over 80 countries. You may write to CCIVS, UNESCO, 1 rue Miollis, 75015 Paris, France, but be sure to include four international postal-reply coupons, available from any U.S. post office, with any request for CCIVS publications.

Another publication on the subject, written primarily for a British audience, is the *International Directory of Voluntary Work*, by David Woodworth. It's available from the publisher, Vacation Work, 9 Park End Street, Oxford, OX1 1HJ, England, for $6.95, plus $1.50 postage if sent to the U.S.

LONG-TERM EMPLOYMENT

Finding a long-term job outside the U.S. is not going to be easy. It can be done, and has been done, but it takes a great deal of patience and perseverance. Most governments are extremely strict about the employment of foreigners in their country. In most countries, before a work permit is issued, the employer must convince his or her government that the job being given to a foreign citizen can be done only by that person and that there isn't a local worker who can do the job. What this means is that your chances of getting a job overseas are related directly to the skills you've acquired before you apply. If you're a doctor, nurse, or teacher, you may be needed. If you've had a liberal arts education with little specialization, you have problems.

There are plenty of horror stories about people who have paid substantial fees to employment agencies that lure people with promises of foreign positions and then do absolutely nothing for them. Very often these organizations go unpunished since they word their advertisements cleverly and are careful not to promise anything at all in writing. Your best bet, whether you decide to use an employment agency or not, is to become informed using some of the directories and other resource materials listed in this chapter.

"Take advantage of any possible experience abroad. . . . Use your personality and your wits. Contacts are of the greatest importance; foreign language facility and an understanding of foreign cultures are also essential."

Jobs With the U.S. Government

The U.S. Department of State, the U.S. Department of Commerce, the U.S. Department of Agriculture, the U.S. Information Agency, and the Agency for International Development all hire personnel for positions abroad. Overseas assignments are made primarily to the 230 diplomatic and consular posts abroad.

Foreign service officers manage overseas posts and perform political, economic, consular, administrative, and cultural functions. They are selected through a rigorous written and oral examination process. Interested applicants for entry-level foreign service positions in the Department of State, the United States Information Agency, and the Department of Commerce's Foreign Commercial Service should write to the Recruitment Division, Department of State, P.O. Box 9317, Rosslyn Station, Arlington, VA 22209.

Other departments of the U.S. government also offer positions overseas. Anyone interested in positions abroad with the Department of Agriculture, for example, should write to the Department of Agriculture, Foreign Agricultural Service, Washington, DC 20520. Those interested in positions overseas with the Agency for International Development (AID) should write to the Agency for International Development, Office of Recruitment, Foreign Service Personnel, Room 1430, SA-1, Washington, DC 20523-0114. Most candidates recruited by AID have graduate degrees and several years of relevant work experience.

The Peace Corps is another government agency that offers positions abroad, and although remuneration is not great, a living allowance is provided. Both generalists and specialists are in demand, including RNs, civil engineers, industrial arts teachers, architects, accountants, and agriculturalists. Peace Corps volunteers undergo 12 to 14 weeks of training, including language study, and then serve for two years. The living allowance is determined by wages in the host country, with an additional $200 per month, payable upon completion of service. Applications for Peace Corps positions are available from Peace Corps, Volunteer Recruitment Services, 806 Connecticut Avenue NW, Washington, DC 20526, from your college placement office, or by calling toll-free (800) 424-8580.

Jobs With International Organizations

There are many nongovernmental organizations active worldwide that hire U.S. citizens for posts abroad. Included are organizations such as American Red Cross and CARE. The best way to investigate employment possibilities in this category is to find out what organizations of this type exist. Check your library for a copy of the most recent edition of the three-volume *Encyclopedia of Associations*, published by Gale Research Company, which contains one of the most complete and best annotated listings of organizations in the United States; check especially the "Public Affairs" and "Foreign Interest" listings.

Designed for current students and recent graduates, the *ODN Opportunities Catalog* lists opportunities with U.S.-based international development organizations. The Overseas Development Network (ODN) is a nonprofit national student organization that, in its own words, "joins students and communities in addressing the fundamental issues of global poverty and injustice." The *Catalog* is available for $8 ($6 for students—include a copy of your current student ID); $2.50 should be added for postage and handling. For further information, write the Overseas Development Network, P.O. Box 2306, Stanford, CA 93409.

Another source of information on long- or short-term employment opportunities with international development organizations is the *Job Opportunities Bulletin*, which is published by the nonprofit TransCentury Recruitment Center, a consulting group based in Washington, D.C., that recruits highly qualified people to work in the Third World on various development projects. A year's subscription to the *Bulletin*, six issues, costs $15. For more information write to the TransCentury Recruitment Center, 1724 Kalorama Road NW, Washington, DC 20009.

Jobs in International Business

It is rare for an American company to hire someone in the U.S. and then send him or her on an overseas assignment. If an overseas job is not filled by a local worker, it is almost always filled by someone who has been working for the company for a number of years in the United States. A company will take very few risks on untried personnel in overseas positions. If you'd like to work for a bank or some other international business operation, you'd better resign yourself first to serving a few years on U.S. soil. Be sure, though, that your employer knows that you'd eventually like to go abroad.

If you want to apply for business positions abroad, the three-volume *Directory of American Firms Operating in Foreign Countries* is an especially useful publication. The *Directory*, which describes more than 3,000 U.S. corporations and their 21,000 subsidiaries operating abroad, is published by World Trade Academy Press, 50 East 42nd Street, New York, NY 10017, and is available in most college as well as many public libraries. Many foreign embassies also put out lists of U.S. companies that have branches in their country.

Jobs in the Health Professions

People with health-related skills are probably the most in demand throughout the world. The American Nurses' Association, a member of the International Council of Nurses, can provide limited information to registered nurses interested in professional visits or work abroad. For information, contact Careers, American Nurses' Association, 2420 Pershing Road, Kansas City, MO 64108.

The American Medical Student Association offers year-long fellowships in developing countries for those in the health field. For further information and applications contact the International Health Project, AMSA Foundation, 1890 Preston White Drive, Reston, VA 22091.

A useful publication for dental personnel is *Suggestions for U.S. Dentists Seeking Employment Abroad*, available free from the American Dental Association, Office of International Affairs, 211 East Chicago Avenue, Chicago, IL 60611. *Overseas Demand for Dental Personnel and Materials: Directory of Programs* can be ordered from the same office for $10.

Teaching Positions

There are two kinds of schools that offer teaching positions abroad to U.S. citizens: one caters primarily to American students and the other to residents of the host or other countries. In most cases a bachelor's degree and at least two years of teaching experience are required. In addition, you should be willing to go wherever you're needed and to stay there for at least one year, more often two. Appointments are made several months before the beginning of the academic year, so start planning early. Salaries will range from subsistence level to the equivalent of U.S. salary and sometimes more.

The U.S. Information Agency (USIA) operates a teacher-exchange program (most assignments are for a full academic year) open to elementary and secondary school teachers, college instructors, and professors. Participating countries include Argentina, Belgium, Brazil, Canada, Chile, Colombia, Cyprus, Denmark, France, Germany (Federal Republic), Hungary, Iceland, Italy, Luxembourg, Mexico, the Netherlands, Norway, the Philippines, Senegal, South Africa, Switzerland, and the United Kingdom. Applicants must be U.S. citizens and have at least a bachelor's degree, three years' teaching experience, and, often, facility in the language of the host country. USIA's annual booklet, *Opportunities Abroad for Educators*, gives details of the opportunities available under this program for qualified U.S. teachers. Also included in the booklet is information about short-term seminars abroad for teachers. Copies are available from the Fulbright Teacher Exchange Branch, E/ASX, USIA, 301 Fourth Street SW, Washington, DC 20547. Applications for these positions should be completed by October 15 of the year preceding the assignment.

Teacher exchanges can also be arranged with the help of the nonprofit Faculty Exchange Center (FEC), which was established in 1973 to help college professors exchange positions and/or houses with colleagues at home or abroad. The FEC acts as a clearinghouse, issuing a catalog with the names of instructors, their qualifications, where they want to teach, and whether they're willing to exchange their homes. A listing in the catalog costs $20. The FEC also publishes a house-exchange supplement to encourage travel and study abroad for teachers and administrators at all levels. To register and receive a current directory, send $20 to FEC, 952 Virginia Avenue, Lancaster, PA 17603.

Another teaching program that has employed many American teachers abroad is operated by the Department of Defense. The DoD maintains 277 elementary, junior, and senior high schools in 20 foreign countries for children of U.S. military and civilian personnel stationed overseas. It is also responsible for staffing these schools with teachers, counselors, librarians, nurses, psychologists, and social workers. Some of the elementary schools are small, and teachers are required to teach more than one grade; some junior high schools require that you teach two or more subjects. Assignments are usually for one or two years. The Department of Defense emphatically insists, however, that applicants must "agree to accept an assignment to any location throughout the world where a vacancy exists and where their services are needed." For more information on openings or to request an application form, write to the Department of Defense, Office of Dependent Schools, Recruitment and Assignment Section, 2461 Eisenhower Avenue, Alexandria, VA 22331.

Teachers interested in positions abroad might find a job opening through the International Schools Services (ISS), a private organization that recruits and recommends personnel for American and international schools abroad. At present ISS serves over 300 schools in Africa, Europe, the Far East, Latin America, the Middle East, and Southeast Asia. Applicants must have a bachelor's degree and at least two years of current, successful experience either at the elementary or secondary level. There is a $50 registration fee and an additional fee if the candidate is placed. For information on registration procedures, contact ISS, 15 Roszell Road, P.O. Box 5910, Princeton, NJ 08543.

Another organization that might be of assistance is the European Council of International Schools (ECIS), which comprises 250 affiliated schools at the pre-university level, chiefly in Europe, but also in other locations. Every fall ECIS publishes an *International Schools Directory* giving detailed descriptions of its member schools and a listing of more than 500 other English-speaking independent international schools throughout the world. The directory may be ordered from Peterson's Guides, P.O. Box 2123, Princeton, NJ 08543-2123; the cost is $16.95 plus $2.75 postage.

The best book on teaching opportunities overseas is *Teaching Abroad*, updated every other year by the Institute of International Education (IIE). This easy-to-use book provides a listing of schools and other educational institutions around the globe that have indicated an interest in hiring U.S. nationals as teachers and administrators. Also included in the book is a section on study abroad opportunities for teachers. You can order it from IIE, 809 United Nations Plaza, New York, NY 10017 ($21.95, including postage and handling).

Another directory that's useful for those seeking teaching positions abroad is *Schools Abroad of Interest to Americans*. Now in its seventh edition, the book is actually meant to describe 900 elementary and secondary schools in 125 countries for parents who wish to send their children to a school abroad, but it also serves as a useful resource for anyone who would like an idea of what kinds of schools exist in other countries. The book is available from the publisher, Porter Sargent Publishers, 11 Beacon Street, Boston, MA 02108, at a cost of $30, plus $1.50 for postage and handling.

Still another book on the subject of teaching abroad is *Educators' Passport to International Jobs*, written by Rebecca Anthony and Gerald Roe and published by Peterson's Guides. According to the authors, it "can take you from your first tentative daydreams about foreign teaching through a step-by-step process of finding information, learning and applying effective job-seeking skills and strategies, preparing to live abroad, and finally returning to stateside employment." The book contains a number of specific contacts for jobs, but for the most part it concentrates on telling the reader how to construct a résumé, how to evaluate a job offer, et cetera. Check your local bookstore for a copy.

If you have a degree in the Teaching of English as a Second or Other Language (TESOL), your skills are needed in several countries and your chances of finding overseas positions are enhanced—although even for these specialists, jobs are tight. Every two months an organization called Teachers of English to Speakers of Other Languages publishes a list of opportunities for people trained in the field. Most of the jobs listed require a master's degree and experience in teaching English as a second language. To receive the listing, TESOL members should send $12 and nonmembers should send $20 ($18 or $24, respectively, if you want it sent outside the U.S.), to TESOL, 1118 22nd Street NW, Washington, DC 20037; (202) 872-1271.

The English Teaching Fellow Program places U.S. citizens with master's degrees in TESOL in positions abroad. Teaching Fellows generally serve as full-time teachers of English as a foreign language but may be assigned to materials development, teacher training, or supervisory activities. Most are placed in Latin America and assigned to binational centers—local, independent associations that promote mutual understanding between the people of the U.S. and the people of the host country. Teaching Fellows also may be placed in other institutions such as national universities and teacher-training institutes. Contracts are for twelve months, with the possibility of a one-year renewal. Salaries vary from one country to another but are sufficient to live modestly on in the host country. Round-trip transportation is provided from the Fellow's U.S. residence; no allowances are provided for dependents. While the USIA publishes announcements and processes applications for the English Teaching Fellow Program, the Fellow is an employee of the binational center or similar local institution, rather than of the U.S. Government, for the duration of his or her contract. For further information, contact USIA, English Teaching Fellow Program, English Language Programs Division (E/CE), 301 4th Street SW, Washington, DC 20547.

Publications on Long-Term Employment Abroad

The *International Employment Hotline* is a monthly newsletter that provides current job listings and advice for "career" international job-seekers. A year's subscription is $29; contact International Employment Hotline, P.O. Box 3030, Oakton, VA 22124.

Employment Abroad: Facts and Fallacies is a useful booklet that realistically covers all the possibilities for long-term employment as well as considerations involved in seeking employment overseas. It's available for $4 from Publications Fulfillment, Chamber of Commerce of the U.S., 1615 H Street NW, Washington, DC 20062.

The *Guide to Careers in World Affairs*, published by the Foreign Policy Association, is a 326-page paperback that includes more than 250 listings of some of the best sources of international employment in business, government, and nonprofit organizations. Published in 1987, it's available for $10.95 from the Foreign Policy Association, 729 Seventh Avenue, New York, NY 10019.

Another source of information on the subject is *Making It Abroad: The International Job Hunting Guide* by Howard Schuman. This book provides helpful suggestions and techniques for finding an international job; however, you won't find the names and addresses of specific organizations or companies with jobs overseas. It's available for $12.95 from John Wiley and Sons, 1 Wiley Drive, Somerset, NJ 08850-1271.

The Overseas List, by David M. Beckmann and Elizabeth Anne Donnelly, is written for "idealistic young people, middle-aged Christians who find their jobs unfulfilling, and retirees looking for a second career," and describes opportunities for working and volunteering in Asia, Africa, or Latin America. The authors' objective is to "offer guidelines in selecting an employer who is worth serving." Published in cooperation with Bread for the World, the book is available by mail from Augsburg Fortress, 426 South Fifth Street, Box 1209, Minneapolis, MN 55440 for $12.95, plus $2.25 postage and handling.

The 223-page *Directory of Work and Study in Developing Countries*, by David Leppard, is divided into three parts—work, voluntary work, and study—and describes nonprofit organizations, employment agencies, government offices, educational institutions, and business firms that provide opportunities in one of these three categories in Third World countries. It's available from the publisher, Vacation Work, 9 Park End Street, Oxford OX1 1HJ, England, for £6.95, plus £1.50 postage if sent to the U.S.

CHAPTER FOUR
STUDYING ABROAD

"Responsibility and awareness confront you head on. You develop new qualities, refine some, and get rid of others. And through it all you also become much more globally aware and culturally sensitive."
—Stacey M. Coito, Turlock, California

There was a time not all that long ago when study abroad was the exclusive privilege of the rich. Now, for many reasons, study abroad has become a possibility for all—and the opportunities are boundless. The number of American students studying abroad continues to grow; figures gathered from colleges and universities across the U.S. indicate that more than 50,000 undergraduate students study abroad each year. Why do they choose to pursue part of their education overseas? A survey commissioned by the Council in the mid-1980s indicates that nearly one-fifth of the participants in study programs abroad sponsored by U.S. institutions said career goals influenced their decision; many felt an overseas experience would add a new dimension to their schooling, improve their foreign-language skills, and help them to become more independent. Of American students preparing for a second trip abroad, the survey found that as a result of their first international experience "an overwhelming number became more interested in international events, saw an improvement in academic performance, and became more self-confident."

The experience of living and studying abroad is one that enhances understanding, helping people see beyond their own world views to sympathize with and really comprehend other cultures. In fact, it was the belief that international understanding would help promote peace and stability that brought about the formation of the Council shortly after the end of the Second World War. Today, in addition to the goal of achieving international peace and understanding, less lofty concerns about the United States' international competitiveness in the global arena of business and finance prompt leaders in business, government, and education to emphasize the need for enhanced foreign-language training and improved international education.

Like everything else, studying abroad means different things to different people. To one student it may mean a three-week course in French culture on the Riviera during July, while for another it may mean a year of research on a doctoral thesis in the stacks of a German library. First, you'll have to decide what kind of study experience you want. Your choice will depend on such things as your field of interest, your capabilities (particularly language skills), the amount of time available to you, and the amount of money you can afford to spend. You should also ask yourself: Am I independent and outgoing? Serious and academic? How organized and academically focused am I? How hesitant am I about going on my own?

Be certain to talk with your academic adviser or with your school's study-abroad adviser early in your planning. Your adviser will help you decide what kind of study-abroad experience is right for you, evaluate program possibilities, and arrange for credit transfers and the continuation of any financial-aid packages you might be benefiting from. If you don't have a study-abroad or academic adviser, make an effort to speak with your school's admissions officer, registrar, or dean of students for help and assistance. Also make an effort to talk to any foreign students on your campus—they are an invaluable source of information about what it is like to study and live in a foreign culture.

Also, think ahead to that day when you return to your home, friends, and school. There's a phenomenon associated with foreign travel that some have termed "culture shock." The process of preparing for a trip and then leaving behind the customs and values familiar to you, as well as family and friends, can be very difficult. In addition, while overseas you may find that you change your outlook about many important things. This may include changing your goals—both personal and educational. Depending on the length and type of experience you have had, you may find readjustment to your old life somewhat trying.

"When I returned home from more than a year in Southeast Asia, I had a terrible time. My year of study was rich in learning, relationships, and self-discovery. It seemed that nothing at home had changed much, and it took a long time for me to sort out what was going on. In that one year I had changed more than in all the rest of my life."

Once you have set your personal and academic goals, you need to look at the study options available to you. Basically, there are two kinds of study-abroad experience: direct enrollment in a foreign university and programs sponsored by a U.S. university or other institution.

Direct Enrollment in a Foreign University

Direct enrollment in a foreign university can be an exacting venture, and is best suited to the independent and highly motivated individuals who already have experience living abroad and are fluent in the language of the country where they plan to study. Others will probably need the support system of a program sponsored by a U.S. institution (see the following section).

Students considering direct enrollment in a university overseas should be well aware that university systems and teaching methods in other countries are very different from those in the United States. For one thing, students entering a university in Europe are, generally speaking, at about the same educational level as college juniors in the U.S. This almost always makes it impossible for a freshman or sophomore in the U.S. to enroll in a university abroad except in a special program of some kind. The American Association of Collegiate Registrars and Admissions Officers (AACRAO) publishes the World Education Series, a series of profiles of foreign educational systems. Although designed for U.S. admissions officers evaluating foreign academic credentials, these publications are also of use to the prospective student. For a complete list of titles, write AACRAO, One Dupont Circle, Washington, DC 20036.

Because of the differences between higher education systems from country to country, credit is not easily transferred from a foreign university to a U.S. university. Students who want to transfer credit earned at an institution abroad to a university in the United States should try to make an arrangement with the U.S. institution *before* going abroad. In general, this is a somewhat risky business; many American students return to the States to find that their home institution will not give them full credit for courses taken at a foreign university.

"My university awarded me nine transfer credits for what should have been eighteen. The registrar didn't seem to understand the way hours work in a

British tutorial system. The loss of credits was my own fault because I didn't get my adviser's assistance before I left."

Besides the problems of adapting to another educational system and transferring credit, there is also the problem of language. Study-abroad advisers at U.S. institutions report that a number of students without proficiency in a foreign language ask about the possibilities of direct enrollment at universities where the language of instruction is not English. According to one adviser: "The fact of the matter is that most Americans do not have sufficient foreign-language skills to qualify for enrollment as a regular student at foreign universities in non-English-speaking countries. Many Americans grossly underestimate the time it takes to acquire the proficiency in a foreign language necessary to follow a formal lecture, take notes, participate in class discussions, and then compete on tests on an equal footing with those students who are native speakers of the language."

Instead of enrolling in regular university courses, you may find it easier to enroll in some of the special courses offered to foreigners, which usually include language classes and courses in the history and culture of the country. Some of these courses are taught during the academic year but most are given during the summer, when foreign universities usually suspend their regular classes. The two best sources to consult for this kind of program are *Vacation Study Abroad* and *Academic Year Abroad*, both published by the Institute of International Education (see "For More Information on Study Abroad" near the end of this chapter).

Another possibility for U.S. students is to study at one of the "American" colleges and universities that have been established abroad. Two of the better-known institutions of this type are the American University in Cairo and Sophia University in Japan. Organized like U.S. institutions, these institutions boast a heterogenous mix of Americans and other students from all over the world, and offer a varied curriculum.

U.S.-Sponsored Programs

Due to the challenges of direct enrollment in a foreign university, most Americans studying abroad choose a program sponsored by a U.S. institution instead. American colleges and universities sponsor hundreds of these programs. In fact, you should first check to see whether your own school sponsors an overseas program or is a member of a consortium (an association of colleges and universities) that sponsors such a program. Going abroad with your own university will ease the problems of transferring academic credit and maintaining any scholarships or loans you might have.

It's possible, though, that your college may not sponsor the type of program you are looking for. If that is the case, don't be discouraged. Of the several hundred U.S. colleges and universities sponsoring overseas study programs, most accept students from other campuses. In fact, there are so many programs to choose from that selecting a course from the listings in *Work, Study, Travel Abroad* or one of the other books described later in this chapter can be a formidable task. Of course, you'll eliminate many of them after taking into consideration things such as language requirements, cost, academic focus, and whether or not your own school will grant academic credit for them. In making your selection, however, be sure to consult the office on your own campus that advises students on foreign study or administers your school's foreign-study programs. People in this office may be personally familiar with some of the programs you are considering and might also be able to direct you to students on campus who were participants at an earlier date.

Programs sponsored by American institutions grant academic credit that is usually quite easy to transfer to your home college or university, but there may still be problems. Be absolutely sure to have your courses approved for credit by your college or university advisers and registrar before you commit yourself to a particular program.

Type of Program

While making a decision about the program that's best for you, carefully consider two important points:

First, what types of courses are provided? Does the program provide American-style courses or does it utilize the regular courses of a foreign university? Some programs, at one extreme, export U.S. professors to teach the same courses they would teach at home (in English, of course); others enroll their students in the large lecture classes typical of foreign universities. In between are a range of compromises: American-style courses taught by foreign professors (some in English, some in the language of the visiting professor); special courses set up by the foreign university for all of their foreign students (occasionally in English); or regular courses with tutorial assistance provided by students from the university. Some programs offer several of these options. Decide what's best for you. Students with language competence and good academic skills may profit most by enrollment in the regular courses of a foreign university, where he or she will meet students of the host country and experience its university system firsthand. Students with more limited language skills or academic backgrounds may be wise to seek a program offering special classes for Americans or other foreigners.

Second, how much will the living arrangements provided as part of the program involve you in the social life of the students of the host country? In this area, too, U.S.-sponsored programs provide a range of possibilities. Some programs arrange for all U.S. students to live together in a hotel or dormitory; others house participants in university dormitories with students from the host country. Still others provide housing in rented rooms or in private homes. Students living with foreign families may face greater difficulties in adapting, but in general they will acquire a better understanding of the host country and its language.

Of course, there are some personal considerations to take into account as well. How do you feel about the size of the host institution? Would you prefer studying in a major city or in a more rural setting? And last (but certainly not least), what should you expect to spend in the way of daily living expenses?

Each section devoted to a specific country in this book contains listings, by subject area, of study programs for undergraduate and graduate students. These programs are sponsored by member colleges, universities, and organizations of the Council on International Educational Exchange. Addresses for the institutions offering these programs appear in Appendix I.

"I didn't get a chance to spend as much time with British students as I would have liked or expected. Our residence halls were just for program students—all Americans. Secondly, the Polytechnic was a commuting school

—there was no campus, and a campus would have been much more conducive to meeting students and forming more solid relationships."

"Live with a family that has children. You'll learn more of the language and there's no better way to understand a culture than to see how children are brought up. Best of all, you'll never be bored."
—Gary Lemons, Albuquerque, New Mexico

Length of Program

How long will you be studying abroad? A summer, a semester, or a full academic year? Or maybe just a month during the winter-term break?

There are a number of factors students should consider in deciding how long to study abroad: timely fulfillment of graduation requirements; pertinence of courses to a particular field of study; degree of strain placed upon personal financial resources; and personal maturity and independence. It is generally assumed that the traditional year abroad (usually at the junior-year level) is the most beneficial. A growing number of students are participating in more than one study-abroad program during their college career, often going for a summer or other short-term experience initially, and then later for a semester or year abroad. It should be pointed out, however, than many programs do not accept college freshmen.

A semester or academic year of study abroad should give you enough time to become involved in the student life of the country. It can also give you enough time to get miserably homesick. After all, being away from home and friends for six months or a year and having to cope with the pressure of another academic system doesn't appeal to everyone.

"Be prepared to feel very small for three months or so, until you really get into the swing of things. It takes that long to learn how to survive and cope. It takes time to establish your own identity."

If you can't, or don't, want to interrupt your regular course of studies and go abroad for a semester or year, a summer program might be best for you. Again, an extraordinary variety of opportunities is available. You can study business and management in Japan; architecture in the Yucatán; or Gandhian philosophy in India. Taking a summer course might also be a good way to find out whether you would like to study abroad for a longer period of time.

More and more colleges and universities have switched to calendars that have an "interim" period between terms. During the interim, usually between the fall and spring semesters, students can select one of a variety of programs, many of which involve an off-campus experience. An example of an interim program might be an architecture tour in which participants spend a week attending classes in London and the rest of the time in an organized "tour" studying important works of architecture in several European countries. Classes are usually taught by professors from the sponsoring school. Students can join such programs arranged either by their own or another school.

In the specific country sections of this book we've arranged the listings into two broad groups: (1) semester and academic-year programs and (2) summer programs. You'll find the interim programs—although they are short-term in character—listed in the "Semester and Academic Year" section, since they can take place at various times during the school year.

Evaluating a Program

Once you've decided to join a study-abroad program, you'll soon discover how many there are to choose from. Chances are that at first they will all sound good to you—and most of them are. But there are some that will not suit your purposes and some that are just not worth the money. Unfortunately, there have been several incidents in which students have enrolled in programs only to find, on the eve of their trip, that the organization has disbanded and there is no program. The U.S. Information Agency often receives complaints from people who have found themselves taking courses of limited academic value as well as complaints from students who have discovered, too late, that they had paid fees far exceeding the value of the services received. Often, if the right questions had been asked *before* the student committed his or her time and money to the program, disappointment would have been avoided.

How to Read an Advertisement

Lily von Klemperer, one of the pioneers in the field of study abroad, wrote an article for the National Association for Foreign Students Affairs (NAFSA) newsletter entitled "How to Read Study Abroad Literature." We have borrowed most of what follows in this section from this now-classic article.

Spend Your Summer in Sunny Spain!
(1) Live in a Medieval Castle or with a Local Family
(2) Learn Spanish at a Renowned Academic Institution
(3) Outstanding Faculty
(4) International Student Body
(5) Academic Credit Available
(6) Limited Enrollment—All Ages Eligible
(7) All-Inclusive Charge
(8) Write to the Director of Admissions, P.O. Box 000, Cambridge, MA.

Above is the text of an imaginary advertisement. How does this program sound? Let's take this mock advertisement line by line and see what it really does and does not say.

First, the emphasis seems to be on spending the summer in sunny Spain. Not an unappealing idea, of course, but if your objective is to learn the language, how will that be accomplished? How serious does the program sound if it uses as its "hook" a travel brochure's view of Spain?

Line 1: A medieval castle sounds great, but how close is it to the place where you will study or to town? Are there places to eat nearby? It may be a castle, but how has it been converted? Will you sleep in a dorm with six other students? And what about the host family? Is it going to turn out, in fact, to be someone who simply wants to make some extra money by having an American boarder?

Line 2: Just what is this famous university? Why isn't it named? Foreign universities *do not* have regular classes during the summer, so what is probably referred to here is a special course for foreigners—not a regular university class. Whenever the ad or brochure uses the words "recognized" or "accredited" to describe a learning institution, find out exactly who does the recognizing or accrediting.

Line 3: This reference to outstanding faculty needs to be explained carefully in any brochures. Their names, titles, and affiliations should be given. This phrase is much too vague.

Line 4: Get specifics on this. The students who are categorized as "international" may actually be sons and daughters of U.S. parents working abroad. Find out how many countries are really represented.

Line 5: This vague reference to credit is of little use, since the transfer of credit is such an individual matter. Whether or not you can get credit where you want it is something that only you can determine. You should, however, ask the sponsor to give you a list of institutions that have granted credit for the program in the past. This will be excellent ammunition if you need to approach your own guidance counselor or academic dean to request credit.

Line 6: How selective is this organization? What are the standards for limited enrollment? Are there, indeed, standards? And if all ages are eligible, how will you like being together with people much younger or older than you? If some are working for credit and others aren't, will that affect the seriousness of the work?

Line 7: "Inclusive charge" is much too vague. This is where the small print comes in. Find out exactly what is included and get an estimate of the total expenses, whether or not they are included.

Line 8: The actual name of a responsible person would be better here. When the backup brochure arrives, it should list (besides the director of faculty) a board of advisers, trustees, et cetera. Don't let the Cambridge address mislead you into assuming that the program is affiliated with Harvard. Remember that anyone can get a post office box anywhere.

We obviously aren't able to give you an all-inclusive qualitative framework for evaluating a program. In the final analysis, you have to decide what's best suited to the goals you have identified for yourself. We do suggest that you judge whether the costs of any particular program seem fair and representative of the course offerings and objectives. If you have questions, ask a study-abroad adviser if he or she has heard about the program.

Scholarships, Loans, and Fellowships

You may be surprised to learn that study abroad (transportation included) is not necessarily more expensive than study in the United States. In fact, studying in many Third World countries, where the U.S. dollar generally has more purchasing power than it does at home, may even be cheaper than studying at your own institution.

Your school may be willing to apply your regular scholarship or loans to the cost of study abroad. Check with your academic dean or financial-aid office. If cost factors are important to you, remember that your tuition costs may be lower if you apply for programs available through public universities in the state of which you are a resident.

The U.S. Department of Education's Office of Student Financial Assistance administers five financial-aid programs for students who are enrolled at least half-time in a regular program of study at a school that participates in the programs. The programs are the Pell Grant, the Supplemental Educational Opportunity Grant, the College Work-Study Program, the Perkins Loans Program, and the Guaranteed Student Loan Program. A student attending a foreign school may receive aid from one of these programs if the school is a branch of an eligible school located in the United States. A student attending school abroad may receive a guaranteed student loan if he or she is attending an eligible foreign institution. To find out if a particular school is eligible, contact the financial-aid office of the school.

A good source of information on how to apply all types of scholarship, loan, and grant programs to overseas study is *Financial Aid for Study Abroad*, by William W. Cressey. While not a listing of individual scholarships and grants, the book provides general information and discusses the application of financial resources provided through major government and private programs to study abroad. Contact the National Association for Foreign Student Affairs (NAFSA), 1860 19th Street NW, Washington, DC 20009, for price and ordering information.

One specific source of scholarship funds is the Rotary Foundation of Rotary International, which offers six types of scholarships:

- undergraduate scholarships for study abroad in any field
- graduate fellowships for graduate study abroad in any field
- vocational scholarships for high school graduates studying in a variety of vocational and professional fields
- scholarships to experienced teachers for study of education of the handicapped
- scholarships to experienced journalists for study in the field of print or broadcast journalism
- grants for university teachers in countries other than their own, especially Third World countries, who have demonstrated excellence in teaching or research in international relations or the fields of political, economic, social, or cultural studies

All six scholarship categories are for a full academic year and require a good working knowledge of the language of the host country. Applications must be made through a local Rotary Club chapter by July 15 (except for the last category, which has an April 15 deadline) of the year preceding the award. Details are available from the Rotary Foundation of Rotary International, 1560 Sherman Avenue, Evanston, IL 60201.

CIEE's ISIC Scholarship Fund, financed in part with revenues from the sale of the International Student Identity Card (ISIC), provides grants to high school and college students planning a study or service experience in a Third World country. Applicants must be sponsored by a nonprofit organization or educational institution. Undergraduates must be students at a CIEE member institution or planning to participate in a program sponsored by a CIEE member institution. However, any high school student at least 16 years old is eligible to apply. Awards are made twice a year. For information and application forms, contact CIEE, Information and Student Services Department, 205 East 42nd Street, New York, NY 10017.

While there are only a limited number of scholarships set aside for undergraduates who wish to study abroad, a greater number of grants are available to graduate students. *Fulbright and Other Grants for Graduate Study Abroad*, a free brochure put out each year in May by U.S. Student Programs, Institute of International Education, 809 United Nations Plaza, New York, NY 10017, describes fellowships and scholarships administered by the Institute of International Education (IIE). The 96-page booklet includes grants offered by foreign governments, universities, corporate, and private donors, as well as U.S. government grants for graduate study funded under the Fulbright-Hays Act.

A number of directories—usually available in college and university libraries—provide information on the specific scholarships, grants, and fellowships available for study abroad. Most of the scholarships and grants in the directories listed below are available only at the graduate level, however:

- A comprehensive source of information on the subject is *Financial Resources for International Study*, which lists hundreds of grants, fellowships, and awards available to U.S. nationals for study and research abroad at all academic levels. A new directory, it was compiled in 1989 by IIE and is available for $36.95 (plus $1.75 postage) from the publisher, Peterson's Guides, P.O. Box 2123, Princeton, NJ 08543–2123.
- *The Grants Register 1989–91* offers a detailed compendium of graduate-level awards offered for study, research, and training for nationals of all countries. Compiled by Ronald Tunner and published by St. Martin's Press, 175 Fifth Avenue, New York, NY 10010, it costs $69.95.
- *The International Scholarship Book*, edited by Daniel Cassidy and published by Prentice Hall in 1988, provides a comprehensive list of scholarships, grants, and internships available in the public and private sector for study in dozens of countries. The author states that $6.6 billion in funds from corporations is unclaimed, "not because people were unqualified, but because no one knew where to look." The cost of the book is $19.95. Prentice Hall's address is 198 Sylvan Avenue, Englewood Cliffs, NJ 07632.
- *Study Abroad* is an international directory of fellowships, scholarships, and awards that can be applied to study and travel opportunities in over 100 countries. The 1988–91 edition, produced by UNESCO, is available from UNIPUB, 4611-F Assembly Drive, Lanham, MD 20706–4391. It costs $19 (order #U1634).
- *Fellowships, Scholarships, and Related Opportunities in International Education* is published by the Center for International Education, 201 Alumni Hall, University of Tennessee, Knoxville, TN 37996–0620. The cost of the most recent edition (1989) is $10, including postage; make checks payable to the University of Tennessee.
- The seventh edition (1989) of the *Fellowship Guide for Western Europe* is available from the Council for European Studies, Box 44 Schermerhorn Hall, Columbia University, New York, NY 10027. The cost is $8 (make checks payable to Columbia University).

A special note for veterans: More than 1,200 university-sponsored programs open to veterans in 64 countries are listed in the Veterans Administration pamphlet entitled *Foreign Training for Veterans, Inservice Students and Eligible Dependents* (#22–72–2). It is available at Veterans Administration regional offices, or from the Director, Vocational Rehabilitation and Education Service (223B), U.S. Department of Veterans Affairs, 810 Vermont Avenue NW, Washington, DC 20420.

For Further Information on Study Abroad

There are several places you can go for additional information on study abroad. Start on campus at the placement office, the office of the academic dean, or the international programs office. If you've already decided where you want to study, you can get information from the consulate, tourist office, or information service of that country. (Lists of these offices can be found throughout this book.)

If you are in or near New York City, you may want to stop at the Information Center of the Institute of International Education (IIE), 809 United Nations Plaza, open Monday through Friday from 10 A.M. to 4 P.M. Volunteers will assist you in utilizing the extensive resources of the Center, which include books, brochures, and audio-visual materials.

The most comprehensive guide to study programs outside the U.S. open to Americans is *Academic Year Abroad*. Updated annually, this IIE publication lists, country by country, over 1,700 semester and academic-year study programs abroad for undergraduates and graduates. Program descriptions offer information on when and where programs take place, as well as how long they last; eligibility requirements; orientation sessions; course descriptions; and where to write for more information. It also includes guidelines for choosing a program, an annotated bibliography, and a field-of-study index. The cost is $24.95, including book-rate postage. Write to IIE, 809 United Nations Plaza, New York, NY 10017.

The companion volume to the above book is *Vacation Study Abroad*, also published annually by IIE. It includes information on 1,300 programs abroad that are open to U.S. students and take place from April to October. The cost is $22.95, including book-rate postage (see above for the address). Most international centers and study-abroad offices at U.S. universities have copies of these two books; in fact, many also have the information listed in these books in the form of a computer database, which can greatly speed your search for the program that's right for your needs.

One of the best and most often overlooked sources of study information on any given country is that country's embassy or consular office in the United States. Most will provide, at no charge, lists of the specific courses available to you and instructions on how to go about enrolling in them. The titles of many of these information sheets are included in the individual chapters of *Work, Study, Travel Abroad*.

Written mainly for Canadian students but also of interest to U.S. students is the *International Educational Travel Planner*, an annual directory of programs offered by 30 Canadian universities around the world. Also included in this 64-page publication are background articles about study and travel abroad. It's available for $2 from Student Services, Box 10,000, Athabasca University, Athabasca, Alberta T0G 2R0.

For students planning to study at a foreign university—either through direct enrollment or by participating in a program sponsored by a U.S. institution—there are several reference works that might by useful. However, since they are quite expensive, you'll probably want to check a library for a copy rather than purchasing your own. The *World Education Encyclopedia* (Facts on File, $175), by George Kurian, provides descriptions of the educational system of every country in the world, from Afghanistan to Zaire. *The World of Learning* (London: Europa Publications, $220), which is updated annually, describes more than 25,000 academic institutions all over the world. Another useful source is *Higher Education in the European Community: A Directory of Higher Education Institutions* (European Community Information Service, 1985, $13).

In addition to these, there a number of publications on specific disciplines such as medicine and engineering that can be of great help to students planning to study abroad.

- **For medical students:** The *World Directory of Medical Schools*, compiled by the World Health Organization (WHO), costs $21 (plus $2 for postage and handling) and is available (prepaid) from WHO Publications Centre,

USA, 49 Sheridan Avenue, Albany, NY 12210. You may also be able to find a copy of the now out-of-print *Barron's Guide to Foreign Medical Schools*, by Carla Fine, in your public library or study-abroad office. *Note*: Some agencies promising to place U.S. students in foreign medical schools charge large fees for their service; the Association of American Medical Colleges warns that these agencies usually charge fees for information that is available without cost from other sources.
- **For business students:** *Management Study Abroad 1989–91*, a new book listing over 500 international business programs for business students and executives, is available for $18.95 (including book-rate postage) from the Institute of International Education, 809 United Nations Plaza, New York, NY 10017.
- **For engineering students:** The *World Directory of Engineering Schools* lists 1,347 institutions in 111 countries as well as the programs offered at each one. It can be ordered from Geographics, Box 133, Easton, CT 06612 for $28.95.

High School Programs

Although the focus of this book is on work, study, and travel opportunities for college students, there is also a rapidly expanding number of programs abroad for high school and junior high school students. Too numerous to be listed here, these programs are described in *The Teenager's Guide to Study, Travel, and Adventure Abroad* (see page 465). You'll also want to check Appendix II of this book for a listing of programs abroad sponsored by CIEE member institutions.

It has become fairly common for students to take off the year between high school and college in order to do something "different" before settling down to a college routine. For those who want to spend this interim year in another country, there are many alternatives. Some of the study-abroad programs listed in the specific country sections of this book are open to graduating high school seniors; *The Teenager's Guide* contains a more complete listing of such opportunities. If you feel you want to take a break from studying, there are other options open to you as well; check the sections on international workcamps, voluntary service, service learning, and field-research projects in Chapter 2 of this book. You'll also find more options of this type in *The Teenager's Guide*.

> *"I do know this year has meant more than just a divergence from the traditional routine, more than a delay of the inevitables, more than a romp in the fields before continuing the climb. Spending some time overseas, I've become more independent, better disciplined, and broader in my own thinking. But mostly, I've developed a genuine desire to learn."*

Continuing Education

The number of educational programs abroad designed specifically for adults is growing by leaps and bounds. At CIEE we receive brochures almost daily describing programs sponsored by museums, alumni organizations, and the continuing education divisions of foreign universities. While the focus of this book is on work, study, and travel opportunities for college students, many of the programs described here are also open to adults not currently attending any type of school. To find these, check through the eligibility requirements for the study and travel programs listed in the specific country sections later in this book. For some ideas for learning vacations, you might also look at Chapter 5 as well as the various sections on workcamps, field-research projects, and voluntary service in Chapter 2.

Traditionally, one of the most popular ways of taking a learning vacation has been to enroll in a language center in a foreign country and spend a few weeks immersed in the study of the language. These language centers exist everywhere. Some are quite well known, like the Instituto Allende in San Miguel de Allende, Mexico. Eurocentres, another such organization, operates 22 language centers in 7 different European countries. Courses range from 2 weeks to 6 months and are designed for the beginning as well as the most advanced student. Among its many programs, French is offered at various locations in France and Switzerland; German in Cologne and Lucerne; Italian in Florence; and Spanish in Barcelona and Madrid. Students can live with host families or in hotel/pension facilities. More information and application details on Eurocentres is available from Council Travel offices across the country (see pages ix–xi), or by writing Eurocentres, Seestrasse 247, 8038 Zurich, Switzerland.

And for people 60 years old or older seeking a learning vacation, there's the popular Elderhostel program, which "combines the best traditions of education and hosteling." Elderhostel was founded on the belief that retirement, rather than mean withdrawal and isolation, can, on the contrary, be an opportunity to enjoy new experiences. Besides an extensive network of Elderhostels in the U.S., where participants spend a week on a college campus studying different topics and enjoying activities in the local setting, the organization sponsors programs in Australia, Bermuda, Canada, France, Germany, Great Britain, Holland, India, Ireland, Israel, Italy, Mexico, Scandinavia, and Spain. International programs usually involve one-week stays at several colleges or universities. For example, in a typical Elderhostel program in Australia, participants spend a week at Dunmore Lang College studying the character of the city of Sydney, a week on Heron Island focusing on the Great Barrier Reef, and a week at the Gippsland Institute in rural Victoria studying the relationship between man and the environment. For details on Elderhostel offerings, write to Elderhostel, 80 Boylston Street, Boston, MA 02116.

The best source of information on unusual educational opportunities for adults is *Learning Vacations* (Peterson's Guides; $9.95), which focuses on short-term "take-your-mind-along" vacations that include a learning experience of some sort—seminars, music tours, art and folk festivals, archaeological digs, et cetera. Although most of these programs are in the U.S., there are some in other countries as well.

"This whole expedition has had a disquieting effect on me. Now I feel like I'll blow up or go crazy if I don't go places and do things. I want excitement and danger, new people and new places. I'm so restless now. It's stirred me up like nothing else I've done."

CHAPTER FIVE
MAKING YOUR TRAVEL PLANS

"International travel broadens the mind, warms the heart, sharpens the senses, and exercises the legs. It will also test your wits and challenge your adaptability. Knowing the language makes the whole experience twice as rewarding."
—Chris Allert, Minneapolis, Minnesota

By now you're ready to see the world, be it as a student, volunteer, or tourist. Whether you plan to trek the Himalayas or simply find your way to a school in London, you need to know a little about the travel options so you can make the best decisions about how to get to where you're going. And once you're there, you'll probably have to make some plans for getting around. Good research and planning can help you make the most of the time you have as well as keep your costs low.

If you live near a Council Travel office, your research will be a bit easier. Council Travel offices are full-service travel agencies that specialize in providing services for students and other budget-minded travelers. There are 28 of them in the United States, as well as a number in Europe and Asia (see pages ix–xi). Many are conveniently located near university campuses, and all are staffed by trained personnel who can answer your questions about student discount fares, rail passes, and other ways to save money traveling. CIEE's other travel subsidiary, Council Charter, is discussed in detail in the "Charter" section of this chapter.

Whether or not you live near a Council Travel office, your research should begin with a copy of the 64-page *Student Travel Catalog*, published annually by the Council on International Educational Exchange. It's available free of charge at Council Travel offices as well as at many college and university study-abroad offices and international centers. Or you can get a copy by writing the Council in New York and enclosing $1 for postage. Once you get it, you'll discover that its pages are filled with information on travel basics such as air fares, car-rental options, and rail-pass plans. Looking at it before going to a travel agency or making your own travel plans will help ensure you get what you want at a reasonable price. Remember: Research is the only way to make your overseas experience an economical one.

GETTING THERE

Finding the Best Air Fare

Over the last several years, the airline industry has seen a number of changes—not uncommon in an industry that's in a seemingly perpetual state of flux. In general terms, international air fares remain competitive, and ticket prices for some international destinations are actually falling. In addition, because of low air fares, more and more travelers are heading to non-European destinations such as Asia, the South Pacific, and South America.

Before you begin researching fares, however, you'll need to make a few decisions about your trip. You should have a rough idea of your general itinerary, your travel budget, how many stopovers you plan to make, what time of year you plan to travel, and the length of time you plan on staying. Then start shopping around. But start early. Many bargain air fares are limited in availability and must be purchased far ahead of your departure date.

Be aware, too, that although some advertised fares may be lower than others, there are usually certain restrictions attached that you'll learn about only by reading the fine print. In some situations you may even be better off buying a more expensive ticket, particularly if you wish to make several stopovers. More expensive fares often allow you a number of "free" stopovers, resulting in an airfare that's better suited to your particular itinerary. As you do your research, keep in mind that inexpensive fares abound; they just require a certain amount of investigation, flexibility, and a good deal of creative planning. Let this be your guiding principle when it comes to air fares: Usually, the more conditions attached to a certain fare, the cheaper it's going to be.

If you're a student, you'll find as you plan your travels that your International Student Identity Card (ISIC) is worth many times what you paid for it. The ISIC entitles you to travel on a student-fare basis to almost any destination in the world at savings of up to 50 percent off regular economy-class fares. Even if you're not a student but are still under 26, you are eligible for many of the same discounts if you get an International Youth ID Card. Educators, too, are eligible for some of these discounts if they have a valid International Teacher Identity Card (see page 9). Council Travel offices can advise you on how these fares apply to your itinerary as well as make the reservations for you.

With all that in mind, it's not possible at press time for us to tell you exactly what international fares will be in the spring of 1990. What we can do, though, is advise you on how to go about getting the latest consumer information on the best fares available. For starters, Council Travel publishes "Airfare Updates," fact sheets that provide the latest information on nearly every type of international air fare; you can get these at a Council Travel office or have them automatically mailed to you as they are published by completing the appropriate form in the *Student Travel Catalog*. In addition, a book that uncovers a treasure trove of money-saving ideas, many that even a seasoned traveler wouldn't have imagined, is *Beat the High Cost of Travel*, by Tom Brosnahan (Prentice Hall, Frommer Books; $6.95). Also check the Sunday travel sections of large metropolitan newspapers such as *The New York Times*, the *Chicago Tribune*, the *Los Angeles Times*, and *The Washington Post*—usually, they are full of ads for competitive air fares and contain the latest travel information in columns or feature articles.

Charter Flights

Charter flights are often the least expensive air-fare alternative. A charter flight is one in which a tour operator has chartered a plane to fly a specific route on certain dates. Unlike the early days of charter travel, however, anyone can now take a charter, regardless of age or student status. Before purchasing your ticket, read the contract that operators are by law required to supply. Knowing your rights and responsibilities beforehand eliminates headaches later.

There are a lot of pros and cons to consider in deciding whether or not you want to take a charter flight. What follows is a list of facts you should be aware of in making a decision:

- You can book many charters on either a one-way or round-trip basis.
- Charters are available to a variety of destinations, but most are to Europe.
- Generally, charters depart only from major cities; some operators do offer low-cost "add-on" fares, however.
- Some charters are available year-round, but others only operate seasonally.
- Many charter operators offer a "mix-and-match" option, allowing you to pick and choose from among several arrival and departure cities.
- There may be delays. Every charter company is occasionally beset by the vagaries of schedule, weather, or aircraft changes. Most can't be predicted; the best advice is to allow some leeway for schedule changes in your itinerary.
- Fuel surcharges and price increases sometimes occur after you have booked a flight; ask the operator about their likelihood.

Taking everything into consideration, charters are still a good option for those people looking for an inexpensive way to get to where they're going. Getting beyond the popular European charter destinations, however, requires further exploration. You may want to combine a charter flight with a regular flight offering a student/youth fare to your final destination, for example. Allow plenty of time for the unexpected when combining two such flights: a delay that causes you to miss your connection may not only be inconvenient but also quite expensive.

Council Charter, the oldest charter company in the U.S., has more than forty years of experience in the budget travel field. Two features that make its service unique are the mix-and-match plan, which lets you fly into one city and return from another, and its trip-cancellation waiver. The latter, an optional waiver, is available for a modest fee at the time of booking and guarantees a full refund of all money paid if the cancellation notice is received anytime up to your scheduled check-in time. In 1989, Council Charter flew to Amsterdam, Brussels, Geneva, London, Madrid, Malaga, Nice, Paris, Rome, and Zurich. Some of its charters operate on a year-round basis. It also offered special low-cost add-on fares to New York from Chicago, Cleveland, Denver, Las Vegas, Los Angeles, Minneapolis, Portland, Salt Lake City, San Diego, San Francisco, Seattle, and Spokane. You'll find fares for Council Charter flights to Europe listed in the "Getting There" section of the chapter on Western Europe. For more information, contact a Council Travel office or call Council Charter's toll-free number: 1-800-223-7402.

Scheduled Flights

The airline industry, as we mentioned earlier, is always in a state of flux. Rules governing fares, promotions, and cancellations vary widely and are likely to continue to do so in the immediate future. The best advice we can give is that you look at every option as far ahead of your planned departure as possible. If you use a travel agent, select one who is interested in selling budget travel. Many agents simply aren't interested in scrolling through their computer databases on your behalf in return for the small commission a budget fare earns them. Similarly, those agents who don't normally devote a good deal of time to reading and studying bargain fares won't be of much help to you.

Give some thought to when you plan to travel. There are often "low" and "high" season cut-off dates that apply to fares; length of stay is another cost factor in fare determination. Below you'll find listed some of the fare possibilities that were available for scheduled flights in 1989:

- **Student/Youth Fares:** For those who are eligible (usually students under the age of 31 and youths under the age of 25), student/youth fares can save you as much as 50 percent over the regular economy fare on a scheduled flight. In order to qualify for a student/youth fare, you must have either an International Student Identity Card (see page 8) or an International Youth ID Card (see page 9). International student/youth fares are quoted in the "Getting There" sections of the chapters that follow. In addition, Council Travel offices will be happy to provide you with current fare information and make bookings.
- **Advance Purchase Excursion (APEX) Fares:** In some ways the airline industry's answer to charters, APEX fares are between 30 and 40 percent lower than regular economy class. Since low fares seem to go hand in hand with restrictions, however, be aware that there are minimum- and maximum-stay requirements, cancellation and change penalties, and stopover restrictions. You must also purchase your ticket anytime from 7 to 30 days in advance. "Super" APEX fares are somewhat cheaper than regular APEX fares but are only in effect on a limited number of routes.
- **Special Bargain or Promotional Fares:** A winter flight from Newark to London recently was advertised for $99 one-way. Bargain fares like this pop up sporadically; usually, they are part of a "quick sale" strategy that airlines use to fill seats during slow periods. One drawback is that they usually require the traveler to act immediately rather than meticulously plan an itinerary ahead of time. However, if you have the luxury of flexibility, promotional and bargain fares can be a dream come true.
- **Economy Fares:** The term "economy," when applied to an airline fare, is a contradiction in terms for anyone but the wealthy. Nonetheless, in a situation where you intend to make a number of stopovers en route to or returning from your final destination, an economy fare may actually be less expensive than an APEX fare. In some cases, it may be the only available option.
- **"Last Minute" Youth Fares:** Most major carriers have replaced their old "standby" fares with what we call their "last minute" youth fares. Usually, these are available to passengers 12–24 years of age on a one-way or, less frequently, round-trip basis. The catch is you can only book your seat within three days of your departure. What can be an attractive fare in low season is much harder to obtain during the high season. If your travel plans are flexible, this may be just your ticket, but if you have a schedule to keep, a serious delay could be a major problem for you.
- **Around the World Passes:** Most major carriers sell "Around the World" passes (the average price was about $2,000 in 1989), which are good for one year of unlimited travel on a particular airline (and, often, a limited group of partner airlines). These can be an economical alternative—if you really intend to be a "world" traveler. Regulations vary slightly depending on the airline, but most require a 14-day advance purchase, allow for unlimited stops (although only one per city), and require that you travel in one continuous direction.

In addition, there are many special low-cost excursion fares on commercial routes connecting countries outside the United States. Many of these can only be sold in the country from which the flight originates and cannot be advertised in the U.S. Check with the airlines wherever you are to see if such fares exist on the route you intend to travel. Certain cities have emerged as excellent places to look for inexpensive air travel. London, Bangkok, and Singapore, for instance, are famous as starting points for inexpensive scheduled and unscheduled flights to other parts of the world. It's possible to do some wheeling and dealing in these three cities and thus end up with real air-fare bargains. But don't forget that it almost always takes time and effort, and that the expenditure of both may not be worth the savings.

Flying as an International Air Courier

International courier companies use regularly scheduled flights on major airlines to ship items such as film, documents, blueprints, advertising material, and canceled checks. Since the packages accompanying the courier are considered personal baggage, they are cleared through customs immediately, thereby considerably reducing the time that would otherwise be required for their shipment. Persons wishing to fly as a courier can either schedule a flight weeks in advance or at the last minute, although last-minute choices as to flight, return date, and destination are limited. Flights as a courier are available from major international airports in the U.S., including those in New York, San Francisco, Los Angeles, and Chicago. In general you pay a registration fee to a courier service, which entitles you to fly at about ⅓–½ of a standard fare. Here are some examples of such round-trip fares: New York–Hong Kong for $459; New York–Mexico City for $175; and New York–Paris for $199. However, couriers are allowed only carry-on luggage. For further information, contact one of the several agencies that screen and select couriers. In New York, one such agency is Now Voyager, (212) 431–1616. Another is Skypack, (516) 745–6656 (10 A.M.–12 noon; 3–4 P.M.). In Los Angeles, try On Board, (213) 642–7700.

Getting There by Ship

People who have time to spare can enjoy the luxury of crossing the ocean by ship. Transatlantic student fares are available through Cunard Lines, (800) 221–4770, and Polish Ocean Lines, (514) 849–6111. There are a lot fewer crossings now than in past years, but you still may be able to find a ship that is leaving around the same time you'd like to go. Rates for one-way passage will vary according to the ship, its departure date and ports of call, and cabin location, but are generally much more expensive than air travel.

Although there are still many freighters operating all over the world, few have room for passengers. In fact, there's only one company, the Gydnia America Line, 39 Broadway, 14th Floor, New York, NY 10006, (212) 952–1280, that operates passenger-carrying freighters between the East Coast and Europe. There are more choices on routes from the West Coast to Asia, from New York to Africa, and from New York or Miami to South America. Accommodations on freighters vary from modest to luxurious. Staterooms on many current American-flag cargo vessels are equal and even superior to rooms on cruise liners, which cost considerably more. Not everyone will be happy on a freighter, however. There is no entertainment except that provided by the six to twelve passengers and the freighter's officers and crew. But if you enjoy the sea, good food (you usually dine with the officers), restful days and peaceful nights, exotic ports, and have plenty of time, then freighter travel can be just what you've been looking for. Note, however: Freighter schedules are changed to meet the demands of cargo; therefore, to enjoy a freighter cruise you must have a very flexible schedule. TravLtips Cruise and Freighter Travel Association (163–07 Depot Road, Flushing, NY 11358) publishes the *Freighter Bulletin* ($15 per year), a compilation of the personal travel experiences of the Association's members. Another useful source of information is *Ford's Freighter Travel Guide and Waterways of the World* (19448 Londeluis Street, Northridge, CA 91324). Published twice a year, it lists freighter cruises, describes ships, gives fares, et cetera. The cost is $8.95 for a single copy, $15 for a year's subscription.

Still another option might be working your way overseas. But, according to the National Maritime Union, "Unless they have very special skills or seniority, nobody can pick up a job on a U.S. ship to earn money during a summer vacation. There are no opportunities for working your way just for transportation on an American flag ship. 'Workaways,' as they are called, are prohibited by union policy and company rules." But a job on a cruise ship may be a possibility. A recently updated book, *Guide to Cruise Ship Jobs* (1989) by George Reilly, describes the different departments on a ship, positions within each department, qualifications needed, and the best way to apply. Copies are $3.95, plus $1 for postage, and are available from the publisher, Pilot Books, 103 Cooper Street, Babylon, NY 11702.

TRAVELING AROUND

Getting the Most Out of Your Trip

Since you're already well into the fifth chapter of this book, you're obviously not like the character in Ann Tyler's *The Accidental Tourist* who, when forced to travel, wanted to know things such as "What restaurants in Tokyo offered Sweet 'n' Low? Did Amsterdam have a McDonald's? Did Mexico City have a Taco Bell? Did any place in Rome serve Chef Boyardee ravioli?" Forget the Holiday Inn slogan, "No surprises"; much of the excitement of an overseas trip is due precisely to the fact that it's different and full of surprises. In fact, if there's any advice we feel it is vital we pass along, it's "keep an open mind" and "expect the unexpected." Trite though these phrases may be, everyone coming back from a good experience abroad gives this advice in one way or another.

> *"For any traveler abroad, an open mind is a necessity. This helps to avoid culture shock and any prejudgmental feelings that may prohibit understanding and enjoyment of the new culture."*
> —Marcie A. Alexander, Barrington, Illinois

> *"Be open and be flexible. Try to meet as many people as you can and try your best to speak the language, because that's the only way to learn it."*
> —Chris Ann D'Alessandro, Dallas, Texas

If you're going to a Third World country, you have to be especially ready to adjust to new ways of doing things. Relax and don't worry if train and bus schedules seem to have little to do with reality. Try to see beyond the poverty you'll encounter to understand and appreciate other aspects of the culture. You may well in fact discover that you "wouldn't want to live there." But, then, no one is asking you to. Instead, enjoy your stay in the country for the positive things it does have to offer.

> *"Forget the lack of progress and respect the traditions instead. Let go of being an American and sit back and watch the people operate in their own world. It's easier to be an observer than a critic."*
> —Heidi Kolk, Fulton, Illinois

Deciding How You Want to Get Around

Because there are so many options for traveling around once you've arrived at your destination, you'll have to make some choices. Do you want to travel by yourself or with a tour group? Do you want to see as much as possible or stay in one place and really get to know it? How do you want to travel—by foot, bus, train, car, boat, or bike?

One of the questions you should ask yourself is if you would feel safer, less isolated, and more at home with a group. Certainly, there is safety in numbers, and a tour means you'll always have somebody to talk to—traveling can be lonely sometimes. And if you take an organized tour, you won't have to worry about planning the logistics of your trip and arranging transportation, accommodations, and meals. But there are disadvantages to traveling in a group, too. A lot of the adventure is planned out of your trip, and since you have to go along with the group, your individual needs may not always be served. And if you really want to meet the people of the country and learn another language, the worst thing you can do is travel with other Americans. Remember, too, that most organized tours are usually more expensive than traveling on your own; tours always have an administrative fee built into them.

In the following sections, we'll discuss some of the options you have as to modes of travel. More specific information on getting around can be found in the following chapters on particular regions.

- **By Train:** In many countries, travel by train is the least expensive, safest, and most convenient way to get around. On a train you can eat, sleep, see the countryside, and meet interesting people. And the train leaves you in the center of the city without having to worry about traffic or parking. Train systems are well developed in the countries of Western and Eastern Europe, as well as in Japan, Australia, and some Third World countries such as Argentina, Thailand, China, and India. Even in nations without extensive rail networks, the train—usually slower and cheaper than the bus—can be one of the most comfortable and interesting ways to get around.

    Most countries with extensive rail systems offer foreigners special rail passes that are good for unlimited travel over a certain period of time. You'll find further information on these in the specific country and region sections of this book. An additional source of information is the *Eurail Guide*, which, in spite of its name, actually covers train travel in 141 countries around the world. The 912-page 20th edition is available for $14.95 in bookstores. To order by mail, send $17 to Eurail Guide Annual, 27540 Pacific Coast Highway, Malibu, CA 90265. Aficionados of train travel will also enjoy reading Paul Theroux's *The Patagonian Express* and *The Great Railway Bazaar*.
- **By Bus:** Buses are the world's most common form of public transportation.

While intercity bus service in Europe is relatively limited, in the Third World buses are often the only means of public transportation. Buses go everywhere—and relatively cheaply—although the level of comfort varies greatly depending on the bus line, the condition of the road, and the number of passengers. Bus passes that provide unlimited mileage over a national system are available in a few countries and regions; you'll find more information about these in appropriate sections of the remaining chapters of this book.

- **By Car:** The independence and flexibility that a car offers when you're traveling cannot be matched. On the other hand, being in your own car will not put you into contact with local people the way public transportation will. And a car that is useful in getting to out-of-the-way places can become a major headache in a traffic-choked city where you don't know your way around.

  You can use your own car to get to and around Canada and Mexico, but traveling by car in most foreign countries means renting one. Fortunately, car rentals are available all over the world. In fact, companies such as Hertz and Avis are now worldwide, and you can get car-rental information just about anywhere by calling their toll-free numbers. Usually, however, local agencies will offer cheaper rates. Finally, Council Travel offers economical car-rental plans in both Europe and the South Pacific.

  Most English-speaking countries allow American citizens 18 years of age and over to drive with a valid U.S. driver's license. Your ordinary U.S. license is also all you need in a number of other countries where American tourists are common, including Belgium, France, Israel, Mexico, the Netherlands, Switzerland, the Scandinavian countries, and most of the Caribbean. However, an International Driving Permit is either required or strongly recommended for driving in most other countries. This document provides an official translation of the information on your regular license, which you must also carry with you. The permit, established by a 1949 United Nations treaty, must be obtained in the country where your regular license is issued. In the United States, the International Driving Permit can be obtained at a local office of the American Automobile Association (AAA), where you'll have to complete an application form and provide two passport-size photos and a fee of $5. If you apply in person, a permit will be issued while you wait; it will take at least a week if you apply through the mail. The International Driving Permit is valid for one year, unless your regular license expires earlier.

- **By Boat:** A wide range of options awaits those who want to travel by water. A barge gliding through the canals of France, a hydrofoil speeding to a Mediterranean island from the mainland, a luxury cruise boat on the Nile, a hovercraft skimming across the English Channel, or a steamer making the 2,000-mile journey down the Amazon—these are just a few of the possibilities. Because it is relatively slow, boat service usually focuses on routes where road and rail transportation is not possible. Unlimited passes similar to those available for rail transportation are not available, but youth or student fares can sometimes be obtained upon presentation of the International Student Identity Card or International Youth Card.

- **By Bicycle:** Bicycling lets you escape the confinement of the motor vehicle's steel shell when you travel, allowing you to enjoy the countryside and its people at a more leisurely pace. Taking your own bicycle on the plane usually is no problem and can be done at little or no extra charge; or you can rent or buy a bicycle abroad.

There are two ways to go if you decide to see a foreign country by bike: on your own or with an organized bicycle tour. On a tour, a group of 20 or so participants and two to three leaders bike a prescribed route, followed by a van carrying luggage and anyone who wants to rest. Sometimes the use of a bicycle is included in the price of the tour. Check the listings of travel programs in the remaining chapters of this book for the bicycle tours abroad offered by American Youth Hostels and Council Travel. Other organizations that offer bicycling programs abroad include Backroads Bicycle Touring (P.O. Box 1626, San Leandro, CA 94577); Breaking Away Bicycle Tours (1142 Manhattan Avenue, Suite 253, Manhattan Beach, CA 90266); Butterfield and Robinson (70 Bond Street, Toronto, Ontario M5B 1X3); Europeds (883 Sinex Avenue, Pacific Grove, CA 93950); the International Bicycle Fund—Bicycle Africa (4247 135th Place SE, Bellevue, WA 98006); and Wilderness Travel (801 Allston Way, Berkeley, CA 94710).

Youth Hostels

At youth hostels all over the world you can spend the night for approximately $8. The hostels in Europe, as in other parts of the world, are designed primarily for use by backpackers and bikers. Accommodations are dormitory style: you are provided with a bed-mattress and blankets. Sleeping sacks are usually required, although some of the larger hostels rent sheets. Different regulations exist for youth hostels in each country, and although they vary, there are certain similarities from country to country. Hostelers usually are expected to share in the cleanup, to abstain from drinking and/or using drugs in the hostel (and smoking in some areas), to stay no more than three days, and to be in the hostel by 10:00 P.M.

In order to stay at hostels around the world you must have a membership card issued by American Youth Hostels (AYH), the U.S. member of the International Youth Hostel Federation. The cost of the AYH membership varies according to age: $10 if you are under 18; $25 if you are over 18 but under 55; and $15 for persons 55 or over. AYH also offers a family membership for $35, which includes all children under the age of 18. Cards are valid for twelve months from the date of purchase. You'll find a listing of hostels by country and information on hostel rules in the annual *International Youth Hostel Handbook*, which is available from AYH in two volumes: Volume I covers Europe and the Mediterranean; Volume II covers Asia, Australia, Africa, and the Americas ($8.95 each, plus $2.00 postage per book). For the AYH membership card, the handbooks, and general information on hosteling, write to American Youth Hostels, P.O. Box 37613, Washington, DC 20013–7613.

Cutting Costs

Perhaps the question we hear most often is "How much will it cost?" Throughout the book to this point, we've tried to give you information on low-cost travel options; in this section you'll find additional tips for people who want to keep the cost of traveling as low as possible. In general, we recommend that you be frugal—but not at the expense of skipping the things you should do to make your trip enjoyable. Also, try to avoid the mistake of overspending during the first few days of your trip, which is easier than you'd think due to the unfamiliar surroundings and the feeling that your foreign currency is "play money."

Whatever your travel plans are, arm yourself with a good guidebook for low-cost travel. Among the best travel guidebooks for students and other travelers on a budget are the *Let's Go* guides (Cambridge, MA: Harvard Student Agencies), the *Real Guides* (New York: Prentice Hall Travel Books), and the *Travel Survival Kits* (Oakland, CA: Lonely Planet Publications). You'll find all three series in good bookstores. In addition, we've made some specific recommendations on guidebooks in the sections on individual regions and countries that follow this chapter.

If you're traveling with a friend, you can save money in hotels and pensiones, where two in a room can mean considerable savings. Purchasing food for two in the local markets is another money-saving technique. Should trains be your chosen mode of travel, a Eurail or comparable train pass is security in itself. You won't need to worry about money for train tickets, and many young travelers short on cash for lodging have found themselves jumping on a midnight train to another city. Finally, be sure to take advantage of the many youth and student discounts that may be available (see page 8 for information about the International Student Identity Card).

We strongly suggest you set aside an emergency money supply—a stash not to be used under any circumstances unless you absolutely have to. Hide it in a place that is safe and dry, as well as a secret from fellow travelers. Also keep with it a list of emergency addresses, phone numbers, and personal medical information in case of an accident.

If you are going to join a program, you will have a pretty good idea of what the whole trip will cost ahead of time and will probably pay for most of it before you leave. Costs vary from program to program. Before you leave on a prearranged program, be sure you understand just what you are expected to pay for and what is going to be paid for you.

Organized Tours

If you're convinced that an organized tour is the way to go, prepare for it by having realistic expectations. There are many different types of tours, from a standard three-week tour of the European capitals to a 23-day grasslands horseback trip in Inner Mongolia. Some are sponsored by nonprofit organizations or universities, others by private agencies and tour operators. Many are designed to give participants the opportunity to see major cultural attractions through a sightseeing program led by a guide. Others are organized around a particular interest shared by members of the group, such as kayaking, wine tasting, or art appreciation. Check the travel programs offered by CIEE member institutions and organizations listed in the chapters that follow. You will also find a wide selection of tours listed in the travel sections of newspapers and travel magazines.

Whatever your choice, be sure it's run by a reliable operator or an institution with proven experience. If possible you should talk to a previous participant. Licensed tour operators should belong to a professional organization with clearly defined operating standards. If you want to avoid the risk of losing your entire vacation budget, try to check them out before putting your money down.

Among the tours worth checking into are those offered by the members of the International Student Travel Confederation (ISTC), a coalition of student travel bureaus located in more than 55 countries. These student travel bureaus organize a number of interesting tours in their individual countries geared especially to students and youths. Here are some examples of those offered recently:

- Hot-air ballooning over Ayers Rock (Australia)
- Hong Kong harbor tour by Chinese junk
- Eight-day bicycle tour of the Netherlands
- One-day cruise to islands off Costa Rica's Pacific coast with fishing and snorkeling opportunities
- Diving to explore the undersea world of the Gulf of Aqaba (Israel)
- Sightseeing tour of Budapest (Hungary)

Holders of the International Student Identity Card receive a discount on tours offered by ISTC members. You'll find the addresses for these student travel bureaus listed in the appropriate country sections. CIEE, the U.S. member of the ISTC, organizes tours to the U.S.S.R., China, and Thailand through its travel subsidiary, Council Travel (see the tour descriptions in the appropriate country sections).

Meeting the People

If you want to spend a short time with a family while you travel, there are organizations in many countries—often government tourist offices—that will arrange an afternoon or evening visit for you. These organizations are listed throughout this book by country or geographic area.

One possibility is SERVAS, an organization that sponsors a worldwide program of person-to-person contacts for travelers in 90 countries, with the ultimate aim of helping to build world peace, goodwill, and understanding. Here's how SERVAS works: You apply and are interviewed; if accepted, you receive a personal briefing, written instructions, a list of SERVAS families in the area you are going to visit, and an introductory letter. Using this introductory letter, you can arrange by letter to stay with families who are listed. The average stay with SERVAS hosts is two nights. One CIEE staff member took advantage of SERVAS's program and came back from Italy and France raving about the wonderful families he had met and excited about the possibility of returning this kind of hospitality to others visiting the United States. For more information write to the U.S. SERVAS Committee, 11 John Street, Room 706, New York, NY 10038. If you use its services, SERVAS asks for a donation of $45 and a refundable deposit for the loan of its list.

Another program with a "meet the people" philosophy behind it is the Friendship Force, a private nonprofit organization that arranges exchange visits between the U.S. and other countries. It works like this: A group of people from an American city flies to a city in another country, where they stay in private homes for one to two weeks. At a later date, a contingent of people from the community visited travels to the U.S. for a similar experience. For information, write to the Friendship Force, 575 South Tower, One CNN Center, Atlanta, GA 30303.

If you'd like a complete listing, with appropriate addresses, of meet-the-people programs in 34 countries, you can order the *International Meet-the-People Directory* ($4.95), compiled by the International Visitors Information Service, 733 15th Street NW, Suite 300, Washington, DC 20005.

Resources for the Traveler

If you're looking for a larger selection of travel books than what's available in your local bookstore, there are a number of travel bookstores that publish mail-order catalogs. Among those that will send a free catalog are: Hippocrene Books (171 Madison Avenue, New York, NY 10016); Forsyth Travel Library (P.O. Box 2975, 9154 West 57th Street, Shawnee Mission, KS 66201); Bradt Enterprises (95 Harvey Street, Cambridge, MA 02140); Wide World Bookshop (401 NE 45th Street, Seattle, WA 98105); and the Traveller's Bookstore (22 West 52nd Street, New York, NY 11019).

Later in this book, you'll find guidebooks and other materials relating to specific countries or areas of the world. For now, however, here are a few books that encompass the four corners of the globe:

- *1989 Adventure Holidays*, by David Stevens, covers all sorts of adventure travel, from scuba diving in the Red Sea, to mountain climbing in Wales, to camel caravaning in the Sahara. It's available in the U.S. for $9.95 from Writer's Digest Books, 1507 Dana Avenue, Cincinnati, OH 45207.
- The *Directory of Low-Cost Vacations with a Difference* was put together by a former chairman of the board of SERVAS (see page 52). A healthy portion of its brief organizational descriptions pertains to homestays; other listings include bed-and-breakfasts, vacation work programs, and home exchanges. It is available for $4.95 from Pilot Books, 103 Cooper Street, Babylon, NY 11702.
- The *International Educational Travel Planner* is a directory of travel programs for students and adults offered around the world by Canadian universities, colleges, and community colleges. Most programs listed are noncredit educational tours that last one to three weeks. Also included in the magazine-style publication are articles about unusual travel experiences. Published each February, it's available for $2.00 from Student Services, Box 10,000, Athabasca University, Athabasca, Alberta T0G 2R0.

There are a growing number of magazines catering to the travelers of the world. One worth investigating—although it may not be on your local newsstand—is *Great Expeditions*, which features firsthand information from travelers, free classified ads, and an information exchange. Some of the recent articles featured in the magazine have included "Biking Baja California," "Fly Cheap as an Onboard Courier," and "Streetsmarts for South America." Six issues cost $18, or you can request a free sample copy from Great Expeditions, Box 8000–411, Sumas, WA 98295–8000. Another good magazine for people looking for an active, outdoor vacation is *Adventure Travel*. Filled with useful information and interesting photos, a recent issue included articles about kayaking in the Queen Charlotte Islands, backpacking in Norway, bicycling in Australia, and a 100-mile walk in England. A one-year subscription (four issues) is $13.97 ($15.97 outside the U.S.); write to Diamandis Communications, 1515 Broadway, New York, NY 10036.

Frommer's Dollarwise Travel Club, headquartered in New York and run by the Prentice Hall Travel division of Simon and Schuster, currently numbers more than 15,000 members, most of whom are interested in traveling as cheaply as possible. Membership costs $18 (U.S.) or $20 (outside the U.S.) per year and includes several free Arthur Frommer guidebooks, substantial discounts on all other books, and a subscription to the club's newsletter, *The Dollarwise Traveler*. Published quarterly, *The Dollarwise Traveler* features requests for traveling companions, announcements of special discounts for members, and news and information for budget travelers. Write to Frommer's Dollarwise Travel Club, Prentice Hall Travel, 15 Columbus Circle, New York, NY 10023.

ATLANTIC OCEAN
NORWAY
SWEDEN
FINLAND
UNITED KINGDOM
IRELAND
DENMARK
NETHERLANDS
BALTIC SEA
BELGIUM
LUXEMBOURG
WEST GERMANY
FRANCE
LIECHTENSTEIN
AUSTRIA
SWITZERLAND
PORTUGAL
ANDORRA
ITALY
SPAIN
MEDITERRANEAN SEA
GREECE
MALTA

CHAPTER SIX
WESTERN EUROPE

Most of you reading this book will be going to Europe. It may be your primary destination, or it may be a stop along the way to Africa or Asia. The first part of this chapter covers transportation to Western Europe and getting around via the many forms of transport available in the region once you're there. Later in the chapter, you'll find work, study, and travel opportunities covered for each individual country of Western Europe. Also included are brief descriptions of the programs sponsored by the member institutions and organizations of the Council on International Educational Exchange. For some countries we've also included some suggested literary works to read and films to see before going abroad.

GETTING THERE

In the previous chapter, we gave you basic information on international travel, including traveling by charter, by regularly scheduled airline, by ship, or as an international air courier. If you want to know what your options for international travel to Europe are—as well as the advantages and disadvantages of each—be sure to read Chapter 5. One thing we will repeat here is that most prices quoted throughout the book are for comparison purposes only, owing to the constantly changing nature of air fares. Fares quoted here were those available in mid-1989. For more up-to-date information, write for a free copy of Council Travel's regularly updated "Airfare Update" fact sheet; you can get these at a Council Travel office, or by completing the form in the *Student Travel Catalog*, which will result in them being mailed to you as soon as they become available.

When making travel plans, you'll need to decide not only what city you want to fly to but also when you want to go. There are usually "high" and "low" seasons in effect that determine air-fare structures to most travel destinations. Transatlantic flights, for example, are most expensive during the period between June 1 and August 31 (sometimes September 15, depending on the airline). If you want to go during the summer, you'll find that planning at least one leg of the trip at an off-peak time may save you money; on the other hand, many airlines base the round-trip fare on the departure date regardless of the return date. Whatever dates you choose, however, plan early: at least seven or eight weeks ahead of your departure if you want to get the lowest fares available.

> "When I took everything into consideration—weather, crowds, cultural events—I decided that Paris in September would be much more desirable than it would be in August (when the Parisians themselves are on vacation and shops are closed). By flying there in the off-season, I saved money and gained some other travel benefits."

Charter Flights

Charters continue to be one of the best bargains in air travel to Europe. In 1989, CIEE's subsidiary, Council Charter, operated charter flights to Amsterdam, Brussels, Geneva, London, Madrid, Malaga, Nice, Paris, Rome, and Zurich. In addition, any Council Travel office (see listing on pages ix–xi) can help you make connections from a starting point in the U.S. to the charter's city of departure. Sample charter fares for the 1989 peak travel season were:

From New York
Amsterdam $538 round-trip
Brussels $558 round-trip
Geneva $538 round-trip
London $538 round-trip
Madrid $578 round-trip
Malaga $598 round-trip
Nice $598 round-trip
Paris $538 round-trip
Rome $618 round-trip
Zurich $538 round-trip

From Chicago
Brussels $598 round-trip

From Boston
Brussels $558 round-trip
Paris $558 round-trip

Student/Youth Fares

Another inexpensive way to get to Europe for students and young people who qualify are student or youth fares on regularly scheduled airlines. Although regulations vary depending on the airline, generally speaking, you must be under the age of 26 or, if a student, under the age of 31. You must also have either an International Student Identity Card (see page 8) or an International Youth ID Card (see page 9). Any Council Travel office can arrange student and youth tickets. Examples of *one-way* youth and student fares for 1989 were:

	Off-Peak Season	Peak Season
New York–London	$189	$245
New York–Paris	$219	$259
Boston–Brussels	$199	$270
Chicago–Amsterdam	$235	$309
Dallas–Frankfurt	$325	$399
Seattle–London	$295	$345

Other Discount Fares

If you watch the Sunday travel section of your newspaper, you're likely to find real bargains in the off-season. Budget-minded travelers going to Europe should also keep in mind Icelandair and Virgin Atlantic, two smaller airlines known for their affordable transatlantic fares. Remember, too, that by making arrangements in advance you can make use of APEX or Super APEX fares, both of which require advance purchase and a stay of at least seven days but less than a year. For more information, see Chapter 5.

By Ship

There was a time when students traveled back and forth across the Atlantic on student ships. Between 1947 and 1969, more than 150,000 students made the trip on liners chartered by the Council specifically for student travel. Today, travel by air is both cheaper and faster. To give you an idea of what a transatlantic voyage might cost you, passage on Cunard's *Queen Elizabeth II* in the summer of 1989 (with a return within 20 days) began at $1,895, including a British Airways ticket from London back to the United States. If you chose to return by sea, the lowest excursion fare in 1989 was $1,420 (fares do not include port taxes of approximately $90 per person). If you would like more information, write to Cunard Line, 555 Fifth Avenue, New York, NY 10017, or contact a Council Travel office.

TRAVELING AROUND WESTERN EUROPE

If you're a student or youth under the age of 26 and you have an ISIC or an International Youth Card, you can benefit from a number of travel discounts offered by student travel bureaus in each country. Refer to Chapter 2 for basic information on who is eligible and how to apply for the cards.

By Air

There are student flights and special student/youth fares on scheduled flights connecting a number of major cities within Western Europe. In many cases, savings can be more than 50 percent off the regular economy fares on the same routes. As with transatlantic student discounts, regulations vary depending on the airline, but generally speaking you must be a student under the age of 31 or a young person under the age of 26 and have either an International Student Identity Card (see page 8) or an International Youth Card (see page 9). Student/youth fares on most of these flights can be booked at a Council Travel office. Sample student/youth fares within Europe that were available in 1989 are listed below:

Route	One-Way Fare
London–Paris	$ 55
London–Athens	$129
Paris–Rome	$ 75
Amsterdam–Nice	$ 70
Rome–Athens	$240

By Train

Train travel in Europe is an unforgettable experience and an unexpected pleasure for Americans, who will have the chance to experience a way of travel quite different from that available in the United States. In Europe, you'll find an international group of fellow travelers on the trains, many of them eager to talk and share their own experiences. Add to that the unsurpassed vistas of country and seaside—like the Mediterranean's waves breaking along the shore on the ride from Rome to Nice—and you get an idea of what's in store for you.

> "The people on trains and in the station were very friendly. Conversations on trains really helped to build my language confidence. Many a language lesson and lunch were shared in second-class compartments."

> "I tried to schedule a lot of long, overnight trips so that I could sleep on the train. This saved wasting travel time during the day, which I needed for sightseeing, and avoided the confusion of arriving in a strange city too late to find a hostel, hotel, or tourist office. It also saved the cost of accommodation for one night. That's why the extra expense of the first-class Eurail versus the Youthpass was worth it to me, especially since the first-class compartments were usually empty and I could sleep in peace. However, sleeping more than two or three nights in a row on the train is very exhausting."

A number of special discount rail-pass options are available that provide unlimited train travel over a specified time period. It's a good idea, however, to compare the cost of any one discount plan to the combined individual ticket prices for your journey before laying out the money for a rail pass. You can do this by consulting the *Eurailtariff Manual* at any travel agency. The general rule of thumb is that you'll save money by buying a Eurailpass if your plans call for visiting more than three countries or covering more than 1,500 miles. In addition, many European countries offer their own national rail passes for travel within that country; you'll find information on this type of pass in the individual country sections later in this chapter. All of the Eurail passes mentioned below must be purchased in the U.S., either at the U.S. offices of the various national railroads, from any Council Travel office, or from your local travel agency.

- **Eurail Youthpass.** If you are under 26, you can purchase the Eurail Youthpass, which entitles you to unlimited *second-class* travel in 17 countries: Austria, Belgium, Denmark, Finland, France, Germany, Greece, Holland, Hungary, Ireland, Italy, Luxembourg, Norway, Portugal, Spain, Sweden, and Switzerland. In 1989, a two-month pass cost $470; a one-month pass cost $360. The Eurail Youthpass is also valid on many lake and river steamers, ferry boats, and buses. There are supplementary fees for seat reservations and special express trains.
- **Eurailpass.** The Eurailpass, which has no age requirement, entitles you to unlimited *first-class* travel in 17 countries—the same ones listed directly above for the Eurail Youthpass. Since some trains get very crowded on certain routes, especially during vacations and summer, comfort-conscious students might want to consider buying the first-class Eurailpass. In 1989, a pass valid for 15 days (beginning on the first day used) cost $320; for 21 days, $398; for one month, $498; for two months, $698; and for three months, $860. A sleeping compartment and meals are not included in the price, but you won't have to pay extra to travel on the European luxury trains. Like the Youthpass, travel on many lake and river steamers, ferry boats, and buses is also included in the price. Details are provided in the Eurail pamphlet you receive at the time of purchase.

- **Eurail Saverpass.** If you plan to travel with companions, the Eurail Saverpass was good for 15 days of unlimited first-class travel for $230 per person in 1989. Three people must travel together and share the same itinerary to be eligible for the pass during the peak travel season; between October 1 and March 31, only two people are required to be eligible for the pass.
- **Eurail Flexipass.** Designed for those who want a more leisurely itinerary, the Flexipass allows unlimited first-class travel for nine non-consecutive days over a 21-day period. The cost in 1989 was $340. Besides the price advantage, rail passes allow for a great deal of flexibility. You could easily decide to leave for Zurich or Stockholm at a moment's notice, for example, without worrying about the cost or hassling with buying a ticket. And there's always the added security of knowing that if you're in another city when your money runs out, you can still get back to the airport to catch your return flight home.

On the other hand, for those planning a less extensive trip, buying individual tickets—rather than a rail pass—may be cheaper. A number of travel agencies in Europe offer the under-26 population what are commonly known as "BIJ" tickets (*Billets Internationals de Jeunesse*). Two of the better-known agencies that sell them are Eurotrain and Transalpino.

- **Eurotrain.** If you're under 26, you may be able to save up to 50 percent off second-class rail fares on routes connecting nearly 500 cities throughout Europe. Information and bookings are available from student travel bureaus in Europe.
- **Transalpino.** Transalpino is a commercial agency that also offers discount point-to-point tickets for young people under the age of 26. There are branches and agents in many major European cities. For information check with the student travel bureaus abroad.

If you are going to be living in Europe for a while before traveling, you may be eligible for the **Inter-Rail Pass**. This pass allows *European* youth a one-month rail plan similar to the Eurail Youthpass offered to non-Europeans. To qualify, you must be able to prove at least six months' residency in Europe and be under 26 years of age; authorities enforce eligibility rules strictly. Inter-Rail Pass holders will receive a 50-percent discount on train fares in the country of purchase and unlimited free travel in all other countries subscribing to the plan. The pass is available at many European train stations as well as at student travel bureaus in Europe.

There are a number of good guidebooks geared especially to train travel in Western Europe. The *Eurail Guide*, by Kathryn Turpin and Marvin Saltzman, highlights 730 one-day excursions from 157 European base cities and includes information on schedules for intercity train travel (see page 49 for ordering information). Another good book on the Eurailpass and how to use it is *Baxter's Eurailpass Travel Guide*, by Robert Baxter, available from Rail-Europe, P.O. Box 3255, Alexandria, VA 22302 for $9.95. *How to Camp Europe by Train*, (1988–89 edition), by Lenore Baken, describes how to combine train travel with stays in any of the thousands of campgrounds throughout Europe. The book is available for $12.95 (plus $2.00 postage) from Ariel Publications, 14417 SE 19th Place, Bellevue, WA 98007. *Europe by Train*, by Katie Wood and George McDonald, covers budget train travel in Europe and includes helpful information on transportation to and from rail stations. Published by Harper and Row, the 1988 edition is available in bookstores for $12.95.

By Bus

Bus travel is not as popular as train travel in Europe primarily because the various national rail systems are so good. As a result, buses are usually used for tour groups rather than intercity transportation. They are fairly cheap, however, and there is one bus plan that will save you money if you have a Eurailpass or Eurail Youthpass. It's administered by Europabus, the motor-coach division of the European railroads, which has 70,000 miles of scheduled lines throughout Europe. Holders of the Eurailpass and Eurail Youthpass are entitled to substantial reductions on most European lines. For information and reservations, contact a travel agent or the ticket offices of the European railroads. You can also check with student travel bureaus (see addresses for ISTC members in the individual country sections later in this chapter).

By Ship

Boats still provide a vital transportation link in Europe. You'll find boats of all types connecting Britain to the Continent as well as to Ireland. In Scandinavia, a number of ferry routes link the various countries to each other and to Britain, Germany, Poland, and the U.S.S.R. But it is probably in the Mediterranean region that travel by boat is most popular. Ferries connect the mainland to numerous islands including Sicily, Sardinia, Corsica, and Crete and provide an economical way to get from Europe to North Africa or Israel. Especially popular with tourists are the boats to the resort isles of the Mediterranean such as Mallorca, Ibiza, Capri, Mykonos, and Corfu. But remember that summertime means crowds, so get your tickets as far ahead as possible.

Several national student travel bureaus offer special student rates on Channel, Baltic, and Mediterranean sailings. For example, an International Student Identity Card entitles you to a discount on ferries between Finland and Sweden, Norway and Denmark, Italy and Greece, and Britain and various countries on the Continent. Information and bookings can be made at any of the student travel bureaus in Europe. Your Eurailpass also entitles you to discounts on many boats and ferries.

By Car

There are numerous options for purchasing, leasing, and renting cars in Europe. If you plan to travel with friends and cover a lot of territory, renting a car may actually be cheaper than travel by train or bus. But remember that gasoline prices are much higher in Europe than in the United States—usually around $3 a gallon. Western European roads are generally in good condition and the network of superhighways is extensive, especially in Germany, where the idea originated.

Car-rental arrangements should be made well before you leave the U.S., since cars (as well as campers, vans, and trailers) are scarce during the peak summer season. In fact, reserving a car before you leave for Europe will often make you eligible for a cheaper rate. Arrangements can be made through most travel agencies or through an international car rental company such as Hertz or Avis. Council Travel offices can arrange leases and rentals from a variety of companies (such as Renault and Kemwel) that offer cars with unlimited mileage at budget rates as low as $30 a day. If you plan to drive around Europe for two or three months, it will actually cost you less to lease a car or to purchase one from a company that will guarantee to repurchase it at the end of your trip. Council Travel's Renault Plan can give you these options.

Be sure to check with individual companies on minimum-age requirements; most rental companies require that drivers be at least 21 (and in some cases 24) years of age. However, Auto Europe (P.O Box 1097, Camden, ME 04843) only requires a minimum age of 18; call (800) 223-5555.

You may need an International Driving Permit (see page 49) in order to drive in Europe. Even if the permit is not required, it's helpful to have it when traveling in a non–English-speaking country where your regular license might not always be understood.

When making car-rental arrangements, be sure to check whether insurance coverage is included in the cost. Most companies take care of this for you; they'll also provide you with the International Insurance Certificate, or "green card," which is required for all European countries. If you buy or lease a car, you can obtain insurance coverage and the green card through the dealer.

By Bicycle

In most European countries the bicycle remains a means of transportation that's embraced by people of all ages, and for good reason. Traveling by bicycle allows you to slow down and enjoy the pleasures of the countryside. It's especially popular where the terrain is relatively flat, such as Holland, Denmark, and France's Loire Valley.

Fortunately, most international carriers allow bicycles on transatlantic flights. You do have to take the pedals off, turn the handlebars sideways, and put it into a special bag, however; the cost varies with the destination and the carrier—check with the airline. If you want to avoid the hassle, you can always buy or rent top-quality bicycles in Europe. For information, check with the local tourist office at your destination. In fact, in most European countries, many rail stations offer bike rentals to travelers; inquire at major train stations once you arrive. For those who prefer an organized, escorted bicycle tour, there are brief descriptions of the various bicycle tours offered by American Youth Hostels under "Organized Tours" later in this chapter.

If you're considering extensive bicycling in Western Europe, the following books might be helpful. *Europe by Bike: 18 Tours Geared for Discovery*, written by Karen and Terry Whitehill during a year of saddle sores and 11,000 miles of bicycling, provides details on tours ranging from 100 to 806 miles in length. The book is available from The Mountaineers Books, 306 2nd Avenue West, Seattle, WA 98119 for $10.95 plus $2.00 for postage and handling. *Biking Through Europe*, available in bookstores for $13.95 (Williamson Publishing, 1987), describes 17 bicycle tours taken by the authors, Dennis and Tina Jaffe.

> *"Biking through Amsterdam at 5:00 A.M., after a great night at the discotheque, engulfed in a deserted sea of mist and labyrinth of canals, proved to be one of my most memorable experiences in this great city!"*

Hiking

For those who want to escape the cities, railways, and highways to enjoy the peaceful beauty of the countryside, mountain trails and cross-country paths can be found throughout Western Europe. In the Swiss Alps, for example, you'll find, in addition to well-maintained scenic mountain trails, a network of comfortable trailside chalets that accept phone reservations in advance. (Information on mountain trails and cross-country hikes is available from tourist organizations and mountaineering clubs across Europe.) For further information on the myriad hiking opportunities, you might pick up a copy of *Tramping in Europe: A Walking Guide* (Prentice Hall, 1984), by J. Sydney Jones, or check the sections on individual countries later in this chapter. If you're interested in hiking with an organized group, you should look into the options offered by American Youth Hostels; brief descriptions of AYH's hiking itineraries in Iceland, Ireland, and the Alps are included under "Organized Tours" later in this chapter.

Hitchhiking

Hitchhiking, or "autostop," as it is frequently called on the Continent, is a popular way for European students to get around. Some people say it's risky and that they will never do it, while others argue that it's both the cheapest and the most interesting way of getting around. For anyone who is going to hitchhike in Europe, here are a few pointers:

- Look legitimate; dress in a way that will make drivers feel they can trust you.
- Find out what the local conditions for hitchhiking are—your best source is the people who are doing it.
- Carry a sign that states clearly the direction in which you are headed along with your destination.
- Women: Don't hitchhike alone. The best team is a man-woman one.
- Travel light—you should be able to jump in and out of a car quickly and not burden the driver with having to find room for your luggage.

A useful book if you're planning to hitchhike in Europe is *Europe: A Manual for Hitchhikers*, by Simon Calder, Colin Brown, and Roger Brown. In addition to tips for hitching around Europe, including how to get out of some of the largest cities, it also gives the addresses of agencies that arrange rides in advance for a fee. The book is available in the U.S. for $9.95, plus 50¢ postage and handling, from Bradt Enterprises, 95 Harvey Street, Cambridge, MA 02140.

> *"If you can be patient enough, try hitching on smaller roads, not motorways and autobahns. You'll meet people who don't see travelers as often. Pass through small towns where you can buy food from a grocery store or stop for a coffee or a beer. Always carry some food with you each day you are hitchhiking. You never know how long you might be waiting in the middle of nowhere."*

Organized Tours

On the other hand, if you prefer the security and companionship offered by an organized tour, there are a wealth of options for you in Western Europe. In fact, a number of CIEE's member institutions and organizations offer organized, escorted tours by bus, bike, or foot in Western Europe. These are listed below. Consult Appendix I for the addresses where you can write for further information.

MORE THAN ONE COUNTRY

American Youth Hostels.
- "Saddlebag Special." Thirty-eight-day cycling trip staying in hostels and visiting such cities as London, Stratford-on-Avon, the Loire Valley, Chartres, Paris, Bruges, and Amsterdam. Summer. Minimum age 15.
- "Heart of Europe." Forty-four-day cycling trip staying in hostels and hotels. Visits London, Paris, Berne, Salzburg, Munich, Amsterdam, and many other cities. Summer. Minimum age 15.
- "European Roundabout." Sixteen-day motor trip staying in hostels throughout Europe. Includes visits to Luxembourg, Amsterdam, Frankfurt, Heidelberg, Munich, Salzburg, Zurich, Dijon, and Paris. Summer. Minimum age 15.
- "European Spotlight." This five-week adventure visits the major cities of Europe by train and foot. Includes trips to London, Paris, Nice, Turin, Bern, Innsbruck, Munich, Amsterdam, and many other cities. Summer. Minimum age 15.
- "The Sound of Cycling." Twenty-two-day cycling tour staying in hostels in Switzerland, Germany, and Austria. Summer. Minimum age 15.
- "Mont Blanc." Sixteen-day hiking trip in region of Europe's highest peak, Mont Blanc, visiting France, Italy, and Switzerland. Summer. Minimum age 15.
- "Mediterranean Odyssey." Sixteen-day motor tour exploring the coasts of Italy, France, and Spain. Summer. Minimum age 15.

Ohio University. "Communications Capitals." New York, London, and Paris. Three-week study tour offered in winter. Focus on news media. College freshmen to graduate students. Apply by October 15. Contact School of Journalism; (614) 593-2590.

Western Michigan University. "The Grand Tour." Art and architecture of Europe's cities. Holland, France, Switzerland, Italy, Austria, and Germany. One-month summer tour offered only in even-numbered years. Freshmen to graduate students, and adults; minimum age 18. Apply by April 1.

BELGIUM

American Youth Hostels. "Flemish Fling." Sixteen-day cycling tour staying in hostels and visiting Brussels, Ghent, Bruges, Antwerp, and parts of Luxembourg and the Netherlands. Summer. Minimum age 15.

FRANCE

American Youth Hostels. "Chateau Country." Sixteen-day bicycling tour staying in hostels and visiting Paris and sites in the Loire valley. Summer. Minimum age 15.

New York University. "International Travel Programs." Short-term, usually two-week tours. Students and adults. Apply two months prior to departure.

Contact: NYU School of Continuing Education, International Programs, 331 Shimkin, Washington Square, New York, NY 10003; (212) 998-7133.

GREECE

Ohio University. "Exploring Greece." Athens, Livadia, Delphi, Sparta. Four-week summer tour. Students, faculty, and adults. Apply by March 30. Minimum age 15. Contact Office of Continuing Education; (614) 593-1776.

ICELAND

American Youth Hostels. "Fire and Ice." Sixteen-day hiking trip staying in hostels throughout Iceland. Summer. Minimum age 15.

IRELAND

American Youth Hostels. "Shamrock Shuffle." Sixteen-day hiking trip staying in hostels. Summer. Minimum age 15.

ITALY

American Youth Hostels. "Rooms with Views." Thirty-day cycling trip through the Alps staying in hotels and hostels. Visits Milan, Venice, Florence, Rome, and other Italian cities, as well as parts of Switzerland. Minimum age 15.

New York University. "International Travel Programs." Short-term, usually two-week tours. All students and adults. Apply two months prior to departure. Contact: NYU School of Continuing Education, International Programs, 331 Shimkin, Washington Square, New York, NY 10003; (212) 998-7133.

NORWAY

Ohio University. "Norway Tour." Oslo, Bergen, and other sites. Two-week summer tour. Students, faculty, and adults. Apply by March 15. Contact Office of Continuing Education; (614) 593-1776.

SPAIN

New York University. "International Travel Programs." Short-term, usually two-week tours. Students and adults. Apply two months prior to departure. Contact: NYU School of Continuing Education, International Programs, 331 Shimkin, Washington Square, New York, NY 10003; (212) 998-7133.

Portland State University. "Summer in Spain." Three-week tour with focus on art, architecture, and history. Various cities in central and southern Spain. Students and adults. Apply by May.

Western Michigan University. "WMU Spain Tour." Two-week summer tour. Students and adults. Apply by April 20.

SWITZERLAND

American Youth Hostels. "Alpine Hike." Sixteen-day hiking trip through the Swiss Alps staying in hostels and mountain huts. Summer. Minimum age 15.

UNITED KINGDOM

American Youth Hostels.
"English Standard." Sixteen-day cycling tour staying in hostels and visiting London and various sites in southern England. Summer. Minimum age 15.
"Great Britain Adventure." Sixteen-day motor tour staying in hostels in England, Scotland, and Wales. Summer. Minimum age 15.

Student Travel Bureaus

In nearly every country of Western Europe you'll find a student travel organization that is a member of the International Student Travel Confederation (ISTC). In the individual country sections that follow we've included the addresses of the headquarters of these organizations. In addition, most have a network of branches around the country, usually in university cities and towns. As ISTC members, these offices issue the International Student Identity Card and arrange discounted tickets for student travel. Many also provide information on travel and accommodations, arrange tours, conduct language courses, et cetera. If you're going to be spending some time traveling in a country, be sure to make use of the information, discounts, and services offered by that country's student travel bureau.

Finding a Place to Stay

You'll be able to find inexpensive accommodations in every country of Western Europe; many of these are listed in either the booklets put out by tourist offices or in the guidebooks mentioned later in this chapter. Besides the regular budget hotels, there's a network of student hostels and youth hostels (see page 50) in Europe. When you arrive in a city that has a student travel bureau, be sure to stop and get information on inexpensive accommodations. In most European cities of any size, you'll also find a general tourist office—usually in or near a railroad station, airport, or some other central location—that not only lists accommodations but will often call and book your stay for you.

"A good way of meeting people and finding a cheap place to stay is to head to the university of the city you are in. There is an international camaraderie among university students and young people out there that is well worth plugging into."

"Youth or student hostels are a good place to buy used camping equipment and get travel information—like what bus to take to get to a place outside of a city to begin hitchhiking."

Camping

There are campgrounds located all over Europe—on the outskirts of large cities, along major highways, and in resort areas at beaches, lakes, and mountains. Many are accessible by foot or public transport, although having a car is usually more convenient. Most are well equipped with hot and cold running water, stoves, electrical outlets, laundry facilities, and a small store. Each person using the campsite will have to pay a small fee per night, plus a nominal charge for a car or motorcycle. Fees range from about $1 to $10. A good guide to use when planning your camping trip is Dennis and Tina Jaffe's *The Camper's Companion to Northern Europe*, published by Williamson Publishing, Charlotte, VT 05445, and available in bookstores for $13.95.

If you are going to camp in Europe, you might want to get an International Camping Carnet, a membership card issued by the National Campers and Hikers Association, 4804 Transit Road, Building 2, Depew, NY 14043. In fact, a few European campgrounds require the card, but you can usually purchase it on the spot. In addition, at some campgrounds it can get you a small discount off the regular charge for a campsite, but unless you're planning to camp for an extended period of time, don't expect to save much money. The card costs $23, which includes membership in the National Campers and Hikers Association.

On the other hand, you don't necessarily need a campground to camp. Most Scandinavian countries permit you to camp for one night anywhere in the countryside except on fenced land. And in the other countries of Western Europe, camping for a night in the open countryside is generally acceptable as long as you're discreet and ask permission before setting up camp on a farmer's land. Not only will you save money, you'll also avoid the crowds found at most European campgrounds during July and August.

House Swapping

You might want to investigate the possibility of temporarily swapping your home in the U.S. with someone else's in another country. There are several organizations that specialize in arranging such swaps: Loan-A-Home, 2 Park Lane, 6E, Mount Vernon, NY 10552 (which specializes in housing for the academic year or semester); Vacation Exchange Club, 12006 111th Avenue, Youngtown, AZ 85363; InterService Home Exchange, Box 387, Glen Echo, MD 20812; and International Home Exchange Service, INTERVAC U.S., P.O. Box 3975, San Francisco, CA 94119. Most of these services charge for a listing and then circulate their directory among subscribers. Then, if anyone is interested in your home, they contact you directly.

Suggestions for Further Reading

Let's Go: Europe, updated each year by the Harvard Student Agencies (1990 edition, $13.95), is the best and most popular guidebook for students going to Europe. It includes information on getting around, the sights to see, and inexpensive places to stay and eat. Published by St. Martin's Press, it's available in bookstores and from Council Travel offices. Other guidebooks for the budget traveler widely available in bookstores are *Europe on $30 a Day*, by Arthur Frommer (1989 edition, $14.95), and *Fielding's Budget Europe*, by Joseph and Judith Raff (1990 edition, $10.95). Also available in bookstores is Fodor's *Budget Europe* (1989 edition, $12.95).

Europe Through the Back Door, by Rick Steves, is designed to prepare the first-time traveler for independent travel to Europe. Included are 34 "back doors," or interesting places to visit off the beaten tourist path. *Europe 101: History, Art and Culture for the Traveler*, by the same author, offers readers a thorough, if somewhat whimsical and anecdotal, education in Europe's rich artistic and cultural history. Both of these books are available in bookstores or can be ordered for $13 each from Europe Through the Back Door, 120 4th Avenue North, Edmonds, WA 98020.

For those specifically interested in the museums of Europe, try *Mona Winks: A Guide to Enjoying the Museums of Europe*, by Rick Steves and Gene Openshaw, which describes 25 European museums, with floor plans for self-guided tours and over 100 photographic reproductions. It's available from Europe Through the Back Door (address above) for $15. Travelers interested in art, architecture, and history might want to purchase the *Michelin Green Guides* or *Baedeker's Travel Guides*, which provide the most comprehensive information about the artistic and historical sights of Western Europe. Michelin and Baedeker guidebooks for individual Western European countries and cities are widely available in bookstores.

STUDYING IN WESTERN EUROPE

The options for study in Western Europe are virtually unlimited. In the individual country sections that follow, you'll find descriptions of academic programs offered by member institutions of the Council on International Educational Exchange. In this section, we've listed only those study programs that take place in more than one country of the region. Consult Appendix I for the addresses of the colleges and universities listed in this section.

SEMESTER AND ACADEMIC YEAR

General Studies

Associated Colleges of the Midwest. "Arts of London and Florence." Eight weeks in each city. Spring semester. Sophomores, juniors, and seniors with 2.75 GPA. Apply six months prior to start of program.

Eastern Michigan University. "European Cultural History Tour—Fall Semester." Travel-study program visiting 45 cities in Western Europe, the Soviet Union, and the Mediterranean. History, art, literature, and political science taught in an interdisciplinary context. Freshmen to seniors. Apply by June 1.

Friends World College. "European Studies." London, with trip to continental Europe. Academic year or semester. European culture, history, politics, and individualized program combining independent study with fieldwork or internships. Sophomores, juniors, seniors. Apply by May 15 for fall and November 15 for spring.

Northeastern University. "Ireland: North and South." A bicultural experience, including social studies at Dublin's Institute of Public Administration and the Queen's University, Belfast, with internships in the Irish Parliament. Fall and winter quarter. Juniors and seniors with 3.0 GPA. Apply by April 15.

University of Pittsburgh. "Semester at Sea." Fall or spring semester. Students, based aboard the S.S. *Universe*, attend classes on board and travel to various countries in Europe, the Middle East, and Asia. Sophomores, juniors, and seniors with 2.75 GPA. Contact: Semester at Sea, 2E Forbes Quadrangle, University of Pittsburgh, Pittsburgh, PA 15260; (412) 648-7490.

German Language and Culture

Macalester College. "Associated Colleges of the Twin Cities German Program." Spring semester. Intensive German language in West Germany during January and February; culture and literature study in Vienna, March through May. Sophomores, juniors, and seniors with two years of college German. Apply by October 15.

Urban Studies

Antioch University. "GLCA European Urban Term." Yugoslavia, the Netherlands, and United Kingdom. Fall quarter. Offered with Great Lakes Colleges Association. Juniors and seniors. Apply by March 1.

Women's Studies

Antioch University. "Women's Studies in Europe." Yugoslavia, the Netherlands, West Germany, and United Kingdom. Fall quarter. Juniors and seniors. Apply by March 15.

SUMMER

Architecture

Southern Illinois University at Carbondale. "Les Impressions de la Culture." Great Britain, France, Italy. Site visits to fashion design and architecture centers in Europe. Freshmen to graduate students, and qualified community members with strong background in related field. Apply by March 1.

Syracuse University. "Le Corbusier: A Journey East." France, West Germany, Greece, Austria, Hungary, Yugoslavia, Romania, Turkey, and Italy. Sophomores to graduate students. Apply by March 16.

Art

Brigham Young University. "Europe for the Artist." Greece, Italy, Switzerland, France, and England. Drawing, water color painting, and readings. All students. Apply by February 1.

University of North Texas. "UNT Summer Art in Europe: Watercolor Painting & Drawing." France, Italy, England, Switzerland. Studio and fieldwork, with emphasis on landscape. Freshmen to graduate students and nonstudents. Apply by February 1.

Business

University System of Georgia/University of Georgia. "International Business Perspectives—London and Brussels." Undergraduate and graduate students with 2.5 GPA and one course in basic marketing and business law. Apply by March 1; applications accepted thereafter on a space-available basis.

Chemistry

Southern Illinois University at Carbondale. "The History of Chemistry." Belgium, France, East and West Germany, Great Britain, Netherlands, Italy, Switzerland, and Czechoslovakia. Visits to science museums and laboratories of historical importance. Juniors to graduate students and teachers. Apply March 1.

Environmental Design

University of Colorado. "Comparative European Environments." England, Switzerland, Italy, Greece. Urban policy and planning in several countries. Juniors and seniors with 3.0 GPA and background in environmental design or related field. Apply by end of January.

Michigan State University. "Interior Design in Europe." London, Paris, and Milan. Study interior design and architecture from the 16th century to present. Contemporary design will be offered in Italy as an option. Juniors, seniors, and graduate students. Apply by April 21.

General Studies

Eastern Michigan University. "European Cultural History Tour—Summer." An intensive travel-study program visiting 35 cities in Western Europe, Eastern Europe, and the Mediterranean. Freshmen to seniors. Apply April 1.

History

Eastern Michigan University. "European Travel Study." Munich and other European cities. High school graduates, college students, and adults. Apply by May 15.

Syracuse University. "The Medieval Pilgrimage Routes from Southern France to Santiago de Compostela: Romanesque Art in the Making." Sophomores to graduate students and professionals. Apply by March 17.

University System of Georgia/Dalton College. "Western Civilization in London and Paris." College students with 2.5 GPA. Apply by March 15.

International Studies

Wittenberg University. "Global Issues and World Churches." Geneva, Rome, West Berlin, and East Berlin. Sophomores to graduate students. For early decision apply January 6; deadline is March 1.

Management

Michigan State University. "Management Program in Sweden, Helsinki, and Geneva." Juniors, seniors, and graduate students. Apply by April 21.

Science

Michigan State University. "Science Museums Study Program." London and Paris. Focus on design, presentations, and educational programs of some of the major science museums of London and Paris. Sophomores to graduate students, and teachers. Apply by April 21.

AUSTRIA

"There are no kangaroos in Austria," declares a popular T-shirt, and one that's indicative of the confusion foreigners sometimes have regarding this historic country. Austria's neighbors include members of NATO as well as Warsaw Pact countries, but the country itself maintains a strict neutrality, and as a result does without trade or defense alliances. In addition, due to its geographic location in the heart of Europe, this small landlocked nation often serves as a crossroads between East and West, and is the site of one of only three United Nations complexes.

From Innsbruck in the west, the Alps stretch east to Austria's capital and most populous city, Vienna. Small towns dot the Alps, their architecture typically Bavarian, the countryside pristine. Inhabitants of the more remote Alpine regions still wear lederhosen, the traditional leather shorts with suspenders, and still dance to ancient melodies, including waltzes. Salzburg, a small picturesque city in the heart of the Alps, overflows each summer with tourists eager to see the medieval city where Mozart was born and where *The Sound of Music* was filmed. To the east lies Vienna, spreading from the Alpine foothills to the Danube and across the riverian plain toward Hungary.

In general, Austria's standard of living is high. Most families can afford cars and electronic equipment imported from Germany and Japan. Austria itself manufactures many products exported to its Eastern European neighbors.

It was the assassination of Franz Ferdinand, an Austrian archduke and heir apparent to the Hapsburg throne, that precipitated the First World War. The archduke was from a dynasty that for hundreds of years had ruled a large central European empire, including all or part of what is now Germany, Italy, Hungary, Yugoslavia, Romania, Czechoslovakia, Poland—and Austria.

Today, Austria is still home to a diverse mix of peoples. Descendants of Bavarians and Swiss reside in the west; descendants of Turks, Slavs, and Hungarian Magyars in the east. Not surprisingly, the various groups are fiercely protective of their ethnicity, but Austrians of all backgrounds resent being thought of as German. As they see it, their country ruled much of Europe more than 500 years before Germany even arose as a nation-state. And while German is Austria's principal language, as spoken in Austria, it is often unfathomable to northern German speakers.

—*Peter Stadtfeld, Ypsilanti, Michigan*

Official name: Republic of Austria. **Area:** 32,375 square miles (about the size of Maine). **Population:** 7,600,000. **Population density:** 235 inhabitants per square mile. **Capital and largest city:** Vienna (pop. 1,650,000). **Language:** German. **Religion:** Roman Catholic. **Per capita income:** US$9,140. **Currency:** Schilling. **Literacy rate:** 98%. **Average daily high/low:*** Vienna: January, 34°/25°; July, 76°/60°. **Average number of days with precipitation:** Vienna: January, 8; July, 9.

TRAVEL

Americans will need a passport to travel to Austria; however, a visa is not required for stays of up to three months. Persons planning a stay longer than three months should check with the Austrian Embassy, 2343 Massachusetts Avenue NW, Washington, DC 20008, for information on specific requirements.

Getting Around

A good deal for anyone who wants to travel around the country via its rail system is the "Austria Ticket." Available to anyone 6–26 years of age at Austrian rail stations, it entitles the holder to four days of travel within a ten-day period for either $37 (second-class) or $53 (first-class). If you're over 26 years of age, consider the "Network Pass," which offers one month's unlimited travel on all "manner of conveyance operated by the Austrian Federal Railways," including trains, some boats, buses, cable cars, et cetera. A second-class pass costs $238, while a first-class one is available for $357 at any Austrian rail station or from the central rail offices in Frankfurt, Munich, or Zurich. Eurail passes are also valid for train travel throughout Austria (see page 58).

Many Austrian railway stations rent bikes to travelers from April to October. Rental fees are approximately $6 per day, with a 50-percent discount if you purchase a ticket to the station where you intend to rent. Pick up a list of participating train stations from any Austrian Federal Railways office. During off-peak periods, bikes are permitted as free hand baggage on Austrian trains.

For those who want to see the Alps as the Austrians do, an Alpine trek from one mountain hut to the next is an energetic option. Huts are open from early July until mid-September, and vary from the extremely basic to ones equipped with hot showers. To help plan your itinerary, *Walking in Austria's Alps, Hut-to-Hut* describes 82 routes for both novices and experienced hikers. The book is available for $10.95 from The Mountaineers Books, 306 2nd Avenue West, Seattle, WA 98119.

---

*all temperatures are Fahrenheit

"Walk! The climate is wonderful and the people are warm and friendly and willing to share Austria with you."
—Paula K. Morris, Deerfield, Illinois

Especially for Students and Young People

Students going to Austria should be aware of two student travel organizations:

- ÖKISTA, a member of the ISTC, provides an accommodation service, daily sightseeing tours, weekend excursions to Budapest and Prague, and student discount tickets for flights and trains. The organization also sponsors language courses, an international youth center, and a sports vacation program during the summer for young people ages 16–30. Also available from the organization are various brochures, including *Skiing in Austria*. ÖKISTA branches are located in Graz, Innsbruck, Linz, Salzburg, Klagenfurt, and Bregenz. For further information, contact ÖKISTA, Turkenstrasse 4, A-1090 Vienna.
- Buro für Studentenreisen (BfSt), also a member of the ISTC, offers a student accommodation service, student discount tickets for flights and trains, and language courses. You can write them at Schreyvogelgasse 3, A-1010 Vienna.

Holders of the International Student Identity Card (see page 8) are entitled to reduced or free admission to many museums, palaces, and historical buildings in Vienna and Salzburg, and up to 50-percent discounts on admission to some concerts and theaters.

For Further Reading

A number of publications, including the *Austria Vacation Kit*, are available from the Austrian National Tourist Office, 500 Fifth Avenue, New York, NY 10110. You can get a copy of *Live*, a brochure written by the staff of a Viennese magazine called *Falter* that's full of information on Austria's cities, including meeting places, cultural events, restaurants, and accommodations, from the same source. The tourist office also distributes listings of moderately priced hotels and pensiones, information about camping, and special brochures with information on Salzburg and Vienna with young people in mind. Up-to-date information on Austria can be found in *Austrian Information*, the monthly newsletter of the Austrian Press and Information Service of the Austrian Consulate General, 31 East 69th Street, New York, NY 10021.

"Bring your musical instrument with you to Salzburg. It is one of the great centers of European musical life and there are orchestras, bands, and choirs for every level of ability. An amateur band, the Eisenbahner Musikverein, which meets once a week and plays occasional concerts, welcomes American students."

WORK

Getting a job

According to the Austrian Consulate General, government regulations regarding employment in Austria have been tightened. Foreigners wishing to work in the country must be in possession of a valid work permit, which are issued for one-year periods by the local State Employment Office upon application by the prospective employer. Whether or not a visa is issued depends on the current status of Austria's domestic unemployment rate. Further information is included in *Employment of Foreigners in Austria*, which is available from the Austrian Consulate General, Austrian Press and Information Service (address directly above).

A fact sheet, *Teaching in Austria*, is available from the Austrian Institute (11 East 52nd Street, New York, NY 10022). The Institute also has a list of the addresses of the various provincial boards of education, and suggests that teaching positions often exist in the smaller provincial cities. They add that "a very good command of the German language is absolutely necessary for anyone to be appointed as a teacher at an Austrian public school."

Internships/Traineeships

Programs offered by members of the Council on International Educational Exchange are listed below. For further information, consult Appendix I for the appropriate addresses.

AIESEC—US. Reciprocal internship program for students in economics, business, finance, marketing, accounting, and computer sciences. See page 18 for further information.

Association for International Practical Training.
"IAESTE Trainee Program." On-the-job training for undergraduate and graduate students in technical fields such as engineering, computer science, agriculture, architecture, and mathematics. See page 18 for more information.
"Hotel & Culinary Exchanges Program." On-the-job training for young people beginning a career in the hotel and food service industries. Participants must have graduated from a university or vocational school and possess at least six months of training or experience in the chosen field. Training usually runs 6–12 months.

Voluntary Service

One possibility for persons interested in voluntary service work in Austria is the "Year Abroad Program" sponsored by the International Christian Youth Exchange. Open to persons 18–24 years of age, it offers voluntary service opportunities in the fields of health care, education, the environment, construction, et cetera. See page 22 for more information.

STUDY

The Austrian Institute (see above for address) distributes helpful publications on study opportunities at Austrian universities. Its *American Educational Programs in Austria* is a free listing of U.S. colleges and universities that sponsor their own programs in Austria and accept students from other schools. The Austrian National Tourist Office (see page 72 for address) distributes *Summer Courses in Austria. Information for Foreign Students Intending to Study at an*

Austrian Institute of Higher Learning is available from the Austrian Press and Information Service, Austrian Consulate General (see page 72 for address).

Listed below are the academic programs offered by member institutions of the Council on International Educational Exchange. Consult Appendix I for the addresses of the colleges and universities listed in this section. In addition to the programs below, Illinois State University, Indiana University, the University of California system, and the University of the Pacific offer programs open only to their own students.

SEMESTER AND ACADEMIC YEAR

Business

Northern Illinois University. "International Business Internship in Salzburg." Spring semester. Internship, plus two courses in economics, business, marketing, or finance. Housing with Austrian families. Sophomores, juniors, and seniors with 2.7 GPA. Apply by November 1.

European Studies

American University. "Vienna Semester." Fall or spring semester. Politics and foreign policy of Austria, Germany, and Switzerland. Internships with international organizations and Austrian agencies. Second-semester sophomores, juniors, and seniors with 2.75 GPA. Apply six months prior to start of program.

Beaver College.
"Vienna Semester Program in Modern European Studies." Fall semester. Offered in cooperation with the Austro-American Institute of Education. Juniors and seniors with 3.0 GPA. Apply by April 20.
"Vienna Semester Program in Southeast European Studies." Spring semester. Offered in cooperation with the Austro-American Institute of Education. Juniors and seniors with 3.0 GPA. Apply by October 5.
"Vienna Semester Program in Soviet and East European Studies." Fall semester. Offered in cooperation with the Austro-American Institute of Education. Juniors and seniors with 3.0 GPA. Apply by April 20.

Northern Illinois University. "European Studies in Salzburg." Semester or academic year. Internships in business available spring semester. Housing with Austrian families. Sophomores, juniors, and seniors with 2.7 GPA. Apply by June 1 for fall and November 1 for spring.

State University of New York at Fredonia. Vienna. Spring semester. Austrian and Central European history, economics, and culture. Juniors and seniors. Some German preferred but not required.

General Studies

Alma College. "Program of Studies in Austria." Vienna. Sophomores, juniors, and seniors. Rolling admissions.

Brigham Young University. "BYU Study Abroad." Vienna. July-December. Sophomores, juniors, and seniors. Some German required. Apply by February 1.

St. Lawrence University. "Vienna Semester Program." Fall or spring semester. Sophomores, juniors, and seniors with 2.8 GPA. No language prerequisite. Apply by February 20 for fall and October 10 for spring.

State University of New York at Binghamton. Graz. Academic year or fall semester. Study at Karl Franzens University. Juniors and seniors with four semesters of college-level German.

University of Arkansas. "Austrian Exchange Program." Graz. Study at Karl Franzens University. Sophomores, juniors, and seniors. Some German required. Rolling admissions.

University of Maine. "New England Study Abroad Program." Salzburg. Academic year or spring semester. Sophomores to graduate students with four semesters of German. Apply by April 15 for academic year and November 15 for spring.

University of Notre Dame. "Foreign Study Program in Innsbruck." Academic year. Focus on German language and Austrian history and philosophy. Priority is given to students at Notre Dame and St. Mary's College. Sophomores and juniors with one year of college German; 2.5 GPA with 3.0 GPA in German. Apply by February 1.

Wilmington College. "Wilmington College in Vienna." Spring semester. Courses in music, art and architecture, history and civilization, economics, and German language. Housing with families. Includes tours in Austria and surrounding countries. Sophomores to seniors. Apply by November 15.

German Language

Adventist Colleges Abroad. Bogenhofen. Academic year, semester, or quarter. Open only to Adventist Colleges Abroad consortium institutions. Freshmen to seniors with 3.0 GPA in German and 2.5 overall GPA. Apply sixty days before beginning of academic term.

Beaver College. "Vienna January Term in Intensive German." Offered in cooperation with the Austro-American Institute of Education. Beginning and intermediate language levels. Sophomores, juniors, and seniors. Apply by November 15.

Central University of Iowa. "Central College in Germany and Austria." Vienna. Semester or academic year. Sophomores, juniors, and seniors with intermediate-level German, 2.5 GPA (3.0 in German). Apply by November 1 for spring and April 15 for fall.

Ohio University. Salzburg. "Spring Quarter in Austria." Freshmen to seniors with two quarters of German. Apply by January. Contact Department of Modern Languages; (614) 593-2765.

University of Minnesota. "German and Austrian Studies in Graz." Fall quarter. Freshmen to graduate students and adults. One year of German required. Apply by June 15.

Photography

Northern Illinois University. "Photography Program in Salzburg." Academic year only; requests for one semester option considered on an individual basis. Housing with Austrian families. Two years of photography required. Apply by June 1.

SUMMER

Austrian Studies

State Universities of New York at Oneonta, Plattsburgh, and Potsdam. Bregenz. Freshmen to seniors. No language requirement. Rolling admissions.

Syracuse University. "Vienna, the Heart of Europe: Literature, Arts, Culture, and the Alps." Sophomores to graduate students and professionals. Two years of German required for those enrolling in selected topics. Apply by April 1.

Chinese Studies

State University of New York at Oneonta. Murau and/or Vienna. International summer institute on China sponsored by Austria's Ludwig Boltzmann Institute for Research on China. A visit to China is also included. Freshman to graduate students, teachers, and adults. Rolling admissions.

General Studies

Hope College. "Vienna Summer School." Freshmen to seniors. Apply by March 1.

Southern Methodist University. "SMU-in-Austria." Salzburg. Liberal-arts studies focused upon Austria and Central Europe. Sophomores, juniors, and seniors. Apply by March 15.

German Language

Eastern Michigan University. "Intensive German Language Program." Vienna. Beginning, intermediate, and advanced German language. Freshmen to graduate students.

Indiana University. "Summer Language Study in Graz." Second-year German. Freshmen to seniors with one year of German. Apply by February 1.

University of Arkansas at Little Rock. "Summer in Austria." Graz. Sophomores, juniors, and seniors with intermediate-level German. Apply by March 1.

EXPLORING AUSTRIAN CULTURE

Literature

There is an Austrian tendency toward dark introspection that stretches back to the moody *fin de siècle* decadence of the last years of the Austro-Hungarian Empire. Austrian literature tends to turn inward on deep personal problems, which perhaps reflects both a preoccupation with the shadow of a glorious past and the search for a new and relevant identity. Peter Handke, perhaps the best-known Austrian writer working today, is preoccupied with these kinds of ideas and has written a number of interesting books that have been translated into English. Handke's *The Goalie's Anxiety at the Penalty Kick* is the story of a former soccer player turned pathological killer.

Ingeborg Bachmann, another contemporary writer, has written many short stories in which she explores different ways of interpreting life in an idiosyncratic stream-of-consciousness style. Thomas Bernhard was a novelist and playwright who wrote about his country in a cynical, pessimistic way that earned him at least as many enemies in his home country as admirers. His novel *The Chalk Factory* is about a misanthropic husband who kills his wife in order to write a study about hearing. Bernhard's *The Ignoramus and the Madman* is a drama about alienated individuals who have lost the ability to be spontaneous. In *Heldenplatz*, a drama written just before his recent death, Bernhard risked a head-on collision with his countrymen, once again bringing up their Nazi past and connecting it with the moral state of the country in the wake of the Waldheim affair.

BELGIUM

Although Belgium has existed as an independent state since 1830, there is no Belgian language and there are no real Belgians. Two cultures—the Flemish and the Walloon—coexist within the state's borders. About 55 percent of the Belgian people speak Flemish, while the remainder are French-speaking Walloons. Today, as the importance of the historic forces that traditionally have unified Belgium (such as a common religion and king) continue to weaken, linguistic battles and other disputes between the two groups have become more pronounced. While an international soccer championship can sometimes unify them so that they do justice to the national motto, *l'union fait la force* (unity is strength), Belgium is evolving into two separate, semi-autonomous regions within a federal system.

The Flemish region (known as Flanders) encompasses the flat lowlands of the northern part of the country. In the late Middle Ages the area produced some of the wealthiest trading cities in the world. Visitors to the cities of Antwerp, Ghent, and Bruges today will find the inhabitants intensely proud of their rich heritage of art and architecture.

Farther south, in the French-speaking area known as Walloonia, the countryside becomes progressively more hilly and scenic. Here travelers enjoy hiking and biking, explore quaint villages and castles, and visit caves and spas (in fact, the Belgian town of Spa gave its name to the whole concept).

In the center of the country lies the booming "Eurocity" of Brussels. Although the capital of Belgium, Brussels is now more important as the headquarters of NATO, headquarters of the European Economic Community, and European headquarters for a growing number of multinational corporations. New high-rise buildings now surround the city, but the Grand Place, the medieval center of the city, retains its charm.

In this small country tucked between France, Germany, and the Netherlands, people are used to dealing with cultural and linguistic differences. Most people speak more than one language and many, especially the young, speak some English.

Paradoxically, Belgium, although split by ethnic rivalry, has consistently been a leading proponent of greater European unity. Such a stand is not surprising. The country's modern industrial economy is dependent on international trade and the nation's very existence depends on friendly relations between its more powerful neighbors. In fact, in greater European unity might be found the final denouement of the country's ethnic rivalry as well as an end to the conflicts between Belgium's neighbors, which have, twice in this century, turned the small nation into a bloody arena for the armies of the world.

—*Vera van Brande, New York, New York*

Official name: Kingdom of Belgium. **Area:** 11,781 square miles (slightly larger than Maryland). **Population:** 9,772,160. **Population density:** 836 inhabitants per square mile. **Capital and largest city:** Brussels (pop. 976,536). **Language:** Flemish, French. **Religion:** Roman Catholic. **Per capita income:** US$7,801. **Currency:** Belgian franc. **Literacy rate:** 98%. **Average daily high/low:*** Brussels: January, 42°/31°; July, 73°/54°. **Average number of days with precipitation:** Brussels: January, 12; July, 11.

TRAVEL

A passport is required for Americans visiting Belgium. A visa is not required for business or tourist stays of up to 90 days. For longer stays, a temporary residence permit is required. For residence authorization, check with the Belgian Embassy, 3330 Garfield Street NW, Washington, DC 20008.

Getting Around

For persons who want to get to know Belgium by train, there are several rail passes to consider. A Belgian Tourrail "B" Pass allows you unlimited travel for five days within any 17-day period. Youths under 26 receive special discounts: BF1,200 (about $30) for second class, BF1,800 (about $45) for first class. Adult passes cost BF1,600 (about $40) for second class, BF2,400 (about $60) for first class. The "16-Day Pass" is good for 16 days' consecutive travel year-round and costs BF2,920 (about $73) for second class, BF4,380 (about $110) for first class. The "Half-Rate Card," which costs BF500 (about $13) for first- or second-class travel and is good for a month, entitles the holder to a 50-percent discount on rail tickets bought in Belgium for travel within the country. There is also a "Benelux Tourrail Pass," valid for travel in Belgium, the Netherlands, and Luxembourg for five days in any 17-day period during certain parts of the year: those under the age of 26 pay BF1,790 (about $45)

---

*all temperatures are Fahrenheit

for second class or BF2,690 (about $68) first class; those over the age of 26 pay BF2,490 (about $63) second class or BF3,740 (about $94) first class. Eurail passes are also valid on the Belgian rail network (see page 58). For further information about rail passes, contact Belgian National Railroads, 745 Fifth Avenue, New York, NY 10501.

For those who want to explore Belgium by bicycle, bikes can be rented year-round at most train stations. They also can be taken on Belgian trains at no extra charge. If your interest leans more toward an organized bicycle tour, you might be interested in the one offered by American Youth Hostels (see page 63).

In Brussels, the Tourist Information Office, rue du Marché aux Herbes, 61 (or, in Flemish, Grasmarkt 61), can help you find accommodations to suit your budget throughout Belgium.

Especially for Students and Young People

One good source of information on student travel in Belgium is the office of ACOTRA (rue de la Madeleine, 51, B-1000 Brussels). Another good source is Connections, which has offices in Brussels (13 rue Marché au Charbon, Kolenmarktstraat, 1000 Brussels) as well as in Ghent and Liège. In Belgium, holders of the International Student Identity Card receive reduced train and plane fares to international destinations as well as discounts on tours offered by ACOTRA. Also free at Connections offices is a handbook describing discounts available to holders of the ISIC.

For Further Information

You can get maps and information on camping, budget hotels, et cetera from the Belgian Tourist Office, 745 Fifth Avenue, New York, NY 10151. Also available from the tourist office is *Windrose*, a listing of accommodations with host families in Belgium. For $3 (to cover postage and handling), the tourist office will send you a copy of Arthur Frommer's *A Masterpiece Called Belgium*.

WORK

Finding a Job

A work permit is required in order to obtain employment in Belgium. The permit is obtained by the employer and sent to the employee, who then applies to the Belgian Consulate General for an authorization of temporary residence. These papers have to be presented at your port of entry.

Internships/Traineeships

There are both AIESEC and IAESTE internship programs in Belgium; see page 18 for additional information.

Voluntary Service

CIEE places volunteers in Belgian workcamps organized by Compagnons Batisseurs (rue Notre-Dame de Grâces, 63, B-5400 Marché-en-Famenne). At these workcamps groups of volunteers from around the world work on a variety of social service and ecological projects. Applicants must be 18 years of age or older. The applications of U.S. residents are processed by CIEE. For more information contact CIEE's International Voluntary Service Department.

For persons interested in longer-term voluntary service work, the "Year Abroad Program" sponsored by the International Christian Youth Exchange offers persons ages 18–24 voluntary service opportunities in the fields of health care, education, the environment, construction, et cetera. See page 22 for more information.

STUDY

For those who want to study in Belgium, the Belgian Embassy (3330 Garfield Street NW, Washington, DC 20008) provides two publications of interest upon request: *University Studies in Flanders (Belgium)* and *The French-Speaking Community in Belgium and Its Universities.*

For predoctoral students wishing to pursue independent study and research in Belgium, the Belgian American Educational Foundation offers a $10,000 fellowship good for a ten-month period. Candidates must speak and read either French or Dutch. The application deadline is December 31. For details write to the Belgian American Educational Foundation, 195 Church Street, New Haven, CT 06510.

Listed below are academic programs sponsored by CIEE member institutions. Consult Appendix I for the addresses where you can write for more information about any of these programs.

SEMESTER AND ACADEMIC YEAR

General Studies

International Student Exchange Program. Direct reciprocal exchange between U.S. universities and the Katholieke Universiteit te Leuven and Université Catholique de Louvain. Semester or academic year. Full curriculum options. Open only to students at ISEP member institutions.

Northern Illinois University. "Academic Internships in Brussels." Fall or spring semester. Students take two courses plus internship. Wide range of internships available for residents of Illinois; more limited selection for residents of other states. Sophomores, juniors, and seniors with 3.0 GPA and two years of French. Apply by April 4 for fall and November 1 for spring.

International Relations

American University. "Brussels Semester." Fall or spring semester. U.S.–Western European relations. Internships with multinational organizations. Second-semester sophomores, juniors, and seniors with 2.75 GPA. Apply six months prior to start of program.

SUMMER

International Relations

Michigan State University. "International Relations in Brussels." For students with an interest in political science, international studies, and international relations. Sophomores, juniors, and seniors. Apply by April 21.

DENMARK

Denmark, a small maritime country, consists of a peninsula and a group of islands that form a bottleneck between the North and Baltic Seas. As a result, no one in Denmark lives more than 35 miles from the sea. From the time of their Viking ancestors, the Danes have been exploring new horizons and trading with the far corners of the earth.

Blessed with a mild climate (although Copenhagen lies farther north than Ketchikan, Alaska), the rich, green countryside is ideal for agriculture. The land is flat—so flat that it is said if you stand on a carton of beer (Denmark's Tuborg or Carlsberg brands will do nicely), you can see from one end of the country to the other. "Danish modern" design—a style recognized and appreciated worldwide—reflects the simple linear beauty of the Danish countryside.

Official Name: Kingdom of Denmark. **Area:** 16,631 square miles (about half the size of Maine). **Population:** 5,100,000. **Population density:** 307 inhabitants per square mile. **Capital and largest city:** Copenhagen (pop. 1,358,540). **Language:** Danish. **Religion:** Lutheran. **Per capita income:** US$11,290. **Currency:** Krone. **Literacy rate:** 100%. **Average daily high/low:*** Copenhagen, January, 36°/29°; July, 75°/55°. **Average number of days with precipitation:** Copenhagen, January, 9; July, 9.

TRAVEL

Americans must have a passport to visit Denmark. However, a visa is not required for stays of up to three months—a period that begins as soon as one enters the Scandinavian region. For specific visa requirements, check with the Royal Danish Embassy, 3200 Whitehaven Street NW, Washington, DC 20008.

Getting Around

If you arrive in Copenhagen and have no place to stay, go straight to the information desk in Central Station or to USE IT at Radhusstraede 13, DK-1466, Copenhagen K. USE IT distributes an excellent newspaper called *Playtime*—"an alternative introduction and guide to Copenhagen especially

---

*all temperatures are Fahrenheit

for low-budget tourists." USE IT also distributes a number of free brochures, provides a mail drop and free luggage storage for travelers, and puts hitchhikers in touch with people driving their way. The bulletin boards at USE IT are full of information, and when the office is closed there's a notice board outside.

Travelers who fly SAS directly between the U.S. and Scandinavia are eligible to purchase a Visit Scandinavia pass. The pass entitles the holder to five economy flights within Denmark, Norway, and Sweden between July 1 and August 14. It must be purchased in the U.S., however, costs $200, and is valid for up to 30 days after your arrival in Scandinavia. In addition, it can be used on any of the three Scandinavian airlines: Danair, Linjeflyg, and SAS (excluding flights to the Faroe Islands and Greenland).

If you plan on traveling extensively by rail in Scandinavia, you should investigate the Nordturist Ticket (approximately $250), which allows 21 days of unlimited second-class travel throughout Denmark, Sweden, Norway, and Finland. It's also good on government-run ferries to Germany and Denmark. Tickets can be purchased at all major train stations. Eurail passes may be used on the Danish rail network (see page 58).

For those who prefer to get some exercise as they travel, bicycles can be rented at major train stations and tourist offices in Denmark for approximately $5 a day or $25 a week. They can also be carried on trains as checked baggage for a small additional fee.

Especially for Students and Young People

Denmark's student travel organization and ISTC member, DIS Travel (Skindergade 28, DK-1159 Copenhagen K), provides a number of useful services for the student traveler, including information on and bookings for transportation, accommodations, and tours. Branch offices are located in Aarhus, Esbjerg, and Odense.

Many museums in Denmark offer discounts to holders of the International Student Identity Card (ISIC); a list is available from DIS Travel in Copenhagen. ISIC holders also often receive discounts on bus, plane, and train travel to European destinations, as well as discounts on ferries to Norway and the United Kingdom.

Meet the People

Through the "Meet the Danes" program, groups can spend an evening in a Danish home in Roskilde. Check well in advance with the Danish Tourist Board (address below) for more information about the program. Friends Overseas is an American-Scandinavian people-to-people program that helps put travelers in touch with Scandinavians who share similar interests. For further information, send a self-addressed stamped envelope to Friends Overseas, 68-04 Dartmouth Street, Forest Hills, NY 11375.

For Further Information

The Danish Tourist Board has a number of free publications geared toward young people, including *Rent a Bicycle in Copenhagen, Inexpensive Accommodations in Copenhagen for Young People, Camping and Youth Hostels in Denmark,* and *Destination Scandinavia: A Guide to Low-Cost Scandinavia.* To obtain any of these, write to the Danish Tourist Board, 655 Third Avenue,

18th floor, New York, NY 10017. Available in bookstores is Frommer's *Scandinavia on $60 a Day* ($13.95), a good source of information for the budget traveler about one of Europe's most expensive regions.

> "Although it may seem absurd to generalize about an entire nation of people, an account of Denmark is criminally incomplete without mention of how kind and hospitable the Danes are. And the customs that are unique to them make the Danes even more fun to be around. The Danes are quick to invite participation in all of their activities. It would be silly not to accept."
> —Jeffrey Seth Jacobson, Hartford, Connecticut

WORK

Getting a Job

At present, work permits for foreign guest workers are not being granted, with the exception of those foreigners possessing special training or skills not readily available in Denmark. In such cases, the employer then applies for the work permit. Contact the Royal Danish Embassy (3200 Whitehaven Street NW, Washington, DC 20008) for further information.

Internships/Traineeships

There are both AIESEC and IAESTE internship programs in Denmark; see page 18 for more information.

In addition, the American Scandinavian Foundation sponsors a program that provides summer training assignments for full-time students majoring in engineering, computer science, horticulture, agriculture, forestry, and chemistry, among others. The deadline for application is December 1. The organization also offers long-term training assignments of up to 18 months in a variety of fields. Recent graduates with at least one year's experience in the field in which training is sought and with competence in Danish are eligible. For long-term assignments, send a résumé specifying the field of training and country desired. Note, however: No traineeships are available in teaching, social work, or medically related fields. Contact the American Scandinavian Foundation, Exchange Division, 127 East 73rd Street, New York, NY 10021.

Voluntary Service

CIEE places young people in Danish voluntary service workcamps organized by Mellemfolkeligt Samvirke (Bogerade 10–14, DK-1300 Copenhagen). Many of these workcamps are organized in cooperation with institutions for the mentally handicapped and involve building playgrounds or interacting with children. Volunteers must be 18 years or over. The applications of U.S. residents are processed by CIEE. Contact the International Voluntary Service Department at the Council's New York office for details.

For persons interested in longer-term voluntary service work, the "Year Abroad Program" sponsored by the International Christian Youth Exchange offers persons ages 18–24 voluntary service opportunities in the fields of health care, education, the environment, construction, et cetera. See page 22 for more information.

STUDY

There are several sources of information on study programs for foreigners in Denmark. The Exchange Division of the American Scandinavian Foundation (127 East 73rd Street, New York, NY 10021) can provide a listing of English-language academic-year and summer programs offered in Scandinavia (including Denmark); ask for *Study in Scandinavia*. In addition, the Royal Danish Embassy (address above) distributes a useful fact sheet called *Studying in Denmark*.

The Danish Cultural Institute (Kultorvet 2, DK-1175 Copenhagen K) is a nonprofit institution that receives an annual grant from the Danish Ministry of Culture. Its aim is to disseminate information about Denmark and improve cultural relations and international understanding. Among its activities are short-term courses and study tours on socio-cultural subjects such as education for children and adults, libraries, social care, architecture, and design. For details, contact the Institute at the above address.

The academic programs sponsored by member institutions of the Council on International Educational Exchange are listed below. Consult Appendix I for the addresses where you can write for more information. In addition to the programs listed below, New York University, Ohio State University, and the University of California system offer programs open only to their own students.

SEMESTER AND ACADEMIC YEAR

General Studies

Scandinavian Seminar. "College Year in Denmark." Individual placement in Danish folk colleges throughout Denmark. Danish language and cultural immersion, with emphasis on liberal arts. College credit granted through University of Massachusetts–Amherst. Sophomores to graduate students. Apply by May 1.

State University of New York/Empire State College. "Semester Program in Denmark." Elsinore and Thy. Semester or academic year. Sophomores to graduate students and adults. Apply by June 15 for fall and November 30 for spring.

Denmark's International Study (DIS) Program at the University of Copenhagen. Copenhagen. Semester or academic year. Architecture and design, Danish language, international business, and liberal arts. Courses conducted in English. Juniors and seniors with 3.0 GPA. Apply through the more than 60 cooperating U.S. colleges and universities; contact the study abroad office or international center at your school for further information.

Social Sciences

Scandinavian Seminar. "Semester Program on Nordic and Global Issues." Helsingør (fall or spring) or Vejen (spring). Focus on global issues from a Nordic perspective, featuring coursework, discussions, and excursions. Sophomores to graduate students and nonstudents. Apply by May 1.

SUMMER

Architecture and Design

Denmark's International Study (DIS) Program at the University of Copenhagen. Copenhagen. Architecture and design. Courses conducted in English. Juniors and seniors with 3.0 GPA. Apply through one of the more than 60 cooperating U.S. colleges and universities, including the University of Oregon.

FINLAND

Nestled in Europe's far north, the land of the midnight sun, Finland has been able to carve out a niche in the struggle between the superpowers. Indeed, the word *Finlandization* has been coined to describe its ability to pursue an independent path without provoking its powerful eastern neighbor, the Soviet Union. Finland has been able to maintain this independence in part due to its formidable expanse of inhospitable terrain and in part due to a special virtue that the Finns call *sisu*—a mixture of perseverance, stamina, and a touch of stubbornness.

Finland is a land of lakes, forests, and thousands of picturesque islands, many uninhabited except in the summer months, when Finns abandon the cities by the hundreds of thousands to enjoy what is probably Europe's last wilderness. Most visitors are enchanted by the country's vast uninhabited countryside, and partake of activities ranging from hiking and saunas to biking, swimming, and sailing on the countless bodies of water that cover much of Finland's surface.

Official Name: Republic of Finland. **Area:** 130,119 square miles (about the size of Montana). **Population:** 4,900,000. **Population density:** 38 inhabitants per square mile. **Capital and largest city:** Helsinki (pop. 530,000). **Language:** Finnish. **Religion:** Lutheran. **Per capita income:** US$12,180. **Currency:** Markka. **Literacy rate:** 100%. **Average daily high/low:*** Helsinki: January, 27°/17°; July, 71°/57°. **Average number of days with precipitation:** Helsinki: January, 11; July, 8.

TRAVEL

Americans will need a passport to visit Finland. However, a visa is not required for a stay of up to three months—a period that begins as soon as you enter the Scandinavian region. Persons planning a longer stay should check with the Embassy of Finland, 3216 New Mexico Avenue NW, Washington, DC 20016.

*all temperatures are Fahrenheit

Getting Around

If you're going to be covering a lot of territory in Finland in a short time, check with Finnair about their Holiday Ticket pass, which allows 15 days of unlimited economy travel within the country. In 1989, the price was $250 ($200 for those under 23 years of age).

The Finnrailpass, which must be purchased before you leave for Finland, entitles the holder to unlimited travel on all passenger trains throughout the country. A second-class pass costs $90 for 8 days, $135 for 15 days, and $166 for 22 days. A first-class ticket is available at about 50 percent more. Tickets may be purchased from Holiday Tours of America, 40 East 49th Steet, New York, NY 10017. Eurail passes may also be used on the Finnish rail network (see page 58).

Finland has an abundance of youth hostels and student dormitories which are used as hotels in summer. The camping season starts in late May or early June, and there are 300 campsites throughout Finland from which to choose. Further information is available in *Finland Camping and Youth Hostels*, which is distributed by the Finnish Tourist Board, 655 Third Avenue, New York, NY 10017.

Especially for Students and Young People

FSTS Travela (Finnish Student Travel Service) is Finland's ISTC member. You can obtain information on travel in Finland and get student and youth discounts on tickets to, from, and within Finland by contacting them at Kaivokatu 10B, 8th floor, 00100 Helsinki (they have branch offices in Jyvaskyla, Oulu, Tampere, and Turku). FSTS also offers a selection of tours to the Soviet Union.

A number of discounts are available to students traveling with the International Student Identity Card, including discounts of 25 to 50 percent on some domestic air fares, discounts of up to 40 percent on international train fares, and discounts of up to 50 percent on ferries to Sweden. In addition, ISIC holders can purchase a Helsinki discount card, which entitles you to free travel on buses, trams, and the metro; free admission to 35 museums; free boat trips; and other discounts. One-day passes cost Fmk 60 (about $15); two-day passes cost Fmk 80 (about $20); and three-day passes cost Fmk 95 (about $24).

Meet the People

Friends Overseas is an American-Scandinavian people-to-people program that puts travelers in touch with Scandinavians who share similar interests. For further information, send a self-addressed stamped envelope to Friends Overseas, 68-04 Dartmouth Street, Forest Hills, NY 11375.

For Further Information

A number of publications geared to the student or budget traveler can be obtained from the Finnish Tourist Board (655 Third Avenue, New York, NY 10017). These include publications on camping, hiking, and youth hostels, as well as maps and a calendar of events. Also available in bookstores is Frommer's *Scandinavia on $60 a Day* ($13.95), a good source of information for the budget traveler in the region.

WORK

Getting a Job

According to embassy personnel, it is very difficult for U.S. citizens to obtain work in Finland. As is the case in many Western European countries, an offer of employment is required before you apply for a work permit. Contact the Embassy of Finland (3216 New Mexico Avenue NW, Washington, DC 20016) for details.

Anyone interested in living as an au pair in a Finnish family should contact the Ministry of Labor, International Trainee Exchanges, P.O. Box 30, SF-00101, Helsinki. The ministry's Finnish Family Program is for young people who are native speakers of English, German, or French and want to learn about Finnish culture by living with a family. Besides teaching English, you are expected to take part in daily family life—domestic or farm work, child care, gardening, et cetera. The summer program lasts a maximum of three months, a minimum of one. During the winter the minimum stay is six months. Participants in the summer program should be 17–22 of age; for the winter program, 18–25.

Internships/Traineeships

Programs sponsored by CIEE member organizations and institutions are listed below; consult Appendix I for the addresses where you can write for more information.

AIESEC—US. Reciprocal internship program for students in economics, business, finance, marketing, accounting, and computer sciences. See page 18 for further information.

Association for International Practical Training.
"IAESTE Trainee Program." On-the-job training for undergraduate and graduate students in technical fields such as engineering, computer science, agriculture, architecture, and mathematics. See page 18 for further information.
"Hotel & Culinary Exchanges Program." On-the-job training for young people beginning a career in the hotel and food service industries. Participants must have graduated from a university or vocational school and possess at least six months of training or experience in the chosen field. Training usually runs 6–12 months.

In addition, the American Scandinavian Foundation sponsors a program that provides summer training assignments for full-time students majoring in engineering, computer science, horticulture, agriculture, forestry, business, and chemistry, among others. The application deadline for summer programs is December 1. The organization also offers long-term training assignments of up to 18 months in various fields. Recent graduates with at least one year's experience in the field in which training is sought and with competence in Finnish are eligible. For long-term assignments, send a résumé specifying the field of training and country desired. No traineeships are available in teaching, social work, or medically related fields. Contact the American Scandinavian Foundation, Exchange Division, 127 East 73rd Street, New York, NY 10021.

Finland's Ministry of Labor also sponsors internship opportunities. Students ages 18–30 with at least one year of study in their field may apply for openings (May to October) in tourism service, forestry, agriculture, horticulture, and a limited number in commerce. In addition, graduates under 30 years of age may apply for six-month openings in commerce, catering, agronomy, horticulture, and language teaching. Deadline for application is March 31. Your campus placement office or international program office may have applications; if not, contact the Ministry of Labor, International Trainee Exchanges, P.O. Box 30, SF-00101 Helsinki.

Voluntary Service

One opportunity for voluntary service in Finland is the "Year Abroad Program" of the International Christian Youth Exchange. The program offers persons ages 18–24 voluntary service opportunities in the fields of health care, education, the environment, construction, et cetera. See page 22 for more information.

STUDY

The Exchange Division of the American Scandinavian Foundation, 127 East 73rd Street, New York, NY 10021, will provide you with a listing of academic-year and summer programs in Scandinavia, including Finland. Also available from the Consulate General of Finland (Finland House, 540 Madison Avenue, New York, NY 10022) are publications on adult-education options in Finland as well as opportunities for Finnish-language study.

The academic programs offered by CIEE member institutions are listed below. The addresses where you can write for further information are provided in Appendix I.

SEMESTER AND ACADEMIC YEAR

General Studies

International Student Exchange Program. Direct reciprocal exchange between U.S. universities and institutions in Helsinki, Espoo, Oulu, and Tampere. Semester or academic year. Full curriculum options. Open only to students at ISEP member institutions.

Scandinavian Seminar. "College Year in Finland." Individual placement in Finnish folk colleges throughout Finland. Finnish language and cultural immersion, with emphasis on liberal arts. College credit granted through University of Massachusetts–Amherst. Sophomores to graduate students. Apply by May 1.

Social Sciences

Scandinavian Seminar. "Semester Program on Nordic and Global Issues." Fall semester in Helsinki and Espoo; spring semester in Hauho. Focus on global issues from a Nordic perspective, with coursework, discussions, and excursions. Sophomores to graduate students and nonstudents. Apply by May 1.

SUMMER

Business

Southern Illinois University at Carbondale. "International Business Operations." Tampere. Field assignments in teams with Finnish firms in addition to classroom presentations and individual readings. Juniors, seniors, graduate students, and qualified adults. Background in marketing, finance, statistics, quantitative methods, and organizational behavior. Apply by March 1.

FRANCE

Some say it was the French who first defined the term civilization. Indeed, for centuries, France has nurtured and subsidized the arts, and the results are visible in its cathedrals, palaces, art, literature, formal gardens, high fashion, gastronomy, and viniculture. Even Julius Caesar lauded the wines. France provides a sumptuous feast for the senses and the mind.

Still, while it is the lure of a 2,000-year-old heritage that attracts millions of tourists each year, the French would rather be praised for their present accomplishments. France is a technologically advanced nation and the fourth leading exporter in the world. Entirely dependent on others for its petroleum —gasoline is costly—it has made the development of hydroelectric and nuclear energy a high priority. A modernized rail system links Paris to the other major French cities, but cycling, backpacking, and hitchhiking are all popular alternatives. France competes with, sometimes envies, and often emulates the U.S., which lessens but does not totally eliminate the cultural shock for most Americans.

The French are prompt to declare that "Paris is not France." While that is indisputable, it is the nation's capital, France's largest city by far, and has been the hub of its highly centralized government for over 900 years. Paris remains the stellar French attraction for most foreign visitors: a cosmopolitan city in which the well-preserved past and the ultramodern present coexist. It is best explored on foot. Tourists flock to its major landmarks and throng its bustling boulevards, but the charm of the *quartiers*, of its meandering streets, of its picturesque surprises and serene parks are reserved for the adventurous stroller. If time is a concern, public transportation such as the metro and the RER suburban railway line is both first-rate and affordable. The city languishes during the summer doldrums after Bastille Day; theaters and concert halls close as Parisians head south to the sea, west to the ocean, and east to the mountains for the six-week peak vacation period that follows.

Hexagonal in shape and relatively small in size, France is nevertheless noted for its diversity. Despite systematic efforts to homogenize its culture and language, strongly ingrained regional traditions endure: Alsace, Brittany, and Corsica are just the most striking examples of the cultural ferment that underlies the country's seeming uniformity. Politically, it is a pluralistic society. Those who know France are prone to conclude that it has a population of 50,000,000 individualists. The wonder is that it has only 366 varieties of cheese.

On the whole, the French are formal and reserved but gracious. Their word *hôte* means both guest and host, implying that there must be a reciprocity of conduct. Off the beaten paths, some knowledge of the language is a necessity.

The effort made to speak French is a courtesy that is always appreciated and is volubly rewarded. And while friendships develop gradually, the French have always been hospitable to students; study opportunities for a full year, a semester, or a summer abound.

—*Alfred F. Massari, Oneonta, New York*

Official name: French Republic. **Area:** 211,208 square miles (about the size of Texas). **Population:** 55,900,000. **Population density:** 265 inhabitants per square mile. **Capital and largest city:** Paris (pop. 2,150,000). **Language:** French. **Religion:** Roman Catholic. **Per capita income:** US$9,280. **Currency:** Franc. **Literacy rate:** 97%. **Average daily high/low:*** Bordeaux: January, 48°/35°; July, 80°/58°. Nice: January, 56°/40°; July, 81°/66°. Paris: January, 42°/32°; July, 76°/55°. **Average number of days with precipitation:** Bordeaux: January, 16; July, 11; Nice: January, 8; July, 2; Paris: January, 15; July, 12.

TRAVEL

Americans going to France will need a passport, but a visa is no longer required for stays of less than three months. Students planning a stay of more than three months should see the special information under the ''Study'' heading later in this chapter. More information on French visa requirements is available from a French consulate office or from the French Embassy, 4101 Reservoir Road NW, Washington, DC 20007.

Getting Around

"Each province in France has its own characteristics and traditions—the country is a patchwork of different cultures."
—*Stephanie Oswald, Saugerties, New York*

Air Inter, which serves 28 cities, offers a Le France pass that entitles the holder to unlimited economy air travel on any seven days of a given month for $210. The pass must be purchased in the U.S., however.

French National Railroads (610 Fifth Avenue, New York, NY 10020) offers a railpass called France Vacances that entitles the holder to unlimited rail travel throughout France in addition to many valuable bonuses, including free airport transfers, a metro pass for a period of unlimited bus and subway travel in Paris, and discounts on car rentals at over 200 railroad stations. A pass for second-class travel costs $99 and is good for four out of fifteen days; it's $160 for nine days of travel in a one-month period. First-class travel costs $134 and $224, respectively. Eurail passes are also valid on the French rail system (see page 58).

On most French trains bicycles are permitted free of charge; you'll know that's the case if there's a bike symbol on the timetable for that particular train. Passengers take their bikes to a special car and load and unload the bikes themselves. It is also possible to rent bicycles at many train stations. Half-day

---

*all temperatures are Fahrenheit

rentals will cost you anywhere from $4.50 to $6, depending on the type of bike; full-day rentals range from $6 to $7.50.

If you're in Paris and interested in ride-sharing to another destination in Europe, call Allostop-Provoya (42-46-00-66). Located at 84, Passage Brady, 75010 Paris, this organization matches persons looking for rides with drivers looking for someone with whom they can share gas costs. You pay an annual membership fee of 150 francs for unlimited ride referrals, or 30 francs per referral for short trips and 60 francs for a longer trip. In addition, there is a charge of 16 centimes per kilometer for both members and nonmembers.

Especially for Students and Young People

CIEE/Council Travel operates travel offices in Paris, Nice, and Aix-en-Provence. You'll find offices at:

- 31, rue St. Augustin, 75002 Paris
- 16, rue de Vaugirard, 75006 Paris
- 51, rue Dauphine, 75006 Paris
- 37bis, rue d'Angleterre, 06000 Nice
- 12, rue Victor Leydet, 13100 Aix-en-Provence

These offices specialize in providing information to and making arrangements for students and other budget travelers. You can also get an International Student Identity Card there, book discount train and plane tickets, arrange for a seat on a transatlantic charter flight, and so on.

Another youth-oriented organization in France that offers a range of useful services is Accueil des Jeunes en France (12 rue des Barres, 75004 Paris). This welcome service provides guaranteed low-cost accommodation in and around Paris (approximately $10 to $14 per person, per night, bed and breakfast) in a variety of youth centers, student residences, and tourist hotels. It has four hospitality and travel offices in Paris, including one at the Gare du Nord.

Students are a privileged class in France and are entitled to many discounts in museums, theaters, cinemas, and restaurants. ISIC holders under 27 and youths under 25 may obtain discounts of 40 to 50 percent on flights within France on the domestic airline Air Inter (except on "red" or commuter flights). Discounts are also available to students under 27 and youths under 22 on international flights from France. Be sure to show your ISIC everywhere. It entitles you to discounts on international bus lines, on domestic and international train service (up to 40 percent on off-peak travel), and on boats to Great Britain, Ireland, and Greece. The ISIC also allows you to eat in *restaurants universitaires* (student restaurants) and to obtain discounts on admission to movies, the theater, and museums. Also be sure to check the prices at any metro station while you're in Paris for the *Carte Orange*, a money-saving subway pass.

Meet the People

There are many reputable organizations that make hospitality arrangements for students who would like to meet with a family for an afternoon or live with a French family as a paying guest. General information on homestays is available from French Cultural Services, 972 Fifth Avenue, New York, NY 10021.

"Americans tend to view the French as being unfriendly, impossible-to-get-to-know people. In some ways this is very true—don't expect them to approach you with open arms, unless they want to practice their English. But once you get to know them, you'll realize how warm and generous they are."
—Sherry Cohen, Huntington, New Jersey

For Further Information

For a comprehensive listing of low-cost accommodations, plus suggestions on what to do and see from a student's point of view, get a copy of *Let's Go: France*. Written by the Harvard Student Agencies and published by St. Martin's Press, it's available for $12.95 in most bookstores and from CIEE (add $1 for postage and handling when ordering by mail).

You'll find an array of guidebooks to France at most bookstores. Especially well known and respected are the *Michelin Green Guides*, which are invaluable for the historical and background information they provide. English-language editions are available for Paris ($10.95) as well as most of the other regions of the country.

General travel information is available from the French Government Tourist Office (610 Fifth Avenue, New York, NY 10020). Among the publications available is *Wish You Were Here*, a listing of French travel packages and tours sold in the U.S. (including student tours). Another free brochure is *Paris à Pied*, which outlines several walking tours in Paris. It can be obtained by sending a stamped self-addressed envelope to Air France, Paris à Pied, Dept. NYCDX, 2039 Ninth Avenue, Ronkonkoma, NY 11779.

A useful book for anyone planning on spending some time in France is *Cultural Misunderstandings: The French-American Experience* by Raymonde Carroll. The book contains revealing vignettes and commentary that bring to light fundamental differences in French and American presumptions about love, friendship, raising children, as well as everyday activities such as using the telephone and asking for information. It's available for $19.95 plus $2 for postage from Intercultural Press, P.O. Box 700, Yarmouth, ME 04096.

"Prepare yourself mentally and emotionally for the French mentality. For it is impossible to separate the museums, the monuments, the shops, the countryside from the people. They have a different way of doing things and they are very proud of it. Extensive traveling in France made me realize that Paris alone does not represent French culture."
—Shanda Gibson, Milpitas, California

WORK

Getting a Job

"Working as a travel agent in France and arranging for pet travel to such exotic places as Izmir, Palerme, and La Nouvelle Orleans, I gained new understanding of the depth of poodle-Parisian relationships. And I had the opportunity to work closely with Dominique, Madeleine, and Frederic, and to explain to client Monsieur Foisy that he could not see all of the United States by car in five days. My work experience was unforgettable."
—Samuel Engel, Philadelphia, Pennsylvania

In recent years a variety of new, quite stringent rules have gone into effect regarding foreigners working in France. In general, nonstudents will find it virtually impossible to find a job in France. With unemployment currently running at unacceptably high levels, the government is anxious to discourage immigration.

For students seeking employment, there are some very specific regulations that must be followed. The best source of information on the subject is the French Cultural Services division of the French Embassy (972 Fifth Avenue, New York, NY 10021), which puts out a helpful information sheet, *Employment in France for Students*. Foreign students who come to France during the summer must do so under the aegis of an organization approved by the government. *Employment in France for Students* lists the organizations, including CIEE, that have received government approval.

> "Many French still adhere strictly to traditional sex roles, not merely shutting women out of traditionally male, high-powered work, but shutting men out of traditionally female, service-oriented work. Many times I arrived for a job interview with a business that had specifically requested American students from CIEE only to be told, 'Mais non, merci. Nous recherchons une femme'—'No thank you. We are looking for a woman.' Even after protesting that I could wash dishes, seat customers, and answer telephones as well as my female colleagues, I usually received a curt, 'Bah, tant pis.' —'Ah, too bad.' Sexism is rampant in the scut sector of the French employment marketplace."
> —Samuel Engel, Philadelphia, Pennsylvania

CIEE can provide you with work authorization, which allows you to seek employment in France for up to three months at any time during the year. To qualify, you must be at least 18 years of age, a full-time college or university student with two years of college-level French, and be a U.S. citizen or permanent resident. The cost of the program is $96. Past participants have taught English in Paris, worked in the vineyards of Bordeaux, and served as lifeguards on the Côte d'Azur. For details and an application form, contact CIEE's Work Exchange Department, 205 East 42nd Street, New York, NY 10017. Additional assistance is available from CIEE's Paris offices on arrival.

Persons seeking a job in France might be interested in *Emplois d'Été en France*, a do-it-yourself guide to job-hunting. Written in French, it can be ordered from CIEE for $11.95, plus $1 postage.

Au Pair

Au pair work, open to young women and men (although men are harder to place), requires that participants help their French "mother" by taking care of the children and helping with light household chores on the average of five hours a day. In return, an au pair receives room and board, pocket money, and, if possible, a room of her/his own. French law requires that au pairs be between the ages of 18 and 30 and that they take courses at a school or university while employed. Although some organizations placing au pairs have summer positions available, most prefer stays of at least six months.

There are four organizations in France that have earned solid reputations for au pair placements. These are listed in *Au Pair Work in France*, compiled by the French Cultural Services division of the French Embassy (address above). You can write to the organizations directly for information on their particular programs: L'Accueil Familial des Jeunes Étrangers, 23 rue du Cherche-Midi, 75006 Paris; Amitié Mondiale, 39 rue Cambon, 75001 Paris; Relations Internationales, 20 rue de l'Exposition, 75007 Paris; and Séjours Internationaux Linguistiques et Culturels, 16002 Angoulême, Cedex.

> "For an insider's view of France and the French, get to know a French family. Becoming involved in family interactions is a wonderful way to experience the national personality—values, customs, lifestyle. I strongly recommend the au pair system because of this."
> —Kris Santiago, Brooklyn, New York

"Jobs in France—especially au pair, tutoring English, and secretarial work—can best be found once you get there. Especially good for au pair jobs is CIDJ (metro stop Bir Hakeim, near the Eiffel Tower). This is a youth center with hundreds of ads on bulletin boards offering jobs, housing, rides, et cetera. The CROUS foreign student office at any French university will usually have a few au pair openings, especially in September-October and January-February. Au pair work is available for guys, but not through the agencies. However, answering an ad in one of the above places might land a guy an au pair job."

Camp Counselor Positions

The YMCA's International Camp Counselor Program has positions open in France; for further information see page 17.

Farm Work

It's possible that you'll be able to find work at grape harvest time without having to prearrange it. But if you prefer to do things ahead of time, you can contact the Maison des Jeunes et de la Culture (25 rue Marat, Bôite Postale 26, 11200 Lézignan, Corbières), which sets up workcamps during the grape harvest in the Languedoc section of France. The harvest begins sometime in late September and lasts from two to three weeks. Students over 16 years of age are eligible. All inquiries must be accompanied by an international postal-reply coupon.

Teaching

The French Government Teaching Assistantships in English offer candidates the opportunity to teach English conversation in French secondary schools for an academic year. Most assignments are to provincial centers. "Strong preference in the competition is given to unmarried candidates under 30 years of age who plan careers in the teaching of French." Contact IIE, 809 United Nations Plaza, New York, NY 10017 for details.

Internships/Traineeships

Opportunities for internships in France include the following programs offered by CIEE member institutions and organizations. In addition, Southwest Texas State University has an internship program open only to its own students.

AIESEC—US. Reciprocal internship program for students in economics, business, finance, marketing, accounting, and computer sciences. See page 18 for further information.

Association for International Practical Training.
"IAESTE Trainee Program." On-the-job training for undergraduate and graduate students in technical fields such as engineering, computer science, agriculture, architecture, and mathematics. See page 18 for further information.
"Hotel & Culinary Exchanges Program." On-the-job training for young people beginning a career in the hotel and food service industries. Participants must have graduated from a university or vocational school and possess at least six months of training or experience in the chosen field. Training usually runs 6–12 months.

Council on International Educational Exchange. "Paris Internship and Study Program." Juniors, seniors, graduates; two and a half years of French, and French course in semester immediately preceding program; 3.0 GPA in French and 2.75 overall. Apply by April 1 for fall and October 1 for spring. Contact Academic Programs Department.

Voluntary Service

CIEE places young people in French voluntary service workcamps organized by the following organizations:

- Concordia (27, rue du Pont-Neuf, B.P. 238, 75024 Paris, Cedex 1) sponsors two- to three-week workcamps during the spring and summer. Projects take place all over France and generally involve construction, restoration work, conservation, or social work. Volunteers must be 16 years of age or older.
- Etudes et Chantiers (18, rue de Chantillon, 75014 Paris) accepts volunteers for workcamps throughout France. Projects include restoring old houses and public buildings, creating playgrounds, maintaining river banks, and protecting sand dunes. Volunteers must be 18 years of age or older.
- Jeunesse et Reconstruction (10, rue de Trevisse, 75009 Paris) specializes in two- to four-week workcamps that involve volunteers in a variety of construction, conservation, and ecology projects. Volunteers must be 16 years of age or older.

A four-week study tour in France that includes a short workcamp experience is offered by International Christian Youth Exchange (ICYE). Persons ages 18–35 are eligible. Application for the summer program should be made by May 1. Contact the Short-Term Programs Department at ICYE (see Appendix I for the address).

In addition, there are a couple of organizations that conduct workcamps for persons interested in restoring historic buildings and monuments in various parts of France.

- R.E.M.P. ART (1, rue des Guillemites, 75004 Paris) organizes workcamps that last anywhere from a weekend to a month or longer. An application fee is charged, and volunteers pay a daily fee (which varies according to location) to cover their food and lodging expenses. Generally, participants must be at least 18 years old.

- Most of the workcamps organized by Club du Vieux Manoir (10, rue de la Cossonnerie, 75001 Paris) function during Easter vacation and from July 2 to September 30; a few operate year-round. During the summer, volunteers are required to stay at least 15 days, beginning on either the 2nd or 16th of the month. Camping facilities are provided at a cost of approximately $8 per day. Anyone over 15 years of age is eligible.

For persons interested in longer-term voluntary service work, the "Year Abroad Program" sponsored by the International Christian Youth Exchange offers persons ages 18–24 voluntary service opportunities in the fields of health care, education, the environment, construction, et cetera. See page 22 for more information.

STUDY

A U.S. citizen who wishes to study at the undergraduate level in France for longer than 90 days must apply for a student visa at the French consulate having jurisdiction over his/her place of residence. Consulates are located in Boston, Chicago, Houston, Los Angeles, Miami, New Orleans, New York, San Francisco, and Washington, D.C.; contact the French Consulate General (934 Fifth Avenue, New York, NY 10021) for further information. Be sure to allow plenty of time, since applications received by mail take at least two weeks to be processed.

The free publications issued by the French Cultural Services (972 Fifth Avenue, New York, NY 10021) are excellent sources of information if you plan to study on your own in France. These include *Courses for Foreign Students in France* and *Selected Programs in France—Summer*. Also available from them is general information on fellowships and assistantships for college graduates.

Listed below are the educational programs offered by CIEE member institutions. Consult Appendix I for the addresses of the colleges and universities listed in this section.

In addition to the programs below, the American Graduate School of International Management, California State University, the College of Charleston, Illinois State University, Lewis and Clark College, New York University, Pennsylvania State University, Stanford University, the University of California system, the University of Rhode Island, the University of Tennessee, and Valparaiso University offer programs open to their own students only.

SEMESTER AND ACADEMIC YEAR

Business

Experiment in International Living/School for International Training. "College Semester Abroad." Toulouse. Fall or spring semester. Intensive language, international business, and French institutions seminar with internship and homestay. Sophomores to graduate students with 2.5 GPA. Apply by May 15 for fall and October 15 for spring.

Critical Studies

Council on International Educational Exchange. "Critical Studies Program at the University of Paris III." Semester or academic year. Juniors, seniors, and graduate students. Two years college French for academic year and fall semester; three years required for spring semester; 3.0 GPA in French and overall. Apply April 1 and October 1. Contact Academic Programs Department.

Drama

New York University. "Experimental Theatre Wing in Paris." Trips to Italy and the U.S.S.R. (optional). Semester or academic year. Offered by Tisch School of the Arts. Juniors and seniors with intermediate French, one year of actor training, and courses in drama or theater history. Audition required. Apply by October 15 for spring and February 15 for fall. Contact: Experimental Theatre Wing/Paris, 721 Broadway, 2nd floor, New York, NY 10003; (212) 998-1854.

French Language and Civilization

Adventist Colleges Abroad. Collonges-sous-Salève. Open only to students at Adventist Colleges Abroad consortium institutions. Academic year, semester, or quarter. Freshmen to seniors with 3.0 GPA in French and 2.5 overall GPA. Apply sixty days before beginning of academic term.

Central University of Iowa. "Central College Paris Program." Academic year or semester. Sophomores, juniors, and seniors with intermediate French and 2.5 GPA (3.0 in French). Introductory program also available. Apply by April 15 for fall and November 1 for spring.

Experiment in International Living/School for International Training. "College Semester Abroad." Tours, Nantes, or Toulouse (depending on language level). Intensive language, life and culture seminar, homestay, and excursions. Students may do both programs in an academic year. Sophomores to graduate students with 2.5 GPA. Apply by May 15 for fall and by October 15 for spring.

Macalester College. "PAAT (Paris, Aix, Avignon, and Toulon) French Program." Spring semester. January orientation in Paris prior to study in Aix, Avignon, or Toulon. Sophomores, juniors, and seniors with two years of college French. Apply by September 15.

Michigan State University. Paris. "French Language, Literature, and Culture in Paris." Spring quarter. Sophomores, juniors, and seniors with two years college-level French. Apply by February 3.

Middlebury College. Paris. Sophomores to graduate students. Fluency in French required. Rolling admissions.

Northern Illinois University. "French Studies in the South of France." Aix-en-Provence or Avignon. Semester or academic year. Courses offered in cooperation with the Institute for American Universities. No language prerequisite. Housing with French families. Sophomores, juniors, and seniors with 2.5 GPA.

Ohio University. "Spring Quarter in France." Tours. Freshmen to seniors with two quarters of French. Apply by January. Contact Department of Modern Languages; (614) 593-2765.

State University of New York at Buffalo. "Study Abroad–Grenoble." Semester or academic year. Juniors to graduate students with intermediate French and 3.0 GPA. Apply by April 1 for fall and October 15 for spring. Contact International Education Services, 409 Capen Hall, Buffalo, NY 14260; (716) 636-2258.

State University of New York at Oswego. Paris. Semester or academic year. Study at University de Paris–Sorbonne and the Institut Catholique de Paris; juniors and seniors with two years of French. Apply by April 15 for fall and November 15 for spring.

State University of New York at Stony Brook. Avignon. Semester or academic year. Juniors and seniors with five semesters of college French. Apply by April 1 for fall and October 15 for spring.

Stetson University. Dijon. Semester or academic year. Sophomores, juniors, and seniors with two years of French and 2.5 GPA (3.0 in major). Apply by March 1 for fall and October 15 for spring.

University of Colorado at Boulder. "Spring Semester in Chambéry." French grammar, literature, conversation, and civilization. Freshmen to seniors with two semesters of college-level French and 2.75 GPA. Apply by October 15.

University of Massachusetts–Amherst. "French Studies in Angers." Spring semester. Sophomores, juniors, and seniors with one semester of college French. Apply by December 1.

University of Minnesota. "French in Montpellier." Fall, winter, or spring quarter. Freshmen to graduate students with one year college-level French and 2.5 GPA. Apply June 15, October 15, and December 15.

University of North Carolina–Chapel Hill. "UNC Year at Montpellier." Academic year. Sophomores to graduate students with 2.7 GPA and two years of pre-college French plus three semesters of college French. Apply by March 1.

University of Notre Dame. "Foreign Study Program in Angers." Academic year (October 15–June 1), with four-week preliminary session in September. Sophomores and juniors with two years of French. Apply by February 1.

University System of Georgia/Georgia College. "Semester/Year Study in France." Caen and Tours. Undergraduate and graduate students with three quarters of college-level French; 2.5 overall GPA and 3.0 in French. Apply by August 15 for fall and December 15 for spring.

General Studies

Alma College. "Program of Studies in France." Paris. Academic year or semester. Study at Alliance Française. Sophomores, juniors, and seniors with 2.5 GPA. Apply by June 15 for fall and October 15 for winter.

American Heritage Association. "Northwest Interinstitutional Council on Study Abroad–Avignon." Fall, spring, and/or winter quarters. Sophomores, juniors, and seniors with two semesters of French and 2.5 GPA. Apply by June 1, November 1, and January 2.

Beloit College. "French Seminar." Rennes. Spring semester. Sophomores to graduate students with a minimum of intermediate French and 2.0 GPA. Apply by November 1.

Brethren Colleges Abroad. Strasbourg. Semester or academic year. Juniors and seniors with two years of college French and 3.0 GPA. Apply by May 1 for fall and November 1 for spring.

Carleton College. "Carleton College Programs at the University of Pau." Two trimesters (January–June). Family homestay. Sophomores, juniors, and seniors with two years of French. Apply by October 15.

Central Washington University. "Northwest Interinstitutional Council on Study Abroad–Avignon." See listing under American Heritage Association.

Council on International Educational Exchange. "Undergraduate Program at the University of Haute-Bretagne." Rennes. Semester or academic year. Sophomores, juniors, and seniors with two years college French for semester program; two and a half years required for academic year. 3.0 GPA required. Apply by February 15 for fall and October 15 for spring. Contact Academic Programs Department.

Davidson College. "Davidson College Junior Year Abroad in Montpellier." Academic year. Two years of French and 2.75 GPA required. Apply by February 1.

Experiment in International Living/School for International Training. "College Semester Abroad." Toulouse. Sophomores to graduate students with 2.5 GPA. Apply by May 15 for fall and November 15 for spring.

Guilford College. "Semester in Paris." Spring. Sophomores, juniors, and seniors with three semesters of college-level French. Apply by September 30.

Hollins College. "Hollins Abroad Paris Program." Semester or academic year. Juniors and seniors with 2.0 GPA and one year of college-level French. Apply by April 1 for fall and September 30 for spring.

Indiana University. "Overseas Study in Strasbourg." Academic year. Limited to students at Indiana and Purdue. Juniors and seniors with two years of French and 3.0 GPA. Apply by first week of November.

Kalamazoo College. Caen, Clermont-Ferrand, or Strasbourg. Fall and winter quarter (September 15–February 15). Juniors and seniors with 20 quarter hours of French and 3.0 GPA. Students are required to spend the summer prior to going abroad at Kalamazoo. Apply by May 1.

International Student Exchange Program. Direct reciprocal exchange between U.S. universities and institutions in Aix-en-Provence, Angers, Besançon, Caen, Chambery, Grenoble, Lyon, Montpellier, Nantes, Nice, Rennes, Saint-Etienne, and Villeneuve d'Ascq. Semester or academic year. Full curriculum options. Open only to students at ISEP member institutions.

Lake Erie College. Semester or academic year. Sophomores, juniors, and seniors with 2.5 GPA. Apply by June 1 for fall and November 1 for spring.

New York University. "NYU in France." Paris. Semester or academic year. Juniors, seniors, and graduate students with at least three semesters of college French and 3.0 GPA. Apply by May 1 for fall and October 1 for spring. Contact: NYU in France, 19 University Place, Room 631, New York, NY 10003; (212) 998-8722.

Purdue University. "Strasbourg Program." Academic year. Priority is given to Purdue and Indiana students. Juniors and seniors with two years of college-level French. Apply by first Friday in November.

Rosary College. "Rosary in Strasbourg." Semester or academic year. Internships also available. Juniors only; two years of college-level French required. Apply by February 1.

Rutgers University. "Junior Year in France." Study in Tours, with six weeks in Paris. Academic year. Juniors with two years of college French and courses in French literature. Apply by March 1.

St. Lawrence University. "France Year Program." Academic year in Rouen, with one-month orientation in Paris. Sophomores to seniors with 2.8 GPA and intermediate college French. Apply by February 20.

Skidmore College. "Junior Year Abroad." Paris. Semester or academic year. Juniors and seniors with 3.0 GPA; intermediate proficiency in French required for single semester, third-year level for academic year. Apply by October 15 for spring and February 15 for fall.

Southern Methodist University. Paris. "SMU-in-Paris." Semester or academic year. Liberal-arts studies focused on French experience. Sophomores, juniors, and seniors with one year college French. Apply by October 15 for spring and by March 15 for fall.

State University of New York at Stony Brook. Paris. Academic year or fall semester. Juniors, seniors, and graduate students with two years of college-level French and 3.0 GPA required. Apply by April 1.

Syracuse University. "Syracuse University in Strasbourg." Fall or spring semester. Sophomores, juniors, and seniors with 3.0 GPA. Apply by March 15 for fall and October 15 for spring.

Tufts University. "Tufts in Paris." Juniors with two years college French and 3.0 GPA. Apply by February 1.

University of Colorado at Boulder. "Study Abroad in Bordeaux." Juniors and seniors with two years college French and 2.75 GPA. Apply by March 1.

University of Connecticut. "Study Abroad Program in France." Rouen or Paris. Academic year. Freshmen to seniors with one year of college French. Apply by February 15.

University of Maryland. "Maryland-in-Nice." Academic year or spring semester. Sophomores, juniors, and seniors with one year college French and 3.0 GPA. Apply by March 15 for academic year and October 15 for spring.

University of North Carolina–Chapel Hill. "UNC Program to Lyon." Academic year. Juniors and seniors. 3.0 GPA and fluency in French required. Apply by February 15.

University of Oregon.
"Northwest Interinstitutional Council on Study Abroad–Avignon." See listing under American Heritage Association.
"OSSHE–Lyon Universities Exchange Program." Academic year. Juniors, seniors, and graduate students with three years college French and 3.0 GPA. Preference is given to Oregon State System of Higher Education (OSSHE) students. Apply by January 2.
"OSSHE–Poitiers Exchange Program." Academic year. Juniors, seniors, and graduate students with two years college French and 2.75 GPA. Preference given to Oregon State System of Higher Education (OSSHE) students. Apply by February 15.

University of Washington. "Northwest Interinstitutional Council on Study Abroad–Avignon." See listing under American Heritage Association.

University of Wisconsin–Madison. Aix-en-Provence. Academic year. Sophomores to graduate students with two years of college French and 3.0 GPA. Open to students at colleges or universities in the state, or Wisconsin residents studying in other states. Apply by February 1.

University System of Georgia/University of Georgia. "Semester/Year Study in France." Paris. Fall or spring semester. Freshmen to graduate students with two years college French and 3.0 GPA. Apply three months prior to beginning of term.

Wesleyan University. "Wesleyan Program in Paris." Semester or academic year. Sophomores, juniors, and seniors with five semesters of college French and 3.0 GPA in French. Apply by March 10 for fall and October 10 for spring.

Western Washington University. "Northwest Interinstitutional Council on Study Abroad–Avignon." See listing under American Heritage Association.

History

Michigan State University. "Paris and the French Revolution." Paris. Fall quarter. Historical, cultural, and literary studies. Sophomores, juniors, and seniors with two years college French. Apply by June 5.

Marketing

University of New Hampshire. "Spring Semester in Grenoble." Study international marketing at the Université de Grenoble II. Juniors and seniors at state universities in New England. Contact Whittemore School of Business and Economics, McConnell Hall, University of New Hampshire, Durham, NH 03824; (603) 862-1981.

Teacher Education

State University of New York at Cortland. "Cortland International Programs–Caen." Academic year at Ecole Normale d'Instituteurs du Calvados. Elementary teaching methods and curriculum. Juniors, seniors, and graduate students with advanced French courses. Apply by February 15.

SUMMER

Art

New York University. "The Culture Industry–Paris." Graduate students. Apply by April 15. Contact: School of Education, Health, Nursing and Arts Professions, 32 Washington Place, 3rd floor, New York, NY 10003; (212) 998-5030.

Business

Ohio State University.
"French Business Language and Environment." Nantes. Business French, French civilization, and France's social and economic environment. French majors between junior and senior year with 2.75 GPA. Apply by April 1. "International Program in Business." Nantes. European civilization, business, and financial environment. Business majors with 2.75 GPA. Apply by April 1.

Monterey Institute of International Studies. "Commercial French." Rouen. Upper division program on the campus of the Institut de Formation a la Vente Internationale. Advanced undergraduates and graduate students. Limited enrollment for students outside the Monterey Institute. Apply by March 15.

Syracuse University. "International Personnel and Organization Management." Strasbourg, with field trips to Germany, Switzerland, and Luxembourg. Juniors, seniors, and graduate students. No language requirement. Apply by March 17.

Foreign Language Education

New York University. "Foreign Language Education." Graduate students. Apply by April 15. Contact: School of Education, Health, Nursing and Arts Professions, 32 Washington Place, 3rd floor, New York, NY 10003; (212) 998-5030.

French Language and Culture

Experiment in International Living/School for International Training. "Summer Academic Study Abroad." Tours and Aix-en-Provence. Intensive language and life and culture seminar. Freshmen to seniors. Apply by March 15.

Illinois State University. "ISU Summer Program at University of Grenoble." Eight weeks. Freshmen to seniors with one year college French. Apply by March 1.

Indiana University. Dijon. "Language Study in France." Freshmen to seniors with one year of college-level French and 2.8 GPA. Apply by mid-February.

Marquette University. "Summer Study Program in France." Limoges. Undergraduates with one year of college French or two years of high-school French. Apply by April 25. Contact: Director, Department of Foreign Languages, Lalumiere Language Hall, Marquette University, Milwaukee, WI 53233.

Mary Baldwin College. "May Term in Paris." Classes conducted in French. Undergraduates with intermediate French. Apply by December 1.

Michigan State University. "French Language, Literature, and Culture in Tours." Sophomores, juniors, and seniors with one year college French. Apply by April 21.

Southern Methodist University. "SMU-in-Tours." Tours. Sophomores, juniors, and seniors. Apply by March 15.

State University of New York at Oswego. Paris and St. Malo. Freshmen to seniors with intermediate-level French. Apply by April 25.

State University of New York at Stony Brook. Avignon. Juniors and seniors with 3.0 GPA and five semesters of French. Apply by April 1.

University of Alabama. "Academic Summer Program in France." Aix-en-Provence. Freshmen to graduate students with two semesters of college French. Apply by April 1.

University of Arkansas at Little Rock. "Summer in France." Strasbourg. Sophomores, juniors, and seniors with intermediate French. Apply by March 15.

University of Massachusetts at Amherst. "Summer Studies in Dijon." Sophomores to graduate students with one year of French (fluency required for graduate students). Apply by February 1.

University of North Carolina–Chapel Hill. "UNC Summer in Montpellier." Sophomores, juniors, and seniors. Apply by February 15.

University System of Georgia/Columbus College. Dijon. Freshmen to seniors with 2.5 GPA. Apply by March 15.

University System of Georgia/Georgia College. Tours. Sophomores to graduate students with three quarters of college-level French or equivalent and 3.0 GPA in French and 2.5 overall GPA. Apply by March 15.

Western Michigan University. "Summer Study in France." Lyon and/or Paris. Sophomores to graduate students with three semesters of French and 2.0 GPA.

General Studies

Alma College. "Program of Studies in France." Paris. Study at Alliance Française. Sophomores, juniors, and seniors with 2.5 GPA. Apply by March 15.

Louisiana State University. "LSU in Paris." Sophomores to graduate students with 2.5 GPA. Apply by April 15.

New York University. "NYU in France." Paris. High-school graduates, freshmen to graduate students with 2.5 GPA. Apply by April 1. Contact: NYU in France, 19 University Place, Rm 631, New York, NY 10003; (212) 998-8722.

Skidmore College. Paris. Juniors and seniors with some knowledge of French. Apply by February 15.

University of Utah. "Molière Vous Invite en Provence." Forcalquier. Acting and intensive course work. Seniors, graduate students, and secondary teachers of French proficient at the graduate level in French. Apply by March 1.

Humanities

New York University. "Humanities." Paris. Graduate students. Apply by April 15. Contact: 32 Washington Place, 3rd floor, New York, NY 10003.

Law

University of Iowa. "International and Comparative Law." Study program in Arcachon, France, followed by law clerk options in Paris, London, Madrid, and Frankfurt. Students at accredited law schools and practicing attorneys. Apply by March 1. Contact: Dean, College of Law.

Marketing

University System of Georgia/Georgia State University. "Marketing in Paris." Open only to business students with minimum 2.5 GPA. Apply by March 1.

EXPLORING FRENCH CULTURE

Literature

Many classics of French literature continue to provide interesting reading for anyone going to France today. Among these are Honoré de Balzac's novel,

La Cousine Bette, which deals with the downfall of the French aristocracy and Gustave Flaubert's *Madame Bovary*, the story of a woman unable to adapt to the provincial life she is forced to lead, a fact which finally leads to self-destruction.

The 1930s saw the emergence of a number of existentialist writers, including Jean Paul Sartre. His *Nausea* tells the story of a man with no friends or family, a man who is disgusted with life and finds the lives of others boring and meaningless. Sartre's *No Exit* takes place in hell—which is depicted as an ordinary hotel room where three people are left together for eternity.

During the 1950s France gave birth to the "new novel." New novelists saw themselves as inventors rather than transcribers of reality. They often portrayed characters without names as Nathalie Sarraute did in *Portrait of an Unknown*. And often their stories were set in unusual time frames, such as that in Alain Robbe-Grillet's *The Erasers*, which takes place within 24 hours, but not in any particular time in history. In *Zazie dans le Metro* Raymond Queneau writes about a girl living in the suburbs whose longtime dream is to ride the metros of Paris.

More recently, Francoise Sagan's first novel *Bonjour Tristesse*, about a young girl living with her widowed father on the Côte d'Azur, and Christiane Rochefort's *Josyanne and the Welfare*, describing life in the projects of Paris, have dealt with more traditional coming-of-age themes.

In addition to producing its own great writers, France has attracted expatriate writers of many nationalities who have gone on to create classics in their own languages. An American heading to France for a vacation or period of work or study might enjoy reading accounts of the English-speaking expatriate community in Paris in the 1920s and 1930s. Among the best of these are Henry Miller's *Tropic of Cancer*, Ernest Hemingway's *A Moveable Feast*, and George Orwell's *Down and Out in Paris and London*.

Film

Since the invention of the movie projector in France by the Lumière brothers, August and Louis, in 1895, French films have been among the world's best-known. This is especially true of the productions made during the 1920s and 1930s, a stylistically mixed period that saw such "classical directors" as Jean Renoir, with his lyrical, witty treatments of contemporary issues in films such as *Grand Illusion, A Day in the Country, The Human Beast*, and *Boudu Saved From Drowning*, as well as the more surrealistic films of avant-garde directors such as Jean Cocteau and René Clair. Even with their disparate aesthetic concerns, the French films of the inter-war period addressed the overlapping issues of industrialization, modernity, class differences, internationalism, and modern warfare.

The French *Nouvelle Vague*, or "New Wave," with its critical devotion to American cinema, has been an internationally influential film movement for the past 30 years. Early New Wave directors such as Jean-Luc Godard, François Truffaut, Alain Resnais, Eric Rohmer, and Agnès Varda have gone on to produce enormously varied oeuvres dealing with themes as different as adolescent coming of age, religious mores and repression, Maoist political philosophy, the objectification of women, and the rationalization of sexual conquest. The principal characteristics linking their work, however, have been a desire to experiment with the language and conventions of cinema as well as an adventurous manipulation of the ways of viewing a subject. Easily found titles include *Breathless* (Godard), *The 400 Blows* and *Shoot the Piano Player* (Truffaut), *Hiroshima Mon Amour* and *Last Year at Marienbad* (Resnais), and *Cleo From 5 to 7* (Varda).

Recent French film releases include productions by original New Wave directors such as Louis Malle (*Au Revoir les Enfants*) and Agnès Varda (*Vagabond*). In addition, a number of younger French directors, including Claude Berri (*Jean de Florette* and *Manon of the Spring*) and Jean-Jacques Beineix (*Diva* and *Betty Blue*), have established themselves as directors to watch in the 1990s.

In addition to the work of the filmmakers discussed above, an enormous variety of French films can be viewed in the U.S. These include Abel Gance's silent masterpiece *Napoléon* (1927), Jean Vigo's *L'Atalante* (1934), and Robert Bresson's *Diary of a Country Priest* (1951). Also of note is the work of documentarist Chris Marker, who has produced numerous influential short films, including *Cuba Si!* (1961), *Description d'un Combat* (1960), and his only fiction film, *La Jetée* (1964).

GERMANY (Federal Republic)

Clichés about Germany abound. Popular-media images of a country of medieval castles, quaint villages, and beer-drinking people in lederhosen exist side by side with those of high-speed autobahns filled with Porsches and Mercedes zipping from one end of the country to the other. Contrasting with these, however, are dark memories of a fascist past that resulted in the deaths of millions of people. Obviously, considering any one set of images out of context is misleading. Germany is not a country that is easy to understand.

Germany's location in the heart of Europe has made it a crossroads of cultures and has produced a variety of German peoples rather than a uniform nationality. German history shows the efforts of these different peoples to accommodate and adapt themselves to their geographical circumstances, fighting to achieve a common cultural identity and create a single political entity.

Diversity may be the foremost characteristic of Germany. The nation encompasses a varied landscape that extends from the flat grasslands of the northern coast to the picturesque valleys of the Rhine and its tributaries, to the Black Forest and Bavarian Alps in the south. Linguistically, Germany is divided into the Low-German dialects of the north and the High-German dialects of the south. Both in terms of culture and mentality you will find great differences between Friesians, Westphalians, Berliners, Swabians, and Bavarians—to name just a few of the German regional groups.

The war also divided Berlin and ended its role as the nation's predominant city. As a result, the traditional regional centers of Germany have regained their importance. On the North Sea coast are the seaports of Hamburg and Bremen, both rich in the traditions of the medieval Hanseatic merchant league. Cologne and Frankfurt are the urban centers of central Germany. Cologne is famous for its medieval city and cathedral, which was reconstructed after it was devastated by Allied bombing during the Second World War. Frankfurt is West Germany's railway, communications, and banking center. In the south there's Stuttgart—the heart of the thriving high-tech state of Baden-Württemburg—and Munich, home of the Hofbrauhaus and capital of Bavaria. And in the middle of communist East Germany is West Berlin, an extraordinarily lively and attractive city that retains much of the cosmopolitan style and energy of the prewar capital.

Modern West Germany, together with Japan, leads the exporting nations of the world, and enjoys a booming economy and a stable currency. In spite of its economic success, however, the unemployment rate has hovered around six to eight percent for most of the last decade. Though an extensive welfare network provides a safety net for those out of work, there is no denying the considerable frustration and unrest among the young, who increasingly face the real possibility of joblessness after graduation.

Except during summer vacation, Germans are generally not very mobile. Come August, however, millions of Germans depart for the beaches of Italy, Greece, and Spain. This exodus makes room for the foreign tourists who flock to Heidelberg, Neuschwansteinl, and other romantic spots made famous in tourist brochures but perhaps less dear to the Germans themselves.

Tourists will find getting around Germany fairly easy. Efficient public rail and bus services exist and hitchhiking is common among students (but not permitted on the autobahns). In addition, ride-sharing agencies can be found in any large city. And if you lose your way, you'll soon find people willing to try their English on you (English is compulsory from middle school onward). In the countryside English-speakers are less common, but the foreigner will find him- or herself in a situation not much different from that of a northern German faced with a Bavarian dialect. The language, people, culture, and history may be difficult to make sense of initially; however, a little effort to get tuned in will prove to be extremely rewarding.

—*Kurt Gamerschlag, Bonn, West Germany*

Official name: Federal Republic of Germany. **Area:** 96,010 square miles (about the size of Wyoming). **Population:** 61,200,000. **Population density:** 637 inhabitants per square mile. **Capital:** Bonn (pop. 292,600). **Largest city:** Hamburg (pop. 1,575,700). **Language:** German. **Religions:** Protestant and Roman Catholic. **Per capita income:** US$10,300. **Currency:** Deutsche Mark. **Literacy rate:** 99%. **Average daily high/low:*** Hamburg: January, 35°/18°; June, 69°/56°. Munich: January, 33°/23°; July, 72°/54°. **Average number of days with precipitation:** Hamburg: January, 12; July, 12. Munich: January, 10; July, 14.

TRAVEL

U.S. citizens need a passport, but a visa is not required for stays of up to three months in West Germany (including West Berlin). For longer stays, check with the Embassy of the Federal Republic of Germany (4645 Reservoir Road NW, Washington, DC 20007) or a West German consulate for specific requirements.

Getting Around

For people planning to travel around West Germany by rail, GermanRail offers a variety of discount plans:

---

*all temperatures are Fahrenheit

- The GermanRail Tourist Card allows unlimited rail travel as follows: four days for $81, nine days for $124, and 16 days for $172, all second class; or four days for $121, nine days for $186, and 16 days for $258, first class.
- The Junior Tourist Card, available to anyone under 26, costs $79 for 9 days and $99 for 16 days, second class only.
- The Tramper Ticket is available to youths under 22 and students under 26, and entitles the holder to one month of unlimited train travel, second class, on the GermanRail network. It must be purchased in Germany; the cost is DM234 (about $138). To qualify you must show proof of age (passport or other ID) and have a passport-size photo.
- The Junior Pass qualifies the holder to 50 percent off regular fares on point-to-point tickets for a period of up to one year. Youths from 18–22 years of age and students under 27 are eligible. The card is available for DM110 (about $65) at rail stations throughout Germany.

Eurail passes are also valid on the West German rail network (see page 58).

On trains with baggage cars, bicycles can be placed aboard the train, provided the passenger has obtained a bike card from the ticket seller ($2.25 to $3.60, depending on trip mileage). Under GermanRail's "Bicycle at the Station" plan, passengers can rent a bicycle for $2.75 a day (non-passengers pay $5.50). Bikes may be dropped off at any of nearly 300 stations participating in the program. Most operate from April to October, while some operate year-round. Brochures listing the participating rental stations can be obtained at GermanRail offices.

"There are a lot of Americans in West Germany—perhaps more than in any other European nation. It is very easy (and tempting during bouts of homesickness) to surround oneself with fellow expatriots and tourists. But anyone who gives in to the lure of familiarity is doing himself a great disservice. Most West Germans are not only fluent in English (for those unwilling or unable to try German), but also eager to introduce interested foreigners to the delights of their country."
—Crystal Mazur, Cheektowaga, New York

"I think the most important thing I learned about Germany, or better, the Germans, is the effect World War II has had on their entire culture. The loss of pride that the Germans felt directly after the war has only begun to fade."
—David G. Barber, Virginia Beach, Virginia

Especially for Students and Young People

The following West German organizations specialize in student travel offering reduced prices on air, rail, and bus travel; all are members of the ISTC.

- Council Travel Service (CTS), Graf-Adolf-Strasse 18, 4000 Düsseldorf
- Reisedienst Deutscher Studentenschaften (RDS), Niederlassung Rentzelstrasse 16, 2000 Hamburg 13
- AStA-Reisen, Keplerstrasse 17, D-7000 Stuttgart 1
- StR Studententreisen Tübingen, Wilhelmstrasse 13 (Mensa), 7400 Tübingen

Other student travel bureaus are located in Frankfurt, Hanover, Kiel, Münster, and Mainz. In West Germany, students with an ISIC can get reduced-fare plane and train tickets both within the country as well as from Germany to points in Europe and beyond. They are also entitled to discounts on West Berlin buses, on admission fees to some museums and historical sites, and to many theaters, opera houses, and concert halls.

For Further Information

The German National Tourist Office (747 Third Avenue, New York, NY 10017) and the German Information Center (950 Third Avenue, New York, NY 10022) are good sources of general cultural and tourist information on West Germany.

Helpful suggestions on budget travel and accommodations can be found in *Let's Go: Europe* ($13.95), *Frommer's Germany* ($14.95), and *Fodor's Great Travel Values: Germany* ($7.95). The *Michelin Green Guide* to West Germany is a comprehensive guide to cultural points of interest. All can be found in most bookstores.

WORK

Getting a Job

The Council's Work in Germany Program is administered through its offices in New York and Bonn. The program enables you to work for a period of five months, from May 15 through October 15. Participants must be U.S. citizens at least 18 years of age and full-time college or university students with a minimum of two years of college-level German. In the 1989 program job options varied, but students found employment in cities from Munich to Hamburg as waiters/waitresses, secretaries, factory workers, bank clerks, and nurse's assistants. The cost of the program is $96. For details, contact CIEE's Work Exchanges Department, 205 East 42nd Street, New York, NY 10017. Students who participate in the program receive overnight accommodations and an orientation from CIEE's Bonn office, which also provides information on living, working, and traveling in Germany.

The Zentralstelle für Arbeitsvermittlung (ZAV), 6000 Frankfurt (Main), Feuerbachstrasse 42–46, the official government labor agency, also places U.S. and Canadian students in summer jobs throughout Germany. In order to be eligible you must be at least 18 years old, have a good command of German (how good depends on the individual job), and agree to work for at least two months. Most jobs are unskilled—you'll probably end up working in a hotel or restaurant as a kitchen helper, chambermaid or dishwasher, or, if your German is good enough, as an assistant waiter or waitress. There is no fee for this service; write to the ZAV for applications. Applications will be accepted until March 1, but the ZAV should receive your application at least three months before you wish to begin work.

CDS International offers a Career Training Program for young professionals with degrees in business, engineering, or a technical field, as well as training in the hotel business or as a bilingual secretary. The program includes intensive language training, followed by a year to 18 months working in a German company. The CDS Internship Program offers U.S. college seniors and recent graduates the opportunity to receive in-depth language training followed by a five-month paid internship with a German company. Applicants for both programs must be U.S. citizens and have a good knowledge of German. For more information contact CDS International, 425 Park Avenue, New York, NY 10022.

Au Pair

Au pair positions can be arranged through the Central Placement Office of the German Federal Labor Agency. Positions are for females 18 to 27 years old with a basic knowledge of German. Au pairs generally spend 10 to 12 months living with a family doing light housework and looking after children in return for room and board and about DM300 (about $176) per month. Interested persons fill out an application form in German; then, families looking for an au pair review the applications and select the person they wish to employ. Applications are available from CIEE's Work Exchanges Department.

Teaching

Teachers of German, as well as anyone else with a college degree and a major in German, may apply for positions as modern language assistants in Germany. Applicants must be under 30 years of age. Teaching assignments are supervised by a master teacher and involve 12 hours of teaching a week for ten months; the salary is approximately DM900 per month. Applications must be received in October for work the following year. For more information, contact U.S. Student Programs, Institute of International Education, 809 United Nations Plaza, New York, NY 10017 or Padagogische Austausch-dienst, Sekretariat der Standigen Konferenz der Kulturminister der Lander in der Bundesrepublik Deutschland, Nassestrasse 8, D-5300 Bonn. Information is also available at the embassy or consular offices of the West German government.

"Being registered at a German University means you receive a work permit allowing you to seek part-time and vacation jobs. One of the most accessible, and lucrative, jobs in Germany is teaching English. If you're in a major city, just drop by any of the various foreign language schools, which are often beset by the problem of too many students wanting to learn American English and an all British faculty. If you're in a small town, or do not have a work permit, put up ads around your school offering to teach American English at a reasonable rate. This could bring you DM15 an hour. Proficiency in German will help your search even more."
—Christopher Spahr, Lake Forest, Illinois

Internships/Traineeships

Programs sponsored by member organizations of the Council on International Educational Exchange are listed below. Consult Appendix I for the addresses of the organizations listed in this section. In addition to the organizations listed below, Southwest Texas State University sponsors an internship program in West Germany that is open only to its own students.

AIESEC–US. Reciprocal internship program for students in economics, business, finance, marketing, accounting, and computer sciences. See page 18 for further information.

Association for International Practical Training.
"IAESTE Trainee Program." On-the-job training for undergraduate and graduate students in technical fields such as engineering, computer science, agriculture, architecture, and mathematics. See page 18 for more information.
"Hotel & Culinary Exchanges Program." On-the-job training for young people beginning a career in the hotel and food service industries. Participants must have graduated from a university or vocational school and possess at least six months of training or experience in the chosen field. Training usually runs 6–12 months.

Voluntary Service

CIEE places young people in West German voluntary service workcamps organized by the following organizations:

- Internationale Jugendgemeinschaftsdienste (Kaiserstrasse 43, D-5300 Bonn 1) sponsors three- to four-week workcamps during Easter vacation and from the end of June to October. Workcamps are organized around historical-preservation projects, environmental-protection projects, and urban-recreation activities. Volunteers must be over 16; knowledge of German is required for some workcamps.
- Internationale Begegnung in Gemeinschaftsdiensten (Schlosserstrasse 28, D-7000 Stuttgart 1) sponsors three-week workcamps from June to September that involve constructing hiking paths, renovation of youth centers, forest conservation, et cetera. Volunteers must be over 18.

The applications of U.S. residents for the workcamps of both organizations are processed by CIEE. Contact the International Voluntary Service Department at the Council's New York office for details.

The YMCA places Americans in West German workcamps organized by Nothelfergemeinschaft der Freunde. English is the common language at these camps, where 15 multinational workers and two group leaders work on assignments ranging from light construction to domestic work. Workcamps last three to four weeks and are operated from July through October. Dormitory housing is provided. The registration fee of 50DM (about $30) is refunded upon completion of the assignment. For more information contact the YMCA International Camp Counselor Program Abroad, YMCA of Greater New York, 356 West 34th Street, 3rd Floor, New York, NY 10001.

Another organization conducting workcamps in West Germany is Christlicher Friedensdienst, deutscher Zweig (Rendelerstrasse 9–11, 6000 Frankfurt 60). Volunteers 17 years of age and older work on three- to four-week projects involving children, the elderly, immigrant groups, and local peace groups. A study theme may also be a major aspect of the camp. Some camps require a good knowledge of German, and other skills may be needed depending on the nature of the camp. U.S. residents may obtain further information and application forms from CMP, 427 Bloor Street West, Toronto, Ontario, Canada M5S 1X7.

For persons interested in longer-term voluntary service work, the "Year Abroad Program" sponsored by the International Christian Youth Exchange offers persons ages 18–24 voluntary service opportunities in the fields of health care, education, the environment, construction, et cetera. See page 22 for more information.

STUDY

An excellent source of information on study and research in Germany is the German Academic Exchange Service, 950 Third Avenue, New York, NY 10022. DAAD (its German initials) puts together and distributes several publications free of charge, including *Academic Studies in the Federal Republic of Germany*, *Grants for Study and Research in the Federal Republic of Germany*, and *Language Courses at German Universities*. DAAD will also answer questions from U.S. students who wish to study in Germany.

Another source of information is the Consulate General of the Federal Republic of Germany (460 Park Avenue, New York, NY 10022). Its publications include *Goethe Institute—Language Courses*, *Summer Courses at German Universities*, and *Academic Studies in the Federal Republic of Germany*.

Listed below are the educational programs offered by member institutions of the Council on International Educational Exchange. Consult Appendix I for the addresses of the college and universities listed in this section. In addition to the programs below, the American Graduate School of International Management, California State University, Illinois State University, Indiana University, New York University, Northern Arizona University, Ohio State University, Pennsylvania State University, the University of California system, the University of Rhode Island, Stanford University, the University of Toledo, and Valparaiso University all offer programs open only to their own students.

SEMESTER AND ACADEMIC YEAR

Business

State University of New York at Cortland. Münster. Includes visits to international firms. Juniors, seniors, and graduate students with two years of college German and 3.5 GPA in major. Apply by March 1.

East-West Relations

Experiment in International Living/School for International Training. "College Semester Abroad." Berlin. Fall or spring semester. Intensive language, seminars, independent-study project, homestays, and excursions to Poland and German Democratic Republic. Sophomores to graduate students with 2.5 GPA. Apply by May 15 for fall and October 15 for spring.

General Studies

American Heritage Association. "Northwest Interinstitutional Council on Study Abroad–Cologne." Fall, winter, and/or spring quarters. Sophomores with one term college German. Apply by June 1 for fall and November 1 for winter.

Beloit College. "German Seminar." Hamburg. Fall semester. Sophomores to graduates with intermediate German and 2.0 GPA. Apply by April 1.

Brethren Colleges Abroad. Marburg. Academic year, and fall or spring semester. Juniors and seniors with two years of college German and 3.0 GPA. Apply by May 1 for academic year and fall, November 1 for spring.

Central Washington University. "Northwest Interinstitutional Council on Study Abroad–Cologne." See listing under American Heritage Association.

Davidson College. "Davidson College Junior Year Abroad in Würzburg." Academic year. Juniors of all majors with two years of German and 3.0 GPA. Apply by February 1.

Guilford College. "Semester in Munich." Fall semester. Sophomores, juniors, and seniors. Apply by October 31.

Heidelberg College. "American Junior Year at Heidelberg University." Academic year, and fall or spring semester. Juniors, seniors, and graduates with two years college German and 3.0 GPA. Apply by April 15 for academic year or semester. Contact American Junior Year at Heidelberg, 310 E. Market Street, Tiffin, OH 44883-2434; (419) 448-2256.

Indiana University. "Overseas Study in Hamburg." Academic year. Limited to students at Indiana, Purdue, and Ohio State. Juniors and seniors with two years of German and 3.0 GPA. Apply by first week of November.

International Student Exchange Program. Direct reciprocal exchange between U.S. universities and institutions in Braunschweig, Bremen, Eichstätt, Giessen, Kassel, Marburg, Munich, and Tarforst. Semester or academic year. Full curriculum options. Open only to students at ISEP member institutions.

Kalamazoo College.
  "Kalamazoo College in Bonn." Study at the University of Bonn. Fall and winter quarter (September 15–February 15). Orientation at Kalamazoo the summer prior to study abroad. Juniors and seniors with 2.75 GPA and 20 quarter-hours of German. Apply by May 1.
  "Kalamazoo College in Erlangen." Fall and winter quarter at the University of Erlangen. Juniors and seniors with 15 quarter hours of German and 2.75 GPA. Apply by May 1.
  "Kalamazoo College in Hannover." Juniors and seniors with 15 quarter hours of German and 2.75 GPA. Apply by May 1.

Lake Erie College. Tübingen. Sophomores, juniors, and seniors with 2.5 GPA. Apply by June 1 and November 1.

Lewis and Clark College. "Junior Year in Munich." Academic year or semester. Sophomores to seniors with two years of German and 3.0 GPA.

Michigan State University. "Junior Year in Freiburg." See program listing under Wayne State University.

Northern Illinois University. "Academic Internships in Bonn/Cologne." Fall semester. Students take two courses plus internship. Wide range of internships available for residents of Illinois; more limited selection for residents of other states. Sophomores, juniors, and seniors with 3.0 GPA and two years of German. Apply by April 4.

Portland State University. "Baden-Württemberg Program." Academic year. Juniors, seniors, graduates, and teachers with two years of college German. Apply by January 31.

Purdue University. "Overseas Study in Hamburg." See program listing under Indiana University.

Rutgers University. "Junior year in Germany." Constance. Academic year. Juniors with two years college German, German literature, and 3.0 GPA. Apply by March 1.

State University of New York at Albany. "Würzburg University Exchange." Academic year, fall and spring semester. Juniors, seniors, and graduates with two years of college German, 2.8 overall GPA and 3.0 in German. Apply by March 15 for academic year and fall and November 15 for spring.

State University of New York at Cortland.
Heidelberg. Fall or spring semester. Sophomores, juniors, and seniors with one year of college German and 3.5 GPA. Apply by March 1 for fall, October 1 for spring.
Tübingen. Spring semester or spring/summer quarter (March 1 to mid-July). Juniors, seniors, and graduates with two years of college German and 3.5 GPA. Apply by November 1.

State University of New York at Oswego. "Georg-August-Universität/SUNY Oswego Exchange Program." Göttingen. Academic year. Junior or senior German majors or education concentrations. Apply by April 15.

State University of New York at Stony Brook. Tübingen. Academic year. Sophomores to graduate students with two years of college German and 3.0 GPA. Apply by April 1.

Syracuse University. "Syracuse in Germany." Marburg. Exchange program with Philipps Universität. Academic year or spring semester. Juniors and seniors with two years college German and 3.0 GPA. Apply by March 15 for academic year, October 15 for spring semester.

Tufts University. "Tufts in Tübingen." Academic year or spring semester. Mainly juniors with two years of college German and 3.0 GPA. Apply by February 1.

University of Colorado at Boulder. "Academic Year in Regensburg." Juniors and seniors with four semesters of college German or equivalent and 2.75 GPA. Apply by February 15.

University of Massachusetts–Amherst. "Freiburg/Baden-Württemberg Exchange." Juniors, seniors, and graduates with 3.0 GPA and fluency in German. Apply by March 1.

University of North Carolina.
"UNC Program to Berlin." Academic year. Juniors and seniors, fluency in German and 3.0 GPA required. Apply by February 12.
"UNC Program to Göttingen." Academic year (see above for eligibility and deadline).
"UNC in Tübingen." Academic year. Sophomores, juniors, and seniors with 3.0 GPA and two years college German. Apply by March 15.

University of Oregon. "Northwest Interinstitutional Council on Study Abroad–Cologne." See listing under American Heritage Association.

University of Washington. "Northwest Interinstitutional Council on Study Abroad–Cologne." See listing under American Heritage Association.

University of Wisconsin–Madison.
Bonn. Academic year at Rheinische Friedrich Wilhelms University. Juniors and seniors with 3.0 GPA and one year of German. Open only to students at a college or university in Wisconsin or to Wisconsin residents studying outside the state. Apply by February 1.
"Junior Year in Freiburg." See program description under Wayne State University.

Wayne State University.
"Junior Year in Freiburg." Academic year at Albert Ludwigs University. Co-sponsored with Michigan State University, University of Michigan, and University of Wisconsin. Program offered mainly to juniors and occasionally to seniors with 3.0 GPA and two years of German. Apply by April 1.
"Junior Year in Munich." Junior standing or seniors on a space-available basis. Two years of German and 3.0 GPA required. Apply by April 1.

Wesleyan University. "Wesleyan University Program in Germany." Heidelberg and West Berlin. Spring semester. Language courses, seminars, and general studies at the University of Heidelberg. Sophomores, juniors, and seniors with three semesters of college German. Apply by November 1.

Western Washington University. "Northwest Interinstitutional Council on Study Abroad–Cologne." See listing under American Heritage Association.

German Language and Civilization

Alma College. "Program of Studies in Germany." Kassel. Academic year or semester. Sophomores, juniors, and seniors with 2.5 GPA. Apply by June 15 for fall and October 15 for winter.

Antioch University. "Antioch in Germany." Tübingen. Academic year or semester. Juniors and seniors with two years of German. Apply by January 15.

Central University of Iowa. "Central College in Germany and Austria." Prien and Murnau. Academic year or semester. Sophomores, juniors, and seniors with intermediate German and 2.5 GPA (3.0 in German). Apply by April 15 for fall and academic year, and November 1 for spring.

Hiram College. "Hamburg Quarter." Academic courses and travel in Germany with a trip to East Germany. Sophomores, juniors, and seniors with one year of German and 2.5 GPA. Apply by January 15.

Kalamazoo College. "Kalamazoo College at Münster." Fall and winter quarter. Juniors and seniors with 15 quarter hours of German and 2.5 GPA. Apply by May 1.

Middlebury College. Mainz. Sophomores to graduates. Fluency in German required. Rolling admissions.

Portland State University. "Spring Intensive Language Program." Tübingen. Limited to students from the Oregon State System of Higher Education. Spring quarter. Freshmen to graduate students with two quarter terms of first-year German and 2.5 GPA. Apply by January 31.

Stetson University. Freiburg. Academic year or semester. Sophomores, juniors, and seniors with two years of German and 2.5 GPA (3.0 in major). Apply by March 1 for fall and academic year and October 15 for spring.

University of Oregon.
"OSSHE–Baden-Württemberg Universities Exchange." Tübingen, Stuttgart, Konstanz, Hohenheim, Freiburg, Karlsruhle. Academic year. Preference given to juniors at schools in Oregon State System of Higher Education (OSSHE). Two years of college German with B average. Apply by January 31.
"OSSHE–Intensive German Language Program." Tübingen. Spring semester. Sophomores to graduate students with two quarters of college German and 2.5 GPA. Preference given to Oregon State System of Higher Education (OSSHE) students. Apply by January 31.

University of Washington. "Northeast Interinstitutional Council on Study Abroad." Cologne. Fall quarter. Sophomores, juniors, and seniors with two semesters of German and 2.75 GPA. Apply by June 1.

University System of Georgia/Georgia Southern College. "Semester Study in Germany." Tübingen. Spring semester. Undergraduates with 2.5 GPA and two quarters of German (but not more than three), 3.0 GPA in those courses. Apply by January 15.

Mechanical Engineering

Michigan State University. "Engineering in Aachen." Study at the Technical University of Aachen, with opportunities to participate in research and explore German industrial activities. Spring quarter. Juniors and seniors with mechanical-engineering background. Apply by February 3.

Physical Education

State University of New York at Cortland. Cologne. Spring. Juniors and seniors with one semester of college German and 3.5 GPA in major. Apply by October 1.

SUMMER

Business

University System of Georgia/Georgia State University. Tübingen. Two weeks in June. Seminar on industry and business practices in Germany. Undergraduates and graduates with 2.5 GPA. Apply by March 1; applications accepted thereafter on a space-available basis.

Communications

New York University. "Media Ecology: Studies in Communication." Mainz, West Germany. Graduate students. Apply by April 15. Contact: School of Education, Health, Nursing and Arts Professions, 32 Washington Place, 3rd floor, New York, NY 10003; (212) 998-5030.

Economics

University System of Georgia/Georgia State University. "Spring Seminar in Germany." Focus on changing role of the German economy in European Community. Graduates and undergraduates. Apply by March 1.

German Language and Civilization

Alma College. "Program of Studies in Germany." Kassel. Sophomores, juniors, and seniors with 2.5 GPA. Apply by April 15.

Illinois State University. "Summer Program in the Federal Republic of Germany." Bonn. Freshmen to graduates. Apply by March 17.

Marquette University. "Marquette University's Language Center in Germany." Rhineland, Berlin, and Hildesheim. Sophomores, juniors, and seniors with one year of German. Apply by February 15. Contact: Dr. E.L. Hudgins, Lalumiere Language Hall, Marquette University, Milwaukee, WI 53233.

Michigan State University. "German Language Program in Mayen." Juniors and seniors with two years college German. Apply by April 21.

North Carolina State University. "Summer Study Tour in Ludwigsburg." Co-sponsored with University of North Carolina–Charlotte. Freshmen to graduates with one year of German. Apply by March 1. Contact Study Abroad Office, Center for International Studies, UNC–Charlotte, NC 28223.

Portland State University. "Summer Study in Schwäbisch Gmünd." Excursions to Stuttgart, Dinkelsbühl, and Nördlingen. Juniors, seniors, graduate students, and teachers with two years of college German.

State University of New York at Albany. "Braunschweig Summer Language Program." Freshmen to graduates with one year of German. Apply by April 15.

University of Colorado at Boulder. "Study Abroad in Kassel." Intensive language program at all levels. Freshmen to seniors with 2.75 GPA. Apply by February 15.

University of Maryland. "Summer in Kassel." Sophomores, juniors, and seniors with 12 credits college German and 3.0 GPA. Apply by March 1.

University of Utah. "Kiel German Language Program." Four weeks of language study, preceded by three weeks of travel in Europe. Freshmen to graduates, and adults. Previous German language study is recommended. Apply by March 1.

University System of Georgia/Georgia State University. Erlangen. Freshmen to seniors with 2.5 GPA and three quarters of college German with 3.0 GPA in those courses. Apply by April 1.

EXPLORING GERMAN CULTURE

Literature

The legacy of the Second World War is a pervasive theme in West German writing. Thomas Mann's *Mario and the Magician* deals with the rise of Nazi Germany. Heinrich Böll, one of the pioneers of postwar German literature, is the author of *The Bread of Those Early Years*, a story about love transforming a cynic in a postwar Rhineland town. Günther Grass, a younger writer, continues to write about the problems and guilt caused by the war. While *The Tin Drum* is his best-known work, he has also written a number of other books addressing the same concerns, including *The Danzig Trilogy*. Siegfried Lenz, another politically oriented writer of Grass's generation, is the author of *The German Lesson* and *Homeland Museum*. Botho Strauss's novels and plays, including *A Rumour* and *The Young Man*, reflect modern German concerns with establishing an identity by looking back at German history, particularly to the Second World War.

Peter Schneider is a young West Berliner whose *Knife in the Head* and *The Wall Jumper* deal with the tensions of living in a divided and politically isolated city. Franz Xavier Kroetz is a Munich writer who depicts the lower depths of Bavarian society in books such as *Agnes Bernauer* and *Maria Magdalena*, the story of a single working-class woman and the problems she encounters when she discovers she's pregnant. Gabriele Wohmann writes about women trying to find themselves in an atmosphere of modern urban angst. In her book *Serious Intention*, for instance, a woman recounts her life during a sickness, in the process addressing the problems of women in modern Germany as well as the conflicts between the older generation that came of age during the Second World War and today's generation. Walter Abish, a modern German-American writer, recently treated the same subject with surprising insight in *How German Is It*.

Film

Early German filmmaking is best represented by the films made between the two world wars, pictures known for their production values and high technical quality. Many of the themes in films such as *Die Nibelungen* by Fritz Lang, *The Student of Prague* by Henrik Galeen, and *The Cabinet of Dr. Caligari* by Robert Wiene call upon German folklore and tradition. Later films of the interwar period delved into the subjects associated with modern urban life: crime; graft, and seduction are the focus of G.W. Pabst's *The Threepenny Opera* (1931); sexual intrigue characterized Josef Von Sternberg's *The Blue Angel*

(1930) and Pabst's *Pandora's Box* (1929); and the life of a pathological child murderer and mob justice was the subject of Lang's *M* (1931).

The American film industry's control of West German film production after the Second World War made it difficult for German filmmakers to distribute their films within Germany. In the early 1960s, a loose-knit group of younger German filmmakers began to explore the funding options available for independent production and soon inaugurated what became known as the New German Cinema. The best known of this group was Rainer Werner Fassbinder, whose *The Marriage of Maria Braun* (1979) was an extended metaphor for postwar Germany, and who linked contemporary Germany with German history in *Berlin Alexanderplatz* (1979) and *Lili Marlene* (1980). This preoccupation with German history and tradition and Germany's peculiar relationship with the U.S. is also found in the films of Hans Jurgen Syberberg, which include *Our Hitler, Parsifal*, and *Ludwig the Mad Bavarian King*, and the work of Wim Wenders, which includes *Wings of Desire* and *The American Friend*. Other recent German films of note include Volker Schöndorf's *The Tin Drum*, the story of a boy who refuses to grow physically as the Nazis take power, and Ulrike Ottinger's *Ticket of No Return*, an investigation into female identity.

GREECE

Greece, the birthplace of Western civilization, is sacred ground to lovers of history, drama, mythology, art, and archaeology. So much of Western civilization has its roots in Greece, in fact, that it is difficult, if not impossible, to list all of the Greek philosophers, dramatists, scientists, poets, and statesmen who have played a part in forming our modern Western world. The ruins of the temples of the Acropolis, of the 2,500-year-old island city of Delos, and of the ceremonial center at Delphi are but a few of many monuments that remind the visitor of this nation's glorious past.

Mountains cover most of Greece, the terrain of which is largely rocky and infertile, and no part of it is more than 85 miles from the sea. As a result, the Greeks have been a seafaring people for thousands of years. Naturally, many ancient Greek legends, including those involving Ulysses and Jason, center around sea voyages, and today Greece has one of the largest merchant shipping fleets in the world.

Although Greece is the birthplace of democracy, the country's history since its emergence from Turkish control in the 19th century has been marked by dictatorships, shaky government, and political confusion. However, since the most recent military regime was deposed in 1974, Greece has enjoyed democratic government and become a member of the European Community.

Official name: Hellenic Republic. **Area:** 50,961 square miles (about the size of Arkansas). **Population:** 10,100,000. **Population density:** 198 inhabitants per square mile. **Capital and largest city:** Athens (pop. 3,027,000). **Language:** Greek. **Religion:** Greek Orthodox. **Per capita income:** US$3,550. **Currency:** Drachma. **Literacy rate:** 95%. **Average daily high/low:** * Athens: January, 54°/42°; July, 90°/72°. **Average number of days with precipitation:** Athens: January, 7; July, 1.

---

*all temperatures are Fahrenheit

TRAVEL

A passport is required for American citizens visiting Greece. However, a visa is not required for stays of up to three months. For regulations regarding residence in Greece over three months, contact the Greek Embassy, 2211 Massachusetts Avenue NW, Washington, DC 20008.

Getting Around

The Greek islands of the Aegean Sea are one of the most popular destinations in Europe for young people from all over the world. Attracted by beaches, warm sunny weather, and some of the cheapest prices in Western Europe, young people fill the ferries that shuttle between the islands. While the historic ruins and picturesque beauty of many of the islands lure both young and old travelers alike, the focus on many of them—especially Ios—is definitely on youth.

Travel by train or ferry in Greece is generally inexpensive, and passes for unlimited travel on the rail system are available: $30 for ten days; $49 for 20 days; and $66 for one month. Eurail passes may be used on the Greek rail network (see page 58) as well.

Greece also offers outstanding opportunities for hiking and mountaineering. *Greece on Foot: Mountain Treks, Island Trails*, by Marc S. Dubin, suggests hiking itineraries to suit almost anyone. You can order it for $10.95 from The Mountaineers Books, 306 2nd Avenue West, Seattle, WA 98119.

Especially for Students and Young People

There are a number of student travel bureaus in Greece:

- USIT, 1 Filellinon Street, Syntagma Square, 105 57 Athens (open summer only)
- ISYTS-International Student and Youth Travel Service, 11 Nikis Street, 2nd floor, Syntagma Square, 105 57 Athens
- CTS Student Travel Centre, c/o Hello Travel, 62 Akadimias, Athens
- VITAL STS, 1 Filellinon Street, Syntagma Square, Athens TT1 18

All of these offer student/youth discounts on ferries, international flights, and international train tickets for holders of the International Student Identity Card (ISIC). A variety of student tours and cruises are also available. With your ISIC you'll be entitled to discounts at many museums, including the Acropolis archaeological site, the National Archaeological Museum, the Temple of Olympian Zeus, and the Theater of Dionyssos, to name a few.

For Further Information

Let's Go: Greece, written by the Harvard Student Agencies, is probably the best guidebook for students and other budget travelers heading to Greece. Published by St. Martin's Press, it is available in most bookstores for $11.95. Another good guidebook for budget travelers is Frommer's *Greece on $30 a Day*, available in bookstores for $12.95. In addition, general information about Greece is available from the Greek National Tourist Organization, 645 Fifth Avenue, 5th floor, New York, NY 10022.

WORK

Getting a Job

Job opportunities in Greece are scarce. A work permit from the Ministry of Labor, 40 Pireos Street, 10437 Athens, is mandatory, but is granted for specialized work only. However, foreign firms located in Greece are allowed to secure work permits for their foreign employees. These firms often place advertisements for staff openings in Athens' English-language newspapers, *The Athens News* and *The Athens Post*. Such openings are usually for long-term positions and require that application be made in person.

"A lot of young people teach English either privately or in a school. Since there are several foreign schools in Athens, they quite regularly are looking for stand-in or permanent teachers. People might check with the American Embassy in Athens or The Athens News.*"*

Internships/Traineeships

There are both AIESEC and IAESTE internship programs in Greece; see page 18 for more information.

STUDY

Contact the Office of Press Information of the Greek Embassy for their eight-page fact sheet entitled *American-Sponsored or Affiliated Educational Programs and Schools in Greece*. It includes elementary- and secondary-school listings, university-level programs, and summer programs.

The following are the educational programs offered by member institutions of the Council on International Educational Exchange. Consult Appendix I for the addresses of the college and universities listed in this section. In addition to the listings below, programs open only to students already enrolled at the sponsoring institution are offered by Pennsylvania State University.

SEMESTER AND ACADEMIC YEAR

General Studies

Experiment in International Living/School for International Training.
"College Semester Abroad." Athens and Thessaloniki. Fall or spring semester. Intensive language, life and culture seminar, urban and village homestays, and independent-study project. Sophomores to graduate students with 2.5 GPA. Apply by May 15 for fall and October 15 for spring.

Greek Studies

Beaver College.
"Semester in Greece: Classical Greece." Athens. Fall or spring. Juniors and seniors with 3.0 GPA. Apply by April 20 for fall and October 5 for spring.

"Semester in Greece: Contemporary Greece." Athens. Fall or spring. Juniors and seniors with 3.0 GPA. Apply by April 20 for fall and October 5 for spring.

SUMMER

General Studies

Southern Illinois University at Carbondale. "Reconstructing the Past: Religion & Science in Archaic Greece." Greece and Turkey. Seminars on the ancient Greek experience. High school graduates to university graduates, and adults with college background. Apply by April 1.

University of North Carolina. "UNC Summer Program to Greece." Excursions to various cities. Sophomores to graduate students.

Greek Mythology

State University of New York at Brockport. Program includes instruction at relevant sites and attendance at Greek theater. Undergraduates and graduates.

ICELAND

Icelanders are quick to point out that their island in the North Atlantic is not all ice. In fact, although Reykjavik is the world's northernmost capital, its average January temperature is warmer than that of New York. Its climate moderated by the Gulf Stream, Iceland stays cool and wet year-round.

Some say that Icelanders have little to do during their long damp winters except read and write. Indeed, Icelanders are proud of their language and literary traditions. In fact, Icelandic is the oldest living language in Europe, and has changed so little over the centuries that Icelanders today can easily read the 12th-century sagas that record the exploits of Norse heros of the 10th and 11th centuries. With a literacy rate over 99 percent, Icelanders are also one of the most educated people in the world, and many are trilingual, speaking Danish and English in addition to Icelandic.

The country's tourist bureau promotes the island as the "land of fire and ice," and it's true that life here can seem a little unearthly at times. The sun hardly sets in summer and shines but an hour in midwinter. Ice sheets cover large areas of the interior, yet the country also contains a number of active volcanoes and more hot springs than any other country in Europe. The barren, rocky interior is virtually uninhabited; most people live in port towns with access to the rich fishing grounds that support the island's leading industry.

Official name: Republic of Iceland. **Area:** 39,709 square miles (about the size of Virginia). **Population:** 224,000. **Population density:** 5.04 inhabitants per square mile. **Capital and largest city:** Reykjavik (pop. 91,394). **Language:** Icelandic. **Religion:** Lutheran. **Per capita income:** US$10,700. **Currency:** New Krona. **Literacy rate:** 99.9%. **Average daily high/low:*** Reykjavik:

---

*all temperatures are Fahrenheit

January, 36°/28°; July, 58°/48°. **Average number of days with precipitation:** Reykjavik: January, 20; July, 16.

TRAVEL

Americans will need a passport to visit Iceland. A visa is not required for stays of up to 3 months (a period that begins as soon as you enter the Scandinavian region—Denmark, Finland, Norway, Sweden, or Iceland itself). For specific requirements, check with the Embassy of Iceland, 2022 Connecticut Avenue NW, Washington, DC 20008.

Getting Around

Iceland has no railroads, but its bus network reaches even the most isolated communities. The Omnibus Passport is a special discount bus ticket, valid for unlimited travel on any scheduled bus route in Iceland within a specified time period: 7 days for $190; 14 days for $240; 21 days for $310; and 28 days for $360. The Full Circle Passport is valid for travel on the island's main road, or "ring route," and there is no time limit, but you have to maintain a continuous direction around the island. It costs $163.

Icelandair offers an "Iceland Air Pass" for $165. The pass entitles you to four domestic flights and is valid for 30 days after the first flight is taken. ISIC holders under 26 years of age are also entitled to 25-percent discounts on flights within Iceland.

Hitchhiking can be fairly easy but traffic is sparse. Be prepared for rain and cold weather.

Especially for Students and Young People

Iceland Student Travel (University Student Center, Hringbraut, 101 Reykjavik) is the nation's student travel bureau and ISTC member. With the International Student Identity Card, you can get a 25-percent student discount on plane tickets within Iceland and a smaller discount on bus passes.

> *"Hotel Gardur in Reykjavik operates as a hotel during the summer only— it's a student dormitory the rest of the year. It's an inexpensive place to stay and has a restaurant, too, where you're sure to meet other students. ISIC holders can get a 50-percent discount."*

For Further Information

Iceland is included in *Let's Go: Europe*, an excellent guide for students and other budget travelers; it's available for $13.95 in most bookstores. One of the few guidebooks focusing on Iceland is *Iceland: The Visitor's Guide*. It's available from the Traveller's Bookstore (75 Rockefeller Plaza, New York, NY 10019) for $19.95, plus $3.75 postage. General tourist information is available from the Icelandic Tourist Board, 655 Third Avenue, Suite 1810, New York, NY 10017.

WORK

Internships/Traineeships

There are both AIESEC and IAESTE internship programs in Iceland; see page 18 for more information.

Voluntary Service

Voluntary service work can be arranged through the "Year Abroad Program" sponsored by the International Christian Youth Exchange. The program offers persons ages 18–24 voluntary service opportunities in the fields of health care, education, the environment, construction, et cetera. See page 22 for more information.

STUDY

The Exchange Division of the American Scandinavian Foundation, 127 East 73rd Street, New York, NY 10021, will provide you with a listing of English-language academic-year and summer programs offered in Scandinavia, including Iceland.

A study program offered by a member organization of the Council on International Educational Exchange is described below. Consult Appendix I for the address you can write for further information.

SUMMER

Geology

Scandinavian Seminar. "Icelandic Geology, Geography, and Culture." Reykjavik. Five-week program in cooperation with University of Iceland and Icelandic Fulbright Commission. Juniors, seniors, and graduate students majoring in geology, geography, or geoscience. Apply by April 15.

IRELAND

If you're looking for an example of the persistence of Hollywood myth, observe the looks of surprise on the faces of many first-time visitors to Ireland touching down at Shannon. As "just another airport" looms into view, images of leprechauns and banshees are quickly dispelled. This is no country of blarney-spouting peasants leaning over half-doors. Modern Ireland has too much on its mind for all that, but you'll be made welcome all the same.

Topographically, Ireland consists of a central plain surrounded by coastal highlands, except for the stretch of the east coast between Dublin and Dundalk, where the plain extends to the sea. The country possesses, especially in its rugged western and southwestern regions, a profound natural beauty. But the isolation of its sparsely populated rural areas is in sharp contrast to the friendly urban bustle of its cities and towns. All of the cities are compact—even Dublin, the capital, has a central area of scarcely one square mile—and can be explored leisurely on foot.

The economy is a typical European "mixed bag." Most sectors are dominated by private enterprise, but the government exercises a shrinking monopoly in others. Agriculture is still the nation's largest industry, although efforts to modernize the economy over the years have concentrated on marketing Ireland as an ideal location for foreign corporations. Due to its small size and the shortage of many essential natural resources, Ireland has had to depend heavily on foreign business. At present, the economy is suffering from an 18 percent unemployment rate and a decline in international competitiveness. This has resulted in a wave of emigration as the nation's youth seek, ironically, greener pastures in Britain, Australia, and the United States.

Economic, social, and religious affairs, of course, provide excellent fuel for debate. There is an unusually keen interest in politics among the Irish, and lively conversations on the subject rage nightly in those hallowed focal points of Irish social life, the pubs. There is no shortage of atmospheric bars in the land; indeed, you may find them impossible to avoid.

Long a literary center, Ireland also boasts an impressive theatrical heritage that is exemplified by the excellent theater groups in its major cities. Much in evidence, as well, is a lively music scene, where traditional practitioners coexist comfortably with a rock and pop scene rejuvenated of late by the international successes of U2, Sinéad O'Connor, and others.

Physically isolated from Europe's mainland, Ireland has a distinctly individual flavor. The Irish do not readily regard themselves as "Europeans." After centuries of occupation by colonial powers and a concurrent suppression of its indigenous culture, Ireland is still busy promoting its independence. As you would expect from a state that has been in existence for less than 50 years, there are political problems still to be ironed out, but the general mood is one of casual optimism.

—*Denis Murphy, New York, New York*

Official name: Republic of Ireland. **Area:** 26,600 square miles (about the size of West Virginia). **Population:** 3,500,000. **Population density:** 132 inhabitants per square mile. **Capital and largest city:** Dublin (pop. 569,000). **Language:** English, Irish. **Religion:** Roman Catholic. **Per capita income:** US$7,480. **Currency:** Irish pound (punt). **Literacy rate:** 99%. **Average daily high/low:*** Dublin, January, 47°/35°; July, 67°/51°. **Average number of days with precipitation:** Dublin: January, 13; July, 13.

TRAVEL

U.S. citizens need a passport, but a visa is not required for tourists staying up to 90 days. Tourists may be asked to show an onward/return ticket or sufficient funds to cover their stay. For residence authorization, consult the Embassy of Ireland, 2234 Massachusetts Avenue NW, Washington, DC 20008.

---

*all temperatures are Fahrenheit

Getting Around

Eurail and InterRail passholders receive free boat passage between France (either Le Havre or Cherbourg) and Rosslare, in southeastern Ireland. Ferries also link Ireland with several ports in Wales and England, with easy connections from there to cities throughout Britain. Discounts on Irish Continental Line ferries between Ireland and ports in France and Britain are available to holders of the International Student Identity Card (ISIC).

If you're thinking of flying to Britain, check the fares of Ryan Air, which flies between the two countries. Within Ireland, ISIC holders receive a 10-percent discount on Aer Arann flights between Galway and the Aran Islands.

Trains connect the major cities of Ireland to Dublin, but other cities are not always well connected with one another. Usually, buses fill in the gaps in rail service. Eurailpasses are valid on trains and some buses in Ireland, and students can save 50 percent on rail and bus travel in Ireland if they have an ISIC with the Travelsave stamp (see "Especially for Students and Young People" below). The same savings apply to ferry service between Galway and the Aran Islands.

A Student/Youth Rambler ticket good for unlimited rail and bus travel within Ireland is available for anyone between the ages of 14 and 26. Rambler tickets for eight days of travel within any 15-day period cost $82; 15-day tickets cost $111; and one-month tickets cost $145. Rambler tickets must be purchased prior to your departure for Ireland, however, and require a minimum of one-month advance notice. Contact CIE Tours International, 122 East 42nd Street, New York, NY 10168.

If standing in the rain doesn't deter you, hitching in Ireland, especially in rural areas, is safe and often the best way to get around. People will generally stop and will usually be interested in tales of your travels.

"Irish people tend to be easygoing, light-hearted, and quick-witted, with a wonderful sense of humor about themselves as well as life in general. About 94 percent of the population is Roman Catholic. Families tend to be large and closely knit. Tradition is much valued, and the Irish place less emphasis on material possessions and status than do Americans. The Irish love sports, both as participants and spectators: rugby, soccer, hurling, Gaelic football, and cycling are some of the more popular pastimes. And, of course, the Irish love to talk and to share their great pride in their beautiful country."
—Katherine Aziz, Winter Park, Florida

Especially for Students and Young People

Any information you might need about Ireland is available at the travel offices of USIT (Union of Students in Ireland—Travel), a member of the ISTC. The main office is at 19 Aston Quay, Dublin 2, but USIT also has offices in Limerick, Belfast, and Waterford, as well as at the universities in Cork, Galway, Jordanstown, and Coleraine. At a USIT office you can get the Travelsave stamp affixed to your International Student Identity Card (ISIC) for £6 (about $10); this entitles you to 50 percent off train and bus tickets for travel within Ireland.

Museums in Ireland are free to everyone. However, the ISIC card will entitle you to a 10-percent discount in some 1,500 shops, restaurants, and nightclubs throughout Ireland. The free National Student Discount Directory lists the participating establishments. Another discount available to ISIC holders is the Student Theatre Stand-By Scheme, which offers reduced-rate theater tickets 15 minutes before a performance. Check with USIT for more information.

For Further Information

For suggestions on budget accommodations in Ireland as well as what to see and how to get around, consult a copy of *Let's Go: Britain and Ireland*. Put together by the Harvard Student Agencies and published by St. Martin's Press, it's available in bookstores for $12.95. Another good book for the budget traveler is Frommer's *Ireland on $30 a Day*, available in most bookstores for $13.95.

General tourist information, including a booklet entitled *Discover Young Ireland*, is available from the Irish Tourist Board, 757 Third Avenue, New York, NY 10017. In addition, persons interested in visiting Northern Ireland can get information from the Northern Ireland Tourist Board, 40 West 57th Street, New York, NY 10019.

"Don't overplan a trip to Ireland—come prepared to enjoy the free and easy way of life that Ireland offers. The climate is temperate year-round, so that fall-type clothing is adequate, with an extra sweater or so in winter."

WORK

Getting a Job

To work in Ireland you must obtain a permit before entering the country. Application for the permit should be made by the employer in Ireland and sent to the employee, who must show it at the port of entry.

The Council will help you secure a work permit good for up to four months any time of the year in Ireland. Full-time college or university students who are at least 18 years of age and permanent residents or citizens of the U.S. are eligible. Once you're in Ireland, the USIT office in Dublin will advise you on the current job situation. There is a $96 fee for the service, which includes one night's accommodation and breakfast. Contact the Council's Work Exchanges Department for more information.

Internships/Traineeships

Programs sponsored by member organizations of the Council on International Educational Exchange are listed below. Consult Appendix I for the addresses where you can write for more information.

AIESEC–US. Reciprocal internship program for students in economics, business, finance, marketing, accounting, and computer sciences. See page 18 for further information.

Association for International Practical Training.
"IAESTE Trainee Program." On-the-job training for undergraduate and graduate students in technical fields such as engineering, computer science, agriculture, architecture, and mathematics. See page 18 for more information.

"Hotel & Culinary Exchanges Program." On-the-job training for young people beginning a career in the hotel and food service industries. Participants must have graduated from a university or vocational school and possess at least six months of training or experience in the chosen field. Training usually runs 6–12 months.

Voluntary Service

CIEE places young people in voluntary service workcamps in Ireland organized by Comhchairdeas (204 Br. Sheinleasa, Seantraibh, Dublin 9). At these workcamps, groups of about 20 people from various countries work on projects such as running recreation programs for inner-city children, restoring historical sites, and building community centers. Workcamps operate from the end of June to the end of September. Volunteers must be 18 or over and willing to work an average of eight hours per day for two or three weeks; they receive room and board in return. The applications of U.S. residents are processed by CIEE. For more information contact the International Voluntary Service Department at CIEE.

STUDY

The Consulate General of Ireland (515 Madison Avenue, New York, NY 10022) distributes an information sheet on universities and other institutions of higher education in Ireland. USIT recommends that students who are planning to study in Ireland contact the Central Applications Office, Tower House, Eglinton Street, Galway, Ireland.

For individuals interested in an Irish study program, CIEE administers the "Encounter Ireland" program on behalf of USIT. "Encounter Ireland" is a one-month summer homestay, study, and travel program for U.S. college students. The first three weeks of the program are spent in Dublin living with an Irish family and attending a special course in Irish Studies at Trinity College. The final week of the program is set aside for students to explore the country on their own. Participants receive an eight-day rail and bus pass good for travel throughout the country. Scholarships are provided by USIT, reducing the cost of the program to $1,890, which includes round-trip transportation between New York and Ireland. Applicants must be at least 18 years of age and full-time students at a U.S. college or university. The application deadline is May 31. Contact CIEE for details.

The following are the educational programs offered by member institutions of the Council on International Educational Exchange. Consult Appendix I for the addresses of the colleges and universities listed in this section. In addition to the programs below, Ohio State University and the University of California system offer programs open only to their own students.

SEMESTER AND ACADEMIC YEAR

Business Management

Beaver College. "Irish University Year at University of Limerick." Academic year, fall or spring program. Juniors and seniors with 3.0 GPA. Apply by April 20 for fall and October 5 for spring.

Drama

Beaver College. "Irish University Year in Drama at Trinity College, Dublin." Academic year. Juniors and seniors with 3.0 GPA. Apply by January 1.

Engineering

Beaver College. "Irish University Year at University of Limerick." Academic year or quarter. Juniors and seniors with 3.0 GPA. Apply by April 20 for academic year and fall quarter; October 5 for spring.

English Literature

Michigan State University. "English Literature in Dublin." Irish history, literature, and culture, with field trips. Spring quarter. Sophomores to graduate students. Apply by February 3.

General Studies

Beaver College.
  "University College, Cork." Academic year. Juniors and seniors with 3.0 GPA. Apply by April 10.
  "Trinity College, Dublin." Academic year. Juniors and seniors with 3.0 GPA. Apply by January 1.
  "University College, Dublin." Academic year or fall term. Juniors and seniors with 3.0 GPA. Apply by April 10.
  "University College, Galway." Academic year or semester. Juniors and seniors with 3.0 GPA. Apply by April 10 for fall and October 5 for spring.
  "St. Patrick's College, Maynooth." Academic year. Juniors and seniors with 3.5 GPA. Apply by April 10.

Northeastern University. "Ireland: North and South." A bicultural experience, including social studies at Dublin's Institute of Public Administration and Queen's University, Belfast, with internships in the Irish Parliament. Fall and winter quarter. Juniors and seniors with 3.0 GPA. Apply by April 15.

Rollins College. "Rollins Fall Term in Dublin." Fall semester. Sophomores, juniors, and seniors with 3.0 GPA. Apply by April 15.

Irish Studies

State University of New York at Cortland. Dublin. Fall or spring semester. Juniors and seniors with 3.5 GPA in major. Apply by March 1 for fall and November 1 for spring.

Peace Studies

Experiment in International Living/School for International Training. "College Semester Abroad." Dublin and Northern Ireland. Fall or spring semester. Academic seminar, field visits, independent study project, and homestay. Sophomores to graduate students with 2.5 GPA. Apply by May 15 for fall and October 15 for spring.

EXPLORING IRISH CULTURE

Literature

The shadow of James Joyce falls across much of Irish literature, sometimes obscuring other important figures. Still, Joyce's *Ulysses* (1922) is the central text of modern literature, its influence extending well beyond the borders of Ireland. *Ulysses* is both a comic masterpiece, a profound exploration of the human psyche, and a celebration of humanity in all its flawed complexity. However, readers sometimes find the novel difficult because of its length and the complexity of Joyce's technique. Other works by Joyce, particularly *Dubliners* (1914) and *Portrait of the Artist as a Young Man* (1916), may offer a less daunting introduction to this great Irish writer.

Characteristic of much Irish literature is its verbal wit and linguistic inventiveness. Oscar Wilde's *The Importance of Being Earnest* (1895) is rich in inversion and comic paradox. Another Irish playwright with a highly developed ear for language and its comic potential is J.M. Synge. His *Playboy of the Western World* (1907) is a rich comedy that precisely captures the cadence of Irish speech. Continuing in this tradition today are playwrights Hugh Leonard and Brian Friel. Leonard's *Da* describes how a son, returning to Ireland for the funeral of his father, comes to terms with their relationship. Friel's *Philadelphia, Here I Come* evokes the rural Ireland of the 1950s on the eve of an only son's emigration to the States.

Witty and poetic literature still abounds in contemporary Ireland. In *The Pornographer* (1979), John McGahern writes comically about a Dubliner whose formula porn stories begin to happen in real life. Christopher Nolan, winner of the Booker prize for literature, examines his life as a victim of cerebral palsy in the moving *Under the Eye of the Clock* (1987). In his first work, *Damburst of Dreams*, Nolan released the poetic outpourings that had remained trapped inside before he had a means to communicate.

The short story is a pervasive form in Irish literature as well. Frank O'Connor's stories provide funny, insightful glimpses into the lives of children in rural Ireland. *My Oedipus Complex and Other Stories* includes one of his best-loved stories, "My First Confession." Other notable collections of short stories by contemporary writers include William Trevor's *The Ballroom of Romance and Other Stories*, Edna O'Brien's *Mother Ireland*, Mary Lavin's *The Shrine and Other Stories*, and Benedict Kiely's *The State of Ireland*.

Ireland also has a long tradition of poetry, from Jonathan Swift through William Butler Yeats to Seamus Heaney, whose contemporary poetry reflects some of the traumas associated with the ongoing political and religious conflict in Northern Ireland. The troubled relationship with Britain has been a recurrent theme in Irish literature, a place where myth, poetry, and politics have tended to be inseparably entwined.

ITALY

Italy today is more than just the repository for many of the great artistic and architectural treasures of the Roman Empire, the Middle Ages, and the Renaissance. Ferrari sport cars, Benetton clothes, and Olivetti computers are a hint of what Italy has become: one of the world's richest industrial economies, with a standard of living on a par with that of France, Japan, and the United States. In contemporary Italy the ancient and modern exist side by side. Historic centers are constantly rejuvenated: a Roman amphitheater houses a trendy restaurant; a Milanese palazzo houses a Giorgio Armani boutique; an Olivetti showroom in Venice is located on the square from which Marco Polo set off on his journeys centuries ago.

Italy has the good fortune of being located on a beautiful, mountainous peninsula that juts into the middle of the Mediterranean Sea. For sheer natural beauty, it is the envy of Europe. To the north are the Alps, and in every other direction are the beaches of the Adriatic and Mediterranean. At the same time, the life of Italy lies in its pulsing cities. The Renaissance center of Florence, the ancient imperial capital of Rome, the fairy-tale island-city of Venice, and the thriving financial center of Milan demonstrate the richness of Italy's urban landscape.

Of course, Italy has its problems, too. Since the Second World War neither of its two major political parties, the Christian Democrats and the Communists (a Western European socialist party), have been able to gain the support of a majority of the voters, thus leaving the country in the hands of weak coalition governments unable to take decisive action. And in spite of years of government efforts to spread the prosperity of northern Italy southward, Sicily and southern Italy remain a land apart—not only much poorer but also more traditional in character—where the Church, the family, and the Mafia retain much of their historic influence.

The Italians are a friendly, gregarious lot. Young Italians are generally fascinated by all that is American, so there is ample opportunity for international contact, and most Americans are surprised by the ease with which they can learn Italian. The Italians appreciate the effort made to speak their language and are more than willing to help foreigners learn their language.

For centuries Italy has been the home of some of the best the world has to offer in art, food, fashion, design, and urban living. In fact, it was the Italians who gave the world the phrase for the good life: *la dolce vita!*

—Randy Epping, Zurich, Switzerland

Official name: Italian Republic. **Area:** 119,764 square miles (slightly larger than Arizona). **Population:** 57,300,000. **Population density:** 492 inhabitants per square mile. **Capital and largest city:** Rome (pop. 2,826,733). **Language:** Italian. **Religion:** Roman Catholic. **Per capita income:** US$12,395. **Currency:** Lira. **Literacy rate:** 97%. **Average daily high/low:*** Florence: January, 49°/35°; July, 89°/63°. Rome: January, 54°/39°; July, 88°/64°. **Average number of days with precipitation:** Florence: January, 9; July, 4. Rome: January, 8; July, 2.

TRAVEL

U.S. citizens will need a passport, but a visa is not required for tourist stays of up to three months. For stays over three months, a visa should be obtained

---

*all temperatures are Fahrenheit

before departure. Check with the Italian Embassy, 1601 Fuller Street NW, Washington, DC 20009 for specific requirements.

Getting Around

Italy has a modern railroad network, and travel on Italian trains is relatively inexpensive. Best of all, Eurail passes are valid for use on the Italian rail network (see page 58). Buses are also a common means of intercity transport and, for short trips in mountainous regions, may be faster than the train, which often takes a more circuitous route.

Italian State Railways (666 Fifth Avenue, New York, NY 10103) offers the B.T.L.C., or "go-anywhere," ticket, which is good for unlimited train travel within Italy. The cost for second-class passes is $107 for eight days, $130 for 15 days, $152 for 21 days, and $186 for 30 days. A first-class B.T.L.C. ticket costs $169 for eight days, $204 for 15 days, $245 for 21 days, and $295 for 30 days. Although available only to nonresidents of Italy, B.T.L.C. tickets can be purchased after arrival in the country.

Throughout Italy (with the exception of certain express trains), bicycles may be taken aboard as checked baggage. You pay an extra charge based on the weight of the bike and the distance traveled, however.

"Traveling within Italy was an integral part of my understanding of a fairly recently unified nation whose citizens still feel a foremost allegiance to their state or region. There is a tremendous diversity of cultures, dialects, and languages—from the Alto Adige to Sicily."
—Elizabeth Alixandre Schijman, New York, New York

Especially for Students and Young People

Centro Turistico Studentesco e Giovanile (CTS) is Italy's student travel bureau and ISTC member, with offices around Rome as well as 30 other Italian cities. You can contact them at CTS Centro Turistico Studentesco, Via Nazionale, 66, 00184 Rome.

Students will find that the International Student Identity Card (ISIC) entitles them to discounts on night flights within Italy; on ferries from various Italian ports to Egypt, Greece, Sardinia, Spain, and Yugoslavia; and on bus, train, and plane travel from Italy to various international destinations. In addition, ISIC holders can get discounts on CTS tours in Rome and reduced admission fees for the Vatican Museum and a number of other museums in Rome as well. A 30-percent discount in cinemas throughout Italy is also available upon purchase of a special cinema discount card (about $2).

For Further Information

Italy—General Information for Travelers, which covers everything you need to know about travel in the country, is available free from the Italian Government Travel Office (ENIT), 630 Fifth Avenue, New York, NY 10111. Also available are maps and hotel lists.

Let's Go: Italy, published by St. Martin's Press and available for $12.95 in most bookstores, contains a wealth of information on where to stay, what to see, and how to get around. The *Michelin Green Guide* for Italy ($10.95) is known for its in-depth treatment of cultural points of interest. You'll find an array of other books on Italy available in most bookstores, including both Fodor's and Birnbaum's guides to the country.

> *"Read about the country, especially the art and architecture. Try to learn at least a few words in Italian. Italians are very, very, friendly and if you show interest in them and their country they will embrace you even more."*
> —Nina Martinez, Takoma Park, Maryland

Meet the People

Several tourist offices in Italy can introduce you to a local Italian host for an afternoon or evening get-together. Although the Italian Government Travel Office (address above) distributes a list of tourist offices in Italy, not all can provide this kind of service. Write ahead and find out whether the office in the town you're going to offers this kind of hospitality service, and if they do, make your arrangements in advance of your arrival in Italy.

WORK

Getting a Job

In Italy, laws regulating work by foreigners are very strict. The Italian Ministry for Home Affairs must first grant the prospective employee a residence permit for work purposes. When the permit has been issued, the employer must then provide a certified declaration that there are no nationals in the area who are able to perform the work in question.

Teaching

American teachers interested in teaching in Italy should write for the booklet *Schools for English-Speaking Students in Italy*. It is available from the Italian Cultural Institute, 686 Park Avenue, New York, NY 10021.

Internships/Traineeships

There are both AIESEC and IAESTE internship programs in Italy; see page 18 for more information.

Voluntary Service

For persons interested in voluntary service work, the "Year Abroad Program" sponsored by the International Christian Youth Exchange offers persons ages 18–24 voluntary service opportunities in the fields of health care, education, the environment, construction, et cetera. See page 22 for more information.

STUDY

There are numerous schools and academies throughout Italy—particularly in Florence—that specialize in the instruction of foreigners in Italian art, language, history, et cetera. *Schools for Foreigners in Italy*, a directory of Italian schools offering programs for foreign students, is available from the Italian Cultural Institute (686 Park Avenue, New York, NY 10021). *The Italian Educational System: A Brief Outline* is also available from the same source.

The following are the educational programs offered by member institutions of the Council on International Educational Exchange. Consult Appendix I for the addresses of the colleges and universities listed in this section. In addition to those listed below, programs open only to students already enrolled at the sponsoring institution are offered by New York University, Northern Illinois University, Pennsylvania State University, Texas A&M University, the University of California system, and the University of Notre Dame.

SEMESTER AND ACADEMIC YEAR

Architecture

Syracuse University. "Masters of Architecture." Florence. Academic year. Graduate program. Apply by March 15.

University of Washington. "Architecture in Rome." Fall and winter quarter. Juniors, seniors, and graduate students in architecture and related fields. Apply by February 19.

Art

Rhode Island School of Design. "European Honors Program." Rome. Academic year of independent studio art. Juniors and seniors with some knowledge of Italian and 3.0 GPA. Apply by December 2.

Syracuse University. "Renaissance Art in Florence." Three-semester program. Fall semester and following spring and fall in Italy. Graduate students only. Some Italian required. Apply by February 1.

Classics

Stanford University. "Intercollegiate Center for Classical Studies in Rome." Fall or spring semester. Juniors and seniors who are classical studies majors with B average. Apply by April 15 for fall and October 15 for spring.

University of Washington. "Classics in Rome." Spring semester. Juniors, seniors, and graduate students in the classics. Apply by November 1.

General Studies

American Heritage Association. "Northwest Inter-institutional Council on Study Abroad–Siena."Fall, winter, and/or spring quarter. Sophomores, juniors, and seniors with 2.5 GPA. Apply by June 1 for fall, November 1 for winter, and January 2 for spring.

American University. "Rome Semester." Most courses supplemented by field trips and excursions. Orientation in Siena. Sophomores, juniors, and seniors with 2.75 GPA. Apply six months prior to start of program.

Drake University. "Drake-ISI Italy." Florence. Semester or academic year. Courses in humanities, art, fashion design, and language at the Istituto di Studi Italiani. Sophomores through graduate students with 2.5 GPA. Rolling Admissions.

Experiment in International Living/School for International Training. "College Semester Abroad." Siena. Fall or spring semester. Intensive language, life and culture seminar, independent-study project, and homestays. Sophomores to graduate students with 2.5 GPA. Apply by May 15 for fall and October 15 for spring.

Gonzaga University. "Gonzaga in Florence." Academic year. Juniors and seniors with 2.5 GPA. Apply by April 1.

Hiram College. Rome. Study at John Cabot International College. Academic year or fall, winter, or spring quarters. Sophomores, juniors, and seniors with 2.5 GPA.

Indiana University. "Bologna Cooperative Studies Program." Academic year. Program offered by consortium of City University of New York, University of Minnesota, University of North Carolina, University of Pennsylvania, and University of Wisconsin. Direct enrollment in University of Bologna. Juniors and seniors with two years of Italian and 3.0 GPA. Apply by January 15.

International Student Exchange Program. Direct reciprocal exchange between U.S. universities and institutions in Rome, Milan, Florence, Pavia, and Urbino. Semester or academic year. Full curriculum options. Open only to students at ISEP member institutions.

Lake Erie College. Florence and Perugia. Sophomores, juniors, and seniors. Programs all year long. Apply by June 1 and November 1.

Rutgers University. "Junior Year in Italy." Florence, with six weeks in Urbino. Juniors with two years college Italian, preferably with some Italian literature courses. Apply by March 1.

State University of New York at Buffalo. "Siena Semester Program." Sophomores, juniors, and seniors with one college Italian course and 2.5 GPA. Apply by April 1 for fall and October 1 for spring.

State University of New York at Stony Brook. Rome. Juniors and seniors with two years of Italian and 2.5 GPA. Apply by April 1.

Syracuse University. "Syracuse in Florence." Sophomores to graduate students with 3.0 GPA. Apply by March 15 for fall and October 15 for spring.

Trinity College. "Trinity College/Rome Campus." Fall or spring semester. All enrolled students must take Italian in Rome. Sophomores, juniors, and seniors. Apply by mid-March for fall and mid-October for spring.

University of North Carolina. "UNC Program to Bologna." Academic year. Sophomores, juniors, and seniors with 3.0 GPA and fluency in Italian. Apply by February 12.

University of Oregon. "Northwest Interinstitutional Council on Study Abroad–Siena." See description under American Heritage Association.

University of Washington. Northwest Interinstitutional Council on Study Abroad–Siena." See description under American Heritage Association.

Western Washington University. Northwest Interinstitutional Council on Study Abroad–Siena." See description under American Heritage Association.

University of Wisconsin–Madison.
Bologna. Academic year. Sophomores to graduate students with 3.0 GPA and two years of college Italian. Open only to students at colleges or universities in Wisconsin and Wisconsin residents studying outside of the state. Apply by February 1.
Florence. Academic year. Sophomores to graduate students with 3.0 GPA. English is language of instruction. Open only to students at colleges or universities in Wisconsin and Wisconsin residents studying outside of the state. Apply by February 1.

Italian Language and Culture

Middlebury College. Florence. Sophomores to graduate students fluent in Italian. Rolling admissions.

University of Massachusetts–Amherst. "Semester in Siena." Spring semester. Sophomores, juniors, and seniors with two semesters of college Italian. Apply by October 15.

University of North Carolina–Chapel Hill. "UNC Program to Siena." Semester or academic year. Sophomores, juniors, and seniors. Apply by March 15 and October 15.

Music

Kent State University. "Kent in Florence." Fall semester. Sophomores to graduate students with 2.5 GPA. Rolling admissions.

SUMMER

Archaeology

Michigan State University. "Prehistoric Archaeology in Italy." Siena. Sophomores to graduate students. Apply by April 21.

Architecture and Design

Syracuse University.
"Architecture: Summer Semester in Florence." Students with three years of architectural design in a B.A. program or two years in an M.A. program. Apply by March 15.
"Environmental Design: Summer Semester in Florence." Sophomores to graduate students.
"Pre-Architecture in Florence." Freshmen to seniors. Apply by March 17.

University of Oregon. "Summer Study in Rome." Sophomores and above. Apply by March 1.

Art History and Studio Art

New York University. "Studio Art in Venice." Graduate students. Apply by April 15. Contact: School of Education, Health, Nursing and Arts Professions, 32 Washington Place, 3rd floor, New York, NY 10003; (212) 998-5030.

Ohio University. "Art in Italy." Rome, Florence. Offered odd-numbered years only. Freshmen to graduate students, and nonstudents. Apply by March 3. Contact Italy Program, School of Art, Ohio University, Athens, OH 45701; (614) 593-4288.

Southern Methodist University. "SMU-in-Rome." Sophomores, juniors, and seniors. Apply by March 1.

Syracuse University. "Visual Arts in Florence." Sophomores to graduate students, and professionals. Apply by March 17.

University of Colorado at Boulder. "Art History in Italy." Formal classroom instruction, with visits to many of the masterpieces of art and architecture. Sophomores to graduate students with 2.75 GPA and some knowledge of fine arts. Applications are accepted from the end of November until program is full.

Western Michigan University. "Studio Art in Italy." Italian Lake District. Freshmen to graduate students, and community members; minimum age 18. Apply by April 1.

Child Care and Development

Syracuse University. "Child Care and Development in Italy: A Comparative Perspective." Florence. Sophomores to graduate students and professionals. Apply by March 16.

European Studies

Syracuse University. "Popular Culture in Early Modern Europe: Its Content and Its Decline." Florence. Sophomores to graduate students, and professionals. Apply by March 17.

General Studies

Brigham Young University. "BYU Study Abroad." Rome. Sophomores, juniors, and seniors with some Italian. Apply by February 1.

Drake University. "Drake-ISI Italy." Florence. Courses in humanities, art, fashion design, and language at the Istituto di Studi Italiani. Sophomores through graduate students with 2.5 GPA. Rolling admissions.

Hiram College. Rome. Study at John Cabot International College. Full course load plus field trips. Sophomores, juniors, and seniors with 2.5 GPA.

Louisiana State University. "LSU in Florence." Excursions to Siena, San Gimignano, and Pisa. Sophomores to graduate students with 2.5 GPA. Apply by April 15.

Michigan State University. "Social Science in Rome." Politics, economics, educational, and cultural aspects of Italy. Freshmen to seniors. Some knowledge of Italian required. Apply by April 21.

New York University. "Gallatin Abroad: Humanities Seminar in Florence." Art and literature of the Italian Renaissance. Freshmen to graduate students. Apply by February 1. Contact Gallatin Division, New York University, 715 Broadway, New York, NY 10003.

Syracuse University. "Humanism and the Arts in Renaissance Italy." Florence, with excursions to other cities. Sophomores to graduate students, and professionals. Apply by April 16.

Italian History and Civilization

Mary Baldwin College. "Renaissance Studies in Italy." May term. Florence, Venice, and Rome, with field trips to Milan, Padua, Mantua, and Siena. Undergraduates. Apply by December 1.

Italian Language and Culture

Indiana University. "Overseas Study in Florence." Studio art also offered. Freshmen to graduate students with 2.8 GPA. Apply by first week in February.

Michigan State University. "Italian Language, Literature, and Culture in Florence." Freshmen to graduate students with previous study of Italian. Apply by April 21.

Portland State University. "A.L.P.S. in Italy—Italian Language Program." Montefalco. Culture excursions to medieval churches, ancient monuments, and museums. All students, but undergraduate credit only. One term of college Italian recommended. Apply by May 1.

Rosary College. "Rosary in Florence." Italian language, with emphasis on literature and art history. Sophomores, juniors, seniors, and others interested in Italian culture. Apply by April 1.

State University of New York at Stony Brook. "Summer in Rome." High school seniors to college seniors. Apply by April 1.

Syracuse University. "Italian Language and Literature." Florence. Sophomores, juniors, seniors, and professionals. Apply by April 15.

University of Oregon. "Summer Study in Perugia, Italy." Sophomores and above. Apply by April 1.

University of Utah. "Siena, Italy: Italian Study Program." Freshmen to graduate students, and others. Some Italian required. Apply by March 1.

University System of Georgia/University of Georgia. Florence. Study at the Centro Linguistico Italiano Dante Alighieri. All students with 2.5 GPA. Apply by April 1.

Music

New York University. Graduate students. Apply by April 15. Contact: School of Education, Health, Nursing and Arts Professions, 32 Washington Place, 3rd floor, New York, NY 10003; (212) 998-5030.

Social Work

Michigan State University. "Social Work in Italy." Santa Maria. Juniors, seniors, and graduate students. Apply by April 21. Internship possible with prior arrangements.

EXPLORING ITALIAN CULTURE

Literature

In contrast with the more socially oriented literature of Italy's prewar years, a more personalized and experimental literature has dominated Italian letters since the Second World War. In his novels *Adolescents* and *The Time of Indifference*, Alberto Moravia takes as his central theme the boredom that springs from failure and poisons the enjoyment of art, love, and life itself. Italo Svevo's best-known and most interesting work is *The Confessions of Zeno*, a diary written in an ironic style that expresses the bitterness of human existence and the inner conflicts provoked by conscience. Cesare Pavese is a writer whose books generally are about the difficulties of coming to terms with life. His *The Moon and the Bonfire* is about its narrator's quest for the truth about both his past and future in a Piedmont village. Pavese's *Selected Works* includes four novels that depict the confining and restricting nature of modern urban middle-class life.

Film

The majority of Italian films prior to the Second World War consisted of either large, lavish spectacles with epic, classical themes, or, during the reign of Mussolini, the aptly described "white telephone" pictures. (The term refers to a succession of rather dull bedroom farces with an ever-present white telephone prop—always a sure sign of affluence.)

However, the postwar rebuilding of Italy also meant the reinvigoration of the Italian film industry. Directors Roberto Rossellini (*Open City*), Vittorio De Sica (*The Bicycle Thief*), and Luchino Visconti (*Ossessione*) made films that fictionalized the drastic disruptions experienced by Italian society as they focused on the daily routines of the "average" Italian. This style, called neorealism, featured a particular mix of nonprofessional actors and a moving, fluid camera technique, and was an important influence on the French *Nouvelle Vague* (New Wave) and *cinéma vérité* movements of the 1960s and 1970s. Well-known Italian filmmakers who started in the neorealistic style include Michelangelo Antonioni and Federico Fellini. Fellini went on to direct some of the most unforgettable films of the Italian postwar cinema, including *La Dolce Vita* (1960), *8½* (1963), and *Amarcord* (1973); travelers going to Rome might be especially interested in Fellini's 1970s portrait of the city, *Roma*.

Other notable postwar Italian filmmakers include Lina Wertmuller—director of *Swept Away* (1974) and *Seven Beauties* (1974)—and Pier Paolo Pasolini—director of *Oedipus Rex* (1967)—both of whom explore the dynamics of sexual politics. Bernardo Bertolucci, another directorial star of the postwar Italian cinema, has concentrated on the darker side of Italian life, both past and present, in such films as *The Conformist* and his epic saga *1900*. But perhaps the most popular Italian movies of the postwar period—if not the most critically acclaimed—have been the so-called "spaghetti Westerns" of director Sergio Leone, including *The Good, the Bad, and the Ugly* and *Once Upon a Time in the West*.

LUXEMBOURG

Nestled between Belgium, France, and Germany, the Grand Duchy of Luxembourg has survived as a small independent country between its often belligerent neighbors. These days, this prosperous, orderly country is enjoying increased importance as the European Community becomes more established and many European businesses and banks move their offices here to take advantage of the country's central location and strict bank secrecy laws.

Luxembourgers use French, German, and English for business, but among themselves they speak Luxembourgish, a dialect that sounds something like Dutch or German but is unintelligible even to people from the Netherlands or Germany. Although smaller than Rhode Island, it offers a varied landscape, from the Ardennes forests in the north to the fertile vineyards of the Mosel Valley in the south. Along the French border, iron ore deposits give the earth a reddish tint and feed the blast furnaces and steel rolling mills that make this tiny nation an important world steel producer.

Official name: Grand Duchy of Luxembourg. **Area:** 999 square miles (about the size of Rhode Island). **Population:** 400,000. **Population density:** 400 inhabitants per square mile. **Capital and largest city:** Luxembourg (pop. 80,000). **Language:** Luxembourgish, French, German. **Religion:** Roman Catholic. **Per capita income:** US$13,988. **Currency:** Luxembourg franc. **Literacy rate:** 100%. **Average daily high/low:*** Luxembourg: January, 36°/29°; July, 74°/55°. **Average number of days with precipitation:** Luxembourg: January, 14; July, 13.

Travel

U.S. citizens will need a passport but not a visa for stays of up to three months. Travelers to Luxembourg also must be in possession of sufficient funds and an onward/return ticket. For specific requirements for stays over three months,

---

*all temperatures are Fahrenheit

check with the Embassy of Luxembourg, 2200 Massachusetts Avenue NW, Washington, DC 20008.

Getting Around

Most travelers who fly Icelandair will arrive in Luxembourg, and from there can take a train or bus to other destinations in Europe. Eurail passes are valid on trains throughout Luxembourg (see page 58). If you decide to stay a while, the country's youth hostel organization, Centrale des Auberges de Jeunesse Luxembourgeoises (18 Place d'Armes, L-1136 Luxembourg), has travel information for students and youths and will be happy to arrange accommodations or local tours.

> *"Appreciate the many activities and chances to get to know the Luxembourgers. It is a small country and at first glance it appears that there is not much to do. There is hiking, kayaking, ice skating, and swimming—the possibilities are endless."*
> —Ann Gardner, Tallmadge, Ohio

Especially for Students and Young People

Holders of the International Student Identity Card (ISIC) get a discount on train travel within Luxembourg as well as from Luxembourg to points all over Europe. The ISIC also entitles you to a 50-percent discount at most museums. For further information on student discounts contact the youth hostel association mentioned above or Voyages Sotour—Tourisme des Jeunes, 15 Place du Theatre, L-2010 Luxembourg.

For Further Information

The Luxembourg Tourist Office (801 Second Avenue, New York, NY 10017) provides general tourist information, including a brochure on camping in Luxembourg.

WORK

Internships/Traineeships

There is an IAESTE internship program in Luxembourg; see page 18 for more information.

MALTA

The small island-nation of Malta, strategically located between the Eastern and Western Mediterranean, has long been a prize for any conquerer wishing to dominate the Mediterranean. Phoenicians, Carthaginians, Romans, Arabs, and the Knights of St. John have all laid claim to the island at one time or another. Under British control during the Second World War, its populace earned Britain's George Cross for refusing to capitulate despite constant Axis bombardment. The George Cross now appears on the flag of Malta, which became an independent nation in 1964 after 150 years of British rule. Malta's language, Maltese, is closely related to Arabic, but also includes elements of the languages spoken by the many different peoples that have dominated these small islands throughout its history. English is also widely spoken.

Official name: Republic of Malta. **Area:** 122 square miles (about one-fifth the size of Rhode Island). **Population:** 400,000. **Population density:** 3,279 inhabitants per square mile. **Capital:** Valletta (pop. 16,000). **Largest city:** Birkirkara (pop. 20,000). **Language:** Maltese, English. **Religion:** Roman Catholic. **Per capita income:** US$4,057. **Currency:** Maltese pound. **Literacy rate:** 83%. **Average daily high/low:*** Valletta: January, 59°/31°; July, 84°/72°. **Average number of days with precipitation:** Valletta: January, 13; July, 1.

TRAVEL

A passport is required for U.S. citizens traveling to the islands. However, a visa is not required for stays of up to three months. Check with the Embassy of Malta, 2017 Connecticut Avenue NW, Washington, DC 20008 for specific requirements.

Getting Around

Ferries link Valletta with several cities of southern Italy; smaller ferries connect Malta to the outer islands of Gozo and Comino, both of which are more rural and relaxed than crowded, bustling Malta. The buses that serve all parts of the island of Malta provide an inexpensive way of getting around. Mopeds, which can be rented at various locations around the island, are another popular means of travel.

Especially for Students and Young People

NSTS—Student and Youth Travel (220, St. Paul Street, Valletta) is Malta's student travel organization and member of the ISTC. NSTS even has a branch office on the small neighboring island of Gozo, one of three islands that make up the tiny nation of Malta. NSTS provides information on travel and accommodations in Malta, offers student tours and cruises, operates a student accommodations center, and runs a water-sports facility. Students with the International Student Identity Card (ISIC) will receive discounts on all of these NSTS services. Other discounts for ISIC holders include those at a number of retail stores, free admission to all government museums, and 60 percent off regular one-way airfares from Malta to numerous international destinations. In addition, NSTS organizes many social activities for visiting young people from June to September; you can contact them for further details.

There are many inexpensive guesthouses on Malta suitable for students. Contact NSTS for further information on accommodations (NSTS requests that people writing for information enclose two international postal-reply coupons).

---

*all temperatures are Fahrenheit

Internships/Traineeships

There are both AIESEC and IAESTE internship programs in Malta; see page 18 for more information.

STUDY

A program offered by a member institution of the Council on International Educational Exchange is listed below. Consult Appendix I for the address where you can write for more information.

SEMESTER AND ACADEMIC YEAR

General Studies

International Student Exchange Program. Direct reciprocal exchange between U.S. universities and the University of Malta. Semester or academic year. Full curriculum options. Open only to students at ISEP member institutions.

THE NETHERLANDS

The Netherlands' proximity to the North Sea, plus the fact that much of the country lies below sea level, are the dominant factors in shaping the character of its people. The Dutch have long been sailors and vigorous entrepreneurs, members of an outward-looking society that takes pride in welcoming and assimilating foreigners. But while the sea is a door opening outward, it is also a source of potential catastrophe. The successful battle to keep it at bay has instilled in the Dutch a strong sense of community, which in turn is the foundation for one of the strongest welfare states in the world. The Dutch pay very high taxes and social premiums; their expectations of government are accordingly much higher than in most countries. The recently completed Delta Project, for example, an elaborate system of dikes and dams designed to protect the low-lying coastline, was publicly financed. Similarly, virtually all education, including religious schools, is state sponsored. By American standards, health care, public transportation, the arts, sports, and social services are all heavily subsidized.

Discussing national and international political issues is a daily pastime for the Dutch, either among family members, with co-workers during the morning coffee break, or with friends in one of the country's pubs and bars. American visitors are encouraged to be well informed about their country's foreign policy, as the topic is likely to come up sooner or later. Such discussion will be in English, which most Dutch speak quite well. (In comparing political systems it is helpful to remember that the Dutch word *liberaal* does not translate into "liberal" in English; *liberaal* refers to laissez-faire economic policy, and the Dutch *liberalen* are considered conservatives, though many do share the views of American liberals on issues such as abortion, gay rights, and so on.)

Current challenges facing Dutch society include the maintenance of its welfare system, which has become a heavy burden on the lackluster Dutch economy of the 1980s. Another challenge is assimilating the growing numbers of ethnic peoples into Dutch society. Since the early 1960s, the Netherlands, like many northern European countries, has become a magnet for migrant workers from the Mediterranean region. In addition, many people from former Dutch colonies such as Suriname and Indonesia have emigrated to the Netherlands. And refugees from all over the world have sought and been granted political asylum there. As a result, the country known for its tolerance now has the difficult task of finding solutions for the problems this influx of newcomers has created.

—*Angelique Dietz, Northfield, Minnesota*

Official name: Kingdom of the Netherlands. **Area:** 16,041 square miles (about twice the size of New Jersey). **Population:** 14,700,000. **Population density:** 916 inhabitants per square mile. **Capital and largest city:** Amsterdam (pop. 679,100). **Language:** Dutch. **Religion:** Roman Catholic, Dutch Reformed. **Per capita income:** US$9,180. **Currency:** Guilder. **Literacy rate:** 95%. **Average daily high/low:*** Amsterdam: January, 34°/40°; July, 59°/69°. **Average number of days with precipitation:** Amsterdam: January, 19; July, 14.

TRAVEL

U.S. citizens will need a passport, but a visa is not required for pleasure or business stays of up to 90 days. The tourist may be asked to show an onward/return ticket or sufficient funds for his or her stay. For residence authorization check with the Embassy of the Netherlands, 4200 Linnean Avenue NW, Washington, DC 20008.

Getting Around

The Dutch railway system is efficient and provides excellent service to all parts of the country. Its Rail Ranger tickets allow unlimited second-class travel within the country: the three-day ticket costs approximately $37; the seven-day ticket $51; and the 30-day ticket $200.

You can also purchase a "Benelux Tourrail Pass," which is valid for travel in the Netherlands, Belgium, and Luxembourg for any five days in a 17-day period during certain parts of the year: those under 26 pay approximately $45 for a second-class pass or $68 for a first-class pass; those over 26 pay approximately $63 for a second-class pass or $94 for a first-class pass. Eurail passes are also valid on the Dutch rail system (see page 58).

The flat lowlands of the country are probably best seen by bicycle. Most streets and highways have separate bike lanes, and bicycle rental agencies are plentiful and include most train stations. There's an extra charge for carrying bikes on trains ranging from $3.75 to $8, depending on distance, the season, and the day of the week.

---

*all temperatures are Fahrenheit

Especially for Students and Young People

Check with NBBS, Holland's student and youth travel bureau (and a member of the ISTC), for travel information, accommodation reservations, and student discounts on international travel by plane or train. In addition to the main office (Schipholweg 101, 2316XC Leiden), NBBS has offices in 16 cities around the country; its two Amsterdam offices are at Dam 17, Dam Square, and Leidsestraat 53. NBBS also offers tours of Amsterdam and an eight-day bicycle tour of the Netherlands; holders of the ISIC get discounts on all NBBS products.

For Further Information

The Netherlands Board of Tourism (355 Lexington Avenue, New York, NY 10017) distributes a number of general publications, including one for young people called *Holland Just for You*. The Netherlands Tourist offices in the U.S. offer what they call the Holland Leisure Card, which costs $10 and includes vouchers for substantial discounts on car rentals, bus and rail fares, et cetera. Another card, the Holland Leisure Card-Plus, entitles the holder to free admission to Holland's 350 museums in addition to the vouchers described above. The card costs $20.

WORK

Getting a Job

A work permit is required, but it is difficult to obtain because there are very few positions open to students. Contact the Embassy of the Netherlands (4200 Linnean Avenue NW, Washington, DC 20008) for further information.

Internships/Traineeships

There are both AIESEC and IAESTE internship programs in the Netherlands; see page 18 for more information.

Voluntary Service

CIEE places young people in voluntary service workcamps in the Netherlands organized by Stichting Internationale Werkkampen (Willemstraat 7, NL-3511 RJ Utrecht). Projects include construction work, forest management, working in homes for the physically disabled, et cetera. Volunteers work for about three weeks during the summer. Room and board are provided, although no wages are paid. Applicants must be between the ages of 18 and 30. The applications of U.S. residents are processed by CIEE. For more information contact the International Voluntary Service Department at the Council.

STUDY

Information on higher education, international courses, and scholarships open to foreign students in the Netherlands is available from the Netherlands Organization for International Cooperation in Higher Education. Its publications include *Basic Data on International Courses Offered in the Netherlands, Living in Holland: Practical Tips for Adjusting to Life Among the Dutch, Dutch Language Courses for Foreign Students*, and *Studying at a University in Holland: Should You*? Write to NUFFIC, Information Department, Badhuisweg 251, P.O. Box 90734, 2509 The Hague, Netherlands for further information. Information is also available through the Press and Cultural Sections of the Netherlands Consulate General in either New York, San Francisco, Los Angeles, Houston, or Chicago, as well as the embassy in Washington, D.C. Another booklet, *Vademecum: A Concise Guide to Studying in the Netherlands for Foreign Students*, is available for f300 (approximately $2) from the Foreign Student Service, Oranje Nassaulaan 5, 1075 AH Amsterdam.

The following are the educational programs offered by member institutions of the Council on International Educational Exchange. Consult Appendix I for the addresses of the college and universities listed in this section. In addition to the programs below, Indiana University offers a program open only to its own students.

SEMESTER AND ACADEMIC YEAR

Business

Michigan State University. "Business Law." Rotterdam. Spring quarter. Juniors and seniors with previous courses in business studies. Apply by February 3.

University of Oregon. "University of Oregon—Netherlands School of Business Exchange." Breukelen. Academic year. Juniors with 2.75 GPA. Preference given students at the University of Oregon. Apply by April 1.

General Studies

Central University of Iowa. "Netherlands Study Program." Leiden. Academic year or semester. Sophomores, juniors, and seniors with 2.5 GPA. Apply by April 15 for fall and November 1 for spring.

International Student Exchange Program. Direct reciprocal exchange between U.S. universities and institutions in Amsterdam, Groningen, Nijmegen, Tilburg, and Utrecht. Semester or academic year. Full curriculum options. Open only to students at ISEP member institutions.

Linguistics

State University of New York at Albany. "Netherlands Exchange Program." Nijmegen. Fall or spring semester. Juniors and seniors with two previous courses in linguistics. Apply by April 1 for fall and October 15 for spring.

Public Policy and Administration

Indiana University.
   Rotterdam. Spring semester at Erasmus University. Juniors and seniors with 3.0 GPA. Apply by October 1.

SUMMER

Business

University of Oregon. "University of Oregon—Netherlands School of Business Exchange." Breukelen. Juniors with 2.75 GPA. Preference given students at University of Oregon. Apply by April 1.

NORWAY

Norway is the northernmost of the Western European nations; in fact, fully a third of the country lies above the Arctic Circle. But Norway's climate is moderated by the Gulf Stream, which keeps its ports—even Hammerfest (the world's northernmost city)—ice-free year-round.

With the North Sea to the south, the Atlantic Ocean to the west, and the Arctic Ocean to the north, Norway is, not surprisingly, dependent on the sea. Since the days of the Vikings, it has been a leader in shipping and shipbuilding, and fishing has long been the principal economic activity of towns and villages all along the coast. But in recent years petroleum—from wells sunk far out in the North Sea—has replaced fish products as the country's number-one export.

Norway is perhaps most famous for its fjords, however, which provide the visitor with one of Europe's most spectacular encounters with nature. These narrow inlets cut into the rugged mountains along the Norwegian coast, so that while the nation extends along the sea for 1,100 miles, it actually has more than 12,000 miles of coastline.

Most of Norway's interior terrain is mountainous, with less than four percent of the land considered suitable for agriculture. But the wealth from the sea, as well as abundant timber resources and hydroelectric power for industry, have helped the nation develop one of the world's highest standards of living in the years since it gained independence from Sweden in 1905. But be prepared: this prosperity has also made Norway one of Europe's most expensive countries.

Official name: Kingdom of Norway. **Area:** 125,049 square miles (about the size of New Mexico). **Population:** 4,200,000. **Population density:** 34 inhabitants per square mile. **Capital and largest city:** Oslo (pop. 488,000). **Language:** Norwegian. **Religion:** Lutheran. **Per capita income:** US$13,900. **Currency:** Krone. **Literacy rate:** 100%. **Average daily high/low:*** Oslo: January, 30°/20°; July, 73°/56°. **Average number of days with precipitation:** Oslo: January, 8; July, 10.

---

*all temperatures are Fahrenheit

TRAVEL

A passport is required for U.S. citizens visiting Norway. However, a visa is not required for stays of up to three months (a period that begins as soon as you enter the Scandinavian region—Finland, Sweden, Denmark, Iceland, or Norway itself). For specific requirements, check with the Royal Norwegian Embassy, 2720 34th Street NW, Washington, DC 20008.

Getting Around

Norway has a variety of transportation systems to choose from—bus, train, or boat. Travelers who fly SAS directly between the U.S. and Scandinavia are eligible to purchase a Visit Scandinavia pass. This pass entitles the holder to five economy flights within Denmark, Norway, and Sweden between July 1 and August 14. The pass must be purchased in the U.S., costs $200, and is valid for up to 30 days after your arrival in Scandinavia. In addition, it can be used on any of the three Scandinavian airlines: Danair, Linjeflyg, and SAS (excluding flights to the Faroe Islands and Greenland).

If you plan on traveling extensively by rail in Scandinavia, you should investigate the Nordturist Ticket (approximately $250), which is good for 21 days of unlimited second-class travel throughout Scandinavia. Eurail passes are also valid on the Norwegian rail network (see page 58). If you have the time you may also want to investigate the legendary coastal steamers that link towns along the coast from Bergen to Kirkenes, near the Soviet border.

Especially for Students and Young People

Univers Reiser (UR), the Norwegian student travel bureau, is a good source of information on travel and student discounts in Norway. Besides its Oslo office (Universitetssentret, Boks 55, Blindern, 0313 Oslo 3), it has offices in As, Bergen, Stavanger, and Tromsö. In Norway, students with the International Student Identity Card (ISIC) get reductions on admission to some museums, discounts on train and plane fares from Norway to a variety of international destinations, and 25-percent discounts in certain hotels in Bergen, Oslo, Stavanger, and Tromsö.

Meet the People

Friends Overseas is an American-Scandinavian people-to-people program that helps put travelers in touch with Scandinavians who share similar interests. For further information, send a self-addressed stamped envelope to Friends Overseas, 68-04 Dartmouth Street, Forest Hills, NY 11375.

For Further Information

The Norwegian Tourist Board (655 Third Avenue, New York, NY 10017) distributes publications on cycling, camping, farm vacations, and hiking in Norway. You'll also find Frommer's *Scandinavia on $60 a Day* ($13.95), a good source of information for the budget traveler about one of Europe's most expensive regions, in most bookstores.

WORK

Getting a Job

For the most part, work permits for long-term work are issued only to a specific few: "Aliens with long-standing and special ties to Norway, scientists, performing artists and musicians, trainees admitted under agreement with other countries, and young people who enter Norway sponsored by any of the youth-exchange programs of the Norwegian Foundation for Youth Exchange [see below]." However, foreigners may work in Norway during the summer for up to three months without obtaining a work permit before entering the country. Unfortunately, holiday jobs are becoming more popular with young Norwegians and there has been an increase in unemployment of late, so that the competition for such jobs is greater now than it used to be. According to the Arbeidsdirektoratet (Directorate of Labor), "The best opportunity for obtaining jobs occurs from May to mid-June and from mid-July to the end of September, as the influx of young Norwegians seeking summer employment is greater during the intermediate period."

Farm Work

Atlantis—Norwegian Foundation for Youth Exchange (Rolf Hofmosgate 18, 0655 Oslo 6) has been granted permission to organize work programs that are not affected by the general regulations for work permits. Atlantis will place young people 18–30 years of age as working guests or au pairs in Norwegian households. Chores may include haying, weeding, milking, picking fruit, and feeding cattle, in addition to normal housework and childcare. Free-time activities include walking tours in the mountains and forests, swimming, fishing, boating, and excursions to famous Norwegian sights. Placement occurs year-round, with a minimum placement of four weeks and a maximum of twelve weeks. Participants receive room and board and approximately $55 per week in pocket money. The registration fee is approximately $45. Enclose two international postal-reply coupons when writing for information.

Internships/Traineeships

There are both AIESEC and IAESTE internship programs in Norway; see page 18 for more information.

In addition, the American Scandinavian Foundation sponsors a program that provides summer training assignments for full-time students majoring in engineering, computer science, horticulture, agriculture, forestry, and chemistry, among others. The deadline for application is December 1. The organization also offers long-term training assignments of up to 18 months in a variety of fields. Recent graduates with at least one year's experience in the field in which training is sought and with competence in Norwegian are eligible. For long-term assignments, send a résumé specifying the field of training and country desired. No traineeships are available in teaching, social work, or medically related fields. Contact the American Scandinavian Foundation, Exchange Division, 127 East 73rd Street, New York, NY 10021.

Voluntary Service

For persons interested in voluntary service work, the "Year Abroad Program" sponsored by the International Christian Youth Exchange offers persons ages 18–24 voluntary service opportunities in the fields of health care, education, the environment, construction, et cetera. See page 22 for more information.

STUDY

Publications on folk high schools and university programs for foreign students are available from the Norwegian Information Service, 825 Third Avenue, 17th floor, New York, NY 10022. The Exchange Division of the American Scandinavian Foundation (127 East 73rd Street, New York, NY 10021) will provide a listing of English-language academic-year and summer programs in Scandinavia, including Norway.

> "I was the only American student at my school and so I spent nearly all of my time with Norwegian students. I learned Norwegian quickly as a result —and also learned much more about their culture and way of life than if I had been in a program of mostly Americans."

The following are the study-abroad programs offered by member institutions of the Council on International Educational Exchange. Consult Appendix I for the addresses of the universities and organizations listed in this section. In addition to those listed below, the American Graduate School of International Management, Ohio University, and the University of California system offer programs open only to their own students.

SEMESTER AND ACADEMIC YEAR

General Studies

Scandinavian Seminar. "College Year in Norway." Individual placement in Norwegian Folk Colleges throughout Norway. Norwegian language and cultural immersion with emphasis in liberal arts. College credit granted through University of Massachusetts–Amherst. Sophomores to graduate students. Apply by May 1.

University of Oregon. "University of Oregon—University of Bergen Exchange Program." Academic year. Juniors with one year of Norwegian and summer intensive program in Norway or two years of Norwegian. Preference given to students at University of Oregon. Apply by April 1.

University of Washington. "The Oslo Year Program." Academic year or semester. Juniors and seniors with one year of Norwegian. Apply by January 31 for fall and academic year and October 15 for spring.

Social Sciences

Scandinavian Seminar. "Semester Program on Nordic and Global Issues." Sogndal or Vesby. Fall or spring semester. Focus on global issues from a

Nordic perspective, with coursework, discussions, and excursions. Sophomores to graduate students and nonstudents. Apply by May 1.

SUMMER

General Studies

University of Washington. "University of Oslo International Summer School." Oslo. Juniors and seniors. Apply by March 1.

PORTUGAL

One of the European Economic Community's newest members, Portugal is also its poorest. Once it was a great seafaring kingdom (Magellan and Vasco de Gama are two of the many Portuguese explorers who ventured to India, the Orient, and the New World). Today, the Portuguese economy is based on manufacturing, farming, wine production, tourism, and the income sent home by a large population of Portuguese workers living in the wealthier countries of Europe (chiefly France).

Portugal was the last European power to hang onto its colonial empire in Africa. After a successful revolution overthrew Portugal's 50-year military regime in 1974 and installed the current democratic government, Portugal finally granted independence to Mozambique, Angola, and its other African colonies. Today, all its formal colonies are gone, with the exception of the tiny enclave of Macao, due to be ceded to China at the end of the century. Yet both the nation's people and fascinating points of interest remind visitors of its past greatness—and, by implication, its future potential.

Official name: Republic of Portugal. **Area:** 34,240 square miles (about the size of Kentucky). **Population:** 10,300,000. **Population density:** 300 inhabitants per square mile. **Capital and largest city:** Lisbon (pop. 831,000). **Language:** Portuguese. **Religion:** Roman Catholic. **Per capita income:** US$2,970. **Currency:** Escudo. **Literacy rate:** 80%. **Average daily high/low:*** Lisbon: January, 56°/46°; July, 79°/63°. **Average number of days with precipitation:** Lisbon: January, 9; July, 1.

TRAVEL

U.S. citizens will need a valid passport; however, a visa is not required for visits of up to 60 days. If you plan a stay of more than two months, contact the Embassy of Portugal, 2125 Kalorama Road NW, Washington, DC 20008 for specific requirements.

Getting Around

Portugal is still one of the least expensive countries to visit in Europe, and is well worth considering when you plan your itinerary.

---

*all temperatures are Fahrenheit

With the exception of the express trains that run between Lisbon and Porto and Lisbon and the Algarve, train travel in Portugal is slow. However, Eurail passes are valid throughout the country (see page 58). The intercity buses are faster and more comfortable, although usually a little more expensive than the train. Unlimited first-class train passes are available for $69 for seven days; $109 for 14 days; and $156 for 21 days.

> *"Trains in Portugal (and many in Spain) are 'country trains.' They plod along at their own speed and stop everywhere. Just because you whistled down from Paris in eight hours flat, don't expect that you're going to reach the Algarve at the same clip."*

The Portuguese Youth Hostel Association, Pousadas de Juventude (Rua Andrade Corvo, 46, 1000 Lisbon) has hostels throughout Portugal. The organization also offers a variety of low-cost tours in mainland Portugal, as well as in the Azores and Madeira. Included are tours by railroad, bus, bicycle, and on foot; also available are seven-day vacation packages featuring a particular activity such as archaeology, canoeing, pottery, tapestry, windsurfing, or scuba diving.

Especially for Students and Young People

The following organizations specialize in student travel; both are members of the ISTC.

- TAGUS-Turismo Juvenil, Praça de Londres 9b, 1000 Lisbon
- ATEJS, Rua Miguel Bombarda 425, 4000 Porto

Both organizations provide travel information, sell discounted train, bus, and plane tickets, and operate sightseeing tours.

Holders of the International Student Identity Card (ISIC) receive a discount of up to 20 percent on buses and a 50-percent discount on train travel within Portugal, as well as discounts on train travel to the rest of Europe. Students with the ISIC also get free admission to more than 30 government museums as well as a number of shopping discounts (both TAGUS and ATEJ provide a list of stores offering discounts).

For Further Information

Brochures available from the Portuguese National Tourist Office (548 Fifth Avenue, New York, NY 10036-4704) include tourist information, camping guides, and a youth hostel list. An excellent guidebook to take along is *Let's Go: Spain, Portugal and Morocco*, published by St. Martin's Press and available in bookstores for $12.95.

WORK

Getting a Job

For regular employment in Portugal (which is very difficult for a U.S. citizen to obtain), a work permit obtained by the employer is a must. After application for the permit is approved by the Ministry of Labor, the employee must get the appropriate visa from the Portuguese Consulate (630 Fifth Avenue, Suite 655, New York, NY 10111).

Internships/Traineeships

There are both AIESEC and IAESTE internship programs in Portugal; see page 18 for more information.

Voluntary Service

CIEE places young people in voluntary service workcamps in Portugal organized by Turicoop (Rua Pascoal de Melo, 15-1 DTO, 1100 Lisbon), which sponsors two- to three-week camps based in small rural towns. Volunteers, who must be 16 or over, are involved in conservation and archaeological projects. The applications of U.S. residents are processed by CIEE. For more information contact the International Voluntary Service Department at the Council.

STUDY

A fact sheet titled *Information on Study in Portugal* is available from the Embassy of Portugal (2125 Kalorama Road NW, Washington, DC 20008). The American Graduate School of International Management and the University of California system offer study programs in Portugal; however, these programs are open only to students already enrolled in these institutions.

SPAIN

The mere mention of Spain conjures up familiar images, even among those who have never been there: visions of spirited bullfights, crowded *tapas* bars, passionate flamenco dancers, sun-drenched castles, and colorful Easter processions, to name a few. This is the Spain, exotic and romantic, that annually attracts some 50 million visitors to a country of only 36 million people. Those who arrive in quest of Don Quixote's Spain will still find enough of it preserved to satisfy their romantic expectations: from the Altamira cave paintings in Asturias to the Roman aqueduct in Segovia, from the Moorish Alhambra in Granada to the Royal Palace in Madrid, the remains of Spain's rich and glorious past are easy to find.

Most visitors, however, will also be struck by the difference between the contemporary realities of Spain and the images featured in travel brochures. The conservative, tradition-bound Spain, which for centuries asserted its uniqueness, has in recent years transformed itself into Europe's most dynamic and rapidly changing country.

Madrid, the thriving capital, has grown to a population of nearly five million. The city is renowned for the variety and energy of its nightlife, especially during the spring and summer, when *Madrileños* young and old wind up an evening at the theater or a restaurant by stopping off at one of the many sidewalk cafés that are open well into the early morning hours. At the same time, within the modern, cosmopolitan city can still be found the more traditional Spanish city, with its bullring, Rastro flea market, world-famous art museum, and old quarter around the Plaza Mayor. A word of caution, however. Madrid's heady plunge into modernity has also transformed it into one of Europe's most expensive capitals.

The change in Spain has not been confined to Madrid. Barcelona, Madrid's long-time commercial and cultural rival on the Mediterranean coast, is thriving as a commercial and industrial center, as well as being the focus of a resurgent Catalan language and culture. Outside the major cities, television, improved transportation, and economic growth have succeeded in spreading modern consumer culture into traditionally isolated areas.

Much of Spain's ongoing transformation can be traced to the emergence of democracy in 1976 after nearly forty years of military dictatorship under General Francisco Franco. Today Spain is a constitutional monarchy. While its king, the popular Juan Carlos I, has little official political authority under the terms of the 1978 constitution, he is generally credited with having saved the young democracy in 1981 when he energetically intervened to help put down an attempted coup by dissatisfied military officers. Now regarded as a stable Western-style democracy, Spain officially ended its many years of political isolation from Europe when it joined NATO and the European Community in 1986.

—*Michael Vande Berg, Kalamazoo, Michigan*

Official name: Kingdom of Spain. **Area:** 194,885 square miles (about ¾ the size of Texas). **Population:** 39,000,000. **Population density:** 200 inhabitants per square mile. **Capital and largest city:** Madrid (pop. 3,160,800). **Language:** Spanish and various regional languages, chief of which is Catalan. **Religion:** Roman Catholic. **Per capita income:** US$5,198. **Currency:** Peseta. **Literacy rate:** 97%. **Average daily high/low:*** Barcelona: January, 56°/42°; July, 81°/69°. Madrid: January, 47°/33°; July, 87°/62°. **Average number of days with precipitation:** Barcelona: January, 5; July, 4. Madrid: January, 9; July, 3.

TRAVEL

A passport is required for U.S. citizens going to Spain. A visa is not required for tourists staying up to six months. You may also be required to show a nontransferable return plane ticket and adequate means of support. For specific regulations, check with the Spanish Embassy, 2600 Virginia Avenue NW, Suite 214, Washington, DC 20037.

Getting Around

Eurail and InterRail passes are valid in Spain (see page 58). However, if you're traveling to Spain by rail, you'll have to change trains at the French border, since most of Spain's railroads are a different gauge than the rest of Europe. Because of its popularity as a summer destination (Spain welcomes more

---

*all temperatures are Fahrenheit

tourists than any other country in the world), trains are almost always crowded in summer. In addition, persons with Eurailpasses are required to make advance reservations for all long-distance trains.

RENFE, the national rail system, sells passes that are good for unlimited travel in Spain. Eight days of second-class travel cost about $95; the price for 15 days is $153; and 22 days cost $195. First-class passes cost about $132, $216, and $252, respectively. Passes may be purchased in the U.S., but are also available in Spain. RENFE also offers the *Tarjeta Joven* to travelers ages 12 to 26. For 2,000 pesetas you receive a 50-percent discount on all train trips over 100 kilometers.

A number of different bus companies provide intercity service in Spain, a travel option that costs about the same, or even more than the train. Along the Cantabrican coast and in the southern region of Spain, however, buses fill in the gaps in the national rail network, providing more direct and convenient service than that available by rail.

Iberia Airlines has a "Visit-Spain" fare that entitles you to unlimited-mileage air travel in Spain as well as to and from the Balearic Islands. The ticket costs $199 for 60 days, and $249 if the Canary Islands are included. You must fly Iberia to Spain to be eligible for the pass, however, and it must be purchased in the U.S. or Canada.

Passenger boats link Spain's Mediterranean ports with the famed Balearic islands of Majorca, Minorca, and Ibiza. However, before hopping on a boat, check the air fare; in many cases, going by plane is actually cheaper. Ferries also link Spain's Mediterranean ports with Spanish enclaves on the African coast (Ceuta and Melilla) and connect Cadiz with ports in the Canary Islands. Numerous boats also make the short trip across the Strait of Gibraltar to Tangiers, Morocco.

Bicycling around Spain is enjoyable but difficult, as most of Spain's secondary roads are rough and uneven, and mountains crisscross the country. However, bikes may be carried on trains as baggage at no extra charge.

"Spain is a very diverse country, and very rich in culture. The typical thoughts of bullfights and flamenco only apply in Andalucía. Every region has its own culture to offer, and some areas, like Galicia, seem like a different world."
—Stacy M. Coito, Turlock, California

"Be sure to take advantage of the siesta. It is a great way to get refreshed and so necessary in order to properly enjoy Spanish nightlife."
—Nathan Kreie, Princeton, Minnesota

Especially for Students and Young People

Check with TIVE, Spain's student travel bureau and member of the ISTC, for information on travel, accommodations, and student discounts. It has offices in Madrid (José Ortega y Gasset, 71, 3rd floor, E-28006 Madrid) as well as 26 other Spanish cities.

In Spain, holders of the International Student Identity Card (ISIC) can get reduced train and bus tickets for travel from Spain to points around Europe, as well as reduced plane tickets to destinations all over the world. They also get a discount on TIVE's tours in Madrid and excursions to Salamanca, Toledo, and El Escorial. Students with ISICs get free admission to state museums, including the Prado, with its unrivaled collections of El Greco, Velasquez, and Goya.

For Further Information

At most bookstores you'll find a wide selection of travel books on Spain. *Let's Go: Spain, Portugal and Morocco* contains useful information on low-cost accommodations, what to see, and how to get around for students and travelers on a budget. It's published by St. Martin's Press and is available at Council Travel offices for $12.95. Also good for budget travelers is Frommer's *Spain and Morocco on $40 a Day* ($13.95). The *Michelin Green Guide* for Spain ($10.95) provides comprehensive information on sites of natural, historical, and artistic interest.

The National Tourist Office of Spain (665 Fifth Avenue, New York, NY 10022) has brochures describing the various regions of Spain, maps, and publications on camping sites, pensiones, et cetera. In addition, every city of Spain has its own tourist office were you can get maps, brochures, and help in finding accommodations.

WORK

Getting a Job

According to the Spanish authorities, employers may obtain a work permit for a U.S. citizen only if there are no Spanish applicants for the job. Young people may be able to find summer employment in resort areas, but the pay is very low. The best place to look for au pair jobs and other positions suitable for English-speakers is the English-language newspaper, *The Iberian Sun*.

Internships/Traineeships

There are both AIESEC and IAESTE internship programs in Spain; see page 18 for more information. In addition, Southwest Texas State University has a program open only to students already enrolled there.

Voluntary Service

CIEE places young people in voluntary service workcamps in Spain organized by Servicio Voluntario Internacional (Calle José Ortega y Gassett, 71, E-28006, Madrid). At these summer workcamps groups of international volunteers work on a variety of projects involving archaeology, forestry, social work, et cetera. Applicants must be between 18 and 26 years of age and have some knowledge of Spanish. The average length of service is 15 to 20 days. The applications of U.S. residents are processed by CIEE. For more information contact CIEE's International Voluntary Service Department.

For persons interested in longer-term voluntary service work, the "Year Abroad Program" sponsored by the International Christian Youth Exchange offers persons ages 18–24 voluntary service opportunities in the fields of health care, education, the environment, construction, et cetera. See page 22 for more information.

Study

For information on studying in Spain, contact the Cultural Office of the Spanish Embassy (2600 Virginia Avenue, Suite 214, Washington, DC 20037) or a consulate in your region. Available are a number of fact sheets, including *Summer Courses for Foreigners, Academic Year Courses for Foreigners,* and *American Programs in Spain.*

The following are the educational programs offered by member institutions of the Council on International Educational Exchange. Consult Appendix I for the addresses of the colleges and universities listed in this section. In addition to the programs below, the American Graduate School of International Management, California State University, Mary Baldwin College, New York University, Ohio State University, Pennsylvania State University, and the University of California system offer study-abroad programs open only to their own students.

SEMESTER AND ACADEMIC YEAR

Business Administration

Council on International Educational Exchange. "Business & Society Program." Seville. Fall or spring semester. Sophomores to graduate students (not for graduate credit) with advanced Spanish, 2.75 GPA, and previous courses in business or economics. Apply by October 15 for spring and April 1 for fall.

General Studies

Alma College. "Program of Studies in Spain." Madrid or Segovia. Sophomores, juniors, and seniors with 2.5 GPA. No language prerequisite for Madrid. Two years of Spanish required for Segovia. Apply by June 15 for fall and October 15 for winter.

Brethren Colleges Abroad. Barcelona. Semester or academic year. Juniors and seniors with two years of college Spanish and 3.0 GPA. Apply by May 1 for fall and November 1 for spring.

Council on International Educational Exchange.
   "Language Area Studies Program." Alicante. Fall or spring semester. Sophomores to graduate students (not for graduate credit) with one semester college Spanish. Apply by April 1 for fall and October 25 for spring. Contact Academic Programs Department.
   "Liberal Arts Program." Seville. Semester or academic year. Sophomores to graduate students (not for graduate credit) with one semester college Spanish. Apply by April 1 for fall and October 25 for spring. Contact Academic Programs Department.

Experiment in International Living/School for International Training. "College Semester Abroad." Granada. Spring or fall semester. Intensive language, life, and culture seminar, village stay, independent-study project, and homestay. Sophomores to graduate students with 2.5 GPA. Apply by May 15 for fall and October 15 for spring.

Georgetown University. "Universidad de Barcelona." Academic year. Juniors with two years of Spanish and 3.0 GPA. Apply by mid-February.

Indiana University. "Overseas Study in Madrid." Academic year. Study at University of Madrid. Limited to students at Indiana, Purdue, and the University of Wisconsin. Juniors and seniors with two years of Spanish and 3.0 GPA. Apply by first week of November.

International Student Exchange Program. Direct reciprocal exchange between U.S. universities and institutions in Madrid and Santiago de Compostela. Academic year. Full curriculum options. Open only to students at ISEP member institutions.

Lake Erie College. Salamanca. Academic year, semester, or quarter. Sophomores, juniors, and seniors with 2.5 GPA. Apply by June 1 or November 1.

Marquette University. "Marquette University Study Center at the University of Madrid." Semester or academic year. Sophomores, juniors, and seniors with 3.0 GPA and one college Spanish course beyond intermediate level. Apply by May 15 for fall and November 30 for spring. Contact: Director, Madrid Study Center, Marquette University, Milwaukee, WI 53233.

New York University. "NYU in Spain." Madrid. Semester or academic year. Undergraduate program and MA programs in Hispanic literature and Hispanic civilization. Juniors and graduate students. Intermediate Spanish and 3.0 GPA required for undergraduates. Major in Spanish required for MA program. Apply by May for fall and by November for spring. Contact: NYU in Spain, 19 University Place, Room 409, New York, NY 10003; (212) 998-7060.

Northern Illinois University. "Academic Internships in Madrid." Fall semester. Students take two courses plus internship. Wide range of internships available for residents of Illinois; more limited selection for residents of other states. Sophomores, juniors, and seniors with 3.0 GPA. Apply by April 4.

Ohio State University. "Study in Spain: the Toledo Program." Semester or academic year. Juniors and seniors with one and a half years of Spanish. Open to students at Ohio schools only. Apply by August 1 for fall and December 15 for spring.

Portland State University. "ISIS Program in Spain." Barcelona. Fall or spring semester. Courses offered by Institute for Social and International Studies. Language of instruction is English. Juniors, seniors, and graduate students with 3.0 GPA. Apply 12 weeks prior to beginning of semester.

Purdue University. "Overseas Study in Madrid." See program listing under Indiana University.

St. Lawrence University. "Spain Year Program." Academic year in Madrid, with orientation in Salamanca and one-month village homestay. Sophomores, juniors, and seniors with intermediate college Spanish and 2.8 GPA. Apply by February 20.

Skidmore College. "Junior Year Abroad." Semester or academic year. Juniors and seniors with intermediate proficiency for single semester, third-year level for academic year; 3.0 GPA required. Apply by October 15 for spring and February 15 for fall.

Southern Methodist University. "SMU-in-Spain." Madrid. Semester or academic year. Liberal arts studies focused on the Spanish experience; courses in international business also available. Sophomores, juniors, and seniors with one year of college Spanish. October 15 for spring and March 15 for fall.

State University of New York at Cortland. Salamanca. Sophomores, juniors, and seniors with two years of college Spanish and 3.5 GPA in major. Apply by March 1.

Syracuse University. "Syracuse University in Madrid." Fall or spring semester. Sophomores, juniors, and seniors with 3.0 GPA. Apply March 15 and October 15.

Tufts University. "Tufts in Madrid." Juniors with two years college Spanish and 3.0 GPA. Apply by February 1.

University of Minnesota. "International Program in Toledo." Freshmen to graduate students. Apply by July 15 for fall and December 1 for spring.

University of New Hampshire. "Study in Granada." Semester or academic year. Sophomores, juniors, and seniors with five semesters of college Spanish; 3.0 in Spanish and 2.5 overall GPA required. Preference given to students from the Universities of New Hampshire, Connecticut, and Rhode Island. Apply by March 1 for fall and October 1 for spring. Contact Department of Spanish and Classics, 209 Murkland Hall, University of New Hampshire, Durham, NH 03824; (603) 862-3120.

University of North Carolina–Chapel Hill. "UNC Year at Seville." Semester or academic year. Juniors and seniors with two years of college Spanish and 2.5 GPA. Apply by March 15 for fall and October 15 for spring.

University of Oregon. "Study in Seville." Winter and spring quarters. Sophomores, juniors, and seniors with two years college Spanish and 3.0 GPA. Apply by October 15.

University of Wisconsin–Madison. "Overseas Study in Madrid." See program listing under Indiana University.

University of Wisconsin–Platteville. "Seville Study Center." Semester or academic year. Study at Spanish-American Institute. Spanish language and literature, liberal arts, and international business. Courses taught in English and Spanish. Sophomores, juniors, and seniors with 2.5 GPA. Apply by April 30 for fall and November 1 for spring.

Social Science

American University. "Madrid Semester." Spring semester. Spanish politics, economics, and foreign policy. Internships with multinationals. Juniors and seniors with two years of college Spanish and 2.75 GPA. Apply six months prior to start of program.

Spanish Language and Culture

Adventist Colleges Abroad. Sagunto. Open only to students at Adventist Colleges Abroad consortium institutions. Academic year, semester, or quarter. Freshmen to seniors with 3.0 GPA in Spanish and 2.5 overall GPA. Apply sixty days before beginning of academic year.

Boston University. "Boston University in Madrid." Semester or academic year. Sophomores, juniors, and seniors with a 3.0 GPA. Apply by March for fall and October for spring.

Brigham Young University. "BYU Study Abroad." Madrid. Spring semester. Sophomores, juniors, and seniors. Some Spanish required. Apply by October 1.

Central University of Iowa. "Central College Spanish Program." Granada. Semester or academic year. Sophomores, juniors, and seniors with intermediate-level Spanish and 2.5 GPA (3.0 in Spanish). Apply by November 1 for spring and April 15 for fall.

Council on International Educational Exchange. "Language & Society Program." Seville. Fall or spring semester. Sophomores to graduate students (not for graduate credits) with intermediate Spanish and 2.75 GPA. Apply by October 15 for spring and April 1 for fall. Contact Academic Programs Department.

Davidson College. "Spring Semester in Spain." Madrid. Spring semester, odd-numbered years only. Freshmen, sophomores, and juniors with intermediate Spanish and 2.75 GPA. Apply by October 3.

Heidelberg College. "The Center for Cross-Cultural Study." Seville. Semester or academic year. Sophomores to graduate students with intermediate college Spanish and 3.0 GPA. Apply by May 15 for fall and November 15 for spring. Contact American Secretary, Center for Cross-Cultural Study, 219 Strong Street, Amherst, MA 01002; (413) 549-4543.

Kalamazoo College. "Kalamazoo College in Madrid." Fall and winter quarter (September 15–February 15). Juniors and seniors with 15 quarter hours in Spanish and 3.0 GPA. Apply by May 1.

Michigan State University. "Spanish Language, Literature, and Culture in Caceres." Spring quarter. Sophomores, juniors, and seniors with two years of Spanish. Apply by February 3.

Middlebury College. Madrid. Sophomores to graduate students fluent in Spanish. Rolling admissions.

North Carolina State University. "Semester in Spain." Santander. Fall semester. Sophomores to graduate students with four semesters of Spanish and 2.5 GPA overall and in Spanish. Apply by March 15.

State University of New York at Albany. Madrid. Semester or academic year. Juniors and seniors with 3.0 GPA and two years college-level Spanish; advanced level courses in language or literature desirable. Apply by March 15.

Stetson University. Madrid. Semester or academic year. Sophomores, juniors, and seniors with 2.5 GPA (3.0 in major). Apply by March 1 for fall and October 15 for spring.

University System of Georgia/Augusta College. "Semester/Year Study in Spain." Seville. Undergraduate and graduate students with one year of Spanish and 2.5 overall GPA (3.0 in Spanish). Apply three months prior to beginning of term.

SUMMER

General Studies

Alma College. "Program of Studies in Spain." Madrid or Segovia. Sophomores, juniors, and seniors with 2.5 GPA. No language prerequisite for Madrid. One year of Spanish required for Segovia. Apply by March 15.

New York University. "NYU in Spain." Salamanca. Undergraduate and graduate program. Elementary Spanish required for undergraduates; major in Spanish or equivalent required for graduate students. Apply by May. Contact: NYU in Spain, 19 University Place, Room 409, New York, NY 10003; (212) 998-7060.

Rollins College. Madrid. "Verano Español." High school graduates, college students, and teachers with two years of college-level Spanish. Apply by March 15.

University of Minnesota. "Toledo Program." Freshmen to graduate students. Apply by April 15.

Spanish Language and Culture

Central Washington University. León. Four-week program. Sophomores, juniors, seniors, and teachers. Apply by April 4.

Experiment in International Living/School for International Training. "Summer Academic Study Abroad." Granada. Intensive language and life and culture seminar. Freshmen to seniors. Apply by March 15.

Illinois State University. "ISU Summer Program in Spain." Salamanca, with excursions to various cities in Spain. Freshmen to seniors with one year of college Spanish. Apply by March 9.

Michigan State University. "Spanish Language, Literature, and Culture in Denia." Sophomores, juniors, and seniors with one year college Spanish. Apply by April 21.

Ohio State University. "Study in Spain: The Toledo Program." Juniors and seniors with one and a half years of Spanish. Open to students at Ohio schools only. Apply by April 1.

Portland State University. "Hispanic Studies Program." Madrid. Excursions to Andalucía and Asturias. High school graduates and college students with one year of college-level Spanish. Apply by May.

State University of New York at Buffalo. "Study Abroad—Salamanca." Freshmen to graduate students with one year college Spanish. Apply by March 15. Contact International Education Services, 409 Capen Hall, Buffalo, NY 14260; (716) 636-2258.

State University of New York at Oswego. Madrid. Freshmen to seniors. Apply by April 25.

University of Alabama. "Academic Summer Program in Spain." Pamplona, with tour to Madrid and other cities. Spanish language, civilization, and literature. Freshmen to graduate students.

University of Arkansas at Little Rock. "Summer in Spain." Sophomores, juniors, and seniors. Some Spanish required. Apply by March 15.

University of Massachusetts—Amherst. "Summer Program in Spain." Juniors, seniors, and graduate students with three years of college Spanish. Apply by April 6.

University of Utah. "Salamanca Spanish Language Program." Freshmen to graduate students and adults. Previous Spanish study required. Apply by March 1.

University System of Georgia/Valdosta College. Salamanca. Graduates and undergraduates with one year of college Spanish and 2.5 overall GPA (3.0 in Spanish). Apply by March 15.

EXPLORING SPANISH CULTURE

Literature

Federico García Lorca, although killed at the age of 37 during the Spanish Civil War, is the leading playwright of 20th-century Spain. Lorca's dramatic works, written in verse, delve deeply into Spanish customs and traditions. *Blood Wedding* (1933) deals with love that defies village tradition and leads to an inescapable tragic end. *The House of Bernarda Alba* (1936) tells of the conflict between a domineering mother and her five daughters, who find themselves imprisoned by Spanish traditions and beliefs.

A more recent view of Spain is presented by Juan Goytisolo, a Spanish writer now living in France, in his autobiography, *Marks of Identity* (1969). *The Heliotrope Wall and Other Stories*, by Ana Maria Matute, is a collection of her best stories, in which the theme of a rural childhood in Spain is rendered in the style that has become known as "magical realism." *Five Hours with*

Mario by Miguel Delibes is the story of the troubled marriage of a politically active novelist and his comfortably middle-class Francoist wife.

The traditions, excitement, and struggles of Spain have attracted a number of noted American and British writers. Hemingway's *The Sun Also Rises* (1926), the story of a group of expatriates in Pamplona for the annual running of the bulls, blends passion and excitement with the violence of bullfighting. George Orwell's *Homage to Catalonia* (1952) deals with the heavy and often savage fighting that took place in the northeastern corner of the country during the Spanish Civil War. James Michener's nonfiction work, *Iberia* (1968), provides an insightful portrait of Spain during the Franco era.

Film

The films of pre-Civil War Spain were, for the most part, popular comedies often based on folkloric themes and romantic dramas marked by a strong Catholic influence. This trend continued after Franco's coming to power in 1936, but with a much heavier dose of official ideology as government censorship became widespread. Films celebrating nationalism, patriotism, and national heroics were the norm until filmmakers such as Juan Antonio Bardem with *Death of a Cyclist* (1955) and *Calle Mayor* (1956) and Luís Buñuel in *Viridiana* (1961) and *Tristana* (1970), began to obliquely criticize Spanish society and government. Only since Franco's death in 1976 have filmmakers been free to delve into themes of Spanish society and government without fear of censorship.

Among the best known contemporary filmmakers of Spain is Carlos Saura, whose films range from the *Garden of Delights* (1970), a satire of Spanish society and human venality, to *Blood Wedding* (1981), a filmed version of Lorca's play told without any dialogue—only music and flamenco ballet. Another noteworthy contemporary Spanish filmmaker is Victor Erice; in *The Spirit of the Beehive* (1973) he explores a child's world of reality and imagination. The years since Franco's death have produced a whole series of raucous, humorous investigations of changing Spanish social and sexual norms. Best known of these in the U.S. are the films of Pedro Almodóvar: *Matador* (1986), *Law of Desire* (1987), and *Women on the Verge of a Nervous Breakdown* (1988).

SWEDEN

Sweden, the third-largest nation in Western Europe (after France and Spain), is one of the world's most prosperous as well. The country's policy of strict neutrality kept it untouched by the two world wars and its cities still retain much of their old-world charm. Because of this neutrality, it has opted not to become a member of the European Community, but its economy and industries remain competitive nevertheless. In fact, Swedish products (steel, cars, appliances, precision equipment, et cctera) have earned a reputation for quality around the world. At the same time, the open-minded Swedes have used their wealth to create one of the world's most successful welfare states.

Official name: Kingdom of Sweden. **Area:** 173,349 square miles (slightly larger than California). **Population:** 8,400,000. **Population density:** 48 inhabitants per square mile. **Capital and largest city:** Stockholm (pop. 1,409,000). **Language:** Swedish. **Religion:** Lutheran. **Per capita income:** US$11,860. **Currency:** Krona. **Literacy rate:** 99.5%. **Average daily high/low:*** Stockholm, January, 30°/13°; July, 71°/57°. **Average number of days with precipitation:** January, 8; July, 9.

TRAVEL

U.S. citizens traveling to Sweden will need a passport; however, a visa is not required for stays of up to three months—a period that begins when entering the Scandinavian region. Check with the Embassy of Sweden, 600 New Hampshire Avenue NW, Washington, DC 20037 for specific requirements.

Getting Around

Travelers who fly SAS directly to Scandinavia are eligible to purchase a Visit Scandinavia pass, which entitles the holder to five economy flights within Denmark, Norway, and Sweden between July 1 and August 14. The pass must be purchased in the U.S., costs $200, and is valid for up to 30 days after your arrival in Scandinavia. It can also be used on any of three Scandinavian airlines: Danair, Linjeflyg, and SAS (excluding flights to the Faroe Islands and Greenland).

The Swedish rail network serves all of southern Sweden and much of the northern part of the country (it even crosses the Arctic Circle). However, trains are expensive. If you plan on traveling by rail in Scandinavia, you should investigate the Nordturist Ticket (approximately $250), which entitles you to 21 days of unlimited second-class travel throughout Sweden, Norway, Finland, and Denmark. It's also good on government-run ferries to Germany and Denmark. Tickets can be purchased at all major train stations. In addition, persons under the age of 26 can get a 45-percent discount on all train fares by purchasing a *rabattkort* (Kr85, about $15); however, it's not valid on Friday or Sunday nights and Saturday or Monday mornings. Eurail passes are valid for train travel in Sweden (see page 58).

Especially for Students and Young People

Check with SFS-RESOR, Sweden's student travel bureau and ISTC member, for information on travel and student discounts in Sweden. In addition to the main office (Kungsgatan 4, 11143 Stockholm), it has offices in Göteborg, Lund, and Umea. Holders of the International Student Identity Card can get discounts on plane and train travel from Sweden to destinations around the world.

> *"Visit in spring to get a real feeling for student life in Sweden. The best time is April–May. Visit Uppsala first, and then maybe Göteborg and also Lund in the south of Sweden."*

---

*all temperatures are Fahrenheit

Meet the People

Friends Overseas is an American-Scandinavian people-to-people program that helps put travelers in touch with Scandinavians who share similar interests. For further information, send a self-addressed stamped envelope to Friends Overseas, 68–04 Dartmouth Street, Forest Hills, NY 11375.

For Further Information

The Swedish Tourist Board (655 Third Avenue, New York, NY 10017) distributes a variety of publications, including *Youth Hostels in Scandinavia* and *Hotels in Sweden*. Available in bookstores is Frommer's *Scandinavia on $60 a Day* ($13.95), a good source of information for the budget traveler in one of Europe's most expensive regions.

WORK

Getting a Job

In order to work full-time in Sweden on a long-term basis you will need to obtain a work permit before entering the country. To be eligible for such a permit you will have to show written proof that your job and living accommodations in Sweden have already been arranged. For more information, contact the Embassy of Sweden (600 New Hampshire Avenue NW, Washington, DC 20037) for a copy of *Employment and Residency in Sweden*.

Internships/Traineeships

There are both AIESEC and IAESTE internship programs in Sweden; see page 18 for more information.

In addition, the American Scandinavian Foundation sponsors a program that provides summer training assignments for full-time students majoring in engineering, computer science, horticulture, agriculture, forestry, and chemistry, among others. The deadline for application is December 1. The organization also offers long-term training assignments of up to 18 months in a variety of fields. Recent graduates with at least one year's experience in the field in which training is sought and with competence in Swedish are eligible. For long-term assignments, send a résumé specifying the field of training and country desired. No traineeships are available in teaching, social work, or medically related fields. Contact the American Scandinavian Foundation, Exchange Division, 127 East 73rd Street, New York, NY 10021.

Voluntary Service

For persons interested in voluntary service work, the "Year Abroad Program" sponsored by the International Christian Youth Exchange offers persons ages 18–24 voluntary service opportunities in the fields of health care, education, the environment, construction, et cetera. See page 22 for more information.

STUDY

The Swedish Information Service (825 Third Avenue, New York, NY 10022) has a number of brochures and fact sheets on studying in Sweden, including *Studying in Sweden, Higher Education for Visiting Students,* and *International Summer Courses in the Swedish Language.* The Exchange Division of the American Scandinavian Foundation (127 East 73rd Street, New York, NY 10021) will also provide you with a listing of English-language academic-year and summer programs offered in Sweden.

The following are the educational programs offered by member institutions and organizations of the Council on International Educational Exchange. Consult Appendix I for the addresses you can write for further information. In addition to the programs listed below, the American Graduate School of International Management, California State University, New York University, Ohio State University, and the University of California system offer programs open only to their own students.

SEMESTER AND ACADEMIC YEAR

General Studies

International Student Exchange Program. Direct reciprocal exchange between U.S. universities and Växjö University. Semester or academic year. Full curriculum options. Open only to students at ISEP member institutions.

Scandinavian Seminar. "College Year in Sweden." Individual placement in Swedish folk colleges throughout Sweden. Swedish language and cultural immersion with emphasis on liberal arts. College credit granted through University of Massachusetts–Amherst. Sophomores to graduate students. Apply by May 1.

University of Oregon. "University of Oregon—University of Linköping Exchange." Fall semester or academic year. Juniors and seniors with two years college Swedish and 2.75 GPA. Apply by March 1.

Social Sciences

Scandinavian Seminar. "Semester Program on Nordic and Global Issues." Fall semester in Skinnskatteberg and spring semester in Sigtuna. Focus on global issues from a Nordic perspective, with coursework, discussions, and excursions. Sophomores to graduate students and nonstudents. Apply by May 1.

SUMMER

Marketing

Michigan State University. "Packaging in Sweden." Lund. Juniors and seniors. Apply by April 21.

EXPLORING SWEDISH CULTURE

Film

Swedish film is closely related to Swedish theater. Many filmmakers, including Ingmar Bergman, have worked regularly in the theater, and many traditional themes of Swedish theater have been explored in their movies. Bergman's films, for example, are usually stark psychological portraits of individuals grappling with the issues of death, religion and faith, sexuality and repression, and are often framed within a series of dreams, flashbacks, and illusions. The weightiness of their intellectual content is complemented by their cinematography, which more often than not evokes an austere, intensely personalized atmosphere. Some of his more readily available films include *The Seventh Seal* (1957), *Wild Strawberries* (1957), *The Magician* (1958), *Persona* (1966), *Hour of the Wolf* (1969), and *Fanny and Alexander* (1982). Another recent Swedish import, *My Life as a Dog* (1987), directed by Lasse Halstrom, tells the story of a young boy's experiences in a small Swedish town and is an extremely witty update of Swedish film tradition.

SWITZERLAND

An American visiting Switzerland for the first time will be amazed at the cleanliness and prosperity that greets one upon arrival in Zurich, Basel, or Geneva. Over the course of the last century, the Swiss have been able to transform a poor federation of small agricultural cantons into one of the world's wealthiest and most stable countries.

Switzerland is a land of amazing natural beauty—mountain peaks, Alpine skiing resorts, and quaint villages alternate with green well-kept meadows. But there is another Switzerland as well, the Switzerland of modern banks and investment houses connected to other world financial capitals via computers and satellite; of highly efficient rail, highway, and air networks; of cities with a healthy blend of old-world charm and high-tech convenience. Where else in the world can one walk into a twenty-four-hour convenience center to change currencies, make account transfers, and even buy gold bullion and coins—all at the push of a button?

It is difficult to find any evidence of poverty in Switzerland. Everyone seems to work; at last count the unemployment rate was less than one percent. The major industries are tourism, watchmaking, precision instruments, banking, and agriculture. Much of the unskilled labor is provided by foreigners, who are allowed to work in Switzerland for limited periods of time.

The young Swiss who have grown up in this idyllic land seem to live a charmed life. Fluent in many languages, they benefit from Switzerland's role as the crossroads of Europe. They eat French food, wear Italian clothes, drive German cars, and are fed a steady diet of American and British rock music through video programs broadcast via satellite. Unfortunately, drug abuse also seems to flourish in affluent countries such as Switzerland.

There is no "Swiss" language; depending on the region of the country, the people speak French, German, or Italian as their native language. The majority speaks German—actually a dialect called Schweizerdeutsch, which is difficult for foreigners, even Germans, to understand. However, most Swiss speak more than one language and many speak English. The Swiss living in the cantons bordering on France are the exception; many of them have adopted the French custom of not really learning any language other than French.

Divided by language and split by geography, it's rather amazing that the country of Switzerland, founded in 1291, exists at all. The world's oldest continuous democracy, Switzerland has a federal system of government much like that of the United States, with most of the actual decision-making power in the hands of the 23 cantons. And, despite its peace-loving image, Switzerland maintains an enormous army for a country its size; the Swiss see military power as a necessary part of their country's policy of strict neutrality, which since 1815 has kept it at peace with its more powerful and often belligerent neighbors.

—*Randy Epping, Zurich, Switzerland*

Official name: Swiss Confederation. **Area:** 15,941 square miles (about the size of Hawaii). **Population:** 6,600,000. **Population density:** 414 inhabitants per square mile. **Capital:** Bern (pop. 137,100). **Largest city:** Zurich (pop. 349,500). **Language:** German, French, Italian. **Religion:** Roman Catholic, Protestant. **Per capita income:** US$14,030. **Currency:** Swiss franc. **Literacy rate:** 99.5%. **Average daily high/low:*** Geneva: January, 39°/29°; July, 77°/58°. Zurich: January, 36°/26°; July, 76°/56°. **Average number of days with precipitation:** Geneva: January, 10; July, 9. Zurich: January, 11; July, 15.

TRAVEL

U.S. citizens need a passport for travel to Switzerland; however, a visa is not required for stays of up to three months. For specific requirements, check with the Embassy of Switzerland, 2900 Cathedral Avenue NW, Washington, DC 20008.

Getting Around

Switzerland has an excellent national railway system comprised mainly of government-run railroads but with a number of privately owned railways as well. Eurail and InterRail passes are valid in Switzerland, but only on the government railroads (see page 58). While travel by train is quite expensive, persons under 26 can purchase the Half-Fare Travel Card, which entitles the holder to a 50-percent discount on all fares charged by both government and private railways; the card costs Sfr100 (about $70) and is good for one year. In addition, a six-day unlimited youth pass costs Sfr150 (about $105). There is also a Swiss Pass Card, which entitles you to unlimited travel on the railway network, lake steamers, and postal buses. For second-class travel, the pass costs approximately $105 for four days, $125 for eight days, $155 for 15 days, and $210 for a month. Comparable first-class passes cost $155, $180, $220, and $300, respectively. For further details contact the Swiss National Tourist Office (608 Fifth Avenue, New York, NY 10020).

One of the most spectacular ways to enjoy Switzerland's natural beauty is to hike its Alpine trails. *Berghotels* or *auberges de montagne* are rustic moun-

---

*all temperatures are Fahrenheit

tain guesthouses—popular with both the Swiss and foreigners—that provide hikers with a meal and a place to stay in incredibly scenic spots far from the nearest road or railway. For more information, pick up a copy of *Walking Switzerland—the Swiss Way*, by Marcia and Philip Lieerman, available for $10.95 from The Mountaineers Books, 306 2nd Avenue West, Seattle, WA 98119.

> *"In Switzerland, the way of life is slower paced, more conservative. It takes time to get used to it. Make every effort to understand the culture. The more you show your understanding, the more open the people will be."*
> —Robert Merino, Stockton, California

Especially for Students and Young People

SSR-Reisen is the student travel bureau and ISTC member in Switzerland. You can contact the organization at Bäckerstrasse 52, 8004 Zurich. In addition, it has 15 other offices around Switzerland where you can get international plane and train tickets, book accommodations, and obtain travel information. SSR operates student hotels in Zurich, Berne, Geneva, Basel, Lugano, Lausanne, and Interlaken as well. It also offers river rafting and canoeing trips.

In Switzerland, students with the International Student Identity Card get discounts on international plane and train fares. They also receive discounts on tours offered by SSR-Reisen, as well as at its member hotels. A *National Student Discount Directory* is also available from SSR-Reisen.

Meet the People

"Meet the Swiss" is what the Zurich Tourist Office calls its hospitality program. You can make arrangements to meet Swiss families of similar backgrounds and interests at the tourist office, Bahnhofplatz 15, CH-8023 Zurich.

For Further Information

The Swiss National Tourist Office (608 Fifth Avenue, New York, NY 10020) can provide a wide range of useful materials, including information on rail travel, camping, and youth hostels, as well as general information about Switzerland. For detailed advice on what to see in Switzerland, get a copy of *Frommer's Switzerland and Liechtenstein* ($14.95) or the *Michelin Green Guide* for Switzerland ($10.95), both available in most bookstores.

WORK

Getting a Job

Anyone who wishes to work in Switzerland must obtain a work permit in advance of arrival; application for the permit is made by the prospective Swiss employer. The possibilities for finding permanent employment in Switzerland are very limited; in general, only applications from specialists or skilled workers are considered.

Internships/Traineeships

The programs run by members of the Council on International Educational Exchange are listed below. Consult Appendix I for the addresses where you can write for further information.

AIESEC–US. Reciprocal internship program for students in economics, business, finance, marketing, accounting, and computer sciences. See page 18 for further information.

Association for International Practical Training.
"IAESTE Trainee Program." On-the-job training for undergraduate and graduate students in technical fields such as engineering, computer science, agriculture, architecture, and mathematics. See page 18 for more information.
"Hotel & Culinary Exchanges Program." On-the-job training for young people beginning a career in the hotel and food service industries. Participants must have graduated from a university or vocational school and possess at least six months of training or experience in the chosen field. Training usually runs 6–12 months.

Syracuse University. "Graduate Internship in International Studies." Geneva. Summer. Graduates with basic knowledge of French or German. Apply by March 1.

Voluntary Service

For persons interested in voluntary service work, the "Year Abroad Program" sponsored by the International Christian Youth Exchange offers persons ages 18–24 voluntary service opportunities in the fields of health care, education, the environment, construction, et cetera. See page 22 for more information.

STUDY

Listed below are the educational programs offered by member institutions of the Council on International Educational Exchange. Consult Appendix I for the addresses where you can write for further information.

SEMESTER AND ACADEMIC YEAR

General Studies

Experiment in International Living/School for International Training. "College Semester Abroad." Zurich. Fall or spring semester. Intensive German language, life and culture seminar, independent study project, homestay, and Geneva U.N. excursion. Sophomores to graduate students with 2.5 GPA. Apply by May 15 for fall and October 15 for spring.

International Student Exchange Program. Direct reciprocal exchange between U.S. universities and the Université de Fribourg and Université de

Lausanne. Academic year. Full curriculum options. Generally only graduate students accepted. Open only to students at ISEP member institutions.

La Salle University. "La Salle-in-Europe." Fribourg. Academic year. Liberal arts, science, international studies; lectures in French, German, and English. Sophomores, juniors, and seniors with one year of college French or German and 2.5 GPA. Apply by May 1.

State University of New York at Cortland. Neuchâtel. Semester or academic year. Sophomores to graduate students with intermediate French and 3.5 GPA in major. Apply by March 1 for fall and February 15 for spring.

International Studies

Experiment in International Living/School for International Training. "College Semester Abroad." Geneva. Fall or spring semester. Intensive French language, academic seminar, including U.N. contributors, independent-study project, and homestay. Sophomores to graduate students with 2.5 GPA. Apply by May 15 for fall and October 15 for spring.

Kent State University. "KSU Semester in Geneva." Fall or spring semester. International relations and the U.N., and all levels of French language. Sophomores, juniors, and seniors with 2.5 GPA. Rolling admissions.

SUMMER

French Language

University of Utah. "Neuchâtel French Language Program." Multilevel French language study for four weeks preceded by three weeks of travel in Europe. Freshmen with some knowledge of French. Apply by March 1.

General Studies

State University of New York at Cortland. Neuchâtel. Sophomores to graduate students with intermediate French and 3.5 in major. Apply by April 1.

University of North Carolina–Chapel Hill. "UNC Program to Switzerland." Thun. Sophomores, juniors, and seniors. Apply by February 1.

Hotel and Restaurant Management

Michigan State University. Lausanne. European food selection, marketing, preparation, and service systems. Juniors and seniors. Apply by April 21.

University of Massachusetts–Amherst. "Summer Program in Hotel, Restaurant, and Travel Administration." Sophomores, juniors, and seniors. Some French required. Apply by January 15.

Political Science

University of Toledo. "Summer Study in Switzerland." Lausanne, Geneva, Bern, Montreux, Zermatt, Gruyeres. High school students to graduate students and nonstudents. Apply by May 1.

Music Composition

Syracuse University. "The Vevey New Music Sessions." Sophomores to graduate students and professionals. Apply by April 27.

UNITED KINGDOM OF GREAT BRITAIN AND NORTHERN IRELAND

Britain frequently is seen through the distorting lens of stereotypes popularized by movies, novels, and songs. But it is neither the fog-bound, subterranean nightmare of Dickens's imagination nor the cheery, quaint landscape of 1950s television comedies, and it is certainly not the trendy playground depicted in so many pop songs. Visitors will look in vain for relics of the Beatles' Britain; even the punks have become a bizarre tourist attraction rather than a representation of real social protest.

The current reality is that, for good or ill, Britain has undergone a quiet revolution in sensibility since Margaret Thatcher became prime minister in 1979. The country has moved closer to an American economic model, with an emphasis on self-reliance and competitiveness. This has lead toward a change in many traditional British beliefs and practices, including a commitment to the welfare state. In many ways Britain is becoming a tougher place to live, a place where the weak are no longer supported and the dispossessed can no longer be sure of a safety net. The thoughtful visitor cannot fail to see that the nation's social and political environment is shifting.

One result of this period of change has been the revival of Benjamin Disraeli's notion of Britain as two nations—rich and poor, South and North. The South, with London as its driving wheel, is relatively prosperous and characterized by high incomes (and high prices). The North of England, in contrast, has suffered most from industrial decline and the resulting unemployment. The two regions are also culturally distinct. For many visitors, an exclusive focus on London obscures the rich variety of English life and customs.

Scotland and Northern Ireland further illustrate the political, social, and cultural complexity of the United Kingdom. Economic problems in Scotland and political/religious disputes in Northern Ireland should not hide the fact that both locations are of considerable interest. As well as being rich in natural beauty, these regions have distinct cultures that are worth discovering. Wales also has a clearly separate identity, with its own language and a strong nationalist movement. In short, the United Kingdom is not a single coherent unit but several distinct cultures coexisting in a sometimes uneasy alliance.

Since 1945 Britain has drifted from the center of world affairs toward its periphery. Adjustment to a post-imperialist role has characterized Britain's foreign policy and has led to some ambiguity in its relationship with other countries. At the same time, the country has become an uneasy member of the European community; England's sense of "Europeaness" is provisional and her commitment to European unity is by no means unanimous. Traditional links with the English-speaking world remain strong in both political and emotional terms. The British may be a part of Europe, but they do not necessarily feel that that is where they belong.

For the U.S. visitor, Britain is a particularly attractive destination. And though the common language allows easy entrance into the culture, it obscures the fact that British society is profoundly different from our own. In comparison to the States, Great Britain is a formal society where status and class continue to be important factors. In a country with a strong sense of its past achievements, there is an inevitable nostalgia for a lost world and the preeminent role the country once played in that world. Still, Britain has one foot in its own past and another in the future, thus maintaining an uneasy balance between the two. It both clings to the symbols of past grandeur while looking toward the high technologies of the future.

There is still cultural dynamism in the country. Postwar immigration from the West Indies and the Indian subcontinent has created a cosmopolitan society that continues to attract immigrants and visitors. A vibrant theater and innovative art scene manage to flourish despite an occasionally inhospitable political climate. Britain is a society of paradox—both aging and forward-looking, traditional and modern, smug and uneasy. And like most paradoxes, it is fascinating and well worth investigating.

—*Michael Woolf, London*

Official name: United Kingdom of Great Britain and Northern Ireland. **Area:** 94,247 square miles (about the size of Wyoming). **Population:** 57,100,000. **Population density:** 606 inhabitants per square mile. **Capital:** London. **Largest city:** Greater London (pop. 6,767,500). **Language:** English, Welsh, Gaelic. **Religion:** Anglican. **Per capita income:** US$8,380. **Currency:** Pound sterling. **Literacy rate:** 99.5%. **Average daily high/low*:** Edinburgh: January, 45°/35°; July, 63°/52°. London: January, 44°/35°; July, 73°/55°. **Average number of days with precipitation:** Edinburgh: January, 18; July, 17. London: January, 17; July, 13.

TRAVEL

U.S. citizens will need a passport; however, a visa is not required for a stay of up to six months. Check with the British Embassy, 3100 Massachusetts Avenue NW, Washington, DC 20008, for specific regulations.

Getting Around

"England is scenically much more beautiful than most people realize. If you are really interested in enjoying your time in England rather than taking pictures of pigeons in London, spend your time in the smaller towns, especially in the north of England. You'll find the people there much more friendly and interested in you."
—Timothy Doyle, Burnsville, Minnesota

---

*all temperatures are Fahrenheit

If you want to travel in Britain by air, you can purchase a Visit UK ticket, which is honored in the ten cities served by Dan Air. Valid for 30 days, the ticket costs $66 for the first segment and $49 for each additional segment; tickets must be purchased in the U.S., however.

Though a comprehensive rail network covers Britain, the Eurailpass is not valid (the InterRail pass is, however). Travel by train is generally more expensive in Britain than on the Continent, but BritRail offers a number of passes and discounts. The Young Person's Railcard, available at most stations, gives holders a 33-percent discount off any train ticket. It costs £15 (approximately $26), and you'll need two photos and proof that you're under 24 years of age or that you are a student (the ISIC is acceptable). Unless you're planning on doing a lot of traveling around Britain, this may be a better deal than the BritRail passes.

The BritRail Youth Pass, for those between 16 and 25, entitles you to eight days of unlimited second-class travel for $149, 15 days for $219, 22 days for $289, and one month for $329. Persons over 25 pay $179, $259, $339, and $389, respectively, for the same options. The first-class version of the BritRail pass is available for $250, $370, $470, and $540, respectively.

BritRail also offers the Flexipass, which allows travel on any 4 out of 8 days for $149 (second class), or $210 (first class); travel for 8 days in a 15-day period costs $219 (second class), or $310 (first class). If you're between the ages of 16 and 25, a second-class BritRail Flexipass will cost $129 for 4 out of 8 days, and $189 for 8 out of 15 days.

All BritRail passes must be purchased before entering the United Kingdom; you can get them at Council Travel offices (see pages ix–xi), from most travel agents, or from Britrail International (630 Third Avenue, New York, NY 10017). There are also a number of regional Rail Rover tickets that allow for a week's travel within one of nine regions of the United Kingdom. These can be purchased for £19 to £44 (about $35 to $75) at the main stations within the region.

"Try to see Wales. Learn a little Welsh and it will steal the Welsh's hearts. The Welsh and the English are very different. I learned especially not to call an Englishman a Welshman, and vice versa."
—Teri Snyders, Ankeny, Iowa

Travel by train is not your only option; express coaches (buses) provide service that's generally a little cheaper and nearly as fast as the trains. The main intercity bus network is National Express/Scottish Citylink, which covers most of Great Britain. If you have an ISIC, a Student Coach Card can be obtained for £3.50 (about $8) and entitles you to a 33-percent discount off the regular fare. Foreign citizens of any age can buy the BritExpress Card and get a 33-percent discount on all trips made on coaches of the National Express/Scottish Citylink network in a 30-day period. The BritExpress Card can be purchased for £8 (about $15) at travel agencies outside Britain or from the National Express office at 13 Regent Street, London SW1.

In addition, you can travel on any number of local buses. For example, if you'd like to travel around rural Scotland cheaply, consider going by mail bus. Run by the postal service, these buses carry passengers as well as mail and their fares are extremely reasonable. There are 130 routes—all of them to areas not serviced by regular buses. You can get route and schedule information from the Post Office Headquarters (Scotland), West Port House, 102 West Port, Edinburgh, EH3 9HS.

Another option in the U.K. is hitchhiking. The fastest hitching is on the expressways, or "motorways," where you are allowed to hitch only on entrance ramps or the exit ramps to the gas station and restaurant service complexes that are located along the road at regular intervals.

"I hitched in Scotland and it was very easy to get rides. Where else would an elderly woman doing her weekly shopping give you a ride? And my longest wait ever for a ride was 20 minutes. Always try thumbing first, because to get to some historical sites, it is pretty near impossible any other way—for example, Cawdor Castle (Macbeth's)."

Rural areas of Britain are ideally suited to bicycling. The secondary roads are smooth and well maintained, and British drivers are more courteous than those you'll encounter on the Continent. As in most European countries, rural people are more hospitable than their urban counterparts. With pubs and lodgings readily available in the villages of the countryside, you'll be well taken care of. *Cyclist's Britain* describes 302 bicycle routes, each traced on an ordnance map complete with a description of the terrain. The book can be ordered from Hunter Publishing (300 Raritan Center Parkway, Edison, NJ 08818-7816) for $12.95 plus $2.50 postage. On most trains (except a few express trains with limited baggage space) you can take your bicycle at no extra charge. However, rules vary from route to route; be sure to ask the ticket collector which trains accept bikes and where they should be taken for loading.

One of the best ways to enjoy the British countryside is on foot. Persons interested in going by foot can get *Walker's Britain*, a guide to 240 walks complete with ordnance maps and descriptions of sights and attractions along the way. The book can be ordered from Hunter Publishing (300 Raritan Center Parkway, Edison, NJ 08818-7816) for $12.95 plus $2.50 postage.

Especially for Students and Young People

A number of student travel bureaus operate in the United Kingdom. For travel information, train, plane, and ferry tickets, and accommodation bookings, you might check with the Council Travel Office at 28a Poland Street, London WIV 3DB.

Student unions on the campuses of colleges and universities throughout Britain issue the International Student Identity Card (ISIC) and serve the needs of the student traveler. Many of these operate bars, restaurants, and recreational facilities, the majority welcome traveling students and all of them serve as a good source of information about accommodations, student discounts, and student life in the area. Many student unions also have an accommodations booking service and, during the summer, arrange accommodations for travelers in student residences. If you would prefer to arrange your accommodation before you leave, Council Travel can arrange dormitory accommodation at British universities starting from about $20 per night.

In Britain, persons with the ISIC can obtain discounts on ferry service to the Continent, on international train and plane fares, and on train and intercity bus travel within the United Kingdom. A Theatre Standby Scheme offers discounted standby tickets at West End theaters; to find out which plays are offering discounts, look for an "S" with a circle around it in the entertainment section of the newspapers or go to the kiosk in Leicester Square.

Meet the People

There is no government-sponsored "meet the people" program in Britain. There are a number of agencies that can make arrangements for a visitor to stay with a family as a paying guest. Stays of a week or more are preferred, but weekend visits can sometimes be arranged. There's a list of these agencies in an information booklet titled *Stay With a British Family*, available from the British Tourist Authority, 40 West 57th Street, New York, NY 10019.

For Further Information

The British Tourist Authority (40 West 57th Street, New York, NY 10019) distributes publications on accommodations, travel, and a wide variety of activities throughout Great Britain. We especially recommend the *Young Britain Guide* for its completeness and usefulness.

There's no lack of tourist guides to the United Kingdom. For students and other young travelers, one of the best is *Let's Go: Britain and Ireland* ($12.95), updated annually by the Harvard Student Agencies. Two other books geared to the budget traveler are Frommer's *Scotland and Wales on $40 a Day* ($12.95) and *England on $40 a Day* ($13.95). The *Michelin Green Guides* are recommended for their comprehensive information on cultural and historical attractions; there are *Green Guides* available for London, England's West Country, and Scotland. If you can't find exactly what you want at your local bookstore, you can obtain a catalog from the British Travel Bookshop (40 West 57th Street, 3rd floor, New York, NY 10019) by writing to their distributor: GHS Inc., Box 1224, Clifton, NJ 07012.

For current information on what is going on in London, buy a copy of *Time Out* magazine, a weekly that lists just about everything that is happening in the city. It's also a good place to check the classified ads for apartment shares, and picking up traveling companions.

In London, you can get all sorts of tourist information from the London Tourist Board and Convention Bureau, which has branches at Victoria Station, Harrods (4th floor), Heathrow Airport, Selfridges (ground floor), and the Tower of London. Another useful London resource is the British Travel Centre (12 Regent Street, London SW1), a booking center for accommodations, tours, and car/rail/air/motorcoach travel. The Centre also has up-to-the-minute information on cultural events and entertainment, and maintains both a bookshop and a currency-exchange service.

WORK

Getting a Job

For almost all types of employment in Britain, the prospective employer must obtain a permit for his foreign employee from the Department of Employment. These permits are issued only in certain job categories for which British workers are not available. The employer is responsible for sending the permit to the employee, who then must present it at his or her port of entry. A permit is issued only for a specific job with a specific employer.

CIEE, in cooperation with BUNAC (British Universities North America Club), can obtain permission for you to work in Great Britain for a period of up to six months any time during the year. In addition to work authorization, CIEE gives participants information on living and working in Great Britain and details on the best way to find work. Jobs are relatively easy to find upon arrival; participants work as secretaries, temps, waiters, et cetera. You can expect to make enough money to cover your daily living expenses and usually save something toward the cost of travel once you finish your job. To be eligible, you must be a U.S. citizen at least 18 years of age, enrolled as a full-time student in an accredited U.S. college or university, and residing in the U.S. at the time of application. Upon arrival in Britain you are required to have proof of round-trip transportation or the equivalent in funds as well as proof of minimum funds of $400 for support until you receive your first paycheck. There is a $96 fee for the service; application forms are available from CIEE's Work Exchanges Department.

Persons thinking about working in the U.K. might want to get a copy of the annually published *Summer Jobs in Britain* (1989 edition, $9.95), which lists the names of employers and describes the jobs available. Copies are available from CIEE (add $1 for book-rate or $2.50 for first-class postage) or Writer's Digest Books, 1507 Dana Avenue, OH 45207 (add $2.50 for postage and handling).

For those who want to teach in Britain, send for a copy of *Teaching in Britain*, a fact sheet put out by the British Information Services (845 Third Avenue, New York, NY 10022).

> *"A naturally shy and introverted person, I was forced out of my shell by having to deal with finding and maintaining employment. I found myself maturing and expanding in my perceptions of human nature and the world. If anything, the program helped me in discovering who I am, my limitations and abilities. As a 'pet Yank' I was exposed to an England few tourists could ever dream of experiencing. As the weeks progressed I even began to feel myself growing 'British' in attitude and manner—I even began to enjoy tea with milk!"*
> —Libatique Prudiel, Simi Valley, CA

Internships/Traineeships

The programs offered by organizations and institutions that are members of the Council on International Educational Exchange are listed below. Consult Appendix I for the addresses where you can write for further information.

AIESEC–US. Reciprocal internship program for students in economics, business, finance, marketing, accounting, and computer sciences. See page 18 for further information.

Association for International Practical Training.

"IAESTE Trainee Program." On-the-job training for undergraduate and graduate students in technical fields such as engineering, computer science, agriculture, architecture, and mathematics. See page 18 for more information.

"Hotel & Culinary Exchanges Program." On-the-job training for young people beginning a career in the hotel and food service industries. Participants must have graduated from a university or vocational school and possess at least six months of training or experience in the chosen field. Training usually runs 6–12 months.

Beaver College. "London Internship Program in Arts Administration, Business, Communications, Government, Science, Social Services." In cooperation with City of London Polytechnic. Fall or spring semester. Juniors and seniors with 3.0 GPA. Apply by April 20 for fall and October 5 for spring.

Syracuse University.
"Fashion Design Internships in London." Summer. Juniors to graduates; portfolio of five slides of work. Apply by March 17.
"Management Internships in London." Summer. Juniors to graduates; three years of college in a program that includes management courses or one year of graduate course work in management; six credits of undergraduate or three credits of graduate accounting.

Voluntary Service

CIEE places young people in voluntary service workcamps in Wales organized by the United Nations Association (Temple of Peace, Cathays Park, Cardiff CF13AP, Wales). At these workcamps, small groups of volunteers from various countries work on a range of community-service projects. Volunteers receive room and board in return for their labor. The applications of U.S. residents are processed by CIEE. For more information contact the International Voluntary Service Department at the Council.

Another short-term voluntary service opportunity is the 41-year-old Winant-Clayton Volunteers program. British students come to the U.S. to do social work (the Claytons) and American students go to England to do the same (the Winants). Participants, who must be 18 or older, are usually placed in central city areas, drug-crisis centers, shelters for the homeless, and rehabilitation centers for the mentally disabled. Participants pay their own way; the cost of the summer program is usually abut $1,600, which covers air fare and personal expenses. Volunteers spend six weeks in service and three weeks traveling on their own. For details, write to the Winant-Clayton Volunteers, St. Bartholomew's Church, 109 East 50th Street, New York, NY 10022.

A number of other types of short-term volunteer work are available. For persons interested in volunteering for an archaeological dig, the Council for British Archaeology (112 Kennington Road, London SE11 6RE) publishes a newsletter called *British Archaeological News* six times a year ($15 surface mail; $25 airmail) that lists information about archaeological projects in Great Britain as well as indicating which ones will accept volunteers. For persons interested in working on a restored narrow-gauge railway, the Ffestiniog Railway Company (Harbour Station, Porthmadog, Gwynedd, North Wales) recruits volunteers for the summer season. And for those interested in farm work, the International Farm Camp (c/o Camp Organizer, Hall Road, Tiptree, Colchester, Essex CO5 0QS) provides room and board for volunteers who want to spend a week or two picking fruit and berries.

"I spent three weeks at a workcamp in England picking gooseberries and strawberries. I didn't participate for the money but to experience an international camp, working and living with people from different nations."

It was a growing and unique experience and helped me in understanding people of other cultures. You can, if you are a quick picker, earn quite a bit of money, but most people had only about £5 left after paying their weekly room and board. Don't expect anything great—you make it what you want it to be."

If you are interested in a longer term of voluntary service, the "Year Abroad Program" sponsored by the International Christian Youth Exchange offers persons ages 18-24 voluntary service opportunities in the fields of health care, education, the environment, construction, et cetera. See page 22 for more information.

Another organization linking potential volunteers with projects that need them in Great Britain and Northern Ireland is Community Service Volunteers (237 Pentonville Road, London, N1 9NJ). No special skills are required, but volunteers must be between the ages of 18-35. Terms of service range from ten weeks in the summer to a full year. About two thousand volunteers are placed each year—150 or so from outside the U.K. A placement fee of £380 (about $700) is required.

There are numerous other opportunities for voluntary service in the United Kingdom. You'll find a listing of British organizations seeking volunteers for all types of community service described in *Volunteer! The Comprehensive Guide to Voluntary Service in the U.S. and Abroad* ($6.95), published by CIEE. Another good source of information is the Scottish Community Education Council (Atholl House, 2 Canning Street, Edinburgh EH3 8EG), which provides information on opportunities for voluntary community work in Scotland. (Be sure to enclose an international postal-reply coupon when writing them, however.)

STUDY

"Studying in England allowed me to see and understand the country for what it really is. It is impossible to develop an accurate insight into the nation without experiencing it firsthand. I formed strong friendships with English people and learned to understand their way of thinking, behaving, and interacting."
—Kathryn L. Dixon, Mateo, California

Anyone interested in studying in Britain should send for *Study in Britain*, which outlines application procedures and gives information about courses, tuition fees, and scholarships and awards. It's available at no cost from British Information Services, 845 Third Avenue, New York, NY 10022. British Information Services also distributes several other fact sheets on the subject, including *Study in Britain*, *University Summer Schools for Overseas Students*, and *Study by Correspondence*.

The following are the educational programs offered by member institutions of the Council on International Educational Exchange. Consult Appendix I for the addresses of the colleges and universities listed in this section. In addition to the programs listed below, Boston University, California State University, Guilford College, Illinois State University, Indiana University, New York University, Northern Illinois University, Ohio State University, Pennsylvania State University, the University of California system, the University of Pittsburgh, the University of Rhode Island, Southern Methodist University, Stanford University, the University of Tennessee, the University of Toledo, and Valparaiso University all offer programs open to their own students only.

SEMESTER AND ACADEMIC YEAR

Art and Design

University of Illinois. "Art and Design in Britain." Various sites in England and Wales. Students from institutions with programs in art and design only. Academic year or semester. Juniors, seniors, and graduate students. Apply by April 1 for fall and October 1 for spring.

Business Studies

Beaver College. "British University Year at Middlesex Polytechnic at Hendon." London. Academic year or fall semester. Juniors and seniors with 3.0 GPA. Apply by April 20.

Economics

Beaver College. "Single-Term Program in the Department of Economics, University College." London. Fall or spring term. Juniors and seniors with 3.0 GPA. Apply by April 20 for fall and October 5 for spring.

University of North Carolina–Chapel Hill. "UNC at LSE." Academic year. Study at London School of Economics. Juniors and seniors with 3.5 GPA. Apply by February 12.

English Literature

Michigan State University. "English Literature." Wimbledon. Fall quarter. Sophomores to graduate students. Apply by August 1.

University of Minnesota. "Literature in London." Spring quarter. Freshmen to graduate students and interested adults. Apply in January.

General Studies

American Heritage Association.
  "Northwest Interinstitutional Council on Study Abroad–Bath." Fall or spring quarter. Sophomores, juniors, and seniors with 2.5 GPA. Apply by June 1 for fall and January 2 for spring.
  "Northwest Interinstitutional Council on Study Abroad–London." Fall, winter, and/or spring quarter. Sophomores, juniors, and seniors with 2.5 GPA. Apply by June 1 for fall, November 1 for winter, and January 2 for spring.

American University. "The London Semester." Internships available. Sophomores, juniors, and seniors with 2.7 GPA. Apply by April 15 for fall and November 15 for spring.

WESTERN EUROPE

Antioch University. "Antioch London." Quarter or academic year. Juniors and seniors. Apply by March 31.

Beaver College.
"London Semester Program at City of London Polytechnic." Fall or spring semester. Juniors and seniors with 3.0 GPA. Apply by April 20 for fall and October 15 for spring.
"British University Year at the University of Birmingham." Academic year, fall, or spring programs. Juniors and seniors with 3.0 GPA. Apply by April 20 for fall and October 5 for spring.
"British University Year at the University of Bristol." Academic year. Juniors and seniors with 3.2 GPA. Apply by March 20.
"British University Year at the University of Essex." Colchester, England. Academic year, fall or spring programs. Juniors and seniors with 3.0 GPA. Apply by April 20 for fall and academic year; October 5 for spring.
"British University Year at Royal Holloway and Bedford New College, University of London." Egham Hill, Surrey, England. Academic year. Juniors and seniors with 3.0 GPA. Apply by March 20.
"British University Year at the University of Surrey." Guilford, England. Academic year. Juniors and seniors. Apply by April 20.
"British University Year at the University of Lancaster." Academic year, fall, or spring programs. Juniors and seniors with 3.0 GPA. Apply by April 20 for fall and academic year; October 5 for spring.
"British University Year at Goldsmiths' College, University of London." Academic year. Juniors and seniors with 3.0 GPA. Apply by April 20.
"Single-Term Program at Imperial College, University of London." Fall or spring term. Juniors or seniors with 3.3 GPA. Apply by April 20 for fall; October 5 for spring.
"British University Year at King's College, University of London." Academic year, fall, or spring programs. Juniors and seniors with 3.0 GPA. Apply by April 20 for fall and academic year; October 5 for spring.
"British University Year at the London School of Economics and Political Science." Academic year, fall, or spring programs. Juniors and seniors with 3.3 GPA. Apply by March 10 for fall and October 5 for spring.
"British University Year at Queen Mary College, University of London." Academic year or semester. Juniors and seniors with 3.0 GPA. Apply by March 10 for fall and October 5 for spring.
"British University Year at Middlesex Polytechnic at Trent Park." Greater London area. Academic year or semester. Juniors and seniors with 3.0 GPA. Apply by April 20 for fall and October 5 for spring.
"British University Year at The City University." London. Academic year, fall, or spring programs. Juniors and seniors with 3.0 GPA. Apply by April 20 for fall and October 5 for spring.
"British University Year at University College." London. Academic year, fall, or spring programs. Juniors and seniors with 3.0 GPA. Apply by March 10 for fall, April 20 for academic year, and October 5 for spring.
"British University Year at Westfield College, University of London." Academic year, fall, or spring programs. Apply by March 10 for fall and October 5 for spring.
"British University Year at the University of East Anglia." Norwich. Academic year, fall, or spring programs. Apply by March 10 for fall and October 5 for spring.

"British University Year at the University of Nottingham." Academic year, fall, or spring programs. Juniors and seniors with 3.0 GPA. Apply by April 20 and October 5.
"British University Year at the University of Reading." Academic year, fall, or spring programs. Juniors and seniors with 3.0 GPA. Apply by April 20 and October 5.
"British University Year at the University of Southampton." Academic year. Juniors and seniors with 3.0 GPA. Apply by April 20.
"British University Year at the University of York." Academic year, fall, or spring programs. Juniors and seniors with 3.0 GPA. Apply by April 20 for fall and October 5 for spring.
"British University Year at the University of Aberdeen." Academic year, fall, or spring programs. Juniors and seniors with 3.0 GPA. Apply by April 20 for fall and October 5 for spring.
"British University Year at the University of Edinburgh." Academic year, fall, or spring programs. Juniors and seniors with 3.0 GPA. Apply by March 20 for fall and October 5 for spring.
"British University Year at the University of Glasgow." Academic year, fall, or spring programs. Juniors and seniors with 3.0 GPA. Apply by April 20 for fall and October 5 for spring.
"British University Year at the University College of North Wales, Bangor." Academic year, fall, or spring programs. Juniors and seniors with 3.0 GPA. Apply by April 20 for fall and October 5 for spring.
"British University Year at the University of Wales, Swansea." Academic year, fall, or spring programs. Juniors and seniors with 3.0 GPA. Apply by April 20 for fall and October 5 for spring.

Brethren Colleges Abroad. Cheltenham, England. Semester or academic year. Sophomores, juniors, and seniors, with 3.0 GPA. Apply by May 1 for fall and November 1 for spring.

Brigham Young University. "BYU Study Abroad." London. Fall semester (July to December). Sophomores, juniors, and seniors. Apply by February 1.

Central University of Iowa.
"Central College London Program." Academic year or semester. Sophomores, juniors, and seniors with 2.5 GPA. Apply by April 15 for fall and November 1 for spring.
"Central College in Wales." Carmarthen, Wales. Semester or academic year (fall quarter option also available). Sophomores, juniors, and seniors with 2.5 GPA. Apply by November 1 for spring and April 15 for fall.

Central Washington University.
"Northwest Interinstitutional Council on Study Abroad–Bath." See listing under American Heritage Association.
"Northwest Interinstitutional Council on Study Abroad–London." See listing under American Heritage Association.

Colorado State University. Aberdeen, Scotland. Semester or academic year. Juniors and seniors.

Experiment in International Living/School for International Training.
"College Semester Abroad." Oxford. Fall or spring semester. Life and culture

seminar, independent-study project, homestays, and excursions to London and York. Sophomores to graduate students with 2.5 GPA. Apply by May 15 for fall and October 15 for spring.

Great Lakes Colleges Association. "GLCA Scotland Program, Wabash College." Aberdeen. Academic year. Sophomores, juniors, and seniors with 3.0 GPA and two faculty references. Apply by March 4. Contact GLCA Scotland Program, Wabash College, Crawfordsville, IN 47933; (317) 364-4410.

Hiram College. "Cambridge Quarter." Fall quarter. Sophomores, juniors, and seniors with 2.5 GPA. Apply by April 1.

Hollins College. "Hollins Abroad London." Fall or spring semester. Juniors and seniors with 2.0 GPA. Apply by March 1 for fall and September 30 for spring.

International Student Exchange Program. Direct reciprocal exchange between U.S. universities and institutions in London, Cardiff, Coleraine (Northern Ireland), Glasgow, Plymouth, Sunderland, and Preston (Lancashire). Academic year. Full curriculum options. Open only to students at ISEP member institutions.

Kent State University. "Kent in England." Leicester. Semester or academic year. Juniors and seniors with 3.0 GPA. Apply by April 15.

Lake Erie College. "Academic Programs Abroad." Semester, quarter, or academic year. Sophomores, juniors, and seniors with 2.5 GPA. Apply by June 1 for fall and November 1 for spring.

Macalester College/Cambridge University. "A Background to Britain." September. Special three-and-a-half-week supplementary program at Cambridge University for students beginning a semester or year abroad at other British universities. Apply by May 1.

Michigan State University. "Humanities and Social Science in England and Scotland." London, Cambridge, York and the Lake District, and Edinburgh. Spring quarter. Freshmen to seniors. Apply by February 3.

Northern Arizona University. "Semester in London." Fall or spring semester. Sophomores, juniors, and seniors with 2.5 GPA. Apply by November 1 for spring and March 15 for fall.

Northern Illinois University. "Academic Internships in London." Semester or academic year. Students take two courses plus internship. Wide range of internships available for residents of Illinois; more limited selection for residents of other states. Sophomores, juniors, and seniors with 3.0 GPA. Apply by April 4 for fall and November 1 for spring.

Rosary College. "Rosary in London." Fall semester. Sophomores and juniors. Apply by February 1.

St. Lawrence University. "London Semester Program." Spring or fall semester. Internships or one-month Oxford course option can be arranged within the program. Sophomores to seniors with 2.8 GPA. Apply by February 20 for fall and October 10 for spring.

State University of New York at Albany.
"University of Glasgow Exchange." Academic year. Juniors and seniors with 3.3 GPA in major and 3.0 overall. Apply by March 15.
"Plymouth Polytechnic Exchange." Academic year. Juniors and seniors with 3.3 GPA in major and 3.0 overall. Apply by March 15.
"University College of Swansea Exchange." Academic year. Juniors and seniors with 3.3 GPA in major and 3.0 overall. Apply by March 15.

State University of New York at Buffalo. "Manchester Polytechnic." Fall semester. Sophomores, juniors, and seniors with 2.5 GPA. Apply by March 1.

State University of New York at Cortland. "Cortland International Programs–London." Fall or spring semester. Sophomores, juniors, and seniors with above average achievement in major. International management internship available. Apply by March 1 for fall and October 1 for spring.

Stetson University. Nottingham. Academic year or semester. Sophomores, juniors, and seniors with 2.5 GPA (3.0 in major). Apply by March 1 for fall and October 15 for spring.

Syracuse University. "Syracuse in London." Fall or spring semester. Sophomores to graduate students with 3.0 GPA. Apply by March 15 for fall and October 15 for spring.

Tufts University.
"Tufts in London." Academic year. Juniors with 3.0 GPA. Apply by February 1.
"Tufts in Oxford." Academic year. Juniors with 3.0 GPA. Apply by February 1.

University of Colorado at Boulder.
"Academic year in Lancaster." Juniors and seniors with 2.75 GPA. Apply by February 15.
"London Semester Program." Fall or spring semester. Freshmen to seniors with 2.75 GPA. Apply by March 1 for fall and October 15 for spring.

University of Evansville. "University of Evansville's Harlaxton College." Grantham. Fall or spring semester. Sophomores, juniors, and seniors. Adviser's permission required. Apply by June 1 for fall semester and October 1 for spring.

University of Maryland. "Study in London." Semester or academic year. Sophomores, juniors, and seniors with 2.5 GPA. Apply by May 1 for fall and October 15 for spring.

University of New Hampshire. "Study Abroad in Regent's College, London." Semester or academic year. Sophomores to graduate students with 2.5 GPA. Apply by mid-April for fall and mid-October for spring. Contact University of New Hampshire London Program, Hamilton Smith Hall; Durham, NH 03824; (603) 862-3962.

University of North Carolina–Chapel Hill.
"UNC Program to Bristol, England." Academic year. Sophomores, juniors, and seniors with 3.0 GPA. Apply by February 12.
"UNC Program to Leeds, England." Academic year. Juniors and seniors with 3.0 GPA. Apply by February 12.
"UNC Exchange Program to Manchester, England." Academic year. Juniors and seniors with 3.0 GPA. Apply by February 12.
"UNC Program to Sussex, England." Academic year. Juniors and seniors with 3.0 GPA. Apply by February 12.
"UNC Program to St. Andrews, Scotland." Academic year. Sophomores, juniors, and seniors. Apply by February 12.

University of North Texas. "Texas London Consortium." Fall or spring semester. Offered through AIFS in conjunction with the University of Texas at Arlington, the University of Houston, and Texas Tech. Open only to students at schools in Texas. Sophomores through graduate students with 2.5 GPA. Apply by June 1 for fall and November 1 for spring.

University of Oregon. "Northwest Interinstitutional Council on Study Abroad–London." See listing under American Heritage Association.

University of Wisconsin–Madison. Coventry. Academic year. Sophomores to graduate students with 3.0 GPA. Open only to students at colleges or universities in the state or Wisconsin residents studying in other states. Apply by February 1.

University of Wisconsin–Platteville. "London Study Centre at Ealing College." Semester or academic year. Liberal arts, business administration, and criminal justice. Sophomores, juniors, and seniors with 2.5 GPA. Apply by April 15 for fall and November 1 for spring.

University of Washington. "Northwest Interinstitutional Council on Study Abroad–London." See listing under American Heritage Association.

University of Wyoming. "London Semester." Spring semester. Second semester freshmen to seniors with 2.0 GPA. Apply by November 1.

University System of Georgia/Georgia Southwestern College. Semester or academic year. Study at King Alfred's College in Winchester or Queen Mary College in London. Juniors and above with 2.5 GPA. Apply three months prior to beginning of term at King Alfred's College; apply to Queen Mary College by April 1 for fall and November 1 for spring.

Western Washington University.
"Northwest Interinstitutional Council on Study Abroad–Bath." See listing under American Heritage Association.
"Northwest Interinstitutional Council on Study Abroad–London." See listing under American Heritage Association.

Humanities

Beaver College. "London Humanities Semesters in Cooperation with City of London Polytechnic." Fall or spring semester. Specially arranged courses for American students, with one-week trip to Paris or Berlin. Juniors and seniors with 3.0 GPA. Apply by April 20 for fall and October 5 for spring.

International Studies

Beaver College. "Oxford Semester Program." Fall or spring semester. Contemporary British and European politics, history, and economics. Juniors and seniors with 3.2 GPA. Apply by April 20 for fall and October 5 for spring.

Law

Beaver College. "Two-Term Spring Pre-Law Program at King's College, University of London." Juniors and seniors with 3.3 GPA. Apply by October 5.

Notre Dame Law School. "The Concannon Program of International Law." Academic year. Study at the Notre Dame London Law Centre. Law students who have successfully completed one year of law study. Contact Notre Dame Law School, Notre Dame, IN 46556.

Nursing

University System of Georgia/Medical College of Georgia. "Nursing in Brighton and London." Two weeks in spring. 2.5 GPA and students enrolled in BSN program or graduates. Apply by January 15; applications accepted thereafter on a space available basis.

Social Sciences

American University. "London Semester." Fall or spring semester. British politics and society. Internships with British and international organizations. Second-semester sophomores, juniors, and seniors with 2.75 GPA. Apply six months prior to start of program.

University of North Carolina–Chapel Hill. London. Academic year. Study at the London School of Economics. Juniors and seniors with 3.5 GPA. Apply by February 12.

Teacher Education

Hiram College. "Education in England." Cambridge. Fall quarter. Includes visits to English schools and cultural field trips. Sophomores, juniors, and seniors with 2.5 GPA. Apply by April 1.

SUMMER

Art and Art History

Michigan State University.
"Art in London." Studio art and art criticism. Sophomores to graduate students. Apply by April 1.
"History of Art." London. Instruction and visits to museums. Sophomores to graduate students. Apply by April 21.

New York University. "Tisch School of the Arts Summer in London." Freshmen to seniors, and graduate students for independent study. Apply by April 15. Contact: TSOA Student Affairs Office, 721 Broadway, 7th floor, New York, NY 10003; (212) 998-1900.

Ohio University. "Art in England." Art education. Freshmen to graduate students and teachers. Contact School of Art; (614) 593-4288.

British Studies

University System of Georgia/Armstrong State College. London. Undergraduates with 2.5 GPA and graduate students with 3.0 GPA. Apply by March 15.

Broadcasting

Syracuse University. "Media Explorations: British Broadcasting." London. Sophomores to graduate students. Apply by March 17.

Southern Illinois University at Carbondale. "British Television Programing, Policy and Production." London, Bristol, Manchester. Seminar focusing on the differences in programming, production, and administration between the British and American broadcasting systems. Sophomores to graduate students, and qualified professionals. Apply by March 1.

University System of Georgia/University of Georgia. London. Focus on evolution of national broadcasting systems into global mass communication network, visits to BBC Radio and Television. Undergraduate and graduate students with 2.5 GPA and previous courses in journalism or communications. Apply by April 1.

Business

Syracuse University. "International Business Environment: A London Perspective on European Integration." Juniors to graduate students. Two years of college courses in accounting, economics, and finance. Apply by March 18.

University of Colorado at Boulder. "London Seminar in International Finance." Undergraduate/graduate seminar focusing on the planned integration of the European Community and its effects on the nations of the Community and on world finance. Juniors to graduate students with previous international finance or international economics. Apply by March 1.

University System of Georgia/Georgia State University. "International Banking and Finance in London." Seniors and graduate students with 3.0 GPA. Apply by March 1; applications accepted thereafter on a space-available basis.

University System of Georgia/University of Georgia. "Entrepreneurship/Small Businesses and the European Market." London. Undergraduate and graduate students with previous courses in accounting, marketing, and finance, with 2.5 GPA. Apply by March 15; applications accepted thereafter on a space-available basis.

Communication

Michigan State University. "Mass Media in Britain." London. Working seminars with British media professionals. Juniors, seniors, and graduate students. Apply by April 21.

Ohio University. "Visual Communication in Scotland." Edinburgh. Photography and international picture usage. Juniors, seniors, and graduate students with photography portfolio. Apply by April 15. Contact School of Visual Communication; (614) 593-4898.

Computer Science

University System of Georgia/Southern College of Technology. "Computer Science in Leicester." Undergraduate and graduate students with 2.5 GPA and previous courses in computer science, including structured programming. Apply by March 15.

Criminal Justice

Michigan State University. "Forensic Anthropology and Human Identification." London and Cambridge. Instruction and field experiences in forensic anthropology in the study of skeletal biology and forensic identification. Juniors, seniors, and graduate students. Apply by April 21.

University System of Georgia/Georgia State University. Graduate students with 3.0 GPA, or juniors and seniors with 2.5 GPA. Knowledge of U.S. criminal justice system required. Apply by March 1.

Drama

Michigan State University. "Acting and Theatre in Great Britain." London and Stratford-on-Avon. Seminars, plays, classes in acting and theater history, and class trips. Sophomores to graduate students. Apply by April 21.

Mary Baldwin College. "Contemporary Theater in London." May term. Undergraduates. Apply by December 1.

New York University. "Educational Theater." Graduate students. Apply by April 15. Contact: 32 Washington Place, 3rd floor, New York, NY 10003; (212) 998-5030.

University of Pennsylvania. "Penn-in-London I & II." British theater and literature. College students and professionals. Apply by March 1.

Economics

Beaver College. "London School of Economics and Political Science International Summer School in Economics—Introductory and Intermediate Levels." Six weeks, end of June to early August. Juniors and seniors with 3.0 GPA. Apply by April 20.

English Literature

University of Massachusetts–Amherst. "Oxford Summer Seminar." Juniors, seniors, and graduate students with 3.0 GPA. Apply by March 31.

Michigan State University. "English Literature in London." The course also involves theater productions and museum resources. Sophomores to graduate students. Apply by April 1.

University of North Carolina–Chapel Hill. "UNC Summer Program to London." Sophomores, juniors, and seniors. Apply by February 1.

Film Studies

Michigan State University. "Film in Britain." London, Bradford, Birmingham, and Edinburgh. Sophomores to graduate students. Apply by April 21.

Syracuse University. "Major British Directors." London. Sophomores to graduate students, and professionals. Apply by March 17.

General Studies

Beaver College. "Summer School at Middlesex Polytechnic, Trent Park." Greater London. Five weeks, July–August. Juniors and seniors with 3.0 GPA. Apply by April 20.

Beloit College. "Exeter Seminar." Sophomores to graduate students with 2.0 GPA. Apply by February 1.

Brigham Young University. "British Literary Masterworks Study Abroad Program." Sophomores, juniors, and seniors. Apply by February 1.

Lake Erie College. "Academic Programs Abroad." Sophomores, juniors, and seniors with 2.5 GPA.

Louisiana State University. "LSU in London." Six weeks of coursework in theater, journalism, and architecture, supplemented by field trips to castles, gardens, museums, and cathedrals. Sophomores to graduate students with 2.5 GPA (3.0 for graduate students). Apply by April 15.

Mary Baldwin College. "Virginia Program at Oxford." Sophomores, juniors, and seniors at Hampden-Sydney College, Mary Baldwin College, Roanoke

College, Sweet Briar College, Virginia Military Institute, and Washington and Lee University who have completed intermediate French. Apply by March 1.

Michigan State University. "Cambridge University International Summer School." Juniors and seniors with 3.0 GPA. Apply by April 21.

New York University. "NYU in London." Freshmen to seniors. Apply by March 25. Contact: English Department, Faculty of Arts and Science, New York University, 19 University Place, 2nd floor, New York, NY 10003; (212) 998-8800.

North Carolina State University.
"The London Experience." Freshmen to graduate students with 2.0 GPA. Apply by March 1.
"A Summer in Oxford." Open only to students at NCSU and University of North Carolina–Ashville. Freshmen to graduate students. Apply by February 1.

Ohio State University. "Oxford Liberal Arts." Sophomores, juniors, and seniors with 2.75 GPA. Apply by April 15.

Southern Methodist University. "SMU-in-Oxford." Sophomores, juniors, and seniors. Apply by March 15.

University of Alabama. "Alabama at Oxford." Four-week study program with course offerings in English and history. Freshmen to graduate students. Apply by March 31.

University of New Hampshire. "A Summer of Study in Cambridge." Freshmen to graduate students. Apply by March. Contact Department of English, Hamilton Smith Hall, University of New Hampshire, Durham, NH 03824; (603) 862-1313.

University of Utah. "Cambridge International Summer School." Students from schools in Utah, Nevada, Arizona, and Wyoming. Sophomores, juniors, and seniors, and community participants. 3.0 GPA required for students, two letters of reference for community participants. Apply by March 20.

University of Wisconsin–Platteville. "Summer Session in London at Ealing College." Courses in theater, art, history, and culture. Sophomores, junior, and seniors with 2.5 GPA. Apply by March 31.

Western Michigan University. "Oxford Seminar." Freshmen to graduate students, and community members (especially teachers). Apply by April 1.

History

New York University. "Cambridge Study Program/Victorian Britain." All students and nonstudents interested in Victorian Britain. Apply by April 28. Contact NYU/SCE, International Programs, 331 Shimkin, Washington Square, New York, NY 10003; (212) 998-7133.

Humanities

Michigan State University. "Humanities in London." A study of Western civilization drawing from the arts, history, literature, philosophy, and religion. Freshmen to seniors. Apply by April 21.

Journalism

Michigan State University. "Journalism Reporting." London. Sophomores to graduate students, also professionals or working journalists. Apply by April 21.

Law

Mary Baldwin College. "Crime and Justice in England." May term. Undergraduates. Apply by December 1.

Notre Dame Law School. "Live and Learn Law in London." Study at Notre Dame Law Centre. Law students who have successfully completed one year of law study. June 26–August 2. Apply by April 1.

Ohio State University.
"Oxford—Law." Graduate students with one year of law school. Apply by April 10.
"Oxford—Pre-Law." Introduction to American law, with emphasis on the heritage of English culture and legal institutions. Juniors and seniors with 3.0 GPA. Apply by April 15.

Marketing

Michigan State University. "Packaging in England." London. Explore packaging and development of packages for the European market. Juniors and seniors. Apply by April 21.

Syracuse University. "Retailing in London Today." Ten-day trip to Paris included. Juniors and seniors. Apply by March 17.

Nutrition

New York University. "Food, Nutrition, and Dietetics." Graduate student program. Apply by April 15. Contact: School of Education, Health, Nursing and Arts Professions, 32 Washington Place, 3rd floor, New York, NY 10003; (212) 998-5030.

University System of Georgia/Georgia State University. London. Examine role of the dietician through field trips to clinical and community facilities. Undergraduates with 2.5 GPA and graduate students with 3.0 GPA, plus one course in physiology. Apply by March 15.

Philosophy

Michigan State University. "Medical Ethics and History of Health Care." London. Program is designed for medical and nursing students as well as students in philosophy, health policy, and international relations. Juniors, seniors, and graduate students. Apply by April 21.

Photography

Michigan State University. "Photo Communication in England and Scotland." London, Bath, York, Bradford, Edinburgh, and Glasgow. Freshmen to graduate students. Apply by April 21.

Political Science

Michigan State University.
"Political Science in London." Sophomores to graduate students. Apply by April 21.
"James Madison/Cambridge Program." Juniors and seniors. Apply by April 21.

Syracuse University. "Politics in England." London. Sophomores to graduate students. Apply by March 17.

Nursing

Michigan State University. "Nursing Program in London." Role and responsibilities of nurses in different health-care organizations. Juniors to graduate students, and professional nurses. Apply by April 21.

Social Sciences

Michigan State University. "Social Science in London." Political, economic, and social processes in the industrial world. Sophomores, juniors, and seniors. Apply by April 21.

Sociology

Michigan State University. "Comparative Health Care Systems." Juniors, seniors, and graduate students. Apply by April 21.

Speech Science

Michigan State University. "Speech-Language Pathology and Audiology in London." Juniors, seniors, and graduate students. Apply by April 21.

Teacher Education

Michigan State University. "Comparative Education." London, Cambridge, and Norwich. Social and historical forces that have shaped British education. Seniors, graduate students, and teachers. Apply by April 21.

New York University.
"Elementary Education." London and Oxford. Graduate students only. Apply by April 15. Contact: School of Education, Health, Nursing, and

Arts Professions. 32 Washington Place, 3rd floor, New York, NY 10003; (212) 998-5030.

"Deafness Rehabilitation." London. Graduate students only. Apply by April 15. Contact: see above.

"English Education." London and Oxford. Graduate students only. Apply by April 15. Contact: see above.

Writing

Michigan State University. "American Thought and Language—Writing." London. Freshmen and sophomores. Apply by April 21.

University of Minnesota. "Summer Writing in England." London and English countryside. Freshmen to graduate students. Apply by April 15.

EXPLORING BRITISH CULTURE

Literature

Social and political issues dominate British writing, making it more concrete and less metaphysical than much European writing. If the French are preoccupied with philosophical issues, the British concern is with social manners and political morality. For example, in *Pride and Prejudice* (1813) Jane Austen explores social convention; in *Hard Times* (1854) Charles Dickens confronts the devastating impact of industrialization on Great Britain; and in *The Mill on the Floss* (1860) George Eliot traces a young woman's efforts to free herself from the restrictive pressures of family life. Alan Sillitoe confronts the mores and institutions of British society in the short story *The Loneliness of the Long-Distance Runner* (1959), a 20th-century example of this type of literature.

Novelists from the United States and the United Kingdom have found the meeting of the two societies a source for both serious cultural exploration and comedies of profound bewilderment. *Changing Places* (1975), David Lodge's novel of Anglo-American academic exchange, is an amusing example of this sort of cultural confusion. So is Malcolm Bradbury's *Stepping Westward* (1965). Alison Lurie's *Foreign Affairs* (1985) provides an example of an American version of the experience.

Perhaps the most interesting development in British literature has been the emergence of a number of younger writers from immigrant backgrounds. Timothy Mo, an Anglo-Chinese novelist, examines the trauma and comedy of one family's cultural adjustment in *Sour Sweet* (1982). Salman Rushdie, the product of an Anglo-Indian background, also represents this aspect of contemporary British writing: a growing cosmopolitanism and a movement away from the purely British landscape to the more complex and dangerous world of intercultural relations. His novel *Midnight's Children* (1981), like *The Satanic Verses* (1988), draws its considerable energy from a sense of being caught between two worlds and feeling at home in neither. Mo, Rushdie, and other writers of immigrant backgrounds have given voice to a new Britain characterized by cultural contrast, ethnic diversity, and, at times, unsettling discord.

Film

Not surprisingly, many of the most memorable films of the early British cinema were based either on British theater productions or works of British literature. Among the best known were recreations of Dickens and Emily Brontë, in particular *Wuthering Heights* (1939), starring Laurence Olivier and Merle Oberon. Other notable films of the period include a couple of Alfred Hitchcock's early thrillers, *The Man Who Knew Too Much* (1934; the first version, starring Leslie Banks and Peter Lorre) and *The Thirty-Nine Steps* (1935).

A number of films made during and immediately after the war by the team of Michael Powell and Emeric Pressburger are worth seeing, among them *One of Our Aircraft Is Missing* (1942), *Stairway to Heaven* (1946), *Black Narcissus* (1947), and *The Red Shoes* (1948). Typically, the films of Powell and Pressburger were marked by a personal, quirky sense of humor and striking cinematography.

Many of the films of the 1950s and 1960s, a period of the disintegration of the British empire, looked back at times of greater glory. David Lean's *Bridge Over the River Kwai* (1957) is the best example of a number of 1950s films that depicted British heroism during the Second World War. This look backward continued in the 1960s with films such as Lean's epic *Lawrence of Arabia* (1962), the story of a enigmatic British adventurer in the First World War, and Tony Richardson's *Tom Jones* (1963), an adaptation of Henry Fielding's novel about the exploits of a rustic playboy in 18th-century England.

Since the early 1970s a great number of relatively low-budget independent films have been produced in Great Britain, many with the help of funding from the BBC. These films often have a curious relationship to current British social ills and the continuing decline of "British eminence." Dennis Potter's fantasy transformation of the "hard-boiled detective" genre, *The Singing Detective*, is a particularly good example. Others also receiving attention in the U.S. are Mike Leigh's *High Hopes*, Stephen Frears's *My Beautiful Laundrette* and *Sammie and Rosie Get Laid*, Neil Jordan's *Mona Lisa*, and Bill Forsyth's *Local Hero* and *Gregory's Girl*.

CHAPTER SEVEN
EASTERN EUROPE

Change is sweeping Eastern Europe: new economic structures defy Communist orthodoxy; the beginnings of pluralistic democracy have taken root in several countries; and trade, people, and ideas now flow across borders where there once was an impermeable "Iron Curtain." Today, making broad generalizations about Eastern Europe is difficult, as each country charts its own political, economic, and cultural course. But this much is certain: the startling changes that have transformed the Warsaw Pact countries and brought down the "Iron Curtain" make Eastern Europe an especially interesting and exciting destination for the 1990s.

> *"What would I tell a student visiting Eastern Europe? Forget any prejudgments created by Western mass media and be interested in another European culture."*

An increasing number of students are going to Eastern Europe to travel, study, and even work. Many are fascinated by the idea of observing an alternative style of social organization and by the prospect of seeing social and political change in the making. These days all Eastern European countries—with the exception of Albania—welcome foreigners; they see tourism as one means to obtain the hard currency needed to pay off international debts and buy Western products.

As a result, travel in most Eastern European countries is really no more difficult than in Western Europe—it's just a bit different. For one thing, you'll need a visa. (You'll find more information on visas in the individual country sections later in this chapter.) Another difference is that in many Eastern European countries you are required to exchange a certain amount of money for every day you spend in the country, or prepay for travel arrangements before you enter that country. This ensures that you will have to change your money at the official exchange rate, which is usually much higher than the black market rate. It also ensures that you will spend a certain amount of money in that country, since most Eastern European currencies cannot be reconverted into Western currencies. We've included specific information on currency regulations in the individual country sections that follow.

Still another difference of traveling in Eastern Europe is that young people cannot be quite as casual about their behavior as they can be in other parts of the world. For instance, generally you are not permitted to just put your sleeping bag down in a park or a field and make that your home for the night. In most countries you will have to stay in an official lodging of some sort—campground, hotel, hostel, et cetera. In the Soviet Union itself, you must have your itinerary and hotels arranged in advance for every night of your stay.

Getting There

There are inexpensive student fares from New York and other U.S. cities to most of the countries of Eastern Europe. These can be booked at any Council Travel office (see pages ix–xi) or at student travel bureaus in Europe. Reg-

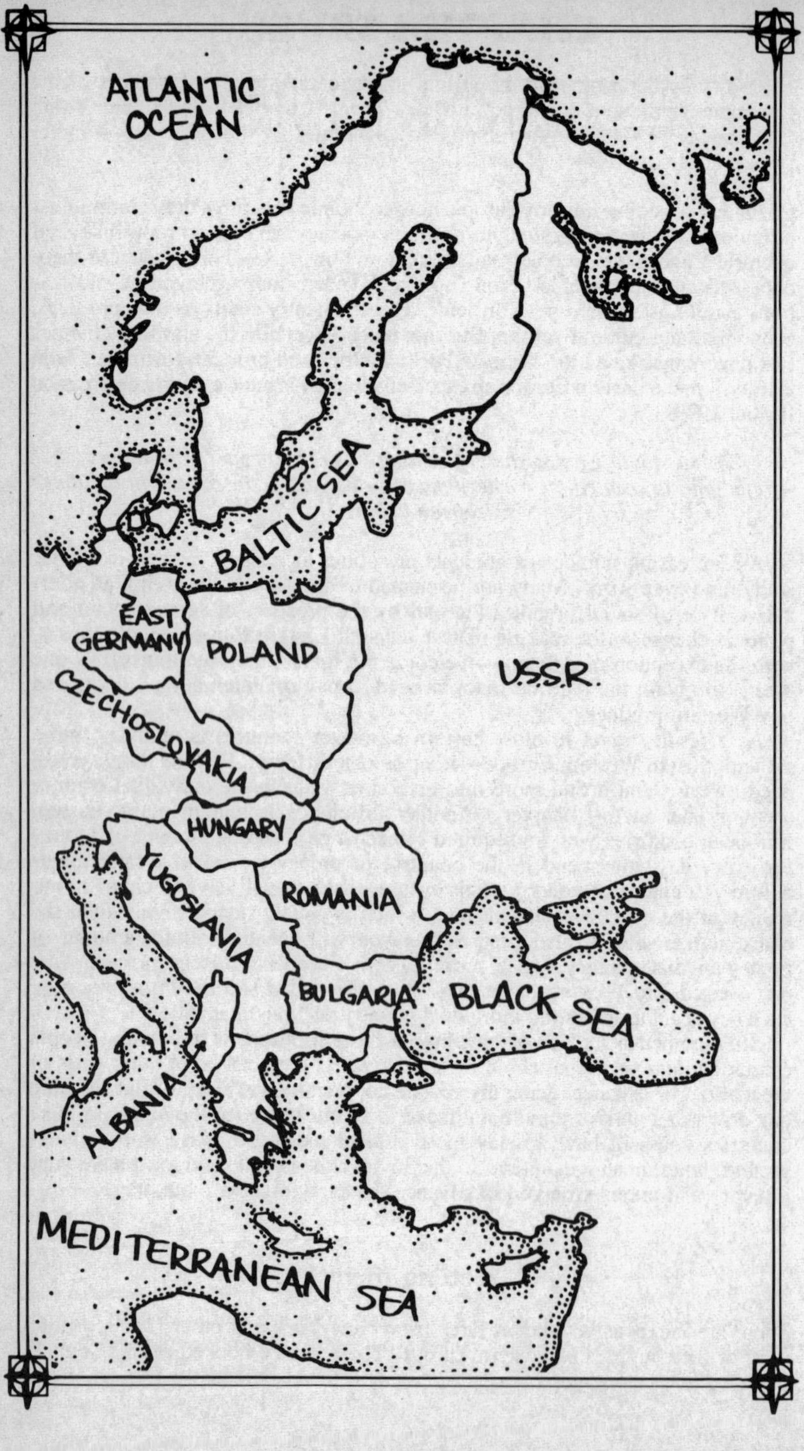
ATLANTIC OCEAN
BALTIC SEA
EAST GERMANY
POLAND
U.S.S.R.
CZECHOSLOVAKIA
HUNGARY
YUGOSLAVIA
ROMANIA
BULGARIA
BLACK SEA
ALBANIA
MEDITERRANEAN SEA

ulations vary depending on the airline, but generally speaking holders of the International Student Identity Card (see page 8) or the International Youth Card (see page 9) are eligible. Sample student fares for the 1989 peak summer season are listed below:

New York–Warsaw $750
New York–Belgrade $750
New York–Moscow $749
Chicago–Budapest $750

Student fares are also offered by several different airlines that service cities in Western and Eastern Europe. A sampling of such student/youth fares valid during summer 1989 are listed below. For more information, contact a Council Travel office.

Paris–Moscow $538 round-trip
London–Budapest $370 round-trip
London–Belgrade $330 round-trip
Frankfurt–Warsaw $290 round-trip

In addition, train crossings or connections can be made from Western to Eastern Europe at a number of border points. In fact, Hungary has recently become the first Eastern European nation to join the Eurailpass network. The more adventurous might want to consider a different rail route to Eastern Europe—traveling west from Asia on the Trans-Siberian Railroad. Check with any Council Travel office for information about a Beijing to Moscow trip by train.

Besides getting there by train or plane, there are a number of other options available, including bus, rental car, and boat. While it's generally quite difficult to rent a car in Eastern Europe—except in Yugoslavia—you can rent a car in Western Europe and then drive into most Eastern European countries. There are also ferries from Greece and Italy to Yugoslavia and from the Scandinavian countries to East Germany, Poland, and the U.S.S.R. Rapid hydrofoils on the Danube River link Vienna, Austria, and Budapest, Hungary. You'll find more information under the "Getting Around" sections in the individual countries later in this chapter.

Traveling in Eastern Europe

One of the first questions the person considering a trip to Eastern Europe must ask is whether to travel independently or with an organized group of some sort. As we said before, traveling independently within Eastern Europe is not difficult as long as you are aware of the visa and currency regulations for each country. However, during peak travel periods (July and August), when tour groups often fill the limited number of available hotels and get priority in restaurants, traveling in some countries of Eastern Europe can be exasperating.

You can join student/youth tours to Eastern Europe that are sponsored by ISTC members in Western Europe and that originate in various Western European cities. Or, if you prefer, you can wait and join a tour in Eastern Europe. For more information on the Council's own student/youth tours to the Soviet Union see page 215.

Student Travel Bureaus

There are student travel offices in every country of Eastern Europe except Albania. Like their Western European counterparts, most of these offices are ISTC members and help students traveling in their country by providing a variety of discounts and services. One exception is SPUTNIK, the international youth travel bureau of the U.S.S.R., which does *not* deal with individual students but, instead, only assists student groups.

In the past, most socialist countries of Eastern Europe have recognized only the international student card issued by the International Union of Students (IUS), a student travel organization formed by the Soviet-bloc countries. However, as a result of the growing cooperation between the nations of Eastern and Western Europe, the International Student Identity Card (ISIC) is now officially recognized in Eastern Europe and persons with the ISIC are entitled to all the student discounts previously available only to holders of the IUS card. As a result, one discount now available to ISIC holders is a fare reduction on trains connecting Eastern European cities. We've provided more information on student/youth discounts in the individual country sections that follow.

Eating and Sleeping

You will find youth hostels or youth centers in all of the countries of Eastern Europe. The *International Youth Hostel Handbook, Volume 1* lists youth hostels in Yugoslavia, Hungary, Bulgaria, Czechoslovakia, and Poland (see page 50 for ordering information). In addition, in Yugoslavia, Hungary, Poland, Czechoslovakia, and East Germany there is a wide range of other inexpensive accommodations, including campgrounds and budget hotels.

For Further Information

There's a growing number of travel books on Eastern Europe and the U.S.S.R. available in bookstores and libraries. *Let's Go: Europe* is the best source of practical information for students and budget travelers. The book has sections on Bulgaria, Czechoslovakia, East Germany, Hungary, Poland, Romania, the U.S.S.R., and Yugoslavia. It's revised annually by the Harvard Student Agencies, is published by St. Martin's Press, and costs $13.95. Following the successful format of its guides to Asia, Lonely Planet Publications (Embarcadero West, 112 Linden Street, Oakland, CA 94607) has released its first guidebook on Europe, *Eastern Europe on a Shoestring*. It's available for $14.95 (plus $1.50 postage) from the publisher. Another guide for budget travelers is Frommer's *Eastern Europe on $25 a Day*, published by Prentice Hall Travel. The 1989–90 edition costs $13.95 and is available in most bookstores.

If you want to know what it's like to travel on your own (by yourself and with no knowledge of the language) in Eastern Europe, read Brian Hall's *Stealing from a Deep Place*, an account of the author's travels by bicycle in Hungary, Romania, and Bulgaria. It sells for $18.95 in most bookstores, and you should add $1.50 for postage and handling if you order it from the publisher (Hill and Wang, 19 Union Square West, New York, NY 10003).

Before you go, you can also get a free copy of *Tips for Travelers to Eastern Europe and Yugoslavia*, which is published by the U.S. Department of State's

Bureau of Security and Consular Affairs. The pamphlet is available for $1 from the Superintendent of Documents, U.S. Government Printing Office, Washington, DC 20402.

Since opportunities for Americans interested in studying or working in Bulgaria, Romania, and Albania are virtually nonexistent, we haven't elaborated on the subject in a separate country section later in this chapter. However, if you are interested in going to one of these countries, the sources of information provided below will be useful.

Bulgaria's student travel organization, ORBITA, has its main office in the capital (45 A Stamboliiski Blvd., 1000 Sofia), but there are also branch offices in Burgas, Ruse, and Varna. The organization, a member of the ISTC, runs more than a dozen student hotels and can make arrangements for anyone interested in vacationing at an international youth center on the Black Sea. The Embassy of the People's Republic of Bulgaria is located at 1621 22nd Street NW, Washington, DC 20008, and the address for the Bulgarian Tourist Office in the United States is 161 East 86th Street, New York, NY 10028.

Romania's student/youth travel bureau is BTTR (Onesti Street 6-8, Bucharest 1). A couple of other useful addresses are the Embassy of the Socialist Republic of Romania (1607 23rd Street NW, Washington, DC 20008) and the Romanian National Tourist Office (573 Third Avenue, New York, NY 10016).

U.S. citizens are no longer forbidden from traveling to Albania; however, the nation admits few tourists and getting a visa and crossing the border will be difficult. Albania has no tourist offices abroad and no diplomatic relations with the United States, so there's no embassy here you can contact. However, for further information you might try writing the Albanian Mission to the United Nations, 320 East 79th Street, New York, NY 10021.

Study in Eastern Europe

It is possible to enroll independently at universities in Eastern Europe. While an American studying in these countries probably would get more political instruction than he or she would at home, admission is not restricted on the basis of political belief. In admitting foreign students, Eastern European educational institutions usually give preference to those from the developing countries of Africa and Latin America. In certain countries such as Hungary and Poland, students of Hungarian or Polish heritage are given priority when applying. In most cases, a high degree of language competence is needed for study in an Eastern European university, and generally speaking study at the graduate level is recommended over undergraduate enrollment. Information on study in any of the Eastern European countries is available from that country's embassy.

The International Research and Exchanges Board (IREX) administers advanced research exchange programs with the U.S.S.R., Bulgaria, Czechoslovakia, Hungary, Poland, Romania, and the German Democratic Republic. Programs are open to graduate students, university faculty, and scholars. For further information, write to IREX (126 Alexander Street, Princeton, NJ 08540-7102) and request the latest program announcement.

In the individual country sections in this chapter, you'll find a number of study programs listed. Below we've listed only the study programs of CIEE member institutions that take place in more than one country of the region. Consult Appendix I for the addresses of these institutions.

SEMESTER AND ACADEMIC YEAR

General Studies

The Experiment in International Living/School for International Training. "College Semester Abroad—East and West Relations." Cracow, Warsaw, and Gdansk, Poland; and sites in East and West Germany. Fall or spring semester. Sophomores to graduate students with 2.5 GPA. Apply by May 15 for fall and October 15 for spring.
"College Semester Abroad—Eastern European Studies." Budapest, Hungary; Cracow and Warsaw, Poland; Vienna, Austria. Fall and spring semester. Sophomores to graduate students with 2.5 GPA. Apply by May 15 for fall and October 15 for spring.

History

Eastern Michigan University. "Discover Russia and Poland." Warsaw and Cracow, Poland; Moscow, Leningrad, and other cities in the Soviet Union. Semester or academic year. Freshmen to seniors. Apply by June 1.

SUMMER

History

University System of Georgia/Georgia State College. "East-Central European History and Culture." Austria, East and West Germany, and Czechoslovakia. Undergraduate and graduate students with 2.5 GPA and some knowledge of German. Apply by March 15.

CZECHOSLOVAKIA

The term *Czechoslovakia* was born in 1918—along with the country—when two nationalities—the Czechs and the Slovaks—were placed by the Treaty of Versailles in a new state that occupied territory that had long been part of the Austro-Hungarian Empire. These two peoples, each with their own language and traditions, continue to live in uneasy coexistence within the modern state.

The nation's short history has been greatly influenced by its location in the heart of Europe between two powerful neighbors—Germany and the U.S.S.R. From 1938 to 1945, Czechoslovakia was occupied by Nazi Germany. Then, in 1948, it was absorbed into the Soviet bloc. In 1968 the attempt of the nation's Communist leadership to de-Stalinize and democratize Communism (a movement known as "the Prague Spring") was crushed by a Soviet invasion. However, during the last months of 1989, the country underwent a startling transformation to a government no longer dominated by the Communist Party and an economy that has begun the process of conversion to a free-market system.

Official name: Czechoslovak Socialist Republic. **Area:** 49,374 square miles (about the size of New York). **Population:** 15,600,000. **Population density:**

316 inhabitants per square mile. **Capital and largest city:** Prague (pop. 1,193,500). **Language:** Czech, Slovak. **Religion:** Roman Catholic, Czechoslovak church. **Per capita income:** US$8,700. **Currency:** Koruna. **Literacy rate:** 100%. **Average daily high/low:*** Prague: January, 34°/24°; July, 74°/58°. **Average number of days with precipitation:** Prague: January, 12; July, 14.

TRAVEL

Regulations

U.S. citizens will need a passport and a Czechoslovak visa. A tourist/transit visa valid for one entry costs $14; two entries cost $28. In addition, two passport-size photos are required. Tourist and transit visas are valid for five months. Recently the government has begun issuing visas at three of the main border crossings from West Germany and Austria. However, it still may be a good idea to get your visa at a Czechoslovak embassy or consulate before arriving at the border. The process takes two to three weeks in North America, but can be done overnight or while you wait at an embassy in Europe. For specific regulations and visa application forms, check with the Embassy of the Czechoslovak Socialist Republic, 3900 Linnean Avenue NW, Washington, DC 20008.

There are mandatory minimum currency-exchange requirements in effect in Czechoslovakia. For every day spent in the country, travelers must change at least DM 30 (about $17), which cannot be reconverted into a Western currency upon departure. Students are only required to change half this amount.

Getting Around

Travel by rail in Czechoslovakia is inexpensive. However, neither Eurail nor InterRail passes are valid in the country. Buses are faster than trains but charge slightly more. Bicycles can be brought across the border, but renting them in Czechoslovakia is difficult. However, for a small charge bikes may be carried on trains as baggage. There are no restrictions on bicycle travel as long as the visitor has a visa.

Especially for Students and Young People

CKM is Czechoslovakia's student/youth travel bureau and ISTC member. Its main office is located at 12 Zitna Ulice, 12105 Prague 2, and it also has an office in Bratislava.

Students with the International Student Identity Card (ISIC) get a 25-percent discount on rail tickets to other Eastern European countries and a 50-percent discount on admission to most museums, galleries, and theaters. ISIC holders will also get a discount in the student/youth hotels and dormitories operated in nine cities by CKM.

---

*all temperatures are Fahrenheit

Meeting the People

Cedok, the Czechoslovak Travel Bureau (Overseas Department, Prikopy 18, 11135 Prague 1), will organize group visits to schools, factories, and cooperative farms; it can also arrange for you to meet people with interests similar to your own. You must write ahead, however, explain what type of visits you would like arranged, and give the office your exact date of arrival. There is a small fee for its services.

For Further Information

The Czechoslovak Travel Bureau (10 East 40th Street, New York, NY 10016) can provide general tourist information for people considering a visit to the country.

WORK

Getting a Job

It is virtually impossible for Americans to get regular paid employment in Czechoslovakia; however, you can contact the embassy (3900 Linnean Avenue NW, Washington, DC 20008) for the complicated regulations on the subject. As an alternative, you might check into an internship or trainee program, or a workcamp (see below).

Internships/Traineeships

There are both AIESEC and IAESTE internship programs in Czechoslovakia; see page 18 for more information.

Voluntary Service

CIEE places young people in voluntary service workcamps in Czechoslovakia organized by the Czechoslovak student/youth travel bureau, Cestovni Kancelar Mladeze (CKM, Zitna 12, 121 05 Prague). At these workcamps, groups of international volunteers get involved in various agricultural or conservation projects. Czechoslovak workcamps are organized during the summer vacation (July through September), and last two to three weeks. Volunteers must be healthy, between the ages of 18 and 35, and able to do hard physical labor. In return for their service, they receive room and board. The applications of U.S. residents are processed by CIEE. For more information, contact the International Voluntary Service Department at the Council.

STUDY

There are no study programs sponsored by CIEE member institutions that take place exclusively within Czechoslovakia. For general information about studying in Eastern Europe, as well as for information about the University System of Georgia's summer program in Austria, Czechoslovakia, and Germany, see the "Studying in Eastern Europe" section above.

EXPLORING CZECHOSLOVAK CULTURE

Literature

Czechoslovakian literature is a somewhat complicated affair. For starters, it actually consists of two distinct literatures in two different languages (i.e., Czech and Slovak). At the same time, the literature of the country is divided into two distinct periods as a result of the impact of the 1948 Communist takeover. The most famous Czech book dating from the pre-1948 era is probably Jaroslav Hasek's *Good Soldier Schwejk* (1921), which presents the absurdities of war and its bureaucratic machinery from the point of view of a common soldier who manages to survive its horrors through imagination and cunning. Among other well-known authors of the pre-takeover period is Karel Capek, whose collection of short stories *Money and Other Stories* and novel *War with the Newts* are available in translation. The acute sense of black humor in these early books also runs through modern Czech works, especially Bohumil Hrabel's stories and novels, such as *Closely Watched Trains* (1981). Its subject is, typically, the tragicomic lives of everyday people, while the plays of Vaclav Havel, especially *The Memorandum*, in the tradition of Beckett and Pinter take a bleak look at modern man's inability to communicate. While only a few Czech books have found their way into English translation, none of the modern Slovak writers, whose works concentrate mainly on rural life and the transition from village to modern city life, have been translated into English. To read Slovak authors such as Razus, Fabry, Urban, or Buncak one will have to turn to German or French translations.

Since 1968, many emigrant and dissident Czechoslovakian writers have received attention in the West. Naturally, their books, including Josef Skvorecky's *The Engineer of Human Souls*, which contrasts Communist Czechoslovakia with an emigrant community in Toronto, Pavel Kohout's *White Book*, and Milan Kundera's *The Joke* (1969), a satire on Czechoslovakian politics, *The Book of Laughter and Forgetting* (1981), and *The Unbearable Lightness of Being* (1975), in which he attempts to overcome the failure of the Prague uprising in 1968 with a somewhat desperate philosophy of acceptance, are marked by their bitterness.

GERMANY (DEMOCRATIC REPUBLIC)

East Germany, or the German Democratic Republic, is the sector of Germany that was occupied and maintained by Soviet forces at the end of the Second World War. Its capital and showcase is East Berlin, but the city is probably most famous for the wall that for three decades separated it from West Berlin. Its proximity to its Western sister city influences most aspects of life in East Berlin through contact with Westerners, a busy black market, and access to West German television programming. The city is one of Eastern Europe's most prosperous, enjoying a disproportionate share of the country's wealth.

Since the mid-1970s, East Germany has enjoyed steady economic growth. In the three decades prior to that it had been recovering from the Second World War, an effort that included not only the rebuilding of its own economy, but also contributing to the recovery of the Soviet economy as a form of war reparation. Today, however, the GDR has one of the stronger economies of the Eastern bloc, and its official spokespeople proudly tell visitors that East Germans can eat meat at every meal if they so desire.

The official image of the West is an integral component of the legitimization of the political and social order of the GDR. The government propaganda line highlights the miseries and follies of unemployment, racism, and militarism in the West, especially in the U.S. Of course this is intended to paint East Germany as a better place to live. However, the citizens do not heed this image so readily and are always interested in a Westerner, especially an American.

Young East Germans are eager to express themselves to foreigners. Older people tend to be a bit more hesitant and deliberate; often, they can remember the postwar days of Stalin, when people were taken away for speaking their conscience, never to be seen or heard from again. Still, the variety of personalities and points of view that the visitor will actually encounter in the GDR is guaranteed to confound the stereotype of Eastern European culture being bland and one-dimensional.

—*Jay Ruby, Hopwood, Pennsylvania*

Official name: German Democratic Republic. **Area:** 41,767 square miles (about the size of Ohio). **Population:** 16,737,000. **Population density:** 397 inhabitants per square mile. **Capital and largest city:** East Berlin (pop. 1,215,586). **Language:** German. **Religion:** Protestant, Roman Catholic. **Per capita income:** US$10,400. **Currency:** East German mark. **Literacy rate:** 99%. **Average daily high/low:*** East Berlin: January, 35°/26°; July, 74°/55°. **Average number of days with precipitation:** East Berlin: January, 10; July, 10.

TRAVEL

Americans must have a passport and visa for travel to East Germany. Transit visas for travel through East Germany to West Berlin or another country are issued at the border. Permission for one-day visits to East Berlin from West Berlin may be obtained at the border without advance application. Visas for a longer stay can be obtained in advance from the Embassy of the German Democratic Republic. A visa can also be issued at a border crossing point if you have travel vouchers proving confirmed hotel accommodations for the nights you will be in the country; tourists arriving by car or plane may make accommodations arrangements and get the necessary travel vouchers at the border crossing point. For further information, contact the Embassy of the German Democratic Republic, 1717 Massachusetts Avenue NW, Washington, DC 20036.

There are mandatory currency-exchange requirements for most Westerners visiting East Germany: about 25 East German marks ($20) for each day you will be in the country. This money cannot be reconverted to a Western currency.

---

*all temperatures are Fahrenheit

Getting Around

Eurail and InterRail passes are not valid in East Germany, including travel between West Germany and West Berlin. However, trains are very inexpensive (make your seat reservations in advance). You can drive into East Germany in a rental car, but you must follow restrictions for foreigners when buying gas. Foreigners are not permitted to hitchhike or rent a bike.

> *"The key to gaining insights about the Germans is to sit in cafés or clubs and relax for a couple of hours. Friends describe their country in a way no book could or would. Germans of the GDR take care of each other; from toddler age on they are taught the importance of community. This philosophy of life is evident on the streets, where a baby carriage is parked outside of a grocery market with the child in it."*
> —Cynthia F. Yoder, Doylestown, Pennsylvania

Especially for Students and Young People

Jugendtourist (Alexanderplatz 5, 1026 Berlin) is East Germany's student/youth travel bureau and ISTC member. Students holding the International Student Identity Card receive a 33-percent discount on rail transportation to most other Eastern European countries. In addition, they are eligible for savings at youth tourist hotels in a number of cities and pay half price for admission to museums.

STUDY

Goshen College offers a study-service program open only to students already enrolled at the school. There are no other study programs based in East Germany sponsored by CIEE members. However, you may want to check the listings for the Federal Republic of Germany, since a number of study and travel programs in that country include a segment in the German Democratic Republic.

EXPLORING THE CULTURE OF EAST GERMANY

Literature

After the Second World War, writers in East Germany had to confront not only the legacy of the war but a new political system and way of life as well. In *A Model Childhood*, Christa Wolf wrote about her childhood in Nazi Germany and of coming to terms with it in later life. *Cassandra*, perhaps her most widely read book, is a very personal and searching look at the complexities of life in East Germany. Her latest book, published in the spring of 1989, is *Breakdown*.

After living abroad during the war, the playwright Bertolt Brecht, a Communist, chose to make his home in East Berlin. His play *Mother Courage* illustrates his vision of communism, while *Stories from Mr. Keuner* is a collection of antiwar stories.

Other modern East German writers include Ulrich Plensdorf, who used a famous work by Goethe (*The Sorrows of Young Werther*) as the basis for a novel dealing with the problems of life in East Germany today, *The New Sorrows of Young Werther*. Herman Kant, whose novels were published mostly in the 1960s and 1970s (*The Assembly Hall* among them) was another critic of life in East Germany, though he believed in the principles on which the government and economy were organized. Another fairly recent novel, *Sleepless Days* by Jurek Becker, describes the monotony of living in an authoritarian society.

HUNGARY

The Hungarians (or "Magyars" as they call themselves) occupy a fertile plain along the Danube River in the center of Europe. In the ethnic puzzle of the region, large Hungarian minorities can also be found in neighboring countries, especially Romania. Among the peoples who inhabit central Europe, the Hungarians are proud of their uniqueness, and are quick to point out that the Magyar language is unrelated to the Germanic, Slavic, and Romance languages of their neighbors.

Liberalization of the Communist political and economic system has occurred gradually since Soviet tanks suppressed a popular revolt in 1956. Since 1968, economic reforms that include decentralization of planning and the encouragement of individual entrepreneurship have helped Hungarians improve their standard of living. More recently, Hungarians have begun to enjoy greater political freedom as the government has legalized a number of opposition parties and moved toward a western-style democracy. As a result, Hungary, although the smallest nation of Eastern Europe, has become a model for reformers (including Gorbachev) who seek less economic and political rigidity in the Communist system.

Official name: Hungarian People's Republic. **Area:** 35,919 square miles (about the size of Indiana). **Population:** 10,711,000. **Population density:** 295 inhabitants per square mile. **Capital and largest city:** Budapest (pop. 2,076,000). **Language:** Magyar. **Religion:** Roman Catholic, Protestant. **Per capita income:** US$7,520. **Currency:** Forint. **Literacy rate:** 98%. **Average daily high/low:*** Budapest: January, 30°/20°; July, 82°/61°. **Average number of days with precipitation:** Budapest: January, 6; July, 7.

TRAVEL

For travel to Hungary, Americans will need both a passport and a visa. A transit visa ($10) is good for a stay of up to 48 hours. An entry visa ($10) permits one entry into the country and a stay of up to 30 days. A multiple-entry visa ($40) is valid up to one year after the date of purchase and is good for stays of up to 30 days. Various other types of visas are also available, and applications for all must be accompanied by two passport-size photos. For further information, contact the Embassy of the Hungarian's People's Republic,

---

*all temperatures are Fahrenheit

3910 Shoemaker Street NW, Washington, DC 20008. There is no mandatory daily currency exchange for visitors to Hungary.

Getting Around

Whether you're traveling by bus, train, or car, the quickest route between any two points in the country will probably be through Budapest, the hub of the nation's transportation system. Hungarian trains are inexpensive and reliable, but travel on the rail system is quite slow. The good news is that Eurail and InterRail passes are valid in Hungary (see page 58). Bus service is also cheap but slower and more crowded than the train. One of the most enjoyable ways to travel (and the most expensive) is on the Danube hydrofoils between Vienna and Budapest. Travel on the domestic airline, Malev, is also quite expensive, but students with the International Student Identity Card can travel standby for about a third of the normal fare.

"Don't be afraid to cross the 'Iron Curtain.' Hungary receives thousands of tourists a year and is a relatively easy country to gain entry into. If you aren't staying with friends, the best way to stay is by renting a room through one of the tourist agencies. Renting a room in a family's apartment is usually very cheap and will give you an idea of how a typical Hungarian family lives. Book early in the day, since in the summer months Budapest fills up with tourists."
—Lisa Hidem, Minneapolis, Minnesota

Especially for Students and Young People

EXPRESS is Hungary's youth and student travel bureau and ISTC member. You'll find the main office, EXPRESS—Budapest, located at Semmelweis utca 4, Budapest 5; it also has offices in seven other Hungarian cities. For students and young travelers, EXPRESS operates 32 hostels and hotels around the country as well as holiday activity centers on Lake Balaton. Vouchers for accommodations at EXPRESS hostels and hotels are available through Council Travel offices.

Students with the International Student Identity Card can get discount standby tickets on domestic flights, a 25-percent discount on rail travel to most other countries in Eastern Europe, and reduced prices at EXPRESS hotels, hostels, and holiday centers. ISIC holders also receive free admission to most museums.

For Further Information

Ibusz Hungarian Travel Bureau, 1 Parker Plaza, Suite 1109, Fort Lee, NJ 07024, can provide general tourist information on Hungary. In addition, you'll find the Frommer *Austria and Hungary* and Fodor's *Hungary* at most bookstores.

WORK

To work at a regular paid job in Hungary you will need to obtain a work permit, which are only granted to foreigners who have been given permission to become permanent residents of the country. Contact the Embassy of Hungary for specific regulations on the subject. As an alternative to regular employment, you might be interested in a trainee program or participation in a workcamp (see below).

Internships/Traineeships

There are both AIESEC and IAESTE internship programs in Hungary; see page 18 for more information.

Voluntary Service

CIEE places young people in voluntary service workcamps in Hungary organized by KISZ KB (Kun B. rkp. 37–38, 1138 Budapest). At the workcamps, groups of volunteers from different countries work on a variety of community-service projects. Volunteers receive room and board in return for their labor. The applications of U.S. residents are processed by CIEE. For more information contact the International Voluntary Service Department at the Council.

STUDY

The following are the educational programs offered by members of the Council on International Educational Exchange. Consult Appendix I for the addresses of the institutions listed in this section. In addition to those listed below, the University of California system offers a program open only to students already enrolled at its various schools.

SEMESTER AND ACADEMIC YEAR

Eastern European Studies

Council on International Educational Exchange. "East European Studies Program." Budapest. Fall or spring semester. Courses taught in English at Karl Marx University. Undergraduates with a 2.75 GPA and six semester hours in economics, history, or social sciences.

Experiment in International Living/School for International Training. "College Semester Abroad." Budapest. Fall or spring semester. Intensive Hungarian language, seminars, independent-study project, excursions to Poland and Vienna, Austria, and homestays. Sophomores to graduate students with 2.5 GPA. Apply by May 15 for fall and October 15 for spring.

General Studies

International Student Exchange Program. Direct reciprocal exchange between U.S. universities and Janus Pannonius University and the Technical University of Budapest. Semester or academic year. Full curriculum options. Open only to students at ISEP member institutions.

University of Massachusetts–Amherst. "Exchange with Janus Pannonius University." Pecs. Fall semester. Sophomores, juniors, and seniors with 3.0 GPA. Apply by March 15.

University of Oregon. "OSSHE—Hungary Exchange Program." Szeged. Academic year. Sophomores, juniors, and seniors with 2.75 GPA. Preference given to Oregon State System of Higher Education (OSSHE) students. Apply by March 1.

University of Wisconsin–Madison. Budapest. Fall semester or academic year. Sophomores to graduate students with 3.0 GPA. No language prerequisite. Apply by February 1.

SUMMER

General Studies

University of Massachusetts–Amherst. "Exchange with Janus Pannonius University." Pecs. Sophomores, juniors, and seniors with 3.0 GPA. Apply by March 15.

POLAND

Everywhere in Poland you can see evidence of both the nation's fascinating history and the profound changes sweeping the country today. You can explore the medieval walled city of Cracow, where Copernicus taught, or visit the Gdansk shipyards where Lech Walesa started Solidarity. You can see the most sacred icon of Catholic Poland, the Black Madonna at Czestochowa, or visit Auschwitz, a symbol of Nazi atrocities still fresh in many Poles' memories.

With the exception of the extreme south, Poland is a flat plain that stretches on into Germany to the west and the Soviet Union to the east. Its geography helps explain why the history of Poland has been one of repeated invasions: Germans, Russians, Tartars, Turks, Swedes, even Genghis Khan all have taken advantage of Poland's lack of natural obstacles at one time or another. And yet, for a brief period in the 16th and 17th centuries, Poland rose to become a leading European power. Polish kings were even credited with saving Western Europe in 1683 by turning back the invading Turks outside the gates of Vienna. Eventually, however, Poland lost its independence—partitioned by Russia, Prussia, and Austria in 1795—and did not regain it until 1918. Twenty years later, the Nazis again made Poland an occupied country; by the time the Second World War ended, in 1945, six million Poles had been killed and the country lay in ruins. Poland officially regained its independence after the war, but has remained under the influence of its "friendly" local superpower, the Soviet Union, for much of the postwar period.

But Polish history is not just the history of military invasions and bitter defeats. Poles are proud of their contributions to science, literature, and the arts, and point to Copernicus, Madame Curie, Chopin, three Nobel prize-winning authors, and other notables in many fields. Two Polish generals, Pulaski and Kosciuszko, played vital roles in helping Americans win their own struggle for independence.

Today, Poland seems to be a country wracked with crises. The political and economic system imposed in 1945 doesn't work, and reforms currently underway won't revitalize the country overnight. The Communist Party now shares power with Solidarity; however, unlike its Communist Eastern European neighbors, the Party has always found its power somewhat less than absolute, diluted by legal and illegal opposition groups, a long-standing tradition of democracy and tolerance, and the power of the Roman Catholic Church. The Pope and Walesa—not Communist officials—have long been the most respected figures in the nation.

In spite of improved East-West relations, Poland does not receive many visitors from the United States. Few Poles speak English, and a trip there will require some initiative and preparation. However, Americans who do travel to Poland will find the people especially friendly. Perhaps it's the mixture of fascination and admiration (and a bit of jealousy) with which they look at the United States. Or perhaps it's the ethnic ties to eight million Polish-Americans. Whatever, a visit to Poland is sure to be an interesting one.

—*Jan Rudomina, New York, New York*

Official name: Polish People's Republic. **Area:** 120,727 square miles (about the size of New Mexico). **Population:** 38,000,000. **Population density:** 315 inhabitants per square mile. **Capital and largest city:** Warsaw (pop. 1,659,400). **Language:** Polish. **Religion:** Roman Catholic. **Per capita income:** US$3,998. **Currency:** Zloty. **Literacy rate:** 98%. **Average daily high/low:*** Warsaw: January, 32°/22°; July, 75°/58°. **Average number of days with precipitation:** Warsaw: January, 8; July, 11.

TRAVEL

U.S. citizens need a passport and visa for travel to Poland. The regular visa issued for tourism, business, and visits to relatives is valid for a stay of up to 90 days and costs $18. A transit visa, valid for only 24 hours, is available for $12. Two passport-sized photos are required for all visa applications. The mandatory currency exchange is $15 per day; exceptions are made for students and persons visiting relatives who are required to exchange only $7 per day. For further information, check with the Embassy of the Polish People's Republic, 2640 16th Street NW, Washington, DC 20009, or the Polish consulates in Chicago or New York.

Getting Around

Travel by train in Poland is inexpensive and the rail network serves almost every town. But be forewarned: ticket lines are long and trains are slow, crowded, and uncomfortable. It's always advisable to make reservations at least a day in advance at an office of ORBIS, the official government travel bureau. Unfortunately, neither the InterRail nor Eurail passes are valid in Poland. However, passes can be purchased at ORBIS for 8, 15, 21, or 30 days of unlimited travel by rail. (The passes are fairly expensive, so you won't save money unless you plan to do a lot of traveling.) International train tickets must also be purchased at ORBIS; holders of the International Student Identity Card (ISIC) get a 25-percent discount on most fares.

---

*all temperatures are Fahrenheit

Buses are slow and crowded—even more so than the trains. ORBIS sells advance tickets, which are often a necessity. Fares on the nation's bus system are about the same as on the train. Faster and more comfortable travel is available on the national airline, LOT, which serves a number of Polish cities. Flights within Poland are quite expensive, but students with the ISIC can pay half-price and fly standby.

Especially for Students and Young People

ALMATUR (ul. Ordynacka 9, 00-364 Warszawa) is Poland's student/youth travel and tourism office; it is also a member of the ISTC. It has offices in Warsaw—the most complete being the ALMATUR Travel Shop, ul. Kopernika 23, 00-359 Warszawa—as well as 16 other Polish cities. ALMATUR offices provide travel information and sell student accommodation vouchers. The organization also offers one-week student holiday packages centered around horseback riding near Zielona Gora or sailing in the Masurian lake country.

In addition to the air and rail discounts noted above, foreign students with the ISIC get a 50-percent discount on compulsory money exchange; reduced fares on Baltic Sea ferries from Poland to Denmark, Sweden, and Finland; reductions on admission fees to most museums and student clubs; and a discount on accommodations in international student hotels in 19 cities during July and August.

For Further Information

The Polish National Tourist Office (342 Madison Avenue, Suite 1512, New York, NY 10173) distributes general information about travel and tourism in Poland. Another useful source of information is the *Insider's Guide to Poland*, published by Hippocrene Books and available in many bookstores for $8.95.

WORK

Foreigners are not allowed regular employment in Poland. As an alternative to regular employment, you might be interested in a trainee program or participation in a workcamp (see below).

Internships/Traineeships

There are both AIESEC and IAESTE internships programs in Poland; see page 18 for more information.

Voluntary Service

CIEE places young people in a voluntary service workcamp in Poland organized by the Bureau for International Youth Exchange (ul. Grzybowska 79, 00-844 Warszawa). At the workcamp, groups of volunteers from various countries are involved in construction or maintenance work at a student holiday center. Volunteers receive room and board in return for their work. The applications of U.S. residents are processed by CIEE. For more information contact the International Voluntary Service Department at the Council.

For those interested in long-term voluntary service work, the "Year Abroad

Program" sponsored by International Christian Youth Exchange offers people ages 18–24 voluntary service opportunities in the fields of health care, education, the environment, construction, et cetera. See page 22 for more information.

STUDY

For information on scholarships, grants, and study programs administered by the Kosciuszko Foundation, write to the Kosciuszko Foundation at 15 East 65th Street, New York, NY 10021. Most of the scholarships are for graduate study only, but there is one exception: study at the summer sessions of the University of Cracow. The deadline for application is January 15.

The following are the educational programs offered by member institutions of the Council on International Educational Exchange. Consult Appendix I for the addresses of the institutions listed in this section. In addition, Stanford University offers a program open only to its own students.

SEMESTER AND ACADEMIC YEAR

East European Studies

Council on International Educational Exchange. "East European Studies Program." Warsaw. Fall or spring semester. Courses in English at the Central School of Planning and Statistics. Undergraduates with a 2.75 GPA and six semester hours in economics, history, or social sciences.

General Studies

American University. "Poland Semester." Poznan. Fall or spring semester. Polish language and liberal arts courses. Second-semester sophomores, juniors, and seniors with 2.75 GPA. Apply six months prior to start of program.

State University of New York at Stony Brook. Warsaw and Wroclaw. Air fare is paid by government grant. Juniors, seniors, and graduate students with one year of Polish or Russian and 3.0 GPA. Apply by April 1.

Polish Language and Culture

University of Massachusetts–Amherst. Poznan. Open only to students at Smith, Mt. Holyoke, Hampshire, and Amherst colleges and the University of Massachusetts. Academic year and semester. Sophomores to graduate students with 3.0 GPA. Apply by January 29 for fall and academic year and September 19 for spring.

SUMMER

East European Studies

University of Minnesota. "Polish in Lublin." Freshmen to graduate students and adults interested in Polish language and culture. Apply by March 1.

Polish Language and Culture

University of Massachusetts–Amherst. Poznan. Open to students at Smith, Mt. Holyoke, Hampshire, and Amherst colleges and the University of Massachusetts. Sophomores to graduate students with 3.0 GPA. Apply by January 29.

THE U.S.S.R.

The grim faces of Muscovite commuters at rush hour, a lunch of overcooked canned peas and gristly meat at a restaurant in Minsk, and a billboard portraying the smiling V. I. Lenin encircled by lifeless toddlers in Kiev are typical of the images of life in the Soviet Union that most travelers bring back. Yet, behind the exterior of an officious, cold, and bureaucratic society is a nation as vast and varied as any country in the world.

The Soviet Union is two and a half times the size of the United States. Stretching from the Baltic Sea across Europe and Asia to the Pacific, it contains an incredibly diverse population speaking dozens of different languages—Armenian and Azerbaijanian, Ukrainian and Uzbek, to name just a few. But although ethnic groups abound, Russians, who once ruled this vast territory under the czars, dominate in both numbers and power.

Both the Slavophile and Orientalist will find architectural treasures in the Soviet Union, including the wooden Russian Orthodox churches of the north and the ancient minarets and mosques of central Asia. Likewise, for the nonspecialist it is an especially exciting time to visit this enigmatic country. Led by one of the world's most dynamic leaders, General Secretary Mikhail Gorbachev, a society that has long suffered economic stagnation and political repression is now being allowed at least a measure of economic choice and political freedoms.

As a result of Gorbachev's policies of *glasnost* and *perestroika*, the Soviet Union is reexamining its past and coming to grips with many of its self-inflicted atrocities. Contemporary theater, literature, and visual arts, which until recently were stilted and contrived because of the didactic notion that all art should serve the political aims of the state, have become far more daring and entertaining. Rock music, once an obscure, underground movement of avant-garde youth, is now a national obsession.

However, it is still that which occurs beneath the official veneer—be it unflinching patriotism or the present "openness"—that is most compelling about the Soviet Union. Among the timeless qualities of the Soviet people are their warm hospitality, their ironic sense of humor, and their boundless faith, which has seen them through the best and worst of times.

—*Julie Raskin, Leningrad, USSR*

Official name: Union of Soviet Socialist Republics. **Area:** 8,649,489 square miles (about two and a half times larger than the U.S.). **Population:** 286,000,000. **Population density:** 33 inhabitants per square mile. **Capital and largest city:** Moscow (pop. 8,714,000). **Language:** Russian, Ukrainian, Tungusic, Altaic, Belorussian, Georgian, Armenian, Turkic. **Religion:** Atheism (official), Russian Orthodox, Islam, Roman Catholic, Jewish, Protestant. **Per capita income:**

US$7,896. **Currency:** Ruble. **Literacy rate:** 99%. **Average daily high/low:*** Leningrad: January, 23°/12°; July, 71°/57°. Moscow: January, 21°/9°; July, 76°/55°. **Average number of days with precipitation:** Leningrad: January, 17; July, 13. Moscow: January, 11; July, 12.

TRAVEL

U.S. citizens will need a passport and visa to enter the Soviet Union. An application for a visa should be completed at least six months in advance (three photos and a photocopy of your passport are required). To get a visa you must make advance travel arrangements, including accommodations for each night you plan to spend in the Soviet Union (see below). For further information, check with the consulates of the U.S.S.R. in Washington (1825 Phelps Place NW, Washington, DC 20008) or San Francisco (2790 Green Street, San Francisco, CA 94123). You can also get a copy of *Tips for Travelers to the U.S.S.R.*, published by the Department of State's Bureau of Security and Consular Affairs, by sending $1 to the Superintendent of Documents, U.S. Government Printing Office, Washington, DC 20402.

"Your visa specifies the dates you will be in the U.S.S.R., the cities you are going to visit, and how long you will be in those cities. You are expected to comply with what is on the visa. It is virtually impossible to extend your stay in any city or to travel to a city that is not on your approved itinerary. It is also next to impossible to extend your stay in the U.S.S.R., so be sure to plan your itinerary carefully before you go."

Getting Around

It is possible to travel independently within the U.S.S.R., but if you choose to travel on your own, you'll have to make all arrangements in advance through a travel agency that is affiliated with the official Soviet travel agency, Intourist (630 Fifth Avenue, Suite 868, New York, NY 10111). Intourist-affiliated travel agencies are listed in *Welcome to the U.S.S.R.*, a booklet available free of charge from the Intourist information office. The agency, with the assistance of Intourist in Moscow, will make arrangements for you to travel independently or, if you prefer, will book you on an Intourist-sponsored tour. Before entering the country, however, you must make housing arrangements for every night you will be there. This usually entails staying at Intourist facilities, which aren't cheap. There are no low-budget options for the independent traveler in the Soviet Union; in other words, you can't simply bum around Moscow looking for a cheap place to stay. Whether you decide to go with a group or make individual arrangements, your plans should be made well in advance, since your visa will not be issued until all arrangements have been duly confirmed by Intourist, Moscow.

Most students choose a third option—an organized youth or student tour —over individual travel or a tour arranged by Intourist. These are planned through SPUTNIK, the Soviet youth travel bureau, and are much less expensive

---

*all temperatures are Fahrenheit

than independent travel or tours arranged through Intourist. Several tours of the U.S.S.R. designed specifically for young people are offered through Council Travel and can be booked at any Council Travel office. These include one- and two-week options encompassing Leningrad, Moscow, the Ukraine, Soviet Central Asia, and the Baltic republics; meetings with Soviet youth are included in the itineraries. Council tours, offered throughout the summer, are available on a land-only basis or with flights from Western Europe included. Other tours of the Soviet Union offered by CIEE members are listed below. Consult Appendix I for the addresses of the institutions listed in this section.

Council on International Educational Exchange. A selection of summer student/youth tours to various parts of the Soviet Union. See information above.

New York University. "International Travel Programs." Short-term, usually two-week tours. Students and adults. Apply two months prior to departure. Contact: NYU School of Continuing Education, International Programs, 331 Shimkin, Washington Square, New York, NY 10003; (212) 998-7033.

University of Tennessee. "Study Tour of the Soviet Union." Contact Department of Germanic and Slavic Languages; (615) 974-0987.

"Even with its rich cultural and historical tradition, the Soviet Union is not rich economically. Everywhere there are people lining up to buy everyday necessities of life such as fruit, meat, vegetables, and bread along with material needs. The traveler to the Soviet Union who must fend for himself will have trouble dealing with the crowds, lines, and frequent shortages, but anything can be gotten used to with a little patience."
—Laura K. Cummings, Old Lyme, Connecticut

Those who really want to see the Soviet Union from one end to the other can travel the Trans-Siberian Railroad, one of the longest and most famous railways in the world. Council Travel can book a train journey from Beijing to Leningrad that includes several days of sightseeing in Irkutsk, Moscow, and Leningrad. Check with any Council Travel office for further information.

"The trans-Siberian trip must be booked in advance during the summertime, and even in mid-winter the reservation process usually takes about ten days to complete. The main complaint of second-class travelers on this route is the lack of showers and the limited toilet facilities. First class, of course, is considerably better outfitted, but is also in a much higher price range. Tourists and Russian nationals are not separated on the trains, though language is usually a common barrier. Food is heavily Russian and paid for in coupons, which are issued via voucher on arrival in the U.S.S.R."

Money Matters

There is no mandatory currency-exchange requirement in the U.S.S.R. However, travelers are prohibited from exchanging currency at any rate other than the official one, as well as from taking rubles in or out of the country. When you enter the U.S.S.R., you'll be given a currency declaration form on which each exchange transaction will be entered during your stay. You must keep this form, together with all receipts from transactions involving the spending or exchange of money, since they will be checked and the form turned in to a customs agent on departure. You can spend your money without changing it into rubles at the Beryozka shops (stores that do not accept rubles, only hard currencies), which offer souvenirs and imported goods not generally available in regular Soviet stores.

> *"The economy has developed increasingly severe problems resulting in shortages of goods, certain foods, and inflated prices. For the visitor this means that their exposure to the massive Soviet 'counter economy' will be intensive and unrelenting. An individual on a two-hour stroll along Nevesky Prospect in Leningrad may be offered the opportunity to trade fifteen or twenty times. Trading (particularly currency exchanges) is against Soviet law and the visitor should always obey all Soviet law. However, it is a fact that many travelers to the U.S.S.R. do trade occasionally for a variety of items and the laws prohibiting such activities are not rigorously enforced. If one should succumb to temptation, then the value of the deal should definitely not exceed $20, since severe penalties can be imposed."*
> —John O. Lindell, Oneonta, New York

Especially for Students and Young People

SPUTNIK (15 Kosygin Street, 117946 Moscow) is the Soviet Union's student travel bureau and ISTC member. It organizes travel for student groups visiting the U.S.S.R., but does not make travel arrangements for individual students. For more information on Council tours organized by SPUTNIK see "Getting Around" above.

Meeting the People

A different type of travel program is the Intercultural Travel Program to the U.S.S.R. sponsored by the Citizen Exchange Council, a nonprofit cultural exchange organization, which enables participants to experience the Soviet Union by meeting its people. Personal contacts are arranged with counterparts in the U.S.S.R., giving participants the opportunity to exchange ideas and experiences with Soviet citizens sharing similar interests. Other features of the program include predeparture orientation, field trips to various Soviet institutions, and special seminars and lectures in each city visited. Participants travel with regularly scheduled groups—some especially for high school or college students or educators, others composed of special-interest groups concerned with the arts, media, and public diplomacy. Programs take place throughout the year and last from two to three weeks. For further details, write to the Citizen Exchange Council, 12 West 31st Street, New York, NY 10001.

> *"The most important thing a visitor to the Soviet Union will experience beyond the history and culture is the deep and almost fanatical interest Soviets have in Americans in the age of glasnost. Language barrier or not, Soviets will find ways to talk with Americans. The subjects range from the war in Afghanistan to the cost of dinner in New York City and what teenagers do for fun after school. Potential travelers to the Soviet Union are cautioned to study up on their own country before leaving."*
> —Laura K. Cummings, Old Lyme, Connecticut

For Further Information

Intourist (630 Fifth Avenue, New York, NY 10111) is the official organization responsible for travel arrangements for foreigners in the U.S.S.R. Contact the New York office for general travel information as well as specific information about tours and travel agents in the United States authorized to work with Intourist. There is a Fodor guide to the Soviet Union and a pocket Berlitz guide for Leningrad and Moscow as well. If you don't speak any Russian, we recommend you get a copy of the Berlitz phrasebook for travelers.

> *"Few people in the U.S.S.R. speak English, so independent wandering, even if it's only to the bread store, would be impossible without a phrasebook like the Berlitz book on Russian for travelers."*

WORK

Americans are not permitted to work in a regular, paid job in the U.S.S.R. As an alternative, you may be interested in a trainee program or workcamp experience.

Internships/Traineeships

There is an AIESEC internship program in the Soviet Union; see page 18 for more information.

Voluntary Service

CIEE places young people in voluntary service workcamps in the U.S.S.R. organized by a variety of youth organizations. At these workcamps, groups of volunteers from different countries work on community-service projects of various types. Volunteers receive room and board in return for their labor. The applications of U.S. residents are processed by CIEE. For more information contact the International Voluntary Service Department at the Council.

STUDY

Persons considering study in the Soviet Union might want to check *A Scholar's Guide to Sources of Support for Research in Russian and Soviet Studies*, by Marc D. Zlotnik. This 144-page book contains information about major sources of funds for predoctoral and postdoctoral research and study, language training, group projects, and conferences. It costs $12.25 and can be ordered prepaid from the American Association for the Advancement of Slavic Studies, 128 Encina Commons, Stanford University, Stanford, CA 94305.

In addition to the programs listed below, there is the option of summer study in the U.S.S.R. in one of several Russian-language seminars arranged by Intourist. These twelve-day seminars, which are held in Sochi and Dyuny, are designed for beginning, intermediate, and advanced students. Tuition covers four hours of lessons per day, with one teacher for every ten students. To supplement the seminars, Intourist provides other activities such as social events, excursions to museums and beaches, and a theater visit.

The following are the educational programs offered by members of the Council on International Educational Exchange. Consult Appendix I for the addresses of the institutions listed in this section. In addition, Lewis and Clark College, Pennsylvania State University, the University of California system, and the University of Tennessee offer programs open only to their own students.

SEMESTER AND ACADEMIC YEAR

Russian Language/Area Studies

Associated Colleges of the Midwest. "Semester in the Soviet Union." Krasnodar. Fall semester. Open only to students at institutions that are members of ACM or the Great Lakes Colleges Association. Juniors and seniors with two years of college Russian. Apply by February 15.

Council on International Educational Exchange. "Cooperative Russian Language Program." Leningrad. Academic year or semester. Sophomores to graduate students with three years of Russian. Apply by March 1 for fall and October 1 for spring. Contact Academic Programs Department.

Experiment in International Living/School for International Training. "College Semester Abroad." Leningrad or Volgograd. Fall or spring semester. Intensive language, life, and culture seminar, independent-study project, excursions, and home hospitality. Sophomores to graduate students with 2.5 GPA and two years college Russian. Apply by May 15 for fall and October 15 for spring.

Kent State University. "Volgograd State University Exchange Program." Spring semester. Juniors and seniors with two years of Russian and 2.5 GPA. Apply by September 15.

Middlebury College. Moscow. Sophomores to graduate students fluent in Russian. Rolling admissions.

State University of New York at Albany. "Thorez Institute Exchange." Moscow. Fall semester. SUNY students only. Juniors and seniors with three years of college Russian. Apply by November 15 for fall.

State University of New York at Albany. "Moscow State University Exchange." Semester or academic year. Graduate students enrolled at a SUNY school only. Three years of college Russian. Apply by November 15.

SUMMER

Economics

Illinois State University. "ISU Summer in the Soviet Union." Various cities. Sophomores, juniors, and seniors. Apply by February 13.

Russian Language and Culture

Council on International Educational Exchange.
"Cooperative Russian Language Program." Leningrad. Sophomores to graduate students with two years of Russian. Apply by January 25. Contact Academic Programs Department.

"Cooperative Russian Language Program for Science Students." Novosibirsk. Freshmen to graduate students with one year of college Russian. Apply by January 25. Contact Academic Programs Department.
"Cooperative Russian Language and Area Studies Program." Kalinin. Freshmen to graduate students with 3–5 semesters of Russian. Apply by January 25. Contact Academic Programs Department.

Indiana University. "Overseas Study in Leningrad." Freshmen to seniors with one year of Russian and 3.0 GPA. Apply by February 6.

University of New Hampshire. "Summer Seminars in Leningrad." Freshmen to graduate students. Apply by February 7 for the first session and March 7 for the second and third sessions. Contact Department of German and Russian, Murkland Hall, University of New Hampshire, Durham, NH 03824-3541; (603) 862-3522.

EXPLORING SOVIET CULTURE

Literature

In the past couple of years, as a result of Mikhail Gorbachev's policy of *glasnost*, literary works that were previously considered "inappropriate" for publication are now being read by the Soviet public. Some of these literary works have already received wide acclaim in the West, such as Boris Pasternak's *Doctor Zhivago*, Alexander Solzhenitsyn's *Gulag Archipelago*, Evgeny Zamyatin's *We*, and Andrei Platonov's *The Foundation Pit*. Others are being published for the first time in both the U.S.S.R. and the West. Anatoly Rybakov's *Children of Arbat*, which tells the story of a group of young adults in Moscow at the outset of the Second World War, is one such example. Another is *Life and Fate*, by Vasily Grossman, which realistically depicts the war. One of the best known of contemporary Soviet writers is Tatyana Tolstaya, the great-grandniece of Leo Tolstoy. Her collection of short stories, *On the Golden Porch*, was translated into English in 1989 to critical acclaim.

Of course, there are many older classics of Russian literature as well. These include Mikhail Bulgakov's *Master and Margarita* and the short stories of Mikhail Zoshchenko. Or you might want to read some of the pre-Revolution works of writers such as Tolstoy, Chekov, or Dostoevsky. These and others will help you grasp the extent of the social and political changes that have swept the country in this century, as well as providing insights into the Russian character.

Film

The cinema has been an integral part of modern Soviet culture. Consistent with the ideas of industrialization, mass culture, and modernity associated with the Russian Revolution, film was idealized as the art form of the proletariat in the decades that followed the overthrow of the czarist order. Montage stylistics, the epitome of machine-age experience, is the hallmark of Sergei Eisenstein's *The Battleship Potemkin* (1925), *October* (1928), and *Que Viva Mexico* (1932), as well as *Man With A Movie Camera* (1929) by Dziga Vertov. In addition to their then-revolutionary technique, these films took an aggressive, confrontational look at the intricacies of class difference, revolution, and the role of cinema.

Governmental restrictions on filmmaking and the rehashing of traditional themes of patriarchy and patriotism faded with the post-Stalinist "thaw" led by Nikita Khrushchev in the 1950s. Characters became contradictory and unpredictable, almost to the extent of resembling human beings as tractors were supplanted in leading roles by flesh-and-blood actors. Good examples of this type of film are *The Cranes Are Flying* (1957) by Mikhail Kalatozov and *Carnival Night* by Eldar Ryazanov.

The "thaw" snowballed into what became known as the "spring" or "ice-breaking" when oppositional stances to socialist realism became the norm. Andrei Tarkovksy's cryptic and fantastic interpretations of personal identity in the modern Soviet Union, with all their beauty and spareness, are mapped out in his films, including *Ivan's Childhood* (1962), *Andrei Rublev* (1966), *Solaris* (1972), and *Mirror* (1975–78).

The Soviet cinema is currently booming both abroad and at home. A multitude of films probing historical questions, the malaise of Soviet youth, the meaning of *glasnost*, and a range of social problems have received international attention. Typical of this trend is Vassili Pitchul's *Little Vera* (1988), a witty look at the bleak prospects for Soviet youth.

YUGOSLAVIA

Yugoslavia is a patchwork quilt of peoples, languages, and customs, as well as a land of incredible scenic beauty. Situated in the heart of the Balkan peninsula along the Adriatic Sea, it has been a strategic crossroads between Europe and the Near East for centuries. As a result, Yugoslavia encompasses amazing contrasts. In a few hours you can travel from the sophisticated boutiques and coffeehouses of Slovenia to the mysterious world of Bosnia, where the five-times-daily Moslem call to prayer transports you to a world far removed from Western Europe.

The enchanting coast and islands of the Adriatic are popular with tourists. More remote and exotic are the villages in the rugged mountains that cover two-thirds of the country. The nation's capital, Belgrade, lies in the fertile lowlands along the Danube River in the eastern part of the country.

Yugoslavia has existed as a nation only since 1919. After the First World War brought about the final collapse of the Austro-Hungarian and Ottoman empires, the two powers that had long dominated the region, Yugoslavia was created by the victorious Allied powers, who decided that the various Slavic peoples of the region should be united in a single country. This state fell apart during the Second World War but was reunited as a new socialist federated republic by the Communist leader Josip Broz Tito in 1945. Since 1948, the country has walked the tightrope between the capitalist West and the Soviet bloc.

The complex history of the region has resulted in a nation of great differences. Today Yugoslavia is made up of six republics (Serbia, Macedonia, Bosnia and Herzegovina, Montenegro, Croatia, and Slovenia) and two autonomous regions (Vojvodina and Kosovo). Serbo-Croatian, Slovenian, and Macedonian are the principal languages of the country, while Islam and Christianity (Orthodox and Roman Catholic) are its most prominent religions. To make it even more confusing—and fascinating—there are numerous minorities: Slovaks, Czechs, Jews, Rumanians, Gypsies, Hungarians, Albanians, and Italians.

In recent years the Yugoslav economy has fallen on difficult times. Extraordinary inflation (275 percent in 1988), severe unemployment, an increasing number of strikes, a renewal of ethnic rivalries, and the weakness of one-party government have all contributed to an impending crisis. While few are suggesting that the whole enterprise is ready to fall apart, most observers believe that the next few years are crucial to the viability of this independent socialist state.

—*Thomas A. Emmert, St. Peter, Minnesota*

Official name: Socialist Federal Republic of Yugoslavia. **Area:** 98,766 square miles (about the size of Wyoming). **Population:** 23,600,000. **Population density:** 239 inhabitants per square mile. **Capital and largest city:** Belgrade (pop. 1,250,000). **Language:** Serbo-Croatian, Slovene, Macedonian. **Religion:** Greek Orthodox, Roman Catholic, Islam. **Per capita income:** US$5,600. **Currency:** Dinar. **Literacy rate:** 85%. **Average daily high/low:*** Belgrade: January, 37°/27°; July, 84°/61°. **Average number of days with precipitation:** Belgrade: January, 8; July, 6.

TRAVEL

A passport and a visa are required for U.S. citizens traveling to Yugoslavia. Visas are valid up to one year and are issued free of charge. Check with the Embassy of the Socialist Republic of Yugoslavia (2410 California Street NW, Washington, DC 20008) for specific requirements. There are no minimum currency-exchange requirements.

Getting Around

An assortment of boats—ferries, hydrofoils, steamers, et cetera—link the cities along Yugoslavia's popular Adriatic Coast with Italy; boats also connect Yugoslavia with Greece. There is also international train and bus service connecting Yugoslavia to the rest of Europe. While Eurail passes are not valid within Yugoslavia, the InterRail pass is. Trains are inexpensive, and although travel on many lines is slow, the rail network extends to all parts of the country. Students also get a discount on the already cheap intercity fares on JAT, the state airline. For those who prefer to exercise as they travel, look for a copy of *Yugoslavia: A Climbing, Walking and Cultural Guide*, published by Hunter Publishing and available in most bookstores for $13.95.

Especially for Students and Young People

Yugotours—NAROM is Yugoslavia's student travel bureau and ISTC member. Their main office is located at Djure Djakovica 31, 11000 Belgrade, and they also have an office in Zagreb. Students with the International Student Identity Card (ISIC) get discounts on domestic and international air fares, as well as on rail travel to other Eastern European countries. They are also entitled to discounts at certain hotels and at many museums and galleries.

For Further Information

For more background information about the country, contact the Yugoslav Press and Cultural Center, 767 Third Avenue, New York, NY 10017. Tourist

---

*all temperatures are Fahrenheit

information is available from the Yugoslav National Tourist Office, 630 Fifth Avenue, New York, NY 10020. In addition, you can purchase Baedeker and Fodor guides to Yugoslavia at most bookstores.

WORK

It is difficult for U.S. citizens to get the work permit needed for regular, paid employment in Yugoslavia. You can contact the embassy of Yugoslavia for specific regulations on the subject, however. As an alternative to regular employment, you might be interested in a trainee program or participation in a workcamp.

Internships/Traineeships

There are both AIESEC and IAESTE internship programs in Yugoslavia; see page 18 for more information.

Voluntary Service

CIEE places young people in voluntary service workcamps in Yugoslavia organized by RK ZSMS—Commission for International Exchange of Volunteers (Dalmatinova ul. 4, YU 61000 Ljubljana). At these workcamps groups of volunteers from various countries work together on projects that involve reforestation efforts, recreation for people with muscular diseases, and conservation of historical sites. Volunteers receive room and board in return for their work. The applications of U.S. residents are processed by CIEE. For further information contact the International Voluntary Service Department at the Council.

STUDY

The following are the educational programs offered by member institutions of the Council on International Educational Exchange. Consult Appendix I for the addresses of the universities listed in this section. In addition, Indiana University offers a program open only to its own students.

SUMMER

General Studies

Michigan State University. "The Roman Frontier in Yugoslavia." Sarkamen. Archaeological field training, research, and lectures on the Roman frontier in Maesia. Juniors, seniors, and graduate students. Apply by April 21.

Serbo-Croatian Language

Portland State University. "Summer in Yugoslavia." Zagreb, Sarajevo, Dubrovnik, Split, and other sites. Improvement of Serbo-Croatian language ability while visiting historical sites. Open to students and nonstudents with previous exposure to the language. Apply by July 21.

CHAPTER EIGHT
THE MIDDLE EAST AND NORTH AFRICA

Strategically located where Europe, Africa, and Asia meet, the Middle East is a region whose boundaries are not well defined. For the purposes of this book we've included southwestern Asia from Iran to Turkey and the Mediterranean countries of northern Africa.

A number of powerful bonds unite this region. Islam is the dominant religion of nearly all of the countries found here, and many of the nations of the Middle East are Arab-speaking ones. Nevertheless, cultural diversity—rather than unity—is the dominant characteristic of the region.

By virtue of its location, the Middle East has long been of strategic importance. The region not only lies at the juncture of three continents but also encompasses a number of vital waterways—the Suez Canal, the Bosporus, the Strait of Gibraltar, and the Strait of Hormuz. As a result of this geography, the Middle East has played a central role in world history, and many of the world's peoples trace the roots of their religion and civilization to the region. Today, the importance of the Middle East is further enhanced by its control of much of the world's petroleum reserves.

Yet in spite of the region's rich history and strategic importance, few U.S. college students work, study, or even travel to the Middle East. Nevertheless, there is a variety of work, study, and travel opportunities available; Americans taking advantage of these will gain insight into an interesting and complex region little understood in the United States.

Getting There

The cheapest fares available from the U.S. to the Middle East are generally APEX fares (see Chapter five for a general explanation of air fares). There are also student fares to a few destinations. Listed below are some examples of *one-way* summer fares that were in effect during 1989. More up-to-date information is available at a Council Travel office near you (see listing on pages ix–xi).

   New York–Istanbul, $309
   New York–Casablanca, $320
   New York–Cairo, $309
   New York–Tel Aviv, $349
   New York–Bahrain, $604

In addition, student/youth flights are available from several European cities to Tel Aviv and other cities in the Middle East. These can be booked at any Council Travel office or at a student travel bureau in Europe. Regulations vary depending on the airline but generally holders of the International Student Identity Card (see page 8) or the International Youth Card (see page 9) are eligible. Listed below are sample *one-way* student fares for the 1989 peak summer season:

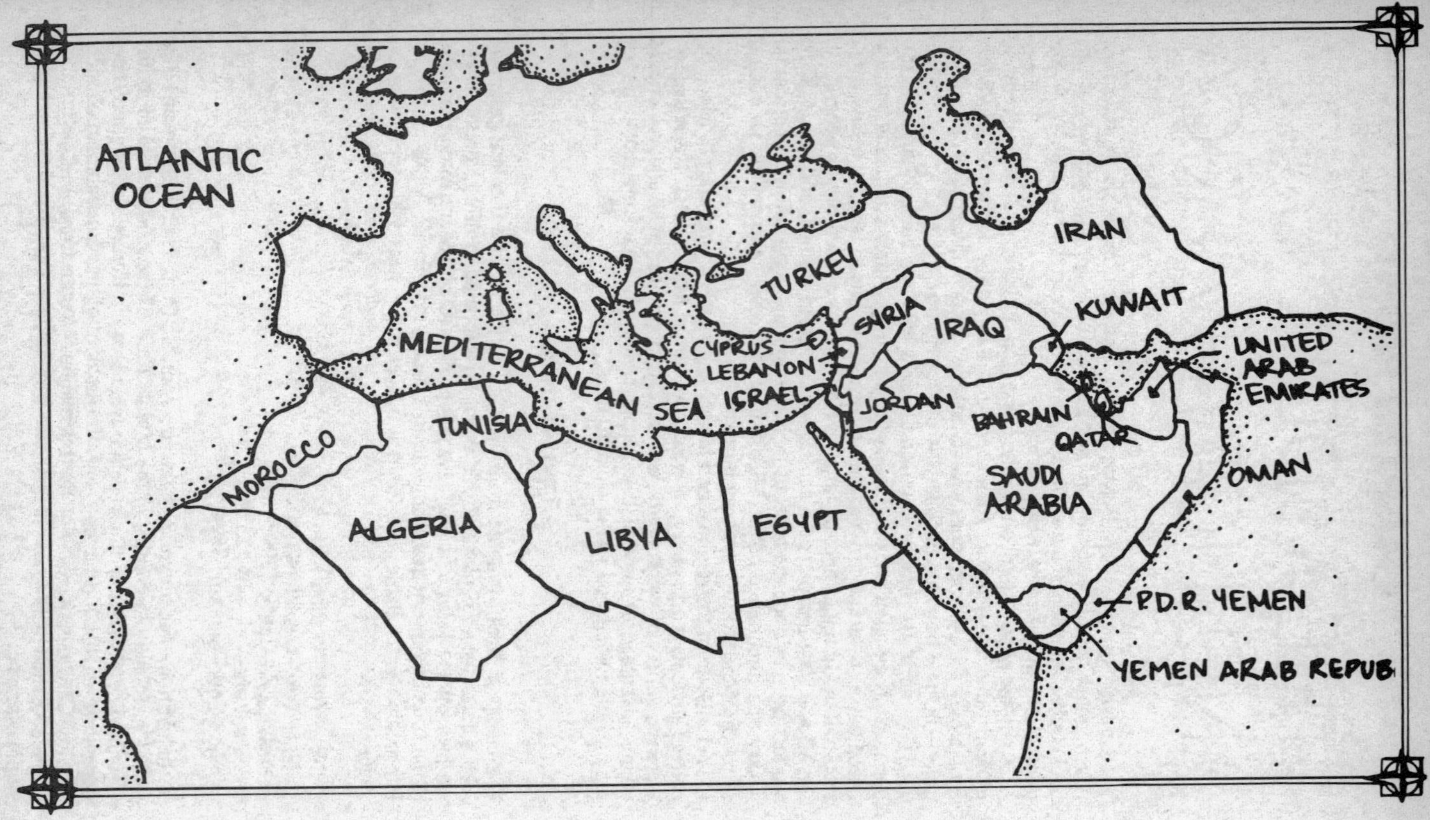
ATLANTIC OCEAN
MEDITERRANEAN SEA
TURKEY
IRAN
KUWAIT
SYRIA
IRAQ
CYPRUS
LEBANON
ISRAEL
JORDAN
UNITED ARAB EMIRATES
BAHRAIN
QATAR
OMAN
SAUDI ARABIA
MOROCCO
TUNISIA
ALGERIA
LIBYA
EGYPT
P.D.R. YEMEN
YEMEN ARAB REPUB

London–Cairo, $219
Paris–Tel Aviv, $185
Paris–Istanbul, $199
Paris–Tunis, $169

An excursion to the Middle East is a quick and easy option for Americans visiting Europe. From Algeciras, Spain, a variety of boats (including car ferries and hydrofoils) depart for the cities of Ccuta and Tangiers on the African continent, little more than an hour away. From Palermo and Trapani (Sicily) you can find various types of passenger boat service to Tunisia. And several Greek islands, including Rhodes and Samos, are only a short boat trip from Turkey's Aegean coast. Ferry service is also available from Greece to Cyprus and from there on to Lebanon and Israel. Student travel bureaus in Europe will be happy to provide you with more information.

Travel in the Middle East

You can obtain a copy of the Department of State's brochure *Tips for Travelers to the Middle East and North Africa* for $1 from the Superintendent of Documents, U.S. Government Printing Office, Washington, DC 20402. According to the brochure, some Arab countries may refuse to admit persons who have Israeli stamps or notations in their passports. However, to avoid this problem, it's possible to have Israeli visa, entry, and exit stamps put on a separate sheet that can be stapled to the passport and removed on departure.

Because of the political climate in the Middle East, the Department of State has issued travel advisories in a number of countries, including Iran, Lebanon, and Libya. Before you go, contact the Citizens Emergency Center (see page 6) at the U.S. State Department for any travel warnings that may be in effect for countries you are considering traveling to.

Algeria has recently changed its policy of discouraging Western tourism and now officially welcomes tourists. However, tourist accommodations are minimal and little has been done to promote the country as a tourist destination. Nevertheless, Algeria is an attractive destination for persons who like more unusual and adventurous travel. A good source of travel information on Algeria is Fodor's *North Africa* (see "For Further Information" below).

Other countries, most notably Saudi Arabia, still discourage tourism and restrict travel by Westerners.

> *"Saudi Arabia and the Gulf States still remain undecided on the benefits of tourism. Outside of Bahrain and Kuwait, which now issue tourist visas, it's extremely difficult to obtain entry visas to the large oil-producing countries. An exception is the 'road transit pass' between Jordan and Kuwait through Saudi Arabian territory, which is sometimes issued by the Saudi Arabian embassy in Amman. Jobs in these countries for Americans have become few and far between with the winding down of construction projects that started in the oil boom years of 1973–76."*

In the more conservative Middle Eastern countries, travelers of both sexes—but women in particular—will feel more comfortable if they are sensitive to local customs and act and dress accordingly. Remember, too, that there is a tremendous difference between the urban and rural areas of the Middle East; what is acceptable in the city may not be acceptable in the country.

"Women should have at least one long-sleeved, loose, ankle-length dress or a tunic/pants outfit with them as well as a large scarf that can be used for a head covering. Besides making them look more respectful of local customs, they'll find that these clothes are also the most suitable for the climate."

While traveling in Moslem countries, you may run into the month-long holiday of Ramadan, during which Moslems fast from dawn to sunset. If you try to get a meal in a restaurant between these hours, you may be frowned upon or even refused service. Fasting includes no eating, drinking, or smoking, and since it is adhered to strictly in a number of Middle Eastern countries, it is a simple matter of respect for a tourist to refrain from breaking the custom in public. If you want to eat, eat in a hotel or an enclosed restaurant.

Most people seem to agree that in most Middle Eastern countries—with some exceptions—women won't be able to go out at night alone without attracting unwanted attention. It is best, then, to bring along a friend; a male friend is preferable, but even another woman will make things more comfortable for you. However, the lack of a traveling companion need not necessarily preclude a visit to the Middle East.

"Though Arab men are certainly friendly, I encountered no problems taking an evening walk in Damascus, Cairo, Baghdad, or Amman. It was definitely safer than my own neighborhood in Seattle. I found the average male, particularly of university age, very protective in attitude toward this lone woman traveler."

For Further Information

Let's Go: Europe, in spite of its title, includes chapters on a number of Middle Eastern countries, including Morocco, Tunisia, Turkey, Cyprus, Israel, and Egypt. As a result, it comes in handy for students traveling in Europe who want to experience—if only for a short time—the non-Western cultures of the Middle East. Written by the Harvard Student Agencies and revised every year, the book is available in bookstores for $13.95.

Guidebooks for countries often visited by tourists, including Egypt, Israel, Morocco, and Turkey (see the individual country sections that follow for some of these books), abound. However, there are few books for travelers planning a trip to more out-of-the way places such as Algeria, Syria, or Yemen. Lonely Planet Publications (Embarcadero West, 112 Linden Street, Oakland, CA 94607) publishes some good guidebooks to several of the less-visited countries of the region, including *Jordan and Syria: A Travel Survival Kit* ($8.95) and *Yemen: A Travel Survival Kit* ($8.95). Add $1.50 postage if ordering by mail. In addition, Fodor's publishes *Jordan and the Holy Land* and *North Africa*, the latter a comprehensive guide to Morocco, Algeria, and Tunisia ($16.95).

For persons interested in staying at youth hostels in the region, volume two of the *International Youth Hostel Handbook* lists hostels in Israel, Lebanon, Morocco, Syria, Tunisia, and Egypt. The government tourist offices of Egypt, Israel, and Turkey will also be happy to send you free hostel information for their countries.

Listed below are addresses where you can write for general information as well as details on visa requirements for Middle Eastern nations we have not covered in a separate country section in the last part of this chapter:

THE MIDDLE EAST AND NORTH AFRICA

- Embassy of Bahrain, 2600 Virginia Avenue NW, Washington, DC 20037
- Embassy of the Democratic and Popular Republic of Algeria, 2118 Kalorama Road NW, Washington, DC 20008
- Embassy of Iraq, 1901 P Street NW, Washington, DC 20036
- Jordan Information Bureau, Suite 1100, 1701 K Street NW, Washington, DC 20006
- Embassy of the Republic of Kuwait, 2940 Tilden Street NW, Washington, DC 20008
- Embassy of Lebanon, 2560 28th Street NW, Washington, DC 20008
- People's Bureau of the Diplomatic Mission of the Socialist People's Libyan Arab Jamahiriya, 1118 22nd Street NW, Washington, DC 20037
- Embassy of Oman, 2342 Massachusetts Avenue NW, Washington, DC 20008
- Embassy of Qatar, 600 New Hampshire Avenue NW, Washington, DC 20037
- Embassy of Saudi Arabia, 1520 18th Street NW, Washington, DC 20036
- Embassy of the Syrian Arab Republic, 2215 Wyoming Avenue NW, Washington, DC 20008
- Embassy of the United Arab Emirates, 600 New Hampshire Ave NW, Washington, DC 20037
- Embassy of the Yemen Arab Republic, 600 New Hampshire Avenue NW, Suite 860, Washington, DC 20037

"It's also important for students en route to the Middle East to make use of the human resources available to them at their U.S. campuses. There are very few U.S. schools that currently have no Middle Eastern students in residence. These students could help American students plan their trips, as well as suggest places and ways to meet local students and families overseas."

Work

For U.S. citizens, the chances of obtaining salaried employment in the Middle East and North Africa are not very good unless they are fluent in the local language. Teaching is one area, however, where there are a few openings for Americans. Anyone interested in teaching in the Middle East should write for a copy of AMIDEAST's *Teaching Opportunities in the Middle East and North Africa*, available for $14.95 from AMIDEAST, 1100 17th Street NW, Washington, DC 20036.

You'll find internships and traineeships in Cyprus, Egypt, Israel, Morocco, Tunisia, and Turkey listed in the individual country sections later in this chapter. In addition, IAESTE has internship possibilities in Iraq, Jordan, Lebanon, Libya, and Syria; see page 18 for more information about this program.

Study

Those who wish to study in this part of the world may write to AMIDEAST (address above) for copies of its publication, *Study and Research Opportunities in the Middle East and North Africa* ($7.95). The book lists over 150 U.S.-based programs in that part of the world, and also includes a listing of grants and other sources of financial assistance for study in the region.

You'll find study programs listed for Cyprus, Egypt, Israel, Morocco, and

Turkey later in this chapter. In this section, we've listed only those study programs offered by CIEE members that take place in more than one country of the region. Consult Appendix I for the addresses of the colleges and universities listed below.

SEMESTER AND ACADEMIC YEAR

General Studies

St. Olaf College.
"Term in the Middle East." Istanbul, Turkey; Cairo, Egypt; Jerusalem, Israel; and Rabat, Morocco. Fall semester plus January. Social and political issues of the contemporary Middle East. Sophomores, juniors, and seniors. Apply by March 1.
"Global Semester." Cairo, Egypt; Bangalore, India; Taipei, Taiwan; and Kyoto, Japan. Fall semester plus January. Cultures and contemporary problems of non-Western world. Sophomores, juniors, and seniors. Apply by March 1.

University of Pittsburgh. "Semester at Sea." Fall or spring semester. Students based aboard the S.S. *Universe*, attend classes on board and travel to various countries in Europe, the Middle East, and Asia. Sophomores, juniors, and seniors with 2.75 GPA. Contact: Semester at Sea, 2E Forbes Quadrangle, University of Pittsburgh, Pittsburgh, PA 15260; (412) 648-7490.

University System of Georgia/Georgia State University. Spring break in Israel and Egypt. Business or arts and sciences emphasis. Undergraduates and graduates with 2.5 GPA. Apply by December 1; applications accepted thereafter on a space available basis.

CYPRUS

The Mediterranean island nation of Cyprus was the site of early Phoenician and Greek colonies. Over the centuries it has fallen prey to numerous other conquerors, the most recent being the British, who seized the island from the Turks in the First World War and held it until 1960, when it was granted independence.

Turkish-Greek animosity on the island is rampant. In fact, the majority of the population regard themselves as either Greeks or Turks, rather than Cypriot nationals. To make matters worse, violence between Greek and Turkish Cypriots has been provoked by the interference of Greece and Turkey in the island's affairs. In 1974, Turkish troops invaded Cyprus in defense of the Turkish minority, and Turkey still controls about a third of the island. Greek Cypriots—most of whom support self-determination for the island (i.e., union with Greece)—have fled to the southern and western parts of the country. Turkish Cypriots, however, have set up a government in the area they control and proclaimed their independence. While the international community still recognizes Cyprus as a single independent state, in actual fact the island is split into two belligerent states, divided by linguistic, religious, and ethnic differences.

Official name: Republic of Cyprus. **Area:** 3,572 square miles (one and a half times the size of Delaware). **Population:** 700,000. **Population density:** 196 inhabitants per square mile. **Capital and largest city:** Nicosia (pop. 123,298). **Language:** Greek, Turkish, English. **Religion:** Greek Orthodox, Islam. **Per capita income:** U.S.$3,270. **Currency:** Cypriot pound. **Literacy rate:** 89%. **Average daily high/low:*** Nicosia: January, 58°/42°; July, 97°/69°. **Average number of days with precipitation:** Nicosia: January, 10; July, less than 1.

TRAVEL

U.S. citizens will need a passport to travel to Cyprus; however, a visa is not required. Check with the Embassy of the Republic of Cyprus (2211 R Street NW, Washington, DC 20008) for specific requirements.

Getting Around

Tourists are prohibited from crossing the militarized border ("Green Line") between the Greek and Turkish sections of the island. Most tourists visit the Greek section, which is linked by plane to Western Europe and the Middle East and by ferry to Greece, Israel, and Lebanon. Good beaches, a warm sunny climate, and inexpensive food and accommodations have made the Greek section popular with tourists in spite of the ongoing conflict between Greeks and Turks.

The routes between the major towns and cities are served by buses and shared taxis. The taxis follow regular routes, departing when they are full and picking up and dropping off passengers along the way. Hitchhiking is relatively easy, and on secondary routes it can be the only alternative. Car rentals can also be arranged (driving on the left side of the road only).

For Further Information

Let's Go: Europe ($13.95), revised and updated annually by the Harvard Student Agencies and published by St. Martin's Press, contains a section on Cyprus, as does *Let's Go: Greece* ($12.95). These guidebooks are designed specifically for the budget-minded student traveler. In most bookstores you'll also find Berlitz's pocket-sized guide to Cyprus, which includes good maps and color photos. General tourist information is available from the Cyprus Tourist Office (13 East 40th Street, New York, NY 10016).

WORK

Internships/Traineeships

There is an IAESTE internship program in Cyprus; see page 18 for more information.

---

*all temperatures are Fahrenheit

STUDY

The following are the educational programs offered by members of the Council on International Educational Exchange. Consult Appendix I for the addresses of the institutions listed below.

SEMESTER AND ACADEMIC YEAR

Business

State University of New York/Empire State College. "Semester Program in Cyprus." Nicosia. Semester or academic year. Business and technology in the Eastern Mediterranean. Sophomores to graduate students and adults. Apply by November 30 for spring and June 15 for fall.

General Studies

International Student Exchange Program. Direct reciprocal exchange between U.S. universities and Frederick Polytechnic University. Semester or academic year. Full curriculum options. Open only to students at ISEP member institutions.

EGYPT

When they envision Egypt, most Americans think of the pyramids, the Sphinx, and King Tut. Indeed, the thousands of American tourists who visit Egypt each year come almost exclusively to visit Pharaonic Egypt. The monuments of ancient Egypt attract even larger numbers of European tourists, who also come for the Egyptian sun and Mediterranean and Red Sea beaches. However, to those who really want to get to know and understand the Arab world, Egypt offers the opportunity to study Arabic and gain insights into Islam, Arab history, and the politics, economics, and culture of the contemporary Middle East.

The roll call of civilizations and cultures in Egypt actually has been much more diverse than simply the Pharaonic and Arab. There are traces of ancient Persia in Egypt; the ancient Greek and Roman civilizations are visible in Egyptian monuments; and the Byzantine and Coptic Christian cultures are evident as well. Indeed, although today 85 percent of the population is Moslem, 15 percent remains Coptic Christian. In fact, the word *Copt* comes from the same root word as Egypt, and the Copts regard themselves as the true Egyptians, undiluted by the intermingling of later Moslem conquerors. Throughout the 19th and early decades of the 20th century, France and Great Britain were the foreign powers that extended their influence over Egypt. Finally, in 1952, after a nonviolent revolution, Egyptians once again ruled Egypt. Thus Egypt, although one of the world's oldest civilizations, is a relatively new independent nation-state.

Though a trite phrase, "Egypt, the gift of the Nile" is essential to understanding the nation. Ninety-six percent of Egyptian territory is uninhabited desert. In the remaining four percent live 50 million Egyptians, making the Nile valley and delta among the most intensely farmed and densely populated areas on earth.

A quarter of all Egyptians live in metropolitan Cairo, which has been described as the ultimate urban experience—one of the noisiest and most crowded cities on earth. It is also a city where the vast majority of citizens are poor; yet there is very little crime. This fact can be ascribed to the importance of the family and religion in Egyptian life. Both Moslem and Christian believe that individual behavior must ultimately be judged by both family and God.

God is in every Egyptian's conversation. "See you tomorrow, *ensha'allah* (God willing)"; "My mother is recovering nicely, *el hamduli'lah* (thanks be to God)"—both Moslems and Christians use the same phrases and acknowledge the same God's influence in their lives. But religion in Egypt is neither puritanical nor gloomy. Egyptians are optimistic, exuberant, possess a sense of humor, and have a great capacity for enjoying themselves.

—*Molly Bartlett, Eugene, Oregon*

Official name: Arab Republic of Egypt. **Area:** 386,900 square miles (three-quarters the size of Alaska). **Population:** 53,300,000. **Population density:** 138 inhabitants per square mile. **Capital and largest city:** Cairo (pop. 12,560,000). **Language:** Arabic. **Religion:** Islam. **Per capita income:** US$690. **Currency:** Egyptian pound. **Literacy rate:** 43%. **Average daily high/low:*** Cairo: January, 65°/47°; July, 96°/70°. **Average number of days with precipitation:** Cairo: January, 1; July, 0.

TRAVEL

U.S. citizens need a passport and a visa. A tourist visa is valid for three months and costs $10. The Egyptian government requires foreigners to exchange a minimum of US$150 on arrival; persons traveling on a prepaid tour are exempt from this requirement. For specific requirements, check with the Embassy of the Arab Republic of Egypt (2310 Decatur Place NW, Washington, DC 20008), or with the Egyptian consulates in Chicago, Houston, San Francisco, or New York.

Getting Around

One of the best ways to get around Egypt is by train. Trains connect Cairo with Alexandria and Port Said and will take you south up the Nile Valley to Luxor and Aswan. Good overnight service with sleeping cars is provided on the longer runs, and discounts are available to students (see "Especially for Students and Young People" below).

Buses are another option between the major cities. Shared taxis, which travel on a fixed route dropping off and picking up passengers along the way, serve virtually every town and village in the Nile Valley. If you hitchhike, you will be expected to pay the equivalent of the shared taxi fare.

You can also rent a car; Hertz, Avis, and Budget are among the companies operating in Egypt. Driving is on the right side of the road, and you will need an International Driving Permit.

---

*all temperatures are Fahrenheit

Probably the most relaxing as well as the most scenic way to get around the country is by traveling on the Nile, which has served as the country's major highway for thousands of years. Numerous passenger boats make the three- to four-day trip between Aswan and Luxor, which has become a standard part of most organized tours to Egypt. However, you can also choose to make this trip by felucca, the traditional sailboats that still provide local transportation up and down the river for many Egyptians.

> *"All transportation within Egypt is heavily crowded. Buses will have people hanging from them while trains have passengers not only in the coaches, but also on top of the cars and on the locomotive. Prices, however, are relatively cheap. Port Said and Alexandria can both be reached from Cairo for only a few dollars."*

Especially for Students and Young People

ESC/STSD (P.O. Box 58, El-Malek El-Saleh, Cairo) provides students and young people with tourist information. Write for further information about travel and student discounts in Egypt. Holders of the International Student Identity Card receive reduced air fares from Egypt to a number of international destinations, a 50-percent discount on train travel (except first class) within Egypt, and discounts on admission to museums and historical sites.

> *"Wherever you are in Egypt, be prepared to haggle over everything from the price of a bottle of water to the availability of space on trains. Haggling is just a way of life and tourists will be treated with more respect if they start by haggling."*

Organized Tours

For persons interested in an organized educational tour to Egypt, a program sponsored by a member of the Council on International Educational Exchange is listed below:

New York University. "International Travel Programs." Short-term, usually two-week tours. Students and adults. Apply two months prior to departure. Contact: NYU School of Continuing Education, International Programs, 331 Shimkin, Washington Square, New York, NY 10003; (212) 998-7133.

For Further Information

Let's Go: Israel and Egypt ($12.95) is one of the best guidebooks for the student or young budget traveler going to Egypt. It's revised and updated annually by the Harvard Student Agencies and published by St. Martin's Press. *Let's Go: Europe* ($13.95) also includes a short chapter on Egypt for those who wish to combine a visit to Egypt with their trip to Europe. Another very good guide to Egypt is Lonely Planet's *Egypt and the Sudan: A Travel Survival Kit*. If you can't find it in a bookstore, you can order it for $7.95 (plus $1.50 postage and handling) from Lonely Planet Publications (Embarcadero West, 112 Linden Street, Oakland, CA 94607). Finally, for the traveler on a budget, Frommer's publishes *Egypt*, available in most bookstores for $14.95.

You'll also want to contact the Egyptian Tourist Authority (630 Fifth Avenue, New York, NY 10111), which can provide you with information on youth hostels, budget hotels, restaurants, and study opportunities in Egypt; there's an Egyptian Tourist Authority office in San Francisco as well.

WORK

Finding regular salaried employment in Egypt is difficult for foreigners. An offer of a contract from an Egyptian company is required for starters, and then you must apply for a work permit at a labor office in Egypt.

Internships/Traineeships

There are both AIESEC and IAESTE internship programs in Egypt; see page 18 for more information.

STUDY

For information on Egyptian universities that offer courses for foreign students in Arabic language, Islamic history, Islamic religion, and Egyptology, contact the Cultural Counselor, Egyptian Educational Bureau, 2200 Kalorama Road NW, Washington, DC 20008.

The American University in Cairo, a private university founded in 1919, welcomes students from American colleges and universities for a semester or full year. The aim of the university is to offer an American-style education to Egyptian, Middle Eastern, African, American, and other students so as to serve "as a bridge of understanding between the U.S. and the Middle East." Eighty percent of its students are Egyptian, and there are normally 150 to 200 American students on campus studying Middle Eastern politics, economics, anthropology and sociology, Egyptology, et cetera. The language of instruction is English, but an intensive Arabic language program is also available. Apply by June 1 for the fall term and November 1 for the spring term. In addition, the American University in Cairo offers summer courses in Arabic language and general studies. Apply by April 30. Consult Appendix I for the address where you can write for more information. In addition to the programs of the American University in Cairo, two other CIEE member institutions, the University of California system and Pennsylvania State University, offer study programs open only to their own students.

EXPLORING THE CULTURE OF EGYPT

Literature

The most internationally recognized of Egypt's contemporary writers is Naguib Mahfouz, winner of the 1988 Nobel Prize for literature. His *Midaq Alley* depicts working-class Cairo. Other books by Mahfouz are *Miramar*, *Fountain and Tomb*, and *Children of Gebelawi*, the latter an allegory about the three great religions that sprouted from the arid soil of the Middle East. Though Mahfouz has the greater international reputation, Yusuf Idris is as widely read and appreciated by Egyptians themselves. A novelist who once worked as a doctor in the Nile delta, his books (try *Rings of Burnished Brass*) are sharp, gritty stories portraying rural life in Egypt. Fathey Ghanem, author of *The Man Who Lost His Shadow*, is a writer of more popular, commercial fiction. The most important Egyptian playwright is Tawfiq Al-Hakim, whose plays include *The Tree Climber* and *Fate of a Cockroach*.

For a vivid portrait of life in Egypt today, you might try one of these biographies. *Shahhat, An Egyptian*, is an account of the life of an Egyptian peasant as told to Richard Critchfield, a Westerner fascinated by the lives of ordinary people in the Third World. In *Khul-Khaal: Five Egyptian Women Tell Their Stories*, Nayra Attiya portrays the strength and spirit of five contemporary women of the lower and lower-middle classes. The perspective of an upper-class woman is related in *A Woman of Egypt*, the autobiography of Jehdan Sadat, the wife of the late Egyptian President Anwar Sadat. Hers is an explanation of the culture and recent history of Egypt written specifically for the Westerner with little knowledge of the country.

Film

Since World War II there has been a rapid expansion of filmmaking in Egypt, particularly of commercial melodramas and farces with dreamy settings. Most of these are stories of love and jealously dripping with wealth and glamour and the usual touch of song and dance. This successful formula may explain the enormous popularity of Egyptian films throughout the rest of the Arab world. Alongside the commercial industry is a relatively small number of independent filmmakers, who, beginning in the 1950s, wanted to make films popular with audiences, but without strictly adhering to the formulaic rigidity of most Egyptian commercial films.

Chief among these independent filmmakers is Youssef Chahine, whose films *Cairo Station* and *Black Waters* are portraits of the workers and lower classes of Egypt. Two of his later films, *The Land* and *The Sparrow*, are insightful, political impressions of conflicting Egyptian social forces. *The Land* is a story about a land and water dispute between a village and a wealthy bey; *The Sparrow* investigates the 1967 war with Israel. The maturation of Chahine's style continues with two of his more recent films, *Alexandra . . . Why?* and *An Egyptian Story*, both heavily autobiographical films detailing the experience of balancing the cultural influences of your own country and those of the dominant Western World.

ISRAEL

Israel, often referred to as the "Holy Land," may hold too much spiritual significance for too many different religions and peoples. For centuries, Muslims, Christians, and Jews have fought to control this small piece of relatively arid land. Today, the continuing struggle pits Arab against Jew for control of the homeland the Arabs call Palestine and the Jews call Israel.

Late in the 19th century, the Zionist movement was founded in Europe with the goal of creating a Jewish state in the land the Hebrews had inhabited in biblical times. During the first half of this century Jews from Europe began immigrating to Israel—an immigration that swelled after 1945 with survivors of the Holocaust. In 1948, the State of Israel was born. Ever since, the politics of the region have been dominated by the competing claims of Arab and Jew to this piece of land situated between the Jordan River and the Mediterranean Sea.

Israel—partly as a result of wars with its Arab neighbors in 1948, 1956, 1967, and 1973—now controls the disputed territory. But Arab Palestinians comprise nearly half the population of the land under Israeli administration (Israel proper and the occupied territories of the West Bank, Gaza, and the Golan Heights). The *intifadeh*, a Palestinian uprising that began in 1987 in the occupied territories, continues to challenge the political and moral authority of the Israeli occupation. The *intifadeh* also serves as a constant reminder of the uncertain future of Israel, a nation that in spite of its impressive military victories still finds security to be an elusive goal.

Today, for a look at the "real" Israel, push and shove your way on to a bus. Each ride presents a microcosm of Israeli society, as varied as the landscape stretching before you. An ultra-orthodox Hasid, dressed in the black garb of his 18th-century Polish ancestors, sits next to a soldier on his way home for a short leave. An Arab woman in white headdress sits next to an *oleh hadash* (new immigrant) from Argentina eating felafel. Suddenly, the multilingual cacophony dies down. Six piercing beeps signal the beginning of the hourly news broadcast. The bus driver raises the volume on his radio so his passengers can follow world events.

With the places along your route—names like Jericho, Jerusalem, Bethlehem, and Masada—serving as constant reminders that this is an ancient land, it is easy to forget that the State of Israel is a relative newcomer to the family of nations. Many Israeli Jews are recent immigrants to the land their ancestors inhabited in ancient times. The new nation absorbed first the Ashkenazi Jews, refugees from Eastern Europe, then the Sephardic Jews of the Middle East and North Africa, and, most recently, the *Falashas*, or Ethiopian Jews. Each group of immigrants has brought with it its own language, food, music, dress, and traditions, but the renaissance of the Hebrew language has done much to unify these disparate groups. In fact, the efforts of the lexicographer Eliezer Ben Yehuda, the "father of Modern Hebrew," to fashion a modern language out of a biblical tongue are celebrated in a popular song.

It may surprise you to know that the overwhelming majority of Israeli Jews are secular. Nevertheless, religion pervades every aspect of life. Part of the reason for this is rooted in Israel's parliamentary democracy. Since no one party ever wins the majority necessary to take control of Israel's 120-seat Knesset, small religious parties holding no more than three or four seats can force concessions that affect the whole country. Their influence has resulted, among other legislation, in no bus sevice being allowed on the Sabbath (except in the northern city of Haifa) and, on the day before Passover, the State of Israel selling the contents of its granaries to a wealthy Israeli Arab so as not knowingly to be in possession of any leavened substance during the eight-day festival.

A trip to Israel offers the chance to visit important religious sites, ancient archaeological digs, and modern cities. You can relax on Mediterranean beaches, explore the Negev Desert, scuba dive in the Gulf of Aqaba, or go skiing in the mountains in winter. It also provides a chance to see firsthand the contemporary struggles of the different peoples who inhabit this ancient land.

—*Carina Klein, New York, New York*

Official name: State of Israel. **Area:** 7,992 square miles (about the size of Massachussetts). **Population:** 4,400,000. **Population density:** 551 inhabitants per square mile. **Capital:** Jerusalem (the United States and most of the international community recognize Tel Aviv as the capital). **Largest city:** Jerusalem (pop. 468,400, including East Jerusalem). **Language:** Hebrew, Arabic, English. **Religion:** Jewish. **Per capita income:** US$6,180. **Currency:** Shekel. **Literacy rate:** 92%. **Average daily high/low:*** Jerusalem: January, 55°/41°; July, 87°/63°. **Average number of days with precipitation:** Jerusalem: January, 9; July, 0.

TRAVEL

A passport, valid for nine months from the date of your arrival, is required for U.S. citizens. Onward or return tickets are also required; however, a visa is not needed for tourist stays of less than three months. For specific requirements, check with the Embassy of Israel (3514 International Drive NW, Washington, DC 20008) or with an Israeli consulate in New York, Chicago, Boston, Houston, Los Angeles, New Orleans, Philadelphia, San Francisco, Detroit, or Newark.

Traveling in Israel itself has been little affected by the Palestinian uprising in the occupied territories. However, travel into the West Bank or Gaza Strip may not be advisable. Before you go, contact the Citizens Emergency Center (see page 6) at the U.S. State Department for any travel warnings that may be in effect. You might also want to become more informed about the *intifadeh* and the political situation in the Middle East. *Conflicts and Contradictions* by Meron Beneviste (an Israeli geographer) is a good examination of the dilemma of Israel/Palestine and the legitimate and powerful claims of two ancient peoples for the same land. One of the best analyses of the Palestinian uprising in the West Bank and Gaza Strip is "Intifadeh," by Don Peretz, in the summer 1988 issue of *Foreign Affairs*.

> *"Living in Israel, I got a much better understanding of a country that is controversial. You get a much different perspective when you're on the other end of the U.S. news stories. It's very interesting to see how people live in a country where war and conflict seem ever-present."*
> —Christopher Shern, New Hope, Minnesota

Getting Around

It's easy to get around Israel; distances are short and there is good and inexpensive bus service. (There is no bus service, however, between Friday afternoon and Saturday night except in Haifa.) In addition, students receive a discount on intercity bus fares (see "Especially for Students and Young People" below). Students also get a discount on train fares, but trains are slower than the buses and the rail network is limited. Another option is the *sherut* taxis that operate between cities and towns, leaving when filled and dropping off and picking up passengers along the way. They are cheaper than regular taxis but more expensive than buses; they also operate on Saturday and late at night, when buses don't.

---

*all temperatures are Fahrenheit

Most people find that the extensive public transportation system makes renting a car unnecessary. Renting a car is fairly easy, however, although you'll need the International Driving Permit (see page 49). The leading car rental agencies are Hertz, Avis, and Eldan; you can get further information by calling the toll-free numbers for Hertz or Avis in the United States.

Especially for Students and Young People

Israel Students Tourist Association (ISSTA), with offices in Tel Aviv (109 Ben Yehuda Street, Tel Aviv 63401), Jerusalem, Haifa, and Beer Sheba, is the nation's student travel bureau and ISTC member. They can provide travel information, book accommodations, and sell plane, train, or bus tickets. You may also have mail sent to you c/o ISSTA Poste Restante at the above address.

Holders of the International Student Identity Card get discounts on international air travel from Israel, on trains and buses within Israel, on ferries to Cyprus and Greece, and on admission to many museums. There is also a discount on tours organized by ISSTA of Israel and Egypt.

Meeting the People

Through the "Meet the Israelis" program, get-togethers are arranged during the day or evening with Israeli families or professionals. The Israeli government tourist offices in Israel can arrange these visits for individual travelers on a day's notice. For a list of addresses of the tourist offices in Israel, write to the Israel Government Tourist Office, 350 Fifth Avenue, New York, NY 10118.

> *"The sabra (a cactus fruit that is hard and prickly on the outside and soft and sweet on the inside) is the nickname for a native Israeli. It is quite appropriate for a nation that has suffered through five wars during its brief existence and centuries of persecution before that. To get through the rugged skin and meet the person inside takes some persistence and patience, but the rewards and insight into the Middle East one gains are worth the effort."*
> —Kenneth L. Milman, New York, New York

For Further Information

For general tourist information, contact the Israel Government Tourist Office (address above), which can provide you with information on camping and youth hostels, among many other topics.

One of the best guidebooks for the independent traveler on a budget is *Israel: A Travel Survival Kit*. If you can't find it in a bookstore, you can order it for $12.95 plus $1.50 postage from Lonely Planet Publications (Embarcadero West, 112 Linden Street, Oakland, CA 94607). More readily available in bookstores is *Let's Go: Israel and Egypt* ($12.95), geared to the student or young budget traveler going to Israel. It's revised and updated annually by the Harvard Student Agencies and is published by St. Martin's Press. *Let's Go: Europe* ($13.95) also includes a short chapter on Israel for those who wish to combine a visit there with a trip to Europe. Another guidebook for the budget traveler is Frommer's *Israel on $40 a Day* ($13.95). Visitors not limited to a tight budget might want to look at Fodor's *Israel* ($13.95).

WORK

"Working in Israel showed me some of the less glamorous aspects of Israel—the Tel Aviv Central Bus Station every morning, trying to stretch each paycheck to pay for everything, and only having one and a half days for the weekend."
—Joanne Abraham, Youngstown, New York

Internships/Traineeships

There are both AIESEC and IAESTE internship programs in Israel; see page 18 for more information.

World Union of Jewish Students Institute is an international graduate center for Hebrew and Jewish students in Arad, Israel. The program is designed to help participants make a decision on immigrating to Israel. Participants spend about five months in formal studies and two to three weeks working on a kibbutz; then, during the final six months of the program, they are given work experience in their profession. Further information can be obtained from the American Zionist Youth Foundation (515 Park Avenue, New York, NY 10022-9918).

Working on a Kibbutz

Kibbutz Aliya (27 West 20th Street, New York, NY 10011) is the U.S. representative for kibbutzim in Israel, and offers young Americans (ages 18 to 32) the opportunity to live and work in one of these unique communities. One option offered by the organization is the Temporary Worker Program, in which participants must make a commitment to remain on the kibbutz for at least one month (the maximum commitment is one year). Another option is the Kibbutz Ulpan Program, one half of which consists of work and the other half of intensive study of Hebrew. The program lasts six months, although a special ten-week course is available in the summer. (Academic credit from Haifa University can also be arranged.) The Kibbutz University Semester Program, an eight- to ten-week kibbutz period and a full semester at Haifa University, is still another possibility. A summer semester combining a month at Hebrew University in Jerusalem and a month on a kibbutz is also available. Further information is available from Kibbutz Aliya upon request.

The American Zionist Youth Foundation (515 Park Avenue, New York, NY 10022–9918) sponsors a variety of programs that bring young people to Israel for periods of a summer, a semester, six months, or a year. The summer programs offer special experiences in the areas of science, nature study, and kibbutz life—all combined with extensive touring of the country. The long-term programs range from six months to a year and combine work with intensive Hebrew language study. Other options include a semester at an Israeli university and a work/study program at a religious kibbutz.

ISSTA (109 Ben Yehuda Street, Tel Aviv) sponsors a kibbutz program of its own; you can start your kibbutz stay at any time of the year between September 1 and May 31. The cost of the program is $60, including room and full board at the kibbutz, one night's accommodation upon arrival in Israel, and the cost of transportation to the kibbutz. Information for this program is available from Council Travel offices.

"The communal experience is quite broadening and you get to meet people with a different viewpoint. At first it's a lonely situation, but after a week I felt completely at home."

Working on an Archaeological Dig

Another work possibility in Israel is volunteering for an archaeological dig. A listing of archaeological excavations open to volunteers is put together each January by the Ministry of Education and Culture, Department of Antiquities (P.O.B. 586, Jerusalem 91004). You must be at least 17 years of age, however, and be prepared to work for at least a week or two. In addition, volunteers must be physically fit and capable of doing strenuous work in a hot climate. The listing of such digs is also available from the Israel Government Tourist Office (350 Fifth Avenue, New York, NY 10118).

STUDY

The Center for Study in Israel coordinates programs in Israel for a number of U.S. colleges and universities. The programs offered include study at major Israeli universities, technical schools, seminaries, and *yeshivot*, as well as service learning and internship opportunities. The center also distributes information on a wide range of study and work programs in Israel and helps students find the particular programs most suitable for them. For further information, write to the center at 60 East 42nd Street, Suite 3318, New York, NY 10017.

If you wish to enroll at an Israeli university, you can contact the New York offices of the following organizations: American Friends of the Hebrew University (11 East 69th Street, New York, NY 10021); American Friends of Tel Aviv University (342 Madison Avenue, New York, NY 10017); American Friends of Haifa University (206 Fifth Avenue, New York, NY 10022); American Technion Society (271 Madison Avenue, New York, NY 10016); American Associates of Ben-Gurion University of the Negev (342 Madison Avenue, Room 1924, New York, NY 10173); and the American Committee for the Weizman Institute of Science (515 Park Avenue, New York, NY 10022).

The following are the educational programs offered by member institutions of the Council on International Educational Exchange. Consult Appendix I for the addresses of the colleges and universities listed in this section. In addition to the programs listed below, Boston University, California State Universities, New York University, Pennsylvania State University, and the University of California system offer programs open to their own students only.

SEMESTER AND ACADEMIC YEAR

General Studies

Friends World College. "Middle East Studies." Jerusalem, with field trip to Egypt. Academic year or semester. Middle East and Israel studies, Hebrew or Arabic, and individualized program combining independent study with fieldwork or internships. Sophomores, juniors, and seniors. Others may participate but will not receive credit. Apply by May 15 for fall and November 15 for spring.

Hebrew University of Jerusalem.
"Freshman Year Program." Open to high school graduates for the first year of college. Apply by April 1.
"One Year Program." Sophomores and juniors. Apply by April 1.
"Graduate Studies." Master's degree program open to students with bachelor's degree. Apply by April 1.

Indiana University. "Overseas Study in Jerusalem." Academic year. Limited to students at the Universities of Illinois, Indiana, and Wisconsin. Juniors and seniors with 3.0 GPA. Apply by the first week of November.

Rutgers University. "Junior Year in Israel." Haifa. Juniors with 3.0 GPA. Apply by March 1.

State University of New York/Empire State College. "Semester Program in Israel." Individualized tutorials and field studies. Internship and voluntary service opportunities available. Sophomores to graduate students and adults.

University of North Carolina–Chapel Hill. "UNC Program to Hebrew University in Jerusalem." Sophomores to graduates with 3.0 GPA. Apply by March 15.

University of Notre Dame. "Foreign Study Program in Jerusalem." Spring semester, with special focus on Arabic, theology, history, and government. Freshmen to graduate students with 2.5 GPA. Apply by October 15.

University of Oregon. "UO—Hebrew University Exchange Program." Sophomores, juniors, and seniors with 3.0 GPA. Apply by April 1.

University of Washington. "Hebrew University—Rothberg School for Overseas Students." Jerusalem. Academic year. Sophomores, juniors, and seniors. Apply by April 1.

University of Wisconsin–Madison. Jerusalem. Academic year. Sophomores to graduate students with two years of college Hebrew and 3.0 GPA. Open only to students at colleges or universities in Wisconsin and Wisconsin residents studying outside of the state. Apply by February 1.

Middle Eastern Studies

Syracuse University. Tel Aviv. Fall or spring semester. Sophomores, juniors, and seniors with 3.0 GPA. Apply by March 15 for fall and October 15 for spring.

SUMMER

Archaeology

University of Massachusetts–Amherst. "Field Program in Israel." Tal Nami. Juniors and seniors. Apply by April 24.

Michigan State University. "Archaeology, Modern Hebrew, and History of Religion." Haifa. Study at Haifa University. Sophomores to graduate students with elementary Hebrew. Apply by April 21.

Communication

Michigan State University. "Mass Media in Israel." Jerusalem, Tel Aviv, and Haifa. Juniors, seniors, and graduates. Apply by April 21.

General Studies

Hebrew University of Jerusalem. Sophomores to graduate students. Apply by May 15 for July and June 15 for August.

University of North Carolina–Chapel Hill. Jerusalem. Sophomores to graduate students with 3.0 GPA. Apply by March 15.

University of Washington. "Hebrew University—Rothberg School for Overseas Students." Jerusalem. Sophomores, juniors, and seniors. Apply by May 15.

EXPLORING THE CULTURE OF ISRAEL

Literature

In 1947, as Israel was fighting for its independence and Jews from all over the world were settling there, Shmuel Agnon, who later won the Nobel Prize for literature, published *In the Heart of the Seas*, about a journey to Israel. Another major Israeli novelist is Abraham B. Yehoshua, whose most recent work, *Five Seasons*, deals with a widower coming to terms with her changed life. *The Fifth Heaven*, by the novelist Rachel Eytan, is the story of a young girl's coming of age in a Tel Aviv orphanage during the Second World War. A best-seller when first published in 1962, it is regularly reissued and still widely read in Israel. Another influential Israeli writer is Amos Oz, whose most recent book, *Black Box*, explores the breakdown of a marriage. Anton Shammas is an Israeli-Arab writer whose *Arabesques* focuses on the Palestinian/Israeli conflict.

MOROCCO

Morocco's distinct cultural personality is a product of a half century of European rule and, before that, of centuries of Arab dominance with strong resistance from native Berbers. In 1956, it achieved its independence from France and Spain, and most of the relatively few Europeans living in Morocco returned to Europe. Today its ethnic makeup is about 35 percent Berber and 65 percent Arab. In religion, however, the country is more homogeneous; about 99 percent of all Moroccans are Sunni Moslems.

The last hereditary monarchy in North Africa, the country is ruled by King Hassan II, who belongs to an Arab dynasty that claims to have descended from the Prophet Muhammad. For the past 15 years, King Hassan has conducted a campaign to annex the region south of Morocco (known as the Western Sahara), which until 1975 was controlled by Spain. However, the Polisario, an insurgent movement supported by Algeria, has resisted Moroccan control of the Western Sahara and seeks, instead, independence for the region.

The essence of Moroccan culture is found less in large modern cities such as Casablanca than in the villages and smaller cities to the north and south. Renting a car or braving the bus system and heading into the Atlas Mountains or the desert of the south and west will expose you to the tribal communities and traditional way of life that is at the heart of modern Morocco. Each village has its own medina, or market, where local crafts and unusual foods are available at low prices to the practiced bargainer. And the desert, with its stunning sunsets and lush oases set amid dusty plains, remains as beautiful and exotic as ever.

Official name: Kingdom of Morocco. **Area:** 117,116 square miles (about the size of New Mexico). **Population:** 25,000,000. **Population density:** 141 inhabitants per square mile. **Capital:** Rabat (pop. 556,000). **Largest city:** Casablanca (pop. 2,158,369). **Language:** Arabic, French. **Religion:** Islam. **Per capita income:** US$750. **Currency:** Dirham. **Literacy rate:** 28%. **Average daily high/low:*** Casablanca: January, 63°/45°; July, 79°/65°. **Average number of days with precipitation:** Casablanca: January, 8; July, 0.

TRAVEL

U.S. citizens will need a passport in order to travel to Morocco; however, a visa is not required for a stay of up to three months. Check with the Embassy of Morocco (1601 21st Street NW, Washington, DC 20009) for specific requirements.

"Morocco generally isn't recommended for women traveling alone, but if you have a high adventure threshold, a low budget, and are willing to leave city comforts behind, a unique experience awaits you."
—Louise Shaughnessy, Ottawa, Ontario

Getting Around

The main north-south rail line connects Tangier, Rabat, Casablanca, and Marrakesh. Another line runs from Casablanca and Rabat to Fez and on to the Algerian border. With the exception of the air-conditioned express trains between Tangier and Casablanca, however, train travel in Morocco is slow; it is also inexpensive. In addition, the InterRail pass is valid in Morocco.

The long-distance bus network in Morocco is more extensive than its rail system. Buses are usually crowded, but they are cheap and a few are air-conditioned. Intercity service is also provided by *grandes taxis* (as opposed to *petits taxis*, which provide service only within city boundaries). Good domestic air transport is provided by Royal Air Inter, which connects all urban centers.

---

*all temperatures are Fahrenheit

Morocco's road system is comprised of generally good but narrow roads, with signs in both Arabic and French. Car rentals are available in major cities from international companies such as Hertz, Avis, and Europcar; if you rent from a local company, you'll have to haggle over price. Hitchhiking is difficult in Morocco and sometimes expensive—offers of a lift may end up costing you more than a bus fare.

"Campgrounds are conveniently located in most cities and cost very little. For those who prefer camping away from regular campgrounds, the southern coast is best. People who really want to get to know Morocco should go south anyway, since the north is full of tourists and people who try to exploit tourists; it is difficult to see how the people really live in that kind of environment."

Especially for Students and Young People

A student travel bureau, UGEM (78 rue Sebou Agdal, Rabat), distributes information on travel in Morocco and sells plane, train, and bus tickets. Holders of the International Student Identity Card are entitled to reduced rates on air fares within the country, as well as from Casablanca and Marrakesh to a number of international destinations. UGEM also arranges accommodations in university residences during the summer vacation (from July 15 to September 15).

Meeting the People

UGEM can arrange for a limited number of foreign students to live with a Moroccan family in either Safi, Marrakesh, Rabat, Fez, or Casablanca for up to four weeks. For further information, write the UGEM office in Rabat (address above) at least two months in advance of your planned visit.

For Further Information

There is no shortage of travel guidebooks written for the young independent budget traveler to Morocco. *Let's Go: Europe* ($13.95), revised annually by the Harvard Student Agencies and published by St. Martin's Press, includes a chapter on Morocco. In the same series, *Let's Go: Spain, Portugal and Morocco* ($12.95) includes more extensive information about the country. One of the best guidebooks for the independent traveler is *Morocco, Algeria and Tunisia: A Travel Survival Kit*. If you can't find it in a bookstore, you can order it for $13.95 plus $1.50 postage from Lonely Planet Publications (Embarcadero West, 112 Linden Street, Oakland, CA 94607). Finally, available in most bookstores are Frommer's *Spain and Morocco on $40 a Day* ($13.95) and the *Real Guide to Morocco* ($12.95), published by Prentice Hall. In addition, general tourist information is available from the Moroccan National Tourist Office (20 East 46th Street, Suite 503, New York, NY 10017).

WORK

It is generally quite difficult for foreigners to get work and obtain the necessary work permit. Application for the work permit must be made by the employer.

Internships/Traineeships

Programs sponsored by members of the Council on International Educational Exchange are described below. Consult Appendix I for the addresses of the institutions listed in this section.

AIESEC–US. Reciprocal internship program for students in economics, business, finance, marketing, accounting, and computer sciences. See page 18 for further information.

University of Minnesota. "Minnesota Studies in International Development." Academic year. Predeparture coursework at the U of M fall quarter, with internship in development-related research or action project in winter and spring quarters. Juniors to graduates and adults with interest in development; 2.5 GPA and French and/or Arabic required. Apply by May 15.

Study

A program offered by a member institution of the Council on International Educational Exchange is described below. Consult Appendix I for the addresses you can write for more information.

SEMESTER AND ACADEMIC YEAR

General Studies

Experiment in International Living/School for International Training. "College Semester Abroad." Rabat. Fall or spring semester. Arabic language study, life and culture seminar, independent-study project, homestay, and field trips. Sophomores to graduate students with 2.5 GPA. Apply by May 15 for fall and October 15 for spring.

TUNISIA

Even the name of Tunisia's main airport, Tunis-Carthage International, reminds arriving visitors that this nation, located at the crossroads of the Mediterranean, has a long and proud history. Phoenicians, Carthaginians, Romans, Arabs, Turks, French—all have left their mark on Tunisia.

Arab conquerers, arriving in the seventh century, called Tunisia "the green land." In fact, the relatively well-watered north, once the granary of Rome, still grows produce such as oranges and olives for the tables of Europe. But today, agriculture has been supplanted by the tourist industry and petroleum from the nearly uninhabited desert that comprises the southern two-thirds of the country as the leading contributor to the economy.

Everywhere you go you'll find streets, schools, mosques, and what-have-you named after Habib Bourguiba, the national hero who led Tunisia in its drive for independence from France in 1956 and then served as president for 31 years. Although ousted from power in 1987, his political legacy lives on in such things as the equal legal status of women and the country's ties with the West.

Today, Tunisia is a North African nation with cultural, racial, and linguistic ties to both Europe and the Middle East. This delicate balance is evident everywhere. The Avenue Habib-Bourguiba, hub of the cosmopolitan capital city of Tunis, is lined with cafés serving mint tea and French pastry, while just a few blocks from the city center is the entrance to the medina and the world of the souks, or traditional outdoor markets, which offer a dizzying array of colors, sights, and smells as well as a chance to test your bargaining skills (most Tunisians speak both Arabic and French).

But you won't want to spend all of your time in Tunis. The electric train known as the TGM is an easy and inexpensive way to get out of the city, and the ride offers a slice of Tunisian life most tourists never see. Your fellow passengers will probably strike up a conversation with you as the train whisks past the ruins of Carthage and the picturesque port city of Sidi Bou Said. The last stop will be the beaches of La Marsa. Don't be surprised to see women in bikinis, or even topless. While Islam is the religion of Tunisia, 75 years of French rule and 1.3 million tourists annually, mostly from Western Europe, have had an impact.

—*Carina Klein, New York*

Official name: Republic of Tunisia. **Area:** 63,379 square miles (about the size of Missouri). **Population:** 7,700,000. **Population density:** 122 inhabitants per square mile. **Capital and largest city:** Tunis (pop. 600,000). **Language:** Arabic, French. **Religion:** Islam. **Per capita income:** US$1,100. **Currency:** Tunisian dinar. **Literacy rate:** 64%. **Average daily high/low:*** Tunis: January, 58°/43°; July, 90°/68°. **Average number of days with precipitation:** Tunis: January, 13; July, 2.

TRAVEL

U.S. citizens will need a valid passport to travel to Tunisia; however, visas are not required for stays of up to four months. Check with the Embassy of Tunisia (2408 Massachusetts Avenue NW, Washington, DC 20008) for specific requirements.

> *"Tunisia is easily reached by ferry from Genoa, Marseille, Palermo, or Trapani. A week here can make the usual trip through Europe more of an adventure."*
> —Matt Lussenhop, Minneapolis, Minnesota

Getting Around

The Tunisian rail network serves all major and many minor cities and links the country to Algeria. Although still somewhat slow by European standards, trains are comfortable and convenient. Buses also provide intercity service,

---

*all temperatures are Fahrenheit

with prices and schedules similar to the trains. You can also travel between cities as a passenger in a *louages*, a regular automobile that serves a fixed route, departing when it is full and dropping off and picking up people along the way. In addition, Tunis Air and Tunisavia offer domestic air service between the main cities and provide transport to the remote desert communities of the south.

The country has a network of roads—both surfaced and unsurfaced—most of which are in relatively good condition. With the exception of the Tunis-Hammanet superhighway, however, they tend to be narrow. Road signs everywhere are in Arabic and French. Renting cars—either self-drive or ones with a driver—is relatively easy, although advance reservations are advisable during the summer tourist season. Bicycles and motorcycles are also available for rental in tourist areas as well as in Tunis.

> *"In Tunisia the people are extremely helpful and friendly. I mostly took buses and often wound up in small towns waiting for a connection for several hours. People would always crowd around me and want to talk. Some would offer to buy me lunch so that they could talk to me alone. In one small town, a little boy ran off to his mother and returned with a delicious steaming hot meal for me. I don't know what it was, but it was great."*

Especially for Students and Young People

Sotutour/STAV (2 Rue de Sparte, Tunis) is Tunisia's student travel bureau and ISTC member. The organization provides information on student travel and offers a variety of one-week tours, including one that involves four days of camel-trekking in the Sahara. Holders of the International Student Identity Card receive a discount on air travel from Tunis to many international destinations.

For Further Information

One of the best guidebooks for the independent, budget-minded traveler is *Morocco, Algeria and Tunisia: A Travel Survival Kit*. If you can't find it in a bookstore, you can order it for $13.95 plus $1.50 postage from Lonely Planet Publications (Embarcadero West, 112 Linden Street, Oakland, CA 94607). More readily available in bookstores are the *Let's Go* guides, geared to the young traveler on a budget. *Let's Go: Europe* ($13.95), revised annually by the Harvard Student Agencies and published by St. Martin's Press, includes only a brief chapter on Tunisia. More extensive information on the country is included in *Let's Go: Italy* ($12.95).

WORK

To hold a regular job in Tunisia, you will need a work permit; a job contract is required before applying. Generally, permits are only granted for those with skills that are not readily obtainable in Tunisia itself.

Internships/Traineeships

There are both AIESEC and IAESTE internship programs in Tunisia; see page 18 for more information.

STUDY

Although there are no study programs offered by CIEE members in Tunisia, a short term of study in the country is easy to arrange, especially at language schools, where you can take courses in French or Arabic.

"The Institut Bourguiba des Langues Vivantes (or 'Bourguiba School') is a good place to study Arabic. I was able to improve my knowledge of Arabic a great deal due to the class but mostly due to my interaction with the people. Another possibility is trading Arabic lessons for English lessons. Contacts can be made at the American Cultural Center or the British Council Library, both in downtown Tunis."
—Matt Lussenhop, Minneapolis, Minnesota

TURKEY

Turkey is a country very much in transition. It is a Muslim country but one receptive to Western influence. On the same beach, you may see a Turkish woman sunbathing in a bikini while nearby another wades in the shallow water fully dressed in heavy layers of clothing, including the traditional head scarf and long, full Turkish pants. Both will point to different interpretations of the Koran to explain their attire—or relative lack thereof. And although bars are still rare in Turkey (in most Muslim countries drinking alcohol is frowned upon), beer and an anis-like liquor called raki are produced and consumed here. For the most part, however, teahouses, rather than bars, are where people gather socially. Traditional teahouses are almost exclusively male, but, especially in the larger cities, there are many that have become used to and even cater to male and female tourists.

Turkey, one of the largest countries in the Middle East, borders on Greece, Bulgaria, the Soviet Union, Iran, Iraq, and Syria. Culturally, it is as varied as the six different countries it adjoins. Istanbul, the former capital of the Ottoman Empire and a gateway connecting Europe and Asia, is a cosmopolitan city, at once an architectural mosaic of ancient mosques and palaces, working-class neighborhoods with traditional wooden houses, and modern areas complete with skyscrapers. In the western part of the country, tourism has become an important part of the economy. This is most noticeable on the Aegean coast, with its impressive beaches and historic ruins. As you head east, the country becomes poorer and more traditional, although Ankara, the capital city located in the center of the country, is a notable exception. The villages along Turkey's northern coast, on the Black Sea, are farming and fishing communities, and the northeast is a rainy mountainous region where most of the tea that is drunk in Turkey is grown. The deserts of the southeast, near Iran and Iraq, are the home of the Kurdish-speaking people.

Though attitudes toward Westerners vary in different regions of the country, in general Turks are friendly and interested in meeting people from other countries. One of the most interesting ways to meet them is to go shopping. There are plenty of interesting goods to be bought in flea markets and shops, including the brightly colored, handwoven carpets for which the country is famous. Many areas in Turkey are known for their characteristic styles of carpets and kilims. If you express interest in one, the owner will most likely invite you to sit down and have tea with him as you discuss the carpet. Turks are great businessmen and love to haggle; you'll want to break out your bargaining skills and match wits with the owner of the carpet. Even if you don't buy it, chances are you'll wind up having a very interesting conversation while learning a lot about carpets. But watch out, you may end up the proud owner of a carpet you never realized you needed!

—Mary Leonard, New York, New York

Official name: Republic of Turkey. **Area:** 300,947 square miles (slightly larger than Texas). **Population:** 52,900,000. **Population density:** 176 inhabitants per square mile. **Capital:** Ankara (pop. 3,462,880). **Largest city:** Istanbul (pop. 5,858,558). **Language:** Turkish. **Religion:** Islam. **Per capita income:** US$1,309. **Currency:** Turkish lira. **Literacy rate:** 80%. **Average daily high/low:*** Istanbul: January, 45°/35°; July, 81°/65°. **Average number of days with precipitation:** Istanbul: January, 12; July, 3.

TRAVEL

A passport is required for U.S. citizens traveling to Turkey; however, a visa is not needed for tourists staying less than three months. Persons traveling to Turkey for reasons other than tourism are required to obtain a visa in advance, regardless of their length of stay. Check with the Embassy of the Republic of Turkey (1606 23rd Street NW, Washington, DC 20008), or with the Turkish consulate in New York or Chicago, for specific requirements.

Getting Around

Travel in Turkey is inexpensive, whether you travel by plane, bus, or train. And students often get an additional discount (see information under "Especially for Students and Young People"). Bus service is quick and comfortable as well as cheap. Train travel is generally slower and there is no service along Turkey's popular western coast. Shared taxis (called *dolmus*) follow fixed routes between cities and allow you to get off and on wherever you like. In addition, domestic fares on Turkish Airlines are reasonable. If you plan to travel to eastern Turkey, flying will allow you to avoid the 36-hour bus trip. Another option is Turkish Maritime Lines, which operates passenger ships along the Black Sea from Istanbul to Trabzon and along the Aegean Sea from Istanbul to Izmir.

> *"Northern Europeans have been flocking to the warm beaches of western and southern Turkey. Many tourists also come for the historical, archaeological, and cultural attractions of this ancient land, which has harbored varied civilizations for 30 centuries."*
> —Ugur Aker, Hiram, Ohio

---

*all temperatures are Fahrenheit

Especially for Students and Young People

There are two student travel organizations in Turkey, both of them ISTC members: 7-TUR Tourism Ltd. (Inonu Cad. 37/2, Gumussuyu-Taksim, Istanbul) and Genctur (Yerebatan Cad. 15/3, 34410 Sultanahmet, Istanbul). Both provide travel information; sell plane, train, bus, and ferry tickets; and book accommodations.

Holders of the International Student Identity Card get discounts on air fares (international destinations only) as well as train tickets (both international and domestic). In addition, they are entitled to discounts on certain tours, car rentals, hotels, museums, cinemas, and ferries to the Greek islands and along the Turkish coast. These two student travel organizations will also make reservations for students at university residences during the summer vacation.

For Further Information

General tourist information is available from the Turkish Government Tourism & Information Office, 821 United Nations Plaza, New York, NY 10017. One useful guidebook for the budget traveler is Frommer's *Turkey on $30 a Day*, which is available in most bookstores for $13.95. Another good guide is *Turkey: A Travel Survival Kit*, which can be ordered from Lonely Planet Publications (Embarcadero West, 112 Linden Street, Oakland, CA 94607) for $14.95 (plus $1.50 postage). *Let's Go: Europe* ($13.95) and *Let's Go: Greece* ($12.95) include much useful information about the entire country, not just the corner actually located in Europe.

WORK

You must enter the country on a special work visa to hold a regular job in Turkey. Application for the visa is made by the employer.

Internships/Traineeships

There are both AIESEC and IAESTE internship programs in Turkey; see page 18 for further information.

Voluntary Service

CIEE places young people in voluntary service workcamps in Turkey organized by Genctur (see address above). At these workcamps, groups of up to 20 people from various countries work on projects involving construction, gardening, or archaeology. Most camps are two weeks in length. For a small fee, workcamp participants may add an optional vacation week organized by Genctur. Volunteers must be at least 18 years old and willing to work an average of eight hours a day for two to three weeks. They receive room and board in return. The applications of U.S. residents are processed by CIEE. For more information contact the International Voluntary Service Department at CIEE.

STUDY

A program offered by a CIEE member institution is listed below. Consult Appendix I for the institution's address.

SUMMER

General Studies

Southern Illinois University at Carbondale. "Reconstructing the Past: Religion & Science in Archaic Greece." Greece and Turkey. (See Greece for description and eligibility.)

EXPLORING THE CULTURE OF TURKEY

Film

Although a large portion of Turkish filmmaking has attempted to re-create the commercial successes of Hollywood, Turkey has also produced a number of adventurous attempts to create its own film culture.

Yilmaz Guney, a leading actor in over 100 Turkish films, many of them Hollywood imitations, was also a prolific screenwriter and director. In his own films he addressed the social concerns of modern-day Turkey. The contradictions and conflicts of values in modern Turkey are the focus of much of his work including *Yol*, *The Herd*, and *The Enemy*. Internal immigration in search of a means of living is a recurring theme in *Elegy, Hope, Anxiety, The Herd*, and *The Father*. Other themes pervading his films are social attitudes toward sexuality, women, revolt, and responsibility.

Other directors attempting to forge a specifically Turkish film culture include Metin Erksan (*Dry Summer* and *I Cannot Live Without You*) and Omer Kavur (*Yusuf* and *Kenan*). In addition, several Turkish filmmakers have taken to making films in exile in response to the political restrictions at home. Significant among these is Tunc Okan whose film, *The Bus*, is a story about migrant Turkish workers in Germany who are swindled by a fellow countryman and end up isolated and deserted in Sweden.

CHAPTER NINE
AFRICA SOUTH OF THE SAHARA

A vast continent, Africa offers the visitor an array of impressions and experiences not easily forgotten. It is a region of immense cultural and linguistic diversity, with more than 800 languages spoken. As a result, African nations—virtually all of which have come into existence as independent states only within the last 35 years—are still struggling to forge a sense of nationhood among the various ethnic groups, many with a variety of languages, cultures, and religious practices, within their boundaries. As these nations have matured, the showy industrial projects of the 1960s and early 1970s have given way to a more realistic emphasis on agrarian development and gradual industrialization. Sadly, economic growth still eludes many of the region's nations; today a disproportionate share of the countries classified by the United Nations as being in the lowest economic bracket lie in sub-Saharan Africa.

Africa offers the perceptive student, volunteer worker, and traveler the chance to experience a radically different way of life while gaining a new perspective on oneself and the world. Among those who have had the chance to experience Africa as more than just a casual tourist, few leave the continent unchanged.

"Nothing can compare to being challenged by an entirely foreign culture and world view. Rather than monuments of the past, life itself is the attraction in Africa. There is nothing like seeing it for oneself."

The Essentials

A trip to sub-Saharan Africa will be a trip off the beaten tourist path and will require some initiative and preparation. One way you can prepare is to talk to people who have traveled there, as well as to Africans who are living and studying in your community. Another way is to read some of the books you'll find recommended in this chapter. These—especially the literary works by African authors—will help put you in touch with the worlds you are about to encounter.

Before traveling to any part of Africa, be sure you understand the political realities of the region or country you're planning to visit. Unfortunately, coverage of African political news in the U.S. press is notoriously poor. Instead, you might need to turn to *Jeune Afrique, Africa News,* and *South,* periodicals that should be available in most libraries. For daily newspaper coverage of events in Africa, we refer you to *Le Monde,* the Manchester *Guardian,* and the *Christian Science Monitor.*

From time to time, the State Department issues travel advisories on the subject of travel in Africa. Borders close, governments restrict travel, borders open, and restrictions are raised. You can contact the department's Citizen's Emergency Center (see page 6) for current travel advisories that may have been issued concerning areas you are planning to visit.

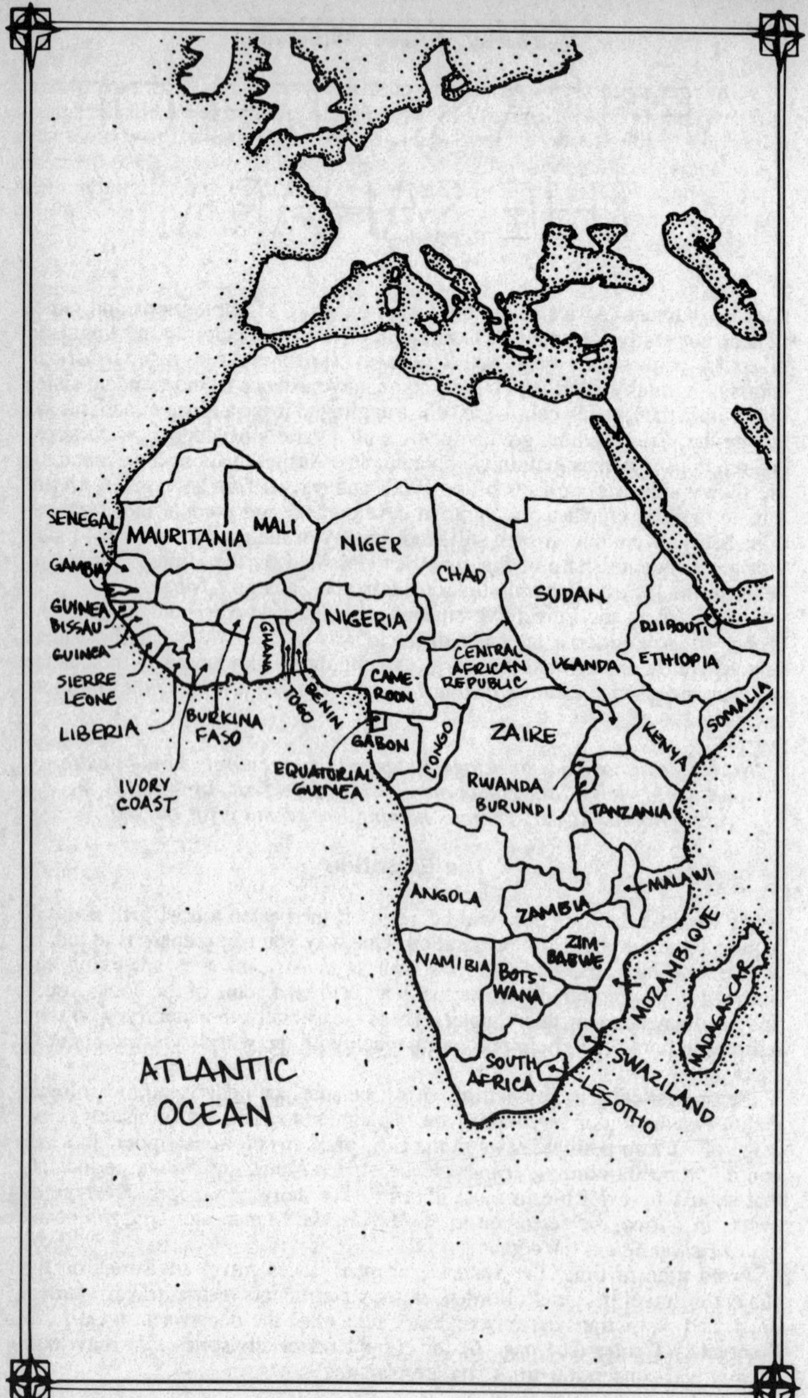
SENEGAL
MAURITANIA
MALI
NIGER
GAMBIA
CHAD
SUDAN
GUINEA
BISSAU
NIGERIA
DJIBOUTI
GUINEA
GHANA
CENTRAL
AFRICAN
REPUBLIC
UGANDA
ETHIOPIA
SIERRE
LEONE
CAME-
ROON
TOGO
BENIN
SOMALIA
LIBERIA
BURKINA
FASO
GABON
CONGO
ZAIRE
KENYA
EQUATORIAL
GUINEA
IVORY
COAST
RWANDA
BURUNDI
TANZANIA
MALAWI
ANGOLA
ZAMBIA
MOZAMBIQUE
ZIM-
BABWE
NAMIBIA
BOTS-
WANA
MADAGASCAR
SOUTH
AFRICA
SWAZILAND
LESOTHO
ATLANTIC
OCEAN

Other preparations you'll need to make involve health. For travel to many of the countries of sub-Saharan Africa, you are required to be vaccinated against smallpox, yellow fever, cholera, typhoid, and polio. It is best to contact your local public health service office for details on the latest health requirements for individual countries; information is also available from the major international air carriers as well as from the consulates of each country. See also the health publications listed in Chapter 2.

"Having been in Africa for some time, I feel a great need to stress health precautions. Often governments out here will not admit that an outbreak of some epidemic exists for fear that it will keep out tourists or show that the government can't cope with health affairs. There are often outbreaks of cholera and polio. Walking barefoot should be discouraged because of the danger of catching hookworms and the Chigoe flea. Furthermore, most fresh water bodies south of the Sahara are infested with bilharzia—you can't just jump in for an impromptu swim. And malaria pills are a must out here."

To gain entry into most African countries, you will also have to show proof of return or onward transportation. An airline ticket will suffice, and in most cases a Miscellaneous Charge Order (MCO), a voucher issued by most airlines and considered equal to a ticket, will also serve as proof.

In addition to your passport, you'll need a visa to enter most countries of sub-Saharan Africa. Visas can be obtained in the United States at the embassy or a consulate of the country you are traveling to; in most cases, your passport must accompany the visa application. Since it may take from 10 days to three weeks for a visa to be processed, you will want to start collecting the necessary visas well before your departure date. It's also possible to obtain visas in some African countries for others; if you plan to apply for visas in Africa, be sure to pack plenty of extra passport photos. You'll find information about visas in the individual country sections later in this chapter. Listed below are the addresses where you can get visa information for countries not covered in the separate sections of this chapter:

- Embassy of the People's Republic of Benin, 2737 Cathedral Avenue NW, Washington, DC 20008
- Embassy of the Republic of Botswana, 4301 Connecticut Avenue, Suite 404, Washington, DC 20008
- Embassy of the Republic of Burkina Faso, 2340 Massachusetts Avenue NW, Washington, DC 20008
- Embassy of the Republic of Burundi, 2727 Connecticut Avenue NW, Washington, DC 20009
- Embassy of the Republic of Cape Verde, 1120 Connecticut Avenue NW, Washington, DC 20036
- Embassy of the Central African Republic, 1618 22nd Street NW, Washington, DC 20008
- Embassy of the Republic of Chad, 1901 Spruce Drive NW, Washington, DC 20012
- Embassy of the Republic of the Congo, 4891 Colorado Avenue NW, Washington, DC 20011
- Permanent Mission of Equatorial Guinea to the United Nations, 801 Second Avenue, New York, NY 10017

- Embassy of Ethiopia, 2134 Kalorama Road NW, Washington, DC 20008
- Embassy of the Gabonese Republic, 2034 20th Street NW, Washington, DC 20009
- Embassy of the Republic of Guinea, 2112 Leroy Place NW, Washington, DC 20008
- Embassy of the Kingdom of Lesotho, 1601 Connecticut Avenue NW, Caravel Building, Suite 300, Washington, DC 20009
- Embassy of the Democratic Republic of Madagascar, 2374 Massachusetts Avenue NW, Washington, DC 20008
- Embassy of the Republic of Mali, 2130 R Street NW, Washington, DC 20008
- Embassy of the Islamic Republic of Mauritania, 2129 Leroy Place NW, Washington, DC 20008
- Embassy of the Republic of Rwanda, 1714 New Hampshire Avenue NW, Washington, DC 20009
- Permanent Mission of Sao Tome and Principe to the United Nations, 801 Second Avenue, Room 1504, New York, NY 10017
- Embassy of the Somali Democratic Republic, Suite 710, 600 New Hampshire Avenue NW, Washington, DC 20037
- Embassy of the Republic of the Sudan, 600 New Hampshire Avenue NW, Washington, DC 20037
- Embassy of the Kingdom of Swaziland, 4301 Connecticut Avenue NW, Washington, DC 20008
- Embassy of the Republic of Uganda, 5909 16th Street NW, Washington, DC 20011
- Embassy of the Republic of Zaire, 1800 New Hampshire Avenue NW, Washington, DC 20009

"Some borders are easy and some are hard. I met someone who was turned back at the Zimbabwe border for insufficient funds—she had $900 and a ticket for an overland truck trip back."

Getting There

There are APEX fares from the U.S. to major African cities such as Lagos and Nairobi. Sample *one-way* fares available during the summer of 1989 are listed below. For more up-to-date information, check with a Council Travel office (see listing of locations on pages ix–xi).

New York–Nairobi, $520
Los Angeles–Nairobi, $600
New York–Lagos, $568
New York–Dakar, $933

However, the least expensive way of getting to most major African cities is via Europe. Students and young people are eligible for special discounted fares between Europe and Africa. These can be booked at any Council Travel office or a student travel bureau in Europe. Regulations vary depending on the airline but generally holders of the International Student Identity Card (see page 8) or the International Youth Identity Card (see page 9) are eligible. Sample *one-way* student fares available during the summer of 1989 are listed below:

London–Nairobi, $435
Paris–Abidjan, $349
Frankfurt–Johannesburg, $534
London–Lagos, $349

Traveling Around Africa

"I spent a great deal of time in West Africa: Senegal, the Ivory Coast, Cameroon, and the Gambia are among the most stable and best organized on the continent. There's a good tourist infrastructure at various price levels throughout these countries. Attractions include the rich tribal traditions maintained in the interior, game preserves, vibrant modern cities, and attractive beaches with camping on some. The confluence of Islam, colonial Western civilization, and a quest for an appropriate indigenous modernity make West Africa especially compelling for visitors."

If you're going to cover long distances within Africa and your time is short, you'll probably have to fly. Air travel within Africa is fairly expensive, so it's important when you make your initial reservation that you book a seat to the farthest point you are traveling to and arrange your intermediary travel via stopovers. If you wait until you're in Nairobi to decide you want to go to Johannesburg, your costs may be double what they'd have been if you'd booked through to Johannesburg with a stopover in Nairobi.

Some countries boast good intercity bus service similar to what you're accustomed to in the United States. However, in most countries crowded vehicles—cars, trucks, vans, or pickups of various types—that collect passengers at a fixed starting point and start their trip when they have a full load serve as the chief means of transport. Following a fixed route, they drop off and pick up passengers along the way. A truck with wooden benches and a roof may not be the most comfortable means of transport, but they're popular with Africans and good places to meet the people of the country you're visiting.

"I like traveling on top of trucks—the fresh air is nice. Just be sure to watch for low-lying branches."

Train travel in Africa is reasonably inexpensive and reliable. The railroads were built for colonial purposes—to transport raw materials from the interior of Africa to the coast, where they could be shipped off to other parts of the world. As a result, you won't be able to travel along the coast by rail, but in most countries you will find lines running from the coastal capital cities into the interior. Some of these lines will treat you to some spectacular scenery along the way. If you want to meet Africans and travel cheaply, trains are perhaps your best bet.

Visitors rarely rent cars in Africa; Kenya and South Africa are the only exceptions. In most countries, if you want a car you'll have to rent one with a driver—usually a relatively expensive option.

"One thing you must have in order to survive a long trip overland in Africa is patience. Things don't run on schedule. People with tight travel schedules will face nothing but frustration. Having to wait for a day or two for a connecting bus, train, or ship is the rule here."

Eating and Sleeping

Africa has an abundance of cheap places to stay, many of which are listed in the guidebooks published by Lonely Planet Publications (see page 258). Another source of information on accommodations in most major cities is the local tourist office, which will be centrally located and easy to find. In addition, the second volume of the *International Youth Hostel Handbook* lists hostels in Kenya and a few other countries (see page 50). For information on youth hostels in South Africa, write to the South African Youth Hostels Association, P.O. Box 4402, Cape Town 8000.

Especially for Students and Young People

Aside from South Africa and Ghana (see information in the individual country sections that follow), there are no national student travel bureaus operating in Africa south of the Sahara. Thus, unless you are going to one of these two countries, you won't find student discount programs specially designated for holders of the International Student Identity Card (ISIC). However, obtaining the card will allow you to take advantage of student air fares from Europe to Africa. And although you certainly won't be able to count on it being as recognized in Africa as it is in Europe, the ISIC may allow you to take advantage of any special discounts for students that you do come across.

Organized Tours

For persons interested in an organized educational tour to Africa, a couple of programs sponsored by a CIEE member are listed below.

Western Michigan University.
"East Africa: Journey of Discovery." Kenya and Tanzania. One-month summer tour. Physically fit adults and students. Apply by March 15.
"Kenya Adventure." Nairobi and various national parks. Two and a half weeks in summer. Adults and students over 18. Apply by April 1.

Work

The ministries of education of the various African countries often have information on teaching positions in their high schools and universities. A university degree is required and teaching certification or experience is helpful; three-year contracts are common. For the address of the ministry of education in the country you are interested in, contact its embassy or a consulate.

"College students interested in teaching should think about the option of teaching in Africa for a few years. African students are hardworking, appreciative, and eager to know about America. Teaching in Zimbabwe, I got valuable teaching experience, an inside look at a fascinating continent, lasting friendships with Africans, and the opportunity to travel to neighboring countries. There were some hardships to face—you have to be resourceful—but, beyond a doubt, it was the most interesting two years of my life."
—Elizabeth Grossi, New York, New York

Another option is voluntary service. To help fill the great need for technical and educational assistance in Africa, a number of organizations based in the United States operate programs there, and many place volunteers in these programs. Some of these are church related, while others are privately run or government agencies. Most of the voluntary service organizations listed in Chapter 3 (including the Peace Corps) make placements in African countries. The Council's publication *Volunteer! The Comprehensive Guide to Voluntary Service in the U.S. and Abroad* (see page 29) will also give you excellent leads on voluntary-service programs in Africa. While some service programs will require you to have technical skills and/or teaching experience, others will accept you without any previous experience.

There are also a number of internship/traineeship possibilities in Africa. In the individual country sections that follow, you'll find information on programs offered by member institutions and organizations of CIEE. In addition to these listings, there are IAESTE trainee programs in Lesotho and the Sudan; see page 18 for more information.

Study

There are a growing number of study programs in Africa sponsored by U.S. institutions and designed primarily for American students. You'll find the study programs of CIEE-member universities listed in the country sections that follow. It's also possible for a well-qualified American undergraduate to enroll directly in an African university. Graduate students planning to conduct research in an African country must notify its government of their plans and obtain the proper visa before going; in most African countries, research is not possible on a tourist visa.

For Further Information

The best guidebooks on Africa are those published by Lonely Planet Publications. *Africa on a Shoestring* ($24.95), by Alex Newton, contains 1,170 pages of detailed information on more than 50 African countries. Like all Lonely Planet publications on Africa, it's geared to independent travelers on a budget. Alex Newton is also the author of *West Africa: A Travel Survival Kit* ($12.95) and *Central Africa: A Travel Survival Kit* ($10.95). Two other Lonely Planet guidebooks of interest are *East Africa: A Travel Survival Kit* ($9.95), by Geoff Crowther, and *Madagascar and the Comoros: A Travel Survival Kit* ($10.95), by Robert Wilcox. There's also *Egypt and the Sudan: A Travel Survival Kit* (described in the Egypt section of the previous chapter). If you can't find these in a bookstore, you can order them (adding $1.50 postage per book) from Lonely Planet Publications, Embarcadero West, 112 Linden Street, Oakland, CA 94607.

CAMEROON

This central African country perhaps offers more diversity than any other nation of Africa. The European powers that divided the continent among themselves in the late 19th century created in Cameroon a nation of more than 150 different ethnic groups. And the land itself varies from rain forest near its muggy Atlantic coast to desert in the north and cool mountain highlands in various areas in between.

Present-day Cameroon is shaped by both its complex ethnic makeup and a long and varied history of colonial rule. Germany unified the region into a protectorate in 1884, and then France and Britain divided the area following the Second World War (giving Cameroon its two official languages). Since independence and the rejoining of the British and French sections of Cameroon in 1961, tribal differences have been used as an excuse for heavy-handed and authoritarian rule by its various presidents.

Official name: Republic of Cameroon. **Area:** 183,569 square miles (about three-quarters the size of Texas). **Population:** 10,500,000. **Population density:** 57 inhabitants per square mile. **Capital:** Yaoundé (pop. 583,500). **Largest city:** Douala (pop. 852,700). **Language:** French and English (both official), Foulbé, Bamiléke, Ewondo, Donala, Mungaka, Bassa. **Religion:** Christianity, Islam, animism. **Per capita income:** US$850. **Currency:** Franc CFA. **Literacy rate:** 55%. **Average daily high/low:*** Yaoundé: January, 85°/67°; July, 80°/66°. **Average number of days with precipitation:** Yaoundé: January, 3; July, 11.

TRAVEL

U.S. citizens visiting the country need a passport and a visa. In addition, a return/onward ticket is required as well as a financial guarantee from a bank. For specific regulations, check with the Embassy of the Republic of Cameroon (2349 Massachusetts Avenue NW, Washington, DC 20008).

Getting Around

Road transportation is generally poor; most roads, even those between major cities, are gravel or packed dirt. As a result, after heavy storms traffic is often held up for three or four hours. Buses are few and far between; public transport consists mainly of shared taxis or trucks. A rail line links Douala and Yaoundé and goes on into the interior; service is slow and infrequent, but provides a cheap and interesting way to travel.

> *"Getting around Cameroon by bus, train, and shared taxi can be tough going, but it's well worth the experience."*
> —Neale MacMillan, Ottawa, Canada

WORK

Internships/Traineeships

There is an AIESEC internship program in Cameroon; see page 18 for more information.

---

*all temperatures are Fahrenheit

STUDY

A program offered by a CIEE member institution is described below. Consult Appendix I for the address where you can write for more information.

SEMESTER AND ACADEMIC YEAR

General Studies

Experiment in International Living/School for International Training. "College Semester Abroad." Yaoundé. Fall or spring semester. French language training, excursions, village stay, seminar on Cameroonian culture, homestay, and independent-study project. Sophomores to graduate students, 2.5 GPA. Apply by May 15 for fall and by October 15 for spring.

GHANA

The first European colony below the Sahara to achieve independence, Ghana was established in 1957 when the British relinquished control of the territory they had called the Gold Coast. The new country was named after an ancient African empire that flourished over a thousand years ago.

The new nation and its charismatic leader Kwame Nkrumah set an inspiring example for the nationalist movements that swept the entire African continent in the years that followed. Sadly, Nkrumah's achievements were offset by corruption and mismanagement, and in 1966 he was overthrown by a military coup. After suffering through a number of incompetent and corrupt governments, the economy all but collapsed. Since 1983, however, Ghana has staged a remarkable turnaround. Today, the government is rebuilding roads and ports, farmers are reclaiming abandoned farms and expanding production, and idle factories have resumed operations.

Official name: Republic of Ghana. **Area:** 92,100 square miles (about the size of Wyoming). **Population:** 14,400,000. **Population density:** 156 persons per square mile. **Capital and largest city:** Accra (pop. 859,600). **Language:** English, Twi, Fanti, Ga, Ewe, Dagbani. **Religion:** Christianity, animism, Islam. **Per capita income:** US$380. **Currency:** Cedi. **Literacy rate:** 45%. **Average daily high/low:*** Accra: January, 87°/73°; July, 81°/73°. **Average number of days with precipitation:** Accra: January, 1; July, 4.

TRAVEL

For U.S. citizens, both a passport and a visa are required. You'll also need an onward or return ticket and a financial guarantee from a bank to cover your stay in the country. Finally, a certificate of immunization against yellow fever

---

*all temperatures are Fahrenheit

and cholera is required. For specific regulations, check with the Embassy of the Republic of Ghana (2460 16th Street NW, Washington, DC 20009).

Getting Around

There are domestic flights from Accra to three interior cities. In addition, a railway network consisting of three lines serves the southern part of the country. Most Ghanaians, however, travel either by bus or "mammy truck." The government-operated bus system provides inexpensive, punctual service on comfortable buses that serve numerous routes throughout the country. Mammy trucks are vans or pickup trucks equipped with unpadded seats and packed with people and all manner of goods; they provide inexpensive if uncomfortable travel to villages and towns all over the country.

Especially for Students and Young People

Ghana is one of the few African countries with a student travel organization. Student and Youth Travel Services (SYTAG), P.O. Box 14337, Accra (located at the Accra Community Centre, High Street, Accra), can book cheap accommodations in several cities in Ghana, issue the International Student Identity Card (ISIC), and arrange local tours. Holders of the ISIC are entitled to reduced domestic and international air fares as well as discounts at some shops, museums, theaters, and cultural events.

WORK

Internships/Traineeships

There are both AIESEC and IAESTE internship programs in Ghana; see page 18 for more information.

Voluntary Service

The International Ecumenical Workcamp, a voluntary-service workcamp in Ghana, provides young people (ages 18–35) from all over the world the opportunity to work on a rural development construction project. The term of service is four weeks. Apply by May 1 to International Christian Youth Exchange (see Appendix I for address).

For persons interested in longer-term voluntary-service work, the same organization's "Year Abroad Program" offers persons ages 18–24 voluntary service opportunities in the fields of health care, education, the environment, construction, et cetera. See page 22 for more information.

EXPLORING THE CULTURE OF GHANA

Literature

A number of novels dealing with the important changes that have swept Ghana in recent years are available in English. One is Margaret Laurence's *This Side of Jordan*, which depicts the language, customs, daily life, and race relations at the time of independence. Ayi Kwei Armah, one of Ghana's most prominent writers, is the author of *Two Thousand Seasons*, in which he reconstructs one thousand years of African history, and *The Beautyful Ones Are Not Yet Born*, which deals with political corruption in a newly independent African nation, among other books. *This Earth, My Brother*, by the poet and novelist Kofi Awoonor, is an allegorical novel in which a lawyer searches for meaning and identity in post-colonial Africa. Her novel *Our Sister Killjoy* is also worth taking the time to track down. For those interested in poetry and theater, there are J.C. DeGrafts's *Beneath the Jazz and Blues* and *Muntu: A Play*.

IVORY COAST

Côte d'Ivoire, or the Ivory Coast, is probably the most cosmopolitan nation in West Africa. Centrally situated on the Gulf of Guinea and dominated by the French for more than three centuries, it was once a major export center for ivory, slaves, and other "commodities." Today its residents include about 30,000 French nationals, many Lebanese and Vietnamese, and even ambassadors from both the P.L.O. and Israel.

In Abidjan, the nation's capital, the shining clusters of skyscrapers, the luxurious hotels, the dozens of European banks, and the superhighways swooping over the estuaries cannot quite obscure the city's slums. No other nation in West Africa so dramatically embodies the contrasts between rich and poor, new and old.

The contrast is particularly dramatic because of the enormous wealth of those who are rich. Imported luxury cars are surprisingly common in the streets of Abidjan. Cash crops such as cocoa, rubber, pineapples, and bananas are grown on giant plantations near the coast—many of them owned by President-for-life Felix Houphouet-Boigny, who is believed to be a billionaire. The president recently has been busy overseeing the relocation of the capital from Abidjan to Yamoussoukro, the former village—now a city—where he was born, and the government is spending hundreds of millions of dollars to make the new capital a monument to his rule. Meanwhile, political groups and the press are struggling for freedom of expression, and no one knows what will happen when the president, who is in his late 80s, eventually dies.

Houphouet's rule has achieved some notable successes, however. Poverty in the Ivory Coast is less severe than in nearby countries such as Guinea and Liberia. Most years, villagers are able to grow ample supplies of staples such as corn and yams, cassavas and tomatoes. In addition, most of the country has electricity, potable water supplies, and well-funded schools run by government-supplied teachers.

The Ivory Coast even has smooth highways linking the different parts of the country together. Part of this has been due to luck; its main export, cocoa, has been more profitable in recent years than the exportable commodities other West African nations rely on.

Ivorians are justifiably proud of their artisanship. They specialize in linen tapestries painted with folk-art animal designs, cotton textiles in bright colors, silver filigree jewelry, and striking wooden sculptures of animals. Abidjan also has some of the largest cassette tape outlets you may ever come across.

Any traveler to the Ivory Coast should try to get out of Abidjan to see the rest of the country. The intercity bus system is excellent. And urban Ivorians will jump at the chance to take a visitor to their ancestral village. Don't turn them down.

—*Jason Zweig, New York, New York*

Official name: Republic of Côte d'Ivoire. **Area:** 124,502 square miles (about the size of New Mexico). **Population:** 11,200,000. **Population density:** 90 inhabitants per square mile. **Capital and largest city:** Abidjan (pop. 686,000). **Language:** French, Diaula. **Religion:** Animism, Christianity, Islam. **Per capita income:** US$772. **Currency:** Franc CFA. **Literacy rate:** 35%. **Average daily high/low:*** Abidjan: January, 88°/73°; July, 83°/83°. **Average number of days with precipitation:** Abidjan: January, 3; July, 12.

TRAVEL

U.S. citizens will need a passport and a visa. An onward or return ticket, a financial guarantee sufficient to cover your stay in the country, and proof of yellow fever vaccination are also required. For specific requirements contact the Embassy of the Republic of Côte d'Ivoire (2424 Massachusetts Avenue NW, Washington, DC 20008).

Getting Around

The Ivory Coast has one of the best internal transportation systems in all of West Africa. Air Ivorie provides good service from Abidjan to the country's other major cities. Luxury buses also link the major cities, which are connected by a relatively well maintained system of roads. Bush taxis—which can be either cars or minibuses—provide service throughout the country. In addition, a single rail line crosses the country north from Abidjan to Ouagadougou in Burkina Faso, and is a good way of getting to many towns in the interior.

WORK

Internships/Traineeships

There is an AIESEC internship program in the Ivory Coast; see page 18 for more information.

STUDY

A study program offered by a CIEE member institution is described below. Consult Appendix I for the address where you can write for more information.

---

*all temperatures are Fahrenheit

SEMESTER AND ACADEMIC YEAR

General Studies

International Student Exchange Program. Direct reciprocal exchange between U.S. universities and the Université Nationale de Côte d'Ivoire. Academic year. Full curriculum options. Open only to students at ISEP member institutions.

KENYA

Friendly people, a stable government, and spectacular natural beauty have made Kenya one of Africa's most popular tourist destinations. Vital to the country's economy, tourism is promoted by the government and fairly well developed. But, while thousands of tourists visit the large game parks, most parts of the country still offer adventuresome travelers the opportunity to explore Africa well off the beaten tourist circuit.

Throughout the country you'll be greeted by a warm and friendly *"Jambo,"* the customary Swahili greeting. Kiswahili is the official language, but English is widely spoken, especially in Nairobi, one of the larger metropolitan centers on the African continent. While most of the population is Christian, many people continue to adhere to traditional religious beliefs and there is a sizable Muslim community along the coast.

Although there are over forty different ethnic groups in the country, political stability has been the rule over the twenty-seven years since Kenya gained its independence from Great Britain in 1963. The first president, Jomo Kenyatta, instituted a policy of *harambee*, or a pulling together of all people, to build a unified independent state, and Kenya emerged as a pro-Western country with a capitalist economy. But poverty is everywhere. There has been, in addition, an enormous population increase, and some experts estimate its rate of population growth to be the highest in the world. Despite its many ties with the West, today Kenya must look inward, examine pressing domestic problems, and find the keys to furthering its economic development while maintaining its natural beauty and ethnic diversity.

—*Liz MacGonagle, Annandale, New Jersey*

Official name: Republic of Kenya. **Area:** 224,960 square miles (slightly smaller than Texas). **Population:** 23,300,000. **Population density:** 104 inhabitants per square mile. **Capital and largest city:** Nairobi (pop. 1,000,000). **Language:** Kiswahili (official), Bantu, Kikuyu, English. **Religion:** Christianity, traditional African religions. **Per capita income:** US$230. **Currency:** Kenyan shilling. **Literacy rate:** 59%. **Average daily high/low:*** Nairobi: January, 74°/54°; July, 69°/51°. **Average number of days with precipitation:** January, 5; July, 6.

---

*all temperatures are Fahrenheit

TRAVEL

U.S. citizens need a passport and a visa. For specific requirements, check with the Embassy of the Republic of Kenya (2249 R Street NW, Washington, DC 20008).

Getting Around

Bus service extends to all parts of the country, and is provided by an array of vehicles, ranging from comfortable air-conditioned buses on a few main routes to *matatus*, rundown and crowded minibuses usually owned by the driver or one of his relatives that provide cheap transportation on local routes. Limited train service is also available, the most famous being the run between Mombasa and Nairobi. In addition, there are a number of small domestic airlines that provide fairly inexpensive service to the various regions of the country.

The majority of people in rural areas travel by flagging down a vehicle—whether it's a *matatu*, a truck, or a car. Generally speaking, when offered a ride you are expected to pay a small amount to the driver. At the other extreme pricewise, you can rent your own car or jeep in Nairobi or Mombasa (the minimum age is usually 23). Your U.S. driver's license is valid in Kenya, but remember to stay on the lefthand side of the road. Kenya's famed game reserves and national parks are accessible to motorists driving their own cars, but most choose to see them as part of an organized tour of some sort.

"Be ready for adventure! Leave your curling irons and hairspray at home. This is a country where material possessions don't matter except for your camera and a lot of film. Be prepared for a challenge. People are friendly and you may find yourself overwhelmed with people willing to give you the shirt off their back. The real challenge is when you find you have to take off your shield and mask in order to learn about these down-to-earth people. The final challenge comes when you have to return home."
—Sean P. Hinchey, Glastonbury, Connecticut

For Further Information

General information is available from the Kenya Tourist Office, 424 Madison Avenue, New York, NY 10017. A good guidebook for adventurous travelers who really want to get to know the country is *The Real Guide to Kenya*, published by Prentice Hall ($12.95). Another useful guidebook is Fodor's *Kenya*, which you'll find in many bookstores.

WORK

The Reformed Church in America, a member organization of CIEE, has elementary school teaching positions available in remote areas of Kenya that involve teaching the children of missionaries. Applicants should be college graduates with a Christian commitment. See Appendix I for the address where you can write for more information.

Internships/Traineeships

Programs sponsored by CIEE members are described below. Consult Appendix I for the addresses of the institutions listed in this section.

AIESEC–US. Reciprocal internship program for students in economics, business, finance, marketing, accounting, and computer sciences. See page 18 for further information.

Association for International Practical Training. "IAESTE Trainee Program." On-the-job training for undergraduate and graduate students in technical fields such as engineering, computer science, agriculture, architecture, and mathematics. See page 18 for more information.

University of Minnesota. "Minnesota Studies in International Development." Nairobi. Academic year. Predeparture coursework at the U of M fall quarter with internship in development-related research or action project in winter and spring quarters. Juniors to graduates and adults with interest in development and 2.5 GPA. Apply by May 15.

Voluntary Service

For persons interested in voluntary service work, the "Year Abroad Program" sponsored by the International Christian Youth Exchange offers persons ages 18–24 voluntary service opportunities in the fields of health care, education, the environment, construction, et cetera. See page 22 for more information.

Persons interested in voluntary service as teachers can contact WorldTeach, a nonprofit program which annually places nearly a hundred recent college graduates in schools in Kenya. Volunteers must commit themselves to a one-year teaching assignment but no teaching training or experience is required. They receive an allowance of $72 a month but pay a program fee of about $3,000 that includes air fare, orientation, and insurance. For more information, contact, WorldTeach, Phillip Brooks House, Harvard University, Cambridge, MA 02138.

STUDY

The following are the educational programs offered by member institutions of the Council on International Educational Exchange. Consult Appendix I for the addresses where you can write for more information. In addition to those listed below, Pennsylvania State University and the University of California system offer programs open to their own students only.

SEMESTER AND ACADEMIC YEAR

Coastal Studies

Experiment in International Living/School for International Training. Lamu, Nairobi, Zanzibar (Tanzania). Fall or spring semester. Intensive Swahili language, academic seminar, independent-study project, village studies, and homestays. Sophomores to graduate students with 2.5 GPA. Apply by May 15 for fall and October 15 for spring.

General Studies

Experiment in International Living/School for International Training. Nairobi. Fall or spring semester. Intensive language study, independent-study project, and seminar in Kenyan life, culture, and rural development. Excursions and homestay. Sophomores to graduate students with 2.5 GPA. Apply by May 15 for fall and October 15 for spring.

Friends World College. "East African Studies." Machakos, Nairobi, and Lamu. Semester or academic year. African studies, Swahili language, and individualized program combining independent study and fieldwork or internships. Sophomores, juniors, and seniors. Others may participate on noncredit basis. Apply by May 1 for fall and November 15 for spring.

International Student Exchange Program. Direct reciprocal exchange between U.S. universities and Kenyatta University. Academic year. Full curriculum options. Open only to students at ISEP member institutions.

Kalamazoo College. "Kalamazoo College in Kenya." Nairobi. Study at the University of Nairobi. Academic year or fall and winter quarter. Juniors and seniors with 3.0 GPA. Residence in Kalamazoo during summer prior to study abroad. Apply by February 15.

St. Lawrence University. "Kenya Semester Program." Nairobi. Fall or spring semester. Includes a one-month internship with a private or public agency. Apply by February 20 for fall and October 10 for spring.

SUMMER

Environmental Studies

Experiment in International Living/School for International Training. "Summer Academic Study Abroad." Nairobi and field sites. Survival Swahili language, academic seminar, homestay, field visits. Freshmen to seniors. Apply by March 15.

EXPLORING THE CULTURE OF KENYA

Literature

A number of Europeans have written about their experiences living in Kenya. Elspeth Huxley's *Flame Trees of Thika*, for example, is about her life growing up as the daughter of British settlers in Thika near Nairobi; *The Mottled Lizard* and *Out in the Midday Sun* are its sequels. *Out of Africa*, by Isak Dinesen, is an autobiographical tale of the Danish writer's experiences as a coffee plantation owner in Kenya early in this century. Another book that looks at the relationships of Africans and Europeans under colonialism, but from the point of view of an African, is Mugu R. Gatheru's autobiography, *Child of Two Worlds*. Gatheru, who is the son of a tribal ritualist, finally was able to become a professor of African history but only after studying in Kenya, India, Britain, and America.

The Mau Mau rebellion, which helped end colonial rule in Kenya, is dealt with in *Mau Mau Detainee*, by J.M. Kariuki, a Kikuyu tribesman and participant in the uprising. Meja Mwangi's *Carcass for Hounds* is also set in the

Laikipia district during the rebellion. More recently, Ngugi Wa Thiong'o's *Matigari* is about a freedom fighter's emergence from the forest after the rebellion to look for the "new" Kenya. In fact, Thiong'o is probably the most important novelist in East Africa today. *A Grain of Wheat*, one of his earlier works, deals with Kenya's struggle for independence. His Marxist views are apparent in *The River Between*, a novel about two young people separated by different beliefs and backgrounds. *Petals of Blood*, perhaps Thiong'o's best known work, presents his view of contemporary Kenya. Still another worthwhile novel for those who want to understand modern Kenya is Ngugi Wa Mirri's *I Will Marry When I Want To*.

In addition, there are a couple of nonfiction works worthy of mention for the insights they present into the lives of today's Kenyans. Tepit Ole Saitoti's *The World of the Maasai* examines the complexities of that traditional society as it struggles to survive in the midst of contemporary Kenya. *Three Swahili Women: Life Histories*, by Sarah Mirza and Margaret Strobel, presents a picture of life in the coastal region of the country.

LIBERIA

Liberia is a product of American "colonizers," freed black slaves from the United States who migrated to Africa in the 19th century. (The name of the country comes from the word *liberty* and its capital, Monrovia, is named after James Monroe.) Not surprisingly, the cultural differences between native Africans and African-American settlers were tremendous. For much of its recent history, the Liberians of American ancestry—who account for only three percent of the population—have dominated the political and economic life of the country. Rioting in 1979 and a military coup in 1980 finally broke the hold of this elite, however, and the country is now ruled by a military strongman from one of the numerous indigenous ethnic groups that comprise the majority of the country's population.

Since 1980, Liberia, which for decades was the most prosperous nation of West Africa, has been in the throes of one of the worst economic declines in Africa. Ethnic tensions and government corruption have compounded the problem. But Liberia's close political, economic, and cultural ties to the United States remain intact. Perhaps because of this, Americans generally find the people of Liberia among the friendliest and easiest to get to know of all the people of Africa.

Official name: Republic of Liberia. **Area:** 43,000 square miles (about the size of Louisiana). **Population:** 2,500,000. **Population density:** 58 inhabitants per square mile. **Capital and largest city:** Monrovia (pop. 425,000). **Language:** English (official), various African languages. **Religion:** Animism, Islam, Christianity. **Per capita income:** US$470. **Currency:** Liberian dollar. **Literacy rate:** 35%. **Average daily high/low:*** Monrovia: January, 86°/73°; July, 80°/72°. **Average number of days with precipitation:** Monrovia: January, 5; July, 24.

---

*all temperatures are Fahrenheit

TRAVEL

U.S. citizens need a passport and a visa. A yellow fever vaccination and medical certificate attesting to the traveler's good health are also required. For specific requirements, contact the Embassy of the Republic of Liberia (5201 16th Street NW, Washington, DC 20011).

Getting Around

Unlike most African countries, intercity bus service in Liberia is almost nonexistent. Instead, public transportation around the country is provided almost exclusively by bush taxis, which may be cars, converted pickup trucks, or small vans or minibuses.

WORK

Internships/Traineeships

There is an AIESEC internship program in Liberia; see page 18 for more information.

Voluntary Service

For persons interested in voluntary service work, the "Year Abroad Program" sponsored by the International Christian Youth Exchange offers persons ages 18–24 voluntary service opportunities in the fields of health care, education, the environment, construction, et cetera. See page 22 for more information.

STUDY

A study program offered by a CIEE member institution is described below. Consult Appendix I for the address where you can write for further information.

SEMESTER OR ACADEMIC YEAR

General Studies

Kalamazoo College. "Kalamazoo in Liberia." Suacoco. Study at Cuttington University College. Fall semester (August 1–December 20). Four weeks orientation at Kalamazoo prior to going abroad. Juniors and seniors with 2.75 GPA. Apply by February 15.

MALAWI

Malawi is a sliver of densely populated land stretching along the western shore of Lake Nyasa (Lake Malawi) in Southern Africa. Although water forms much of its border, the country is nevertheless landlocked, with no direct access to the ocean. Due to an ongoing civil war in Mozambique and erratic rail and road transport in Tanzania, most of Malawi's international trade (including its chief export, tobacco) must pass in a circuitous route through Zambia, Zimbabwe, and South Africa.

Dr. H. Kamuzu Banda, who has taken the title of president-for-life, has led the country since it gained its independence from Britain in 1964. Under his leadership, the country has emphasized agricultural rather than industrial development. As a result, Malawi produces an adequate supply of food for its people and has not been as adversely affected by problems of debt, economic recession, and malnutrition as have most African countries.

Official name: Republic of Malawi. **Area:** 45,747 square miles (about the size of Pennsylvania). **Population:** 7,700,000. **Population density:** 168 inhabitants per square mile. **Capital:** Lilongwe (pop. 202,900). **Largest city:** Blantyre (pop. 378,100). **Language:** English (official), Chichewa. **Religion:** Christianity, traditional African religions, Islam. **Per capita income:** US $170. **Currency:** Kwacha. **Literacy rate:** 25%. **Average daily high/low:*** Zomba: January, 85°/65°; July, 72°/53°. **Average number of days with precipitation:** Zomba: January, 21; July, 3.

TRAVEL

U.S. citizens need a passport; however, a visa is not required for stays of up to one year. There are regulations regarding women's dress and men's hair length. For specific requirements, check with the Embassy of the Republic of Malawi (1400 20th Street NW, Washington, DC 20036).

Getting Around

In general, roads are good, with most primary roads paved and served adequately by buses. There is also a limited rail system, but trains are slow, overcrowded, and often uncomfortable. An increasingly popular way to see the country is on the steamers that run the length of Lake Malawi.

"Lake Malawi is very beautiful and is safe to swim in. There's a boat service on the lake that departs twice a week. The trip, with many stops, takes about three days and is probably the best way to travel the length of the country. Since many of the lake communities do not have road access, the appearance of the boat is the big event of the week."

STUDY

A program sponsored by a CIEE member institution is described below. Consult Appendix I for the address where you can write for further information.

---

*all temperatures are Fahrenheit

SEMESTER AND ACADEMIC YEAR

General Studies

Indiana University. "Overseas Study in Malawi." Zomba. Academic year at University of Malawi. Juniors and seniors with one year of Chichewa preferred and 3.0 GPA. Apply by first week in November.

NIGERIA

Nigeria is not for the faint of heart. The incessant barrage of intense heat, color, sounds, and tastes tests the culture shock threshold of all but the most resilient. The country—Africa's most populous—shows the strains of a large population competing for scarce resources at almost every turn; however, in this somewhat hostile environment you'll also see an aggressive enjoyment of life.

The Niger and Benue Rivers form a Y that divides the country into north and south, and the south into distinct southeastern and southwestern regions. The south is home to the traditional capital, Lagos (soon to be moved to the more central city of Abuja), as well as most of the country's larger cities; it is also the focus of the government's efforts toward social and economic development. Each of the major regions is populated by different ethnic groups, the chief of which are the Yoruba in the southwest, the Ibo in the southeast, and the Hausa-Fulani in the north. Nigeria has struggled with these ethnic divisions since its amalgamation into one territory under British control, but especially since independence in 1960. In 1967 ethnic animosities culminated in a civil war that left an estimated one million Nigerians (mostly Ibos) dead. Today Nigeria maintains a fragile national unity, but the federal government remains shaky—six military coups since independence, a record for Africa.

Although Nigeria is the second largest African oil-producing nation (after Libya), massive migration from rural to urban areas, a shaky industrial base, rampant inflation, and governmental corruption and mismanagement have created immense poverty and one of the most precarious economies in Africa. Social reform has been frustratingly slow, and the cities to which rural migrants flock have become dangerous, overcrowded, and out of control.

Despite these modern ills, Nigeria has succeeded in preserving its traditional cultures. Indigenous beliefs are much in evidence, although most contemporary Nigerians profess to be adherents of Islam or Christianity. And despite the influx of Western-style stores, the Nigerian love of bargaining is still on display in the open-air markets. You will also have the opportunity, especially in the south, to experience colorful traditional festivals on every occasion, be it a birth, a funeral, the time for planting, or the harvest. In fact, no matter how much you learn about Nigeria before your departure, prepare to be surprised by its contradictions and amazing diversity.

—*Sarah Wood, Brooklyn, New York*

Official name: Federal Republic of Nigeria. **Area:** 356,700 square miles (about three times the size of Nevada). **Population:** 111,900,000. **Population density:** 314 inhabitants per square mile. **Capital and largest city:** Lagos (pop.

1,097,000). **Language:** English (official), Hausa, Yoruba, Ibo. **Religion:** Islam, Christianity. **Per capita income:** US$400. **Currency:** Naira. **Literacy rate:** 42%. **Average daily high/low:*** Lagos: January, 88°/74°; July, 83°/74°. **Average number of days with precipitation:** Lagos: January, 2; July, 16.

TRAVEL

U.S. citizens need a passport and a visa. An onward/return ticket is also required. For specific requirements check with the Embassy of the Federal Republic of Nigeria (2201 M Street, NW Washington, DC 20037) or the Nigerian consulate in New York, San Francisco, or Atlanta.

Getting Around

Nigeria's road system is one of the best in Africa and includes an expressway linking Ibadan and Lagos, the country's two largest cities. Buses connect the main cities, but the fastest means of transport is provided by shared taxis (cars and minibuses), which speed along fixed routes, leaving when full and picking up and dropping off passengers along the way. Hitchhiking is relatively easy but the driver will expect anyone hitching to pay something for the ride. A limited rail system provides a cheap but slow alternative for those with more time.

> *"If you plan to travel cheaply, you may want to bring your own mosquito net for the south and prepare for bucket baths (no running water in the more inexpensive places to stay), but no matter what, plan for an exciting adventure."*
> —Kelly Thompson, Hull, Quebec

WORK

Internships/Traineeships

There is an AIESEC internship program in Nigeria; see page 18 for more information.

Voluntary Service

For persons interested in voluntary service work, the "Year Abroad Program" sponsored by the International Christian Youth Exchange offers persons ages 18–24 voluntary service opportunities in the fields of health care, education, the environment, construction, et cetera. See page 22 for more information.

---

*all temperatures are Fahrenheit

STUDY

The following are the educational programs offered by members of the Council on International Educational Exchange. Consult Appendix I for the addresses of the institutions listed in this section.

SEMESTER AND ACADEMIC YEAR

General Studies

Experiment in International Living/School for International Training. "College Semester Abroad." Lagos. Fall or spring semester. Intensive language study, seminar on Nigerian life, culture, and development, independent-study project, homestay, and educational tour. Sophomores to graduate students with 2.5 GPA. Apply by May 15 for fall and October 15 for spring.

International Student Exchange Program. Direct reciprocal exchange between U.S. universities and the University of Ibadan. Semester or academic year. Full curriculum options. Open only to students at ISEP member institutions.

EXPLORING THE CULTURE OF NIGERIA

Literature

Nigeria has produced many of the more popular African writers writing in English today. Chinua Achebe, probably the most famous African novelist, is best known for *Things Fall Apart*, which explores what happens to traditional life as it falls under the influence of Western culture; *Arrow of God* and *No Longer of Ease* continue the exploration of this theme, while *Man of the People* is a novel about politics and government corruption in the Nigeria of the 1960s.

Wole Soyinka, winner of the 1985 Nobel Prize for literature, also addresses the problems of contemporary life. A good selection of his work is included in his *Collected Plays*. In addition, the autobiography of his childhood, *Ake*, provides a window onto the complexities of a life lived between the traditional and "contemporary" worlds.

Amos Tutuola should also be included in any list of prominent African writers. His *The Palm-Wine Drinkard* (1954) is a Nigerian folktale drawn from Yoruba myths and legends, while *My Life in the Bush of Ghosts* (1970), perhaps his most popular book, is the story of a small boy in the bush who faces many of the spirits of African mythology.

Among younger writers, Buchi Emecheta and Flora Nwapa are two of many who have distinguished themselves. Emecheta's *In the Ditch*, about the problems of a Nigerian woman living in London, and *Second Class Citizen*, which tells the story of the same woman's early years in Nigeria, have found a large audience in Nigeria and abroad. Flora Nwapa writes about unconventional African women in books such as *Efuru*.

Those who seek to understand something of the civil war that tore at Nigeria's fabric in the 1960s should read Cyprian Ekuensi's novel *Survive the Peace*. The same author vividly portrays Nigerian city life in *Lokotown* and *Jagua Nana* and his *Burning Grass* is about the herding peoples of northern Nigeria.

SENEGAL

Senegal, the westernmost nation on the African mainland, was the point of embarkation for slaves being shipped to the New World. Today it is the point of arrival for most travelers to West Africa.

Until independence in 1958, France controlled Senegal for the better part of three centuries. The French colonial agenda, however, was only a partial success. Today, while many Senegalese speak French and are Catholic, most are Muslims who speak African languages such as Wolof, Malinke', or Pulaar. Unfortunately, the most visible legacies of French colonialism are also the most tragic: the slave warehouse on the island of Goree' and an environment ravaged by the French focus on the cultivation of peanuts.

The central district of Dakar, Senegal's capital, is clean and open to the sun and sea. It bears the imprint of Leopold Senghor, the nation's president for its first 20 years of independence. Senghor, who loved France, had many of the public buildings designed in French style and named the streets after French heroes. But the rest of Dakar—and the rest of Senegal—are marked by its African heritage. Herds of goats pass through city streets, urban dwellers cook over open charcoal stoves, and brightly dressed nomads drive their flocks through the sandy northern savannah.

The transformation of Senegal into a multiparty democracy in 1983 has encouraged political activity and a freer press. There are several independent newspapers, and European and American papers are often available in Dakar.

The Senegalese love music, and a few of their stars—reggae performer Alpha Blondy and rock star Youssou N'Dour among them—are already well known in the United States. In Senegal itself, cassette tapes play everywhere and the periodic village festivals are full of music and dance. Much of the music is unforgettably beautiful.

Sadly, in the extreme north, along the Senegal River, the savannah is being transformed into desert. In the 19th century the French covered northern Senegal with peanut farms. This had the effect of turning the Senegalese away from traditional farming methods and crops of vegetables and grains and, ultimately, turning thousands of acres of rich land into desert. Seeing this is essential to understanding one of Senegal's most pressing problems.

If your French is weak, get a visa to enter the Gambia, a tiny English-speaking country entirely surrounded by Senegal. An express bus links Dakar and Banjul, the Gambian capital. The Gambia is a sliver of a nation, 200 miles long and as little as 10 miles wide, that stretches along the banks of the River Gambia in central Senegal and boasts fine beaches, picturesque towns reminiscent of the Caribbean, markets buzzing with commerce, and villages with a lively traditional life.

—*Jason Zweig, New York, New York*

Official name: Republic of Senegal. **Area:** 75,954 square miles (about the size of Utah). **Population:** 7,000,000. **Population density:** 92 inhabitants per square mile. **Capital and largest city:** Dakar (pop. 975,000). **Language:** French (official); Wolof, Serer, and other regional languages. **Religion:** Islam. **Per capita income:** US$370. **Currency:** Franc CFA. **Literacy rate:** 23%. **Average daily high/low:**[*] Dakar: January, 79°/64°; July, 88°/76°. **Average number of days with precipitation:** Dakar: January, 0; July, 7.

---

[*]all temperatures are Fahrenheit

TRAVEL

U.S. citizens need a passport and a visa. For specific requirements, check with the Embassy of the Republic of Senegal (2112 Wyoming Avenue NW, Washington, DC 20008).

Getting Around

Senegal has a fairly good network of roads, many of which are paved and in good condition. Main routes are served by a plentiful supply of buses and taxis. There is also a limited rail network that runs from Dakar north to St. Louis and east into Mali.

WORK

Internships/Traineeships

Programs sponsored by members of the Council on International Educational Exchange are described below. Consult Appendix I for the addresses of the institutions listed in this section.

AIESEC–US. Reciprocal internship program for students in economics, business, finance, marketing, accounting, and computer sciences. See page 18 for further information.

University of Minnesota. "Minnesota Studies in International Development." Dakar. Academic year. Predeparture coursework at the U of M fall quarter, with internship in development-related research or action project in winter and spring quarters. Juniors to graduates and adults with interest in development; 2.5 GPA and two years of French. Apply by May 15.

STUDY

A program sponsored by a CIEE member institution is described below. Consult Appendix I for its address.

SEMESTER AND ACADEMIC YEAR

General Studies

Kalamazoo College. "Kalamazoo College in Senegal." Dakar. Academic year at University of Dakar. Summer orientation at Kalamazoo prior to going abroad. Juniors and seniors with twenty quarter hours of French and 3.0 GPA. Apply by February 15.

EXPLORING THE CULTURE OF SENEGAL

Literature

Leopold Sedar Senghor, the first president of Senegal, was also a founder of the "negritude" school of literature, which became important in the French-speaking African countries during the 1960s and 1970s. The idea behind "negritude" was to establish a literature separate from traditional French literature that reflected the lives and concerns of black Africans. More recently, black writers have gone beyond this rather moderate approach. For example, Camara Laye, born in Guinea but now living in neighboring Senegal, has written *The Dark Child* (also translated as *The Black Child*), an autobiographical novel about growing up in Guinea. He is also author of *The Guardian of the World: Kouma Lafolo Kuoma*, a historical novel about the great Mali Emperor Sundiata narrated by a *griot*, a kind of African troubadour.

Another Senegalese writer worth reading is Sembene Ousmane. His novel *Xala* is about a Senegalese businessman caught between the traditional way of life and the modern world. In *God's Bits of Wood*, considered a classic, Ousmane looks at Africa through the prism of a 1948 railroad strike on the Senegal-Niger. And his recently reissued book of short stories, *Tribal Scars and Other Stories*, illustrates Ousmane's social conscience as well as his irony and wit.

SIERRA LEONE

Sierra Leone (which means "Mountain Lion") was named by Portuguese explorers. Both self-interest and good intentions led the British to establish their presence in this West African coastal region late in the 18th century: philanthropists were anxious to establish a homeland for freed slaves and merchants wanted to expand trade with West Africa.

Today, some eighteen different ethnic groups call Sierra Leone home, but since independence in 1961, its politics have been characterized by a struggle between the two largest groups, the Temnes and the Mendes, which are about equal in number. The result has been political instability, including a high incidence of civil violence and military coups.

Sierra Leone is noted for its lush tropical vegetation, beautiful mountains, and unspoiled beaches. Tourism has grown rapidly along the mountainous Freetown peninsula, where during the winter season the limited number of resort hotels fill to capacity with Europeans seeking warm weather, beaches, and cheap prices. However, you'll encounter few tourists in other areas of the country, including the mountainous interior, where roads are poor and tourist facilities are virtually nonexistent.

Official name: Republic of Sierra Leone. **Area:** 27,925 square miles (slightly larger than West Virginia). **Population:** 4,000,000. **Population density:** 143 inhabitants per square mile. **Capital and largest city:** Freetown (pop. 500,000). **Language:** English (official); Mende, Temne, Creole. **Religion:** Animism, Islam, Christianity. **Per capita income:** US$380. **Currency:** Leone. **Literacy rate:** 24%.

TRAVEL

U.S. citizens need a passport and a visa. A return or onward ticket and proof of financial support from a bank or employer is also required. In addition, currency restrictions are enforced: a minimum of $100 must be changed by all adult travelers over the age of 16 upon entry. For specific requirements, contact the Embassy of the Republic of Sierre Leone (1701 19th Street NW, Washington, DC 20019).

Getting Around

Despite its small size Sierra Leone is not always easy to get around, especially in the rainy season. The main form of transport is by bus, and service is reasonably good between Freeport and the larger population centers. Pickup trucks and vans are other frequently encountered forms of transportation, but these can be crowded and uncomfortable. Roads (not entirely paved and sometimes impassable) connect Sierra Leone to the neighboring countries of Liberia and Guinea.

WORK

Internships/Traineeships

There is an AIESEC internship program in Sierra Leone; see page 18 for more information.

Voluntary Service

For persons interested in voluntary service work, the "Year Abroad Program" sponsored by the International Christian Youth Exchange offers persons ages 18–24 voluntary service opportunities in the fields of health care, education, the environment, construction, et cetera. See page 22 for more information.

STUDY

The following are the educational programs offered by members of the Council on International Educational Exchange. Consult Appendix I for the addresses of the institutions listed in this section.

SEMESTER AND ACADEMIC YEAR

General Study

Kalamazoo College. "Kalamazoo College in Sierra Leone." Freetown. Study at Fourah Bay College (University of Sierra Leone). Fall and winter quarter, with summer orientation at Kalamazoo College. Juniors and seniors with 2.75 GPA. Apply by February 15.

University of Wisconsin–Madison. Freetown. Academic year at Fourah Bay College. Sophomores to graduate students with 3.0 GPA. Open only to students at colleges or universities in Wisconsin and Wisconsin residents studying in other states. Apply by February 1.

SOUTH AFRICA

The complexity and tragedy of the Republic of South Africa begins with the fact that it is the only country in Africa where a white minority—comprising only 16 percent of the population—holds a monopoly on political and economic power. This is a country deeply divided by race; there are over 20 million blacks, about four and a half million whites, two and a half million "coloreds" (persons of mixed race), and a million Asians. But instead of trying to unify this multiracial nation, the white minority government has adopted a policy of apartheid—a term that has become synonymous with racism and injustice throughout the rest of the world. Apartheid is based on racial segregation and is defined as "separate development." In practice, it has deprived nonwhite South Africans of political, economic, and social equality.

Fueled by abundant natural resources and a cheap labor pool, South Africa is the industrial colossus of the continent. Its mineral wealth alone is enormous: it is the world's leading producer of gold, gem diamonds, chromite, and platinum, and also produces large quantities of manganese, uranium, coal, iron ore, and asbestos. This mineral wealth, combined with the productive agricultural and industrial sectors of its economy, has allowed the nation to ignore the world community's attempts at economic sanctions. White South Africans enjoy the highest standard of living on the continent and are quick to point out that even blacks in their country are economically better off than the populations in most African countries.

South Africa offers the traveler a varied landscape, beautiful beaches, fascinating wildlife reserves, and modern cities. More important, the visitor to South Africa also has the chance to better understand this complex society and the racial injustice inherent in it.

Official name: Republic of South Africa. **Area:** 472,359 square miles (almost three times larger than California). **Population:** 35,100,000. **Population density:** 80 inhabitants per square mile. **Capital:** Pretoria (pop. 823,000). **Largest city:** Cape Town (pop. 1,912,000). **Language:** Afrikaans, English, various Bantu languages. **Religion:** Protestant, Roman Catholic. **Per capita income:** US$1,560. **Currency:** Rand. **Literacy rate:** 99% (whites), 32% (Africans). **Average daily high/low:*** Cape Town: January, 78°/60°; July, 65°/45°; Johannesburg: January, 78°/58°; July, 63°/39°. **Average days with precipitation:** Cape Town: January, 3; July, 10. Johannesburg: January, 12; July, 1.

Note: In protest of the government's policy of apartheid, few U.S. institutions sponsor programs in South Africa. If you are considering going to South Africa for a work, study, or travel experience, we recommend you become informed,

---

*all temperatures are Fahrenheit

carefully consider the consequences of a visit, and then make your decision accordingly.

TRAVEL

U.S. citizens need a passport and visa. Proof of onward or return transportation is also required. For specific regulations, check with the Embassy of the Republic of South Africa (3051 Massachusetts Avenue NW, Washington, DC 20008).

Getting Around

South Africa has a good modern system of highways ranging from expressways to an extensive network of secondary roads, most of which are paved. There are numerous bus companies, but few of them offer long-distance service. South Africa is also said to be one of the easiest countries to hitchhike in; this, however, is true only if you are white. While South Africa has an extensive railway network, apart from a limited number of express trains rail travel is generally slow. Here, too, the color of your skin will make a difference. If you are white you can only travel first or second class; third class is off-limits and reserved for blacks and "coloreds." Another option for getting around is South African Airways' comprehensive system of flights between the country's major cities.

> "If you go to South Africa, visit the black townships and poverty-stricken rural areas as well as the big tourist draws (beaches, wildlife parks, et cetera). Read about South Africa before you go—there's more critical literature outside than in. Talk to people as you eat, relax, and sightsee. Everyone will tell you their opinions on politics. . . . It's an interesting and beautiful country but come prepared."

Especially for Students and Young People

SASTS (Box 1655, Johannesburg 2000) is the student travel organization and ISTC member for South Africa. There are SASTS offices in Johannesburg (Merbrook House, 1st floor, 123 Commissioner Street, Johannesburg 2000), as well as Cape Town, Durban, Grahamstown, and Pietermaritzburg. All of these offices provide a variety of services, including booking accommodations, providing travel information, and selling plane, train, and bus tickets. In South Africa, holders of the International Student Identity Card receive discounts on international and domestic air fares.

For Further Information

General tourist information is available from the South African Tourist Corporation, 747 Third Avenue, New York, NY 10017.

WORK

Internships/Traineeships

There are both AIESEC and IAESTE internship programs in South Africa; see page 18 for more information. For further information, consult Appendix I for the appropriate addresses.

EXPLORING THE CULTURE OF SOUTH AFRICA

Literature

In South African fiction, as in South Africa as a whole, apartheid is a dominant issue. The late Alan Paton's *Cry the Beloved Country* was one of the first internationally acclaimed books to deal with apartheid, and was followed by his *Ah! But Your Land Is Beautiful*, about an anti-apartheid protest of the 1950s. Athol Fugard, a contemporary playwright, also addresses the tensions and hypocricies in the relationships between whites and blacks in his *Master Harold and the Boys*. Still another white South African whose works are important to an understanding of apartheid is Nadine Gordimer, author of *A Soldier's Embrace* and *July's People*. Afrikaners writing on the subject include Breyton Breytenbach (*Memoirs of an Albino*), and Andre Brink (*A Dry White Season*).

For a historical perspective on South Africa, read Thomas Mofolo's *Chaka*. Still, contemporary issues dominate most works by prominent African writers. Among these are Eskial Mphahlete's *Down Second Avenue*, Peter Abrahams's *Tell Freedom* and *Mine Boy*, and Alex La Guma's *Time of the Butcherbird* as well as his short stories, "A Walk in the Night" and "The Stone Country." A sampling of more recent works should include J.M. Coetzee's *Waiting for the Barbarians*, Sipho Sepamla's *A Ride on the Whirlwind*, and Mongane Serote's *To Every Birth Its Blood*. Finally, you might want to read *Ushaba: The Hurtle to Blood River*, by Jordan K. Ngubane, South Africa's leading Zulu-language novelist.

TANZANIA

Tanzania is a land of rare beauty and unusual interest, boasting such world famous sites as Mount Kilimanjaro, Lake Victoria, the Great Rift Valley, Olduvai Gorge, and the Serengeti Plain. It also has a variety of ethnic groups, the most widely known being the Masai, who have proudly retained their nomadic lifestyle. But the attraction for which Tanzania is most famous is neither its topography nor its people, but its wildlife. In fact, more than a quarter of the country's area is protected as national parks and game preserves. Yet, in spite of these well-known attractions, little has been done to develop tourism and only a few adventurous travelers stray from the beaten path to visit Tanzania.

For most of the last five hundred years, Tanzania has been dominated by foreign powers—Arab, Persian, Portuguese, German, and British. After gaining its independence from Britain in 1961, Tanganyika annexed the island of Zanzibar off the East African coast and became Tanzania in 1964.

For most of its short history as an independent nation, Tanzania was led by Julius Nyerere, or *Mwalimu* (teacher) as he was often called. Under Nyerere's leadership, Tanzania experimented with an African style of socialism called *Ujamaa*. Major corporations were nationalized and private enterprise discouraged. And Tanzanians, a diverse group of over 120 tribes, each with its own language and culture, were encouraged to further national unity by learning Swahili, a language that has long served as a lingua franca among traders on the East African coast. Ironically, a language that developed in conjunction with the Arab and Persian exploitation of Africans has become the language of an African nation trying to assert its freedom and identity.

The Tanzanian socialist experiment, however, has not been notably successful. In spite of receiving the highest per capita foreign assistance in Africa, Tanzania is one of the 25 poorest countries in the world. Agriculture dominates the economy and over 90 percent of the population lives in rural areas. But under the leadership of Ali Hassan Mwinyi, who assumed the presidency after Nyerere stepped down in 1985, the country has gradually moved toward a more open economic system, with positive results.

Tanzanians are a peaceful and friendly people who rarely criticize one another either publicly or privately. They treat each other, and especially the elderly, with respect. Women are regarded as subservient to men and do most of the work. And the lives of most Tanzanians are heavily influenced by witchcraft, spirits, and magic.

—Erna Loewen-Rudgers, Mbeya, Tanzania

Official name: United Republic of Tanzania. **Area:** 364,900 square miles (three times the size of New Mexico). **Population:** 24,300,000. **Population density:** 67 inhabitants per square mile. **Capital and largest city:** Dar es Salaam (pop. 1,400,000). **Language:** Swahili, Arabic, English. **Religion:** Christianity, Islam, animism. **Per capita income:** US$270. **Currency:** Tanzanian shilling. **Literacy rate:** 85%. **Average daily high/low:*** Dar es Salaam: January, 87°/77°; July, 83°/66°. **Average number of days with precipitation:** Dar es Salaam: January, 8; July, 6.

TRAVEL

U.S. citizens are required to have a passport that is valid for at least six months beyond your date of entry as well as a visa. Return or onward transportation plus proof of financial support is also required. For specific requirements, check with the Embassy of the United Republic of Tanzania (2139 R Street NW, Washington, DC 20008).

Getting Around

Major urban centers within Tanzania are connected by roads; however, due to the economic situation in the country, maintenance of roads has been neglected. In addition, a shortage of fuel and spare parts for vehicles has severely affected public transport. Be prepared for long delays whether traveling by bus, plane,

---

*all temperatures are Fahrenheit

or train. Three main rail lines radiate out from Dar es Salaam north to Arusha (near Mount Kilimanjaro and the Kenyan border), west to Lake Tanganyika, and southwest into Zambia. In addition, ferries operate on Lake Victoria and Lake Tanganyika, as well as between the mainland and the islands of Zanzibar and Pemba just off the coast in the Indian Ocean.

For Further Information

General tourist information is available from the Tanzania Tourist Corporation, 201 East 42nd Street, New York, NY 10017.

STUDY

A study program offered by a CIEE member institution is described below. Consult Appendix I for its address.

SEMESTER AND ACADEMIC YEAR

General Studies

International Student Exchange Program. Direct reciprocal exchange between U.S. universities and the University of Dar es Salaam. Academic year. Full curriculum options. Open only to students at ISEP member institutions.

TOGO

Togo is a pencil-thin strip of land tucked between Ghana and Benin. It was part of Germany's only West African colony until it came under French control after the First World War. (Part of the German colony was given to Britain and is now part of Ghana.) The French granted Togo independence in 1960.

Togo's small population of a little over three million people is divided among almost 40 ethnic groups. But political stability—in spite of numerous coup attempts—has been the rule, with one man, General Gnassingbe Eyadema, in control for most of the last 30 years.

Lomé, the nation's capital, is one of West Africa's most interesting and prosperous cities. It is also the center of a growing tourist industry. Tourists come chiefly for the city's markets and nearby beaches. However, Togo offers much more; anyone interested in exploring African cultures will be well rewarded by the diversity and the richness of its traditional ethnic cultures.

Official name: Republic of Togo. **Area:** 21,925 square miles (about the size of West Virginia). **Population:** 3,300,000. **Population density:** 151 inhabitants per square mile. **Capital and largest city:** Lomé (pop. 285,000). **Language:** Ewe, Mina, Kabye, Cotocoli, French (official). **Religion:** Animism, Christianity, Islam. **Per capita income:** US$340. **Currency:** Franc CFA. **Literacy rate:** 18%.

TRAVEL

U.S. citizens need a passport, but Togo is one of the few African countries that does not require a visa for stays of up to three months. However, the government does require yellow fever vaccinations. For specific regulations, check with the Embassy of the Republic of Togo (2208 Massachusetts Avenue NW, Washington, DC 20008).

Getting Around

Main roads in Togo are excellent. Paved roads link the different regions of the country, making it possible to drive from Lomé to the capital cities of neighboring Benin or Ghana in just a few hours. Traveling these roads is cheap and comfortable, with minibuses being the chief means of public transport. There are also two short rail lines from Lomé into the interior, but trains are infrequent and slow. Except for small chartered planes, there is no domestic air service in Togo.

WORK

Internships/Traineeships

There is an AIESEC internship program in Togo; see page 18 for more information.

STUDY

The following are the educational programs offered by member institutions of the Council on International Educational Exchange. Consult Appendix I for the addresses where you can write for more information. In addition to those listed below, the University of California system offers a program open only to students enrolled at its various schools.

SEMESTER AND ACADEMIC YEAR

General Studies

International Student Exchange Program. Direct reciprocal exchange between U.S. universities and the Université du Benin in Lomé. Semester or academic year. Full curriculum options. Open only to students at ISEP member institutions.

SUMMER

French Language

North Carolina State University/Raleigh. "Summer in Togo." Lomé. Sophomores to graduate students with 2.0 GPA; no language prerequisite. Apply by April 1.

ZAMBIA

Zambia was originally organized by the British South Africa Company as Northern Rhodesia during the late 19th century. But, as was so often the case, the country's strange butterfly-shaped borders unified neither tribal nor linguistic groups. However, in this century a nationalistic movement was able to transcend internal differences and bring about the eventual bloodless revolution that resulted in the creation of an independent Zambia in 1964.

More than twenty-five years after independence Zambia still sees itself as a "front-line" state battling the legacies of colonialism—most notably poverty—while at the same time risking its own security and economic stability to help neighboring countries—Zimbabwe in the 1970s and now black South Africans—achieve their independence. Today, the same man who led Zambia to independence, Kenneth Kaunda, is president under a "one-party participatory democracy."

Official name: Republic of Zambia. **Area:** 290,586 square miles (about three times the size of Oregon). **Population:** 7,500,000. **Population density:** 26 inhabitants per square mile. **Capital and largest city:** Lusaka (pop. 650,000). **Language:** English (official), various African languages. **Religion:** Christianity, animism. **Per capita income:** US$390. **Currency:** Kwacha. **Literacy rate:** 55.5%. **Average daily high/low:*** Lusaka: January, 78°/63°; July, 73°/49°. **Average number of days with precipitation:** Lusaka: January, 21; July, 1.

TRAVEL

U.S. citizens visiting Zambia need a visa and passport. For specific requirements, check with the Embassy of the Republic of Zambia (2419 Massachusetts Avenue NW, Washington, DC 20008).

Getting Around

The main roads are quite good but many of the rural routes are impassable in the rainy season. Hitchhiking is relatively easy but you may be expected to pay for the ride. Renting a car with a driver is a good but expensive way to get around the country; renting a car without a driver is generally not an option. Zambia Railways runs passenger trains from Lusaka north to Zaire, northeast to Tanzania, and south to Victoria Falls and Zimbabwe. Zambia Airways serves all major cities and tourist centers.

> *"For a sense of the Zambian people—there are some 74 different tribal groups—time is better spent in the rural areas than in Lusaka, a capital city that's not especially known for its character. Victoria Falls is both vast and stunning and should not be missed. The unusual wildlife in Luangwa and Katue parks make them well worth the visit."*
> —Denis Choiniere, Hull, Quebec

---

*all temperatures are Fahrenheit

For Further Information

General tourist information is available from the Zambian National Tourist Board, 237 East 52nd Street, New York, NY 10022.

STUDY

A study program offered by a CIEE member institution is described below. Consult Appendix I for the address where you can write for more information.

SEMESTER AND ACADEMIC YEAR

General Studies

International Student Exchange Program. Direct reciprocal exchange between U.S. universities and the University of Zambia. Academic year. Full curriculum options. Open only to students at ISEP member institutions.

ZIMBABWE

Zimbabwe, a landlocked country in Southern Africa, is peaceful now but still bears the scars of a bloody interracial war. Zimbabwe was the British colony of Southern Rhodesia until 1965, when white Rhodesians declared independence from Britain and formed a government dominated by whites. Blacks, who comprise over 95 percent of the population, fought a guerrilla war against the white Rhodesian regime, until a 1980 settlement renamed the nation Zimbabwe and ruled by a black majority government headed by Robert Mugabe. Today, blacks and whites work alongside each other. Although racial tensions persist, one is more likely to encounter a widespread feeling of reconciliation and determination to build a better country together.

An American may be surprised by the lingering British influence on the customs, language, and school system in Zimbabwe. Many Zimbabweans still celebrate British holidays such as Boxing Day and take their tea with milk, and English is still the primary language taught in high schools and used in newspapers (in part because the two main ethnic groups, the Shona and Ndebele, speak different languages). In addition, the capital, Harare, is quite cosmopolitan and boasts nightclubs, large hotels, department stores, and public gardens.

But in the countryside, where over three-quarters of the black population lives, Zimbabwe's traditional way of life is much more evident. Most rural blacks are farmers or livestock herders, their life an economic struggle. The majority government's efforts to live up to its promises of education, health care, and other basic services for all are hindered by its dependence on the military and industrial giant to the south. Zimbabwe relies on South Africa for most of its trade as well as for access to the ports necessary for its imports and exports. (Mozambique, to the east, has good harbors but is crippled by war and famine.)

Despite economic hardships, however, Zimbabweans are proud of their past and eager to show visitors the beauty of their country. The tropical savannah landscape encompasses some stunning highlights, including Victoria Falls, an abundance of ancient cave paintings, and game parks alive with elephants, lions, and giraffes. The ruins of Great Zimbabwe, capital of a 14th-century gold-trading empire, are also a spectacular sight. Traveling to these spots is made easy by a network of reliable buses.

Zimbabweans are family-oriented; a visit to someone's home usually includes a hearty meal and plenty of conversation. While foreigners can get by without fluency in Shona or Sindebele, communication in the rural areas is easier if you can manage a simple conversation. And, as is true in most African countries, Zimbabweans will appreciate your efforts to learn their language. They will also share with you the struggles of the past and their hopes for the country's future. For a new nation that enjoys internal stability and increasing economic growth based on agriculture, gold, and chromium, that future looks promising.

—*Elizabeth Grossi, New York, New York*

Official name: Republic of Zimbabwe. **Area:** 150,699 square miles (about the size of Montana). **Population:** 9,700,000. **Population density:** 64 inhabitants per square mile. **Capital and Largest City:** Harare (pop. 681,000). **Language:** English (official), Ndebele, Shona. **Religion:** Christianity, traditional African religions. **Per capita income:** US$260. **Currency:** Zimbabwean dollar. **Literacy rate:** 77%. **Average daily high low:*** Harare: January, 78°/60°; July, 70°/44°. **Average number of days with precipitation:** Harare: January, 18; July, less than 1.

TRAVEL

U.S. citizens need a passport (but not a visa) for travel in Zimbabwe. An onward or return ticket and sufficient funds to cover your stay are also required. For specific requirements, check with the Embassy of Zimbabwe (2852 McGill Terrace NW, Washington, DC 20008).

> *"Come with an open mind, but be aware of the history of Zimbabwe. You should come knowing something about its recent liberation struggle, the impact of apartheid in South Africa on Zimbabwe, and the role the U.S. has played in the region."*

Getting Around

A good rail network connects the major regions of the country and links Zimbabwe to South Africa. There is also an extensive road system, most of which is well maintained. Various types of buses serve the country, providing everything from intercity express service to local service in the cities and countryside. In addition, Air Zimbabwe connects the country's major urban centers and tourist attractions, including Victoria Falls.

---

*all temperatures are Fahrenheit

WORK

Persons interested in teaching in Zimbabwe can contact the Steve Katz Foundation (P.O. Box 5, Harare, Zimbabwe), which provides placement services and limited financial support for volunteer teachers in the nation's school system.

Internships/Traineeships

There is an AIESEC internship program in Zimbabwe; see page 18 for more information.

STUDY

A program sponsored by a CIEE member institution is described below. Consult Appendix I for the address. In addition, Michigan State University offers a study program open only to its own students.

SEMESTER AND ACADEMIC YEAR

General Studies

Experiment in International Living/School for International Training. "College Semester Abroad." Harare. Fall or spring semester. Language training, seminar in Zimbabwe life and culture and southern Africa studies, independent-study project, homestay, and educational tour. Sophomores to graduate students with 2.5 GPA. Apply by May 15 for fall and October 15 for spring.

EXPLORING THE CULTURE OF ZIMBABWE

Literature

Among the many books that explore the colonial period and its injustices is Wilson Katiyo's *A Son of the Soil*, about a black boy growing up in colonial Rhodesia. Doris Lessing's *The Grass Is Singing*, also set in colonial Rhodesia, describes what happens to a white woman's comfortable life when she marries a man who takes her to live on his isolated farm. The underside of colonial Rhodesia is starkly presented in Dambudzo Marechera's *The House of Hunger*.

Since independence, more of an interest has emerged in books that deal with modern Zimbabwean issues as well as in books that reinforce Zimbabwean identity by celebrating its history, culture, and heroes. Solomon Mutswairo's *Chaminuka: Prophet of Zimbabwe* is a historical novel about Zimbabwe's legendary 19th-century man of peace. In a similar vein, Mutswairo's *Mapondera: Soldier of Zimbabwe* tells the story of this man's struggle against the British in the 19th century. *The Polygamist*, by Ndabaningi Sithole, is an essentially autobiographical novel that tells the story of a man who returns to his people (the Ndebele) as a converted Christian.

CHAPTER TEN
SOUTH ASIA

South Asia, separated from the rest of Asia by the Himalayas, is a landmass so vast it is often called the Indian subcontinent. The region is dominated by India, a nation that, at its present rate of growth, is projected to become the world's most populous early in the next century. India contains a great diversity of peoples, religions, languages, and cultures, as well as some of the world's greatest topographic and climatic extremes. The smaller nations on its borders—Bangladesh, Bhutan, Nepal, and Pakistan—as well as the island-nation of Sri Lanka, add to the rich cultural diversity of the region. This diversity, while a source of much that is honored and cherished, has also been at the root of the civil and political strife that has produced a number of wars both within and between the nations of the region—all of which (with the exception of landlocked Nepal and Afghanistan) have come into existence as independent states only in the last 45 years. At press time, internal strife in Sri Lanka and Afghanistan made travel in these regions dangerous; be sure to check with the Citizens Emergency Center at the U.S. State Department (see page 6) before traveling to these countries.

Getting There

Food, lodging, and land transportation in South Asia are inexpensive; your main expense will be transportation to the region. From the U.S., the cheapest air fares to South Asia are APEX or other excursion fares. You'll find up-to-date information on such fares at Council Travel offices. To give you some idea of cost, we've listed sample *one-way* fares in effect during the summer of 1989 below:

Los Angeles–Bombay, $1,069
New York–Delhi, $1,469
San Francisco–Calcutta, $989

From Europe, special student/youth fares, which enable you to save up to 50 percent of regular commercial fares, are available from several European cities to destinations in South Asia. These can be booked at any Council Travel office or a student travel bureau in Europe. Regulations vary depending on the airline, but generally holders of the International Student Identity Card (see page 8) or the International Youth Card (see page 9) are eligible. Sample *one-way* fares in effect during 1989 are listed below:

Frankfurt–Delhi, $380
London–Karachi, $375
Frankfurt–Bombay, $380
Paris–Delhi, $360

Special student/youth fares that give up to 50 percent off regular fares are available from a number of other cities in Asia. You must meet the same eligibility requirements as those described above, however. For further information, contact a Council Travel office. Sample *one-way* fares in effect during 1989 are listed below:

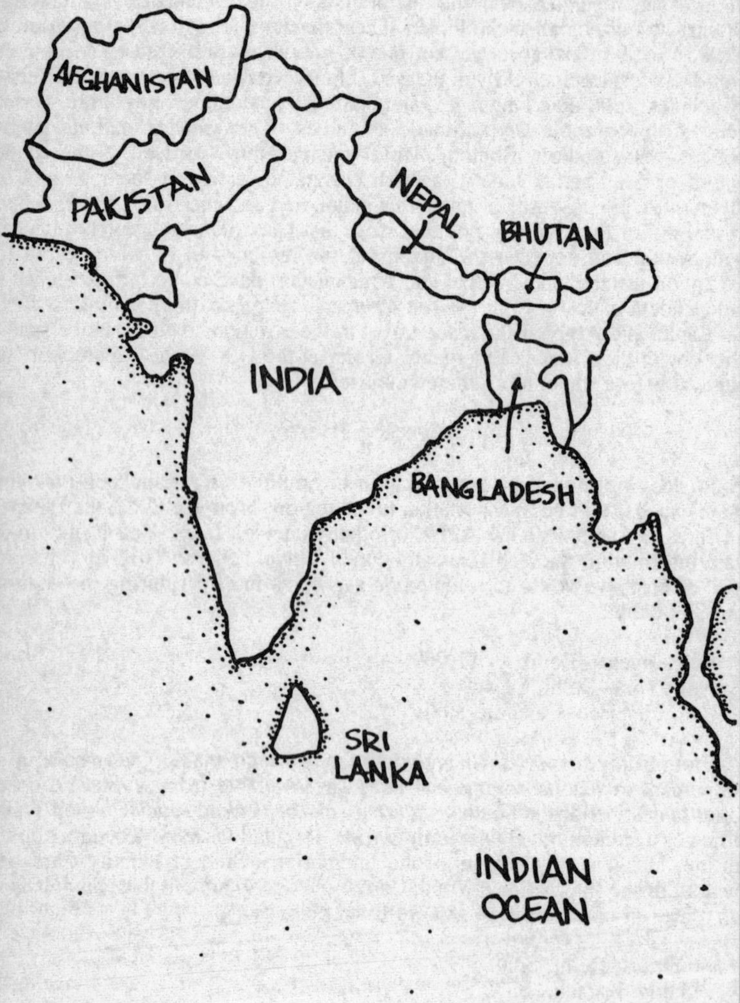
AFGHANISTAN
PAKISTAN
NEPAL
BHUTAN
INDIA
BANGLADESH
SRI
LANKA
INDIAN
OCEAN

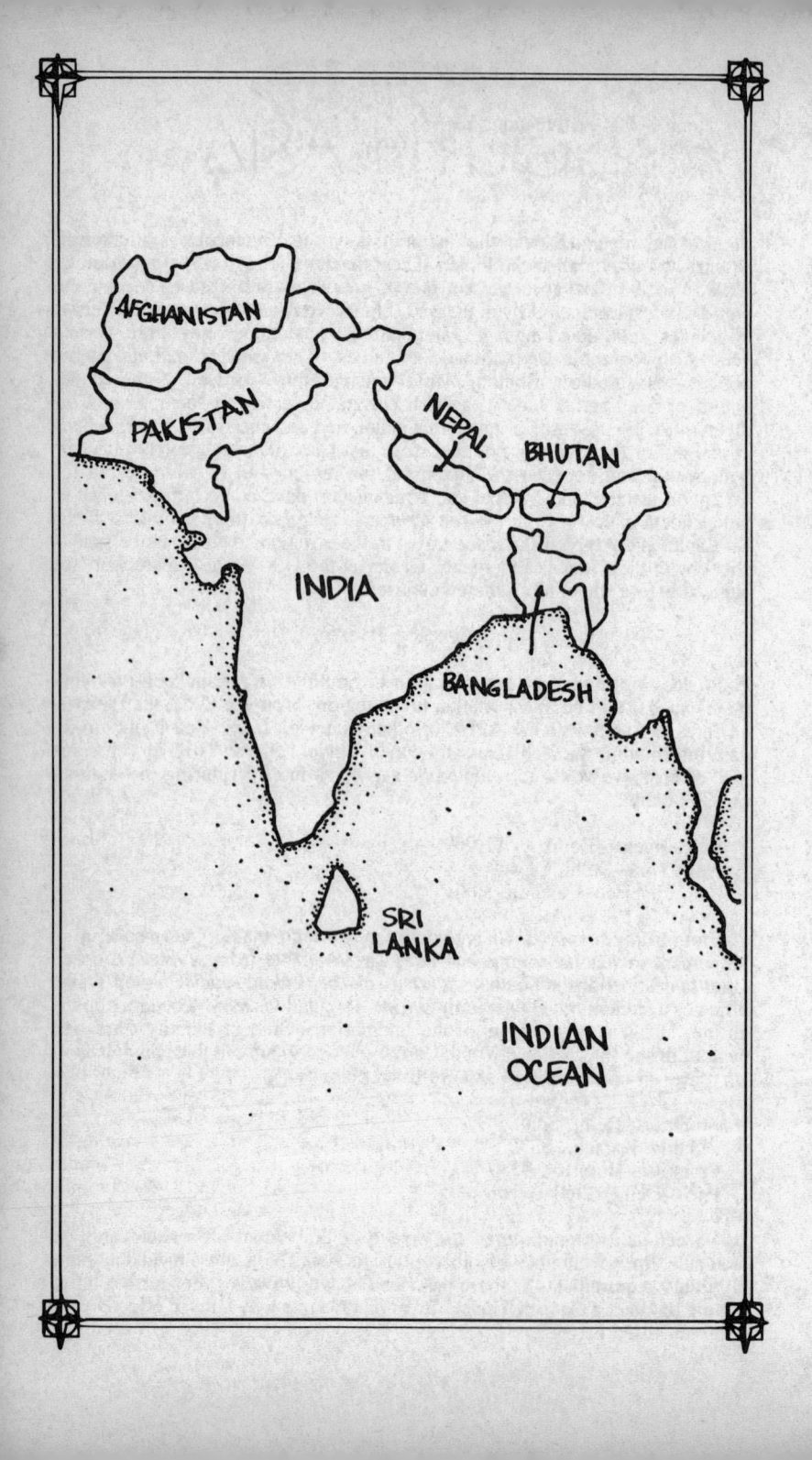

Hong Kong–Kathmandu, $365
Bangkok–Calcutta, $145
Hong Kong–Delhi, $340
Bangkok–Kathmandu, $210

Overland trips from Europe to India and Nepal were once quite popular among more adventurous travelers. "Overlanding" is still an option, although Americans would be wise to overfly Iran and Afghanistan. Many of these tours are British-run and start from London. For more information contact Trailfinders Travel Center (42–48 Earl's Court Road, London W8, England). You can also write them to obtain a free copy of their magazine, *Trailfinder*, which focuses on unusual adventure travel tours around the world.

Getting Around South Asia

India comprises more than half of South Asia and is, geographically speaking, the most important country in the region. For the most part, getting around in South Asia involves travel in India. For further information about travel in India, see the individual section on it later in this chapter.

The best book on budget travel in the country bordering India to the west is *Pakistan: A Travel Survival Kit*. It's available from Lonely Planet Publications (Embarcadero West, 112 Linden Street, Oakland, CA 94607) for $8.95 (plus $1.50 postage). A visa is required for U.S. citizens traveling to Pakistan; contact the Embassy of Pakistan (2315 Massachusetts Avenue NW, Washington, DC 20008) for further information.

For Bangladesh, India's eastern neighbor, the most useful book for budget travelers is *Bangladesh: A Travel Survival Kit*, available from Lonely Planet Publications (address above) for $7.95 (plus $1.50 postage). A visa is not required for stays of up to two weeks in Bangladesh. For further information, contact the Embassy of the People's Republic of Bangladesh (3421 Massachusetts Avenue NW, Washington, DC 20037).

"Having worked as a volunteer for a year in Bangladesh, I realize that it is not a recommended stopover for the casual tourist interested mostly in sightseeing. However, the mere fact that it represents a number of extremes, both cultural and economic, makes it of considerable interest to the more serious and concerned type of traveler."

Political and climatic conditions permitting, you may want to visit the island nation of Sri Lanka. There's ferry service from Rameswaram in southern India to Talaimannar, with bus and train connections from there on to Colombo, Sri Lanka's capital. The three-hour ferry runs are usually suspended in November and December during the monsoon season, however. Americans visiting Sri Lanka will not need a visa unless they're planning to stay more than a month. For further information, contact the Embassy of Sri Lanka (2148 Wyoming Avenue NW, Washington, DC 20008). A good book on budget travel to Sri Lanka is *Sri Lanka: A Travel Survival Kit*, by Tony Wheeler, and available for $8.95 (plus $1.50 postage) from Lonely Planet Publications (address above). Another helpful book is the pocket-sized Berlitz guide to things to see and do in Sri Lanka.

For those of you who prefer to get around South Asia by plane, we've listed some sample one-way fares in effect during 1989 below:

Delhi–Kathmandu, $210
Calcutta–Karachi, $285
Delhi–Dhaka, $90
Kathmandu–Colombo, $190

"Leave the cities of South Asia and you find life as it has always been—a struggle to feed one's family and constant days of hard work for very little money or a meager crop."

For Further Information

A useful guide that covers a number of countries in the region is *West Asia on a Shoestring*, by Tony Wheeler, published by Lonely Planet Publications ($8.95, plus $1.50 postage). Almost half the book is devoted to India and the other countries of South Asia, while the rest deals with countries further west (from Iran to Turkey). Another guidebook filled with useful information on countries in the region is Fodor's *India, Nepal, and Sri Lanka*, published by Random House and available in most bookstores for $16.95.

Travelers interested in staying in youth hostels in South Asia might want to take a look at volume two of the *International Youth Hostel Handbook* (see page 50), which lists hostels in India, Sri Lanka, Pakistan, and Nepal.

Study in South Asia

You'll find a number of study programs listed in the individual country sections later in this chapter. In the section below we've listed only the study programs of CIEE member institutions that take place in more than one country of the region. Consult Appendix I for the addresses where you can write for more information.

SEMESTER AND ACADEMIC YEAR

General Studies

St. Olaf College. "Global Semester." Cairo, Egypt; Bangladore, India; Taipei, Taiwan; and Kyoto, Japan. Fall semester plus January. Cultures and contemporary problems of non-Western world. Sophomores, juniors, and seniors. Apply by March 1.

Tibetan Studies

Experiment in International Living/School for International Training. New Delhi and Dharamasala, India; Kathmandu, Nepal; and Tibet (conditions permitting). Fall or spring semester. Intensive language, seminar in Tibetan studies, field study, village excursions and homestay, and independent-study project. Sophomores to graduate students with 2.5 GPA. Apply by May 15 for fall and October 15 for spring.

INDIA

The quiet inside of a temple contrasts with the chaos of traffic outside. Highrise office buildings coexist with slums. Nuclear power plants stand beside fields plowed by oxen. As a traveler, you will undoubtedly be struck by the contrasting landscapes, cultures, and ways of thinking that India encompasses.

Perhaps the best way to understand India's provocative contrasts is to look at its history. The subcontinent has experienced a series of invasions, beginning in 1,500 B.C. with the Aryan invasion and finally ending in 1947 when the British granted the country its independence. Each successive group brought changes to the subcontinent, enriching its culture with new religions, forms of government, customs, and art. Aryans introduced the caste system as well as a variety of religious practices and beliefs that influenced Hinduism. Moghal invasions beginning in the 16th century ushered in a long period of Muslim rule, with new architectural, artistic, and governmental forms. British colonial rule built the bureaucracy, cemented India's ties with the West, and left a legacy readily seen in the nation's educational system and parliamentary democracy.

As a result of these foreign influences, India is home to many religions: Islam, Hinduism, Parsi, Sikhism, Christianity, Buddhism, and Jainism. There is always a festival or celebration going on, and Westerners are welcomed into most temples and mosques—but don't take photos and take off your shoes! Inside, you can observe the daily prayers, and probably talk with an English-speaking guide about the details of the religious rituals.

Equal to the importance of religion in Indian society is the dominance of the family unit, which is extended to include perhaps three or four generations. The family is a critical social component in India; family members rely on and care deeply about each other.

Indians are friendly toward foreigners; learn to be patient and to put aside inhibitions about accepting invitations. The bazaar gives foreigners an opportunity to see most Indians in their element. Tea stalls, sweet shops, vegetable stands, and cold drink counters are colorful, fragrant, and delicious.

Whether exploring the Ganges plain, climbing the Himalayas, or visiting the Taj Mahal, the Westerner will everywhere encounter the unique and exotic. Visiting the land of Mahatma Gandhi and Mother Teresa will expose the traveler not only to the nation's religious, language, cultural, and class differences, but also to one of the world's oldest and most dynamic civilizations.

—*Laryn E. Callaway, St. Louis, Missouri*

Official Name: The Republic of India. **Area:** 1,229,737 square miles (about one-third the size of the U.S.). **Population:** 816,800,000. **Population density:** 664 inhabitants per square mile. **Capital:** New Delhi (pop. 619,417). **Largest city:** Calcutta (pop. 9,194,018). **Language:** Hindi and English. **Religion:** Hinduism, Islam, Christianity, Sikhism, Jainism. **Per capita income:** US$260. **Currency:** Rupee. **Literacy rate:** 36%. **Average daily high/low:*** Bombay: January, 83°/67°; July, 85°/77°; New Delhi: January, 70°/41°; July, 96°/81°. **Average number of days with precipitation:** Bombay: January, 1; July, 21. New Delhi: January, 2; July, 8.

---

*all temperatures are Fahrenheit

TRAVEL

U.S. citizens traveling to India will need a passport and visa. The visa, valid for stays of up to three months, must be obtained before your arrival in the country. For this you'll need three photographs, your passport, and proof of onward transportation. Be sure to request a multiple-entry visa if you wish to visit neighboring countries and then return to India. For specific requirements, check with the Embassy of India (2107 Massachusetts Avenue NW, Washington, DC 20008) or an Indian consulate in New York, Chicago, or San Francisco. (Note: Holders of a three-month tourist visa are given a liquor permit, which allows them to purchase liquor in some of the "dry" states of India.)

Keep all official bank receipts for money exchanged so that you'll be able to convert your rupees back into American dollars when you leave. When you pay in rupees for your transportation out of India, you'll be asked to show a receipt to prove that you have obtained your rupees officially.

Getting Around

Domestic air service is provided by Indian Airlines, which connects more than 70 cities around the country. If you have only a little time to spend and want to see a lot of the country, you can purchase a See India pass, which entitles you to 21 days of unlimited travel on Indian Airlines for $400. Another option, the Tour India pass, offers six flights over a 14-day period for $300. Indian Wonderfare passes, valid for seven days, provide unlimited travel within one of four major regions in the country for $200. Passes are available only to foreigners, however, and must be purchased outside the country in conjunction with your plane ticket to India. For further information, contact a Council Travel office.

India has an excellent rail network that connects even the most remote areas of the country (except Kashmir). Since rail travel is popular among Indians, it's a good way to meet the people and experience the diversity of India's different cultures. Although there are no student discounts on train travel in India, you can purchase an Indrail Pass, which entitles you to unlimited travel at low cost. Indrail passes can be purchased only by foreigners and must be paid for in U.S. dollars, although they may be purchased within India itself. For further information, contact the Government of India Tourist Office (30 Rockefeller Plaza, Suite 15, North Mezzanine, New York, NY 10112). The following prices were in effect in 1989 for Indrail passes, including night-sleeper charges (but excluding the reservation fee):

Period	Air-Conditioned Class	First Class	Second Class
7 days	$190	$ 95	$ 45
15 days	230	115	55
21 days	280	140	65
30 days	350	175	75
60 days	520	260	115
90 days	690	345	150

It is possible to stay overnight in most Indian railroad stations, either for a fee in the "retiring rooms" (beds and private rooms) or for free on couches in the first-class or second-class waiting rooms.

> *"Indians traveling on trains always bring enough food with them to last for days, and sooner or later they will ask you to share some with them. Don't refuse, as it is always delicious and may win you a new friend. If you are carrying any fruit or other food yourself, be sure to offer it to the people traveling with you. They may refuse because of their strict dietary rules but will appreciate the gesture, and this, too, may lead to a new friend."*

Buses in India are used primarily for local transportation. In urban areas, crowded buses are the primary component of the mass transit system. In rural areas, buses complement the rail system, fanning out to villages from train stations. An increasing number of air-conditioned long-distance buses are linking the country's major cities, providing a comfortable alternative for getting around India.

Rental cars are not readily available in India; however, cars with drivers can be arranged. The price, which may be negotiable, depends on the size of the car, the time spent, and the distance covered.

In the major cities, taxis are readily available. An alternative to taxis are "scooters," three-wheel vehicles that are usually metered, with fares running about half those of regular taxis. In addition, pedal trishaws still operate in many cities and smaller towns. And nearly everyone has a bicycle—perhaps the most efficient way to travel locally.

Especially for Students and Young People

India's student travel organization and ISTC member is the Student Travel Information Centre (Hotel Imperial, Room 6, Janpath, New Delhi 110001), with branch offices located in Bombay, Calcutta, and Madras. STIC issues Indrail Passes, distributes lists of inexpensive hotels and guesthouses, and has information on low-cost flights within India and the region. In India, the International Student Identity Card entitles the holder to discounts on some accommodations and on STIC-operated tours.

Eating and Sleeping

Accommodations and meals in India are inexpensive. Cheap or modest hotels can be found in most towns, and are listed in the various publications of the government tourist offices in addition to more expensive Western-style hotels. In addition, you'll find accommodations in Ys in major cities, and Salvation Army guesthouses in Calcutta, Bombay, and Madras are popular with foreigners as well. The Government of India Tourist Office (30 Rockefeller Plaza, Suite 15 North Mezzanine, New York, NY 10112) can also provide you with a list of youth hostels set up by the Department of Tourism.

> *"It may take some time for your stomach to get accustomed to the spicy food of India. If the food is too hot for you at first, try mixing curd or yogurt with everything. If you must eat Western food, you'll find it in most major cities, though prices will be much higher than for Indian food."*

Meeting the People

The Government of India Tourist Office sponsors a "Meet the People" program. For further information, contact any of the following tourist offices upon arrival: 123, Maharishi Karve Road, Churchgate, Bombay; Embassy No. 4

Shakespeare Sarani, Calcutta; 88 Janpath, New Delhi; and 154 Anna Road, Madras. These offices also have a list of paying guest accommodations in Indian homes.

> *"Indians feel that since you are a guest in their home, it is their duty to take care of you and protect you, so it's best to just relax and let yourself be taken care of. If you have a very limited amount of time to spend with a family in a certain town, be sure to let your host know so that you can see and do those things which are most important to you. The pace of life is very different and may require you to slow down and accommodate yourself to a different sense of time."*

> *"The kind of familiarity with which most Westerners regard each other is usually not encountered in India. With some families, you would not speak to unmarried family members of the opposite sex."*

For Further Information

The Government of India Tourist Office (30 Rockefeller Plaza, Suite 15 North Mezzanine, New York, NY 10112) has brochures on places to see and stay throughout India.

India—A Travel Survival Kit, by Geoff Crowther, Prakesh A. Raj, and Tony Wheeler, is a good book for the budget traveler. It's available for $17.95 (plus $1.50 postage) from Lonely Planet Publications (Embarcadero West, 112 Linden Street, Oakland, CA 94607). Lonely Planet also publishes *Kashmir, Ladakh, and Zanskar: A Travel Survival Kit* ($10.95, plus $1.50 postage), by Margaret and Rolf Schettler, which provides practical information on all three Himalayan regions. For descriptions of trekking routes, Lonely Planet also publishes *Trekking in the Indian Himalayas* ($7.95, plus $1.50 postage). Another good book for the budget traveler is Frommer's *India on $25 a Day*, available in most bookstores for $12.95.

WORK

A work permit is not required for India. However, any money you earn cannot be taken out of the country.

Traineeships

Programs sponsored by members of the Council on International Educational Exchange are described below. Consult Appendix I for the address of the institutions listed in this section.

AIESEC–US. Reciprocal internship program for students in economics, business, finance, marketing, accounting, and computer sciences. See page 18 for further information.

University of Minnesota. "Minnesota Studies in International Development." Pune. Academic year. Predeparture coursework at the U of M fall quarter, with internship in development-related research or action project in winter and spring quarters. Juniors to graduates and adults with interest in development and 2.5 GPA. Apply May 15.

STUDY

The American Institute of Indian Studies (AIIS) is a cooperative organization comprised of 40 American colleges and universities with a special interest in Indian studies. The organization offers a variety of research fellowships to graduate students, researchers, and university faculty members. AIIS also operates a nine-month intensive language training program from September to May. For further details, write AIIS, 1130 East 59th Street, Chicago, IL 60637.

The following are the educational programs offered by member institutions of the Council on International Educational Exchange. Consult Appendix I for the addresses of colleges and universities listed in this section. In addition, the University of California system offers a program open only to students already enrolled at any of its various schools.

SEMESTER AND ACADEMIC YEAR

Buddhist Studies

Antioch University. "Comparative Buddhist Studies." Bodh Gaya. Fall quarter. Courses in philosophy, contemporary culture, history, beginning Hindi or Tibetan, and meditation. Orientation held in London. Sophomores to graduate students in good academic standing. Apply by March 15.

Gandhian Philosophy and Practice

Lisle Fellowship. "Alternatives to Violence: The Role of Women in Nonviolent Social Change." Three-week program offered in January. Co-sponsored by Gandhi Peace Foundation, Institute for Total Revolution, and Center for Women and Religion. Open to women who are recent high school graduates, college students, or adults. Apply by October 1.

General Studies

Associated Colleges of the Midwest. "India Studies." Pune. Spring term at Carleton College and six months in India. Priority given ACM students. Freshmen to graduate students, with priority to sophomores or juniors. Apply by April 1; final deadline is November 1.

Experiment in International Living/School for International Training. "College Semester Abroad." New Delhi, Udaipur, Rajsthan. Fall or spring semester. Intensive Hindi language, life and culture, rural development and environment seminar, village studies, homestays, and independent-study project. Sophomores to graduate students with 2.5 GPA. Apply by May 15 for fall and October 15 for spring.

Friends World College. "South Asian Studies." Bangalore, with trips to other locations in India and Nepal. Academic year or semester. South Asian studies, language, and individualized program combining independent study with fieldwork or internships. Sophomores, juniors, and seniors. Others may participate without credit. Apply by May 15 for academic year and fall semester and November 15 for spring semester.

University of Wisconsin–Madison. Madurai, Varanasi, or Waltair. Academic year. Sophomores to graduate students with 3.0 GPA. Participants normally complete summer course in Tamil, Hindu, or Telugu at Madison prior to departure. Apply by February 1.

South Asian Studies

Davidson College. "Davidson College Fall Semester in India." Madras. Fall only (in odd-numbered years). Juniors and seniors with 2.75 GPA. Preference given to those with previous course work relating to South Asia. Apply by February 1.

SUMMER

Gandhian Philosophy and Practice

Lisle Fellowship. "Alternatives to Violence: Cultural Interaction and Nonviolent Living." Co-sponsored by Gandhi Peace Foundation. Six weeks in mid-summer. Open to recent high school graduates, college students, and adults. Apply by May 1.

EXPLORING INDIAN CULTURE

Literature

For almost 3,000 years Indian priests, historians, and poets have been writing in the various languages of the Indian subcontinent. Noteworthy among the authors who have been translated into English is Thakathi Pillai, whose novels are mostly set in the state of Kerala on India's southwest coast. They include *The Unchaste*, which addresses the problems women face in Indian society, and *Rungs of the Ladder*, a story of simple people corrupted by the desire for power. Also available in translation is Bibhutibhushan Banerjee's *Pather Panchali*, the realistic story of a poverty-stricken family in the state of Bengal.

Indian literature written in English, however, is a quite modern development. Ruth Prawer Jhabvala has chosen as one of her themes the conflicts between Indian life and Western civilization. It's instructive to compare her book *Travellers* with E.M. Forster's classic *A Passage to India* for the insights a different perspective offers. Jhabvala's other books include *The Householders*, a witty novel about a newlywed couple in modern New Delhi, and *How I Became a Holy Mother*, a collection of short stories about Indians belonging to various castes and communities. R.K. Narayan's books concern the lives of middle-class people in the imaginary town of Malgudi. In *The Dark Room* he deals with the problems faced by a traditional Hindu wife; *The Guide* explores the transformation of a guide into a guru despite his wishes; and *The Vendor of Sweets* contrasts the world views of an older man who is a strong believer in the ideas of Gandhi and his son who has just returned from the United States. Anita Desai's *Clear Light of Day* is about a middle-class Hindu family forced to confront an increasingly problematic world and how they must change in order to survive as human beings. Finally, Kamala Markandaya's *Nectar in a Sieve* is a powerful and sensitive novel about a family surviving on the margins of human existence in rural India.

Easily the most famous—or infamous—of today's Anglo-Indian writers is Salman Rushdie, who began his career with *Midnight's Children*, a highly imaginative and critical view of modern Indian history since independence. In *The Satanic Verses* Rushdie provocatively tackled another taboo—the life of the prophet Mohammed and the birth of Islam. He has been in hiding from Moslem extremists since the late Ayatollah Khomeini decreed that Rushdie should die because of his novel's alleged blasphemy against Islam.

Film

India's movie industry, supported by the world's largest film-going public, annually produces more films (over 700) than any other country in the world. In the opinion of many Westerners, it also produces the world's worst films; however, this judgment as often as not indicates a misunderstanding of the cultural roots of commercial Indian cinema. Indian films, predominantly produced in the Hindi language, emphasize spectacular and emotional excess at the expense of strong story lines and narrative realism, and are usually grouped under the following genres: mythologicals, historicals, song and dance, and super-hero films. Two particularly popular and typical examples of the latter category are Manmohan Desai's super-heroic *Naseeb* (1981) and Mehboob Khan's more folklorically tinged *Mother India* (1957). In addition, many of the song-and-dance spectacles can be found on cable television's arts and culture channels on Sunday mornings.

Since the early 1950s more and more Indian films have been made in opposition to the economic and cultural dominance of the commercial tradition, with a number of independent filmmakers following the example of Satyajit Ray, India's most internationally renowned filmmaker. Ray's own "Apu Trilogy"—*Pather Panchali* (1955), *The Unvanquished* (1956), and *The World of Apu* (1959)—presents the stories of a succession of young rural characters trapped between Indian traditions and Western ideas. Other well-known figures in the "New Indian Cinema" are Ritwak Ghatak, who explored rural and urban social attitudes in *Ajantrik*, and Shyam Benegal, whose *The Role*, ostensibly the biography of a popular female film star, is an important commentary on the position of women in Indian culture as well as an encapsulation of the history of Indian film genres.

NEPAL

A rapidly developing tourist industry has brought far-reaching changes to this once isolated kingdom, situated between India and China in the middle of the Himalayan Mountains. As a result, today you can find five-star hotels and Western restaurants serving pizza and linguine in Kathmandu, the country's capital. While these amenities bring the comforts of home to the Westerners who visit Nepal, they can also shelter the traveler from the rustic but far more interesting conditions typical of the country.

By Western standards, Nepal is an impoverished country, its average annual per capita income only approximately $120 per year. However, this poverty is rarely oppressive, and few sick or starving people wander the streets. Kathmandu is bustling, muddy, and polluted; yet it remains a beautiful city filled with temples, open-air markets, and merchants peddling mangoes and oranges on their bicycles. Bare-footed, bare-bottomed children run through the streets playing with discarded bicycle tires and asking unsuspecting tourists for "one rupee," "pen," or "balloon." Women in colorful saris, *lungis*, or Punjabi suits battle the flies for the perfect tomato or head of cauliflower. Many of the side streets reek of rotting meat, courtesy of the merchants who sell chunks of fresh goat and buffalo to loyal customers, and major thoroughfares are filled with dilapidated taxis, bicycles, rickshaws, cows, and city buses overflowing with gaudy decorations and passengers who sit on the dashboard, hang out of windows, or stand on the bumpers.

Despite the crowds and often oppressive smells of the city, the most pervasive feeling in Kathmandu is one of warmth and friendliness. The Nepalese people exude goodwill and will do anything to help a confused visitor. Perhaps it's due to the influence of the two dominant religions in Nepal, Hinduism and Mahayana Buddhism, with most people practicing a unique combination of the two.

The countryside beyond Kathmandu is even more rustic, friendly, and beautiful. In the monsoon season, from July to mid-September, the white-capped Himalayas are obscured by mist and clouds. Even then, however, breathtaking scenery is provided by the green-terraced hillsides that the locals plant with rice paddies and banana trees.

Much of the country is inaccessible by road. Instead, the footpaths that crisscross the mountains are literally the highways of Nepal. Not surprisingly, the Nepalese people are exceptionally strong and surefooted, and even small children scramble along the mountain paths with fifty-pound loads of firewood and fodder on their backs. People will think nothing of walking several days to visit a friend or relative. Tea shops dot the roadsides, and weary travelers are always welcome to sit down to the typical Nepalese meal of *dal bhaat*, which consists of rice, lentils, and vegetables such as potatoes or green beans.

The friendliness of the Nepalese people is as overwhelming as the mountains that attract most visitors to Nepal. And the lack of electricity, running water, and toilet paper hardly seems to matter in this small country with an enormous heart.

—*Victoria R. Clawson, Bernardsville, New Jersey*

Official name: Kingdom of Nepal. **Area:** 54,463 square miles (about the size of Wisconsin). **Population:** 18,300,000. **Population density:** 306 inhabitants per square mile. **Capital and largest city:** Kathmandu (pop. 400,000). **Language:** Nepali (official), Newari, Bhutia. **Religion:** Hindu. **Per capita income:** US$140. **Currency:** Nepalese rupee. **Literacy Rate:** 23%. **Average daily high/low:*** Kathmandu: January, 65°/35°; July, 84°/68°. **Average number of days with precipitation:** Kathmandu: January, 1; July, 21.

TRAVEL

U.S. citizens need a passport and a visa. A visa valid for 30 days can be obtained before leaving the United States from the Nepalese embassy. Short-term visas for seven days are also issued on arrival at the Kathmandu airport.

---

*all temperatures are Fahrenheit

For specific information contact the Royal Nepalese Embassy (2131 Leroy Place NW, Washington, DC 20008) or any Nepalese embassy abroad.

Getting Around

Nepal has no railroads and a limited number of roads passable to motor vehicles. However, if there's a road leading where you want to go, you can be sure there's a bus going there. Bicycles are an excellent way of seeing the towns and countryside in the area around Kathmandu, and can be rented in Kathmandu itself. Rental cars are unknown here, but cars with drivers can be hired. If you're in a hurry, Royal Nepal Airlines operates flights to all areas of the country. While in Kathmandu, you can get around by bus, taxi, or rickshaw; but because the city is quite compact, perhaps the best—and certainly the cheapest—alternative is simply to walk.

"Nepal is both very simple and very complex at the same time. The lifestyle is a simple one that includes hard work as well as fun and playful times, with a great emphasis on family. It is also a place with complex hierarchical structures that foreigners may not be able to fully understand. The country is small but exploding with the many castes, ethnic groups, and varying religions of its diverse people, who incredibly have learned to coexist peacefully."
—Cari Spahn, Petaluma, California

Trekking

Trekking in Nepal is an unforgettable experience; the scenery is beautiful, the paths are safe, and villagers are hospitable. It is hard work, though, so you should be in good health and should try to travel with as little as possible. Although it's possible to trek alone, you'll need to get a permit in Kathmandu. All your trekking equipment—down jacket, pack, boots, and bags—can be rented right in Kathmandu or Pokhara (30 minutes by air from the capital).

The Royal Nepalese Embassy (address above) has a brochure for prospective trekkers called *Nepal—A Walker's Guide to Pokhara*. Another valuable source of information is *A Guide to Trekking in Nepal*, by Stephen Bezrucha, and available from the Mountaineers Books, 306 2nd Avenue West, Seattle, WA 98119 ($10.95). The book includes maps of various treks and lists items you'll need to take with you. *Trekking in the Nepal Himalayas*, by Stan Armington, provides route descriptions as well as recommendations for equipment. It's available for $7.95 (plus $1.50 postage) from the publisher, Lonely Planet Publications (Embarcadero West, 112 Linden Street, Oakland, CA 94607). Another guide to trekking in Nepal is *The Nepal Trekker's Handbook*, published by Mustang Publishing and available in bookstores for $8.95.

For Further Information

A useful guide to Nepal is *Kathmandu and the Kingdom of Nepal*, written by Prakash Raj, a former Nepalese student and journalist. It's available in the U.S. for $7.95 (plus $1.50 postage) from Lonely Planet Publications (address above).

WORK

Work permits are required for Nepal, and obtaining one is extremely difficult. Generally, they are only issued to embassy staff, to those working on government projects, or to foreigners working with the airlines.

STUDY

The following are the educational programs offered by member institutions of the Council on International Educational Exchange. Consult Appendix I for the addresses of the colleges and universities listed in this section.

SEMESTER AND ACADEMIC YEAR

General Studies

Experiment in International Living/School for International Training. Kathmandu. Fall or spring semester. Intensive language, life and culture seminar, village homestays, and independent-study project. Sophomores to graduate students with 2.5 GPA. Apply by May 15 for fall and October 15 for spring.

Pitzer College. "Experience in Nepal." Kathmandu. Fall or spring semester. Intensive language study, homestay, trek, community development project, and independent study. Sophomores, juniors, and seniors with 2.5 GPA. Apply by March 15 for fall and October 15 for spring.

University of Wisconsin–Madison. Kathmandu. Academic year. Participants normally complete a summer course in Nepali and Tibetan at Madison prior to departure. Sophomores to graduate students with 3.0 GPA. Apply by February 1.

CHAPTER ELEVEN
EAST ASIA

East Asia encompasses a diversity of peoples that now accounts for more than a quarter of the world's population. Terms such as "the Orient" or "Far East" still conjure up images of the mysterious and exotic, but increasingly these are being replaced by terms such as the "Pacific Rim," which suggests links and connections rather than differences. It is because of these links that the American government, business establishment, educational system, and public are all focusing increasing attention on the region. More and more young people are traveling, studying, and working in East Asia. In part, the interest in Asia's Pacific Rim is the result of the growing economic power of Japan and the "Asian tigers"—South Korea, Hong Kong, and Taiwan—that seem to be following Japan's model of export-led economic development. In fact, U.S. trade with East Asia now exceeds its trade with Europe. But the growing interest in the Pacific Rim goes beyond economics to encompass a wide range of fields. The United States is beginning to realize that it is as much a Pacific as an Atlantic nation, and that its future depends to a large extent on how well it is able to develop and manage its many economic, political, and cultural ties to its East Asian allies.

Getting There

Today, a variety of excellent air fares have brought down the price of travel to Asia. Many carriers to Asia offer APEX and promotional fares, and student fares are available to a number of cities. Sample *one-way* fares from the U.S. to Asia in effect for the summer of 1989 are listed below. For more up-to-date information on fares to Asia, contact any Council Travel office (see pages ix–xi).

   Seattle–Tokyo, $389
   San Francisco–Hong Kong, $389
   New York–Beijing, $909
   Los Angeles–Seoul, $799

From Europe, persons with the International Student Identity Card (see page 8) or the International Youth Identity Card (see page 9) can get special discounted fares on scheduled flights from a number of European capitals to Hong Kong, Osaka, Seoul, Taipei, or Tokyo. Sample *one-way* student/youth fares in effect during 1989 are listed below:

   London–Hong Kong, $415
   London–Tokyo, $695
   Amsterdam–Taipei, $629

Many of these flights allow stopovers in Bangkok, Thailand. Contact a Council Travel office or a student travel bureau in Europe or Asia for complete information.
   Student/youth fares (same eligibility as above) are also available on scheduled flights connecting East Asian cities with cities in South and Southeast

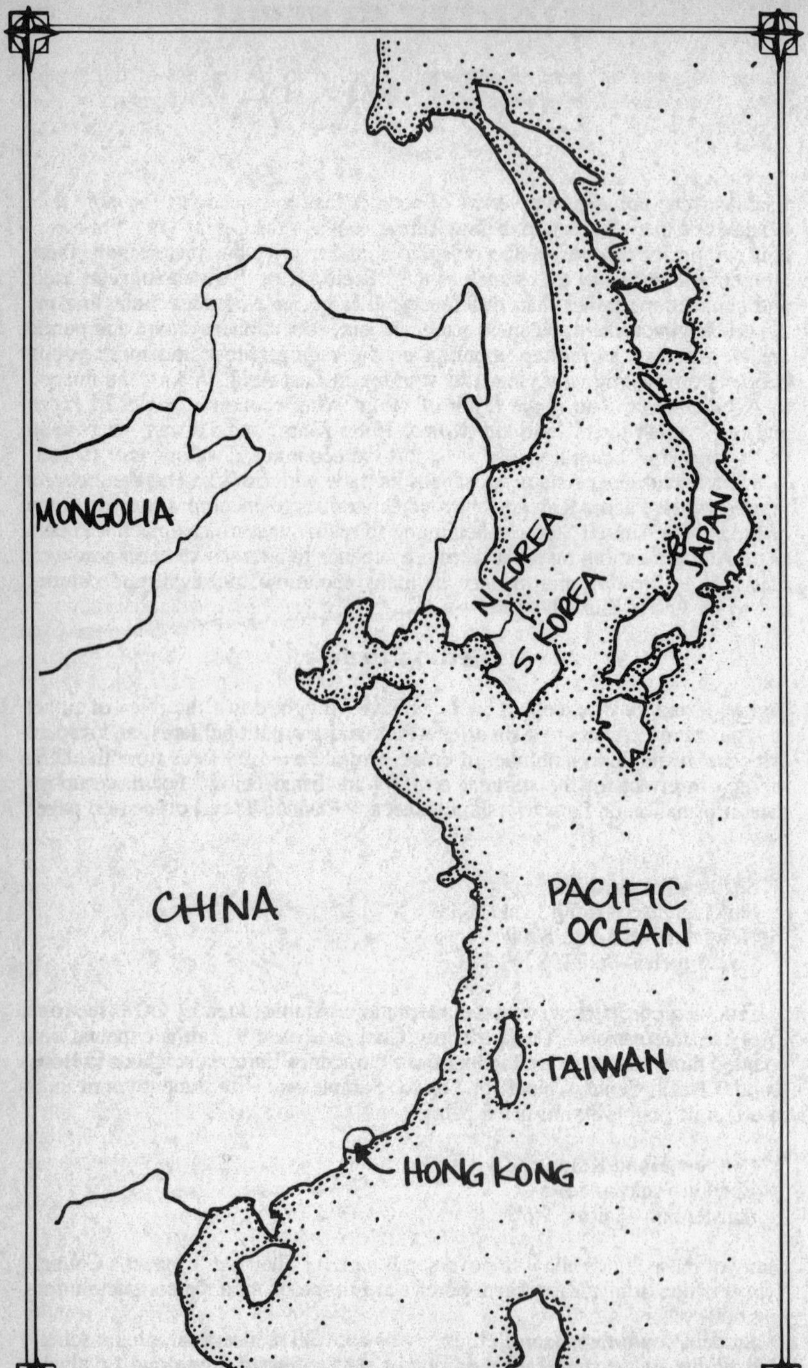
MONGOLIA
N. KOREA
S. KOREA
JAPAN
CHINA
PACIFIC OCEAN
TAIWAN
HONG KONG

Asia. On some of these flights you'll save up to 50 percent of the regular fares. Sample *one-way* student/youth fares in effect during the summer of 1989 are listed below:

Bangkok–Tokyo, $355
Bangkok–Hong Kong, $155
Hong Kong–Singapore, $255

If you want to travel overland between Europe and East Asia, you might consider traveling through the Soviet Union on the Trans-Siberian Railroad. This, the world's longest train route, makes 91 stops, takes you one-quarter of the way around the globe, and passes through seven time zones and 100 degrees of longitude. Nonstop, the trip takes eight days.

Traveling Around East Asia

Largely because of geography, but also because of politics, most travel between the countries of East Asia is by plane. Since the border between North and South Korea remains closed to trade and travel, South Korea is for all practical purposes an island nation like Japan and Taiwan. Of the five nations covered at length in this chapter, only China and Hong Kong share a common border. Thus, for the most part, train, bus, and private automobile—although options within individual countries—are simply not options for international travel in the region. Travel by boat, however, is an option for those traveling between Japan and Korea, with frequent ferry service connecting Pusan, Korea, and Shimonoseki, Japan.

Air service between the nations of East Asia is convenient and fairly inexpensive for persons eligible for student/youth fares; eligibility for these fares is the same as for the student fares discussed above. Sample fares in effect for 1989 are listed below. Updated information is available from Council Travel offices.

Tokyo–Hong Kong, $205
Osaka–Taipei, $180
Seoul–Hong Kong, $245
Beijing–Tokyo, $445

The United States government does not recommend travel to North Korea by U.S. citizens. Although the government does not forbid citizens from visiting the country, such travel is difficult to arrange due to restrictions imposed by the North Korean government and regulations on the activities of U.S. travel agents imposed by the U.S. Treasury Department. U.S. citizens interested in traveling to North Korea must apply for a visa at a North Korean embassy in a third country such as Denmark, Egypt, Malaysia, Norway, Pakistan, or Singapore.

For Further Information

Because the Pacific Rim countries of Asia have become popular destinations for both business and vacation travelers, guidebooks to the region are now plentiful. *North-East Asia on a Shoestring* is full of practical advice for the traveler to China, Hong Kong, Japan, Macao, South Korea, and Taiwan.

Geared to the budget traveler, it can be ordered from Lonely Planet Publications (Embarcadero West, 112 Linden Street, Oakland, CA 94607) for $11.95 (plus $1.50 postage). The *All-Asia Guide*, compiled by the Far Eastern Economic Review, is packed with practical information on all the countries of Asia, and is available from the Charles E. Tuttle Company (26-30 Main Street, Rutland, VT 05701) for $12.95. Under the appropriate country sections later in this chapter, you'll find a discussion of guidebooks to specific nations in the region.

Since the countries and cultures of East Asia are so different from those Americans are accustomed to, travelers may find a cultural introduction as useful as a travel guide. One such introduction is *Asia Through the Back Door*, by veteran travel writers Rick Steves and John Gottberg, available from John Muir Publications (P.O. Box 613, Santa Fe, NM 87504) for $11.95 (plus $1.75 for postage).

Persons interested in staying in youth hostels in East Asia will find volume two of the *International Youth Hostel Handbook*, which lists nearly 500 youth hostels in Japan as well as in Hong Kong and South Korea, indispensable.

The Asia Society, a nonprofit organization dedicated to increasing Americans' understanding of Asian civilizations and cultures, is an excellent source of information and publishes a number of useful publications. For a publications catalog and information about the organization and its services, write to the Asia Society (725 Park Avenue, New York, NY 10021).

Studying in East Asia

You'll find a number of study programs listed in the individual country sections later in this chapter. In the section below we've listed only the study programs of CIEE member institutions that take place in more than one country of the region. Consult Appendix I for the addresses of the colleges and universities listed in this section.

SEMESTER AND ACADEMIC YEAR

General Studies

St. Olaf College. "Term in the Far East." Japan, Taiwan, China, and Thailand. Fall semester plus January. Cross-cultural experience with academic study of non-Western world, including three-month family stay in Chaing Mai, Thailand. Sophomores, juniors, and seniors. Extensive application and interview required. Apply by March 1.

"Global Semester." Cairo, Egypt; Bangalore, India; Taipei, Taiwan; and Kyoto, Japan. Cultures and contemporary problems of non-Western world. Fall semester plus January. Sophomores, juniors, and seniors. Apply by March 1.

University of Pittsburgh. "Semester at Sea." Fall or spring semester. Students, based aboard the S.S. *Universe*, attend classes on board and travel to various countries in Europe, the Middle East, and Asia. Sophomores, juniors, and seniors with 2.75 GPA. Contact: Semester at Sea, 2E Forbes Quadrangle, University of Pittsburgh, Pittsburgh, PA 15260; (412) 648-7490.

Special Education

Southern Illinois University at Carbondale. "Special Education in Japan and Hong Kong." Program features site visits to facilities for the mentally and physically handicapped. Juniors, seniors, graduate students, and special education teachers. Apply by April 1.

SUMMER

Asian Studies

New York University. China and Hong Kong. Interaction of tradition and modernity. Graduate students, teachers, and specialists. Apply by April 15. Contact: School of Education, Health, Nursing and Arts Professions, 32 Washington Place, 3rd floor, New York, NY 10003; (212) 998-5030.

Humanities

New York University. Hong Kong, Taiwan, and People's Republic of China. Graduate students. Apply by April 15. Contact: School of Education, Health, Nursing and Arts Professions. 32 Washington Place, 3rd floor, New York, NY 10003; (212) 998-5030.

CHINA

China, the world's oldest living civilization, has an indomitable heritage, culture, and tradition. The foreigner visiting China today will find him or herself witness to a major turning point in the nation's long history, as the government continues to support far-reaching social and economic changes while repressing demands for democracy and political change. The Yellow River, a symbol of Chinese civilization, flows through the heartland of China to the open sea. However, we have yet to see if, after a history of isolation and backwardness, China will arrive, without further setback, at the open sea of internationalism and modernity.

Much of the turmoil of Chinese history is written on the faces of the Chinese people. The older generation remains fearful and cautious of politics. In 1949, the Communist government under Mao Tse-tung declared a Chinese nation at last independent of foreign domination and internal chaos. But domestic politics soon turned to repression, particularly during the Cultural Revolution of the late 1960s and '70s. As a result, older Chinese have witnessed family and friends being subjected to accusations, jailed, shipped off to labor camps for political "incorrections," and in many cases killed. Now young people, too —as a result of the government's bloody repression of the student prodemocracy movement in 1989—have become victims of a party leadership intent on enforcing its claim to authority. The Chinese people have been numbed by innumerable swings of the political pendulum and masterful manipulation of "truth" for political ends. If fear and apathy seem to be dominating the nation's political life at the moment, it is because the Chinese are tired of sacrificing for the political elite in the name of China.

Over the last decade, greater economic freedom has resulted in an improved standard of living and more contact with the outside world. The young have been at the forefront of this trend. Free markets, black markets, "strange" clothes, "decadent" ways, and foreign ideas, music, and language have been heartily embraced. (The world's largest Kentucky Fried Chicken outlet was built 100 meters from Mao's memorial.) Material rewards have also been adopted to provide incentive for higher economic productivity. Slowly and expensively, the Chinese are being introduced to the luxuries of TVs, refrigerators, and washing machines.

Social changes are also evident. Lovers, previously invisible in public areas, crowd parks, benches, boating houses, and any space they can find—something that would not have been possible a few years ago. More fundamental social change is resulting from the government's strict enforcement of the controversial one-child-per-family policy implemented to control population growth —a policy that challenges the age-old Chinese tradition of the extended family.

However dramatic China's economic and social reforms have been, political reform has lagged behind. This fact fueled much of the popular frustration that led to the student prodemocracy movement in the spring of 1989. TV images of Chinese citizens in open defiance of the regime granted the world an opportunity to transform its stereotypical preconceptions of China. No longer are the Chinese seen as a vast passive population, a people who are undistinguished in all but their reliance on the glories of their past.

The foreigner drawn to China should try to understand China's attraction to the West as well as the history behind its urgency to "catch up" to its Western counterparts. China was once the world's leading civilization. When it reopened its doors to the world in the late 19th century, however, it was stunned to discover that the industrial civilizations of the West had long surpassed it in almost every dimension. Nor was this discovery without its irony. It was, after all, the Chinese who invented the compass, which enabled the European powers to extend their empires and cultural influence all over the globe. It was the Chinese who invented gun powder as well, which armed the West to conquer and colonize. And it was also the Chinese who invented paper currency, which facilitated international trade and the growth of capitalism. Today, the awakened sleeping giant that is China is reaching another vital juncture. The course it will take, both in pace and direction, is yet unpredictable but of critical importance to the rest of the world.

—*Ching-Ching Ni, Oberlin, Ohio*

Official name: People's Republic of China. **Area:** 3,691,521 square miles (slightly larger than the U.S.). **Population:** 2,108,700,000. **Population density:** 294 inhabitants per square mile. **Capital:** Beijing (pop. 9,330,000). **Largest city:** Shanghai (pop. 11,940,000). **Language:** Chinese (Mandarin, Cantonese, Wu, Kan-Hakka, Amoy-Swatow, Foochow). **Religion:** Officially atheist. **Per capita income:** US$330. **Currency:** Renminbi (yuan). **Literacy rate:** 76%. **Average daily high/low:*** Beijing: January, 35°/15°; July, 89°/71°. **Average number of days with precipitation:** Beijing: January, 3; July, 13.

---

*all temperatures are Fahrenheit

TRAVEL

U.S. citizens will need both a passport and a visa for travel to China. Travel arrangements are usually made by China International Travel Service (CITS), the agency with exclusive responsibility for all foreign tourism in China (excluding Chinese people living abroad). CITS tours may be booked through travel agencies and airlines in the United States and abroad. Visas for tour group members are usually obtained by the travel agents as part of the tour package.

It is also possible for individuals to travel on their own in China. Visa applications may be submitted to the Embassy of the People's Republic of China (2300 Connecticut Avenue NW, Washington, DC 20008) or the Chinese Consulates General in Houston, New York, or San Francisco. The current visa fee is $7, and two passport-size photos are required. Allow at least three weeks for processing. *Tips for Travelers to the People's Republic of China* is published by the U.S. Department of State's Bureau of Security and Consular Affairs. The pamphlet is available for $1 from the Superintendent of Documents, U.S. Government Printing Office, Washington, DC 20402.

Tourism in China

"Patience, flexibility, and cultural sensitivity are golden virtues in China. Observe and think before you speak; try to develop an understanding of the relationships involved in the family, the bureaucracy, et cetera. Look for cultural similarities as well as differences. Reserve judgment and keep an open mind."

During the past decade China's interest in attracting Western currency and the interest of many Americans in a long-inaccessible nation rich in culture and history have combined to produce skyrocketing growth in tourism in China. The Chinese government continues to encourage tourism from the West, although at press time the effect of the suppression of the student protest in Tiananmen Square on the flow of tourists from the West was uncertain.

Tourism in China has always focused on seeing the sights and seldom involves significant contact between foreigners and Chinese. Contact is limited both by language and cultural barriers as well as government policies. Tourists—as well as students, businessmen, and diplomats—are generally placed in accommodations exclusively for foreigners rather than being allowed to mingle freely with Chinese.

"You will always be foreign in China. You must accept your status and, at the same time, try to mix with the Chinese. It is a very wide gap to bridge, but persist and you will most likely be rewarded with friendship."

A special currency has been developed for foreigners in China. Renminbi (people's money) is the currency of China, but foreign-exchange certificates (FECs) are supposed to be used by foreigners for all expenses. In practice, FECs must be used for accommodations, train and plane tickets, restaurants in hotels, and Friendship stores, while renminbi can be used for everything else. If a person insists, renminbi will sometimes be accepted when they shouldn't be. Both FEC and renminbi are made up of fen, jiao, and yuan. Ten fen equals one jiao, ten jiao equals one yuan.

The host of most tourist programs in the PRC is the China International Travel Service (CITS—the Chinese name is Luxingshe), located at 6 East Ch'ang-an Street, Beijing. In New York, the China National Tourist Office (60 East 42nd Street, Suite 3126, New York, NY 10165) handles China's promotion and information activities. Recently the All China Youth Federation has also entered the China travel field. Although its services are more limited than CITS's, the tours it offers are more economical and designed to appeal to the youth market. Council Travel offices can help schools and other educational groups develop a tour through either of these two organizations.

Organized Tours

"All China is organized into various groups. Independent initiative as Americans understand it takes on a whole new meaning in China."

Council Travel, in cooperation with the Hong Kong Student Travel Bureau, offers a number of tours to China, ranging from a few days to several weeks, with regular departures throughout the year. These include traditional "grand" tours that visit the main tourist destinations of Beijing, Shanghai, Ghanzhou, Luoyang, and Xi'an to ones that focus on special interests such as bicycling or living on an agricultural commune. Tours are designed especially for students but are also open to non-students of any age. Council Travel offices (see pages ix–xi) have details and will make bookings.

The Council on International Educational Exchange conducts a summer program for educators interested in visiting schools and meeting with their counterparts in the People's Republic of China. In addition, participants in the U.S.-China Educator Exchange visit sites of historic and cultural interest in various cities and regions throughout China. The program is offered every other year; in alternate years the Council hosts a delegation of Chinese educators in the United States. For more information, contact the Professional and Secondary Education Programs Department at the Council.

Travel programs organized by members of the Council on International Educational Exchange are listed below. Consult Appendix I for the addresses of the universities listed in this section.

New York University. "International Travel Programs." Short-term, usually two-week tours. Students and adults. Apply two months prior to departure. Contact: NYU School of Continuing Education, International Programs, 331 Shimkin, Washington Square, New York, NY 10003; (212) 998-7133.

Ohio University. "Chinese Art and Architecture." Beijing and Xi'an. Four-week summer tour. Students, faculty, and adults. Apply by April 1. Contact Office of Continuing Education; (614) 593-1776.

Michigan State University. "Exploring Contemporary China." Various cities. Two-week summer tour. Seniors, graduates, and adults. Apply by April 21.

Getting Around

Westerners can travel around the country with a minimum of restrictions. However, from a practical point of view, Westerners unable to speak Chinese will find independent travel difficult. Learning a little Chinese—even a limited number of phrases—will make things easier.

China has an efficient railway network that extends to most areas of the country and is generally easy to use. Intercity trains have two classes of service—hard seat and soft seat. Hard seats are wood or vinyl-covered benches seating three across; soft seats are linen-covered seats in a private car or compartment. Soft-seat prices are double that of hard seats. Overnight trains have hard sleeper and soft sleeper in addition to seats. Foreigners are charged about 70 percent more for tickets than locals and are usually directed into special lines at train stations. Students studying in China may be allowed to pay the local price. It should also be noted that a person can only buy tickets for trains originating in that city (i.e., you can't buy a ticket from Shanghai to Nanjing in Beijing).

Air China provides air transport to the major cities of the nation. However, flights are often late and service onboard is minimal. Regular tickets are fairly inexpensive but foreigners must pay twice the regular fare on domestic flights.

The bicycle is probably the most popular form of transportation in China. Chinese bicycles are basic, unsophisticated models, but they can be rented everywhere by the hour, day, or week. They can also be loaded on the luggage racks on top of buses with no questions asked; taking them on a train will involve more red tape.

"In order to broaden my experience of life in China, I ventured out into the city, away from campus, as frequently as I could. I often rode my bicycle through the city, coasting through different neighborhoods. Several times a week I strolled through the free markets (free enterprise street markets) near the university. Whenever I stopped to buy some small item, such as some fruit or a peasant toy, a crowd would gather around to watch and listen to a foreigner speak Chinese. Often a small group would follow me down the street. This kind of scrutiny can be discomforting, but most of the people were just curious and friendly. I was able to have many interesting conversations in the market. The peasants just in from the countryside to sell fresh produce had lots of questions to ask me about the price of produce, farming, and life in general in America as well as about my background."

Eating and Sleeping

Lodging for foreigners and Chinese are separate, either by hotel, as is usually the case, or by rooms or floors in a single hotel. At least one hotel in each city provides dormitory-style accommodations for a small fee per night.

"Dormitory rooms are clean and sometimes luxurious. Being surrounded by other independent travelers in the dorm room, one is able to get lots of current information on cities and find traveling companions."

"In China two unmarried people of different sexes requesting a double room are assumed to be married. In some hotels the desk clerks inquire about marital status. If unmarried is replied, they will not permit a couple to have one room; all rooms, however, have two single beds."

Especially for Students and Young People

The People's Republic of China does not have an ISTC-member organization promoting student travel and student travel discounts, nor is the International Student Identity Card recognized for special discounts in China. However, noting that you are a "poor" student may be a useful bargaining tool in obtaining cheaper prices.

For Further Information

The National Committee on U.S.-China Relations, 777 United Nations Plaza, New York, NY 10017, has developed a *Briefing Kit on the People's Republic of China* ($20) designed to meet the special interests of the individual visitor or delegation going to China. It includes three sections: (1) a travel guide, which provides basic information on sightseeing, food, hotels, and transportation; (2) a collection of background materials such as annotated bibliographies, maps, a profile on the economy, and biographies of Chinese leaders; and (3) reprinted articles on topics of concern. Because these kits are individualized, allow four weeks for their preparation in advance. Orders should include the dates of your trip, your itinerary, and any special interests in China that you may have.

Budget travelers will find *China: A Travel Survival Kit* the most helpful guidebook to take along. It's published by Lonely Planet Publications (Embarcadero West, 112 Linden Street, Oakland, CA 94607), and is available for $17.95 (plus $1.50 postage).

Communicating with China, edited by Robert A. Kapp for the China Council of the Asia Society, is a compilation of essays on "down-to-earth problems of language and communication with the People's Republic of China." It includes an excellent bibliography for people willing to do their "homework" in preparation for a trip to China. Published by Intercultural Press, it is available from the publisher at P.O. Box 768, Yarmouth, ME 04096 for $6.95 (plus $1.50 postage).

Information on sightseeing in China is readily available in a number of other guidebooks. *The China Guidebook*, updated annually and published by Eurasia Press (168 State Street, Teaneck, NJ 07666), is available for $16.95. Fodor's *People's Republic of China* is readily available in bookstores for $16.95.

If you want to read contemporary works by Chinese authors, write to China Books and Periodicals (2929 24th Street, San Francisco, CA 94110) for a publications catalog.

"The more you read about China, both historical and contemporary, the more you will understand why the Chinese do what they do."

WORK

Westerners are not permitted to work in China unless they are teachers or technicians working under contract with an agency related to the Chinese government. Chinese institutions of higher learning offer year-long teaching posts to foreign applicants in the fields of English language and linguistics, literature, basic and engineering sciences, finance, business and management, law, et cetera. Applicants should have a master's degree or higher and at least five years' teaching experience. For further information, contact the Consulate General of the People's Republic of China, 3417 Montrose Boulevard, Houston, TX 77006.

Voluntary Service

For persons interested in voluntary service work, the "Year Abroad Program" sponsored by the International Christian Youth Exchange offers persons ages 18–24 voluntary service opportunities in the fields of health care, education, the environment, construction, et cetera. See page 22 for more information.

Persons interested in voluntary service as teachers can contact WorldTeach, a nonprofit program which places recent college graduates in schools in China. Volunteers must commit themselves to a one-year teaching assignment but no teaching training or experience is required. They receive an allowance of $72 a month but pay a program fee of about $3,000 that includes air fare, orientation, and insurance. For more information, contact WorldTeach, Phillip Brooks House, Harvard University, Cambridge, MA 02138.

In addition, Goshen College offers a study-service term open only to Goshen students.

STUDY

At press time, a number of fall 1989 study programs in China were being temporarily relocated to Taiwan or Hong Kong as a result of the uncertain situation caused by the government's suppression of student protest movements at Chinese universities. Most U.S. universities operating study programs at schools in the People's Republic of China expect to resume programs shortly; however, students should be sure to check with the respective institution for the latest information. CIEE's study programs at universities in Beijing, Nanjing, and Shanghai are in operation. Options include language study in Beijing, Nanjing, or Shanghai as well as a program in Chinese business and society in Beijing. For further information on CIEE-sponsored study opportunities, see the program listing below.

A publication that might be of help to persons planning to study in China is *An Introduction to Education in the People's Republic of China and U.S-China Educational Exchanges*. Although designed primarily for college administrators setting up programs with Chinese universities, it also provides useful general information on the Chinese educational system. The book is available for $12.95 from the National Association for Foreign Student Affairs, 1860 19th Street NW, Washington, DC 20009. *China Bound: A Guide to Academic Life and Work in the PRC* is written for Americans traveling to China to live and work in an academic setting. Although it's designed mainly for graduate students, researchers, and professors, it is also useful for undergraduate students. *China Bound* is available for $14.95 from the National Academy Press (2101 Constitution Avenue NW, Washington, DC 20418). If you're thinking of enrolling in a Chinese university, contact the Consulate General of the People's Republic of China (address above) for its fact sheet on the enrollment of foreign students in China.

The following are the educational programs offered by members of the Council on International Educational Exchange. Consult Appendix I for the addresses of the institutions listed in this section. In addition to the programs listed below, the American Graduate School of International Management, Lewis and Clark College, Northern Arizona University, Ohio State University, the University of the Pacific, and the University of California system offer study programs open only to their own students.

SEMESTER AND ACADEMIC YEAR

Business

Council on International Educational Exchange. "Cooperative Chinese Business and Society." Beijing. Courses at the University of International Business and Economics. Spring or fall semester. Sophomores to graduate students with two years Mandarin and basic business courses. Apply by February 15 for fall and October 10 for spring.

University System of Georgia/Georgia State University. "Management and Culture in China." Beijing. Business students with a 2.5 GPA. Apply by April 15; applications accepted thereafter on a space-available basis.

Chinese Language and Culture

AFS Intercultural Programs. "Academic Study Program." Options at universities in nine cities. Academic year. Persons ages 18–35 with one year of Mandarin. Apply by June 1.

Beloit College. "Fudan Exchange Program." Shanghai. Academic year or fall semester. Sophomores to graduate students with a minimum of intermediate-level Chinese and a 2.0 GPA. Apply by April 1.

Brethren Colleges Abroad. Dalian. Semester or academic year. Sophomores, juniors, and seniors with 3.0 GPA. Apply by December 1 for spring and May 1 for fall.

Council on International Educational Exchange.
"China Cooperative Language and Study Program." Beijing. Semester or academic year. Study at Peking University. Sophomores to graduate students with two years of Mandarin. Apply by February 15 for fall and October 10 for spring. Contact Academic Programs Department.
"China Cooperative Language and Study Program." Nanjing. Fall or spring semester. Study at Nanjing University. Sophomores to graduate students with one year college Mandarin. Apply by February 15 for fall and October 10 for spring. Contact Academic Programs Department.

State University of New York at Albany. Beijing and Tianjin, Nanjing, Shanghai, Taipei. Academic year. Juniors, seniors, and graduate students with one year of Chinese. Apply by February 15.

State University of New York at Oswego. Beijing. Semester or academic year. Undergraduates with 2.8 GPA. Apply by April 1 for fall and November 1 for spring.

University of Massachusetts—Amherst. "University of Massachusetts in China." Beijing and Shaanxi. Juniors, seniors, and graduate students with two years of college-level Mandarin. Apply by January 20.

University of North Carolina–Chapel Hill. "UNC Program to China at Beijing." Academic year. Juniors and seniors; previous Chinese language courses required. Apply by February 12.

University of Oregon.
 "OSSHE Beijing Program." Fall semester. Sophomores above with 2.75 GPA. Preference given to Oregon State System of Higher Education (OSSHE) students. Apply by March 1.
 "OSSHE Fujian Program." Winter and spring terms. Sophomores, juniors, and seniors with one year of Chinese and 2.75 GPA. Preference given to Oregon State System of Higher Education (OSSHE) students. Apply by November 1.

East Asian Studies

Indiana University. "Introduction to China." Hangzhou. Spring semester. Sophomores, juniors, and seniors with a 3.0 GPA. Apply by first week in October.

General Studies

American University. "Beijing Semester." Fall semester. Intensive Mandarin and courses on Chinese politics, business, culture, and civilization. Juniors and seniors; knowledge of Mandarin preferable. Apply six months prior to start of program.

Brigham Young University. "BYU Study Abroad." Nanjing. Spring semester. Sophomores, juniors, and seniors with some knowledge of Chinese. Apply by February 1.

Friends World College. "Chinese Studies." Hangzhou (Zhejiang province), with three-week orientation in Hong Kong; optional semester on Taiwan. Academic year; semester option for language study. Chinese studies, Mandarin, TESL, and individualized program combining independent study and field research. Juniors and seniors. Apply by May 15 for fall and November 15 for spring.

State University of New York at Cortland. Beijing. Semester or academic year. Juniors, seniors, and graduate students with one year of Mandarin and 3.5 GPA in major. Apply by March 1 for fall and October 1 for spring.

Physical Education

State University of New York at Cortland. Beijing. Semester or academic year. Juniors, seniors, and graduate students with one year of Mandarin and 3.5 GPA in major. Apply by March 1.

SUMMER

Business

Council on International Educational Exchange. "Cooperative Chinese Business and Society." Beijing. Courses at the University of International Business and Economics. Juniors to graduate students with two years Mandarin and basic business courses. Apply by February 10. Contact Academic Programs Department.

Chinese Language and Culture

AFS Intercultural Programs. "Chinese Studies." Six-week program in Kunming. Three-week program in Shanghai and Hangzhou. Undergraduates, graduates, and adults. Apply by May 1.

Council on International Educational Exchange. "China Cooperative Language and Study Program." Study at Fudan University in Shanghai or Peking University in Beijing. Sophomores to graduate students with two years college Mandarin for program in Beijing, one year for program in Shanghai. Apply by February 10. Contact Academic Programs Department.

Michigan State University. Shanghai. "Intensive Chinese Language and Culture Studies Program." Summer. Juniors, seniors, and graduate students with one year college-level Chinese. Apply by April 21.

North Carolina State University/Raleigh. "NCSU-Liaoning University Summer Institute of Chinese Language." Shenyang and Liaoning province. Sophomores to graduate students and others. Apply by May 10.

Syracuse University. "China: Past & Present." Tianjin. Sophomores to graduate students and professionals. Apply by March 17.

University of Minnesota. "Minnesota-Nankai Summer Intensive Chinese Language Institute." Tianjin. High school students to college graduates. Nonstudents can also apply. One year of standard Chinese required. Apply by February 24. Contact Minnesota-Nankai Institute, 113 Folwell Hall, 9 Pleasant St. SE, Minneapolis, MN 55455; (612) 624-0386.

University of Notre Dame. "Foreign Study Program in Tianjin." Excursions to Beijing and other Chinese cities. Freshmen to graduate students and faculty. Apply by March 1.

University System of Georgia/Kennesaw State College. "Culture in Yangzhou." Freshmen to graduate students. Apply by March 15.

Engineering

University of Illinois at Urbana—Champaign. "International Programs in Engineering." Hefei. Priority given to engineering students. Freshmen to graduate students. Apply by March 1.

General Studies

Portland State University. "Summer Session in Zhengzhou, China." Month-long program designed for intensive language acquisition and cultural immersion. High school graduates to graduate students and nonstudents.

Music

University System of Georgia/Georgia State University. "Music and the Arts in China." Study at the Shanghai Conservatory of Music. Freshmen to graduate students with 2.5 GPA. Apply by March 15.

University of Toledo. "Summer Study in China." Beijing, Shanghai, Hangzhou, Xi'an, Guilin, and Guangzhou. Study Chinese political system through lectures by government and party officials and by Chinese professors. High school students, college students, and adults. Apply by May 1.

Teaching English as a Second Language

University System of Georgia/Georgia State University. Beijing. For graduate students studying to be ESL teachers and for undergraduates majoring in Foreign Languages and English. Apply by April 2.

EXPLORING CHINESE CULTURE

Literature

There have been two particularly fertile periods in 20th-century Chinese literature. The first, ushered in by the May Fourth Movement of 1919, was characterized by a new cultural freedom that allowed many social issues to be addressed. *Family*, by Pa Chin, is an epic saga written during this period that contrasts traditional Chinese values with the modern ideas of the Nationalist May Fourth Movement. Mao Dun's *Midnight*, written in 1933, deals with corruption in prerevolutionary Shanghai. *Masterpieces of Modern Chinese Fiction 1919–1949* is a collection of stories that brings together most of the important Chinese writers of the period, including Ding Ling, one of the first Chinese writers to explore women's thoughts and feelings in fiction, and Lu Hsun, whose "The True Story of Ah Q" is a particularly well-known and critical examination of Chinese culture.

After the death of Mao in 1976, there was another flowering of cultural expression, as Chinese writers began to reflect on the country's recent history. *Chrysanthemums and Other Stories*, a collection of stories by Feng Ji Cai, examines the lives of ordinary people and how they were affected by the Cultural Revolution. *Roses and Thorns: The Second Blossoming of the Hundred Flowers in Chinese Fiction 1979–80*, an anthology of post-Mao writing, shows the evolution of the politically oriented writing of the Mao era to a more personal and experimental type of writing. Gu Hua's *A Small Town Called Hibiscus* shows the effect of larger political events on ordinary country people, starting in the early 1960s and ending with the fall of the "Gang of Four" in the late 1970s. Wang Anyi, an important younger writer, addresses the problems of young people returning to the cities after many years of "reeducation" in the countryside during the Cultural Revolution in *Lapse of Time*. Also providing insights into life in China since the Cultural Revolution is *The Chinese Western*, a collection of eight short stories by writers from China's northwestern provinces.

A more recent picture of the political ferment in China can be found in *Seeds of Fire: Chinese Voices of Conscience*. Published in 1989, it is an anthology of protest and political commentary in various forms, including stories, essays, cartoons, and rock lyrics, organized into sections dealing with different contemporary issues.

HONG KONG

If you want to take a rickshaw ride in Hong Kong, you'd better hurry—there are only six of them left. That's because the rickshaws have been replaced by somewhat more modern means of transport, including a high-speed subway system, wall-to-wall double-decker buses, and long lines of luxury automobiles. In fact, Hong Kong has more Rolls Royces per capita than anywhere else in the world, and nothing better captures the pace at which this island colony is changing than the one-generation leap from rickshaw to Rolls.

Except for majestic Queen Victoria Peak, a regal backdrop to one of the world's best natural seaports, the city of Hong Kong is physically unrecognizable to someone who may have visited it only a few years ago. Over the past 30 years, Hong Kong has been a frenzied construction site. The results have been spectacular, not only in the physical development of this British colony but also in the growth of its economy and the improvement in the quality of life of its inhabitants.

Hong Kong is now a pace-setting metropolis of some 5.6 million people, with a worldwide reputation for its vigor, vibrant commercial life, and investment climate. Its standard of living has increased four to five times in a generation and the rate of economic development continues at a rapid pace.

But amidst the constant din of the riveters' guns, Hong Kong faces an uncertain political future. Currently administered as a British colony, Hong Kong's sovereignty will revert to China effective July 1, 1997, placing one of the world's most successful capitalist showcases directly under the control of the world's most populous Communist nation. Not since the French Revolution has the world seen a political transformation as rich with irony as Hong Kong's current situation.

There are two popular ways to interpret this state of affairs. Some see dire implications for Hong Kong's free economy, predicting that the Chinese will be unable to avoid damaging it no matter how hard they try to preserve it. Others are continuing to put their money squarely on Hong Kong's future.

If one had to sum up Hong Kong in a single word, that word would surely be confidence. Built on a rock, with no natural resources other than its people,

Hong Kong's only choice is to exude confidence—even if the situation doesn't merit it. Without confidence, the people of Hong Kong would soon flee to other shores. With it, the people have something to hope for, namely, continued prosperity and security.

—*Jay Henderson, Hong Kong*

Hong Kong is a dependency of the United Kingdom. Area: 398 square miles (about one-quarter the size of Rhode Island). **Population:** 5,600,000. **Population density:** 14,326 inhabitants per square mile. **Capital and largest city:** Victoria (pop. 501,700). **Language:** English (official), Chinese (Cantonese). **Religion:** Buddhism, Taoism, Christianity. **Per capita income:** US$4,210. **Currency:** Hong Kong dollar. **Literacy rate:** 75%. **Average daily high/low:*** January, 64°/56°; July, 87°/78°. **Average number of days with precipitation:** January, 4; July, 17.

TRAVEL

U.S. citizens are required to have a passport; however, a visa is not required for stays of up to one month with proof of onward transportation by sea or air. For study or work, a visa is required in addition to a passport. For specific requirements, check with the Embassy of Great Britain (3100 Massachusetts Avenue NW, Washington, DC 20009) or with any British consulate.

Getting Around

Hong Kong has a comprehensive public transportation system, but walking is probably the best way to get around. Hong Kong fairly vibrates with commerce, which means there is practically no piece of earth that is not used by someone trying to make a living. You won't find the standard tourist sights here (e.g., monuments, churches, et cetera). What you will see are people going about the business of life in a crowded, bustling city set amidst beautiful natural surroundings.

> *"Hong Kong is a city of business and trading that never seems to rest. Just as the traffic noise starts to die down, it starts up again. Its alleyways and byways are some of the most interesting in the world, though it's a perfect place to simply watch the interaction of people going about their day-to-day lives."*

If you get tired of the pace of the city and want a change, you can take a ferry ride to some of Hong Kong's outer islands, where you can spend some time in a sedate farming village. Or, if you prefer, you can take a train to the border of China and enjoy the view of the countryside along the way. Another fascinating trip popular with tourists is the ferry to Macao, a tiny Portuguese outpost on the coast of China scheduled to revert to Chinese control in 1999.

---

*all temperatures are Fahrenheit

"Macao is one of the most fascinating places to visit in Asia—lots of history but quite inexpensive, too. Most people never see anything beyond the gambling tables of Macao, but if you make the effort, you'll be delighted. Try bicycling your way around—you'll find plenty of places to rent a bike."

For persons interested in seeing Hong Kong as part of a group tour, the Hong Kong Student Travel Bureau (see address in "Especially for Students and Young People" below) offers a selection of tours available throughout the year. Options include half-day and one-day tours by bus, ferry, or junk. The organization also offers an array of tours into the People's Republic of China geared to students and young people; details are available at Council travel offices.

Hong Kong has several youth hostels as well as Ys that provide inexpensive accommodations for students and young people; Hong Kong Student Travel Bureau has a list of other inexpensive accommodations in the city. In addition, the Hong Kong Tourist Association (590 Fifth Avenue, New York, NY 10036) distributes a free brochure entitled *Places of Interest by Public Transport*.

Especially for Students and Young People

The Hong Kong Student Travel Bureau (Room 833, Star House, 3, Salisbury Road, Tsimshatsui, Kowloon, Hong Kong) has five offices scattered about the city. This ISTC member performs a variety of services for student/youth travelers, including providing information, arranging tours, booking accommodations, and selling plane, rail, and bus tickets.

Holders of the International Student Identity Card (ISIC) get reduced fares on international flights from Hong Kong and discount rates on a selection of accommodations, including the YMCA International House, the student travel bureau's hostel, and a number of hotels. In addition, a number of retail stores and restaurants offer discounts of up to 40 percent to ISIC holders; a list of these discounts is available at Hong Kong Student Travel Bureau offices. The organization also distributes free maps and lists of cultural events.

Meeting the People

There are several organizations in Hong Kong that can help you meet people with interests similar to your own. The Hong Kong Tourist Association (35th Floor, Jardine House, 1 Connaught Place, P.O. Box 2597, Central, Hong Kong) has further information.

For Further Information

A useful guide to budget travel in Hong Kong is Lonely Planet Publications' *Hong Kong, Macau, and Canton: A Travel Survival Kit*. It's available in many bookstores, or you can order it for $7.95 (plus $1.50 postage) from the publisher (Embarcadero West, 112 Linden Street, Oakland, CA 94607).

WORK

U.S. citizens interested in regular employment in Hong Kong will need a work permit. Applications for permits can only be made by employers wishing to hire foreigners residing outside the colony. Review of applications requires six to eight weeks.

One possibility for Americans interested in spending a month teaching English in Hong Kong is the Summer with a Purpose (SWAP) program of the Reformed Church in America. Program participants teach in a Christian residential summer camp for Chinese youth located in Hong Kong; applicants must be college upperclassmen or graduate students with a Christian commitment. The application deadline date is February 15. See Appendix I for the address where you can write for more information.

Internships/Traineeships

There is an AIESEC internship program in Hong Kong; see page 18 for more information.

STUDY

The following are the educational programs offered by members of the Council on International Educational Exchange. Consult Appendix I for the addresses of the institutions listed in this section. In addition to the programs listed below, the California State University system and New York University offer programs open only to their own students.

SEMESTER AND ACADEMIC YEAR

General Studies

Associated Colleges of the Midwest. "Chinese Studies." Priority given to students at schools that are members of the Associated Colleges of the Midwest or Great Lakes College Association. Juniors to graduate students with 3.0 GPA. Chinese study is strongly recommended. Apply by February 1.

International Student Exchange Program. Direct reciprocal exchange between U.S. universities and the Chinese University of Hong Kong. Academic year. Full curriculum options. Open only to students at ISEP member institutions.

JAPAN

Japan is both democratic and authoritarian, religious and secular, internationalist and provincial, financially rich and yet lacking in amenities for many of its citizens. Because of these and other paradoxes, as well as because of the vast cultural differences between Japan and the United States, Americans often find Japan to be a perplexing—but also extremely interesting—place.

Whether the setting is family, school, or office, Japanese society maintains an important distinction between "insiders" and "outsiders." Outsiders are treated politely but with reserve while intimacy is saved for insiders. The foreigner, or *gai jin* (literally "outside person"), is the ultimate outsider. To see Japan from an insider's point of view requires enormous effort; the foreigner must persevere despite frequent frustrations, coping at times with what may seem to be overt racism and sexism.

In seeming contradiction to the Japanese attitude toward foreigners, there is an obvious fascination in Japan with things Western. Baseball is the most popular sport in the country, McDonald's outlets are everywhere, and Mickey Mouse reigns at the Disney theme park outside Tokyo. Fascination with the West is especially evident among the young, who are among the world's most devoted fans of American and European music and fashion. In fact, Japan has a long tradition of assimilating and adapting from other cultures, taking what it finds attractive and molding it into something quite different and ultimately very Japanese.

The Japanese believe in the primary importance of education and work. These beliefs have served the country well; travelers cannot help but be impressed with the evidence of Japan's recovery from wartime devastation, becoming in the process perhaps the world's most respected—and feared—economic power. Japan has attracted the attention of both the West and the Third World, and both are busy trying to learn the "secret" behind the Japanese success story.

Another very Japanese trait is a penchant for collective decision-making. Group consciousness is central to Japanese social psychology; the importance of the group (family, fellow workers, et cetera) over the individual can be seen throughout Japanese society. Elementary school children undertake classroom assignments by working in teams rather than competing as individuals. Likewise in professional baseball the team always takes precedence over shows of individual skill.

Another set of values that permeates Japanese society is that of the aristocratic warrior tradition: loyalty, sincerity, discipline, duty, and self-denial. The visitor to Japan will find these values animating people everywhere—from students preparing for exams and workers in offices or factories to participants in sports as different as baseball and sumo. It is these traditional values that account, in part, for the civility and respect for others which amaze Western visitors to Japan.

For the conscientious visitor, a stay in Japan can provide valuable insight into how and why this island nation has become one of the world's great economic powers while remaining one of its most enigmatic.

—*Hallam Shorrock, Tokyo, Japan*

Area: 143,574 square miles (about the size of Montana). **Population:** 122,700,000. **Population density:** 854 inhabitants per square mile. **Capital and largest city:** Tokyo (pop. 8,354,615). **Language:** Japanese. **Religion:** Shintoism, Buddhism. **Per capita income:** US$12,923. **Currency:** Yen. **Literacy rate:** 99%. **Average daily high/low:*** Tokyo: January: 47°/29°; July, 80°/70°. **Average number of days with precipitation:** Tokyo: January, 5; July, 10.

---

*all temperatures are Fahrenheit

TRAVEL

A passport is required, but U.S. citizens no longer need a visa for stays of up to 90 days. Check with the Embassy of Japan (2520 Massachusetts Avenue NW, Washington, DC 20008) or with Japanese consulates for specific requirements.

Money Matters

Japan is one of the most expensive countries in the world, although precisely how expensive it will be depends on the fluctuating rate of exchange between the dollar and the yen. This fact presents a real challenge to the budget traveler, who will have to take advantage of the information we've provided on hostels, rail passes, hitchhiking, et cetera in order to keep expenses to a minimum.

Surprisingly, Japanese-made goods are not necessarily cheaper in Japan than in the United States. But don't miss the experience of a Japanese department store.

"I recommend a visit to a department store for the cultural experience. Japanese department stores are mammoth and they provide all kinds of extra services, including a variety of restaurants, galleries, babysitting facilities, and amusement parks on the roof. The philosophy behind this is that these are places to go and spend time, not just to shop. They have variable closing days, but most are open on Sunday. For English speakers, there's a special desk for help and usually you can find a store guide published in English."

Getting Around

Trains are one of the most popular modes of transportation in Japan. The nation's rail system is excellent and a wide range of prices and types of services are available. The cheapest are the local trains, which stop at every station; then come the express trains, the limited express trains, and the *shinkansen*, or "Bullet Trains," which travel at speeds of up to 130 miles per hour. A ride on one of the *shinkansen*, which depart Tokyo for Osaka and beyond every five or ten minutes during the day, can be a highlight of a trip to Japan. Another unique rail experience is the 33-mile trip through the tunnel that connects the islands of Honshu and Hokkaido.

The Japan Rail Pass offers unlimited travel on Japan Rail's trains, ferries, and buses for periods of 7, 14, or 21 days. In addition, passes can be purchased for either of two classes of travel—Ordinary or Green (luxury). The following were the 1989 prices for the Ordinary class pass: 7 days, $224; 14 days, $356; and 21 days, $454. Passes are available only to foreign visitors and must be purchased *before* your arrival in Japan; you can buy vouchers (exchanged for the actual pass upon arrival in Japan) through Japan Airlines or a travel agent. Contact a Council Travel office for more information. (Persons traveling to Japan on a student visa are not eligible for a Japan Rail Pass.)

Buses operate throughout Japan on feeder routes leading to rail stations, and provide the final link for most people going from the city to mountain resorts or ski areas. In addition, buses operating over Japan's expressways and major highways serve as an alternative system of intercity transport. Since few bus drivers speak English, however, travel by bus may be difficult for those who don't speak the language.

You'll also find frequent air service between Japanese cities. Japan Airlines concentrates on providing service between the major cities, while two other carriers, All Nippon Airways and Toa Domestic Airlines, provide more comprehensive service to both major cities and the smaller provincial centers.

More and more Japanese are taking to the highways. Japan has a good highway system that includes many toll expressways. (You can rent a car in Japan but will find few signs in English.) In addition, numerous ferries link the four major and many smaller islands of the Japanese archipelago; there's also ferry service to Korea and China.

Many students traveling in Japan recommend bicycling and hitchhiking as good ways to get around.

"Hitchhiking in Japan is the best in the world. Though the Japanese won't be seen doing it themselves (they consider it a form of begging, which they wouldn't stoop to except in an emergency), they are quick to help out a foreigner who has lost his way. Quite often you'll find yourself being taken to the local railway station, but never mind; walk back out onto the road and continue your trip! Remember to travel with an English-Japanese phrase book. Many of your benefactors will be eager to try out their English."

"Bicycling is, of course, an excellent way of getting around the less populated areas. The popularity of cycling in Japan lies in the fact that Japan is relatively small and well populated and there is always a town or city within a day's ride. The major highways are not very wide and, in most cases, do not have shoulders. When trucks approach there are usually rice paddies to dive into, but this is not suggested as a frequent maneuver. Fortunately, in many areas long-distance bicycle paths are being constructed."

Japanese-made bicycles are extremely expensive in Japan. Better alternatives are shipping your own bicycle to Japan or, for short trips, renting a bicycle at one of the rental shops found near the larger railroad stations.

Eating and Sleeping

"Japan is one country where, because of the high cost of travel, it's important to have a hostel card."

There are over 450 youth hostels in Japan. About 75 of these are government-run and the rest are privately operated. A map that includes a complete listing of both types of hostels, "Youth Hostels Map of Japan," is available on request from the Japan National Tourist Organization (630 Fifth Avenue, New York, NY 10111). Likewise you'll find a complete listing of Japanese youth hostels in the second volume of the *International Youth Hostel Handbook*. Some are Japanese-style hostels, with mattresses or mats on the floor; others are Western-style. Generally speaking plan to spend up to $14 a night, or $25 with two meals. For information about hosteling and getting a youth hostel card see page 50; if you arrive in Japan without a hostel card but want to stay in a hostel, contact Japan Youth Hostels, Hoken Kaikan 3F, 1–2 Sadohara-cho Ichigaya, Shinjuku-ku, Tokyo 162.

"The youth hostels are found almost everywhere. They may be dormitories, Buddhist temples, shinto shrines, small hotels, or even private homes. All will have the youth hostel sign out front. Two good purchases to make if you plan on using the hostels are a copy of the International Youth Hostel Handbook *and a sheet-type sleeping bag. Both are usually available at the larger hostels in Japan. The* Handbook *lists all hostels in Japan with their description, a map showing how to find them, and a picture of the building so you don't end up walking past it. The sheet sleeping bag is mandatory in all hostels. You can either rent it or buy it. The hostels are usually heavily crowded in the school vacation period of mid-July through August. During this time you must phone several days in advance to make reservations."*

In addition to youth hostels there are a few other inexpensive kinds of accommodations, including people's lodges (*kokumin shukusha*) and national vacation villages (*kokumin kyuka mura*). There are 297 government-run and about 150 privately operated people's lodges located in peaceful, natural settings throughout Japan. The average cost of one night's lodging, with two meals included, is approximately $32. The national vacation villages are popular resorts that focus on recreation (skiing or water sports for example). A one-night stay will cost about $35 to $60, with two meals included in the cost. Make reservations through the Japan Travel Bureau for either the people's lodges or the national vacation villages—they're very popular, especially at vacation time.

You may also stay at *minshuku*, or family inns, which cost less than a hotel. Run by family members, *minshuku* allow you to enjoy the comfortable and relaxed atmosphere of living with a Japanese family. The cost is usually about $35, with two meals included. However, you are advised to make reservations ahead of time at either a *minshuku* center or a sightseeing information center (located in most railway stations). The Japan National Tourist Organization in New York has a list of approximately 270 "international" *minshuku*, all with Western-style plumbing and many where some English might be spoken. (You're advised to carry a phrase book anyway.)

"If you do nothing else in Japan, take the opportunity to stay at a Japanese-style inn and soothe your cares away in a Japanese bath—there is no better panacea in all the world."

Another possibility that might appeal to you—especially if you're interested in Japan's religious life—is an overnight stay in a Buddhist temple. You'll find it easier to find room in a temple located in the countryside, however, since many of the temples in the larger cities have waiting lists. In most cases, if you stay in a temple you will be expected to participate fully in the life of the temple. This may include getting up at three A.M., helping to clean the temple and its grounds, and participating in meditation. If you don't speak Japanese, you should really try to have someone with you who does. Also, if at all possible, make arrangements ahead of time.

If you find yourself in a situation where you do not have reservations and need a place to stay, you'll find an information booth in nearly every train station in Japan—even in the smaller towns. The people staffing these booths are usually very helpful, and in many cases will call to arrange a room for you; usually, you can pay for it right at the desk.

There are few organized campgrounds in Japan, so finding an isolated spot to readily pitch a tent or drop a sleeping bag can be difficult. Camping is not popular among the Japanese; instead, the need for cheap accommodations is well supplied by the abundance of youth hostels.

> *"Those who are used to dropping a sleeping bag in any open space must remember that the Japanese are among the most efficient users of land in the world. The observant traveler will notice that there simply are no unused, clear, flat spaces of land in Japan. The only real possibilities for camping are along the beaches in some of the coastal areas. Anyone spending the night on what appears to be a remote, rural beach, however, should not be surprised to wake up at sunrise in the midst of a large crowd of villagers hauling in the shore nets."*

Especially for Students and Young People

Japan's student travel organization and ISTC member is the National Federation of University Cooperative Associations of Japan (NFUCA). Their main office is located in the Sanshin-Hokusei Building, 2-4-9 Yoyogi, Shibuya-ku, Tokyo 151, and they also have an office in Osaka. NFUCA issues the International Student Identity Card (ISIC) in Japan, sells plane and ferry tickets, books accommodations, and provides information on student discounts.

CIEE's Tokyo office (Sanno Grand Building, Room 102, 2-14-2 Nagata-cho, Chiyoda-ku, Tokyo 100) is another good source of student travel information. It also issues the ISIC and can book airline tickets for you.

Unfortunately, there are a limited number of discounts available for ISIC holders in Japan. However, ISIC holders can take advantage of student fares on flights from Tokyo or Osaka to other parts of Asia. Students are also eligible for a 35-percent discount if they fly standby on domestic routes and receive a discount on most ferries between Japan's various islands. In addition, student discounts are available for some cultural and sporting events as well as at selected hotels, museums, and shops. Contact NFUCA for further information.

Meeting the People

The Home Visit System, which is now operating in 11 cities, gives foreigners a chance to visit a typical Japanese home and talk to the family for a few hours after the evening meal. Although there is no charge for a home visit, a small gift is appreciated. (The Japanese love to give and receive gifts.) The gift needn't be expensive, just a token of thanks to the family for their hospitality. If you'd like to participate in the Home Visit System (you can even bring up to three friends with you), you should contact one of the local tourist information offices after you've arrived in Japan. A list of offices is included in the brochure *Home Visit System*, available from the Japan National Tourist Office (630 Fifth Avenue, New York, NY 10111). You'll have to visit the tourist office in advance, however, in order to fill out an application form and allow the office time to make the arrangements.

> *"When in Japan you may be called upon to make adjustments. The best rule to follow is to watch what others are doing. The Japanese are loath to embarrass you by telling you something you are doing is wrong. Your hosts may tend to overentertain or overschedule you—'honor you with a loss of privacy.' Whereas in the U.S., it is good form to leave a guest alone, it is not so in Japan."*

"Because the Japanese underestimate the ability and the interest that a foreigner has in learning their language, they tend to be overwhelmingly responsive to the slightest effort on your part to understand things from their viewpoint. Begin by learning to say the place names you visit, the names of people you meet, et cetera."

For Further Information

CIEE's Japan program staff has put together a booklet designed for first-time travelers to Japan. *Japan: An Orientation for Travelers* covers your preparation, getting around in Japan, getting used to the language, and helpful information for anyone who plans to stay in a Japanese home. The recently updated second edition of the booklet is available for $3.95 (plus $1 for postage and handling) from CIEE in New York.

The Japan National Tourist Organization will provide advice on transportation within the country. It also operates a toll-free telephone line, the Japan Travel-Phone System, designed to help English speakers who need travel information or emergency medical aid. In Tokyo, the number is 502–1461; in Kyoto, it's 371–5649; outside these two cities, dial 0120–222–800 for information on eastern Japan or 0120–444–800 for information about the western part of the country.

Several helpful brochures on Japan are available free of charge from the Japan National Tourist Organization, which has offices in four U.S. cities in addition to its New York office (630 Fifth Avenue, New York, NY 10111). Of particular interest to students are *Economical Travel in Japan*, *Youth Hostels in Japan*, and a listing of *minshuku* or family-inn-type lodgings in Japan.

The best guidebook for the budget traveler is probably *Japan—A Travel Survival Kit*, by Ian McQueen, available for $13.95 (plus $1.50 postage) from Lonely Planet Publications (Embarcadero West, 112 Linden Street, Oakland, CA 94607). A practical how-to-do-it guide for the Westerner traveling independently is *Japan Solo* ($15), complete with numerous maps and detailed instructions for getting around. You can order it from the Charles E. Tuttle Company (28 South Main Street, Rutland, Vermont 05701). Perhaps the most comprehensive guide is the *Japan Handbook*, available for $12.95 from Moon Publications (722 Wall Street, Chico, CA 95928). In addition, you'll find *Fodor's Great Travel Values: Japan* (Random House, $6.95) and Baedeker's *Japan* ($16.95) in most bookstores. A more in-depth analysis is provided in *The Japanese*, by Edwin O. Reischauer, which is not a guidebook per se but an introduction to Japanese culture. Already a classic, it's published by the Belknap Press of Harvard University and is available in bookstores.

The Japan Information Center is located in the Japan Consulate General (299 Park Avenue, 18th Floor, New York, NY 10171). The center has an auditorium for film showings and lectures, a library and reading room, a photo and film library, and a number of free publications. Another organization devoted to promoting an understanding of Japan in the United States is the Japan Society (333 East 47th Street, New York, NY 10017), a private nonprofit organization that arranges various events for its members and the general public, including lectures, classes, demonstrations, films, and concerts. You can write either of these organizations for specific information about their public education programs and publications.

WORK

Getting a Job

Foreigners need a work visa in order to land full-time paid employment in Japan. Unfortunately, obtaining a work visa is a complicated process that involves finding a Japanese company or school willing to offer you a job and sponsor your application for a work visa. Among other requirements, your prospective employer must convince the Japanese government that the position you are taking cannot be filled by a Japanese national. English teachers usually have little trouble getting the necessary work visa; for others, it may be more difficult. Persons interested in working in Japan can enter as tourists, look for work, and, if a position is found, apply for a work visa in Japan. Positions for English-speaking persons are often listed in the help-wanted sections of English-language newspapers such as the *Japan Times* and the *Asahi Evening News*.

If you're seriously considering working in Japan, get a copy of *Jobs in Japan*, a 266-page guide for English-speaking foreigners seeking work in Japan. Written by John Wharton, it's available for $9.95 (plus $1 postage) from Global Press (1510 York Street, Suite F-204, Denver, CO 80206).

Teaching English

There are a number of possibilities for people interested in teaching English in Japan, including both regular salaried employment and informal tutoring. For those interested in either possibility, *Teaching Tactics for Japan's English Classrooms*, also written by John Wharton and available from Global Press (address above), is a useful primer filled with basic information on English-teaching methodologies as well as tips on popular classroom activities, on dealing with Japanese students, et cetera. The book costs $6.95 (plus $1 postage).

> "I taught basic English for a few weeks, privately, to a doctor. Although I had a student visa, every foreign student teaches English, and as long as you are discreet, no one cares. I decided to work just to get some extra yen. I actually taught very little (two hours a week) but was paid very well."

Persons considering teaching in Japan should be aware of the Japan Exchange and Teaching Program, which offers 12-month positions as assistant English teachers assigned to public or private schools or local boards of education; participants are assigned duties related to English education at the secondary-school level. Applicants must have a B.A. degree and excellent English-speaking skills. Some Japanese language ability and study of or living experience in Japan is preferred, in addition to some background in the teaching of English as a second language. The program is co-sponsored by the Ministry of Foreign Affairs, the Ministry of Education, the Ministry of Home Affairs, and the local governments of Japan. For further information, contact the Embassy of Japan (Office of JET Program, 2520 Massachusetts Avenue NW, Washington, DC 20008).

For most salaried positions in language institutes you will need to be a native speaker of English with experience or training in teaching English as a second language. If you meet these requirements, a couple of institutions where you might want to apply are the Language Institute of Japan (4-14-1 Shiroyama, Odawara-shi, Kanagawa-ken 250) and the International Education Center (Nichibei Kaiwa Gakuin; 1-21 Yotsuya, Shinjuku-ku, Tokyo, 160). For a more complete list of the hundreds of English schools in Japan, see *Teaching Tactics for Japan's English Classrooms* (described above).

English teaching positions offered by CIEE member organizations are described below. Consult Appendix I for the addresses where you can write for further information.

- Earlham College's Teaching English in Japan program involves two-year English teaching assistant positions in rural junior high schools. Applicants should be college graduates with Japanese language preparation and some knowledge of TESOL principles.
- Jobs involving the teaching of English are available in two-year stints at YMCA language schools throughout Japan. A basic salary and housing are provided. Write to the Overseas Service Corps, International Division, YMCA, 101 North Wacker Drive, Chicago, IL 60606.
- The Reformed Church in America offers English teaching positions at church-affiliated high schools. Applicants must be college graduates and members of the denomination interested in becoming involved in the life of a local congregation of the United Church of Christ in Japan.

Internships/Traineeships

There are both AIESEC and IAESTE internship programs in Japan; see page 18 for more information.

Voluntary Service

Service Civil International (2-31-16 Minami-urawa, Urawa-shu, Saitama-ken, 336, Tokyo) sponsors summer workcamps in Japan open to both Japanese and foreigners. Workcamp projects include working with mentally and physically disabled persons for three weeks or agricultural work. No special skills are required, but the minimum age for volunteers is 18.

For persons interested in longer-term voluntary service work, the "Year Abroad Program" sponsored by the International Christian Youth Exchange offers persons ages 18-24 voluntary service opportunities in the fields of health care, education, the environment, construction, et cetera. See page 22 for more information.

STUDY

Admission to Japanese universities is based almost entirely on entrance examinations given by the respective institution. It should come as no surprise that it's very difficult for foreign students to compete with Japanese students in these entrance examinations. There are, however, a few national and private universities that will admit foreigners as long as they can prove that their command of the Japanese language is good enough to enable them to take courses given exclusively in Japanese. There are also several private universities in Japan—including International Christian University, Obirin University,

Sophia University, Waseda University, Nanzan University, Kansai Gaidai University, Keio University, Nagoya Gakuin University, and Seinan Gakuin University—which offer special language programs and courses in Japanese and English for foreigners. (For more information about the programs of International Christian University, see the program listings at the end of this section.)

> *"Students who come to Japan to study should understand that after the rigorous secondary education and college entrance examinations, the academic demands on university students (except some women's colleges and science and engineering institutions) give way to an emphasis on personal and social development. Learning tends to be left up to the individual."*
> —Hallam C. Shorrock, Tokyo, Japan

Monbusho—the Ministry of Education, Science, and Culture of the Government of Japan—offers scholarships to those who want to pursue Japanese studies or study at a Japanese university as a research student. For further information, contact the Embassy of Japan (2520 Massachusetts Avenue NW, Washington, DC 20008).

Other possibilities for study in Japan include enrollment in one of the many institutions that offer intensive language instruction for foreigners who want to learn Japanese. Up-to-date information on language schools in Japan is available from the Japanese Language Division, Agency for Cultural Affairs, 3-1-1 Kasumigaseki, Chiyoda-ku, Tokyo 100. Another option is studying full or part time at one of the many cultural arts schools in Japan, which offer different courses—either in English or Japanese—in such subjects as martial arts, flower arrangement, tea ceremony, calligraphy, Zen, and shiatsu. Tourist information centers around Japan can provide information on the courses available and how to apply.

The following are the educational programs offered by member institutions of the Council on International Educational Exchange. Consult Appendix I for the addresses where you can write for further information. In addition to the programs listed below, the American Graduate School of International Management, California State University, Guilford College, Mary Baldwin College, New York University, Ohio State University, Pennsylvania State University, Stanford University, the University of California system, the University of Notre Dame, the University of Oregon, and the University of Rhode Island offer study programs open only to their own students.

SEMESTER AND ACADEMIC YEAR

Business

Brethren Colleges Abroad. Sapporo. Japanese economics, independent studies, and internships in business. Academic year or semester. Sophomores, juniors, and seniors with 3.0 GPA. Apply by December 15 for academic year or spring, by May 1 for fall.

Council on International Educational Exchange. "Cooperative Japanese Business and Society Program." Tokyo. Courses at Obirin University. Fall or spring semester. Sophomores to graduate students with basic business courses and 2.75 GPA. Apply by March 25 for fall and October 25 for spring. Contact Academic Programs Department.

University of Oregon. "OSSHE—Aoyama Gakuin University Exchange." Tokyo. Japanese academic calendar, April–November. Sophomores with one year college Japanese and 2.75 GPA. Preference given to students at schools in Oregon State System of Higher Education. Apply by November 15.

General Studies

Associated Colleges of the Midwest. "Japan Study." Tokyo. Limited to students at institutions that are members of the Associated Colleges of the Midwest or Great Lakes Colleges Association. Academic year. Freshmen to graduate students with one year of Japanese and 2.5 GPA. Apply by February 1.

Experiment in International Living/School for International Training. "College Semester Abroad." Tokyo. Fall or spring semester. Intensive language, life and culture seminar, independent-study project, homestays, and excursions. Sophomores to graduate students with 2.5 GPA. Apply by May 15 for fall and October 15 for spring.

Friends World College. "Japanese/East Asian Studies." Kyoto. Academic year or semester. Japanese history, culture, and language; individualized program combining independent study with fieldwork or internships. Sophomores, juniors, and seniors. Others may participate but will not receive credit. Apply by May 1 for fall, and November 15 for spring.

Great Lakes Colleges Association. See program listed under Associated Colleges of the Midwest.

International Christian University. Tokyo. Academic year of study as regular student at ICU. Wide range of courses available; Japanese and English are languages of instruction. Sophomores, juniors, and seniors with 3.0 GPA. Apply by April 1. Graduate program and undergraduate degree program are also available to qualified U.S. students.

Michigan State University. "Year in Japan." Kobe. Academic year at Konan University. Juniors and seniors. Apply by March 1.

Southern Methodist University. "SMU-in-Japan." Nishinomiya. Language, liberal arts, and business courses at Kwansei Gakuin University. Academic year or fall semester. Sophomores, juniors, and seniors. Apply by March 15.

State University of New York at Albany. Osaka. Juniors and seniors with 3.0 GPA. Apply by March 1.

State University of New York at Buffalo. "Kansai Gaidai." Osaka. Academic year. Juniors and seniors with 3.0 GPA. Apply by March 1.

University of North Carolina–Chapel Hill. "UNC in Kansai Gaidai." Academic year. Sophomores, juniors, and seniors with 3.0 GPA. Previous Japanese helpful. Apply by February 12.

University of Oregon.
"Meiji University Exchange Program." Tokyo. Japanese academic year (April to February). Juniors and seniors with 3.0 GPA and three years college Japanese. Preference given to University of Oregon students. Apply by November 1.
"OSSHE—Waseda University Exchange." Tokyo. Sophomores with 2.75 GPA. No language prerequisite. Preference given to Oregon State Schools of Higher Education (OSSHE) students. Apply by February 15.

University of Pittsburgh. "A Year in Japan." Kobe. Academic year. Juniors and seniors with 2.75 GPA. Apply by March 1. Contact Department of East Asian Languages and Literatures, 1501 Cathedral of Learning, University of Pittsburgh, Pittsburgh, PA 15260.

Japanese Language and Culture

Brigham Young University. "Spring Term in Japan." Tokyo. Sophomores, juniors, and seniors. Some Japanese required. Apply by October 1.

Michigan State University. "Japan Center for Michigan Universities." Shiga. Academic year or semester. Program sponsored by consortium of public universities in Michigan. Open only to sophomores, juniors, and seniors at public colleges and universities in Michigan. Apply by February 1.

Stanford University. "Kyoto Center for Japanese Studies." Academic year. Sophomores, juniors, and seniors with one year college Japanese. Apply by January 31.

Urban Planning

Michigan State University. "Real Estate Development in Japan." Tokyo. Technical and cross-cultural aspects of real estate development critical to building and living in cities in highly urbanized societies. Spring quarter. Juniors to seniors. Apply by February 3.

SUMMER

Art

Southern Illinois University at Carbondale. "Stencil Printing & Natural Dyes: An On-Site Studio in Japan." Kyoto. Freshmen to graduate students, and craftspeople with related interests. A background in art, graphics, or textiles required. Apply by April 1.

Business

Council on International Educational Exchange. "Cooperative Japanese Business and Society Program." Tokyo. Courses at Obirin University. Juniors to graduate students with previous business courses and 2.75 GPA. Apply by March 1. Contact Academic Programs Department.

Japanese Language and Culture

International Christian University. Tokyo. Six-week intensive Japanese language program. College students and graduates. Apply by April 1.

Michigan State University. "Intensive Japanese Language Study." Hikone and Otsu. Language and culture. Juniors and seniors with two years of college Japanese. Apply by April 1.

Portland State University. "Summer Session in Sapporo." High school graduates to graduate students and nonstudents.

University of Utah. "Kobe Japanese Study Program." Some Japanese language study recommended; minimum age 18. Apply by March 1.

Management

Syracuse University. "Management and Ethics in Japan." Tokyo. Sophomores to graduate students and professionals. Apply by March 17.

EXPLORING JAPANESE CULTURE

Literature

While Japan has evolved rapidly into a modern society, it continues to maintain strong links to its historical and cultural traditions. Japanese literature often reflects these links while at the same time examining the important historical events of the 20th century and the ways in which modern life coexists with tradition. Junichiro Tanizaki's novel *The Makioka Sisters*, for example, tells the story of four Japanese sisters as they try to adjust to the rush of events leading up to the Second World War. In *Black Rain: A Novel* Masuji Ibuse depicts the experiences of a man who was near Hiroshima when the bomb was dropped and what happens to him and his daughter in the aftermath of that terrible event. *Snow Country*, by the Nobel laureate Yasunari Kawabata, is written in the compressed style of a haiku poem and tells the story of a doomed love affair between a geisha and the man who visits her at a mountain resort. Kawabata was the mentor of the flamboyant Yukio Mishima, whose novels explore the difficulty of reconciling traditional ideas of empire and honor with postwar reality. His four-volume *The Sea of Fertility* and *The Temple of the Golden Pavilion* are among Mishima's most popular works; *Death in the Afternoon*, a collection of his short stories, is also evocative of contemporary Japanese society and the tensions underlying its seemingly placid surface.

Among Japan's prominent writers today is Yuko Tsushima, whose novel *The Shooting Gallery* looks at the changing roles of women in Japan today. Another contemporary author, Kobo Abe, writes about the all-too-familiar themes of deracination, alienation, and loss of identity in urban life in novels such as *The Face of Another, The Woman in the Dunes*, and *The Box Man*. Shiga Naoya's *Paper Door and Other Stories* includes his masterpiece "The Razor," in addition to other well-crafted vignettes of Japanese life.

Indicative of the increasing North American interest in the Japanese way of life is a crop of novels written by young American authors who have spent time in Japan. In fact, book critic Michiko Kakutani, writing in *The New York*

Times, suggests that Japan may be replacing Europe "as an esthetic pit stop" for young American writers. In Brad Leithauser's *Equal Distance* a 22-year-old American law student takes a year off from his studies to visit Kyoto, where he hangs out with other expatriates and attempts to sort out his hopes and fears. *Ransom*, by Jay McInerney, relates the adventures of a young man who travels to Japan looking for "something more vital than the pallid choice of career." And in *Bicycle Days*, by John Burnham Schwartz, a recent Harvard graduate takes a job in Tokyo in an effort to begin a new life on his own, free of his family and past.

KOREA (SOUTH)

Korea is a divided nation, split after the Second World War into a Communist state in the north supported by the Soviet Union and a U.S.-backed state in the south. Although a slight thaw in relations may be occurring, the People's Democratic Republic of Korea in the north and the pro-Western Republic of Korea in the south remain bitter enemies.

Japanese colonialism (1910–1945) and the Korean War (1950–1953) left Korea a decimated nation. However, over the past two decades South Korea has undergone an "economic miracle" that has resulted in an incredible rate of growth. Today, it is one of the world's fastest-developing countries and the model after which many Third World nations are looking to fashion their own economic growth.

Politically, South Korea is in a sensitive and important stage of transition. After mass student-led demonstrations in June 1987 against the authoritarian rule of former president Chun Doo-Hwan, direct democratic elections were held for the first time in Korea's history. Chun's handpicked successor and the newly elected president, Roh Tae-Woo, is in the process of implementing democratic reforms and opening up South Korea's foreign relations. But Roh faces opposition from a small yet vocal group of leftist students intent on pushing the pace of change.

The media has tended to portray student-led demonstrations in South Korea as dangerous, chaotic events. While this is not really the case, neither are they completely safe. However, they should not deter those interested from visiting the country. In fact, if you keep a reasonable distance from the demonstrations and observe, it becomes clear that they are actually carefully orchestrated events that present no real danger to the cautious.

Approximately a quarter of South Korea's population resides in the capital of Seoul, making it one of the most populated cities in the world. It is also a city of marked contrast and change, one where modern technology and centuries-old traditions exist side by side. Huge skyscrapers and beautifully constructed ancient palaces and temples can be found in every part of the city, creating a varied and exciting atmosphere.

Koreans are an emotional and sincere people. They are concerned about their country's welfare and cultural heritage as Western influences penetrate and alter their society. Today, South Korea is a nation in transition, striving to become a major economic power, while at the same time trying to cope with the political, social, and cultural changes brought about by its amazing strides toward accomplishing that goal.

—*Eugene W. Suh, Glenn Head, New York*

Official name: Republic of Korea. **Area:** 38,031 square miles (about the size of Virginia). **Population:** 42,600,000. **Population density:** 1,120 inhabitants per square mile. **Capital and largest city:** Seoul (pop. 9,600,000). **Language:** Korean. **Religion:** Buddhist, Protestant, Roman Catholic. **Per capita income:** US$2,850. **Currency:** Won. **Literacy rate:** 95%. **Average daily high/low:*** Seoul: January, 35°/15°; July, 87°/71°. **Average number of days with precipitation:** Seoul: January, 8; July, 16.

TRAVEL

U.S. citizens need both a passport and a visa to visit South Korea. A tourist visa is valid up to 90 days, allows multiple entries, and costs nothing. A photo and affidavit of support are required as part of the application process. Fifteen-day transit visas are also available. Check with the Embassy of the Republic of Korea (2370 Massachusetts Avenue NW, Washington, DC 20008) for specific requirements.

Getting Around

Train service between the major cities of South Korea is good, but in many cases bus service is as good if not better (particularly on the east coast). Trains and buses cover most areas of the country, with ferry boats operating along the southern coast between Pusan and Mokp'o via Korea's "inland sea."

There is a good youth hostel organization in Korea as well as numerous small hotels usually located near bus and railway stations. Youth hostels in South Korea are privately owned and provide simple, inexpensive accommodations. The Korean National Tourism Corporation (460 Park Avenue, Suite 400, New York, NY 10022) distributes a list of hotels and YMCAs in South Korea.

"Koreans are usually very friendly people and few travelers get through the country without being invited into a local home. Because of the long-standing U.S. military presence, English is often understood by students and many people working with the public."

Especially for Students and Young People

KIYSES (Room 505, YMCA Building, 9 Chongro 2-ka, Seoul) is the student travel bureau and ISTC member in South Korea. It provides a variety of services to students, including selling plane and ferry tickets, booking accommodations, and supplying tourist information.

Holders of the International Student Identity Card receive a discount on domestic flights in South Korea, as well as reduced air fare on international flights. There is also a discount for ISIC holders on the ferries to Japan from Pusan. In addition, cardholders get a 10- to 30-percent discount in selected hotels, hostels, and inns in Seoul, Taegu, Pusan, and Naksan; for further information contact KIYSES. The organization also distributes a booklet that

---

*all temperatures are Fahrenheit

lists specific museums, shops, restaurants, theaters, health clubs, hairdressers, et cetera that provide discounts to ISIC holders.

Meeting the People

KIYSES also has a homestay program through which short stays with a Korean family can be arranged. The price for one week is approximately $150; for two weeks, the cost is $200.

For Further Information

General tourist information is available from the Korean National Tourism Corporation (460 Park Avenue, Suite 400, New York, NY 10022). The *South Korean Handbook* is one of the most complete guides to the country, and includes black-and-white photos, maps, a glossary of Korean terms, and a bibliography. You might find it in better bookstores; if not, you can order it for $14.95 from Moon Publications (722 Wall Street, Chico, CA 95928). Another useful guide for the budget traveler is *Korea: A Travel Survival Kit*, available from Lonely Planet Publications (Embarcadero West, 112 Linden Street, Oakland, CA 94607) for $8.95 (plus $1.50 postage).

WORK

U.S. citizens need a work permit in order to hold regular employment in South Korea. To apply, you must have prearranged employment but cannot be already residing there. The application process takes about two months. For further information, contact the Embassy of the Republic of Korea (2370 Massachusetts Avenue NW, Washington, DC 20008).

Internships/Traineeships

There are both AIESEC and IAESTE internship programs in Korea; see page 18 for more information.

Voluntary Service

For persons interested in voluntary service work, the "Year Abroad Program" sponsored by the International Christian Youth Exchange offers persons ages 18–24 voluntary service opportunities in the fields of health care, education, the environment, construction, et cetera. See page 22 for more information.

STUDY

For information on higher education in South Korea, contact the Korean Cultural Service at the Korean Consulate General (460 Park Avenue, New York, NY 10022).

The following are the educational programs offered by member institutions of the Council on International Educational Exchange. Consult Appendix I for the addresses of the colleges and universities listed in this section. In addition to the programs listed below, Lewis and Clark College and the University of California system offer study programs open only to their own students.

SEMESTER AND ACADEMIC YEAR

General Studies

Brigham Young University. "Spring Term in Korea." Language, international relations, Asian studies, and selected internships. Sophomores, juniors, and seniors. Apply by October 1.

International Student Exchange Program. Direct reciprocal exchange between U.S. universities and Korea University and Yonsei University. Full curriculum options. Semester or academic year. Open only to students at ISEP member institutions.

State University of New York at Stony Brook. Channam. Juniors, seniors, and graduate students with one year of Korean language and 3.0 GPA. Apply by April 1.

University of Oregon. "OSSHE—Yonsei and Ewha Universities Exchange Programs." Seoul. Sophomores, juniors, and seniors with 2.75 GPA. No language prerequisite. Preference given to Oregon State System of Higher Education (OSSHE) students. Apply by March 1.

TAIWAN (REPUBLIC OF CHINA)

With the retreat of Kuomintang partisans to the island of Taiwan after their defeat by the Chinese Communists in 1949, Taiwan officially became the Republic of China. While on the mainland the Communists ruled over the People's Republic of China, the most populous nation on earth, it was Taiwan that was recognized as the official representative of Chinese civilization by the Western world. Today, however, few nations continue to support the Taiwanese government's claim to be the legitimate ruler of all of China.

The practical effect of Chinese history since 1949 has been to make Taiwan—which has been part of China since 1684—a separate nation. Since the Communists' victory, Taiwan and mainland China have pursued radically different social, economic, and political agendas, all of which pose fundamental obstacles to reunification. For their part, the Chinese of Taiwan are slowly relinquishing their dream of returning victorious to the mainland and are instead beginning to adapt their policies and actions to present realities.

Taiwan, with the support of the West, has enjoyed booming economic growth and now boasts the second highest standard of living in Asia (only Japan's is higher). The young people of Taiwan are strongly attracted to Western lifestyles, particularly Western music, clothing, and ideas, although most still receive a very traditional Chinese education infused by Confucian ethics. Nevertheless, friction exists between the native Taiwanese and recent immigrants from the mainland, who, although in a minority, control the island's economy, government, and social structure.

Official name: Republic of China. **Area:** 13,895 square miles (about twice the size of Hawaii). **Population:** 19,800,000. **Population density:** 1,425 inhabitants per square mile. **Capital and largest city:** Taipei (pop. 2,507,620). **Language:** Chinese (Mandarin and other Chinese dialects). **Religions:** Chinese folk, Buddhist, Christian. **Per capita income:** US$3,750. **Currency:** New Taiwan dollar. **Literacy rate:** 92%. **Average daily high/low:*** Taipei: January, 66°/54°; July, 92°/76°. **Average number of days with precipitation:** Taipei: January, 9; July, 10.

TRAVEL

U.S. citizens need a passport and visa for travel to Taiwan. Visitor visas are good for stays of up to two months and may be renewed twice. There is no charge for a visa but two photos are required. The U.S. does not have official diplomatic relations with the Republic of China; instead of an embassy or consulate, its interests in the United States are represented by the Coordination Council for North American Affairs (4201 Wisconsin Avenue NW, Washington, DC 20016). Additional offices are located in Atlanta, Boston, Chicago, Honolulu, Houston, Kansas City, Los Angeles, New York, San Francisco, and Seattle.

Getting Around

Taipei, Taiwan's capital, is served by a comprehensive bus system, but the best way to see the city is on foot, especially in the Wanhua, the oldest district of the city. Here a proliferation of markets, unusual shops, and old houses hint at the history that underlies Taipei's increasingly modern exterior.

For getting out of the capital to the mountains, the fertile western coastal plain, or the smaller cities of the island, Taiwan has both an excellent bus system and railroad network. Buses serve all parts of the island and can be anything from local buses packed with people that make frequent stops to comfortable air-conditioned buses that run the length of the island (Taipei-Kaohsiung) nonstop along a modern expressway. The main rail line runs from Taipei along the coastal plain to Kaohsiung in the south. Trains vary from locals to high-speed luxury expresses that travel the length of the island in four hours. You'll find all Taiwanese trains to be prompt, clean, and inexpensive, however.

Few car rental agencies provide short-term rentals. While it's possible to rent a car and drive it yourself (you'll need an International Driving Permit), few foreigners do so. Unless you can read the Chinese road signs and are willing to battle heavy traffic, you'll be better off renting a car with a driver.

> *"A little Chinese will get you a long way in terms of starting to break the ice. If you eat at the food stands, people are very easy to meet. They are always amazed to see an American doing commonplace things like taking a local bus."*

Especially for Students and Young People

Taiwan does not have a student travel bureau that is a member of the ISTC. As a result, there is no program of student discounts designed specifically for

---

*all temperatures are Fahrenheit

holders of the International Student Identity Card. However, your card will help identify you as a student and allow you to take advantage of any student discounts that are available.

For Further Information

Lonely Planet Publications (Embarcadero West, 112 Linden Street, Oakland, CA 94607) publishes *Taiwan: A Travel Survival Kit*. If you can't find it in a bookstore, you can order it from the publisher for $8.95 (plus $1.50 postage).

WORK

Foreigners need a work permit for regular paid employment in Taiwan. For further information on working in Taiwan contact the Coordination Council for North American Affairs (address above).

Teaching English

English teachers are especially in demand in Taiwan, where to a large extent the economy depends on international trade and commerce.

"Teaching English in Taiwan is a breeze—go to Nanyang Street and check out any of the many 'preparatory schools' or pu-hsi-pan—schools for students who want to brush up on something like English conversation. The pay is good and it's basically easy (although boring) work. You meet interesting people, though, and you receive all the respect that the Chinese traditionally give to their teachers. In addition to this, Chinese people will probably just walk up to you and ask you for instruction. Also, if you go to the bulletin boards at National Taiwan Normal or look in the Mandarin Daily News, *there might be jobs posted."*

One possibility for Americans interested in spending a year teaching English in Taiwan is the Teaching in Taiwan program of the Reformed Church in America. Program participants teach at the college level and work with student ministries (Christian commitment required). The application deadline is February 15. See Appendix I for the address where you can write for more information.

Internships/Traineeships

There is an AIESEC internship program in Taiwan; see page 18 for more information.

STUDY

For information on study in Taiwan, write to the Cultural Division, Coordination Council for North American Affairs (address above), indicating at what level you wish to study. The following are the educational programs offered by member institutions of the Council on International Educational Exchange. Consult Appendix I for the addresses of the universities listed in this section.

In addition to the programs below, the California State Universities, Pennsylvania State University, and the University of California system offer programs open only to their own students.

SEMESTER AND ACADEMIC YEAR

Architecture

Michigan State University. "Landscape Architecture in Taiwan." Taichung. Spring quarter. Study at Tunghai University, with emphasis on analysis of the natural and cultural physical environment in Taiwan. Juniors and seniors with background in landscape architecture. Apply by February 3.

SUMMER

Chinese Language

University of Massachusetts–Amherst. "Summer at Tunghai." Sophomore to graduate students and recent graduates (for undergraduate credit only). One year college Mandarin and 3.0 GPA required. Apply by March 1.

CHAPTER TWELVE
SOUTHEAST ASIA

According to the statistics, only a small percentage of young Americans going abroad travel to Southeast Asia. In fact, you'll find fewer work, study, and travel programs listed here than in any other chapter of this book. But for the college student willing to venture off the beaten path—and for any resourceful person undaunted by the challenge presented by the unusual—the rewards of an experience in Southeast Asia will be great. This part of the globe is rich in cultural diversity, natural beauty, and adventure.

Southeast Asia hasn't always been such a low priority on American agendas. In fact, for the first half of this century the Philippines was a U.S. colony and the focal point of American efforts to build a Pacific empire. And, of course, in the 1960s and early 1970s, the United States was preoccupied with its involvement in Vietnam. While the American media gives little attention to the region today, the growing importance of Asian economies such as Singapore and Thailand, as well as the largely untapped potential of nations such as Indonesia—the world's fifth most-populous country—promise an important future role for the region.

Getting There

At press time many international carriers were offering APEX and/or budget fares from several U.S. cities to Bangkok, Manila, and Singapore. One such bargain was Thai International Airlines' student fares, currently available from a number of U.S. cities to Bangkok. Sample *one-way* fares in effect for the summer of 1989 are listed below. For more up-to-date information on available fares, contact a Council Travel office (see listing on pages ix–xi).

Seattle–Bangkok, $899
Los Angeles–Bangkok, $699
Dallas–Singapore, $1175
New York–Manila, $949

From the East Coast one of the cheapest ways to get to destinations in Southeast Asia is via Europe. Holders of the International Student Identity Card (see page 8) or the International Youth Card (see page 9) may take advantage of special youth/student fares on scheduled flights connecting various European cities with Bangkok, Kuala Lumpur, Singapore, Jakarta, Manila, and Penang. These fares are excellent bargains. Sample *one-way* student fares that were in effect for the summer of 1989 are listed below. Council Travel offices have more information and can also book these flights for you.

London–Bangkok, $389
London–Singapore, $495
Frankfurt–Bangkok, $440
Paris–Jakarta, $575

In the East Asia and South Asia chapters, we've listed sample fares from cities in these regions to destinations in Southeast Asia. For fares between Southeast Asia and Australia, check the chapter on Australia that follows.

BURMA
LAOS
THAILAND
CAMBODIA
VIETNAM
SOUTH CHINA SEA
PHILIPPINES
BRUNEI
MALAYSIA
MALAYSIA
SINGAPORE
INDONESIA

Traveling Around Southeast Asia

Bus and train service extends along the length of the Malay peninsula, linking Singapore, Malaysia, and Thailand. To get to the islands of the Philippines or Indonesia, the most convenient (and perhaps the cheapest) means of travel is by plane. In Bangkok particularly, it's possible to get especially good bargains on flights to other cities in the region. Even if you're not eligible for student/youth fares, you may be able to arrange a special budget, standby, APEX, or midweek fare that's as low as a student fare. Sample *one-way* student/youth fares that were in effect for the summer of 1989 are listed below; eligibility requirements are the same as for the student/youth fares from Europe described above. Check with a Council Travel representative for more information.

Bangkok–Singapore, $135
Bangkok–Jakarta, $225
Bangkok–Manila, $215

Later in this chapter you'll find more detailed information about travel, work, and study in Indonesia, Malaysia, the Philippines, Singapore, and Thailand. Travel to most other countries in the region, however, is fairly difficult. We've provided basic information below.

Burma: At press time the U.S. State Department warned against travel to Burma (now in the process of changing its name to the Union of Myanmar) due to an "uncertain security situation"; it was also warning against travel on Burmese aircraft. For updated information, contact the Citizens Emergency Center (see page 6).

Burmese government restrictions on foreign tourism only allow travel on individual or group tours organized by the government through its tourism agency, Tourist Burma. For further information (including a list of U.S. travel agents that work with Tourist Burma), contact the Embassy of Burma (2300 S Street NW, Washington, DC 20008) or the Consulate General of Burma (10 East 77th Street, New York, NY 10021). Council Travel offices can book individuals on tours to Burma offered by Thailand's youth travel agency, the Educational Travel Centre (ETC). For budget travelers heading to Burma, a useful guidebook is *Burma: A Travel Survival Kit*, by Tony Wheeler. It's available for $8.95 (plus $1.50 postage) from the publisher, Lonely Planet Publications (Embarcadero West, 112 Linden Street, Oakland, CA 94607).

Vietnam: The U.S. State Department does not consider travel to Vietnam unsafe. However, it warns that U.S. citizens traveling there will not have diplomatic protection, since the U.S. and Vietnam do not have diplomatic relations, nor are U.S. interests represented by a third party there. A visa must be obtained from a Vietnamese embassy in a third country and is generally available only to members of a tour group approved by the Vietnamese government. U.S. Treasury Department restrictions prohibit U.S. travel agents from booking persons on such tours. U.S. citizens wishing to travel to Vietnam can join a tour organized in a third country (such as Canada, Thailand, or the Philippines); in addition, Council Travel offices can book individuals on tours to Vietnam organized by Thailand's student travel organization, the Educational Travel Centre (ETC).

Cambodia: According to the U.S. Department of State, the security of travelers in Cambodia cannot be guaranteed by the Cambodian government.

In addition, U.S. citizens traveling there will not have diplomatic protection, since there are no diplomatic relations between the two countries and no third country represents U.S. interests there. A visa must be obtained from a Cambodian embassy in a third country such as Thailand. U.S. government restrictions similar to those in effect regarding Vietnam require that Americans make travel arrangements through a third country. At press time, international tours to Angkor Wat and Phnom Penh were being offered by only one firm, Diethelm Travel in Thailand (140/1 Kian Gwan Building, Wireless Road, Bangkok 10500).

Laos: At press time, no warnings from the U.S. State Department against traveling in Laos were in effect. However, the Laotian government does not promote tourism and the country is seldom visited by Westerners. U.S. citizens wishing to go to the country need a passport and a visa (apply well in advance). For details write to the Embassy of Laos, 2222 S Street NW, Washington, DC 20008.

Brunei: It isn't difficult to travel to this tiny independent sultanate tucked between the Malaysian provinces of Sarawak and Sabah on the island of Borneo. Though it has relatively few people (about 300,000), Brunei does have a great deal of petroleum, which results in it having one of the world's highest per capita incomes and makes the ruling sultan perhaps the world's richest man. Flights link the capital city, Bandar Seri Begawan (population about 60,000), with major Southeast Asian cities as well as with Darwin, Australia. It is also possible to reach the country by boat from neighboring Malaysia. However, a visit to this small nation won't be cheap, with the prices of food and lodging particularly expensive. U.S. citizens need a passport and a visa to enter the country; contact the Embassy of Brunei (Suite 300, 2600 Virginia Avenue NW, Washington, DC 20037) for more information.

For Further Information

One of the most comprehensive guides to this part of the world is *Southeast Asia on a Shoestring*, which covers travel in 11 Southeast Asian countries. Written by Tony Wheeler, it's available for $14.95 (plus $1.50 postage) from Lonely Planet Publications (Embarcadero West, 112 Linden Street, Oakland, CA 94607). Fodor's *Southeast Asia*, another helpful guidebook, is available in most bookstores for $16.95.

Persons interested in staying in youth hostels in Southeast Asia will find volume two of the *International Youth Hostel Handbook*, with its listings of hostels in Brunei, Malaysia, the Philippines, and Thailand, useful.

INDONESIA

Tourists in Indonesia frequently remark upon the apparent timelessness of the cultural traditions they encounter. Yet a discerning traveler is likely to be equally taken by the country's cultural dynamism and the rapid changes transforming Indonesian society. In the forty-odd years since it declared its independence from colonial rule, Indonesia has emerged as a major Southeast Asian political force, experienced tremendous economic growth, and managed to foster a palpable—albeit arguably fragile—atmosphere of social unity.

These achievements are particularly striking in a land where hundreds of ethnic groups, speaking more than 250 distinct languages, are scattered over an archipelago comprising nearly 14,000 islands. Subjected to 350 years of colonial rule, Indonesians have only recently come to envision themselves as a unified nation. Five major faiths are recognized within the country and various animist religions and mystical, spiritual sects have their adherents as well. Though approximately 90 percent of the population claims to be Muslim, that figure includes a broad spectrum ranging from the devoutly orthodox to those who are merely Muslims "on paper." "Unity in Diversity," the slogan emblazoned on the national seal of the Republic of Indonesia, is, then, more than a motto. It is a challenge that is continually negotiated by the modern state and its citizenry.

Due partly to increased exports of natural commodities, Indonesia has recently become the focus of much world attention. As in the past, when the islands of Indonesia were known to Europeans as the Spice Islands, foreign commercial interests play an important role in the country's fortunes. Ancient maritime empires based in Java and Sumatra carried on trade with Chinese, Indian, and, later, Arab merchants. In time, the Portuguese established a niche in the archipelago. Among the most important foreign influences was that of the Dutch, who created an expansive colonial empire known as the Netherlands East Indies. Indonesia's revolution and the eventual capitulation and expulsion of the Dutch remains a major theme in official rhetoric and the "Spirit of '45" still figures importantly in the popular imagination.

Today executive power in Indonesia lies in the hands of the president. The incumbent, Suharto, has run unopposed since being elected acting president in 1967. Prior to assuming office Suharto commanded the armed forces, which continue to play a major role in local and national politics. Opposition to state policies is strongly suppressed.

Though the world's fifth most-populous country, Indonesia is rarely on the itineraries of American travelers. Those who do visit generally go only to the most populated island, Java, or the neighboring island of Bali. But visitors with more time and the inclination to experience the less familiar might also want to venture to such islands as Sumatra, Kalimantan (Indonesian Borneo), or Irian Jaya (New Guinea). Obviously, a longer stay will enable the traveler to make a deeper exploration into the richness of the complex cultures that make up Indonesia.

—*Anne Schiller, Malang, Indonesia*

Official name: Republic of Indonesia. **Area:** 735,268 square miles (about three times larger than Texas). **Population:** 177,400,000. **Population density:** 241 inhabitants per square mile. **Capital and largest city:** Jakarta (pop. 7,636,000). **Language:** Bahasa Indonesia (official), Dutch, English, and other regional languages. **Religion:** Islam. **Per capita income:** US$450. **Currency:** Rupiah. **Literacy rate:** 64%. **Average daily high/low:*** Jakarta: January, 84°/74°; July, 87°/73°. **Average number of days with precipitation:** Jakarta: January, 18; July, 5.

---

*all temperatures are Fahrenheit

TRAVEL

U.S. citizens need a passport for travel to Indonesia (valid six months beyond the date of arrival), but a visa is not required for stays of less than two months. You must also have an onward or return ticket. Check with the Embassy of the Republic of Indonesia (2020 Massachusetts Avenue NW, Washington, DC 20036) or the Indonesian consulate in New York for further details.

Getting Around

There are several options for ground transportation in Indonesia. Railways connect the main cities of Java and there are three unconnected local rail lines on the island of Sumatra; however, in most other parts of this vast nation, rail transport is not an option. Throughout the country, both express intercity coaches and local buses serving the countryside are a common form of transport. For the most part, rental cars are not available, although cars with a driver can be readily obtained on Bali or in Jakarta. You'll also find jeeps and motorcycles for rent on Bali (an International Driver's Permit is required—see page 99).

In the cities, transportation is provided by taxis, buses, and minibuses. In some cities you'll find *becaks*, bicycle rickshaws that can be hired by the hour or according to the distance traveled; you should bargain and decide on a price before you get in, however.

Since Indonesia is a nation of islands, much of its transportation system is comprised of ferries. The national shipping line, PELNI, operates large passenger ships with regular sailings between the major seaports of the archipelago. In addition, many cargo ships offer passengers cabin or deck space. A faster mode of transport between the islands is provided by several domestic airlines.

If you're going to spend some time traveling around Indonesia, don't expect to live your life by the clock. A boat scheduled to take you from one Indonesian port to another may be held over a day or two, while you'll be left to fend for yourself during the delay. Your only option in such situations will be patience.

> *"Indonesian rail travel is not for the impatient. Two-hour stops in the middle of rice fields in the hottest part of the day are common. On a trip from Denpasar to Jakarta, I sat on an uncushioned wooden seat for 52 hours. This was on third class and one of my fellow passengers was a goat. I recommend that others invest the few extra dollars and travel first- or second-class instead."*

The Republic of Indonesia consists of thousands of islands, but 70 percent of its population lives on one of them—Java. Tourists usually head for the island of Bali, with most flying in and then flying out a few days later. However, Bali has much to offer, and a visitor willing to spend more time there will not be disappointed.

> *"Bali is the hottest tourist spot in the Indonesian islands, but it has, nonetheless, many unspoiled sights and incredibly low prices. Though it's hard to pull yourself away from Kuta Beach with its lovely beach and hopping nightlife, you should explore the rest of the island, including the lakes, temples, and volcanoes of the northern half of the island. You won't*

have any trouble making friends in Bali—there are young people of all nationalities there."

Especially for Students and Young People

Since there isn't an ISTC-affiliated student travel organization in Indonesia, discounts for holders of the International Student Identity Card tend to be few and far between. However, ISIC holders can get a discount on international flights from Indonesia, as well as discounts at certain hotels in Denpasar and Jakarta.

STA, a student travel organization based in Australia, has offices at the Kuta Beach Club Hotel in Denpasar (Bali) and in Jakarta at Indo Shangrila Travel, Jalan Gaja Mada No. 219G. At both locations you can get discounted plane tickets, book accommodations, or make arrangements for local tours.

For Further Information

The most comprehensive travel guide to the country is the *Indonesia Handbook*, by Bill Dalton, published by Moon Publications; it's available for $17.95 from the publisher (722 Wall Street, Chico, CA 95927). Two guidebooks for the budget traveler are *Indonesia: A Travel Survival Kit* ($14.95) and *Bali and Lombok: A Travel Survival Kit* ($10.95), which can be ordered from Lonely Planet Publications (Embarcadero West, 112 Linden Street, Oakland, CA 94607). Add $1.50 each for postage.

WORK

Foreigners need a work permit to hold regular employment in Indonesia. Application is made to both the Foreign Affairs Department and the Department of Manpower. Getting a permit for casual work is impossible; for long-term employment, the applicant must have a skill that is not available locally.

Internships/Traineeships

AIESEC arranges internships in Indonesia; see page 18 for more information.

STUDY

The following are the educational programs offered by member institutions of the Council on International Educational Exchange. Consult Appendix I for addresses of the organizations listed in this section. In addition to the programs listed below, Lewis and Clark College and the University of California system offer programs open only to their own students.

SEMESTER AND ACADEMIC YEAR

General Studies

Experiment in International Living/School for International Training. "College Semester Abroad." Bali. Fall or spring semester. Intensive Indonesian language study, seminar on Indonesian and Balinese culture, village homestay, and independent-study project. Sophomores to graduate students with 2.5 GPA. Apply by May 15 for fall and October 15 for spring.

Southeast Asian Studies

Council on International Educational Exchange. "Cooperative Southeast Asian Program." Malang. Fall or spring semester. Sophomores, juniors, and seniors with one year college Indonesian. Apply by May 1 for fall and November 1 for spring. Contact Academic Programs Department.

SUMMER

Southeast Asian Studies

Lisle Fellowship. "Bali." Exploration of Balinese culture and Hindu Ashram principles, with special focus on interaction between tradition and modernization. Three weeks. Open to recent high school graduates, college students, and adults. Apply by May 1.

EXPLORING INDONESIAN CULTURE

Literature

In light of the fact that Indonesia was colonized by the Dutch, it should come as no surprise that the first novels about the archipelago were written by Dutch writers. Douwes Dekker's *Max Havelaar*, first published in 1860, depicts the exploitation of the Javanese peasant under the colonial system. *Country of Origin*, by E. du Perron, and Louis Couperus's masterpiece of psychological fiction, *The Hidden Force*, are also excellent portraits of life in colonial Indonesia. Maria Dermout, a Dutch writer born in Java, is the author of *The Ten Thousand Things*, a haunting novel set in Indonesia's Moluccan Islands. First published in 1955, it has lost none of its timeless appeal.

In *The Fugitive*, Pramoedya Ananta Toer portrays the revolution against Dutch colonial rule from an Indonesian point of view. Pramoedya was imprisoned by the Dutch authorities for his involvement in the fight for independence, and his novel was smuggled out of prison by sympathetic Dutch intellectuals. T.B. Simatupang, another Indonesian author, deals with the same turbulent period in *Report From Banaran: The Story of the Experiences of a Soldier During the War of Independence*.

Twilight in Djakarta, by Lubis Mochtar, is a disturbing novel about political corruption in post-independence Indonesia. Finished in jail in 1957, Mochtar's book paints a vivid portrait of the seamier side of life in the Indonesian capital. Ismail Marahimin is another contemporary Indonesian author who has received international recognition. In *And the War Is Over*, published in 1977 but set at the end of the Second World War, Marahimin brilliantly portrays three cultures—each alien to the other—in an ironic story of Javanese and Dutch prisoners plotting an escape from their Japanese captors.

Ring of Fire, by Lawrence and Lorne Blair, is the companion volume to an acclaimed BBC television series of the same name. Published in 1988, this nonfiction account of the authors' ten-year journey of exploration and adventure across the Indonesian archipelago captures much of the diversity and excitement of modern Indonesia, especially its most isolated islands and primitive tribal peoples.

MALAYSIA

The large majority of Malaysians live on the Malay Peninsula, but more than half the area of the country lies across the South China Sea on the island of Borneo. This unlikely arrangement was created by Britain in 1963 when it withdrew from its colonies of Sarawak and Sabah on Borneo and linked them with Malaya (which gained its independence in 1957).

As a result of this politically expedient solution, Malaysia today is a country where ethnic conflict often simmers. Muslim Malays form the majority, but there are also large groups of Indians and Chinese, the latter originally imported to work the tin mines and rubber plantations of the Malay Peninsula. Eventually the Chinese came to dominate commerce and manufacturing in the cities, while the majority of the Malays remained village farmers. The economic disparities, religious differences, and political disputes between the various ethnic groups strain the fabric of this otherwise relatively prosperous nation in Southeast Asia.

Official name: Federation of Malaysia. **Area:** 128,328 square miles. **Population:** 17,000,000. **Population density:** 133 inhabitants per square mile. **Capital and largest city:** Kuala Lumpur. **Language:** Malay, Chinese, Tamil, English. **Religion:** Islam, Buddhism, Hinduism, Christianity. **Per capita income:** US$2,040. **Currency:** Ringgit. **Literacy rate:** 75%. **Average daily high/low:*** Kuala Lumpur: January, 90°/72°; July, 90°/73°.

TRAVEL

A passport (which is valid at least a month beyond the end of your declared stay) is required for U.S. citizens entering Malaysia. A visa is not required for stays of up to three months; a visa is required, however, if you're planning to work, do research, or study at an educational institution in Malaysia. For specific requirements, check with the Embassy of Malaysia (2401 Massachusetts Avenue NW, Washington, DC 20008) or with a Malaysian consulate in New York or Los Angeles.

Warning: While in Malaysia, remember that the Malaysian government

---

*all temperatures are Fahrenheit

has strong views on drugs. The penalties for trafficking and possession—even of minuscule amounts—are severe and include death.

Getting Around

Malayan Railways operates a network of modern trains, many with air-conditioning, sleeping compartments, and dining cars. But while service extends to much of the country, the system provides little coverage of the peninsula's east coast or of Malaysian Borneo. (The famous train journey from Singapore to Bangkok takes you through Kuala Lumpur and along the populous west coast of the country.) Malayan Railways has also introduced a rail pass that's available to foreign visitors; a 10-day pass costs approximately $35 and a 30-day pass is $75. The passes may be purchased at railway stations in Malaysian cities, at the station in Singapore, or at any student travel office.

The roads in peninsular Malaysia are among the best in Southeast Asia. Buses run on all the main roads, including long-distance express buses between the major cities. This highway network, which provides access to the beautiful beaches and tropical rain forest of the peninsula's east coast, also makes the country a good one for those persons wanting to rent a car. Ferries fill in many gaps by providing service between resort islands and mainland towns. However, the roads are not as good in Malaysian Borneo and bus service is often provided by trucks or four-wheel drive vehicles. Hitchhiking is popular, and generally fairly easy along the more traveled roads of Malaysia's west coast.

The national airline, Malaysian Airlines, provides domestic service linking the major cities of Malaysia, including flights between the Malay Peninsula and East Malaysia on the island of Borneo. For those with the time, it's also possible to reach Borneo by passenger/cargo ships.

"Malaysian Borneo is a trip off the main road in Southeast Asia; Kuching, in Sarawak, is a movie set right out of Lord Jim, *while in Sabah, to the north, you can climb Southeast Asia's highest mountain, Mount Kinabalu, at 13,455 feet. There are good air connections with the Malaysian mainland and Singapore—or you can climb aboard one of the small passenger-cargo ships of the Straits Steamship line for a more leisurely crossing."*

Especially for Students and Young People

Malaysia's student travel organization and ISTC member is MSL Travel SDN BHD. You'll find offices in Kuala Lumpur (1st floor, South East Asia Hotel, 69, Jln Hj Hussin, 50300 Kuala Lumpur) and on the resort island of Penang (Ming Court Hotel Lobby, Macalister Road, 10400 Penang). You'll find that these offices provide a full range of services, including providing information, booking accommodations, and selling bus, rail, and plane tickets.

Students with the International Student Identity Card get a discount on international air fares from Kuala Lumpur and reduced rates at certain hotels in Penang, Kuala Lumpur, and a number of other cities and resorts. There is also a discount on tours of Kuala Lumpur and Penang for ISIC holders. Contact MSL Travel for more information.

For Further Information

General tourist information is available from the Malaysian Tourist Information Centers in Los Angeles (818 West Seventh Street, Los Angeles, CA 90017-

3432) and New York (420 Lexington Avenue, New York, NY 10170). The best guidebook for the budget traveler is *Malaysia, Singapore and Brunei: A Travel Survival Kit*. It can be ordered for $9.95 (plus $1.50 postage) from Lonely Planet Publications (Embarcadero West, 112 Linden Street, Oakland, CA 94607).

WORK

Foreigners are required to have a work permit in Malaysia. You'll also need a Malaysian who agrees to assure your maintenance and repatriation.

Internships/Traineeships

There is an AIESEC internship program in Malaysia; see page 18 for more information.

THE PHILIPPINES

About 500 miles off mainland Southeast Asia is a small archipelago comprised of 7,100 islands and islets known as the Philippines. Because of the physical characteristics of Philippine geography, there are noticeable changes in dialect, language, and even styles of clothing as one moves through the different regions of the archipelago. Despite these differences, however, there has been a concerted effort to develop a national identity and move the country out from under the shadows of its Spanish- and American-influenced past.

The Spanish ruled the Philippines from 1521 to 1898, and were so successful in introducing Catholicism to the islands of the archipelago that the Philippines today is the only predominately Roman Catholic country in Asia. (The Muslim south was able to fight off Spanish attempts at Christianization and has retained its Islamic identity.) Aside from religion, the Spanish introduced Western technology, Western economic and political institutions, and a public education system, all of which aided the spread of nationalism among the Filipinos.

When the archipelago was ceded to the United States in 1898, Filipinos were more than happy to be relieved of their Spanish masters and welcomed the professed commitment of the United States to Philippine independence. However, it took the U.S. government 48 years to make good on its promise. In the interim, the Philippines became acquainted with political democracy and equal economic opportunity. English became the medium of instruction, and remains the language of education, business, and government transactions. The Philippines became the first Southeast Asian country to have an elective legislative body. And when the Philippine constitution was drawn up in 1935, it closely resembled its American model.

Today, the country is recovering from a period of economic instability and political turmoil that reached its peak with the 1986 coup against Ferdinand Marcos. Despite guarantees, however, the new Philippine government under Corazon Aquino has yet to fulfill its promises of improvement. Nevertheless, Filipinos are filled with hope about their future.

It is the Filipino's basic nature not to dwell on the negative but rather to adapt to new situations. In the past two years, there has been a proliferation of restaurants, boutiques, discos, and resorts all over the country. This is characteristic of the Filipino's innate desire to enjoy, to entertain, and to be entertained. It is not uncommon to find a Filipino, whether living in a modest nipa hut in the remote province of Vigan or in a grand home in the bustling city of Manila, celebrating the arrival of a guest. The numerous foreigners who come to the Philippines are always moved by the enthusiastic welcome they receive. It is the immense pride of the Filipinos in their culture and country that compels them to receive guests with open arms, exclaiming "Welcome . . . Mabuhay!''

—Moyen F. Lagdameo, Franklin Lakes, New Jersey

Official name: Republic of the Philippines. **Area:** 115,830 square miles (about the size of Arizona). **Population:** 63,200,000. **Population density:** 546 inhabitants per square mile. **Capital and largest city:** Manila (pop. 1,728,400). **Language:** English, Tagalog (and its official form, Pilipino), Arabic, Cebuano, and others. **Religion:** Christianity (Roman Catholic), Islam. **Per capita income:** US$580. **Currency:** Philippine peso. **Literacy rate:** 88%. **Average daily high/low:*** Manila: January, 82°/69°; July 88°/75°. **Average number of days with precipitation:** Manila: January, 6; July, 24.

TRAVEL

U.S. citizens need a passport (which is valid at least six months beyond the date of your entry) to enter the Philippines. If arriving at the Manila airport, an onward or return ticket is required but a visa is not necessary for stays of up to 21 days. For stays of over 21 days, U.S. citizens need a visa (no charge) as well as onward or return tickets. For requirements at other points of entry, check the Embassy of the Philippines (1617 Massachusetts Avenue NW, Washington, DC 20036) or the Consulate General of the Philippines (556 Fifth Avenue, 3rd floor, New York, NY 10036).

Getting Around

The natural barriers of mountains and sea make getting around the islands somewhat slow unless you travel by plane. The most common form of land transportation is bus, with over 20 major companies providing some of the world's cheapest bus service; the most popular routes out of Manila feature luxury air-conditioned buses. Rail service is virtually nonexistent except on Luzon, the largest island in the Philippines, where there are two rail lines from Manila—one going north and the other south. An expensive alternative is to rent a car from a company such as Hertz or Avis in Manila, Cebu City, or Davao City. In cities throughout the Philippines, however, cars with drivers can be hired at rates that may be cheaper than renting a self-drive car.

There are several options for getting around the islands. The national airline, PAL (Philippine Air Lines), provides domestic service to points throughout the archipelago. Most service is from the Manila Domestic Airport, but Cebu's airport is also an important hub. Regularly scheduled ferries provide convenient transportation on some of the more heavily traveled routes. However, getting

---

*all temperatures are Fahrenheit

to many of the islands means making arrangements with one of the many local shipping companies that transport cargo as well as passengers between Manila and ports around the archipelago. Information can be obtained by consulting the Yellow Pages and making some calls or by simply going to the port area (the domestic shipping terminals of the North Harbor area in Tondo, Manila) and making arrangements in person.

> *"Some of the coastal towns served by steamers can hardly have changed since Conrad's day. Arriving in port where the entire local population seems to turn out to greet you is a real travel experience."*
> —Mark Thompson, Rochester, New York

Especially for Students and Young People

YSTAPHIL is the student/youth travel organization and ISTC member in the Philippines. You'll find its office beside the Excelsior Hotel at 4227 Tomas Claudio Street, Paranaque, Metro Manila. The organization provides information and a range of student/youth travel services, including a number of organized tours of the archipelago. YSTAPHIL is also the secretariat of the local youth hostel association and sells the IYHF Card and the *International Youth Hostel Handbook* (see page 50).

In addition, holders of the International Student Identity Card (ISIC) can obtain a discount at a number of hotels in Manila, Baguio, Cebu, Legaspi City, and La Union when the booking is made through YSTAPHIL. The organization will also give you a list of establishments (shops, restaurants, bars, clubs, et cetera) that offer discounts to ISIC holders. Students with the ISIC get a discount on international air fares from the Philippine Railways as well as on some inter-island ferries.

For Further Information

General travel information is available from the Philippine Ministry of Tourism, which has offices in New York (556 Fifth Avenue, New York, NY 10036), Los Angeles (3460 Wilshire Boulevard, Suite 1212, Los Angeles, CA 90010), and Chicago (30 North Michigan Avenue, Suite 1111, Chicago, IL 60602).

The Philippines: A Travel Survival Kit is one of the better guidebooks for the budget traveler. It's available for $8.95 (plus $1.50 postage) from Lonely Planet Publications (Embarcadero West, 112 Linden Street, Oakland, CA 94607).

WORK

Foreigners are required to have a work permit for regular employment in the Philippines. Application is made by the employer after a job has been offered. Generally speaking, work permits are only granted when the foreigner has a needed skill that is not available locally.

Traineeships

There are both AIESEC and IAESTE internship programs in the Philippines; see page 18 for more information.

STUDY

A program offered by a member institution of the Council on International Educational Exchange is listed below. Consult Appendix I for its address.

SEMESTER AND ACADEMIC YEAR

General Studies

International Student Exchange Program. Direct reciprocal exchange between U.S. universities and institutions in Manila, Iloio City, Miag-ao, and Quezon City. Semester or academic year. Full curriculum options. Open only to students at ISEP member institutions.

EXPLORING THE CULTURE OF THE PHILIPPINES

Film

During the American occupation of the Philippines in the first half of this century, most films produced were patterned after boy-meets-girl formats of early Hollywood movies. Even long after the Philippines attained its independence, the American influence prevailed. Love themes camouflaged in vaudeville-type productions have long attracted wide audiences, although none of these films have received much attention outside the country.

Changes in the social norms and shifts in political currents are reflected in many of the films produced in the 1970s and 1980s. As the society became less traditional, filmmakers started experimenting with new ideas that exposed the darker side of life in the Philippines. An array of soft-core pornographic films called "bomba" movies went beyond the boundaries of exploration to the point of exploitation. One such movie which won rave reviews nationally was *Burlesque Queen*. In spite of the fury of the religious sector and the censorship board, the graphic depiction of the life of a female stripper won the approval of the film community, allowing movies with similar themes to dominate the industry in the 1970s. Films such as *Manila by Night, Kontrobersyal*, and *Brutal* followed the same lines, each one creating a scandal, only to encourage production of movies more intense and pornographic.

The revolutionary spirit in the 1980s didn't escape the already unconventional film community. *Sister Stella L.* is a movie about a nun who led a popular protest of blue-collar workers against a powerful corporate magnate. In a similar vein, *Balweg* is a true story of a rebel priest who joined the Communist insurgents in the mountains during the Marcos era. *Bulaklak ng City Jail* attacks the legal establishment by showing the violent experiences of an incarcerated woman. Another noteworthy movie, *Gabi na, Kumander*, explores the contrasts of Filipino society and ideology, depicting the conflict between a military man and his radical brother.

SINGAPORE

On a brief visit, this small island nation may look like any prosperous, cosmopolitan city in the West, but to anyone lucky enough to stay longer, Singapore hides many surprises behind her modern façade.

Situated just off the southern tip of the Malay Peninsula in the South China Sea, Singapore's colonial history began when Sir Stamford Raffles of the British East India Company established a trading post at the mouth of the Singapore River in 1819 and implemented a policy of unrestricted immigration and free trade. In time, settlers came from all over the region, including China, India, Malaysia, and Indonesia, and Singapore evolved into a racially mixed and tolerant society. Although today English is the lingua franca, the majority of the population is of Chinese descent and speaks either Mandarin or a regional dialect of Chinese; others speak Malay or Tamil languages. This variety of languages is matched by a diversity of religions—Buddhism, Hinduism, Islam, and Christianity, to name just the most prominent. As a result, walking downtown from one block to the next can be like walking from one country to another.

Singapore celebrates its 25th year of independence in 1990, and its people are proud of their nation's achievements. Lee Kuan Yew heads the one-party parliamentary democracy, and his People's Action Party controls every government seat. Although his strict control over the lives of his people has sometimes been criticized, the country has achieved a level of economic and social success few other Asian nations have been able to match. And Singapore, although the fourth most-densely populated country in the world, has one of the smallest percentages of people living in poverty.

This entrepôt nation offers a unique chance to sample some of Asia's different cultures, and the cheap and modern public transport system is an excellent way to explore the island and discover its more out-of-the-way places. Singapore is also the geographic hub of Southeast Asia, and an ideal launching point for excursions to nearby Malaysia, Indonesia, and Thailand.

—*Mark A. Bridges, Nassau, Bahamas*

Official name: Republic of Singapore. **Area:** 240 square miles (about one-quarter the size of Rhode Island). **Population:** 2,600,000. **Population density:** 10,924 inhabitants per square mile. **Capital and largest city:** Singapore (pop. 2,600,000). **Language:** Malay, Chinese (Mandarin), Tamil, English. **Religion:** Islam, Christianity, Buddhism, Hinduism, Taoism. **Per capita income:** US$14,435. **Currency:** Singapore dollar. **Literacy rate:** 86%. **Average daily high/low:*** January, 86°/73°; July, 88°/75°. **Average number of days with rainfall:** January, 17; July, 13.

TRAVEL

A passport is required for U.S. citizens traveling to Singapore; however, a visa is not required for tourist stays or social visits of up to 90 days. Visas

---

*all temperatures are Fahrenheit

are required for other purposes. Check with the Embassy of the Republic of Singapore (1824 R Street, NW, Washington, DC 20009) for specific requirements.

Getting Around

There are a number of ways to get around this small island-nation, which is comprised chiefly of the city of Singapore. Taxi, bus, or by foot are the most popular. Most road signs are in English and you'll be able to rent a car without any problem (an International Driving Permit is required); driving is on the left-hand side of the road. For those who want to travel north, a causeway connects the island with the Malaysian mainland, and there is both bus and train service from Singapore to Kuala Lumpur.

Singapore boasts of being the cleanest city in Asia, so it is not surprising that a city making such a claim is also not tolerant of long hair, beards, or disheveled-looking clothing. If you want to be welcome in Singapore and not be bothered by the authorities, you will just have to conform to their standards and customs.

"Did you ever give any thought to why a country that is 75 percent Chinese has a 'Chinatown'? The government keeps Chinatown in part just to appease the tourists. The great masses of Singaporeans live in tremendous housing complexes where Chinese, Indians, Malays, even Europeans, live together and hopefully intermingle. Singapore is in the process of nation building—that means living together, finding a common language (quite a problem when even the Chinese don't all speak the same language) and a common culture. It's also an incredibly clean city—there's about a $200 fine for littering—that's $200 U.S.! So good advice is not to litter—the law's enforced."

Accommodations in Singapore are generally the most expensive of any city in Southeast Asia. Students with the International Student Identity Card can get special rates in several tourist-class hotels, but even then they are not cheap. There are also several Ys in Singapore where relatively inexpensive accommodations can be found. Check at the STA office (see address below).

Especially for Students and Young People

There's an office of STA, Australia's student travel organization, in Singapore (02-17 Ming Court Road, 1 Tanglin Road, Singapore 1024). Students who have the International Student Identity Card (ISIC) can get reduced air fares on international flights from Singapore here. You'll also be able to arrange student discounts at several hotels (and the YMCA on Orchard Road) through STA. However, there aren't many other discounts available to holders of the ISIC in Singapore.

For Further Information

General information on tourism can be obtained from the offices of the Singapore Tourist Promotion Board in Los Angeles (8484 Wilshire Boulevard, Suite 510, Beverly Hills, CA 90211) and New York (342 Madison Avenue, New York, NY 10173). The best guidebook for the budget traveler is *Malaysia,*

Singapore and Brunei: A Travel Survival Kit. It can be ordered for $9.95 (plus $1.50 postage) from Lonely Planet Publications (Embarcadero West, 112 Linden Street, Oakland, CA 94607). You can also purchase Fodor's *Singapore* for $8.95 at most bookstores.

WORK

Nonresidents must have a work permit. Applicants for the permit must be sponsored by an employer, who must prove that the skills needed for the position are not available among the country's work force.

Internships/Traineeships

There is an AIESEC internship program in Singapore; see page 18 for more information.

STUDY

A program offered by a member institution of the Council on International Educational Exchange is listed below. Consult Appendix I for its address. In addition to the program listed below (open to students at all institutions), Indiana University offers a program open only to its own students.

SEMESTER AND ACADEMIC YEAR

General Studies

State University of New York at Albany. Academic year. Liberal arts and business administration at the National University of Singapore. Juniors and seniors with 3.0 GPA. Apply by February 15.

THAILAND

Thailand literally means "Land of the Free." It is one of the few nations of the Third World that, for the most part, managed to escape domination by a European power in the 19th and 20th centuries and remain a kingdom based on its own native traditions. Since a 1932 military coup, however, the king has been a figurehead and, with the exception of the Second World War, when it was occupied by Japan, Thailand has been ruled by a succession of democratic governments and military strongmen.

Thai culture is rich in myth and religion. The splendor of Buddhism flourishes in an abundance of religious temples and monuments. And until recently, every Thai male, including the king, was expected to devote three months of his life to becoming a monk and studying and practicing Buddhism.

Because of its varied natural resources, Thailand's economy is booming. In fact, international investment in industrial production for export is expanding so rapidly that Thailand hopes to follow in the footsteps of Korea, Taiwan,

Hong Kong, and Singapore and emerge as the latest Asian economic "miracle."

Official name: Kingdom of Thailand. **Area:** 198,455 square miles (about twice the size of Wyoming). **Population:** 54,700,000. **Population density:** 276 inhabitants per square mile. **Capital and largest city:** Bangkok (pop. 5,174,682). **Language:** Thai (Siamese), Chinese, English. **Religion:** Buddhist. **Per capita income:** US$800. **Currency:** Baht. **Literacy rate:** 85.5%. **Average daily high/low:*** Bangkok: January, 89°/68°; July, 90°/76°. **Average number of days with precipitation:** Bangkok: January, 1; July, 13.

TRAVEL

U.S. citizens need a passport to enter Thailand; however, a visa is not required for visitors arriving and departing by air, staying 15 days or less, and possessing an onward/return ticket. A transit visa is $10 and is good for stays of up to 30 days; a tourist visa is good for stays of up to 60 days and is available for $15. Non-immigrant and business visas are $20 and permit the holder to stay in the country for up to 90 days. For specific requirements, check with the Royal Thai Embassy (2300 Kalorama Road NW, Washington, DC 20008) or with Thailand's consulates in New York, Los Angeles, or Chicago.

Getting Around

An efficient network of trains is run by the State Railways of Thailand, which offers service to most parts of the country. (You can also get trains from Bangkok to Kuala Lumpur and on to Singapore.) Bus service is crowded but inexpensive and is available throughout the country. Minibuses or vans that operate between cities and towns, waiting to depart until they are full and dropping off and picking up people along the way, are another option. An enjoyable alternative to land transport is the passenger boat service from Bangkok north along the Chao Phya River to Ban Pan and Ayutthaya, the ancient capital of the Kingdom of Siam. Thai Airways provides frequent service from Bangkok to the other major cities as well as to Phuket, an island off Thailand's west coast that is being rapidly developed as an international tourist destination.

The chief means of getting around Bangkok used to be via the city's many canals. However, while canals are still prevalent in certain parts of the city, more and more they are being filled in to allow the construction of modern roads. Today, Bangkok is a bustling city that seems to contain far more than its share of traffic jams and new construction projects.

"The Western world seems to have crept around from both east and west. Although it has left India relatively untouched, in Bangkok it's all there, in honking horns and chrome trim."

Council Travel offers a variety of tour options in Thailand, including trekking in the mountains of the north and visits to important historical, archae-

---
*all temperatures are Fahrenheit

ological, and scenic sites. Some tour itineraries also include Burma and other parts of Southeast Asia. Contact a Council Travel office for more information.

Especially for Students and Young People

Thailand's student travel organization and ISTC member is the Educational Travel Center (ETC), Room 318, Royal Hotel, 2 Rajdamnoen Avenue, Bangkok 10200. Their office provides travel information, books accommodations, and buys plane, bus, and train tickets. STA (Australia's student travel organization) also has an office in Thailand; it's located at the Vieng-tai Hotel, 78 Prachatipatai Road, Bangkok 10200.

Holders of the International Student Identity Card get a discount on international air fares from Bangkok as well as discounts at a number of hotels in Bangkok, Phuket, Chiang Mai, and Pattaya. Reduced rates are also available for a wide range of tours, from a half-day boat tour of Bangkok's floating market to a four-day river rafting trip on the River Kwai to a ten-day trekking adventure in northern Thailand. Inquire at ETC and STA offices for details.

"Prices in Thailand are not high but much depends on one's ability to bargain. There's no set price for anything and it's normal to charge twice the value of an object, assuming the buyer will bargain the price down. One of the first things to do is learn to count in Thai."

For Further Information

For general tourist information, contact the Tourism Authority of Thailand in New York (5 World Trade Center, Suite 2449, New York, NY 10048) or Los Angeles (3440 Wilshire Boulevard, Suite 1101, Los Angeles, CA 90010). As with many Asian countries, the best guidebook for budget travelers is published by Lonely Planet Publications (Embarcadero West, 112 Linden Street, Oakland, CA 94607); *Thailand: A Travel Survival Guide* is available for $8.95 (plus $1.50 postage). An interesting book for anyone expecting extensive interaction with the people and culture of Thailand is *A Common Core: Thais and North Americans* by John Paul Fieg. The book can be obtained for $11.95 (plus $1.50 for shipping) from the publisher, Intercultural Press (P.O. Box 700, Yarmouth, ME 04096).

WORK

In order to work in Thailand, you will need a non-immigrant visa (rather than a tourist visa). Then, to get a work permit, you will need to apply at the Department of Labor and have an employment contract in which your prospective employer specifically states the terms and length of employment. Foreigners seeking casual employment should not expect to be able to find work or obtain the necessary work permit.

Internships/Traineeships

There are both AIESEC and IAESTE internship programs in Thailand; see page 18 for more information.

Voluntary Service

Persons interested in voluntary service as teachers can contact WorldTeach, a nonprofit program which places recent college graduates in schools in Thailand. Volunteers must commit themselves to a one-year teaching assignment but no teaching training or experience are required. They receive an allowance of $72 a month but pay a program fee of about $3,000 that includes air fare, orientation, and insurance. For more information, contact WorldTeach, Phillip Brooks House, Harvard University, Cambridge, MA 02138.

STUDY

The following are the educational programs offered by member institutions of the Council on International Educational Exchange. Consult Appendix I for addresses where you can write for further information. In addition to the programs listed below (which are open to students at different institutions), the University of California system offers a program open only to students at its own schools.

SEMESTER AND ACADEMIC YEAR

General Studies

Experiment in International Living/School for International Training. "College Semester Abroad." Chiang Mai. Fall or spring semester. Intensive language, seminar in Thai life and culture, field study, village excursions and homestay, and independent-study project. Sophomores to graduate students with 2.5 GPA. Apply by May 15 for fall and October 15 for spring.

International Student Exchange Program. Direct reciprocal exchange between U.S. universities and Thammasat University in Bangkok. Semester or academic year. Full curriculum options. Open only to students at ISEP member institutions.

St. Olaf College. "Term in the Far East." Japan, Taiwan, China, and Thailand. Fall semester plus January. Cross-cultural experience with academic study of the non-Western world, including three-month family stay in Chiang Mai, Thailand. Sophomores, juniors, and seniors. Extensive application and interview required. Apply by March 1.

University of Wisconsin–Madison. Chiang Mai. Academic year. Participants normally complete a summer course in Thai language and culture at Madison prior to departure. Sophomores to graduate students with 3.0 GPA. Apply by February 1.

CHAPTER THIRTEEN
AUSTRALIA AND THE SOUTH PACIFIC

In the last decade Australia and the South Pacific have become much less remote from the United States, with more flights—including nonstop ones now linking the West Coast and Australia and New Zealand—than ever before. And because air fares have actually gone down, the number of Americans traveling to the region has skyrocketed. Young people especially are flocking to see such attractions as Australia's Great Barrier Reef and the legendary Outback. At the same time, Australia is also becoming an increasingly popular destination for those studying abroad.

A number of newly independent nations, formerly colonies of Britain and France, have also emerged in the region in recent years. Many of their names—Kiribati, Vanuatu, Tuvalu—are still unfamiliar to Americans. But as travel to Australia and New Zealand has increased, so, too, has tourism on many of the small islands of the South Pacific. And others such as Tahiti and the Fiji Islands have supported large-scale tourist industries for quite some time. However, there are still many remote and "unspoiled" South Sea islands awaiting the traveler who prefers an escape from civilization.

Getting There

APEX and promotional fares are offered by most carriers flying between the U.S. and Australia. Some fares even include stopovers in Honolulu, Tahiti, Fiji, or other South Pacific islands. Sample *one-way* fares from the U.S. to the South Pacific region in effect during the summer of 1989 are listed below. For more up-to-date information, contact any Council Travel office (see listing on pages ix–xi).

San Francisco–Sydney, $1,090
Los Angeles–Auckland, $830
Los Angeles–Fiji, $745
Honolulu–Sydney, $870

Holders of the International Student Identity Card (see page 8) or the International Youth Card (see page 9) are eligible for reduced air fares from several major European cities to points in Australia and the South Pacific; sometimes these rates can be a real bargain. For example, in July 1989 the student/youth *one-way* fare from London to Sydney was $830. Another bargain was the *one-way* fare from Paris to Tahiti, $729. And with some student/youth fares, stopovers in Asian cities along the route are even permitted. Council Travel offices have up-to-date information.

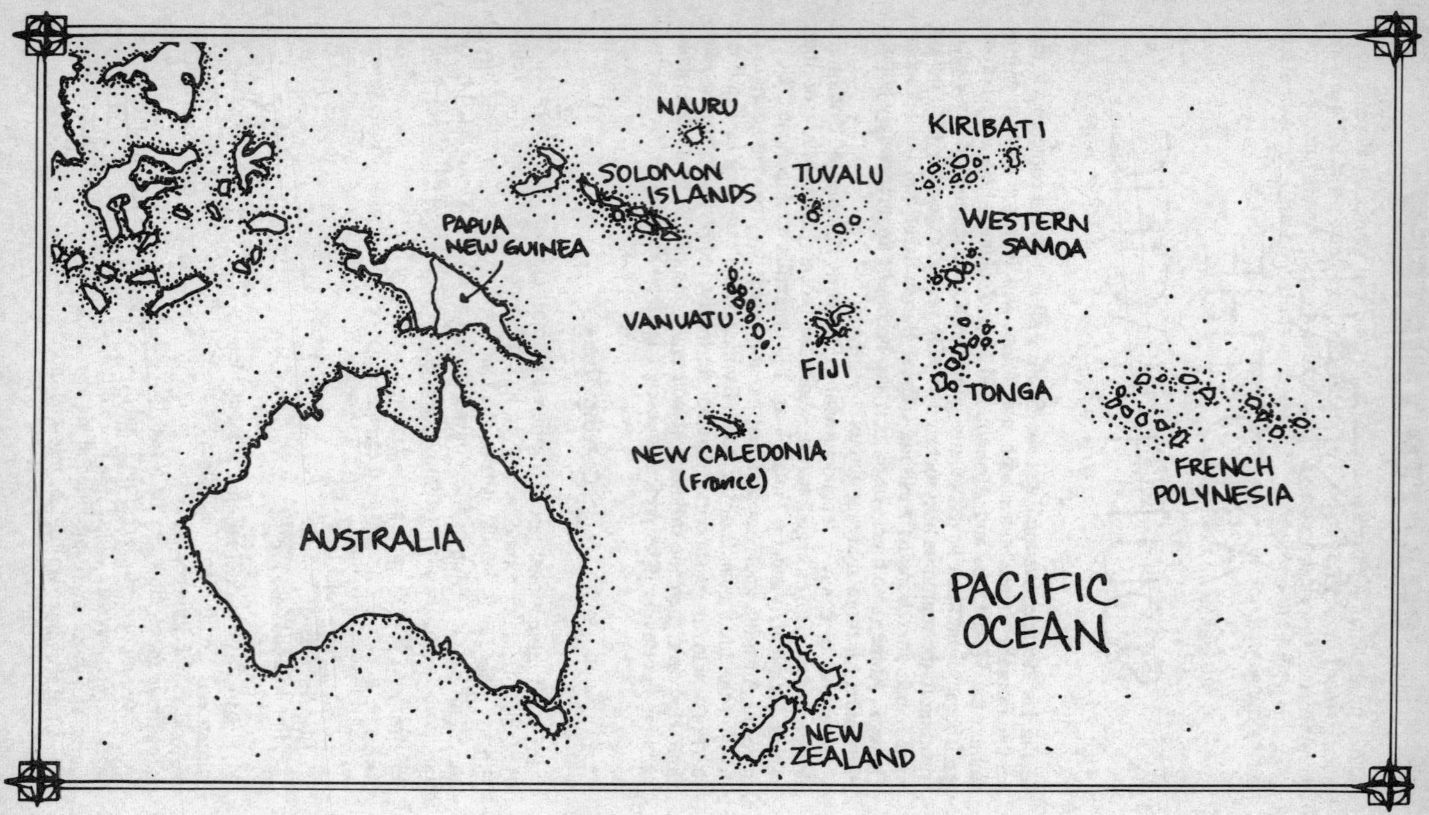
NAURU
KIRIBATI
SOLOMON ISLANDS
TUVALU
PAPUA NEW GUINEA
WESTERN SAMOA
VANUATU
FIJI
TONGA
NEW CALEDONIA (France)
FRENCH POLYNESIA
AUSTRALIA
PACIFIC OCEAN
NEW ZEALAND

If you're departing from a city in Asia, you can also take advantage of student/youth fares to Sydney. To be eligible, you must meet the same requirements as those described above for youth/student fares from Europe. These fares can be booked through any Council Travel office. Sample fares in effect during the summer of 1989 are listed below:

Bangkok–Sydney, $395
Singapore–Sydney, $369
Hong-Kong–Sydney, $525

Getting Around

The South Pacific is so immense and its islands so dispersed that flying is the only truly practical way to travel in the region. In fact, since no two nations in the region share a common border, the only option other than flying is to go by boat. While you'll find passenger and cargo boats connecting some of the more populated islands, it may be difficult to locate ships heading to the more remote and less populated island groups. Sample air fares in effect for the region during the summer of 1989 are listed below; more up-to-date information is available at Council Travel offices.

Sydney–Auckland, $305 (round-trip)
Auckland–Fiji, $490 (round-trip)
Sydney–Tahiti, $818 (round-trip)

For those of you considering spending some time in the South Pacific, you might check into Polynesian Airways' "PolyPass." Valid for 30 days of travel, the pass costs about $799 and is good for unlimited travel over the airline's South Pacific routes. In addition, it includes one round-trip each from Western Samoa to Australia and New Zealand. Travel can not *start* in January or December, however. Passes can be bought in the U.S., Australia, or Fiji.

You'll find information on getting around Australia, New Zealand, and Fiji in the individual country sections later in this chapter. But these three nations by no means represent the only worthwhile destinations in the region.

Papua New Guinea is one of the most exotic destinations on earth. Here the traveler will encounter people and a way of life still closely related to the Stone Age. You'll find more information in *Papua New Guinea: A Travel Survival Kit* ($11.95, plus $1.50 postage), written by Mark Wheeler and published by Lonely Planet Publications (Embarcadero West, 112 Linden Street, Oakland, CA 94607). For general information as well as specific entry regulations (visas are not required for visitors spending less than 30 days in the country), contact the Embassy of Papua New Guinea (1140 19th Street NW, Washington, DC 20039).

Names like Tahiti and Bora Bora immediately conjure up images of paradise on earth. Modern-day Papeete, Tahiti, is a bustling, noisy city, but you can still find an abundance of natural beauty and tranquillity on most of the other 130 islands of French Polynesia. *Tahiti and French Polynesia: A Travel Survival Kit* is the best guide to the area of the South Pacific, which, as its name suggests, is still under French control; it's available for $9.95 (plus $1.50 postage) from Lonely Planet Publications (Embarcadero West, 112 Linden Street, Oakland, CA 94607).

For Further Information

There is a plentiful supply of guidebooks for travelers heading to this part of the world. A good general guidebook to the region is Fodor's *Australia, New Zealand, and the South Pacific* ($15.95), which can be found in most bookstores. Frommer's *South Pacific* ($14.95) is full of practical information for budget travelers destined for the region. The comprehensive *South Pacific Handbook* ($12.95) is available from Moon Publications (722 Wall Street, Chico, CA 95928). Finally, a *Practical Guide to the Pacific* ($12.50) can be obtained from the Charles E. Tuttle Company (28 South Main Street, P.O. Box 410, Rutland, VT 05701-0410).

A good source of information for anyone considering staying in youth hostels in the region is volume two of the *International Youth Hostel Handbook*, which lists about 50 youth hostels in New Zealand and nearly 90 in Australia. (See page 50 for information about staying in youth hostels and getting a copy of the handbook.)

Listed below are addresses where you can write for general information as well as details on visa requirements on some of the smallest and least-visited nations in the region:

- Nauru Consul, Davies Pacific Center, 841 Bishop Street, Suite 506, Honolulu, Hawaii 96813
- Embassy of Solomon Islands, 910 17th Street NW, Suite 331, Washington, DC 20008
- Mission of Western Samoa to the United Nations, 820 2nd Avenue, New York, NY 10017
- Tonga Consulate General, 2900 Vallejo Street, San Francisco, CA 94123

AUSTRALIA

If not for the movie *Crocodile Dundee*, would the immense interest in Australia ever have occurred? Whatever the cause, an increasing number of U.S. students and travelers are heading for Australia, the only continent occupied by a single nation. Of course, American enthusiasm for Australia is at least partly the result of the two countries sharing a common language and heritage. Travelers are also attracted by the country's natural beauty, temperate climate, recreational opportunities, and hospitable people.

The Aboriginal people occupied the island-continent of Australia for at least forty thousand years before the first British settlement was established in Sydney in 1788. Living in harmony with their natural environment, the Aborigines developed a rich spiritual life that was reflected in their songs, stories, dances, drawings, and handicrafts. It is only in recent decades, however, that Australians of European descent have begun to appreciate the cultural heritage of the Aborigines and, through government initiatives, returned such sacred sites as Uluru (Ayers Rock) to Aboriginal ownership.

A member of the British Commonwealth, Australia recognizes Queen Elizabeth II as its official head of state, but is governed by a prime minister and parliament seated in Canberra, a planned city created to serve as the nation's capital. Its constitution brings together elements of the British, American, and Swiss systems—the last evident in the referendum system that is used to amend the constitution. Australia's two major political parties, Liberal and Labor, have orientations similar to the Republican and Democratic parties in the U.S., and the Australian economy is a hybrid of free-enterprise capitalism and socialism, a mix that is generally accepted by both parties.

Most of Australia's 16.5 million people live in a few large urban centers located along the coast; in fact, 27 percent of the continent's population is concentrated in just two cities, Sydney and Melbourne. Spacious parks, attractive museums, good theaters, convenient public transportation, and a safe, clean environment all contribute to the high quality of life enjoyed by Australia's city-dwellers.

Beyond the cities, national parks, beaches, and nature reserves provide abundant opportunity to enjoy Australia's vast open spaces and unique wildlife. Whether you want to hike, surf, snorkel, or pet a koala, you'll find the information and assistance you need at one of the many state-run tourist bureaus.

Australia is much influenced by American culture, and you will find the people quite knowledgeable about U.S. politics and policies. But beware of assuming that Australians are "just like Americans." Part of the fun of getting to know Australia is learning to appreciate the differences between its culture and that of the U.S.

—*Patricia Lancaster, Winter Park, Florida*

Official name: Commonwealth of Australia. **Area:** 2,966,150 square miles (about three-quarters the size of the U.S.). **Population:** 16,500,000. **Population density:** 6 inhabitants per square mile. **Capital:** Canberra (pop. 281,000). **Largest city:** Sydney (pop. 3,472,700). **Language:** English. **Religion:** Roman Catholic, Protestant. **Per capita income:** US$10,860. **Currency:** Australian dollar. **Literacy rate:** 99%. **Average daily high/low:*** Melbourne: January, 78°/57°; July, 56°/42°. Perth: January, 85°/63°; July, 64°/48°. Sydney: January, 78°/65°; July, 60°/46°. **Average number of days with precipitation:** Melbourne: January, 9; July, 17. Perth: January, 3; July, 19. Sydney: January, 14; July, 12.

TRAVEL

U.S. citizens will need a passport and visa to enter Australia. A visitor visa is valid for an unlimited number of visits of up to six months over a five-year period. Proof of onward or return transportation is required for each entry, however. For specific details check with the Australian Embassy (1601 Massachusetts Avenue NW, Washington, DC 20036) or with an Australian consulate in San Francisco, New York, Chicago, Honolulu, Los Angeles, or Houston.

Getting Around

Keep in mind that Australia is a very large country, with much of it sparsely populated. Most of the nation's population is concentrated in five state

---

*all temperatures are Fahrenheit

capitals—Sydney, Melbourne, Brisbane, Adelaide, and Perth. The traveler will have to cross long distances between these population centers.

> *"If time in Australia is short, plan the holiday carefully so as to include at least some of the Outback areas of the country. The cities are exciting, but the Outback is extraordinary."*

Due to the great distances involved, Australians (or Aussies as they generally call themselves) often travel by air. Two domestic carriers, Ansett and Australia Air, offer "Visit Australia Fares" to non-Australian residents that are equivalent to 25 percent off regular economy fares; they must be purchased in conjunction with your international ticket to or from Australia, however, and all travel must be completed within 60 days after your arrival in Australia. You can obtain tickets in Australia within 30 days of your arrival or buy them in the U.S. before you leave. East-West Airlines, another domestic carrier, offers East-West Airpasses good for either 14 or 60 days. Four types of pass are available, each restricting the pass holder to a specific direction or travel itinerary. For example, the Sun Airpass costs AUS$769 (approximately $620) and permits travel up to 60 days in a circular routing around the perimeter of the continent.

Australia's rail system is both a slower and cheaper alternative for getting around the country. The rail network links the five state capitals and serves Alice Springs in the Northern Territory as well. The famous trans-Australian run from Adelaide to Perth covers some 1,316 miles and takes two days and two nights. Going all the way across the continent from Sydney to Perth takes even longer. A good bargain for anyone planning to travel around Australia by train is the Austrian Budget Pass which entitles you to unlimited rail travel for 14 days ($320), 21 days ($411), one month ($502), two months ($714), or three months ($822). The pass must be purchased before entering Australia, however.

> *"Book ahead for the Sydney–Perth train trip. It's a popular journey that takes you through industrial, farming, and desert areas, and spends four hours in the mining town of Broken Hill."*

Bus travel is generally faster and almost as cheap as the train. There are two major bus companies, Pioneer Express and Greyhound Australia. Pioneer offers the Aussiepass and Greyhound has the Bus Pass, both of which entitle you to unlimited bus travel anywhere in Australia served by that particular line. The Greyhound Bus Pass is sold in 7-, 10-, 15-, 21-, 30-, or 60-day versions; at press time the seven-day pass cost $154.05, the 15-day pass $260.70, and the 30-day pass $497.70. The Aussiepass comes in a 15-day option that costs AUS$295 (approximately $236) or a 21-day option for AUS$425 (approximately $340).

Renting a car in Australia costs about the same as renting one in the United States; you drive on the left-hand side of the road, however. The biggest car rental companies in Australia are Hertz, Avis, Budget, and Thrifty, and you can get rates and make reservations by calling their toll-free numbers in the U.S.

Hitchhiking is common. As long as the hitchhiker stands off the road, it is legal in all states of Australia except Queensland. In Perth, Travelmate hostels provides a matching service for people interested in sharing rides on interstate trips. Gas costs are split between the driver and passengers. For more information, contact Travelmate, 496 Newcastle Street, West Perth, Western Australia 6005.

"Women shouldn't hitchhike alone, and hitchhiking in Queensland should be avoided altogether, since it is illegal there and carries a hefty fine. I hitched with another girl from Sydney to Melbourne and we made it in 13 hours, met some terrific people, and saw some interesting countryside."

Especially for Students and Young People

Student Travel Australia (STA) has offices in Sydney (1a Lee Street, Sydney, New South Wales 2000), as well as in Adelaide, Brisbane, Canberra, Melbourne, and Perth. STA is the travel arm of SSA (Student Services Australia), an ISTC member, and provides a wide range of services for student travelers, including plane or bus tickets, accommodation bookings, local tour sign-ups, and travel information. A number of unique adventure tours are also offered by STA, including "Reef and Jungle Exploring" (16 days), "Hot-Air Ballooning Over Ayers Rock" (2 days), and "White Water Rafting" (2 days).

The International Student Identity Card is good for a number of discounts in Australia, including reduced fares on international flights from Australia as well as discounts with certain companies on rental cars, bus transportation, and hotels. Contact STA for further information and ask for their free brochure listing student discounts.

Eating and Sleeping

There are a number of options for travelers seeking inexpensive accommodations in Australia. Possibilities include:

- Hostels: The Australia Youth Hostel Association (60 Mary Street, Surry Hills, Sydney, New South Wales 2010) has a brochure that lists the many hostels throughout the country and provides a map showing how to get to them.
- YMCAs and YWCAs: For a *YWCA of Australia Accommodation Directory*, write to National Headquarters, YWCA of Australia, P.O. Box 59, East Melbourne, Victoria 3002. YMCAs and YWCAs are also listed in Frommer's *Australia on $30 a Day* (see "For Further Information" below).
- University dormitories: The Australian Tourist Commission can provide you with a booklet entitled *Campus Accommodations* that lists university accommodations available during vacation periods—December–February, May, and August–September. These accommodations are open to all, not just students. With an ISIC you also can get access to cafeterias and student union facilities—gyms, libraries, et cetera.

If you're planning on staying in one place for a while, another possibility is to go to the nearest university housing office or youth hostel bulletin board and check listings to see who is seeking a roommate to share a flat.

"Flats in Sydney are very economical, often cheaper than hostels if you plan to stay awhile. My friend and I shared a three-bedroom flat on Bondi Beach with two Australians and a European for less than $30 a week per

person. We were only a half block from the beach on one side and had a bus stop and a market on the other. Check the youth hostel bulletin boards for flats and roommates."

There are a number of commercial campgrounds around the country—one of the cheapest accommodation alternatives. Most of these, however, lie far from the center of towns and therefore are not very practical unless you have a vehicle. Campgrounds generally cater to "caravaners" (people with trailers or campers) rather than tent campers. But you can still pitch a tent and take advantage of the hot showers, laundry facilities, drinking water, et cetera. Most tourist offices in Australia have a list of campgrounds.

"Outside the major cities, Australia is one big campout. It is a good country to travel in with a sleeping bag, as there is always a place to throw it in relative safety."

Meeting the People

In each state there are coordinating committees catering to overseas students and university student clubs that also have home hospitality lists. For further information and the addresses of these committees, write to the Australian Development Assistance Bureau, P.O. Box 887, Canberra City, A.C.T. 2601.

"So much of Australia's social life centers around the pub that anyone wanting to meet students should head directly for a pub in a university town."

For Further Information

For general tourist information, contact the Australian Tourist Commission (636 Fifth Avenue, Suite 467, New York, NY 10111). There are several guides designed especially for the budget traveler in Australia: *Australia: A Travel Survival Kit* is one of the best. You can order it for $19.95 (plus $1.50 postage) from Lonely Planet Publications (Embarcadero West, 112 Linden Street, Oakland, CA 94607). Another such guide is Frommer's *Australia on $30 a Day*, which can be picked up at most bookstores for $12.95. In both books you'll find information on getting around and cheap places to stay and eat, as well as historical and sightseeing information. A good guide for those interested in hiking in various regions of Australia is Lonely Planet's *Bushwalking in Australia*, available for $8.95 (plus $1.50 postage).

WORK

If you want to work in Australia, you must apply to the consulate for a resident visa, which will enable you to seek employment in the country whether you intend to stay for a while or not. Allow at least four to six months for processing of the visa. Prospective employees without relatives in Australia will need to be sponsored by an employer. At the present time, the unemployment rate is high and only skilled workers have any chance of finding a position.

Qualified teachers may apply for positions in primary, secondary, and technical schools in Western Australia, where temporary teaching positions for foreigners are sometimes available in special areas of need. Positions lasting up to 12 months can be found in secondary or technical schools but there is little likelihood of employment in primary schools. Applicants who have obtained a valid work visa should contact the Ministry of Education after their arrival in Western Australia in order to complete an application for employment and arrange a personal interview. Originals or certified copies of documents providing details of qualifications and previous teaching experience need to be produced at such an interview. Applications should be made to the Education Department of Western Australia (151 Royal Street, East Perth, Western Australia 6000).

Internships/Traineeships

AIESEC and IAESTE offer trainee positions in Australia; see page 18 for details.

Voluntary Service

For persons interested in voluntary service work, the "Year Abroad Program" sponsored by the International Christian Youth Exchange offers persons ages 18–24 voluntary service opportunities in the fields of health care, education, the environment, construction, et cetera. See page 22 for more information.

STUDY

Persons considering applying to an Australian institution of higher education should write an Australian consulate to get a copy of their information packet *Study in Australia*, which provides basic information on visas, fees, application procedures, exchange programs, et cetera. Another good publication is *Australian Study Opportunities*, a 142-page annual that provides general information about studying in Australia as well as information about the various programs of specific schools. Most Australian consulates have a copy available for reference, or you can write the International Development Program of Australian Universities and Colleges, GPO Box 2006, Canberra, A.C.T. 2601.

Students considering direct enrollment should be aware that Australian students entering a university are generally at a higher educational level than their American counterparts. (The sophomore or junior year of an American university is considered the equivalent of the first year at an Australian university.)

The school year in Australia extends from early March to late November. In general, student life in Australia is lived with zest. You will be welcomed warmly and should have no trouble being accepted. Regulations allow full-time students with a student visa to work up to 20 hours a week on a casual basis during their course of study, and during vacations overseas students can work full time.

The following are the educational programs offered by member institutions of the Council on International Educational Exchange. Consult Appendix I for the addresses where you can write for further information. In addition to the programs listed below, California State University, Colorado State University, Lewis and Clark College, New York University, Pennsylvania State University, the University of California system, and the University of Oregon offer programs open to their own students only.

SEMESTER AND ACADEMIC YEAR

Australian Studies

Gustavus Adolphus College. "Gustavus at Melbourne." Semester or academic year. Juniors and seniors with 2.75 GPA. Apply by October 1 for spring and March 1 for fall.

Engineering

University of Illinois at Urbana-Champaign. "International Programs in Engineering." Sydney. Academic year. Priority given to engineering students. Freshmen to graduate students. Apply by March 1.

General Studies

Experiment in International Living/School for International Training. "College Semester Abroad." Spring or fall semester. Melbourne, with visit to Queensland and Sydney. Seminar in Australian life and culture, homestay, and independent-study project. Sophomores to graduate students with 2.5 GPA. Apply by May 15 for fall and October 15 for spring.

International Student Exchange Program. Direct reciprocal exchange between U.S. universities and institutions in Sydney, Geelong (Victoria), Toowoomba (Queensland), and Bedford Park (South Australia). Semester or academic year. Full curriculum options. Open only to students at ISEP member institutions.

Rollins College.
"Rollins Fall Term in Melbourne." Sophomores, juniors, and seniors with 3.0 GPA. Apply by March 1.
"Rollins Fall Term in Sydney." Sophomores, juniors, and seniors with 3.0 GPA. Apply by March 1.

University of North Carolina–Chapel Hill. "Australia, Wollongong." Semester or academic year. Sophomores, juniors, seniors, and graduate students with 2.7 GPA. Apply by November 1 for spring and April 1 for fall.

Natural and Human Environment

Experiment in International Living/School for International Training. "College Semester Abroad." Spring or fall semester. Cairns, Queensland, with visits to Sydney and Melbourne, and field trip to ecologically important sites. Seminars, independent-study project, and homestay. Sophomores to graduate students with 2.5 GPA. Apply by May 15 for fall and October 15 for spring.

Teacher Education

State University of New York at Buffalo. Adelaide. Fall semester. Teacher education and liberal arts courses. One-for-one exchange with the South Australian College of Advanced Education. Sophomores, juniors, and seniors with 3.0 GPA. Apply by January 15.

EXPLORING AUSTRALIAN CULTURE

Literature

A number of recent Australian books have dealt with contemporary moral issues. Randolph Stowe's *To the Islands*, for example, is the surreal saga of a disillusioned missionary who embarks on a voyage of self-discovery through the desert to the Aboriginal islands of the dead. Thomas Keneally, a Catholic writer, deals with the problems that arise when a half-caste Aborigine tries to integrate into mainstream Australian society in *The Chant of Jimmie Blacksmith*. In *An Item from the Late News*, Thea Astley explores the conflicts that result when a man, convinced that a nuclear attack is imminent, takes refuge in a small town.

Along with the examination of moral and social issues, contemporary Australian literature is marked by a strong interest in the past. Peter Carey's *Oscar and Lucinda*, a novel set in the 1890s, exemplifies this trend and became the most read book in Australia in 1988. Patrick White's *Voss* (1957), at times a metaphysical account of a German explorer leading an expedition deep into the hostile continent, also looks backward into Australian history.

Peter Carey is also the author of a well-known collection of stories entitled *The Fat Man in History* in which he offers a relentless critique of modern Australian society. In addition, two of his stories are included in *The Faber Book of Australian Short Stories* (edited by M. Bail, 1980), along with stories by many other noteworthy Australian writers.

Film

Beginning in the 1970s, a flurry of Australian filmmaking activity has produced a variety of films. Perhaps dominant among these, at least in terms of popularity and visibility outside Australia are the "ocker" movies. An "ocker" is slang for the archetypical uncultivated Australian working man, boorish, uncouth, and chauvinistic, but always a good mate with a wonderful sense of humor. Bruce Beresford's *The Adventures of Barry McKensie* (1972) is a classic example of this type of film; more recent examples are the *Crocodile Dundee* films (1986, 1988) and Yahoo Serious's *Young Einstein* (1988).

Nationalism is a prime topic of Australian film and can often be found hand-in-hand with the concept of Australian "mateship." Peter Weir's *Gallipoli* (1981) is a historical drama about the World War I massacre of Australian soldiers by the Turks (and the British). Bruce Beresford's *Breaker Morant* (1979) is an anti-imperialist film about the British using three Australian soldiers as scapegoats during the Boer War. Both of these films frame an attitude toward the British colonial period through its effects on Australia's young men.

Australia's "Aboriginal question" is detailed in several films. Fred Schepisi's *Chant of Jimmie Blacksmith* (1978) focuses on an Aborigine trying for acceptance in the white world resulting in an ax murder, a manhunt, and finally, an execution. In contrast, *The Last Wave* (1977) by Peter Weir, represents the distance between the Aborigine and white worlds evidenced by a group of Aborigines living in caves below Sydney. Nicholas Roeg's *Walkabout*

(1971) formulates a comparison and contrast of the two cultures through the interaction of a young Aboriginal male and two suburban, white children.

FIJI

Fiji has been an independent nation since 1970, when Britain relinquished its control over the Fiji Islands, a group of about 300 islands—about 100 of which are inhabited. The major island, Viti Levu, is a major communications and transportation hub of the South Pacific.

Slightly more than half of the islands' inhabitants are Indians, the descendants of laborers who were brought from India to work on sugar plantations in the late 19th and early 20th century. Today, the Fijian minority owns most of the land in an economic system still dominated by the production of sugarcane. Since a military coup ousted the Indian-dominated democratic government in 1987, the government of the nation has been in the hands of Fijians.

In 1987 nearly 200,000 tourists visited Fiji, attracted by the pleasant climate and natural beauty of the islands. However, recent political instability and racial conflict have shattered the image of a South Sea paradise; tourism, as a result, although still a leading industry, has declined.

Area: 7,078 square miles (about the size of New Jersey). **Population:** 700,000. **Population density:** 99 inhabitants per square mile. **Capital and largest city:** Suva (pop. 75,000). **Language:** Fijian, Hindustani, English. **Religion:** Christian, Hindu, Islam. **Per capita income:** US$1,700. **Currency:** Fijian dollar. **Literacy rate:** 86%. **Average daily high/low:*** Suva: January, 86°/74°; July 79°/68°. **Average number of days with precipitation:** Suva: January, 18; July, 14.

TRAVEL

A passport and onward or return ticket are required for U.S. citizens traveling to Fiji. For holders of U.S. passports, a visa is issued upon arrival and is good for stays of up to 30 days; visas can be extended to a maximum of six months. For specific requirements, check with the Embassy of Fiji (2233 Wisconsin Avenue NW, #240, Washington, DC 20007).

Getting Around

Air shuttle service links the main islands, and a variety of small shipping companies provides freight and passenger service between the various inhabited islands. In addition, buses run on the two major islands, Viti Levu and Vanua Levu. A number of rental car agencies, including Avis, Budget, Hertz, and Thrifty, also have operations on the two major islands; driving is on the left-hand side of the road.

---

*all temperatures are Fahrenheit

Especially for Students and Young People

There is no student travel organization on Fiji and no special discounts have been developed for holders of the International Student Identity Card.

For Further Information

A comprehensive guidebook for the traveler who really wants to get to know the islands is *Fiji: A Travel Survival Kit*. It's available for $7.95 (plus $1.50 postage) from Lonely Planet Publications (Embarcadero West, 112 Linden Street, Oakland, CA 94607).

STUDY

A study program offered by a member institution of the Council on International Educational Exchange is listed below. Consult Appendix I for the address.

SEMESTER AND ACADEMIC YEAR

General Studies

International Student Exchange Program. Direct reciprocal exchange between U.S. universities and the University of the South Pacific. Semester or academic year. Full curriculum options. Open only to students at ISEP member institutions.

NEW ZEALAND

New Zealand is not a suburb of Australia. In fact, with well over a thousand miles of Tasman Sea separating it from the island-continent to the northwest, New Zealand is the most geographically isolated of the advanced industrial countries of the world.

Two major islands—North Island and South Island—comprise this nation where nature still seems unthreatened by modern industrial civilization. Snow-covered mountains and majestic fjords are the dramatic natural features of South Island, while volcanoes and hot springs dot the North Island. Few Maoris, a Polynesian people who inhabited New Zealand long before the Europeans finally got around to colonizing this distant land in the 19th century, remain. Today, most inhabitants are of British or Australian descent.

British control gradually was transformed into self-government and some interesting "firsts" for New Zealand. In 1893, the country became the first modern democracy to grant women the right to vote. And about the same time, New Zealand became the first country to institute a system of old-age pensions for its citizens. Today the government takes a stong environmentalist stand and is the leading proponent of a nuclear-free zone in the South Pacific. The latter stand—which has had the practical effect of excluding U.S. military vessels from New Zealand waters since 1984—has ended the long-standing military alliance between the two countries.

While New Zealand has just over three million people, it boasts over 70 million sheep and eight million cattle. Unlike Australia, however, New Zealand has no important mineral deposits, and its economy remains heavily dependent on agricultural exports such as wool, mutton, and dairy products. In recent years economic growth has been elusive, and the nation is now trying to achieve greater economic diversification.

Area: 103,884 square miles (about the size of Colorado). **Population:** 3,300,000. **Population density:** 32 inhabitants per square mile. **Capital:** Wellington. **Largest City:** Auckland (pop. 797,000). **Language:** English. **Religion:** Protestant, Roman Catholic. **Per capita income:** US$7,410. **Currency:** New Zealand dollar. **Literacy rate:** 99.5%. **Average daily high/low:*** Wellington: January, 69°/56°; July, 53°/42°. **Average number of days with precipitation:** Wellington: January, 10; July, 18.

TRAVEL

U.S. citizens will need a passport (valid for three months beyond your entry date) and an onward or return ticket; for stays of less than three months, a visa is not required. For specific requirements, check with the New Zealand Embassy (37 Observatory Circle NW, Washington, DC 20008) or with a New Zealand consulate in New York, Los Angeles, or San Francisco.

Getting Around

There is a limited rail network linking Auckland, Wellington, Christchurch, Invercargill, and Greymouth. New Zealand Railways operates an extensive bus system that supplements the rail network, with buses operating from various train stations, making for convenient connections. New Zealand Railways also operates ferry service between the North and South islands. The New Zealand Travelpass entitles the holder to unlimited travel on the railways, buses, and ferries of New Zealand Railways. Passes cost $160 for 8 days, $205 for 15 days, or $255 for 22 days, and can be purchased in the U.S. at Council Travel offices or at any rail station in New Zealand.

> *"The beauty and diversity of the land is probably unmatched anywhere in the world. In a country the size of Colorado you will find farmlands, volcanoes, geysers, snow-capped mountains, fjords, forests, lakes, and glaciers. New Zealand preserves the characteristic traditions of both its British and Polynesian peoples and remains one of the last unspoiled frontiers of the world."*

The main air carriers in New Zealand are the nationally owned Air New Zealand and Ansett New Zealand. Mt. Cook, another airline, flies mainly to tourist destinations such as Mount Cook and Rotorua. A variety of special air fares and passes are available to foreigners visiting the country; contact any Council Travel office for more information.

---

*all temperatures are Fahrenheit

- Visit New Zealand coupons must be purchased *outside* the country in conjunction with an international flight on Air New Zealand. For NZ$395 you can get coupons entitling you to travel on any four domestic flights offered by Air New Zealand, Mt. Cook Airline, or Mt. Cook bus; NZ$550 entitles you to travel on six domestic flights.
- The New Zealand Airpass offers a similar deal on Ansett New Zealand flights, but visitors can purchase this pass in conjunction with a flight to New Zealand on any airline.
- The Kiwi Air Pass provides one trip in each direction on all Mt. Cook Airline routes. The pass costs US$489, is valid for one calendar month, and must be purchased before your arrival in New Zealand.

New Zealand has a good road system and rental cars are readily available in cities around the country. Driving around on your own will be no problem, since traffic is generally light and roads are well marked. But remember, driving is on the left-hand side of the road. Gasoline prices are high but controlled by the government so that the price is the same at every station in the country. The major car rental firms are Avis, Budget, Hertz, Thrifty, Dollar, and Southern Cross; in some cities you'll be able to find cheaper rates at a local rental agency.

Bicycling is becoming an increasingly popular way to see New Zealand. The terrain is hilly but the country is compact and the climate is mild. Bicycles may be rented by the hour or the day in most cities, or you can bring yours with you (contact the airlines for more information). For persons preferring to bicycle with an organized group, a 42-day cycling tour through the North and South islands is offered by American Youth Hostels (see Appendix I for their address).

> *"I just returned from a month-long bicycle tour of New Zealand, which proved to be one of the most ideal bike-touring countries in the world. You may safely tell anyone that New Zealand is absolutely tops for bicycle touring."*

Hitchhiking is popular with students in New Zealand (helpful New Zealanders often give young people rides). Another way to see parts of New Zealand, and one that's popular among young people, is walking, or "tramping" as New Zealanders call it.

> *"New Zealand has some of the world's best backpacking. The most famous trails are the Milford Track (November-March only), which has to be booked through the chief ranger at Fiordland National Park; the Routeburn Track, summer only unless you're experienced; and the Heaphy Track near Waikaremoana. All these require good boots, cooking gear, sleeping bags, and waterproof and woolen clothing."*

Especially for Students and Young People

The Student Travel Services (NZ) is the country's student travel organization and ISTC member. The main office is located at 10 High Street, 1st floor, Auckland, but they also have offices in Christchurch, Dunedin, Hamilton, Palmerston North, and Wellington. These offices can provide general information, book local tours, arrange accommodations, and sell plane and bus tickets.

Students with the International Student Identity Card (ISIC) can get a 50-percent discount on standby fares on most domestic routes as well as discounts on international flights from New Zealand. There are also special fares available to ISIC holders on the routes of certain bus companies and discounts at a number of shops and movie theaters. The offices of the Student Travel Bureau distribute a complete listing of student discounts.

Eating and Sleeping

The Youth Hostels Association of New Zealand (YHANZ) administers a network of large and small hostels scattered throughout the country. Hostels are situated in most urban centers as well as near beaches, ski areas, and national parks. YHANZ National Reservations Centre can arrange bookings for all hostels as long as they have 14 days' notice; November to March is the busiest time. YHANZ also offers a series of "go it alone" tours combining public transportation and accommodations in YHA hostels. For further information, write to YHANZ, P.O. Box 436, Christchurch, New Zealand. See Chapter 5 for more general information about staying in youth hostels.

Students visiting New Zealand during summer vacation can usually take advantage of available space at university hostels. This kind of accommodation is inexpensive and the hostels are usually near the center of town. Travel information offices can direct you to local dormitory accommodations.

For Further Information

Probably the most comprehensive guidebook for the budget traveler is *New Zealand: A Travel Survival Kit*, by Tony Wheeler, which includes information on how to get around, where to go, and where to stay, as well as a special section on tramping and skiing. It's available for $11.95 (plus $1.50 postage) from Lonely Planet Publications (Embarcadero West, 112 Linden Street, Oakland, CA 94607). *The New Zealand Handbook* by Jane King contains 512 pages of information, including 107 photos and 82 maps. It can be ordered for $14.95 from the publisher, Moon Publications (722 Wall Street, Chico, CA 95928). Another good guide for the budget traveler is Frommer's *New Zealand on $40 a Day* ($12.95), available in most bookstores.

WORK

CIEE's Work in New Zealand program gives the independent college or university student the opportunity to seek temporary employment (up to six months between April 1 and October 31) in New Zealand. The program is conducted through an agreement with the Immigration Division of the Department of Labour of New Zealand and the Student Travel Bureau of the New Zealand University Students Association (NZUSA). To qualify, an individual must be at least 18 years of age, a college or university student, and a U.S. citizen or permanent resident. The cost of the program is $96.

Since the work exchange began in 1979, over fifteen hundred U.S. students have participated, with most finding unskilled outdoor work such as shearing sheep, picking fruit, or working at a ski resort.

"I worked full time for eight weeks and had two jobs, one as a cook for a camping tour around New Zealand and the other as a helper on a sheep station. Working on the tour was hard—cooking for 35 passengers in camp

facilities—but it was a great way to see the country and go on boat launches and tours for free. In fact, with room and board provided on both jobs, I was able to save all my salary and to see the whole country twice for free."

Internships/Traineeships

AIESEC places students in internships in fields such as economics, business, finance, marketing, accounting, and computer sciences. See page 18 for details.

Voluntary Service

For persons interested in voluntary service work, the "Year Abroad Program" sponsored by the International Christian Youth Exchange offers persons ages 18–24 voluntary service opportunities in the fields of health care, education, the environment, construction, et cetera. See page 22 for more information.

STUDY

The school year in New Zealand extends from early March to late November. According to the New Zealand consulate in New York, the admission of overseas students to New Zealand educational institutions is limited due to the heavy domestic demand for available spots. Enrollment in undergraduate courses and medical schools is generally not available to U.S. students. However, at the postgraduate level, study and research in New Zealand is possible.

Only one study program in New Zealand is offered by a CIEE member, and that program is open only to students already enrolled in the University of California system. Students at one of the schools in the system should check with the study abroad office on their campus.

EXPLORING THE CULTURE

Film

The last ten years have seen a burgeoning production of full-length fiction and documentary films in New Zealand. These films focus on many of the same themes which currently garner attention in films throughout the world; however, many also deal with questions of race, national identity, and cultural colonialism that are specific to New Zealand.

Two films, *Skin Deep* by Geoff Steven and *Came a Hot Friday* by Ian Mune, provide perspectives on small-town New Zealand. *Skin Deep* exposes the inner-workings of a local community through a satire on civic pride. *Came a Hot Friday* steps back to 1949 to give a stylized impression of the small town which combines two con men with guns, fast cars, fast women, liquor, and a dash of cultural colonialism.

As with Native Americans and Australian Aborigines, the societal status of New Zealand's Maori is an important and sometimes volatile topic. *Utu* by Geoff Murphy is a historical fiction about a Maori warrior rebellion in connection with the Anglo-Maori wars of the 1870s. The documentary *Patu* by Merata Mita, on the other hand, takes a more contemporary stance by documenting the 1981 Springbok Tour of New Zealand and the opposition, attitudes, and violence it provoked.

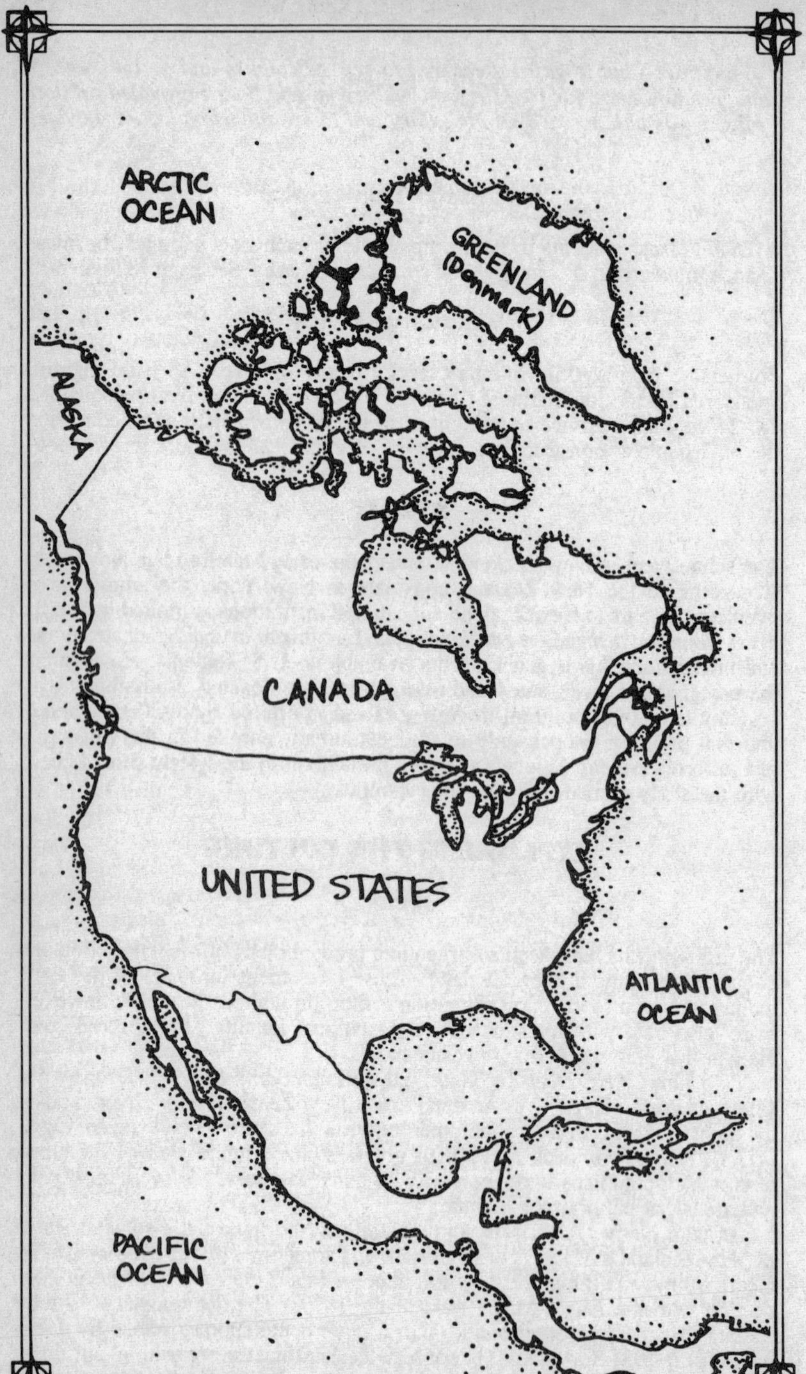

ARCTIC OCEAN
GREENLAND (Denmark)
ALASKA
CANADA
UNITED STATES
ATLANTIC OCEAN
PACIFIC OCEAN

CHAPTER FOURTEEN
CANADA

Although Canada has sometimes been maligned as Europe's spoiled child or called America's 51st state, visitors soon become aware of the unique, refreshing qualities of this beautiful and diverse country.

True, the United States and Canada have a lot in common, including many of the same natural features: the fjords of the Pacific coast, Rocky Mountain peaks, craggy Atlantic Ocean inlets, as well as the wheat fields, forests, and lakes in between. But when asked to define their national identity, most Canadians will launch into an explanation of how they differ from Americans. Whether this is symptomatic of an ingrained sense of inferiority or superiority is debatable, but it usually reflects Canadians' sheer practicality more than it does any overt anti-Americanism; while Canada shares much with the U.S., an awareness of the differences between the two countries will help us to understand Canada's unique qualities.

Larger than the U.S. in total area but only a tenth its size in terms of population, Canada is one of the world's largest but least populated nations. This fact, combined with a European sense of social responsibility, is reflected in its high standard of living and clean, well-organized cities. The latter boast heavily subsidized cultural offerings, excellent public transportation, and little of the homelessness and poverty that plague many large American cities.

Someone once quipped that while Canada could have benefited from French culture, British government, and American know-how, it unfortunately was shaped by American culture, French government, and British know-how. Although this is an obvious oversimplification, it is true that Canada's close ties with all three countries are still very much apparent.

In fact, one of the most striking aspects of Canadian society is its diversity. While the American "melting pot" tends to blur cultural differences, Canadian society and governmental legislation have encouraged the country's many immigrant groups to nurture their customs and languages. Established by colonists loyal to the British Empire, Canada has long since dispersed with its political accountability to England, even as English-speaking Canadians maintain great respect for this heritage. At the same time, Canada's official bilingual French-English status has helped keep the French joie de vivre alive and well in the French province of Quebec, the Acadian communities of the Maritime provinces, and other smaller pockets across the country. But the country is more than just a mix of French, British, and U.S. influences; other cities and regions have become cultural centers for peoples from the Caribbean, Central and Eastern Europe, and the Pacific Rim.

Geography has also shaped Canada's diversity. The remote Yukon and Northwest Territories have a frontier atmosphere to this day. French Canada's geographic and political center, Quebec City, has the pulse and personality of a European capital. And Toronto, Canada's fast-paced financial center, is often compared to New York City.

This diversity means that whether your objective is to experience another culture, enjoy stunning scenery, or join in the excitement of a dynamic city, Canada has much to offer. And it's all just across the border.

—*Sarah Wood, Brooklyn, New York*

Area: 3,851,809 square miles (slightly larger than the U.S.). **Population:** 26,100,000. **Population density:** 7 inhabitants per square mile. **Capital:** Ottawa (pop. 819,263). **Largest city:** Toronto (pop. 3,427,168). **Language:** English, French. **Religion:** Roman Catholic, Protestant. **Per capita income:** US$13,700. **Currency:** Canadian dollar. **Literacy rate:** 98%. **Average daily high/low:*** Montreal: January, 21°/6°; July, 78°/61°. Vancouver: January, 41°/32°; July, 74°/54°. Winnipeg, January, 7°/−13°; July, 79°/55°. **Average number of days with precipitation:** Montreal: January, 15; July, 12. Vancouver: January, 20; July, 7. Winnipeg: January, 12; July, 10.

TRAVEL

Entering Canada is easy enough for a U.S. citizen. As long as you don't intend to stay longer than three months, you won't need either a passport or a visa. But the U.S. government recommends that you carry personal identification of some type such as a birth or naturalization certificate or a valid or expired passport. U.S. citizens entering Canada from a third country are required to have a valid passport. Student authorization is required for persons seeking to enter Canada to attend an educational institution (see "Study" later in this chapter). Check with the Canadian Embassy (1746 Massachusetts Avenue NW, Washington, DC 20036) or a consulate for specific details. Canadian consulates are located in Atlanta, Boston, Buffalo, Chicago, Dallas, Detroit, Los Angeles, Minneapolis, New York, Philadelphia, Pittsburgh, San Francisco, Seattle, and Washington, D.C.

Getting There

Most major U.S. airlines as well as several Canadian airlines provide service between the two countries. As with domestic travel within the two countries, air fares are constantly changing—you'll have to shop around a little to get the lowest fare. Council Travel offices can provide more information and make arrangements for you. Sample *one-way* fares in effect during the summer of 1989 are listed below:

San Francisco–Vancouver, $188
New York–Montreal, $143
Chicago–Toronto, $120
Denver–Vancouver, $280
Denver–Montreal, $336

Charter flights have never accounted for much of the air traffic between the U.S. and Canada. However, Wardair, Canada's largest charter carrier, offers charter flights between Montreal and Toronto and various Florida cities, as well as between Vancouver and Toronto and Hawaii. While these flights are mainly geared toward Canadians looking to escape cold winters, Americans living in Florida or Hawaii will also find them to be the cheapest way of getting to Canada. Hawaiians and Floridians should check the travel sections of their Sunday newspapers for advertisements.

---
*all temperatures are Fahrenheit

Most visitors from the U.S. arrive by automobile; crossing the border usually involves few formalities and is done in a few minutes. It's a good idea to pick up a Nonresident Interprovincial Motor Vehicle Liability Insurance Card from your insurance agent before you go, however. Although it is not required by law, it's a help if you run into any problems while you're in the country.

For persons wishing to travel by train, Amtrak provides service from the Eastern seaboard to Montreal and Toronto, where connections can be made to Via Rail, Canada's national railroad system. If you want to travel by bus, Greyhound provides service across the border at various points. Call Amtrak or Greyhound for schedules and fares, or check with a travel agent. You'll find information about bus and rail travel within Canada under "Getting Around" below.

Getting Around

Canada's airline industry has recently gone through the same deregulation that the American industry did early in the 1980s—a process that has produced bargain fares on certain routes. At press time, the two largest carriers, Air Canada and Canadian Airlines International, were being challenged by Wardair, a smaller airline trying to become Canada's third national carrier. A number of smaller regional airlines also operate in Canada. The fare structure, including travel restrictions on discounted tickets, is similar to that in the United States. Book in advance to obtain the cheapest (but also most restricted) fares. For the up-to-date information, check with a travel agent or call the airlines directly: Air Canada, (800) 422-6232; Canadian Airlines International, (800) 387-2737; and Wardair, (800) 237-0314.

One way to get a good look at all of Canada is to cross it by train. The 3,000-mile trip from Montreal to Vancouver takes four days and three nights. Other interesting rail trips can be made across the vast wilderness areas of Canada's north; one such trip is from Winnipeg to Churchill (famous for its polar bears) on the icy shores of Hudson's Bay. Service is also available to New Brunswick and Nova Scotia. If you plan to travel extensively in Canada by train, inquire about Canrail passes (at press time it was uncertain whether these would continue to be offered in 1990). In 1989 students under 24 could obtain 15 days of unlimited travel on the nation's rail system for Can$239 or 30 days of travel for Can$314. Prices for Canrail passes for those over 24 were Can$299 for 15 days, Can$434 for 30 days. Contact Via Rail for further information, (800) 361-3677.

Buses provide the nation's most comprehensive system of public transportation. In general, travel by bus is slower but also cheaper than travel by train. The three largest bus companies in Canada are Greyhound Lines of Canada (which serves Canada west of Toronto), Gray Coach (in Ontario), and Voyageur (in Ontario and Quebec). One of the most inexpensive ways to get around Canada is the Ameripass, which allows unlimited travel on Greyhound routes (over 100,000 miles) in the U.S. and either the eastern or the western region of Canada for a period of 7 days ($135), 15 days ($214), or 30 days ($299). Prices change depending on the time of year. You can get current prices by phoning any Greyhound terminal or travel agency.

The largest car rental firm in Canada is Tilden Rent-A-Car; for information, call its U.S. affiliate, National Car Rental. Avis, Budget, and Hertz are other major car rental companies in Canada. In Canada most cars rent for a per-day (sometimes a per-week) fixed fee that includes a limited number of free kilometers. However, because unlimited mileage rates are generally not available in Canada, renting a car can be an expensive proposition if you plan to cover a lot of miles. A cheaper alternative might be to rent one in the U.S., where a number of companies still offer unlimited mileage options, and then cross into Canada (make sure the rental contract allows you to take the car across the border).

Bicycling can be an enjoyable experience in Canada. Just as in the U.S., you should try to avoid major roads and use secondary routes. The best source of information is the Canadian Cycling Association (1600 James Naismith Drive, Gloucester, Ontario K1B 5N4). This organization's free brochure lists the titles and prices of its own publications as well as those of the various provincial bicycle clubs. Publications available include *The Complete Guide to Bicycling in Canada* ($12.95), *The Canadian Rockies Bicycling Guide* ($8.95), *The Great Canadian Bicycle Trail* ($15.35), and *Newfoundland by Bicycle* (free); add 15% for postage.

For those who like the great outdoors, another option is hiking or backpacking in Canada's spectacular national parks and vast wilderness areas. *The Complete Guide to Backpacking in Canada* ($9.95), which is available in most bookstores, can help you plan hiking tours in each province. For those interested in other outdoor adventures, Moon Publications (722 Wall Street, Chico, CA 95928) publishes the *British Columbia Handbook*, by Jane King, for $11.95. Organizations that offer backpacking or camping trips include the Sierra Club of Western Canada (314-620 View Street, Victoria, BC V8W 1J6) and the Alpine Club of Canada (P.O. Box 1026, Banff, Alberta T0L 0C0).

Hiking, bicycling, and canoe trips in Canada offered by member organizations of the Council on International Educational Exchange are listed below. Consult Appendix I for the addresses where you can write for further information.

American Youth Hostels.

"Canada's Great Divide." Sixteen-day hiking tour in the Canadian Rockies. Overnights in hostels. Summer. Minimum age 14.

"Canadian Breakaway." Three-week bicycle tour in Quebec, Vermont, and New York state. Overnights camping or staying in hostels. Summer. Minimum age 14.

"Mainly Canadian Pleasure." Four-week bicycle tour in Nova Scotia, New Brunswick, and Maine. Overnights camping or staying in hostels. Summer. Minimum age 14.

"Bay of Fundy Loop." Three-week bicycle tour in New Brunswick, Nova Scotia, and Prince Edward Island. Overnights camping or staying in hostels. Summer. Minimum age 14.

"On the Border." Sixteen-day bicycle tour around Lake Ontario. Overnights camping or staying in hostels. Summer. Minimum age 14.

"Erie Breeze." Sixteen-day bicycle tour around Lake Erie. Overnights camping or staying in hostels. Summer. Minimum age 14.

Association of Student Councils. Travel CUTS, the association's student travel subsidiary, sponsors several summer wilderness trips in Ontario, including the Algonquin Park Canoe Trip and the Killarney Park Wilderness Tours. Tours depart from Toronto. Contact any Travel CUTS office (see page 382).

Eating and Sleeping

You'll find a listing of Canadian hostels in the *International Youth Hostel Handbook*, Volume 1 (see page 50 for ordering information). For information on the activities of the Canadian Hosteling Association, contact them at 1600 James Naismith Drive, Suite 608, Gloucester, Ontario K1B 5N4. Inexpensive lodging can also be found at most YMCAs and YWCAs across Canada. A directory listing their facilities is available from the YWCA of Canada (80 Gerrard Street East, Toronto, Ontario M5B 1G6) or the National Council of YMCAs of Canada (2160 Yonge Street, Toronto, Ontario M4S 2A9). In addition, most Canadian universities have residence halls open to travelers from mid-May to mid-August; you can get information on these from Travel CUTS offices or from provincial government tourist offices (addresses below).

There are virtually unlimited opportunities for camping in Canada. You can get specific information on sites and facilities from the various national and provincial government tourist offices in the United States.

Especially for Students and Young People

The Association of Student Councils/Canadian Federation of Students—Services is an ISTC member and the major student travel organization in Canada. At the organization's Travel CUTS (Canadian Universities Travel Service) offices you can get information about student/youth discounts, accommodations, and air fares. Travel CUTS also sponsors summer wilderness tours and canoe trips in wilderness areas in Ontario. You can contact Travel CUTS at 187 College Street, Toronto, Ontario M5T 1P7; Travel CUTS offices are also located in Burnaby, Calgary, Edmonton, Guelph, Halifax, Montreal, Ottawa, Quebec City, Saskatoon, Sudbury, Vancouver, Victoria, Waterloo, and Winnipeg.

By flying on a standby basis, holders of the International Student Identity Card (ISIC) are eligible for a discount of up to 45 percent on domestic air fares. Students with the ISIC also get discounts on air travel from Canada to destinations around the world. In addition, over 6,000 retail establishments, museums, and theaters give discounts of 10 to 20 percent; a directory of these establishments and institutions is available free upon presentation of an ISIC at any Travel CUTS office.

For Further Information

There are branches of the Canadian government's Office of Tourism in 14 U.S. cities—the same cities in which there are Canadian consulates (see listing above). These offices have a number of useful brochures covering all aspects of travel in Canada. For specific information on any particular province, you can contact the provincial tourist office in Canada:

- Travel Alberta, (800) 661-8888
- Tourism British Columbia, (800) 663-6000
- Travel Manitoba, (800) 665-0040, ext. 20
- Newfoundland and Labrador Tourism, (800) 563-6353
- Travel Arctic, (800) 661-0788
- Nova Scotia Tourist Information Office, (800) 341-6096
- Ontario Travel, (800) 668-2746

- Department of Tourism and Parks of Prince Edward Island, (800) 565-9060 (eastern U.S. only)
- Tourisme Quebec, (800) 443-7000 (eastern U.S. only)
- Tourism Saskatchewan, (800) 667-7191
- Tourism Yukon, (403) 667-5340

Most bookstores in the U.S. carry a number of travel guides on Canada. Particularly good are Birnbaum's *Canada* (Houghton Mifflin, $12.95) and *Canada: A Travel Survival Kit* (Lonely Planet Publications, Embarcadero West, 112 Linden Street, Oakland, CA 94607; $12.95, plus $1.50 postage). At most bookstores you'll also find Fodor's *Canada* (Random House, $14.95) and Frommer's *Canada* (Prentice Hall, $14.95).

WORK

Getting a Job

A work permit is required for regular full-time employment in Canada; application must be made from outside the country. The permit will not be granted unless it is determined that no permanent resident of the country is qualified for the job. However, employment authorization will be given to persons who have arranged temporary work before arriving at the border. For the specific requirements, contact the Canadian embassy or any Canadian consulate.

"When we hitched into Canada we made the mistake of telling the immigration officials that we were considering looking for work in Canada, so they put us through a 30-minute interrogation. Our advice is not to expect to work in Canada—jobs are scarce and the cost of living is very high."

Internships/Traineeships

There are both AIESEC and IAESTE internship programs in Canada; see page 18 for more information.

Voluntary Service

CIEE places young people in voluntary service workcamps in Canada organized by the Canadian Bureau for International Education (CBIE), 85 Albert Street, Suite 1400, Ottawa, Ontario K1P 6A4. At these workcamps, volunteers from various countries work together on projects such as helping disabled children and the blind, providing social services, or helping with the maintenance and construction of recreational facilities. Volunteers receive room and board in return for their labor. The applications of U.S. residents are processed by CIEE. For more information contact the International Voluntary Service Department at the Council.

Frontiers Foundation/Operation Beaver, 2615 Danforth Avenue, Suite 203, Toronto, Ontario M4C 1L6, sponsors voluntary service projects throughout the year. The projects, which last from 2 to 18 months, usually involve construction (low-cost housing, community centers, schools), farming, or child care. Participants from all countries are eligible, but you must be at least 18 years old. Room, board, and transportation (within Canada) to and from the project site are provided.

STUDY

Many U.S. students enroll in Canadian universities and colleges each year. If you're planning on becoming one of them, you'll need a special "Student Authorization." You can get one from the Immigration Division of any Canadian consulate, but first you must present a letter of acceptance from the Canadian school that you will be attending in addition to proof of funds. If you are going to study in the province of Quebec, a certificate of acceptance from the Quebec Immigration Service is also required.

General information on Canada's higher education system, including admission, costs, and immigration requirements, can be found in Reference Paper #36, "University Study in Canada," which is published by Canada's Department of External Affairs, 125 Sussex Drive, Ottawa, Ontario K1A 0G2, and is available at Canadian consulates abroad. More detailed information about Canadian universities and their course offerings is contained in the *Directory of Canadian Universities*, published biennially by the Association of Universities and Colleges of Canada (AUCC). To order, contact the Publications Office, AUCC, 151 Slater Street, Ottawa, Ontario K1P 5N1; when ordered from the U.S. it costs $17 (prepayment required; for first-class mail, add $3). The publication is also available for reference at any Canadian consulate.

Students should remember that Canada is a bilingual country. Most universities and colleges outside Quebec function entirely in English; at most of the institutions in Quebec, on the other hand, the instruction is in French. Many universities and colleges offer immersion or intensive French language training courses however. CBIE (85 Albert Street, Suite 1400, Ottawa, Ontario K1P 6A4) distributes a free directory of such courses entitled *Apprendez le Français au Canada/Learn French in Canada*.

Another useful publication is CBIE's *International Students Handbook*, which includes information on everything from food to law enforcement in Canada. It can be ordered for $4 from CBIE (address above).

The Canadian Embassy has established a Canadian Studies Graduate Student Fellowship that enables doctoral candidates to complete their dissertation in Canada. Details are available from the Academic Relations Section, Canadian Embassy, 1771 N Street NW, Washington, DC 20036.

The following are the educational programs offered by member institutions of the Council on International Educational Exchange. Consult Appendix I for the addresses of colleges and universities listed in this section. In addition to those listed below, programs open only to students already enrolled at the sponsoring institution are offered by the California State Universities, the University of California system, and the University of Rhode Island.

SEMESTER AND ACADEMIC YEAR

International Student Exchange Program. Direct reciprocal exchange between U.S. universities and institutions in Calgary, Charlottetown (P.E.I.), Regina, St. Catharines (Ontario), and Sudbury (Ontario). Semester or academic year. Full curriculum options. Open only to students at ISEP member institutions.

SUMMER

Cinema and Television Production

Syracuse University. "The Film Business: Cinema & Television Production in Canada." Toronto and Montreal. Sophomores to graduate students and professionals. Apply by March 17.

French Language

Brigham Young University. "Summer Term in Quebec." Sophomores, juniors, and seniors. Apply by February 1.

University System of Georgia/North Georgia College. Quebec. Special French language program for speakers of other languages at Laval University. All students with minimum 2.5 GPA. Apply by March 10.

General Studies

Michigan State University. Toronto, Ottawa, Montreal, and Quebec City. "Social Science in Canada." An examination of social, political, and economic issues in Canada. Freshmen to seniors. Apply by April 21.

Natural Science

Michigan State University. Branff, Jasper, Kootenay, and Yoho National Parks. Day trips from base camps and backpacking trips to observe geology and ecology of the region. Freshmen to seniors. Apply by April 21.

EXPLORING CANADIAN CULTURE

Literature

Many Americans feel that Canadians are very much like themselves in outlook. But Canadians are quick to point out the differences between themselves and their neighbors to the south. Still, Americans and Canadians have in common a frontier-oriented history that continues to capture the imagination of Canadian writers. A couple of fairly recent novels that examine the Canadian idea of the frontier are Rudy Wiebe's *The Temptations of Big Bear* (1973), which focuses on the last Indian rebellion on the Canadian prairie, and Robert Kroetsch's *Badlands* (1975), the story of a man obsessed with the past as he searches the Canadian wilds for dinosaur bones.

To find out how different Canadian literature really is, you need only to read one of its classics. Try, for starters, *Settlers of the Marsh* (1925), by F.W. Grove; *The Two Solitudes* (1945), Hugh McLennan's famous novel about French and English Canada; Sinclair Ross's *As for Me and My House* (1941), the best prairie novel around; or one of Margaret Lawrence's Manawaka novels, especially *The Stone Angel* (1964).

Margaret Atwood is probably Canada's best-known contemporary writer. Her novel *Surfacing* (1972) presents one woman's search for identity, a quest which takes her literally and psychologically into the wilderness. *The Handmaid's Tale* (1986) projects a North America dominated in the future by religious fundamentalists. Alice Munro, by contrast, writes about life in small rural Ontario towns in books such as *Lives of Girls and Women* (1971) or *Who Do You Think You Are?* (1978). Finally, Robertson Davies, the grand old man of Canadian literature, uses Canada and the character of its people in such novels as *Fifth Business* (1970), *The Rebel Angels* (1982), and *What's Bred in the Bone* (1985) as metaphors for the modern world and its more bizarre and disturbing aspects.

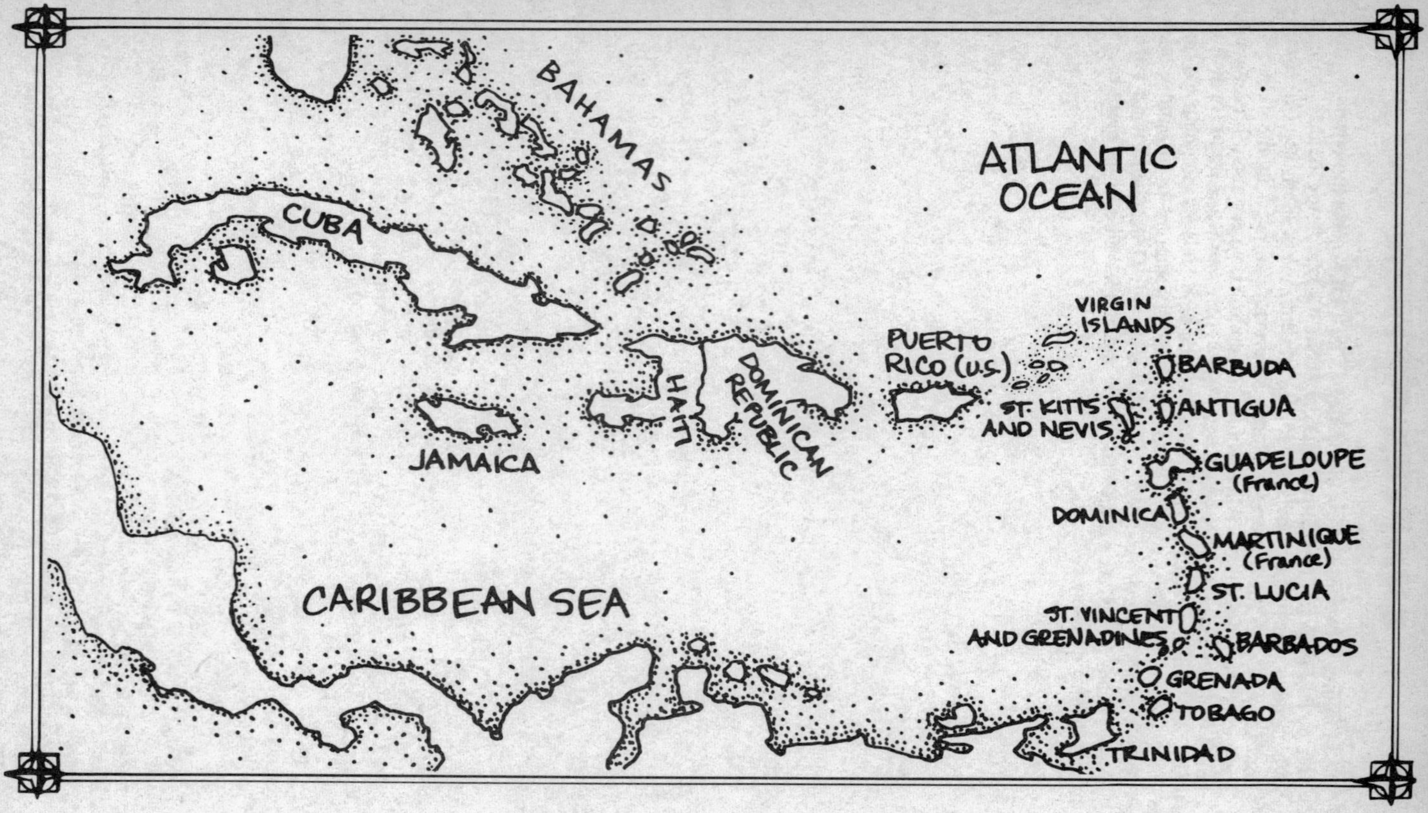
ATLANTIC OCEAN
BAHAMAS
CUBA
JAMAICA
HAITI
DOMINICAN REPUBLIC
PUERTO RICO (U.S.)
VIRGIN ISLANDS
BARBUDA
ANTIGUA
ST. KITTS AND NEVIS
GUADELOUPE (France)
DOMINICA
MARTINIQUE (France)
ST. LUCIA
ST. VINCENT AND GRENADINES
BARBADOS
GRENADA
TOBAGO
TRINIDAD
CARIBBEAN SEA

CHAPTER FIFTEEN
THE CARIBBEAN

Each island of the Caribbean offers its own unique blend of African, native American, Asian, and European cultures. Each island also has a unique history, although they all share a common legacy of hundreds of years of European rule. In fact, there are still islands in the region under British, French, and Dutch (as well as U.S.) control. However, more of the islands of the Caribbean are becoming independent states, and there are now thirteen independent island-nations in the region, the newest being Antigua and Barbuda; St. Kitts and Nevis; St. Lucia; and St. Vincent and the Grenadines.

Once this part of the world brought great wealth to the colonial masters whose slave labor produced tropical agricultural products (like sugar) for consumption in Europe. Today, agriculture has been supplanted by tourism as the number one source of income on most of the islands. One exception is Cuba, where frigid diplomatic relations still keep Cuban products out of the U.S. and U.S. tourists out of Cuba.

In contrast to the popularity of the islands as a vacation destination, relatively few Americans head to the Caribbean for a study or work experience. Perhaps this is due to the fact that the area, with less than one percent of the world's land area and population, is relatively unimportant in world affairs. Or perhaps it is due to a paternalistic attitude on the part of Americans that makes it difficult for them to take the small nations of the region seriously. Nevertheless, a variety of study and work options exist in the Caribbean, and the American electing to take advantage of them will be rewarded by a greater understanding of the nations of this beautiful and culturally interesting region.

Getting There

It's easy to get a flight to the Caribbean from the United States; several U.S. airlines provide nonstop service to a number of the larger islands. (To get to some of the smaller, less visited islands you may have to fly to a major international hub such as San Juan, Puerto Rico, and make a connection.) APEX fares are one of the cheapest ways to go (see Chapter 5 for a general explanation of air fares), but be sure to check the ads in the travel section of a large Sunday paper for special promotional fares. Sample *one-way* fares in effect during the summer of 1989 are listed below. More up-to-date information is available at Council Travel offices (see listing on pages ix–xi).

   Miami–San Juan, $292
   Miami–Nassau, $72
   New York–Santo Domingo, $335
   New Orleans–Kingston, $313

For persons planning a short-term stay (one week or less) at a tourist destination in the Caribbean, the cheapest way of traveling is to buy a package that includes air fare, transfers, and hotel. Most airlines serving the Caribbean offer a wide variety of packages; some even include low-cost car rentals. Packages are generally cheaper than making your own arrangements, since tour operators can make discount volume purchases. In addition, Council Travel arranges special low-cost spring vacation packages geared toward students and teachers interested in making their spring-break getaway an international experience. Check at a Council Travel office or look in the Sunday travel section of any metropolitan newspaper for more information on a wide range of Caribbean packages.

Another way of getting to the Caribbean is by ship. A number of cruise ships depart for Caribbean destinations from Miami, Fort Lauderdale (Port Everglades), and other U.S. ports. Although cruise ships no longer cater just to the retired and wealthy, they are definitely not for those who want maximum contact with local cultures.

Getting Around

Island-hopping in the Caribbean can be done by either airplane or boat. A number of small and large airlines serve the larger islands and the major tourist destinations, and smaller airlines provide scheduled service to even the smallest and most remote islands. While over 300 cruise ships ply the Caribbean, passenger boats providing simple transportation (rather than the "total vacation" of cruise ships) are harder to find. However, a few islands are connected by regular local boat service, including Tortola (British Virgin Islands) and St. Thomas (U.S. Virgin Islands) and St. Maarten (Netherlands Antilles) and St. Barthelemy (French West Indies).

Arrangements can be easily made to visit any country of the region except Cuba. While Americans are not barred from traveling to Cuba, Treasury Department restrictions on U.S. travel agents, airlines, and individual citizens have made travel to Cuba so difficult that it is practically nonexistent. Journalists, some researchers, and graduate degree candidates, as well as people with family on the island, are exempt from these restrictions and can make arrangements through Marazul Tours (250 West 57th Street, Suite 1311, New York, NY 10107), the only travel agency in the U.S. authorized to arrange travel to Cuba. Others will need to make their travel arrangements through a travel agency or airline in a third country such as Canada or Mexico. To obtain a visa to visit Cuba, U.S. citizens need to apply to the Cuban Interests Section of the Embassy of the Czechoslovak Socialist Republic (3900 Linnean Avenue NW, Washington, DC 20008). A travel guidebook, *Getting to Know Cuba*, by Jane McManus, an official with the Cuban government, has recently been published by St. Martin's Press ($14.95).

For Further Information

The most comprehensive guidebook to the region is the *Caribbean Islands Handbook* ($15.95) published by Prentice Hall and available in most bookstores. Another good guide for the budget traveler is Frommer's *Caribbean* ($14.95). In addition, a number of travel guidebooks not specifically geared to the budget traveler are readily available at bookstores, including Fodor's *Caribbean* ($14.95) and Birnbaum's *Caribbean, Bermuda, and the Bahamas*. ($13.95).

Many islands of the Caribbean have tourist offices in the United States. We've listed these offices in the individual country sections later in this chapter. For those not dealt with in a separate country section, we've listed the addresses where you can write for general tourist information below:

- Aruba Tourist Authority, 521 Fifth Avenue, 12th floor, New York, NY 10175

- Barbados Tourist Board, 800 Second Avenue, New York, NY 10017
- Curaçao Tourist Board, 400 Madison Avenue, Suite 311, New York, NY 10017
- French West Indies Tourist Board, 610 Fifth Avenue, New York, NY 10022
- Haiti Government Tourist Office, 1270 Avenue of the Americas, Room 508, New York, NY 10020
- Trinidad and Tobago Tourist Board, 400 Madison Avenue, Suite 712-714, New York, NY 10017

Few nations of the Caribbean region require visas for U.S. citizens visiting as tourists for less than a month or two. However, study, work, or a longer stay on one of the islands may require a visa or residence permit. We've provided more information in the individual country sections that follow. For other countries, contact the embassies and/or consulates listed below for more information:

- Embassy of Antigua and Barbuda, Intelsat Building, 3400 International Drive NW, Washington, DC 20008
- Embassy of Barbados, 2144 Wyoming Avenue NW, Washington, DC 20008
- Embassy of Grenada, 1424 16th Street NW, Washington, DC 20036
- Embassy of Haiti, 2311 Massachusetts Avenue NW, Washington, DC 20008
- Embassy of St. Kitts and Nevis, Washington, DC 20036
- Embassy of St. Lucia, 2100 M Street, NW, Suite 309, Washington, DC 20037
- Consulate of St. Vincent and the Grenadines, 801 Second Avenue, 21st Floor, New York, NY 10017
- Embassy of Trinidad and Tobago, 1708 Massachusetts Avenue NW, Washington, DC 20036

Study in the Caribbean Region

In the individual country sections that follow, you'll find additional study programs listed. In this section we've listed only the study programs of CIEE member institutions that take place in more than one country of the region. Consult Appendix I for the addresses where you write for further information.

SEMESTER AND ACADEMIC YEAR

Science

Michigan State University. "Natural Science in the Caribbean." British and U.S. Virgin Islands. Environmental field studies by direct observation in the field and from text and lectures. Winter break (mid-December to first week of January). Freshmen to seniors. Apply by November 15.

SUMMER

International Relations

Michigan State University. "Summer School in the Caribbean." Barbados, Trinidad, Tobago, and Guyana. Political science, sociology, and international relations. Sophomores, juniors, and seniors. Apply by April 21.

Science

Portland State University. "Natural History of the Virgin Islands." U.S. and British Virgin islands. Various facets of reef and shore biology and dynamics. Four quarter credits in biology or geography. High school seniors to university graduates. Apply by May 9.

BAHAMAS

Contrary to popular belief, this nation made up of 700 low-lying coral islands scattered southeast of Florida's coast is not in the Caribbean but in the Atlantic. No matter. Each year millions of American tourists are attracted to the Bahamas. In fact, tourism is the leading contributor to the country's economy. Most tourists, however, go only to the large hotels and gambling casinos of Nassau or Freeport, leaving the outer islands quiet and less commercial.

Western history books date the discovery of the western hemisphere to the first voyage of Christopher Columbus, whose initial landfall is believed to have been on the island of San Salvador in the Bahamas. Over the centuries, possession of the islands has been exchanged between the Spanish and British, and it was Britain that formally granted the Bahamas its independence in 1973.

Sadly, racial inequality has been pervasive throughout the history of the islands. Although more than 85 percent of the country's population is of African descent, it was not until 1956 that black Bahamians could legally patronize most theaters, hotels, and restaurants. Today, a democratic parliamentary system of government promotes racial equality, but social equality has proven more elusive.

Official name: Commonwealth of the Bahamas. **Area:** 5,380 square miles (slightly larger than Connecticut). **Population:** 223,000. **Population density:** 37 inhabitants per square mile. **Capital and largest city:** Nassau (pop. 139,000). **Language:** English. **Religion:** Protestant, Roman Catholic. **Per capita income:** US$7,950. **Currency:** Bahamian dollar. **Literacy rate:** 89%. **Average daily high/low:*** Nassau: January, 77°/65°; July, 88°/75°. **Average number of days with precipitation:** Nassau: January, 6; July, 14.

TRAVEL

U.S. citizens do not need a passport or a visa for stays of up to eight months. However, proof of citizenship (a birth certificate, passport, or voter registration card) is required, as is an onward or return ticket. A passport and a residence/work permit are required for residence, business, or missionary work. For specific details, contact the Embassy of the Bahamas (600 New Hampshire Avenue NW, Washington, DC 20037) or a Bahamian consulate in New York or Miami.

---

*all temperatures are Fahrenheit

Getting Around

The Bahamas is probably the most accessible country to travelers from the United States after Canada and Mexico. Grand Bahama, for example, is only 60 miles from the east coast of Florida, and numerous flights and boats (ranging from hydrofoils to cruise ships) link Florida to the islands. (In fact, from some islands it's easier to get to Florida than to Nassau, the nation's capital and largest city.)

Getting around the Bahamas, on the other hand, is not easy except by air. Even by air, however, service to some of the less-visited islands is infrequent and often means going through either Nassau or Miami. A number of small private companies—Bahamas Air, Mackey, Chalk's, Helda Air, and Shawnee—operate scheduled flights between various islands. In addition, ferry service (which takes 15 to 16 hours) connects Nassau (New Providence Island) and Freeport (Grand Bahama), the nation's two main cities and tourist centers. Another slow but interesting way of getting to other islands is via the mail boats, which carry passengers, mail, and merchandise.

Cars can be rented in the main tourist resorts, as can bicycles, mopeds, and motorcycles. Bicycles are especially well-suited for the islands, since most are small and the terrain is flat. Driving is on the left-hand side of the road.

For persons considering making a vacation trip to the Bahamas an educational experience as well, there's a one-week December study-tour offered by Ohio University. "Marine and Tropical Field Studies" on Andros Island is open to college students and secondary school teachers; apply by November 1. Additional information is available from Dr. Weldon Witters, 427 Irvine Hall, Ohio University, Athens, Ohio 45701.

Especially for Students and Young People

There is no student travel organization in the Bahamas and no special discounts have been developed for holders of the International Student Identity Card.

For Further Information

General tourist information is available from the Bahamas Tourist Office (150 East 52nd Street, New York, NY 10022). Some, but not all, guidebooks to the Caribbean include information about the Bahamas, which (as noted above) is technically not located in the Caribbean. One of the better ones is Fodor's *The Bahamas*, which comes in both a pocket-sized ($6.95) and regular edition ($8.95).

STUDY

A program offered by a member institution of the Council on International Educational Exchange is described below. Consult Appendix I for its address.

SEMESTER AND ACADEMIC YEAR

Oceanography

State University of New York at Brockport. San Salvador. January. Designed for biology, earth science, and geology majors. Juniors, seniors, and graduate students. Apply by April 15.

DOMINICAN REPUBLIC

According to its tourism bureau, the Dominican Republic, which occupies the eastern two-thirds of the island of Hispaniola, is "the best-kept secret in the Caribbean." And, in fact, in comparison to other Caribbean islands, the Dominican Republic is a relative latecomer to the tourist industry. As a result, it retains much of its intrinsic character and charm. But things are changing. Sugar, once its principal export, has been surpassed by tourism as the country's primary income generator, and a growing number of assembly plants, built by multinational companies attracted by low labor costs, are transforming the nation's economic base. There are now nine duty-free industrial parks in the Dominican Republic, many housed in former sugar refineries.

A relatively stable democratic system has been in place since the American Marine occupation of the country ended in 1966. Despite a long history of U.S. intervention, however, anti-American sentiment is not pronounced. Dominicans have a comfortable, quasi–Puerto Rico-like relationship with the U.S.; in fact, after Santo Domingo, New York City could be considered the country's second-largest city, thanks to its large Dominican population.

Discovered by Columbus in 1492, the Dominican Republic boasts the first Spanish settlement in the New World, the first cathedral, and the oldest university. For three hundred years the island was controlled by Spain, and for briefer periods after that was controlled by France and Haiti (which occupies the western part of the island). It nearly came under U.S. control in 1904 when a shaky Dominican government requested American statehood, a motion that was narrowly defeated in the U.S. Senate. Still, the U.S. has not hesitated to exert its political influence and the Marines have occupied the country twice in this century. In 1966, after the most recent U.S. intervention, Joaquin Balaguer was elected president. Power has since alternated between his rule (re-elected three times) and parties of the center-left.

The Dominican people are primarily of African and Spanish descent (the native population was virtually exterminated in the 16th century), and baseball (not soccer) and *merengue* dancing are their passions. The population is fairly evenly divided between urban and rural areas, with Santo Domingo the political capital and Santiago, the second-largest city, the center of the nation's agricultural production.

In spite of a recent economic downturn, the last decade has been one of healthy economic growth. The booming tourist industry and foreign investment in new clothing and textile industries are signs that the Dominican Republic is a nation in transition.

—*Nancy Robinson, Santiago, Dominican Republic*

Area: 18,704 square miles (about twice the size of Vermont). **Population:** 6,900,000. **Population density:** 369 inhabitants per square mile. **Capital and largest city:** Santo Domingo (pop. 1,410,000). **Language:** Spanish. **Religion:** Roman Catholic. **Per capita income:** US$858. **Currency:** Peso. **Literacy rate:** 68%. **Average daily high/low:*** Santo Domingo: January, 84°/66°; July, 88°/72°. **Average number of days with precipitation:** January, 7; July, 11.

TRAVEL

U.S. citizens need a passport and tourist card, the latter issued upon their arrival, to enter the Dominican Republic. The tourist card costs $5 and is valid for 60 days. Check with the Embassy of the Dominican Republic (1715 22nd Street NW, Washington, DC 20008) for specific details.

Getting Around

Several companies offer long-distance bus service between the country's cities and resorts, including Autobuses Metro, Terrabus, and Caribe Tours. Local buses, called *guaguas*, provide slow but very inexpensive service to virtually every village in the country. In addition, public transport is provided by cars called *públicos*, which travel on major highways picking people up and dropping them off along a specified route. Rail transport is virtually nonexistent.

Renting a car is another option for getting around the country. Main roads are generally well maintained, driving is on the right-hand side of the road, and a U.S. driver's license is valid. Budget and Hertz are among those outfits with operations in the Dominican Republic; you can check rates and minimum-age requirements by calling their toll-free numbers in the U.S. A number of local companies also operate in Santo Domingo and resort areas such as Puerto Plata.

Especially for Students and Young People

ODTE is the student travel organization and ISTC member in the Dominican Republic. In addition to its main office at Avenida Bolivar 456, Apt. 2-B, Ens. Gascue, Santo Domingo (mailing address: P.O. Box 25135, Santo Domingo), there are also offices in Santiago and San Pedro de Macoris. The organization arranges city and beach tours in Santo Domingo, and offers one-week packages (including accommodations and meals) at various beach resorts. Students with the International Student Identity Card get a discount on international air fares from Santo Domingo as well as discounts at some shops. Contact ODTE for more information.

For Further Information

General tourist information is available from the Dominican Republic Tourist Information Center (485 Madison Avenue, New York, NY 10022). In addition,

---

*all temperatures are Fahrenheit

guidebooks to the Caribbean region invariably include a section on the Dominican Republic.

WORK

Internships/Traineeships

AIESEC places students in internship positions in fields such as economics, business, finance, marketing, accounting, and computer sciences. See page 18 for details.

STUDY

The following are the educational programs offered by member institutions of the Council on International Educational Exchange. Consult Appendix I for the addresses where you can write for more information. In addition to those programs listed below, Goshen College offers a study-service term open only to students already enrolled there.

SEMESTER AND ACADEMIC YEAR

Spanish Language and Caribbean Area Studies

Council on International Educational Exchange. "Spanish Language and Caribbean Area Studies Programs." Santiago. Fall or spring semester. Sophomores, juniors, and seniors with four semesters of Spanish. Apply June 1 for fall semester and November 1 for spring. Contact Academic Programs Department.

Experiment in International Living/School for International Training. "College Semester Abroad." Santo Domingo. Fall or spring semester. Intensive Spanish, Caribbean studies seminar, independent-study project, and one-week village homestay. Sophomores to graduate students with 2.5 GPA. Apply by May 15 for fall semester and October 15 for spring.

International Student Exchange Program. Direct reciprocal exchange between U.S. universities and the Universidad Católica Madre y Maestra. Semester or academic year. Full curriculum options. Open only to students at ISEP member institutions.

Michigan State University. "Spanish Language, Literature, and Culture in the Dominican Republic." Santiago. Winter quarter. Sophomores, juniors, and seniors with two years college-level Spanish. Apply by November 23.

JAMAICA

For three centuries the small but heavily populated island of Jamaica was the centerpiece of the British empire in the Caribbean. Since gaining its independence in 1962, Jamaica has maintained a lively parliamentary democracy in which power has alternated between the Jamaican Labor Party and the People's National Party. But neither party has made noticeable progress in alleviating social inequality on the island, and Jamaica continues to suffer from a debilitating combination of inflation, unemployment, and poverty.

Although Jamaican Creole (or patois)—a blend of African languages and English—is the language of communication in informal situations, English still serves as the official language of government, the educational system, and the mass media.

In spite of centuries of British rule, few Jamaicans trace their ancestry to Britain; instead, over 90 percent of Jamaicans are descendants of Africans imported as slaves to work in the sugarcane fields. This African influence enlivens the cultural life of the country. The heartbeat of Jamaica is its music, which ranges from folk ballads and Protestant revivalist hymns to reggae, Jamaica's most famous contribution to the international language of music.

Area: 4,411 square miles (about the size of Connecticut). **Population:** 2,500,000. **Population density:** 567 inhabitants per square mile. **Capital and largest city:** Kingston (pop. 117,000). **Language:** English. **Religion:** Protestant, Roman Catholic. **Per capita income:** US$1,090. **Currency:** Jamaican dollar. **Literacy rate:** 76%. **Average daily high/low:**[*] Kingston: January, 86°/67°; July, 90°/73°. **Average number of days with precipitation:** Kingston: January, 3; July, 4.

TRAVEL

For visits of up to six months, U.S. tourists do not need either a passport or a visa if they are arriving directly from the United States, Puerto Rico, or the U.S. Virgin Islands. However, tourists must have a return or onward ticket and proof of citizenship, along with a photo ID and sufficient funds. A tourist card is issued on arrival and is returned to immigration authorities on departure.

Visas *are* required for Americans going to the island for business or study. For specific requirements, check with the Embassy of Jamaica (1850 K Street NW, Suite 355, Washington, DC 20006) or at a Jamaican consulate in either New York, Miami, Atlanta, Chicago, or Los Angeles.

Getting Around

One of the most interesting and least expensive ways of seeing more of Jamaica than its beaches is to take the train between Kingston and Montego Bay. The five-hour trip across the heart of the island provides beautiful scenery as well as a glimpse of the everyday life of Jamaicans. Another cheap way of getting around are the local buses that serve most areas of the island. (However, travel after dark by bus is not recommended.) In addition, there are minibuses that serve the most popular routes between the island's cities and resorts; these operate as *collectivos*, leaving only when full and picking up and discharging passengers anywhere along the route.

Most international flights arrive at the Montego Bay airport. From there

---

[*]all temperatures are Fahrenheit

many tourists, especially those who have no desire to see little more than their resort hotel, take air shuttles to tourist resorts such as Ocho Rios and Negril. In these resort areas, as well as at the international airport in Kingston, you'll find a variety of car rental companies. Due to the slow and unreliable nature of public transportation in Jamaica, many visitors elect to rent a car; your U.S. driver's license is valid (most agencies insist on a minimum age of 25) but remember that driving is on the left-hand side of the road. The largest car rental firms operating in Jamaica are Avis, Budget, and Hertz; you can call their toll-free numbers in the U.S. to compare rates or find out about minimum-age requirements. Bicycle, moped, and motorcycle rentals are also available in tourist areas.

For those who prefer traveling on an organized tour, American Youth Hostels offers a nine-day trip that focuses on one-day hikes radiating out from the tour's home base, a chalet in the Blue Mountains of Jamaica. Hikers explore local villages as well as the island's beautiful mountains, lakes, waterfalls, and tropical forests. The tour, called "Hidden Jamaica," is offered a number of times each winter.

"It can be hard for an outsider to envision how the huge phenomenon of reggae music came out of a country only 144 by 49 miles in size. Reggae is the root of Jamaican culture and in many ways the people epitomize their music, which is vibrant, rhythmic, and colorful. Reggae is everywhere and a concert such as Reggae Sunsplash should not be missed."
—Sara Hirsch, Sunnyside, New York

Especially for Students and Young People

Jamaica's student travel organization and ISTC member is JOYST (Jamaica Organization of Youth and Student Tourists). Their office is located at 9 Ripon Road, Kingston 5. With the International Student Identity Card (ISIC), students can get discounts on Air Jamaica flights (except those to Toronto, Miami, and New York) as well as reduced rates at some hotels, museums, and theaters. Contact JOYST for more information.

For Further Information

General tourist information is available from the Jamaican Tourist Board (866 Second Avenue, New York, NY 10017). There are also tourist board offices in Chicago, Miami, and Los Angeles. You'll find information about Jamaica in guidebooks to the Caribbean. One focusing exclusively on the country is the Berlitz pocket-sized guide to Jamaica, with good maps and color photos.

WORK

Getting a Job

CIEE's Work in Jamaica program gives college or university students the opportunity to seek employment in Jamaica during the summer vacation period (June 1 to October 1). The program is conducted with the cooperation of JOYST, which meets participants upon arrival, provides an orientation on working in Jamaica, and assists with any problems that may arise. Students are responsible for finding their own jobs; however, JOYST uses local contacts and listings from previous Work in Jamaica participants to locate potential employers. Participants should realize that the summer job market in a Third World country such as Jamaica will be quite different from that of the United States. While you should not expect to find employment related to your field of study, jobs are available in the tourist and service industries. To qualify, an individual must be at least 18 years of age, a college or university student, and a U.S. citizen or permanent resident. The cost of the program is $96.

"Jamaica has a lot more to offer than sunny Caribbean beaches for winter or spring break. Living and working in Jamaica will give you a glimpse of the Caribbean lifestyle that cannot be seen by the ordinary tourist."
—Linda Samuels, Cleveland, Ohio

Internships/Traineeships

A program offered by a member of the Council on International Educational Exchange is described below. Consult Appendix I for its address.

University of Minnesota. "Minnesota Studies in International Development." Academic year. Predeparture coursework at the U of M fall quarter, with internship in development-related research or action project in winter and spring quarters. Juniors to graduates and adults with interest in development and 2.5 GPA. Apply by May 15.

STUDY

A program offered by a member institution of the Council on International Educational Exchange is listed below. Consult Appendix I for its address.

SUMMER

Agriculture

Louisiana State University. "International Agriculture in Jamaica." Kingston. Two-week program of on-site study of tropical agriculture. Sophomores to graduate students with 2.5 GPA. Apply by April 1.

CHAPTER SIXTEEN

MEXICO AND CENTRAL AMERICA

Many people travel to Mexico and Central America for no other reason than its warm weather and beautiful beach resorts like Acapulco and Cancún. Others, however, become more deeply involved. Americans are traveling to the region not only as tourists but also as volunteers to help fight poverty, as scientists to help preserve the rain forest, as students to understand the region's language and culture, as businessmen to help develop industry and commerce, and as archaeologists to explore the mysteries of ancient cities that still rise as testimony to the great empires that flourished long before Columbus's arrival in the Americas. Whatever the reason, few travelers are disappointed.

For nearly 300 years Mexico and the republics of Central America were all part of the Spanish empire. Because of this, these nations share a common heritage and many common characteristics. But making sweeping generalizations would be a serious error. For example, while most of these nations use Spanish as the official language, Belize uses English. The largest population group in the region is the *mestizo*—a mixture of Spanish and Indian ancestry—but Guatemala remains predominantly Indian. Dictatorship or one-party rule are the norm but Costa Rica has a long-standing, two-party democracy. And while you can expect tropical weather in coastal areas, most cities of the region—including Mexico City, Guatemala City, and San José—lie inland far above sea level and enjoy surprisingly temperate climates.

Mexico and Central America are closely linked to their powerful neighbor to the north. As home of the Panama Canal, market for U.S. products, supplier of food and raw materials (including petroleum), and a major source of legal and illegal immigration, the region plays a major role in our economy and society. Study, work, or travel in the region offers the chance to get to know countries that, in spite of their proximity and importance to the U.S., remain little understood by the American public.

Today, merely mentioning Central America brings to the minds of most North Americans images of violence and strife. And it is certainly true that political, social, and economic problems plague the region. However, the image of political instability and violence is not entirely accurate; Mexico and Costa Rica are examples to the contrary. In these two countries, you'll find a wide variety of study, work, and travel programs sponsored by U.S. institutions and organizations. And you need not avoid other countries in the region such as Guatemala or Honduras; they, too, can provide fascinating experiences. Even in Nicaragua, the problems for U.S. travelers are chiefly ones of inconvenience—power blackouts or fuel shortages, for example—rather than life-threatening security problems. However, before going, check with the Citizens Emergency Center at the U.S. State Department (see page 6) for any travel advisories that may be in effect. At press time, the State Department

GULF OF
MEXICO
MEXICO
BELIZE
HONDURAS
NICARAGUA
PANAMA
GUATEMALA
EL SALVADOR
COSTA RICA
PACIFIC
OCEAN

was warning against travel in El Salvador as well as certain areas of Nicaragua and Guatemala.

The Essentials

A tourist card is enough to allow you to enter Mexico and most Central American countries. However, even if a U.S. passport isn't actually required, it's good to have it with you as proof of your citizenship. Most countries of the region also have an onward transportation requirement that may be enforced somewhat arbitrarily. Especially when confronted with young travelers, officials may ask for proof of a ticket out of the country or sometimes just sufficient funds to buy such a ticket. Check with the embassy or consulate for further information.

You'll find entrance requirements and embassy addresses given in the individual country sections that follow. Addresses for the embassies of countries not covered in a separate section of this chapter are listed below:

- Embassy of Belize, 1575 I Street NW, Suite 695, Washington, DC 20005
- Embassy of El Salvador, 2308 California Street NW, Washington, DC 20008
- Embassy of Guatemala, 2220 R Street NW, Washington, DC 20008
- Embassy of Nicaragua, 1627 New Hampshire Avenue NW, Washington, DC 20009
- Embassy of Panama, 2862 McGill Terrace NW, Washington, DC 20008

Getting There by Air

The cheapest fares from the U.S. to Mexico and Central America are generally APEX fares (see Chapter 5 for a general explanation of air fares). Below are some examples of *one-way* fares in effect during the summer of 1989. More up-to-date information is available at Council Travel offices (see listing on pages ix–xi).

New York–Mexico City, $170
Los Angeles–Mexico City, $190
Houston–Mexico City, $155
New York–Guatemala City, $175
Miami–San José, $120

For persons planning a short-term stay (anywhere from four days to a couple of weeks) the cheapest way of traveling may be to buy a vacation package that includes air fare, transfers, and hotel. Generally speaking, packages are available to Mexico City, Guadalajara, Mérida, and beach resorts such as Cancún, Acapulco, Puerto Vallarta, Mazatlán, and Ixtapa. Packages range from budget to luxury, and can be booked through travel agents in the U.S. or through airlines flying to Mexico from the U.S. (including the Mexican carriers Mexicana and Aeroméxico). Packages are generally cheaper than making your own arrangements, since tour operators can mass-book hotels and make volume purchases. Council Travel arranges special low-cost spring vacation packages geared toward students and teachers interested in making their spring-break getaway an international experience (Cancún was a 1989 option). Contact a Council Travel office for more information.

Other Means of Travel

Millions of Americans cross the border by car into Mexico each year. In fact, before civil war broke out in El Salvador, you could drive from the United States all the way to Panama via the Pan American Highway. While it is still possible to do this (in theory) by bypassing El Salvador (going over poor roads directly from Guatemala to Honduras), attempting the journey to Panama by automobile is not advisable at the present time. As we go to press, there are not only State Department warnings against travel in certain parts of the region, but also severe shortages of gasoline and areas where the road is virtually impassable due to lack of maintenance.

While there are many options for getting from the U.S. to Mexico—including car, train, bus, or plane—the options for traveling to the countries of Central America are more limited. While some Central American countries have railroad systems, these systems usually connect capital cities to ports and little else. As a result most travel between the republics of Central America is by bus or plane. You'll find more information about traveling around Costa Rica, Honduras, and Mexico in the country sections that follow.

Organized Tours

For persons interested in an organized tour to Mexico or Central America, several programs sponsored by CIEE members are listed below. Consult Appendix I for the addresses where you can write for further information.

American Youth Hostels.
"South of Two Borders." Sixteen-day bus trip through Mexico and Guatemala. Winter. Minimum age 15.
"You-Can-Yucatan." Sixteen-day cycling tour visiting cities, beaches, and Mayan ruins. Winter. Minimum age 15.
"Mexican Mysteries." Sixteen-day bus trip staying in hostels and hotels with opportunities for snorkeling and other water sports. Winter. Minimum age 15.

Ohio University. "Study Tour of Belize." Includes various sites in Belize plus trip to Flores, Guatemala. Two-week winter tour. Students, faculty, and adults. Apply by October 15. Contact Sociology Department; (614) 593-1383.

Various nonprofit groups in the U.S. sponsor educational tours of Central American nations designed to increase public awareness of the region and its problems. The Center for Global Education at Augsburg College (731 21st Avenue South, Minneapolis, MN 55454) offers a variety of public awareness tours tailored to specific professional, church, and student groups. Another nonprofit organization, the National Educators Committee on Central America (P.O. Box 43509, Washington, DC 20010-9509), conducts organized tours to El Salvador, Guatemala, and Nicaragua. Its tours, geared toward teachers, administrators, and education majors, involve visits to schools and meetings with representatives of various organizations and government agencies concerned with education in the country. A good source of information on public awareness tours sponsored by various groups across the U.S. is the publication, *Travel Programs in Central America* (see page 402).

Eating and Sleeping

You'll find an abundance of inexpensive hotels in Mexican and Central American cities. In addition, the student travel offices listed for Costa Rica and Mexico can help you find inexpensive places to stay. For a listing of youth hostels in Mexico, go to the Asociación Méxicana de Albergues de la Juventud (Madero No. 6, Suite 314, Mexico 1, D.F.).

Work

Except for Costa Rica, where CIEE's work abroad program makes summer employment a possibility for U.S. students, stringent labor regulations and high unemployment rates make it almost impossible for foreigners to obtain employment in Mexico or Central America. Nevertheless, resourceful persons fluent in Spanish can find informal employment (mostly as English tutors) once they've arrived in the region. Persons with a degree in TESOL should check Chapter 3 for teaching opportunities in Latin America.

You'll find internship possibilities for Mexico and Costa Rica listed in the individual country sections later in this chapter. In addition, AIESEC offers internship possibilities in Guatemala and Panama; see page 18 for additional information about this program.

Study

Persons considering study in Latin America might want to take a look at *Funding for Research, Study, and Travel: Latin America and the Caribbean*, edited by Karen Cantrell and Denise Wallen (Phoenix: Oryx Press, 1987), even though most of the grants and scholarships listed in this 300-page reference work are for graduate study. The book is expensive ($37.50), so look for it in your college library.

For Further Information

Probably the most comprehensive guidebook to Latin America is the *South American Handbook*, published in Britain and distributed in the United States by Prentice Hall. In spite of its name, the book includes extensive information about Mexico and Central America. The 1,390-page manual isn't cheap, but it's worth the $29.95 price, especially if you're planning to visit several countries in the region.

Anyone interested in hiking should also take a look at *Backpacking in Mexico and Central America*. The book, complete with maps and photos, can be obtained for $11.95 plus $1.50 for book-rate postage from Bradt Enterprises, 95 Harvey Street, Cambridge, MA 02140.

Numerous budget travel guides are available for Mexico; check the Mexico section later in this chapter for a brief rundown. In contrast, there are few guidebooks to republics of Central America. Of the travel guides available, one of the better ones is Fodor's *Central America* ($15.95), which has extensive information on what to see and how to get around; however, the hotels and restaurants listed tend to be on the more expensive side.

Persons considering a trip to Central America in order to become more actively involved in its internal struggles will be interested in *Travel Programs in Central America*. This publication contains information about short- and long-term volunteer projects, study programs, and educational travel programs in the region. Put out by the Central America Information Center (P.O. Box 50211, San Diego, CA 92105) three times a year, it costs $12 for a yearly subscription or $5 for a single issue.

COSTA RICA

Costa Ricans see their Central American nation as a rose among thorns. Led by a democratically elected president, Oscar Arias Sanchez, who was awarded the Nobel Peace Prize in 1987, Costa Rica offers democracy, social stability, and relative economic prosperity in a region where all three are generally lacking.

The people of Costa Rica value their two-party democracy, tradition of nonviolence, and educational system. They also prize the traditional family structure that remains the central focus of their lives. A strong sense of history has helped keep these attitudes alive in the "Tico" (the name by which the Costa Rican is often called), and he or she will point with pride to the establishment of free and mandatory education for all citizens in 1869, the abolition of the death penalty in 1882, and the disbanding of a standing army in 1949.

But Costa Rica is not entirely immune to the maladies that plague the region. Rapid population growth, deforestation, and external debt (the highest per capita debt of any Third World nation) are among the problems confronting the country. And some question whether Costa Rica can continue to avoid the political strife and economic ills experienced by many of its Central American neighbors.

Although the country is officially neutral, Costa Ricans are strongly pro-American and view the United States as a friend and ally. Much economic support is gained by this relationship, both through the public and private sectors, and an increasing number of U.S. firms are locating their Latin American headquarters or branch offices in Costa Rica because of the nation's political and economic stability as well as the availability of an educated and hard-working labor force. Also visible are a growing number of retired Americans who have settled here to enjoy the good quality of life and pleasant climate at an economical price. Americans—whether businessmen, retirees, students, or travelers—generally find Costa Rica safer, more comfortable, and less "foreign" than other Latin American nations.

—*G. Bernard Yevin, Rockford, Illinois*

Official name: Republic of Costa Rica. **Area:** 19,652 square miles (about twice the size of Maryland). **Population:** 2,900,000. **Population density:** 148 inhabitants per square mile. **Capital and largest city:** San José (pop. 278,500). **Language:** Spanish. **Religion:** Roman Catholic. **Per capita income:** US$1,352. **Currency:** Colón. **Literacy rate:** 90%. **Average daily high/low:*** San José: January, 75°/58°; July, 77°/62°. **Average number of days with precipitation:** San José: January, 3; July, 23.

---

*all temperatures are Fahrenheit

TRAVEL

U.S. citizens need a passport to enter Costa Rica (although other proof of U.S. citizenship is sometimes sufficient). Upon your arrival you will be issued a tourist card valid for 30 days. The tourist card may be extended an additional 90 days by permission of Costa Rican immigration authorities. Longer stays require a visa. For specific details, check with the Embassy of Costa Rica (2112 S Street NW, Washington, DC 20008) or with the Costa Rican consulate in New York.

Getting Around

Traveling around Costa Rica is fairly easy, both because the country is compact and because it has one of the region's best transportation systems. Separate rail lines link the capital with Puerto Limón on the Caribbean and Puerto Arenas and Puerto Caldera on the Pacific. In addition, the Pan American Highway extends the length of the country, and express highways radiate from San José, connecting the capital to the other major cities of the central plateau as well as to Pacific ports and beaches. There are numerous companies in San José offering car and jeep rentals, including major U.S. companies such as Hertz, Avis, Budget, National, and Dollar.

Especially for Students and Young People

The student travel organization and ISTC member in Costa Rica is OTEC (Organización Turística Estudiantil y Juvenil). Its main office is in San José (Avenida 3 Calle 3 y 5, Edificio Victoria, 2do piso) but there are also offices in Cartago, Heredia, and Alajuela. At OTEC offices you can get information, buy international air tickets, book accommodations, sign up for tours, or enroll in a Spanish language course. Tours offered by OTEC include a one-day Pacific island cruise, a one-day white-water rafting trip on the Reventazón River, and a three-day "jungle tour" in Tortuguero National Park.

In Costa Rica, students with the International Student Identity Card are entitled to reduced air fares on international routes from San José, discounts at some hotels, and free or reduced admissions to several museums and theaters. OTEC will supply a list of restaurants, shops, discos, et cetera that provide discounts to ISIC holders.

For Further Information

General tourist information is available from the Costa Rica Tourist Board, 3540 Wilshire Boulevard, Suite 707, Los Angeles, CA 90010.

WORK

Getting a Job

CIEE's Work in Costa Rica program allows U.S. college students to receive authorization to accept temporary employment in Costa Rica for up to four months during their summer vacation (June 1 to October 1). Participants are responsible for finding their own jobs; the most likely categories of employment include unskilled work in the service industries (especially tourism) as well as manual labor (especially agriculture). The program is conducted with the cooperation of OTEC, which meets participants upon arrival, provides an orientation, and assists with problems that may arise. Participants should realize that the summer job market in a Third World country like Costa Rica will be quite different from that of the United States. Salaries may be low compared to the U.S. but should cover the cost of daily expenses. To qualify, an individual must be at least 18 years of age, a college or university student, and a U.S. citizen or permanent resident. The cost of the program is $96. For more information, contact the Work Exchanges Department at CIEE.

Internships/Traineeships

AIESEC places students in internship positions in Costa Rica. See page 18 for further details.

Voluntary Service

The "Year Abroad Program" sponsored by the International Christian Youth Exchange offers persons ages 18–24 voluntary service opportunities in the fields of health care, education, the environment, construction, et cetera. See page 22 for more information.

Persons interested in voluntary service as teachers can contact WorldTeach, a nonprofit program which places recent college graduates in schools in Costa Rica. Volunteers must commit themselves to a one-year teaching assignment but no teacher training or experience is required. They receive an allowance of $72 a month but pay a program fee of about $3,000 that includes air fare, orientation, and insurance. For more information, contact WorldTeach, Phillip Brooks House, Harvard University, Cambridge, MA 02138.

In addition, Goshen College offers a study-service term in Costa Rica that is open only to Goshen students.

STUDY

The following are the educational programs offered by member institutions of the Council on International Educational Exchange. Consult Appendix I for the addresses where you can write for further information. In addition to the programs listed below, the University of California system offers a study program that is open only to students at its own schools.

SEMESTER AND ACADEMIC YEAR

General Studies

Associated Colleges of the Midwest. "Tropical Field Research: Natural and Social Sciences." San José. Academic year or spring semester. Sophomores, juniors, and seniors with social science and natural science courses and one year of college Spanish. Apply by March 15 for full year and November 1 for spring.

Friends World College. "Latin American Studies." San José, with trip to Nicaragua. Academic year or semester. Latin American studies, Spanish, and individualized program combining independent study with fieldwork or internships. Sophomores, juniors, and seniors; others may participate but will not receive credits. Apply by May 15 for fall and November 15 for spring.

International Student Exchange Program. Direct reciprocal exchange between U.S. universities and the Universidad Nacional de Heredia. Academic year or semester. Full curriculum options. Open only to students at ISEP member institutions.

Latin American Studies

Associated Colleges of the Midwest. San José. "Latin American Culture and Society." Fall semester only. Sophomores, juniors, and seniors with at least one year of college Spanish. For early response apply by November 1; final deadline is March 15.

SUMMER

Biology

Council on International Educational Exchange. "Program in Tropical Biology." Monteverde. Sophomores, juniors, and seniors with previous college-level biology courses and 2.75 GPA. Apply by April 1. Contact Academic Programs Department.

General Studies

State University of New York at Albany. San José. Juniors, seniors, and graduate students with at least two years of college-level Spanish and 3.0 GPA. Apply by April 1.

HONDURAS

Mountainous Honduras, in comparison to its neighbors—Nicaragua, El Salvador, and Guatemala—remains an island of relative stability and safety. Its strategic location in the heart of Central America with both Pacific and Caribbean coastlines has made it a key U.S. ally in the region. However, largely due to the press coverage of conflict in Central America in the last decade, there is little organized tourism to Honduras. As a result, you won't find crowds or high prices even at its most famous tourist destinations—the Mayan ruins at Copán and the pristine beaches of the Bay Islands off the nation's Caribbean coast.

Honduras is often thought of as a "banana republic." This derogatory term was coined early in this century to describe a country whose economy is so dependent on one item produced by foreign economic interests that its own sovereignty is compromised. And while it's true that the economic well-being of Honduras still depends on bananas produced mainly by large U.S.-based corporations operating along the nation's Caribbean coast, the power of these foreign-owned corporations has been diminished by a government organization that now oversees the banana industry. At the same time, the country is rapidly diversifying its exports to include beef, coffee, and cotton.

So far Honduras has not been subjected to the civil wars and political upheavals that have torn apart its neighbors. But the same root causes of unrest in these countries also exist in Honduras and the country's long-term stability remains uncertain.

Official Name: Republic of Honduras. **Area:** 43,277 square miles (about the size of Tennessee). **Population:** 4,800,000. **Population density:** 111 inhabitants per square mile. **Capital and largest city:** Tegucigalpa (pop. 571,400). **Language:** Spanish. **Religion:** Roman Catholic. **Per capita income:** US$700. **Currency:** Lempira. **Literacy rate:** 56%. **Average daily high/low:*** Tegucigalpa: January, 77°/56°; July, 83°/63°. **Average number of days with precipitation:** January, 1; July, 8.

TRAVEL

For U.S. citizens planning on traveling to Honduras, a passport (valid for at least six months after the date of entry), a visa, and an onward or return ticket are required. Visas, which are issued for stays of up to 30 days at no charge, can be obtained upon arrival. For specific regulations, check with the Embassy of Honduras (4301 Connecticut Avenue NW, Washington, DC 20008).

Getting Around

As a result of an aggressive road-building program, roads now link most parts of the country, making getting around by car or bus much easier than it used to be. Frequent buses travel the country's main route, which connects the nation's commercial center of San Pedro Sula with Tegucigalpa, the capital. Buses serve most of the rest of the country as well, except for parts of the Mosquito Coast, which are still not accessible by road. Cars can be rented in San Pedro Sula or Tegucigalpa. The country's limited railroad network is confined to the banana-producing areas of the coast and transports a lot of bananas but not many people.

Especially for Students and Young People

There is no student travel organization in Honduras and no special discounts have been developed for holders of the International Student Identity Card.

For Further Information

General tourist information is available from the Honduras Tourist Bureau, 1140 Fremont Avenue, South Pasadena, CA 91030.

---

*all temperatures are Fahrenheit

WORK

The Reformed Church in America, a member organization of CIEE, has elementary school teaching positions available in remote areas of the country that involve teaching the children of missionary workers. Applicants should be college graduates with a Christian commitment, and an elementary education degree is preferred. See Appendix I for the address to write for more information.

Voluntary Service

For persons interested in voluntary service work, the "Year Abroad Program" sponsored by the International Christian Youth Exchange offers persons ages 18–24 voluntary service opportunities in the fields of health care, education, the environment, construction, et cetera. See page 22 for more information.

MEXICO

A 2,000-mile border—sometimes a shallow river but more often just an imaginary line in the desert—separates Mexico and the United States. While the border itself is crossed legally and illegally by thousands of people every day, the real division is a linguistic, economic, historic, and cultural one that is not so easily crossed. Nowhere else does the Third World rub shoulders so closely with one of the world's wealthiest nations. And while the two nations coexist—peacefully but uncomfortably—each of them tries as much as possible to ignore the other. Yet as much as Americans and Mexicans might each like to be rid of their backyard neighbor, the futures of the two countries are inextricably linked.

In the 16th century the Spanish defeated the Aztecs, took their land and silver, and enslaved or killed much of the native population. In the 19th century Mexico gained its independence from Spain, but little changed for the average Mexican. Early in this century the Mexican revolution brought far-reaching changes, including land redistribution and an end to the power of the traditional elite—the landed aristocracy, the church, and the military. But its promise of power to Mexican workers and *campesinos* was never realized; Mexico remains split by stark class differences.

Since 1982, Mexico has been in the throes of a financial crisis that has left the country demoralized and with a standard of living lower than that of ten years ago. This crisis was brought about by a drop in the price of petroleum on world markets and Mexico's resultant inability to make the required payments on its foreign debt. One result of the crisis has been increased emigration—legal and illegal—across the U.S. border. Another has been challenges from both the left and right to the PRI, the political party that has controlled Mexico since the end of the Revolution. President Carlos Salinas de Gortari has promised to give a greater role to the opposition and enforce fair elections. But the political stability of Mexico—like its economic future—is uncertain.

Nowhere is this uncertain future more evident than in Mexico City, the economic, political, and cultural heart of the country. With nearly 20 million people, the metropolitan area is by most counts the world's largest city. Not surprisingly, rapid population growth has strained the infrastructure of the city, producing overcrowding, pollution, and sprawling slums. But in spite of its problems, Mexico City—once the capital of New Spain and before that of the Aztec empire—remains one of the world's most lively and interesting cities. And rising on the northern edge of the city are the ruins of Teotihuacán, once the center of a great empire that reached its zenith a millennium before the arrival of the Aztecs. Even now, Teotihuacán's Pyramids of the Sun and Moon are among the world's most impressive sights.

Although power radiates from Mexico City, it is in the villages of Mexico where the spiritual heart of the country beats. Here the pace of life is slower and traditional ties to the land, the church, and family are strong. Visitors to the highlands of central Mexico will encounter picturesque villages and a way of life that is attractive because it seems unaffected by the ills of modernity. But a closer examination will also reveal that these villages are not lost in time; like all Mexican society today, they are products of the dynamic interplay between ancient Indian ways, the legacy of Spanish colonialism, and the contemporary cultural, political, and economic influence of Mexico's powerful northern neighbor.

Whether you come for unsurpassed beach resorts such as Acapulco or Cancún, the ruins of ancient Indian civilizations, or the natural beauty of its mountains, jungles, and deserts, strike out on your own and explore Mexico's cities, villages, and countryside. Your efforts will be richly rewarded as you develop a new perspective on the U.S.-Mexican relationship and encounter a way of life that's just across the border but a world away.

—*Del Franz, New York, New York*

Official name: United Mexican States. **Area:** 761,600 square miles (almost three times the size of Texas). **Population:** 83,500,000. **Population density:** 110 inhabitants per square mile. **Capital and largest city:** Mexico City (pop. 20,000,000). **Language:** Spanish, various Indian languages. **Religion:** Roman Catholic. **Per capita income:** US$1,950. **Currency:** Mexican peso. **Literacy rate:** 81%. **Average daily high/low:*** Acapulco: January, 85°/70°; July, 89°/75°; Mérida: January, 83°/62°; July, 82°/73°; Mexico City: January, 66°/42°; July, 73°/53°. **Average number of days with precipitation:** Acapulco: January, 0; July, 11; Mérida: January, 8; July, 20; Mexico City: January, 4; July, 27.

TRAVEL

U.S. citizens do not need a passport or a visa to enter Mexico. Tourist cards, which are required, are issued free of charge upon presentation of proof of citizenship (a birth certificate, passport, or naturalization papers). They can be obtained at immigration offices at points of entry along the border, at Mexican consulates and tourist offices, or from airlines serving Mexico. The tourist card is valid for three months and can be extended an additional three months. For entry for purposes other than tourism, check with the Embassy

*all temperatures are Fahrenheit

of Mexico (2829 16th Street NW, Washington, DC 20036) or with one of the nearly fifty Mexican consulates in the U.S.

Getting Around

Mexico's hundreds of bus companies lend credence to the saying that in Mexico where there's a road, there's a bus. Buses range from comfortable air-conditioned intercity buses to trucks with wooden benches, and half of the excitement of visiting a remote village may be the bus trip there. Traveling by bus is cheap and immerses you in Mexican culture in a way that is not possible if you drive or fly.

Mexico also has a well-developed rail network, although it's not nearly as comprehensive as the bus system. Generally speaking, trains are slower and subject to more frequent delays than buses. On the other hand, they are usually more comfortable and even cheaper than the buses. Trains with sleeping cars provide overnight service between Mexico City and the other major cities of central Mexico, while long-distance trains link Mexico City to cities along the U.S. border—a journey that can take a couple of days, depending on the route selected.

Air service is provided by several domestic airlines, the best known of which are Aeroméxico and Mexicana. In Mexico, travel by plane is safe and convenient and a popular alternative for travelers covering long distances.

In this country of few navigable rivers, travel by boat is generally not an alternative. An exception are the car ferries that cross between the Baja Peninsula and various cities on the Mexican mainland.

Mexico will accept a U.S. driver's license without any further documentation. However, persons planning to drive in Mexico should be aware that Mexican roads are characterized by unpredictable hazards that most U.S. drivers are not accustomed to, including animals, slow-moving carts, people, and potholes. Mexican driving habits are also quite different; for example, passing is done with less margin of safety and little attention is paid to the concept of traffic lanes (which are seldom marked on the wider roads). Unleaded gasoline, used only by tourists with U.S. vehicles, can be found only in large towns and resorts. Remember, too, that U.S. auto insurance generally is not valid in Mexico; Americans driving their own cars will have to buy Mexican auto insurance to protect themselves while they are south of the border. In spite of these obstacles, thousands of Americans drive in Mexico. A car provides comfort and independence and can be an enjoyable means of getting around, especially in northern Mexico, where traffic is light. Cars can also be rented in cities and tourist centers throughout Mexico. In addition, hitchhiking is socially acceptable and done by both Mexicans and foreigners.

Especially for Students and Young People

SETEJ México (Hamburgo 273, Colonia Juárez, 06600 México D.F.) is Mexico's student travel organization and ISTC member. There are branch offices in eight other cities, including Acapulco, Cancún, Guadalajara, Mérida, and Monterrey. At most SETEJ México offices you can get travel information, book accommodations, and buy international train and plane tickets. SETEJ México also operates youth hostels in Acapulco and Mexico City, and conducts tours for students and young people. Contact SETEJ México for more information.

In Mexico, holders of the International Student Identity Card (ISIC) receive discounts on international air fares from Mexico City. Some museums, theaters, shops, and hotels also offer discounts to students with the ISIC. A listing of participating establishments is available at SETEJ México offices throughout the country.

Meeting the People

SETEJ México can help arrange a homestay with a Mexican family. Homestays are generally several weeks in length. Contact SETEJ México's main office in Mexico City for more information.

For Further Information

Quite a few guidebooks to Mexico are available; among the best is *Mexico: A Travel Survival Kit* ($17.95), published by Lonely Planet Publications. The same outfit also publishes *Baja California: A Travel Survival Kit* ($8.95). Both are geared toward the independent budget traveler and include comprehensive information about what to see, how to get around, and where to eat and sleep. If you can't find them in bookstores, you can order them (include $1.50 postage per book) from Lonely Planet Publications, Embarcadero West, 112 Linden Street, Oakland, CA 94607. Other good guidebooks for budget travelers interested in exploring Mexican culture and history on their own are *Let's Go Mexico* ($12.95) and *The Real Guide: Mexico* ($11.95). Most bookstores should also carry Frommer's *Mexico on $35 a Day* ($13.95), which covers Guatemala and Belize as well. Among the standard guidebooks less geared to budget travelers, Birnbaum's *Mexico* ($13.95) and Fodor's *Mexico* ($13.95) are good bets.

In addition, general tourist information is available from the Mexican Government Office of Tourism (405 Park Avenue, New York, NY 10022). The Mexican government also has tourist offices in a number of other U.S. cities.

Carl Franz's *The People's Guide to Mexico* ($14.95) is not a guidebook in the traditional sense, in that it does not describe hotels to stay in or the most interesting towns to visit; what it does do is provide, through a series of anecdotes, one of the best pictures of what travel in Mexico is all about. While most informative for the first-time visitor, the book also makes for interesting and enjoyable reading for the seasoned traveler. If you can't find it in bookstores, you can order it from John Muir Publications, P.O. Box 613, Sante Fe, NM 87501 (add $2.75 for postage). Another interesting book for anyone considering travel in Mexico is *Nothing to Declare: Memoirs of a Woman Traveling Alone*, by Mary Morris (Penguin Travel Library, $7.95).

The uneasy relationship between Mexico and the United States is sure to enter into discussions you have with Mexicans. A recent book, *Limits to Friendship: The United States and Mexico*, by Jorge G. Castañeda ($10.95), provides a Mexican perspective on the political, economic, and cultural issues that divide the two countries. If you can't find it in bookstores, you can order it from Random House (400 Hahn Road, Westminister, MD 21157; add $1.50 for postage). A good, concise analysis of foreign policy options from a U.S. point of view is provided by Peter H. Smith in *Mexico: Neighbor in Transition* ($4, plus $1.50 for postage), published by the Foreign Policy Association (729 Seventh Avenue, New York, NY 10019). Another look at the relationship from a U.S. perspective can be found in *Distant Neighbors* (Viking, $8.95) by *New York Times* correspondent Alan Riding.

WORK

Obtaining regular salaried employment in Mexico is nearly impossible for foreigners; employment of foreigners is not allowed unless specifically requested by a Mexican company—a request that is granted only in unusual circumstances.

Internships/Traineeships

Internship programs offered by member institutions and organizations of the Council on International Educational Exchange are described below. Consult Appendix I for the addresses where you can write for further information.

AIESEC–US. Reciprocal internship program for students in economics, business, finance, marketing, accounting, and computer sciences. See page 18 for further information.

Association for International Practical Training. "IAESTE Trainee Program." On-the-job training for undergraduate and graduate students in technical fields such as engineering, computer science, agriculture, architecture, and mathematics. See page 18 for more information.

Brigham Young University. "Spring Term Internship in Mexico." Internships teaching literacy, basic health, and nutrition. Health-related majors with beginning Spanish. Apply by February 1.

Voluntary Service

The "Year Abroad Program" sponsored by the International Christian Youth Exchange offers persons ages 18–24 voluntary service opportunities in the fields of health care, education, the environment, construction, et cetera. See page 22 for more information. You should also check the latest edition of *Volunteer! The Comprehensive Guide to Voluntary Service in the U.S. and Abroad* ($6.95, plus $1 postage), published by CIEE.

> *"Living in a materialistic society such as the United States, one sometimes forgets how important human relationships are to a full life. Mexicans have not neglected this important area of life. Mexico taught me the importance of living a simpler life, one unhampered by an excess of material possessions and monetarily motivated career goals."*
> —Shannan Mattiace, Cedar Rapids, Iowa

STUDY

The following are the educational programs offered by member institutions of the Council on International Educational Exchange. Consult Appendix I for the addresses of the colleges and universities listed in this section. In addition to the programs listed below, the American Graduate School of International Management, California State University, the University of Oregon, the University of Pittsburgh, and Valparaiso University offer study programs open to their own students only.

SEMESTER AND ACADEMIC YEAR

Education

University of Iowa. "Iowa/Yucatán Semester Study Abroad." Spring semester. Spanish, anthropology, and education aimed at undergraduates preparing to teach. Sophomores to graduate students with 2.5 GPA. Apply by October 10. Contact: Associate Dean, College of Education, N459E Lindquist Center, University of Iowa, Iowa City, IA 52242.

General Studies

Alma College. "Program of Studies in Mexico." Mexico City. Academic year and semester. Sophomores, juniors, and seniors with three semesters of Spanish and 2.5 GPA.

Central University of Iowa. "Central College in Yucatán." Mérida. Fall, winter, or spring quarter. Freshmen to seniors with 2.5 GPA. Apply two months prior to beginning of term.

Central Washington University. Morelia. Liberal arts curriculum, including history, literature, and language. Homestay. Undergraduates and teachers. 2.5 GPA, two quarters of college coursework, and one Spanish course required.

Experiment in International Living/School for International Training. "College Semester Abroad." Cuernavaca and Guanajuato. Fall or spring semester. Intensive language, Mexican life and culture seminar, field-study seminar, independent-study project, and village homestay. Sophomores to graduate students with 2.5 GPA. Apply May 15 for fall and October 15 for spring.

International Student Exchange Program. Direct reciprocal exchange between U.S. universities and institutions in Guadalajara, Mexico City, Monterrey, and Puebla. Semester or academic year. Full curriculum options. Open only to students at ISEP member institutions.

Northern Illinois University. "Mexican and Latin American Studies." Mexico City. Semester or academic year. Courses, offered through the Universidad Autónoma de México, are taught in Spanish by Mexican faculty. Apply by June 1 for fall and November 1 for spring.

Portland State University. "Study in Guadalajara." Winter quarter. Includes excursions to Guanajuato, Mexico City, and Morelia. Sophomores to graduate students (not for graduate credit) with one term of Spanish language. Apply by October 15.

Rutgers University. "Junior Year in Mexico." Mexico City. Juniors with two years college Spanish, Spanish literature, and 3.0 GPA. Apply by March 1.

Rollins College. "Rollins Spring Term in Mérida." Sophomores, juniors, and seniors with 3.0 GPA. Apply by November 1.

University of Arkansas at Little Rock. "Mexican Exchange Program." Guadalajara. Open to students at schools in the state of Arkansas. Sophomores, juniors, and seniors. Rolling admission.

University of North Carolina–Chapel Hill. "UNC Program to Mexico City." Semester or academic year. Study at Universidad Autónoma de México. Juniors and seniors. Rolling admissions.

University of Minnesota. "Spanish in Cuernavaca." Fall, winter, or spring quarter. Beginning and intermediate Spanish language. Students and nonstudents. Apply by June 15 for fall, October 15 for winter, and December 15 for spring.

University of Notre Dame. "Foreign Study Program in Mexico City." Semester or academic year. Spanish language, Spanish and Latin American literature, and Latin American civilization. Sophomores and juniors with two years of Spanish and 2.5 overall GPA (3.0 in Spanish). Apply February 1 for fall and October 15 for spring.

University of Wisconsin–Platteville. "Mexico Study Center." Puebla. Academic year or semester at Universidad de las Americas. Sophomores, juniors, and seniors with two years of Spanish and 3.0 GPA. Apply by April 15 for fall and academic year, November 1 for spring.

Latin American Studies

Colorado State University. "Latin American Studies in Mexico." Puebla. Academic year or semester at Universidad de las Americas. Sophomores, juniors, and seniors.

Mexican Studies

Guilford College. "Semester in Guadalajara." Fall. Sophomores, juniors, and seniors with one year college Spanish. Apply by October 31.

Spanish Language and Mexican Culture

Brigham Young University. "Spring Term in Mexico." Spring semester. Includes excursions and two-week study tour to Chiapas and the Yucatán. Sophomores, juniors, and seniors with some knowledge of Spanish. Apply by October 1.

Davidson College. "Spring Semester in Mexico." Guadalajara. Spring semester in even-numbered years only. Sophomores and juniors with intermediate Spanish and 2.75 GPA. Apply by November 1.

Northern Arizona University. "Study Abroad in Mexico." Cuernavaca. Fall semester. Sophomores to graduate students. One semester of Spanish recommended. Apply by June 1.

Ohio University. "Winter Quarter in Mexico." Mérida and Yucatán. Freshmen to seniors with one year of Spanish. Apply by early September. Contact Department of Modern Languages; (614) 593-2765.

Portland State University. "Winter in Guadalajara." Winter term. High school graduates to graduate students with one term of college Spanish. Apply by October 15.

State University of New York at Oswego. "Oswego–Mexico City Program." Freshmen to graduate students with two years of college Spanish and 2.5 GPA. Apply by April 30.

University of Colorado at Boulder. "Semester in Guadalajara." Fall or spring semester. Freshmen to seniors with three semesters of college Spanish and 2.75 GPA. Apply by October 15 for spring and March 1 for fall.

University of Utah. "Cuernavaca Spanish Language Program." Spring quarter (end of March to end of May). Freshmen with one or two quarters of Spanish. Apply by January 1.

University of Washington. "Foreign Student Studies Center." Guadalajara. Fall, winter, or spring quarter. Freshmen to graduate students. Deadline is one month prior to start of program.

Western Washington University. "Study in Mexico." Morelia. Semester or quarter options. Open to high school students with 15 hours of college-level classes, high school graduates, and college undergraduate and graduate students with 2.5 GPA. Apply one month prior to beginning of the program.

SUMMER
General Studies

Alma College. "Program of Studies in Mexico." Mexico City. Study at Universidad Iberoamericana. Sophomores, juniors, and seniors with 2.5 GPA. Apply by March 15.

Central Washington University. Morelia. Liberal arts curriculum, including history, literature, and language. Homestay. Undergraduates and teachers. 2.5 GPA, two quarters of college coursework, and one Spanish course required.

Spanish Language and Mexican Culture

Eastern Michigan University. "Intensive Spanish Language Program." Cuernavaca. Freshmen to seniors. Apply by May 15.

Indiana University. "Overseas Study in Mexico." Mexico City. Freshmen to seniors with one year of Spanish and 2.8 GPA. Apply by early March.

Louisiana State University. "LSU in Mexico." Mexico City. Sophomores to graduate students with one year of college Spanish. Apply by April 1.

New York University. "NYU in Mexico." Mexico City. One-week graduate seminar on culture and society in contemporary Mexico. Some Spanish required. Contact Department of Spanish and Portuguese, Faculty of Arts and Science, 19 University Place, Room 400, New York, NY 10003; (212) 998-8770.

North Carolina State University/Raleigh. "Mexico Summer Program." Morelia. Freshmen to graduate students, and elementary and secondary teachers. One semester of high school Spanish and 2.0 GPA is required. Apply by February 15.

State University of New York at Oswego. "Oswego–Mexico City Program." High school juniors and seniors, college freshmen to graduate students. Apply by April 30.

University of Arkansas at Little Rock. "Summer in Mexico." Guadalajara. Sophomores, juniors, and seniors. Students must register for three-week seminar offered prior to departure. Apply by April 15.

University of Oregon. "Summer in Mexico." Querétaro. Sophomores, juniors, and seniors with one year college-level Spanish and 2.75 GPA. Apply by April 1.

University System of Georgia/Augusta College. "Spanish Language and Mexican Culture in Puebla." Undergraduates with 2.5 GPA. Some Spanish preferred for language students. Apply by March 15; applications accepted thereafter on a space-available basis.

Western Washington University. "Study in Mexico." Morelia. Open to high school students with 15 hours of college-level classes, high school graduates, and college undergraduate and graduate students with 2.5 GPA. Apply one month prior to beginning of the program.

Wichita State University. "Summer Program in Puebla." Freshmen to graduate students with two years high school Spanish or two semesters college Spanish. Apply by May 15.

EXPLORING MEXICAN CULTURE

Literature

Both a poet and a cultural critic, it has been said of Octavio Paz that his different literary roles are just two sides of a single soulful outlook on Mexico, a subject he never tires of writing about. *The Labyrinth of Solitude*, an analysis of the Mexican psyche from the Spanish Conquest to the 20th century, is perhaps his best-known book and a wonderful example of his prose style.

Carlos Fuentes, the son of a Mexican diplomat assigned to Washington, spent his early years in the United States. As a result, when he returned to Mexico, he had to rediscover his homeland and his identity as a Mexican. The novels of the mature Fuentes reflect this preoccupation with what it means to be Mexican, part of the larger preoccupation with history and identity that often surfaces in recent Latin American writing. *The Death of Artemio Cruz*, Fuentes's first and perhaps most popular novel, is the story of a man's life remembered as he is about to die. In his most recent work, *Christopher Unborn*, Fuentes presents an insightful yet humorous picture of his country in a story narrated by an unborn fetus and set in 1992, the 500th anniversary of Christopher Columbus's famous voyage.

The late Juan Rulfo wrote about Jalisco, the state in western Mexico from which he hailed. In *The Burning Plain and Other Stories* Rulfo explored the poverty and forlorn lives led by many of the people of his home state in lean, vivid prose. *Pedro Páramo*, probably his most popular work internationally, is a surrealistic view of life and death in rural Mexico.

Film

Although the typical image of Mexico to emerge from American films is of a world of poverty plagued by corruption and violence, the long Mexican film tradition is characterized by infinitely more insightful explorations of the intricate mix of Mexican community and family relations.

Originally known for popular melodramas such as *Maria Candelaria* (1943), by Emilio Fernandez, that dominated the Latin American market, the Mexican film industry also harbored Luis Buñuel for much of the second half of his career. During his years in Mexico Buñuel made several classics including *The Young and the Damned* (1950), an extremely brutal look at life in the slums of Mexico City.

In recent years Paul Leduc has made several innovative films based on historical and cultural themes. *Reed: Insurgent Mexico* provides a twist on the leftist journalist's account of the Mexican Revolution and also serves as a larger metaphor for Mexican-American relations. Leduc's most recent film, *Frida*, is a beautiful biography of the life and work of Mexican painter Frida Kahlo. Presentations of her paintings are interspersed with fictionalized accounts of her relationships with her husband Diego Rivera, Leon Trotsky, Mexican communism, and her own vibrant approach to life.

VENEZUELA
GUYANA
SURINAME
FRENCH GUIANA
COLOMBIA
ECUADOR
PERU
BRAZIL
BOLIVIA
PARAGUAY
CHILE
ARGENTINA
URUGUAY
PACIFIC
OCEAN
ATLANTIC
OCEAN

CHAPTER SEVENTEEN
SOUTH AMERICA

In spite of widespread economic problems—most conspicuous of which are debt, inflation, and poverty—democracy is currently on the rise in much of South America. While only a decade ago military dictatorships were the rule, today nearly all the countries of the region have popularly elected governments of some sort. This move toward democracy, especially in Argentina, Brazil, and Chile, has fostered a new climate of social and political freedom that enlivens everyday discussions, invigorates educational institutions, and nourishes the arts. As a result, young people from the United States interested in becoming exposed to South American life can expect an especially rewarding experience. Interested North Americans will soon become drawn into discussions of the economic, political, and environmental issues that affect the continent. And, as fellow inhabitants of the double continent 16th-century explorers called the New World, North and South Americans generally will find a surprising amount of common ground between them.

South America offers the visitor enormous physical and cultural variety, from the tropical rain forest of the Amazon Basin to the cold, windy desert of Patagonia, and the ancient Indian way of life that still flourishes in the high valleys of the Andes to the modern European atmosphere of Buenos Aires. While the continent has traditionally been overlooked as a destination by U.S. students going abroad, a growing number of young people are now taking advantage of the possibilities available for studying, working, or simply traveling in the countries of South America.

The Essentials

Usually a passport and a tourist card are enough to gain you entry to most South American countries, but some, including Brazil and Argentina, require visas as well. Most South American countries also require proof of onward transportation such as a return plane ticket, although this rule is often enforced somewhat arbitrarily. Check with the specific embassy or consulate for further information. You'll find entrance requirements and embassy addresses given in the individual country sections that follow. To get more information on entrance requirements for countries not covered in a separate section of this chapter, contact:

- Embassy of Guyana, 2490 Tracy Place NW, Washington, DC 20008
- Embassy of Paraguay, 2400 Massachusetts Avenue NW, Washington, DC 20008
- Embassy of Suriname, 2600 Virginia Avenue NW, Washington, DC 20037

Getting There

The cheapest fares from the United States to South America are generally APEX fares (see Chapter 5 for a general explanation of air fares). Sample *one-way* fares in effect during the summer of 1989 are listed below. More up-to-date information is available at Council Travel offices (see listing on pages ix–xi).

New York–Rio de Janeiro, $375
Los Angeles–Santiago, $490
Miami–Lima, $253
New York–Buenos Aires, $389
Miami–Caracas, $120

For persons planning a short stay (anywhere from four days to a couple of weeks), the cheapest way to go may be to buy a vacation package that includes air fare, transfers, and hotel. Generally speaking, packages ranging from budget to luxury are available to Rio de Janeiro, Buenos Aires, and Caracas; they can be booked through travel agents in the U.S. or through airlines flying to South America. Packages are generally cheaper than making your own arrangements, since tour operators can mass-book hotels and make volume purchases. Check the advertisements in the Sunday travel section of your local newspaper for special packages available from your area, or contact a Council Travel office or other travel agent for more information.

Getting Around

The ease—or difficulty—in getting around South America varies by country. In Argentina, Chile, or southern Brazil, traveling by car or bus is as easy and convenient as it is in the U.S.—once you are accustomed to the slightly different customs and procedures of each individual country. On the other hand, in the Andean countries (Colombia, Ecuador, Peru, and Bolivia) natural barriers and poorly developed road and rail systems make traveling by land time-consuming and often uncomfortable. However, the rewards, in the form of spectacular scenery and contact with colorful native cultures, generally make the effort well worthwhile.

Traveling by train is one of the most interesting ways to see South America. However, with the exception of Argentina, you won't find much in the way of integrated national railway systems; most countries have only one or two lines with passenger service and Venezuela and Uruguay have none. Throughout the continent equipment is antiquated and travel is slow. Although not known for speed and efficiency, South American trains allow you to slow down, enjoy the scenery, and come into contact with workers and *campesinos*.

Buses are the most popular form of transportation in South America, and they range from luxury air-conditioned intercity express buses to trucks with wooden benches. No matter where you might want to go, however, if there's a road there, then there's a bus that travels it. For anyone interested in traveling around the continent by bus, the Amerbuspass is a single ticket good for up to 10,000 kilometers of travel on the routes of 17 cooperating Latin American bus companies over a 99-day period. For price and other information, contact Autobuses Sudamericanos, S.R.L., Bernardo de Irigoyen 1370, 1138 Buenos Aires, Argentina.

Hitchhiking is fairly easy and safe in most parts of Latin America. Of course, females should not hitchhike alone, and everyone will find it easier to get rides if they look neat and clean. Don't be surprised if the driver who gives you a ride asks for a fee. Also, as in other areas of the world, it's best to get your information on hitchhiking from someone who has done or is doing it.

In most countries, it's also quite easy to rent a car; while there are certain advantages to this mode of transportation, it is an expensive alternative and tends to remove the traveler from contact with the people. If you do plan to drive in South America, you'll need to get a driving permit. All South American countries recognize the Inter-American Driving Permit; Argentina, Chile, Ecuador, Paraguay, and Venezuela also recognize the International Driving Permit. You can get either of these permits at an office of the American Automobile Association in the United States; however, you must be 18 years of age, have a valid U.S. driver's license, and pay a fee of $5 (see page 49).

Air travel is certainly the fastest and most convenient way of covering long distances in South America. Nearly all the countries of the continent have air passes of some sort that allow foreigners unlimited travel in that country over a specified period of time. Generally speaking, these passes are good—even exceptional—bargains for anyone planning to visit several regions of a country. You'll find more information on these passes in the individual country sections that follow.

There are also two passes that allow international air travel throughout the continent:

- AeroPeru offers the Visit South America pass, which is valid for 45 days. The pass entitles the holder to air transportation from the United States to Lima, unlimited international travel within South America on AeroPeru, and then a return trip to the U.S. The pass also includes one round-trip flight from Lima to any city in Peru. In South America, AeroPeru serves Bogotá, Buenos Aires, Caracas, Guayaquil, La Paz, Lima, Rio de Janeiro, Santiago, and São Paulo. The only real problem with the Visit South America pass is that you'll have to do a lot of backtracking; for example, flying between Rio and Buenos Aires requires a connection through Lima. The fare from Miami, the only U.S. city served by AeroPeru, is $759 during the low season and $909 during the high season.
- Líneas Aéreas Paraguayas (LAP) also offers a special fare called the Visit South America pass. While it's similar to AeroPeru's pass, it is valid for only 30 days. LAP serves Asunción, Buenos Aires, Lima, Montevideo, Rio, Santa Cruz (Bolivia), Santiago, and São Paulo, and although that's fewer cities than AeroPeru serves, you'll have to do less backtracking, since Asunción is more centrally located. The price from Miami, the only U.S. city served by LAP, is $899.

Organized Tours

For persons interested in an organized tour to South America, programs sponsored by CIEE members include:

American Youth Hostels.
"South American Treasures." Sixteen-day tour using public transportation and staying in hostels in Peru and Bolivia. Winter. Minimum age 15.
"Viva Venezuela." Sixteen-day adventure trip staying in hostels and hotels. Hiking, windsurfing, and a visit to Angel Falls, the world's highest falls. Winter. Minimum age 15.

Eating and Sleeping

You'll find an abundance of inexpensive hotels in South American cities. The student travel offices listed under the individual country sections later in this chapter can often help you find inexpensive places to stay. In addition, volume two of the *International Youth Hostel Handbook* lists a limited number of hostels in Argentina, Chile, and Uruguay. For a listing of hostels in Brazil, write to the Fundação Casa do Estudante do Brasil (Praça Ana Amelia, 9, 22220 Rio de Janeiro).

For Further Information

The most comprehensive guidebook to Latin America is the *South American Handbook*, which is updated annually and distributed in the U.S. by Prentice Hall. Designed especially for travelers who want to get off the beaten tourist path and explore South America on their own, the 1,390-page manual isn't cheap—$29.95—but it's worth the price, especially if you're planning to visit several countries in the region.

Another excellent guidebook for independent travelers, especially those trying to keep costs to a minimum, is *South America on a Shoestring* ($14.95), by Geoff Crowther. Published by Lonely Planet Publications (Embarcadero West, 112 Linden Street, Oakland, CA 94607), the book is available in most bookstores or can be ordered directly from the publisher (add $1.50 for postage).

Frommer's *South America on $35 a Day*, by Arnold and Harriet Greenberg, is a good guide for the budget traveler to South America's capital cities. It doesn't have much information, however, for those who want to explore beyond the ten cities covered in the book. You'll find it in most bookstores for $13.95.

Fodor's *South America*, on the other hand, is quite comprehensive, although the hotels and restaurants listed tend to be toward the more expensive end of the spectrum. Included in the book are good introductory essays on the history and culture of each country. It's available in most bookstores for $14.95.

Bradt Enterprises (95 Harvey Street, Cambridge, MA 02140) publishes several books designed for the adventurous traveler. *Backpacking in Venezuela, Colombia, and Ecuador* ($7.95) describes 12 hikes that will take you through a variety of climates and terrains. *South America River Trips* ($8.95) contains information on a range of trips available on nine South American rivers. *Backpacking in Chile and Argentina* ($7.95) is filled with information on hikes in these two countries as well as the Falkland/Malvinas Islands. All can be ordered from the publisher; postage rates are $2.50 per item for first-class mail, or $1.50 per item for book rate.

Work

Stringent labor regulations and high unemployment rates make it difficult for foreigners to obtain employment in South America. Nevertheless, resourceful persons with some knowledge of Spanish or Portuguese often find informal employment, mostly as English tutors or translators. Persons with a degree in TESOL should check Chapter 3 for teaching opportunities in Latin America.

You'll find the internship and voluntary service opportunities offered by members of the Council on International Educational Exchange listed in the individual country sections later in this chapter. Anyone interested in further exploring volunteer options in South America should contact the voluntary service organizations described in Chapter 3.

Study

Persons seeking scholarships or grants for study in South America might want to take a look at *Funding for Research, Study, and Travel: Latin America and the Caribbean* (see page 403).

You'll find the study programs offered by members of the Council on International Educational Exchange listed in the country sections that follow. Here we've listed only those programs that take place in more than one country of the region. Consult Appendix I for the addresses of the universities listed in this section.

SUMMER

Business

University System of Georgia/Georgia State University. Recife and Rio de Janeiro, Brazil; and Buenos Aires, Argentina. Undergraduate and graduate students with 2.5 GPA. Apply by April 15.

Latin American Studies

University of Pittsburgh. "Latin American Studies Field Seminar." Country in which seminar takes place varies each year. Open only to students in Pittsburgh area schools. Juniors and seniors. Proficiency in Spanish required.

ARGENTINA

No one could blame visitors walking through Buenos Aires, the capital of Argentina, for forgetting they're in South America. The wide boulevards are reminiscent of Paris, the outdoor cafés bring to mind Rome, and that group of giggling blond-haired blue-eyed teenagers would look just as at home in Munich. Elsewhere, bejeweled matrons sip afternoon tea among potted palms and string quartets, while their husbands shoot billiards or sip brandy, and students debate politics, art, and everything else in hundreds of coffee shops and *whiskerías*. But for all its charm, sophistication, and fast pace—best expressed perhaps in the rhythms of the tango—Argentina has not been spared the problems of its South American neighbors. Unstable governments, military rule, civil war and foreign intervention, a boom-or-bust economy, dictators and demagogues, and a frustrating inability to find solutions have plagued the country since the 18th century. Most recently, Argentina emerged in 1983 from nearly a decade of military rule, and its young and fragile democracy is struggling to break this pattern. That such a rich land should have so many problems is both a paradox and a warning.

Although Buenos Aires is its nerve center, Argentina is also the land of the pampas, incredibly fertile grasslands whose cattle herds supply beef for the nation and much of Europe. Here lives the gaucho, that mythic combination of cowboy and outlaw who holds a cherished place in Argentine history and art.

The southern region of Argentina, known as Patagonia, is a sparsely populated windswept expanse of forbidding, semi-arid terrain. But the current government looks toward this region as an answer to the concentration of people, industry, and power in Buenos Aires. There have been calls for building a new capital city in Patagonia, as well as establishing free trade zones there, but a huge foreign debt and an entrenched Buenos Aires bureaucracy and business establishment have so far ensured that these proposals remain at the level of serious discussion only.

The Andes form the country's western border with Chile, and it is in this region that Spanish colonial architecture, vineyards, and mountainous splendor compete for foreign visitors' attention. The reversal of seasons between northern and southern hemispheres gives ski buffs a chance to glide down the slopes in the middle of July at world famous ski resorts such as Bariloche and Las Leñas. And in the north on the border with Brazil is magnificent Iguazú Falls, a natural wonder that draws tourists from around the world.

As diverse as its geography, so are the roots of its people. Argentina, unlike the rest of South America, is a nation of immigrants, mainly European. They are a proud (critics say arrogant), conservative, inward-looking people, and are eager to assert their uniqueness as a nation on a continent better known for Indian, Afro-Caribbean, and *mestizo* influences. Nevertheless, they are not reluctant to accept responsibility for the endemic political and economic problems that haunt this rich and potentially powerful country.

—*Joseph Colletti, Brooklyn, New York*

Official name: Argentine Republic. **Area:** 1,072,067 square miles (about one-third the size of the U.S.). **Population:** 32,000,000. **Population density:** 29 inhabitants. **Capital and largest city:** Buenos Aires (pop. 3,000,000). **Language:** Spanish. **Religion:** Roman Catholic. **Per capita income:** US$2,130. **Currency:** Austral. **Literacy rate:** 94%. **Average daily high/low:*** Buenos Aires: January, 85°/63°; July, 57°/42°. **Average number of days with precipitation:** January, 7; July, 8.

TRAVEL

U.S. citizens will need a passport and a visa to enter Argentina. A tourist visa is valid up to four years from the date of issue and allows multiple entries. For specific regulations, check with the Embassy of the Argentine Republic (1600 New Hampshire Avenue NW, Washington, DC 20009) or with an Argentine consulate in Baltimore, Chicago, Houston, Los Angeles, Miami, New Orleans, New York, San Francisco, or San Juan.

Getting Around

Argentina, the eighth-largest country in the world, stretches from the tropics to the islands of Tierra del Fuego, and, not surprisingly, boasts a variety of far-flung points of interest: there's Iguazú Falls in the north, the Andes resort of Bariloche in the west, the glaciers of Lago Argentino in the south, and the sea mammals and penguins of the Península Valdés on the eastern coast. Because of the great distances involved, most tourists interested in seeing different regions of the country end up doing some flying. Foreigners can purchase Visit Argentina air passes that entitle them to inexpensive air travel within the country. The Visit Argentina I pass is good for 30 days of unlimited air travel and costs $290. The Visit Argentina II ticket allows stops at any three cities over a two-week period and costs $199. Visit Argentina passes are

---

*all temperatures are Fahrenheit

offered by all three airlines operating domestic flights in Argentina (Aerolíneas Argentinas, Austral, and LADE); however, all flights with the pass must be made on the same airline. Visit Argentina tickets (or vouchers) can be purchased from a travel agent or directly from the airline before your arrival in Argentina.

Argentina has an extensive network of paved highways. A variety of bus lines serve all parts of the country, providing comfortable and reliable service. But remember that distances are great: express buses from Buenos Aires to Iguazú Falls take 24 hours; Buenos Aires to Bariloche is a 22-hour trip. Hitchhiking is popular and fairly easy throughout the entire country, except in the south, where traffic is light. All Argentine cities have rental car agencies. Avis, Hertz, and National are among the car rental companies operating in Argentina; you can get more information on rates and age requirements by calling their toll-free numbers in the United States. U.S. motorists should obtain either the Inter-American Driving Permit or the International Driving Permit (see page 49), both of which are recognized in Argentina.

Argentina has the best and most comprehensive rail network of any country of South America; however, it does not extend to the Brazilian frontier and Iguazú Falls in the northeast or cover much of the sparsely populated southern region of the country. The system, built with British investment in the late 19th and early 20th centuries, fans out across the pampas to Bariloche and Mendoza in the west and into Bolivia and Paraguay in the north. Travel by train is inexpensive and comfortable. However, trains are slower than the bus; the trip from Buenos Aires to Bariloche, for example, takes 30 hours. Rail passes are available for unlimited first-class train travel within the country; a 30-day pass costs $63, a 60-day pass $105. Passes are available only to foreigners and must be purchased abroad. Check with a Council Travel office or other travel agent for further information.

Especially for Students and Young People

Argentina has two student/youth travel organizations, both members of the ISTC.

ATESA (Av. Callao 1062, Piso 2, Oficinas C y D, 1023 Buenos Aires) and AAAJ—Associación Argentina de Albergues de la Juventud (Talcahuano 214, Piso 2, Oficina 6, 1013 Buenos Aires) issue air, rail, and bus tickets and also provide an accommodation booking service. In addition to its Buenos Aires office, ATESA has offices located in Córdoba, Rosario, and Salta; AAAJ has branch offices in La Plata, Mar del Plata, and Rosario. AAAJ also offers a Buenos Aires city tour, a ten-day excursion to Bariloche, and a six-day tour to Iguazú Falls.

Holders of the International Student Identity Card (ISIC) are entitled to reduced air fares to various destinations in Latin America, the U.S., and Europe. Students up to 20 years of age can get a discount of up to 50 percent on domestic flights to the southern part of the country. Student discounts are also available for train and bus travel. Information regarding these discounts and those available at a number of individual shops, theaters, museums, and youth hostels can be obtained at AAAJ and ATESA offices.

"Spend time in the parks and squares, where it's easy to meet Argentines. Americans and Argentines have a lot in common; most obviously they are both descendants of immigrants from Europe."
—Jill Strauss, New York, New York

For Further Information

General tourist information is available from the Argentine National Tourist Information Office (12 West 56th Street, New York, NY 10019). Surprisingly, there isn't a single guidebook available in the U.S. that focuses exclusively on Argentina; for travel information to the country check one of the South American guidebooks listed earlier in this chapter.

WORK

Getting regular salaried employment in Argentina is difficult for foreigners, and work visas are granted only to individuals sponsored by an Argentine company.

Internships/Traineeships

There are both AIESEC and IAESTE internship programs in Argentina; see page 18 more information.

STUDY

"Studying in Argentina, I gained an understanding of a people, who although they live in Latin America, have a very European mentality. And living in this economically troubled country gave me a better understanding of economics from a Latin American perspective."
—Alvin Realuyo, Jersey City, New Jersey

The following are the educational programs offered by member institutions of the Council on International Educational Exchange. Consult Appendix I for the addresses of the colleges and universities listed in this section. In addition to the listings below, Lewis and Clark College offers a program open only to its own students.

SEMESTER AND ACADEMIC YEAR

General Studies

University of North Carolina–Chapel Hill. "UNC Program to Belgrano." Semester or academic year. Juniors and seniors fluent in Spanish and 3.0 GPA. Apply by February 12.

International Student Exchange Program. Direct reciprocal exchange between U.S. universities and institutions in Buenos Aires and Córdoba. Semester or academic year. Full curriculum options. Open only to students at ISEP member institutions.

Social Science

American University. "Buenos Aires Semester." Fall semester. Focus on Argentine politics, economics, and culture. Internships with multinational agencies. Juniors and seniors with two years of college Spanish and 2.75 GPA. Apply six months prior to start of program.

SUMMER

General Studies

University of Massachusetts—Amherst. Buenos Aires. Sophomores, juniors, and seniors with proficiency in Spanish. Apply by March 1.

EXPLORING ARGENTINE CULTURE

Literature

Argentina's best-known literary figure in this century was Jorge Luis Borges. In books such as *Labyrinths* and *Fictions*, Borges created unusual existential situations characterized by their erudite verbal pyrotechnics. His *Six Problems for Don Isidro Parodi* is a collection of six detective stories that Borges wrote "as a challenge to the frenetic action of American detective stories" and the "cold intellectualism of the British school."

Julio Cortazar also plays with the reader's perception of reality. His novel *Hopscotch*, for instance, is divided into chapters that can be read in different orders, each arrangement suggesting a different meaning.

Manuel Puig, the author of, among other novels, *Heartbreak Tango* and *Betrayed by Rita Hayworth*, is a younger writer whose surreal visions of modern life reveal the influence of Hollywood and American cartoons. *Kiss of the Spiderwoman*, his most famous work (thanks to the success of the movie version), is the story of two prisoners, one a political dissident and the other a homosexual, and provides a vividly realistic picture of the mechanisms of political repression that were employed by the military government during its "Dirty War" against the Argentine left in the 1970s. In a nonfiction vein, Jacobo Timmerman's *Prisoner Without a Name, Cell Without a Number* is based on the well-known newspaper editor's imprisonment during the same period.

While few tourists visit the remote region of Argentina known as Patagonia, as one of the world's last frontier regions it has captured the interest of a number of writers from around the world. The late Bruce Chatwin's *In Patagonia* is a classic account of the author's travels through that harsh landscape. In the same vein, be sure to check out Paul Theroux's *Patagonia Revisited*.

BOLIVIA

Few nations can equal the geographical diversity found in Bolivia, a country that encompasses both dry barren plains and verdant mountain valleys, snowcapped mountain peaks, and tropical rain forests. And although it's landlocked, Bolivia still campaigns quixotically through diplomatic channels to get Chile to return the corridor to the sea, which it lost in a military campaign more than a century ago.

On a dry, windswept plain more than 10,000 feet above sea level La Paz, the nation's modern capital, coexists with indigenous villages where ancient Indian languages and customs still prevail. Ironically, the nation that produced much of the world's gold and silver now has South America's lowest standard of living. First the deposits of gold, then the silver, and now its tin have been depleted, forcing the nation to look to agriculture (chiefly cotton and cattle) for its economic viability.

Historically, Bolivia, perhaps more than any other Latin American nation, has been plagued by political and economic instability. Recently, however, the country has enjoyed unusual stability. For the first time in memory, power is being transferred peacefully from one elected leader to another. And the inflation rate, which hit an astronomical 24,000 percent a few years ago, has declined to about 6 percent.

Official name: Republic of Bolivia. **Area:** 424,162 square miles (about two and a half times larger than California). **Population:** 6,900,000. **Population density:** 16 inhabitants per square mile. **Capital and largest city:** La Paz (pop. 992,592). **Language:** Spanish, Quechua, Aymara. **Religion:** Roman Catholic. **Per capita income:** US$400. **Currency:** Peso. **Literacy rate:** 75%. **Average daily high/low:*** La Paz: January, 63°/43°; July, 64°/33°. **Average number of days with precipitation:** La Paz: January, 21; July, 2.

TRAVEL

U.S. citizens need a passport to enter Bolivia; for tourist stays of less than 90 days, a visa is not required. For specific requirements, check with the Embassy of Bolivia (3014 Massachusetts Avenue NW, Washington, DC 20008).

Getting Around

Poorly developed road and railway systems make air travel an attractive alternative in Bolivia, which is characterized by a topography that makes traveling by land difficult and uncertain. Lloyd Aéreo Boliviano, the national airline, serves most Bolivian cities. Its Visit Bolivia air pass is good for unlimited travel within the country for a period of 28 days and costs $119. It is sold only in the U.S. to travelers flying to Bolivia on Lloyd Aéreo Boliviano (from Miami) and should be purchased at the same time as your international ticket to Bolivia.

A surprising number of rail lines cross Bolivia; however, equipment is antiquated and service is slow and infrequent. Trains are even less expensive than the bus and offer views of interesting scenery as well as contact with the rural population of the country. Rail lines connect most highland cities and link Bolivia to Chile, Peru, Argentina, and Brazil, but fail to connect Bolivia's two main cities, Santa Cruz and La Paz.

---

*all temperatures are Fahrenheit

Buses are the most frequently used form of transportation in Bolivia, and service between the major cities is generally good. During the rainy season, however, buses providing service on unpaved roads are subject to frequent delays. Rental cars are not available, although taxis can be rented by the hour or day; four-wheel drive vehicles can be rented in La Paz.

Especially for Students and Young People

There is no student travel organization in Bolivia and no special discounts have been developed for holders of the International Student Identity Card.

For Further Information

Bolivia: A Travel Survival Kit ($10.95) is the best guidebook for the independent traveler on a budget who really wants to get to know the country. If you can't find it in bookstores, it can be ordered from the publisher, Lonely Planet Publications, Embarcadero West, 112 Linden Street, Oakland, CA 94607 (add $1.50 for postage).

WORK

Voluntary Service

The "Year Abroad Program" sponsored by the International Christian Youth Exchange offers persons ages 18–24 voluntary service opportunities in the fields of health care, education, the environment, construction, et cetera. See page 22 for more information.

BRAZIL

Brazil, the only Portuguese-speaking country in Latin America, occupies more than half the land area of South America. With a population of some 150 million, it is both the largest Latin and Catholic country in the world.

All too often, Brazil is seen by outsiders through the prism of one or more exotic stereotypes. The annual Carnival extravaganza in Rio de Janeiro, the popular tourist beaches of Ipanema and Copacabana, and the colorful tropical flora and fauna of the Amazon rain forest no doubt do a great deal to foster these images. Indeed, it is no simple task to penetrate beyond these images, to see Brazil and Brazilians on their own terms. But to do so will be exceedingly rewarding.

Since gaining its independence from Portugal in 1822, Brazil has experienced monarchy, democracy, and military rule. Along the way, it was one of the last countries to abolish slavery, finally doing so in 1888. In this century, Brazil has seen two lengthy dictatorships, the second of which brought the military to power in 1964 and ended only in 1985 with the installation of a civilian government.

Sadly, since the early 1980s the country has experienced severe economic hardships and a soaring crime rate as a result of a crushing foreign debt burden. Brazil is now the Third World's largest debtor country, and many experts feel that if a solution is not forthcoming, the country's fledgling democracy will be imperiled. Although it would be a mistake to minimize the seriousness of the current situation, Brazil, more than most of its neighbors, has a history of meeting adversity with optimism, of boldly confronting seemingly hopeless predicaments.

It is, to be sure, a nation ridden with contrasts, paradoxes, and inequities. Despite its standing as the world's eighth-largest market economy, it has failed to eradicate the abject poverty of a large segment of its citizens, who live in the hillside *favelas* of Rio and other cities. Nor has it been able to measure up to the ideal of a "racial democracy," as it has often been characterized. The vibrancy of African culture in Brazil, which has permeated everything from its food and music to its speech and religious beliefs, has not been able to erase the legacy of four-and-a-half centuries of racism. And the destruction of Indians and their traditional ways of life has shamefully continued into the present day. Yet in other respects—most notably in their self-confidence, flair for compromise, and inventiveness—Brazilians are worthy of emulation by other peoples.

The Brazilian spirit is alive, then, not only in the exuberant rhythms of samba and Carnival but also in the country's faith in its ultimate ability to solve its own problems, however difficult they may appear. Neither entirely European nor wholly African or Amerindian in its ways, it can be understood only in its pluralism and in the seeming contradictions that such pluralism often engenders.

—Bobby J. Chamberlain, Pittsburgh, Pennsylvania

Official name: Federative Republic of Brazil. **Area:** 3,286,470 square miles (about the same size as the U.S.). **Population:** 144,400,000. **Population density:** 44 inhabitants per square mile. **Capital:** Brasilia (pop. 1,576,657). **Largest city:** São Paulo (pop. 10,099,086). **Language:** Portuguese. **Religion:** Roman Catholic. **Per capita income:** US$1,976. **Currency:** Cruzado. **Literacy rate:** 74%. **Average daily high/low:*** Rio de Janeiro: January, 84°/73°; July, 75°/63°. Manaus: January, 88°/75°; July, 89°/75°. São Paulo, January, 81°/63°; July, 71°/49°. **Average number of days with precipitation:** Rio de Janeiro: January, 7; July, 8. Manaus: January, 20; July, 8. São Paulo: January, 19; July, 6.

TRAVEL

Both a passport and a visa are required for U.S. citizens traveling to Brazil. In addition, tourists must have an onward/return ticket or bank introduction letter attesting to their financial capability. For specific regulations, check with the Embassy of Brazil (3006 Massachusetts Avenue NW, Washington, DC 20008) or a Brazilian consulate in New York, Miami, Atlanta, Houston, Dallas, New Orleans, San Francisco, or Los Angeles.

The U.S. State Department warns that all tourists are at risk of robbery at all times of the day or night, especially on buses or at beaches and sightseeing

---

*all temperatures are Fahrenheit

locations. Travelers checks, a cheap camera, and no jewelry are the best policy, especially in Rio.

Getting Around

Since Brazil is larger than the 48 contiguous states of the United States and long-distance travel via road and rail networks is slow, most travelers intent on visiting different regions of the country generally resort to air transport for at least part of their journey. Fortunately, Brazil's domestic air transport network is among the world's best, providing comfortable and reliable service to even the most remote areas of the country. Brazil's major airlines with domestic routes—Varig/Cruzeiro do Sul, TransBrasil, and VASP—all offer comparable passes that permit unlimited air travel within the country. The standard version is good for 21 days and costs $330; a 14-day version that allows visits to four cities is available for $250. Both represent exceptional values for anyone who wants to see different parts of the country in a limited amount of time. Passes are available only to foreigners, however, and must be purchased from a travel agent or directly from the airline before your arrival in Brazil.

> *"Most Americans never get beyond Rio and miss most of the other equally interesting attractions of this country. For example, Salvador, a city full of color, activity, and rhythm, is the center of Afro-Brazilian culture and one of the most interesting cities of Brazil. It was the first capital of Portuguese Brazil and still has beautiful, if somewhat rundown, historical neighborhoods dating from colonial times."*
> —Sandra A. White, Hartford, Connecticut

Brazil's railroads were built to transport freight from the interior to the coast. As a result, while there are thousands of miles of track, most of it is not integrated into a national system; in fact, there are five different track gauges in use in Brazil! And even where rail lines do exist, there is not always passenger service. The relatively few passenger trains in operation are used mainly for local transportation in the more densely populated areas. However, there is good intercity rail service between Rio and São Paulo, Belo Horizonte, and Brasilia. But remember that distances are great; even the "short" trip between Rio and São Paulo will take about ten hours, and traveling from São Paulo to Brasilia by train takes about 24 hours.

On the other hand, Brazil has a rapidly expanding highway network. In the south, this network is well developed and includes a number of expressways. In other regions of the country, roads are not as good and travel is slower. But even in the Amazon region travel by road is now a realistic option, with paved roads extending as far as Manaus in the heart of the Amazon basin. Numerous bus companies provide comfortable and frequent service between the major cities of Brazil. Less comfortable buses service even the most remote towns, although bus service on the unpaved roads of the Amazon basin is subject to frequent delays in the best of conditions, and is especially unreliable in the rainy season. It is also possible to rent a car in most Brazilian cities; both Hertz and Avis have extensive operations in the country. Drivers in Brazil are required to have the Inter-American Driving Permit (see page 49), however.

The best way to see the Amazon region of Brazil is by boat. Riverboats still provide most of the transportation in this vast, developing region, allowing you to travel the 2,000 miles up the Amazon to Iquitos, Peru, or simply make a short hop between neighboring towns. The trip between Manaus and Belem, the two metropolises of the Amazon basin, takes five or six days, with stops at cities and towns along the way.

> "Be prepared to ease up on many different levels. Time is often less constraining and regimented. Relationships among friendly acquaintances are warmer—kisses, handshakes, and abraços are part of the greeting routine. Yet the insecurities caused by the tremendous social disparities in wealth are apt to make one tighten up. For example, due to high crime rates in the cities, you'll have to keep any valuables you have to carry with you in a travel safe sack at all times."
> —Miguel Carter, Minneapolis, Minnesota

Especially for Students and Young People

The student travel organization and ISTC member from Brazil is CONTEJ (Rua do Catete, 243, 22220 Rio de Janeiro). At its main office in Rio and its branch office in São Paulo (Rua Vergueiro 2485) you can get travel information, buy international air tickets, book accommodations, and sign up for tours.

Students receive a discount on plane and bus tickets. In addition, holders of the International Student Identity Card get reduced admission to many museums and theaters and discounts in hundreds of retail stores. Contact CONTEJ for a free national discount guide listing specific establishments where reductions are available.

> "Don't miss a Brazilian soccer game. Soccer is an unquestioned basic value of Brazilian society, much like wine is to the French. Boys begin kicking soccer balls around as soon as they can walk. Go to any park or any beach and you'll find a soccer game going on; if you stop and watch for a few minutes, you'll probably be invited to join in. In Rio go to Maracana, the world's largest soccer stadium, where the generally good-natured but passionate crowd is one of the most exciting spectacles in the world of sport."
> —Mark Falango, New York, New York

For Further Information

Probably the best guidebook for the independent traveler on a budget is *Brazil: A Travel Survival Kit* ($14.95). If you can't find it in bookstores, it can be ordered from the publisher, Lonely Planet Publications, Embarcadero West, 112 Linden Street, Oakland, CA 94607 (add $1.50 for postage). Frommer's *Brazil* ($14.95) can be found in most bookstores. Another useful guidebook, especially for its background information on Brazilian history and culture, is Fodor's *Brazil* ($8.95), although the hotels and restaurants it recommends tend to be on the expensive side. General tourist information is available from the Brazilian Tourist Information Office—EMBRATUR (551 Fifth Avenue, Suite 421, New York, NY 10176).

WORK

Getting regular salaried employment in Brazil is difficult for foreigners, with work visas only issued upon presentation of a work contract certified by the Brazilian Ministry of Labor.

Internships/Traineeships

There are both AIESEC and IAESTE internship programs in Brazil; see page 18 for more information.

Voluntary Service

For persons interested in voluntary service work, the "Year Abroad Program" sponsored by the International Christian Youth Exchange offers persons ages 18–24 voluntary service opportunities in the fields of health care, education, the environment, construction, et cetera. See page 22 for more information.

STUDY

"Studying in Rio de Janeiro was more about facing the crude realities of the Third World than living the life of a happy tourist. There is so much more to Rio than carnival and Copacabana. I saw firsthand the explosive effects that can arise in a society of boiling social contradictions. The day bus fares were raised (to keep up with an annual inflation rate of 900 percent), office workers and laborers rioted in downtown Rio and set fire to 40 buses. Living through the madness and hallucinations of a society in deep crisis was something I could have only experienced by being there— the best books and lectures would never have conveyed the same message. And my studies at Rio's Catholic University helped me develop a more coherent and critical perspective upon which to pursue my studies and develop my understanding of Latin American politics and society. The overall experience strengthened my belief in and appreciation for the importance of social and political activism."
—Miguel Carter, Minneapolis, Minnesota

The following are the educational programs offered by member institutions of the Council on International Educational Exchange. Consult Appendix I for the addresses where you can write for more information. In addition to the programs listed below, the American Graduate School of International Management, the University of California system, and the University of Tennessee offer programs open only to their own students.

SEMESTER AND ACADEMIC YEAR

Ecology

Experiment in International Living/School for International Training. "College Semester Abroad." Belem, Santarem, and Manaus. Language study, seminar on Amazon studies and ecology, field visits, homestay, and independent-study project. Sophomores to graduate students with 2.5 GPA. Apply by May 15 for fall and October 15 for spring.

General Studies

Brigham Young University. "Internship in Brazil." Spring quarter (May 1 to June 22). Eight credit hours of Portuguese language, with internships in business, education, health services, etc. Sophomores, juniors, and seniors with two semesters of college Portuguese. Apply by February 1.

Council on International Educational Exchange. "Inter-University Study Program in Brazil." São Paulo. Academic year. Juniors and seniors with 3.0 GPA and two years college-level Portuguese or Spanish (or one year of each language). Apply by March 1. Contact Academic Programs Department.

Experiment in International Living/School for International Training. "College Semester Abroad." Study in Fortaleza, with tours to Recife, Ceara, Amazonia, Minas Gerais, and Bahia. Language study, seminar on Brazilian life and culture, field study, homestay, and independent-study project. Sophomores to graduate students with 2.5 GPA. Apply May 15 for fall and October 15 for spring.

International Student Exchange Program. Direct reciprocal exchange between U.S. universities and the Pontifícia Universidade Católica de Minas Gerais and Ponitifícia Universidade Católica do Rio de Janeiro. Semester or academic year. Full curriculum options. Open only to students at ISEP member institutions.

State University of New York at Albany. Brasilia and Campinas. Juniors, seniors, and graduate students with two years of college-level Portuguese and above average academic record. Apply by April 15.

State University of New York at Oswego. "Oswego—São Paulo Program." Spring semester. Language of instruction is English. Juniors, seniors, and graduate students with 2.5 GPA. Apply by November 1.

University of Maryland. "Study in Brazil." Rio de Janeiro. Fall semester. Sophomores, juniors, and seniors with two semesters of Portuguese. Apply by May 1.

University of North Carolina–Chapel Hill. "UNC Program to Rio de Janeiro." Juniors, seniors, and graduate students fluent in Portuguese and with 2.7 GPA. Apply by February 12.

University of Wisconsin–Madison. São Paulo. Academic year. Sophomores to graduate students with two years of Portuguese and 3.0 GPA. Open only to students at colleges or universities in the state or Wisconsin residents studying in other states. Apply by February 1.

Teacher Education

State University of New York at Brockport. Rio de Janeiro. Semester. Elementary or secondary school teaching. Open to students eligible for student teaching in New York State.

SUMMER

Engineering

University of Illinois at Urbana-Champaign. "International Programs in Engineering." Recife. Priority is given to engineering schools. Freshmen to graduate students with 3.0 GPA. Apply by March 1.

Portuguese Language

University of Illinois at Urbana-Champaign. "Portuguese Language." Basic through advanced Portuguese. Freshmen to graduate students with 3.0 GPA. Apply by March 1.

EXPLORING BRAZILIAN CULTURE

Literature

Most Brazilian authors are closely identified with a particular region of the country, a fact that reflects the strong regional identities found in this vast and diverse country. Jorge Amado, the country's best-known contemporary novelist, writes about the northeast. His books include *Gabriela, Clove and Cinnamon*, the entertaining story of a young migrant worker whose beauty and cooking skill make her the most sought-after woman in town; *Dona Flor and Her Two Husbands*, a farce about a woman whose dead ex-husband comes back to visit her after she has remarried; and *Showdown*, a multigenerational saga set in the cacao-producing heartland of Amado's home state of Bahia.

A number of other Brazilian authors are also worth noting. Marcio Souzas writes about the Amazon region in novels such as *The Emperor of the Amazon* and *Mad Maria*. Raquel de Querios, like Jorge Amado, writes about the northeast; in *The Three Marias*, he explores the problems faced by women and men in a country where *machismo* is still very much a part of everyday life. Inácio de Loyola Brandão offers a dark vision of 21st-century São Paulo in *And Still the Earth*. Finally, less focused on a particular region, *Celebration*, by Ivan Angelo, deals with Brazil's recent political past, specifically with the censorship imposed by the military government during the 1970s.

Film

Closely linked to the country's music, dance, and carnival traditions, Brazilian film is often vibrant, witty, and entertaining, while simultaneously satirical and politically aggressive.

In the 1960s, a group of young filmmakers began producing a series of low-budget independent films that initiated Cinema Nôvo (literally, New Cinema), Brazil's best-known film movement. In its initial stage, Cinema Nôvo revolved around the lives, trials, and tribulations of rural people and their communities. Glauber Rocha's *Barravento* (1961), for example, is a rhythmic but jolting presentation of the hardships, religion, and myths of a rural fishing village. Rocha's *Black God—White Devil* (1964) also looks at the mythic traditions of rural regions. Other films within this vein include *Vidas Secas* (1962), by Nelson Pereira dos Santos, and *Ganga Zumba*, by Carlos Diegues.

Among more recent Brazilian films is *Pixote* (1981), by Hector Babenco (who also directed the film adaptation of Manuel Puig's *Kiss of the Spiderwoman*), the story of an orphan growing up in the streets of Rio. *Dona Flor and Her Two Husbands* (1978) by Bruno Barreto is the movie version of Jorge Amado's novel about a woman torn between her dead irresponsible husband who keeps returning to earth and her considerate but dull second husband. Carlos Diegues's *Bye Bye Brazil* (1980), in addition to being a comedy-drama about a troup of traveling entertainers touring Brazil's small towns, also provides a good travelogue of the country. Also noteworthy are two films by Pereira dos Santos: *Tent of Miracles*, an interesting look at Brazilian racial problems and religions in the state of Bahia, and *How Tasty Was My Little Frenchman*, a critique of the Brazilian government.

Perhaps the best-known film about Brazil, however, is *Black Orpheus* (1959), by the French director Marcel Camus, a hauntingly beautiful and witty combination of Brazilian carnival and Greek mythology.

CHILE

Geographic diversity is the most obvious feature of Chile, which stretches some 1,800 miles from the tropics to Punta Arenas, the world's southernmost city. Squeezed between the Pacific Ocean to the west and the Andes mountains to the east, Chile encompasses deserts and rain forests, farmlands and fjords, mountain peaks and grassy plains. Nearly half the country's inhabitants reside in Santiago, the capital city, which not surprisingly dominates the political, economic, and cultural life of the country. Most of the rest live in central Chile between Santiago and Puerto Montt, while the southern forests and copper- and nitrate-rich northern desert remain only sparsely populated.

Chile is now in the process of returning to democratic rule after 16 years under the military dictatorship of General Pinochet. Some fear that democracy, with Chile's wide spectrum of political parties and divided electorate, will be difficult. Others, more optimistic, point to the 46 years of uninterrupted constitutional democracy before Pinochet's violent overthrow of the Marxist President Salvador Allende in 1973. Regardless, observers agree that Chile, the last major country of South America to reject military government, is entering an interesting and crucial stage of its history.

Official name: Republic of Chile. **Area:** 292,132 square miles (slightly larger than Texas). **Population:** 12,600,000. **Population density:** 43 inhabitants per square mile. **Capital and largest city:** Santiago (pop. 4,804,200). **Language:** Spanish. **Religion:** Roman Catholic. **Per capita income:** US$1,330. **Currency:** Peso. **Literacy rate:** 96%. **Average daily high/low:*** Santiago: January, 85°/53°; July, 59°/37°. **Average number of days with precipitation:** Santiago: January, 0; July, 6.

---

*all temperatures are Fahrenheit

TRAVEL

U.S. citizens need a passport to enter Chile; however, a visa is not required for stays of up to three months. For specific regulations, check with the Embassy of Chile (1732 Massachusetts Avenue NW, Washington, DC 20036).

Getting Around

The Pan American Highway is the main travel artery through Chile. Paved all the way from the Peruvian border, it links the main cities of Chile as far south as Puerto Montt. While there are no roads extending south from Puerto Montt, passenger boat service is available to Punta Arenas on the Strait of Magellan. Intercity bus service along the Pan American Highway is inexpensive and frequent, and a range of bus service links Chile to Argentina. It is also possible to rent cars in major Chilean cities, with Hertz, Budget, and Avis among the major car rental companies operating in the country.

Chile's network of railroads is used mainly for the transport of cargo. Passenger trains link Santiago and Valparaiso, and provide somewhat infrequent service from Santiago as far south as Puerto Montt. Passenger service is also available between Bolivia and Chile's northern seaports of Arica and Antofagasta. However, passenger service from Santiago to northern Chile, as well as over the Andes between Chile and Argentina, has been discontinued.

For tourists wishing to venture far from Santiago—to Antofagasta in the north or Punta Arenas in the south—the most popular way of travel is by plane. Accordingly, a number of air-pass options are available to foreigners on either of Chile's domestic airlines, LanChile and LADECO. LADECO's 21-day Visit Chile pass allows stopovers in up to 12 cities for $299; if a round-trip to Easter Island is included, the price jumps to $520. LanChile offers four different air passes, the cheapest being a $299 pass that allows stopovers in nine Chilean cities but does not include travel to Easter Island. Air passes offered by LanChile and LADECO must be purchased before your arrival in Chile.

Especially for Students and Young People

The student travel organization in Chile is Fundación de Desarrollo para la Juventud (Holanda 286, Santiago), but few discounts have been developed for holders of the International Student Identity Card; students do receive a 20 percent reduction on train travel between Santiago and Puerto Montt, however.

For Further Information

Chile and Easter Island: A Travel Survival Kit ($8.95) is a comprehensive guide for budget travelers interested in getting to know Chile. If you can't find it in your local bookstore, it can be ordered from Lonely Planet Publications, Embarcadero West, 112 Linden Street, Oakland, CA 94607 (include $1.50 for postage). General tourist information is available from the Chilean National Tourist Board, 510 West Sixth Street, Los Angeles, CA 90014.

WORK

Internships/Traineeships

There is an AIESEC internship program in Chile; see page 18 for more information.

STUDY

A program sponsored by a member institution of the Council on International Educational Exchange is described below. Consult Appendix I for the address.

SUMMER

Latin American Studies

University of Iowa. "Summer Social Science Program." Santiago. Introduction to Latin American scholars and contemporary social science issues. Juniors, seniors, graduate students, and elementary and secondary school teachers. Two years of college-level Spanish required. Apply by March 15. Contact: Director, Latin American Studies Program.

EXPLORING THE CULTURE OF CHILE

Film

Cinema in Chile moved to the cultural and political forefront during Salvador Allende's Unidad Popular government of the early 1970s. The unexpected election of Allende's socialist government lent credibility to a group of young political filmmakers who took as their main focus the recent changes in Chilean society and attempted to create a style of narrative that reflected the leftist political attitudes of the period. *The Promised Land* and *The Jackal of Nahueltoro*, by Miguel Littin, both explore the trials and tribulations of landless peasants, workers, and rural communities as they contend with the country's governing bodies, industry, and the military. Perhaps the most symbolic film of the Allende period is Patricio Guzman's epic documentary *Battle of Chile*, which attempts, in no uncertain terms, to investigate the political, cultural, and economic forces that eventually resulted in the military overthrow of Salvador Allende's government and the assassination of Allende himself. Filmed under remarkable circumstances, the footage had to be smuggled bit by bit out of Chile and was not completely edited until several years after the coup.

Since the fall of Allende a number of exiles have been working actively in Europe and elsewhere in Latin America. Most prolific of these filmmakers is Raoul Ruiz, who has produced over 70 films in 15 years. Ruiz' films are informed by an intricate mix of subjective fantasy and historical episodes, cultural references and political critique. Best known are *Tres Tigres Tristes, Three Crowns of a Sailor, Hypothesis of a Stolen Painting*, and *Of Great Events and Ordinary People*.

COLOMBIA

For many Americans, Colombia brings to mind violent drug lords turning Colombian cities into combat zones. Others think of quaint coffee pickers on sleepy mountain plantations (like "Juan Valdez" of the coffee advertisements). Still others think of guerrillas sacrificing innocent civilians to the political causes of both the right and left. While it's true that all these people exist in Colombia, such stereotypes present a grossly misleading picture of one of Latin America's most complex societies.

One of the striking themes of novelist Gabriel García Márquez' *One Hundred Years of Solitude*, a mystical chronicle of one hundred years in the life of a Colombian family, is the role that nature plays in the life of the family. Certainly, the unusually diverse geography of Colombia has contributed to the shaping of the nation. Bordered by both the Atlantic and the Pacific and intersected on a north-south axis by three ranges of the Andes Mountains, Colombia encompasses everything from tropical swamps to snow-dusted volcanoes. Regionalism, the result of mountain barriers, has discouraged unity throughout Colombia's history and even today the country revolves around numerous regional centers such as Medellín, Cali, and Barranquilla in addition to the national capital of Bogotá. Close proximity to the equator means that each city has roughly the same climate year-round, although cities at different altitudes experience radically different climates. Always a land of contradictions, this climatic predictability is unsettled all too often by earthquakes and volcanic eruptions.

Colombia's 16th-century settlers came in search of gold. A visit to the Gold Museum (Museo de Oro) in Bogotá—an awesome vault of pre-Columbian artifacts—is proof that those pioneers found what they were looking for. Today, the country still owes its relative prosperity to its abundant natural resources. Exports of agricultural products, textiles, coal, oil, and precious stones—as well as illicit drugs—are responsible for providing the hard currency that has made Colombia one of the few countries of Latin America to keep pace with the payments on its foreign debt.

Despite the sense that Colombia's government is out of control, an impression strengthened recently by a wave of political assassinations and bombings, Colombia is in fact one of South America's oldest democracies, and has learned to deal creatively with recurring and violent power struggles. Some thirty years ago, for example, several years of bloodshed between members of the Liberal and Conservative parties ended with a power-sharing agreement that provided for alternating Liberal and Conservative governments from 1958 to 1974. However, international factors over which Colombia has little control, including the demand for illicit drugs and the prices on world markets for its exports, have added to the difficulties in resolving the current conflicts. It is possible that Colombia will be destroyed this time around by those who want too large a share of the pie. More likely, the intense national pride of the warring factions will eventually bring them to some sort of reconciliation.

In fact, Colombians have much to be proud of, and the visitor who is willing to avoid involvement in the country's political conflicts will find much to enjoy. The nation's spectacular mountains, forests, and coastline are obvious attractions. So, too, are its people and culture. And everywhere the visitor travels, exuberant Latin American hospitality and Colombian pride will welcome them.

—*Sarah Wood, Brooklyn, New York*

Official name: Republic of Colombia. **Area:** 455,355 square miles (almost three times the size of California). **Population:** 30,600,000. **Population density:** 67 inhabitants per square mile. **Capital and largest city:** Bogotá (pop. 4,208,000). **Language:** Spanish. **Religion:** Roman Catholic. **Per capita income:** US$1,430. **Currency:** Peso. **Literacy rate:** 88%. **Average daily high/low:*** Bogotá: January, 67°/48°; July, 64°/50°. **Average number of days with precipitation:** Bogotá: January, 6; July, 18.

TRAVEL

U.S. citizens need a passport and a tourist card to enter Colombia. The tourist card can be issued by the airline at the time of your departure from the United States. An onward or return ticket is also required. For specific regulations, check with the Embassy of Colombia (2118 Leroy Place NW, Washington, DC 20008).

At press time, the U.S. State Department was warning against travel in various parts of Colombia, although Bogotá and the Caribbean resort of Cartagena were among the areas considered safe for foreign visitors. Travelers in all parts of the country are cautioned against walking alone at night, and due to a high incidence of thefts, should not wear jewelry or carry valuables with them in the street. Current information is available from the Citizens Emergency Center at the U.S. State Department (see page 6).

Getting Around

Colombia, because of its formidable natural barriers, has developed one of the best domestic air systems in South America. Avianca, a privately owned carrier, operates the most domestic flights (as well as the most international flights to and from Colombia). Its Know Colombia visitor ticket allows for stops at ten Colombian cities over a 30-day period and costs $325; if the purchaser is willing to forgo visits to Leticia, Colombia's Amazon port, as well as to the island of San Andrés in the Caribbean, the price drops to $224. Avianca's Colombia Unlimited visitor ticket, good for eight days, costs $190 (or $112 if visits to Leticia and San Andrés are not included). Visitor tickets are not valid for travel in June, July, August, or September, and must be purchased before your arrival in Colombia.

Ground transportation has greatly improved in recent years. Highways link the cities of the interior with each other as well as with coastal ports, and the new Trans-Caribbean Highway greatly improves connections between the cities along Colombia's northern coast. Highways also connect the country to Venezuela and Ecuador, but no roads cross Colombia's borders with Panama, Peru, or Brazil. Within Colombia, buses are the principal means of transportation. Bus service between the major cities is good, while in more remote areas local buses provide interesting but usually slow and uncomfortable transportation. Alternatives to the buses include *busetas* (minibuses) and *collectivos* (shared taxis that leave when full). Car rental agencies can be found in the

---

*all temperatures are Fahrenheit

major cities; more information can be obtained by calling the toll-free numbers in the United States for Avis, Hertz, National, General, Budget, or Dollar— all of which have operations in Colombia. An Inter-American driving permit is required for foreigners, however (see page 422).

Colombia has only a few rail lines. Passenger service is provided between the interior cities of Bogotá and Medellín and the Caribbean port of Santa Marta. However, few passenger trains are in service, and most people prefer the bus, which is much faster. The trip from Bogotá to Santa Marta—barring frequent delays—takes 29 hours.

While the Magdalena River continues to be a main transportation artery, scheduled ferry service on the river has been discontinued. However, it is possible to travel by riverboat from Colombia's Amazon port of Leticia to either Peru or Brazil.

For Further Information

Colombia: A Travel Survival Kit ($11.95) is the best guidebook for the independent traveler on a budget. If you can't find it in bookstores, it can be ordered from the publisher, Lonely Planet Publications, Embarcadero West, 112 Linden Street, Oakland, CA 94607 (add $1.50 for postage). General tourist information is available from the Colombia Government Tourist Office, 140 East 57th Street, New York, NY 10022.

Anyone planning on spending time in the country might be interested in *Living in Colombia*, by William Hutchison and Cynthia Poznanski. The book was published in 1987 by Intercultural Press (P.O. Box 768, Yarmouth, ME 04096), and is available for $15 (plus $1.50 postage).

WORK

Persons wishing to hold regular salaried employment in Colombia need a work visa. However, work visas are only granted for jobs for which no citizen of Colombia has the required training or skills.

Internships/Traineeships

Programs sponsored by members of the Council on International Educational Exchange are described below. Consult Appendix I for the addresses of the organizations and institutions listed in this section.

AIESEC–US. Reciprocal internship program for students in economics, business, finance, marketing, accounting, and computer sciences. See page 18 for further information.

Association for International Practical Training. "IAESTE Trainee Program." On-the-job training for undergraduate and graduate students in technical fields such as engineering, computer science, agriculture, architecture, and mathematics. See page 18 for more information.

University of Minnesota. "Minnesota Studies in International Development." Bogotá. Academic year. Predeparture coursework at the U of M fall quarter, with internship in development-related research or action project in winter and spring quarters. Juniors to graduates and adults with interest in development; 2.5 GPA and two years of Spanish required. Apply May 15.

Voluntary Service

For persons interested in voluntary service work, the "Year Abroad Program" sponsored by the International Christian Youth Exchange offers persons ages 18–24 voluntary service opportunities in the fields of health care, education, the environment, construction, et cetera. See page 22 for more information.

STUDY

The following are the educational programs offered by member institutions of the Council on International Educational Exchange. Consult Appendix I for the addresses to where you can write for further information.

SEMESTER AND ACADEMIC YEAR

General Studies

International Student Exchange Program. Direct reciprocal exchange between U.S. universities and institutions in Bogotá, Cali, and Barranquilla. Full curriculum options. Open only to students at ISEP member institutions.

Great Lakes Colleges Association. "Latin America." Bogotá. Semester or academic year. Sophomores to graduate students with intermediate Spanish and 2.5 GPA overall and in Spanish. Apply by May 15 for fall and October 15 for spring. Contact GLCA Latin America Program, Kenyon College, Gambier, OH 43022.

SUMMER

Great Lakes Colleges Association. "Latin America." Bogotá. Internships; workshops for teachers. Sophomores to graduate students with 2.5 GPA. Apply by April 15. Contact GLCA Latin America Program, Kenyon College, Gambier, OH 43022.

EXPLORING THE CULTURE OF COLOMBIA

Literature

In *One Hundred Years of Solitude*, Gabriel García Márquez presents his image of a Latin American world of myth, sensuality, violence, and conspiracy. Since this novel was published in 1947 it has given birth to a movement in Latin American literature known as "magical realism" and made García Marquez the preeminent novelist of Latin America. Less famous but perhaps equally fascinating are his more recent works, including *The Autumn of the Patriarch*, in which he describes the thoughts of a dying Latin American dictator who has ruled for two centuries; *Chronicle of a Death Foretold*, the story of a man whose imminent murder is known to everyone in town except himself; and *Love in the Time of Cholera*, a love story set at the turn of the century on a Caribbean island.

ECUADOR

Ecuador derives its name from the equator, which bisects the nation; but in spite of its tropical location, the nation encompasses a wide variety of climates. Hot, humid rain forest characterizes the northwest coast and the Amazon basin that makes up the eastern half of the country. However, equally characteristic of Ecuador are snowcapped mountains and cool plateaus. The Andes Mountains, whose peaks rise to more than 20,000 feet, run on a north-south axis through the country. In Ecuador, climate depends on altitude.

The country's geographic diversity is matched by its cultural diversity, with the population of the country including a large number of Indian tribes, each of which retains its own clothing, way of life, and, in some cases, language. As numerous as the Indians are *mestizos*, descendants of both Indians and the Spaniards who conquered the region in the 16th century. About 10 percent of the population is of European descent and an equal number are blacks, whose ancestors were brought as slaves by the Spanish.

Spain, during nearly 300 years of colonial domination, left a strong imprint on Ecuador. Spanish is the official language of the country and the one most commonly spoken. Similarly, Catholicism is the religion of nearly all Ecuadorians. Churches from the colonial period are centerpieces of large cities and small villages alike. But perhaps the most interesting evidence of the Spanish conquest can be found in Ecuadorian art—a mixture of Spanish and Indian motifs, techniques, and styles. Such art continues to flourish in the handicrafts sold in busy markets in cities, towns, and villages.

The Spanish domination generated a sharp division between the upper and lower classes that continues to exist today. Richly blessed by nature, Ecuador has been at different times one of the world's leading exporters of cacao, bananas, rice, and, currently, shrimp. However, the country's wealth—and power—have traditionally been concentrated in the hands of a few leading families. In recent years, the development of petroleum resources in the Amazon basin has enabled the government to carry out programs beneficial to the population at large—one reason why Ecuador has not suffered the bloody social upheavals and political violence that have affected many other countries of the region.

For centuries Ecuador has also been divided by the conflict between its two major cities, Guayaquil and Quito, each of which represents different economic interests, social groups, and regional ties. Guayaquil dominates the coastal region and is the country's leading port, largest city, and economic center. Quito—more isolated and more traditional—is the hub of the Andean region and the nation's capital.

No introduction to Ecuador can be complete without mentioning the Galapagos Islands. Just as Darwin was, visitors to the Galapagos are still amazed by the plant and animal life of these remote and sparsely populated islands.

—Hector Correa, Pittsburgh, Pennsylvania

Official name: Republic of Ecuador. **Area:** 109,484 square miles (about the size of Nevada). **Population:** 10,200,000. **Population density:** 93 inhabitants per square mile. **Capital:** Quito (pop. 1,137,705). **Largest city:** Guayaquil (pop. 1,572,615). **Language:** Spanish, Quechua, Jibaro. **Religion:** Roman Catholic. **Per capita income:** US$1,140. **Currency:** Sucre. **Literacy rate:** 84%. **Average daily high/low:*** Guayaquil: January, 88°/70°; July, 84°/67°. Quito: January, 72°/46°; July, 72°/44°. **Average number of days with precipitation:** Guayaquil: January, 20; July 2. Quito: January, 16; July, 7.

TRAVEL

For stays of less than three months, U.S. citizens need a passport and a return or onward ticket. For specific regulations, check with the Embassy of Ecuador (2535 15th Street NW, Washington, DC 20009).

Getting Around

Frequent air service links the Pacific port of Guayaquil with Quito, which is located high in the Andes nearly 10,000 feet above sea level; the flight takes about 40 minutes (compared to a day-long bus journey). Flights are also available from Quito and Guayaquil to other major cities in Ecuador, as well as to several outposts in the Oriente, the eastern half of the country located in the Amazon basin.

Passenger and freight service remains suspended on most of the rail line between Guayaquil and Quito as a result of heavy rains and flooding in 1982–83. The government, however, is in the process of reconstructing Ecuador's lone rail route—and one of the world's most spectacular—and expects to reopen it in 1990.

Most transportation is provided by buses, which provide frequent service throughout the country except in the Oriente, where transportation by small boat is the rule. Ecuador's road system provides easy access to the cities and points of interest in the Andean and coastal regions of the country. The road network also extends from the Andes eastward to river towns, where people and goods are transferred to boats going to points farther east. Car rentals can be readily arranged in Quito and Guayaquil. Hertz, Avis, Dollar, and Budget are among the car rental agencies with operations in Ecuador; call their toll-free numbers in the U.S. for more information.

For anyone with an interest in nature, one of the world's most fascinating destinations is the Galapagos Islands. Most visitors arrive by plane, although a dual pricing system makes the flight expensive for foreigners. A daily flight connects Guayaquil with a landing strip on the uninhabited island of Baltra, where passengers are then picked up by boats. However, you can't simply fly to the islands on your own and look around. The Ecuadorian government restricts the number of visitors and requires that they be accompanied by a guide. Arrangements must be made through a tour operator authorized to conduct tours to the islands; the largest of these is Metropolitan Touring (C.P.O. Box 2542, Quito).

---

*all temperatures are Fahrenheit

Especially for Students and Young People

There is no student travel organization in Ecuador and no special discounts have been developed for holders of the International Student Identity Card.

For Further Information

Probably the best guidebook for the independent traveler on a budget is *Ecuador and the Galapagos Islands: A Travel Survival Kit* ($10.95). It's available in most bookstores or can be ordered from the publisher, Lonely Planet Publications, Embarcadero West, 112 Linden Street, Oakland, CA 94607 (add $1.50 for postage). General tourist information is available from the government tourism office, FEPROTUR (Box 526632, Miami, FL 33152).

WORK

Regular salaried employment in Ecuador is possible only if you are being brought in by an Ecuadorian company for professional reasons; a work permit is required.

Internships/Traineeships

There is an AIESEC internship program in Ecuador; see page 18 for more information.

STUDY

The following are the educational programs offered by member institutions of the Council on International Educational Exchange. Consult Appendix I for the addresses of the colleges and universities listed in this section.

SEMESTER AND ACADEMIC YEAR

Ecology

Experiment in International Living/School for International Training. "College Semester Abroad—Comparative Ecology." Fall or spring semester. Intensive language, seminars, field study, homestays, and independent project. Sophomores to graduate students with 2.5 GPA. Apply by May 15 for fall and October 15 for spring.

General Studies

Beloit College. "Ecuador Seminar." Quito. Fall semester. Sophomores to graduate students with intermediate Spanish and 2.0 GPA. Apply by April 1.

Experiment in International Living/School for International Training. "College Semester Abroad." Quito and Cayambe. Fall or spring semester. Intensive language, seminar in Ecuadorian life and culture, field study, homestays, and independent project. Sophomores to graduate students with 2.5 GPA. Apply by May 15 for fall and October 15 for spring.

Latin American Culture and Civilization

University of Oregon. "OSSHE Ecuador Exchange." Fall term or academic year. Sophomores, juniors, and seniors with two years college Spanish and 2.75 GPA. Apply by March 1.

SUMMER

Ecology

Experiment in International Living/School for International Training. "Summer Academic Study Abroad." Andes and Galapagos. Intensive language and ecology seminar, including field trips. Freshmen to seniors. Apply by March 15.

Science

Eastern Michigan University. "Galapagos Islands Adventure." Quito, Galapagos Islands, and Amazon rain forest. Freshmen to graduate students. Apply by May 1.

PERU

An Andean country of breathtaking natural wonders, Peru reflects the intermingling of Spanish and Indian heritages. In 1532, Spanish conquistadores led by Francisco Pizarro began their conquest of Tahuantinsuyu, the vast Inca empire that encompassed all of present-day Peru as well as parts of Ecuador, Bolivia, Argentina, and Chile. The rich cultural heritage of the Incas and their predecessors can be seen today not only in museums and archaeological sites but also in the everyday clothing, utensils, language, and way of life of rural Peru. In modern times, the Spanish and Indian cultures have blended to produce a nation that is remarkable in its cultural diversity.

The country is divided geographically into three distinct regions: an arid coastal plain, the magnificent Andean mountain range, and the interior tropical forest. Each region contains its own distinct population.

On the coast, the capital city of Lima is a cosmopolitan center of over four million inhabitants. Founded as the seat of the Spanish government in the 16th century, today it is the political, economic, and educational center of the country, its population a *mestizo* mix of Spanish, Indian, Asian, and black heritages.

In the highlands, where the population is predominantly Indian, one is drawn to the city of Cuzco, which is characterized by a foundation of Incan architecture overlaid with Spanish colonial and modern embellishments. A bustling center of tourism, Cuzco maintains a distinct Indian flavor in its colorful arts and crafts, foods, and, most of all, in the faces of its peoples. Cuzco is also the base for travelers who want to visit the mysterious ancient citadel of Machu Picchu.

Further inland, one enters a region of exuberant flora and fauna, the *selva*, or tropical forest. Here one can enjoy the abundance of tropical fruits and encounter pioneers who have spent a lifetime confronting the "green wall" of a seemingly never-ending forest.

Currently, the government is faced with many problems—economic, political, and social. Shortages of basic foods, interruptions in power and the water supply, and the activities of guerrilla groups (such as the Sendero Luminoso, or "Shining Path") require one to become informed before going to Peru. But regardless of its problems, the people of Peru continue to be graciously helpful to their guests. And travelers continue to leave with feelings of warmth for its people and awe for its natural wonders.

—*Shirley A. Kregar, Pittsburgh, Pennsylvania*

Official name: Republic of Peru. **Area:** 496,222 square miles (about four times the size of Arizona). **Population:** 21,300,000. **Population density:** 43 inhabitants per square mile. **Capital and largest city:** Lima (pop. 5,330,800). **Language:** Spanish, Quechua. **Religion:** Roman Catholic. **Per capita income:** US$970. **Currency:** Inti. **Literacy rate:** 72%. **Average daily high/low:*** Lima: January, 82°/66°; July, 67°/57°. **Average number of days with precipitation:** Lima: January, less than 1; July, 1.

TRAVEL

U.S. citizens will need a passport and an onward/return ticket; a visa is not required, however. For specific regulations, check with the Embassy of Peru (1700 Massachusetts Avenue NW, Washington, DC 20036).

At press time, the U.S. State Department was warning against travel in many parts of Peru due to attacks by the Shining Path guerrillas. Cuzco and Lima are still considered relatively safe, although because of both street crime and terrorist activity, visitors are warned against traveling after dark in Lima or on the roads around Lima. Current information is available from the Citizens Emergency Center at the U.S. State Department (see page 6).

Getting Around

Two airlines, AeroPeru (state owned) and Faucett (privately owned), provide service to most of Peru's provincial cities from Lima. Both AeroPeru and Faucett offer Visit Peru passes, which are valid for 30 days of unlimited travel within the country. (All flights must be on the same airline.) The pass costs $180 if purchased in conjunction with an international ticket to Lima on the same airline, or $250 if purchased separately, and must be purchased before your arrival in Peru.

In general, intercity highways are paved in the coastal region of Peru, are gravel in the Andes, and are virtually nonexistent in the Amazon region (which comprises about half the country). The best road in Peru is the Pan American Highway, which stretches the entire length of the coast; a paved road also runs from the coast to Cuzco, the ancient capital of the Incan empire, which is

---

*all temperatures are Fahrenheit

situated in a valley over 11,000 feet above sea level. Roads also connect Peru with Bolivia, Chile, and Ecuador, but none cross the border to Brazil or Colombia. Buses of various types provide the most common means of transportation for Peruvians. Shared taxis, called *colectivos*, serve the same routes, and although they are faster and more comfortable, they are also more expensive. It is also possible to rent a car in Lima and a few other cities; an Inter-American driving permit is required, however (see page 422).

Peru has a handful of rail lines that connect a few cities of the interior to port cities on the Pacific. In addition, a railroad from Cuzco provides access to Machu Picchu, the spectacular mountaintop city of the Incas and one of the leading tourist attractions in South America. Another of the world's most interesting railway journeys is the trip from Lima to Huancayo, which takes the traveler over 16,000 feet above sea level. However, at press time service on this route had been discontinued due to terrorist attacks.

In the eastern half of Peru, transport is mainly by small boat. In fact, Iquitos (pop. 200,000), the biggest city in Peru's Amazon region, can be reached only by plane or by boat. From Iquitos boats provide frequent passenger service down the Amazon into Brazil, stopping at towns along the way.

Especially for Students and Young People

INTEJ (Av. San Martin 240, Barranco, Lima) is Peru's student/youth travel bureau and ISTC member. Students with an International Student Identity Card receive a discount on some domestic flights and bus routes in Peru. In addition, they are eligible for discounts at a limited number of hotels, restaurants, and discos. More information is available at INTEJ.

For Further Information

Peru: A Travel Survival Kit ($12.95), a guidebook designed for the independent traveler interested in really getting to know the country, is probably the best one on the market. If you can't find it in bookstores, it can be ordered from the publisher, Lonely Planet Publications, Embarcadero West, 112 Linden Street, Oakland, CA 94607 (add $1.50 for postage). General tourist information is available from Peru's tourist office in the U.S., FOPTUR (50 Biscayne Boulevard, Suite 123, Miami, FL 33132).

WORK

Internships/Traineeships

There is an AIESEC internship program in Peru; see page 18 for more information.

STUDY

The following are the educational programs offered by member institutions of the Council on International Educational Exchange. Consult Appendix I for the addresses where you can write for further information. In addition to the programs listed below, the California State Universities, Pennsylvania State

University, and the University of California system offer programs open only to their own students.

SEMESTER AND ACADEMIC YEAR

General Studies

Indiana University. "Intercollegiate Study Center—Lima." Academic year at Catholic University in Lima. Co-sponsored by University of California and University of Wisconsin. Juniors and seniors with two years of Spanish and 3.0 GPA. Apply by February 1.

State University of New York at Stony Brook. Lima. Fall semester or academic year. Study at Universidad de Lima and Universidad Católica del Perú; internships available. Juniors, seniors, and graduate students with 2.5 GPA and two years of college Spanish. Apply by April 1.

University of North Carolina. "UNC Program to Lima." Academic year. Sophomores, juniors, and seniors fluent in Spanish with 3.0 GPA. Apply by February 12.

University of Wisconsin–Madison. "Intercollegiate Study Center—Lima." See program listing under Indiana University.

URUGUAY

Uruguay, one of South America's smallest nations, is often overshadowed by its two neighboring giants—Brazil and Argentina. In fact, Uruguay owes its existence to the stalemate between its two neighbors over which one should control the area. Today, more than half the population of Uruguay lives in a single city, Montevideo, which dominates the political, economic, and cultural life of the country. Other interesting cities include the world famous beach resort of Punta del Este and Colonia, which is known for its well-preserved Portuguese colonial architecture.

The European immigrants who settled in Uruguay created an agricultural economy that generated one of the world's highest standards of living early in this century. Over the decades, however, unable to make the transition to a successful industrial economy, the standard of living slowly eroded. In the 1970s and early 1980s, hundreds of thousands of Uruguayans emigrated to Argentina, Brazil, and Spain in order to escape economic hardship and political repression. However, since 1985, when the military government turned over power to a popularly elected civilian government, attempts to revitalize the country's economy and political system have met with limited success.

Official name: Oriental Republic of Uruguay. **Area:** 72,172 square miles (about the size of Minnesota). **Population:** 3,000,000. **Population density:** 42 inhabitants per square mile. **Capital and largest city:** Montevideo (pop. 1,325,000). **Language:** Spanish. **Religion:** Roman Catholic. **Per capita income:** US$2,500. **Currency:** Peso. **Literacy rate:** 94%. **Average daily high/**

low:* Montevideo: January, 83°/62°; July, 58°/43°. **Average number of days with precipitation:** Montevideo: January, 6; July, 7.

TRAVEL

U.S. citizens will need a passport to enter Uruguay; a visa is not required for stays of up to three months. For specific regulations, check with the Embassy of Uruguay (1918 F Street NW, Washington, DC 20006).

Getting Around

The rail system, built by the British in the late 19th century, had slowly decayed, providing increasingly inadequate service, until the economically hard-pressed government abandoned it entirely in 1988. Persons wishing to travel within the country are now limited to planes, automobiles, or buses. Three bus companies provide comfortable service throughout the country, and cars can be rented in Montevideo or Punta del Este. Domestic flights are offered by PLUNA, which provides service from Montevideo to a limited number of other Uruguayan cities. In addition, a variety of boats (including hydrofoils) link Colonia, about three hours west of Montevideo, with Buenos Aires across the Río de la Plata.

Especially for Students and Young People

AUTE (Asociación Uruguaya de Turismo Estudiantil, Andes 1358, Of. 405, Montevideo) is the student travel bureau and ISTC member in Uruguay. Their office provides tourist information, international air tickets, and books accommodations. Holders of the International Student Identity Card (ISIC) are entitled to reduced air fares on certain international flights; discounts with some bus, hydrofoil, and ferry companies; and reduced rates at several hotels and hostels in Montevideo. In addition, AUTE distributes a list of shops that offer discounts to ISIC holders.

WORK

Internships/Traineeships

There are both AIESEC and IAESTE internship programs in Uruguay; see page 18 for more information.

STUDY

A program sponsored by a member institution of the Council on International Educational Exchange is described below. Consult Appendix I for its address.

---

*all temperatures are Fahrenheit

SEMESTER AND ACADEMIC YEAR

General Studies

International Student Exchange Program. Direct reciprocal exchange between U.S. universities and the Universidad Católica del Uruguay in Montevideo. Semester or academic year. Full curriculum options. Open only to students at ISEP member institutions.

VENEZUELA

The discovery of oil early in this century has given Venezuela the highest standard of living in South America. Oil revenues made possible grandiose industrial, development, transportation, mining, and agricultural projects. And the expanding economy was fertile soil for the development of South America's oldest and most stable democracy. Yet all have not benefited equally: fully a third of the population still lives at the subsistence level. And in recent years falling oil prices have brought an end to economic prosperity and begun to threaten the nation's political stability, proving that Venezuela is not immune to the problems of the Third World.

Travelers to Venezuela will find a modern nation with glass-and-concrete office blocks, shopping malls, traffic jams, and urban air pollution. But as one gets farther away from Caracas and the industrial cities of the north, the picture changes. The Caribbean beaches of Margarita Island and the world's longest and highest cable car system, which ascends the snow-covered Andean peaks near Mérida, offer other images of Venezuela. For those who really want to get off the beaten path, southern Venezuela contains unexplored "cloud" forests, Stone-Age tribes, unmapped mesas, and remote waterfalls, including Angel Falls, the world's highest. Venezuela has even taken steps to preserve its southern wilderness; a national park the size of Belgium stretches from the diamond-strewn Caroni River to the borders of Brazil and Guyana.

Official name: Republic of Venezuela. **Area:** 352,143 square miles (about three times the size of Arizona). **Population:** 18,800,000. **Population density:** 53 inhabitants per square mile. **Capital and largest city:** Caracas (pop. 3,000,000). **Language:** Spanish. **Religion:** Roman Catholic. **Per capita income:** US$3,200. **Currency:** Bolivar. **Literacy rate:** 88.4%. **Average daily high/low:*** Caracas: January, 75°/56°; July, 79°/61°. **Average number of days with precipitation:** January, 6; July, 15.

TRAVEL

U.S. citizens will need a passport and a tourist card to enter Venezuela. Tourist cards valid for 60 days are issued by the airlines serving Venezuela (provided the traveler has purchased a return or onward ticket). For specific requirements,

---

*all temperatures are Fahrenheit

check with the Embassy of Venezuela (2445 Massachusetts Avenue NW, Washington, DC 20008) or a Venezuelan consulate.

Getting Around

Avensa, the country's main domestic air carrier, offers a pass that provides for unlimited travel in Venezuela. The price is $110 for 7 days, $125 for 14 days, or $139 for 21 days. The pass, which can be purchased through any of the international airlines serving Venezuela, must be purchased before your arrival in Venezuela, however.

There is an excellent road system extending to all areas of the country except the south. Roads also connect Venezuela with Colombia, but there are no roads across the border to either Brazil or Guyana. Buses form the backbone of the nation's transportation system. Other alternatives are *por puesto* cars (shared taxis that leave when full) or car rentals (Avis, Budget, Hertz, and National are among those agencies operating in the country). Passenger train service is virtually nonexistent.

Venezuela has become a popular destination for travelers who want to explore remote rain forests, see "lost" mesas, or climb Andean peaks. Angel Falls, located in a remote wilderness in the southern part of the country, always tops the lists of destinations for travelers seeking an "adventure" experience in the country and there are a number of companies operating adventure tours—camping, backpacking, canoeing, mountain climbing, horseback riding, and so on. Tours can be booked through travel agents in Venezuela; arrangements can also be made through many travel agents in the United States.

Especially for Students and Young People

ONTEJ (Parque Central, Avenida Lecuna, Edificio Catuche, Nivel Bolivar, Oficina 37, P.O. Box 17696, Caracas 1015-A) is the student travel organization and ISTC member in Venezuela. Holders of the International Student Identity Card (ISIC) can obtain reduced air fares to numerous international destinations from Venezuela. For travel within the country, they receive discounts on Aeropostal flights as well as long-distance public buses. Students also receive free admission to some museums and reduced admission to several theaters in Caracas. ONTEJ distributes a full list of the 800 shops that offer discounts to ISIC holders.

For Further Information

General tourist information is available from the Venezuela Government Tourist Center, 7 East 51st Street, New York, NY 10022.

WORK

A work visa is required for regular salaried employment in Venezuela; application is made by the Venezuelan company seeking permission to hire a foreigner. Work visas can be issued for 60 days, 120 days, or a year.

Internships/Traineeships

There is an AIESEC internship program in Venezuela; see page 18 for more information.

APPENDIX I

MEMBERS OF THE COUNCIL ON INTERNATIONAL EDUCATIONAL EXCHANGE

Adelphi University
International Student Services
South Avenue
Harvey Hall, Room 216
Garden City, NY 11530
(516) 663-1134

Adventist Colleges Abroad
Board of Higher Education
General Conference of SDA
6840 Eastern Avenue, NW
Washington, DC 20012
(202) 722-6423

AFS International/Intercultural
 Programs
313 East 43rd Street
New York, NY 10017
(800) AFS-INFO

AIESEC–US
841 Broadway, Suite 608
New York, NY 10003

Alma College
International Office
Alma, MI 48801-1599
(517) 463-7247

American Center for Students and
 Artists
29 rue de la Sourdiere
75001 Paris
France

American Graduate School of
 International Management
Thunderbird Campus
Glendale, AZ 85306
(602) 978-7133

American Heritage Association
Program Development
P.O. Box 425
Lake Oswego, OR 97034
(800) 654-2051

American Council on the Teaching of
 Foreign Languages (ACTFL)
6 Executive Boulevard
Yonkers, NY 10701
(914) 963-8830

American University
Tenley Campus
Study Abroad Programs
Washington, DC 20016
(800) 424-2600

American University in Cairo
866 United Nations Plaza
New York, NY 10017
(212) 421-6320

American Youth Hostels
Travel Department
National Office
P.O. Box 37613
Washington, DC 20013-7613

Antioch University
Antioch Education Abroad
Yellow Springs, OH 45387
(513) 767-1031

Associated Colleges of the Midwest
International Programs Associate
18 South Michigan Avenue, Suite 1010
Chicago, IL 60603
(313) 263-5000

Association for International Practical Training
AIESTE Training Program
10480 Little Patuxent Parkway, Suite 370
Columbia, MD 21044-3502

Association of Student Councils
171 College Street, 2nd floor
Toronto, Ontario M5T 1P7
Canada
(416) 977-3703

Association of College Unions-International
400 East Seventh Street
Bloomington, IN 47405
(812) 332-8017

Bates College
312 Lane Hall
Lewiston, ME 04240
(207) 786-6222

Beaver College
Deputy Director
Center for Education Abroad
Glenside, PA 19038
(215) 572-2901

Beloit College
Director, World Outlook Program
700 College Street
Beloit, WI 53511
(608) 365-3391

Boston College
Chestnut Hill, MA 02167
(617) 736-3480

Boston University
143 Bay State Road
Boston, MA 02215
(617) 353-5403

Brandeis University
Kutz Hall/215
Waltham, MA 02254
(617) 736-3480

Brethren Colleges Abroad
Box 184, Manchester College
North Manchester, IN 46962
(219) 982-5238

Brigham Young University
BYU Study Abroad
204 HRCB
Provo, UT 84602
(801) 378-3308

Brown University
Box 1973
Providence, RI 02912
(401) 863-3555

Bucknell University
Lewisburgh, PA 17837
(717) 524-1336

Canadian Bureau for International Education
85 Albert Street, 14th floor
Ottawa
Ontario K1P 6A4
Canada
(613) 237-4820

California State University
Office of International Programs
400 Golden Shore, Suite 300
Long Beach, CA 90802-4275
(213) 590-5655

Carleton College
Director, Off-Campus Studies
Northfield, MN 55057
(507) 663-4332

Carroll College
100 North East Avenue
Waukesha, WI 53186
(414) 547-1211

Central University of Iowa
International Studies Office
Pella, IA 50219
(515) 628-5287

Central Michigan University
Mt. Pleasant, MI 48859
(517) 774-4308

Central Washington University
Ellensburg, WA 98926
(509) 963-3612

Chapman College
Office of International Programs
333 N. Glassell
Orange, CA 92666
(714) 997-6829

College of Charleston
International Programs
Charleston, SC 29424
(803) 792-5676

College of St. Thomas
International Education Center
P.O. Box 4036
2115 Summit Avenue
St. Paul, MI 55105
(612) 647-5693

Colorado State University
315 Aylesworth Hall
Fort Collins, CO 80523
(303) 491-5917

Cornell University
Center for International Studies
474 Uris Hall
Ithaca, NY 14853-7601
(607) 255-6224

Council on International Educational
 Exchange
Academic Programs Department
205 East 42nd Street
New York, NY 10017
(212) 661-1414

Dartmouth College
Hanover, NH 03755
(603) 646-3753

Davidson College
Office for Study Abroad
P.O. Box 1719
Davidson, NC 28036
(704) 892-2250

DIS at the University of Copenhagen
Vestergade 7
DK-1456 Copenhagen K, Denmark

Drake University
Drake-ISI Italy

Meredith Hall 123
Des Moines, IA 50311
(800) 443-7253 ext. 3984

Earlham College
Institute for Education on Japan
National Highway West
Richmond, IN 47374
(317) 983-1324

Eastern Michigan University
Office of International Studies
333 Goodison Hall
Ypsilanti, MI 48197
(313) 487-2424

Ecole Centrale de Paris (Ecole
 Centrale des Arts et Manufactures)
Grande Voie des Vignes
92295 Chatenay-Malabry
France
(46) 836246

Elmira College
Park Place
Elmira, NY 14901
(607) 734-3911

Empire State College
Office of International Programs
1 Union Avenue
Saratoga Springs, NY 12866
(518) 587-2100 ext. 249

Escuela Superior de Administración y
 Direccion de Empresas (ESADE)
Avda. de Pedralbes 60–62
08034 Barcelona
Spain
(343) 203-7800

Experiment in International Living/
 School for International Training
Admissions Office, College Semester
 Abroad
Kipling Road
Brattleboro, VT 05301-0676
(800) 451-4465 or (802) 257-7751

Fontainebleau Fine Arts and Music
 Schools Association
350 West 85th Street
New York, NY 10024-4402
(212) 580-0210

Friends World College
Admissions Office
Plover Lane
Huntington, NY 11743
(516) 549-1102

Fudan University
220 Handan Road
Shanghai 200433
China
(86-021) 483-962

Georgetown University
Office of International Programs
ICC 307
Washington, DC 20057
(202) 687-5867

Gonzaga University
Coordinator, Gonzaga-in-Florence
Spokane, WA 99258-0001
(800) 523-9712 or (509) 328-4220

Goshen College
Admissions Office
Goshen, IN 46526
(219) 535-7535

Great Lakes Colleges Association
2929 Plymouth Road, Suite 207
Ann Arbor, MI 48105-3206
(313) 761-4833

Grinnell College
Box 805
Grinnell, IA 50112
(515) 269-4000

Guilford College
Off-Campus Education
5800 W. Friendly Avenue
Greensboro, NC 27410
(919) 292-5511 ext. 125

Gustavus Adolphus College
Office of International Education
St. Peter, MN 56082
(507) 931-7545

Hampshire College
West Street
Amherst, MA 01002
(413) 549-4600 ext. 542

Hartwick College
Oneonta, NY 13820
(607) 432-4200

Hebrew University of Jerusalem
Office of Academic Affairs
11 East 69th Street
New York, NY 10021
(212) 472-2288

Heidelberg College
310 E. Market Street
Tiffin, OH 44883
(419) 448-2256

Hiram College
Director, Extra Mural Studies
Hiram, OH 44234
(216) 569-5160

Hollins College
Hollins Abroad Programs
P.O. Box 9597
Roanoke, VA 24020
(703) 362-6307

Hope College
International Education Office
Holland, MI 49423
(616) 394-7605

Illinois State University
Office of International Studies and
  Programs
105 McCormick Hall
Normal, IL 61761-6901
(309) 438-5361

Indiana University
Office of Overseas Study
Franklin Hall, 303
Bloomington, IN 47405
(812) 855-9304

Institute of International Education
809 United Nations Plaza
New York, NY 10017
(212) 894-5314

International Christian University
10-2, Osawa 3-chome
Mitaka, Tokyo, 181
Japan
(0422) 33-3131

International Christian Youth
  Exchange
134 West 26th Street
New York, NY 10001

COUNCIL ON INTERNATIONAL EDUCATIONAL EXCHANGE

International Student Exchange
  Program
Georgetown University
1242 35th Street NW
Washington, DC 20057

Iowa State University
Ames, IA 50011
(515) 294-4111

Japan International Christian
  University Foundation
475 Riverside Drive, Room 1848
New York, NY 10027
(212) 870-2893

Kalamazoo College
Study Abroad Office
Kalamazoo, MI 49007
(616) 383-8470

Kansas State University
Manhattan, KS 66509
(913) 532-6900

Kent State University
Center for International &
  Comparative Programs
124 Bowman Hall
Kent, OH 44242-0001
(216) 672-7980

Lake Erie College
Academic Programs Abroad
391 W. Washington Street
Painesville, OH 44077
(216) 352-3361 ext. 357

LaSalle University
LaSalle-in-Europe
Philadelphia, PA 19141

Lewis & Clark College
Office of Overseas and Off-Campus
  Programs
Campus Box 11
Portland, OR 97219

Lisle Fellowship
433 West Sterns Road
Temperance, MI 45192
(313) 847-7126

Louisiana State University
Academic Programs Abroad
365 Pleasant Hall

Baton Rouge, LA 70803-1522
(504) 388-6801 or (800) CALL LSU

Macalester College
International Center
1600 Grand Avenue
Saint Paul, MN 55105
(612) 696-6310

Marquette University
Milwaukee, WI 53233
(414) 224-6832

Mary Baldwin College
Staunton, VI 24401
(703) 885-0811

Miami University
Oxford, OH 45056
(513) 529-5628

Michigan State University
Office of Overseas Study
108 International Center
East Lansing, MI 48824-1035
(517) 353-8920

Middlebury College
Language Schools
Middlebury, VT 05753
(802) 388-3711 ext. 5510

Millersville University of
  Pennsylvania
Millersville, PA 17551
(717) 872-3526

Monterey Institute of International
  Studies
Dean's Office, Language Studies
425 Van Buren Avenue
Monterey, CA 93940

National Association for Foreign
  Student Affairs
1860 19th Street NW
Washington, DC 20009
(202) 462-4811

National Association of Secondary
  School Principals
1904 Association Drive
Reston, VA 22091
(703) 860-0200

458 COUNCIL ON INTERNATIONAL EDUCATIONAL EXCHANGE

New York University
Office of Academic Affairs
Elmer Holmes Bobst Library, Room 1104
70 Washington Square South
New York, NY 10012
(212) 998-2300

North Carolina State University at Raleigh
Study Abroad Office, Box 7344
Raleigh, NC 27695-7344
(919) 737-2087

Northeastern University
400 Meserve Hall
Boston, MA 02115
(617) 437-3980

Northern Arizona University
Office of International Studies
P.O. Box 5598
Flagstaff, AZ 86011
(602) 523-2409

Northern Illinois University
Foreign Study Office
Wirtz House
305 Normal Road
DeKalb, IL 60115-2854
(815) 753-0304

Northern Michigan University
Marquette, MI 49855
(906) 227-5212

Northfield Mount Hermon School
International Programs Office
Northfield, MA 01360

Oberlin College
Oberlin, OH 44074
(216) 775-8650

Obirin University
3758 Tokiwa-cho, Machida-shi
Tokyo 194-02
Japan

Ohio University
Center for International Studies
56 East Union Street
Athens, OH 45701-2979
(614) 593-1840

Ohio State University
Center for International Studies
308 Dulles Hall
230 West 17th Avenue
Columbus, OH 43201
(614) 292-9660

Open Door Student Exchange
P.O. Box 71
Hempstead, NY 11551
(800) 366-6736

Pace University
Pace Plaza
New York, NY 10038
(212) 488-1962

Pennsylvania State University
University Office of International Programs, Education Abroad
222 Boucke Building
University Park, PA 16802
(814) 865-7681

Pitzer College
External Studies
Claremont, CA 91711
(714) 621-8289

Portland State University
International Exchange Programs
P.O. Box 751
Portland, OR 97207
(800) 547-8887 or (503) 464-4081

Pomona College
350 College Way
Oldenborg Center
Claremont, CA 91711
(714) 621-8154

Purdue University
Programs for Study Abroad Office
AGAD Room #3
West Lafayette, IN 47907
(317) 494-2383

Reed College
Office of International Programs
3203 SE Woodstock Boulevard
Portland, OR 97202
(503) 771-1112

Reformed Church in America
Box 803

Orange City, IA 51041
(712) 737-4952

Rhode Island School of Design
2 College Street
Providence, RI 02903

Rochester Institute of Technology
One Lomb Memorial Drive
Rochester, NY 14623
(716) 475-2293

Rollins College
International Programs
Box 2759
Winter Park, FL 32789
(407) 646-2466

Rosary College
International Studies
River Forest, IL 60305
(312) 366-2490

Rutgers University
Study Abroad Office
Room #205 Milledoler Hall
New Brunswick, NJ 08903
(201) 932-7787

St. Olaf College
Office of International Studies
Northfield, MN 55057
(507) 663-3069

St. John Fisher College
3690 East Avenue
Rochester, NY 14618
(716) 385-8215

St. Lawrence University
Office of International Programs
Canton, NY 13617
(315) 379-5991

St. Peter's College
Foreign Study Programs
2641 Kennedy Boulevard
Jersey City, NJ 07306
(201) 915-9273

Scandinavian Seminar
24 Dickinson Street
Amherst, MA 01002
(800) 828-3343

School Year Abroad
Phillips Academy
Dept. WWH
Andover, MA 01810
(508) 475-1119

Scripps College
Office of Off-Campus Study
1030 Columbia
Claremont, CA 91711
(714) 621-8306

Skidmore College
Junior Year Abroad
Saratoga Springs, NY 12866
(518) 584-5000 ext. 2383

Southern Illinois University at
  Carbondale
International Programs and Services
Carbondale, IL 62901
(618) 453-7670

Southern Methodist University
105 Fondren Library West
International Programs Office
Dallas, TX 75275-0391
(214) 692-2338

Southwest Texas State University
Center for International Education
San Marcos, TX 78666

Spelman College
Study Abroad Office
350 Spelman Lane SW
Atlanta, GA 30314
(404) 681-3643

Springfield College
International Center
263 Alden Street
Springfield, MA 01109
(413) 788-3215

Stephens College
P.O. Box 2053
Columbia, MO 65215
(314) 876-7153

Stanford University
P.O. Box L
Stanford, CA 94309

State University of New York at Albany
International Programs LI-84
Albany, NY 12222
(518) 442-3525

State University of New York at Buffalo
International Education
1300 Elmwood Avenue
Buffalo, NY 14222
(716) 878-4620

State University of New York at Cortland
International Programs
P.O Box 2000
Cortland, NY 13045
(607) 753-2209

State University College of New York at Oswego
International Office
102 Rich Hall
Oswego, NY 13126
(315) 341-2118

State University of New York at Stony Brook
Central Hall 101
Office of International Programs
Stony Brook, NY 11794-2700
(516) 632-7030

Stetson University
Office of International Exchange
Box 8412
DeLand, FL 32720
(800) 345-4280

Syracuse University
Division of International Programs Abroad
119 Euclid Avenue
Syracuse, NY 13244-4170
(315) 443-3471

Texas A & M University
Study Abroad Office
161 Bizzell West
College Station, TX 77843-3262

Texas Tech University
Office of International Programs
P.O. Box 4248
242 West Hall
Lubbock, TX 79409-5004
(806) 742-3667

Trinity College
Educational Services
300 Summit Street
Hartford, CT 06106
(203) 297-2437

Tufts University
Tufts Programs Abroad
Medford, MA 02155
(617) 381-3290

Tulane University
1229 Broadway
New Orleans, LA 70118
(504) 865-5339

United Negro College Fund
500 East 62nd Street
New York, NY 10021
(212) 326-1100

Universidad Autonoma de Guadalajara
Av. Patria 1201 Lomas del Valle, 3ra Seccion
Guadalajara 44100
Jalisco
Mexico

Université de Bordeaux III
Domaine Universitaire
Talence Cedex 33405
France
56-80-84-83

University College London
Gower Street
London WCIE 6BT
England
01-387-7050

University of Alabama at Birmingham
318 University Center
University Station
Birmingham, AL 35294
(205) 934-5643

University of Alabama at Tuscaloosa
Capstone International Program Center
P.O. Box 870254
Tuscaloosa, AL 35487-0254
(205) 348-5292

University of Arkansas at Little Rock
Office for International Programs
Little Rock, AR 72204
(501) 569-3374

University of British Columbia
Language Institute
Centre for Continuing Education
5997 Iona Drive
Vancouver V6T 2A4
Canada

University of California
Systemwide Education Abroad
  Program
Hollister Research Center
Santa Barbara, CA 93106

University of Colorado
Office of International Education
Campus Box 123
Boulder, CO 80309-0123
(303) 492-7741

University of Connecticut
Study Abroad Program in Rouen
U-ST Arjona 228
337 Mansfield Road
Storrs, CT 06268

University of Denver
2050 East Evans
Driscoll Center South, Room 56
Denver, CO 80208
(303) 871-3584

University of Essex
Wivenhoe Park, Colchester
Essex CO4 3SQ
England
(0206) 873333

University of Evansville
Harlaxton Coordinator
1800 Lincoln Avenue
Evansville, IN 47722
(812) 479-2146

University of Illinois at Urbana-
  Champaign
310 Coble Hall
801 South Wright Street
Champaign, IL 61820
(217) 333-6168

University of Iowa
International Education
Iowa City, IA 52242
(319) 335-0336

University of International Business
  and Economics
He Ping Li
Beijing
China
(861) 421-2022

University of Kansas
Office of Study Abroad
203 Lippincott Hall
Lawrence, KS 66045
(913) 864-3742

University of Lancaster
University House
Lancaster LA1 4YW
England
44-524-65201

University of Louisville
School of Urban Policy
102 Brigman Hall
Louisville, KY 40292
(502) 588-6482

University of Maine at Orono
Dept. of Foreign Languages
201 Little Hall
Orono, ME 04469
(207) 581-2096

University of Maryland
Study Abroad Office
2109 Skinner Building
College Park, MD 20742
(301) 454-8645

University of Massachusetts
International Programs
William S. Clark International Center
Amherst, MA 01003
(413) 545-2710

University of Michigan
International Center
603 East Madison Street
Ann Arbor, MI 48109-1370
(313) 764-9310

University of Minnesota
The Global Campus
202 Wesbrook Hall
Minneapolis, MN 55455
(612) 626-2223

University of New Hampshire
Center for International Perspectives
New England Center Administration
  Building
Durham, NH 03824-3596
(603) 862-2398

University of North Carolina at
  Chapel Hill
Office of International Programs
207 Caldwell Hall 009A
Chapel Hill, NC 27514
(919) 962-7001

University of North Texas
International Studies Office
Box 13795
Denton, TX 76203
(817) 565-4122

University of Notre Dame
Foreign Study Programs
420 Administration Building
Notre Dame, IN 46556
(219) 239-5882

University of Oklahoma
601 Elm Room 142
Norman, OK 73019

University of Oregon
Office of International Services
330 Oregon Hall
Eugene, OR 97403
(503) 686-3206

University of the Pacific
Office of International Programs
3601 Pacific Avenue
Stockton, CA 95211
(209) 946-2591

University of Pennsylvania
Office of International Programs
133 Bennett Hall
Philadelphia, PA 19104
(215) 898-4661

University of Pittsburgh
UCIS Study Abroad Office
4G32 Forbes Quadrangle
Pittsburgh, PA 15260

University of Rhode Island
Study Abroad
Kingston, RI 02881
(401) 792-5546

University of South Carolina
606 Byrnes Center
Columbia, SC 29208
(803) 777-7797

University of Southern California
Overseas Studies, FIG
Los Angeles, CA 90089-1261
(213) 743-5356

University of Sussex
Falmer, Brighton
East Sussex BN1 9QN
0273-606755

University of Tennessee
Center for International Education
205 Alumni Hall
Knoxville, TN 37996-0621
(615) 974-6992

University of Texas at Austin
Drawer A
University Station
Austin, TX 78713
(512) 471-1211

University of Toledo
2801 West Bancroft
Toledo, OH 43606

University of Utah
International Center
159 Union Building
Salt Lake City, UT 84112
(801) 581-5849

University of Vermont
Living/Learning Center, Box #8
Burlington, VT 05405
(802) 656-4296

University of Virginia
102 Cabell Hall
Charlottesville, VA 22903
(804) 924-3548

University of Washington
Foreign Study Office
572 Schmitz Hall PA-10
Seattle, WA 98195
(206) 543-9272

University of Waterloo
200 University Avenue West
Needles Hall
Waterloo, Ontario N2L 3G1
Canada

University of Wisconsin at Madison
International Studies and Programs
Madison, WI 53706
(608) 262-2851

University of Wisconsin at Platteville
Institute for Study Abroad Programs
308 Warner Hall
1 University Plaza
Platteville, WI 53818-3099
(608) 342-1726

University of Wisconsin at River Falls
Study Abroad Programs
River Falls, WI 54022
(715) 425-3992

University of Wyoming
International Programs
P.O. Box 3707
Laramie, Wyoming 82071-3707
(307) 766-5193

University System of Georgia
International-Intercultural Studies
    Programs
Box 653 GSU University Plaza
Atlanta, GA 30303

Valparaiso University
International Studies
Valparaiso, IN 46383

Volunteers in Asia
Box 4543
Stanford University
Stanford, CA 94305
(415) 723-3228

Wake Forest University
Reynolds Station
Winston-Salem, NC 27109
(919) 761-5000

Washington State University
Bryan Hall 108
Pullman, WA 99164-5110
(509) 335-4508

Wayne State University
Junior Year in Germany
471 Manoogian Hall
Detroit, MI 48202
(313) 577-4605

Wesleyan University
Program Abroad
300 High Street
Middletown, CT 06457
(203) 347-9411 ext. 2271

Western Michigan University
International Education & Programs
2090 Friedmann Hall
Kalamazoo, MI 49008-5011
(616) 387-3951

Western Washington University
Foreign Study Office
Old Main 400
Bellingham, WA 98225

Westminster College
Market Street
New Wilmington, PA 16172-0001
(412) 946-7123

Wichita State University
Office of International Programs
Box 8
Wichita, KA 67208
(316) 689-3730

Wilmington College
Director, International Education
Wilmington, OH 45177

Wittenberg University
Global Studies Program
P.O. Box 720
Springfield, OH 45501

World College West
101 S. San Antonio Road
Petaluma, CA 94952
(707) 765-4500

YMCA of the USA
International Program Services

356 West 34th Street, 3rd floor
New York, NY 10001
(212) 563-4595

Youth for Understanding International Exchange
3501 Newark Street NW
Washington, DC 20016
(800) 424-3691 or (202) 966-6800

APPENDIX II
HIGH SCHOOL PROGRAMS

If you're a high school student considering a trip abroad, you'll have some special things to think about as you begin to plan. Although all of the travel opportunities and student discounts described in this book are open to you, most of the programs are not. (This book focuses on programs for college students.) But don't be discouraged—although many of these programs are closed to you, many others are not.

Most high school students choose to join a tour, study program, or voluntary service project. What you choose will depend on a careful evaluation not only of the program but also of your own maturity. Are you ready for an experience abroad? Would it be better to put it off a year or so, or is now the time for you to go? Traveling abroad is a wonderful experience when done at the right time and under the right conditions, but it can be a grave disappointment if it's not carefully planned.

To help in planning your trip to another country, you might want to pick up a copy of *The Teenager's Guide to Study, Travel, and Adventure Abroad*, written by the Council and published by St. Martin's Press (an updated edition of the guide is produced every two years). Written specifically for students between the ages of 12 and 18, *The Teenager's Guide* anticipates and addresses potential questions and concerns about international travel and study experiences. The book's early chapters cover preparation—practical, emotional, and intellectual—including such information as how to write your first letter to the sponsors of the program, how to get academic credit, how to understand different concepts of time, and how to confront cultures vastly different from your own. It also provides guidelines and self-evaluation instruments, as well as interviews with past participants, to help teenagers decide what's best for them. You can order *The Teenager's Guide* from the Council for $9.95 (plus $1 for book-rate or $2.50 for first-class postage). It's also available in bookstores and at Council Travel offices (see pages ix–xi).

Nearly 200 organizations that sponsor international programs for high school students are described in *The Teenager's Guide*. Listed below are those programs sponsored by member organizations or institutions of the Council on International Educational Exchange. Only a brief outline can be provided here; if a program sounds interesting, be sure to write or call for more information well before the application deadline.

AFS Intercultural Programs.
"Year Program." High school students live with a family and attend a local high school. Programs in 57 countries. High school sophomores, juniors, or seniors with 2.6 GPA. Departure in January, February, or March for study in countries of the southern hemisphere and July or August for countries in the northern hemisphere.
"Semester Program." Same as above but only a semester. Options in five countries.

"Summer Program." Options include family homestay, language study, outdoor skills education, sports, cultural studies, and work programs. Programs in 56 countries. High school sophomores, juniors, or seniors; for cultural study, outdoor skills education, and work programs, applicants must be in excellent physical condition. Apply by March 1. Address: 313 East 43rd Street, New York, NY 10017; (212) 949-4242 or (800) AFS-INFO.

American Heritage Association. Programs custom-designed to suit group needs. Options can include homestays, study, and travel. Most groups travel in summer or during spring break. Programs arranged for junior high and high school groups. Address: P.O. Box 425, Lake Oswego, Oregon 97034; (503) 635-3702 or (800) 654-2051.

American Youth Hostels. International bicycling, hiking, and motorcoach tours in Canada, Europe, and Latin America. Two to six weeks. Most tours operate in summer. Youth tours open to persons ages 15 to 18. Address: 1332 "I" Street NW, Suite 800, Washington, DC 20005.

Council on International Educational Exchange.
"School Partners Abroad." Reciprocal exchange of student groups for three- to four-week program of school attendance and homestay. Partner schools in eleven countries. Selection of participants by home school.
"Youth in China." Summer program in which U.S. students study Chinese language, history, and culture while living with Chinese roommates studying English. Students ages 15–18 with one year of Chinese. Apply by April 15.
Address: Professional and Secondary Education Programs, CIEE, 205 East 42nd Street, New York, NY 10017.

Experiment in International Living. Summer programs range from four to six weeks and include orientation, homestay, and sightseeing. Two weeks of language courses and academic seminars for college credit included in some programs. Other programs include special interest activity such as bike touring or mountaineering. Programs in 28 countries. Ages 14–22. Apply by April 1. Address: Kipling Road, Brattleboro, VT 05301.

International Christian Youth Exchange. High school participants live with families and attend high school in the host country. Choice of 26 countries. Ages 16–24. The experience abroad begins in July and lasts for one year. Apply by March 15. Address: 134 West 26th Street, New York, NY 10001.

Northfield Mount Hermon. "Summer Abroad." Homestay, study, and travel included in six-week summer program. Choice of China, France, and Spain. For France and Spain, two years of appropriate language study required; one year of Chinese required for China. Sixteen- and seventeen-year-olds with good academic records. Apply by February 1. Address: Northfield Mount Hermon School, International Programs Office, East Northfield, MA 01360.

Open Door Student Exchange.
"Semester Abroad." Participants stay with families and attend high school. Programs in 13 countries. Fall semester only. Ages 15–18. Two years

language study required for programs in French-, Spanish-, and German-speaking countries. Apply by April 15; early application recommended.
"Academic Year Abroad." Same as above except for entire academic year (September to May). Programs in seven countries.
"Summer Homestay Experience" and "Summer Homestay/School Program." Four to six weeks living with a family. Summer homestay programs in 12 countries of the northern hemisphere; homestay with school attendance programs available in eight countries of the southern hemisphere. Special programs include a homestay/arts program in Japan and a journalism program in Latin America. Ages 15–18. Apply by April 15; early application recommended.
Address: 250 Fulton Avenue, P.O. Box 71, Hempstead, NY 11551; (516) 486-7330.

School Year Abroad. Homestay with rigorous academic program. High school credit and college preparation. Options in Barcelona, Spain, or Rennes, France. Fall semester or full academic year. High school students entering eleventh or twelfth grade with two years of Spanish or French. Apply by March 1. Address: School Year Abroad, Dept. WWH, Phillips Academy, Andover, MA 01810.

Syracuse University. "Introduction to Architecture for High School Students." Summer program in Florence, Italy. High school juniors and seniors. Apply by April 15. Address: Syracuse University, Department of International and Public Affairs, 119 Euclid Avenue, Syracuse, NY 13244-4170.

Youth for Understanding International Exchange.
"YFU Academic Year." Homestays and high school attendance. Programs in 21 countries. Ages 14–19, with 3.0 GPA. Apply by April 1; early applicants are more likely to receive their country choice.
"YFU Semester." Same as above except for a semester. Programs in seven countries. Apply by April 1 for fall and October 15 for spring.
"Summer Program." Homestays of six to eight weeks. Programs in 22 countries. Ages 14–19, with 2.0 GPA. Apply by April 1.
"Sport for Understanding." Adult coach and 12 to 16 U.S. students are hosted by a sports club and its coaches in another country. Options include 27 different sports. Ages 14–19, with average or better sports abilities and 2.0 GPA.
Programs generally take place in summer and last up to a month. Address: 3501 Newark Street NW, Washington, DC 20016; (800) 424-3691 or (202) 966-6800.

INDEX

Academic Studies in the Federal Republic of Germany, 112
Academic Year Courses for Foreigners, 157
Academic Year Abroad, 32, 39
Adelphi University, 453
Adventist Colleges Abroad, 75, 97, 160, 453
1989 Adventure Holidays, 53
Adventure Travel, 54
Africa on a Shoestring, 257
AFS, 312, 314, 465
AIESEC—U.S., 18, 73, 79, 83, 87, 95, 110, 127, 133, 143, 145, 149, 153, 165, 170, 177, 202, 208, 211, 217, 222, 229, 233, 238, 244, 246, 249, 260, 262, 268, 271, 274, 276, 279, 282, 286, 319, 327, 334, 337, 345, 349, 351, 355, 357, 367, 375, 382, 394, 405, 412, 426, 438, 441, 445, 448, 450, 452
Alabama, University of, 103, 190
All Asia Guide, 304
Alma College, 74, 99, 104, 115, 117, 157, 161, 413, 415, 453
American Association of Collegiate Registrars and Admissions Officers (AACRAO), 31
American Automobile Association (AAA), 49
American Educational Programs in Austria, 73
American Friends Service Committee, 19
American Graduate School of International Management, 96, 150, 166, 312, 328
American Heritage Association, 99, 112, 134, 180, 466
American Institute of Indian Studies (AIIS), 295
American Medical Association, 25
American Nurses Association, 25
American Programs in Spain, 157
American Scandinavian Foundation, 83, 87–88, 124, 149, 165–166
American Sponsored or Applied Educational Programs and Schools in Greece, 121
American University, 74, 80, 134, 159, 180, 186, 212
American University in Cairo, 32
American Youth Hostels, 16, 49, 63, 421, 453
American Zionist Youth Foundation, 238
Amigos de las Americas, 19, 65
Antioch University, 68, 115, 180, 181, 295, 454
Archaeological Fieldwork Opportunities Bulletin, 21
Archaeological Institute of America (AIA), 21
ARGENTINA, 23, 27, 48, 423–427
Arkansas, University of, 75, 103, 162, 414, 416
Asia Society, 304
Asia Through the Back Door, 204
Associated Colleges of the Midwest, 218, 295, 329, 405, 454
Association for International Practical Training, 18, 73, 79, 87, 95, 110, 127, 133, 143, 145, 149, 153, 165, 170, 176, 177, 202, 208, 211, 222, 229, 233, 238, 246, 249, 257, 260, 265, 279, 327, 334, 351, 357, 367, 382, 412, 426, 441, 450
Association of Student Councils, 380–381
Association of Universities and Colleges of Colorado, 383
AUSTRALIA, 12, 15, 17, 22, 48, 359–371

Australia: A Travel Survival Kit, 375
Australia Accommodations Directory, 365
Australia Youth Hostel Association, 365
Australian Study Opportunities, 367
AUSTRIA, 17, 22, 58, 70–77
Austrian Institute, 73
Austria ticket, 71
Austria Vacation Kit, 72

Backpacking in Mexico and Central America, 402
Baedeker's Japan, 325
Baedeker's Travel Guides, 67
Baja California: A Travel Survival Kit, 411
Bali and Lombok: A Travel Survival Kit, 345
Bangladesh: A Travel Survival Kit, 345
Barron's Guide to Foreign Medical Schools, 40
Basic Data on International Courses Offered in the Netherlands, 146
Beat the High Cost of Travel, 43
Beaver College, 74–75, 121, 128–129, 180–181, 186, 189
BELGIUM, 19, 22, 27, 49, 56–58, 63, 77–80
Beloit College, 99, 112, 189, 312
Benelux Tourrail Pass, 78, 144
Biking Through Europe, 61
Birnbaum's Guides: *Carribean, Bermuda and the Bahamas*, 388
  Mexico, 411
BOLIVIA, 8, 22 430–432
Boston University, 160
BRAZIL, 22, 27, 429–436
Brethren Colleges Abroad, 99, 112, 157, 182, 189, 312, 328
Brethren Volunteer Service, 22
Briefing Kit on the People's Republic of China, 310
Brigham Young University, 68, 75, 137, 160, 182, 313, 330, 335, 384, 412, 414
British Archaeological News, 178
British Columbia Handbook, 380
British Universities North America Club (BUNAC), 176
BritRail, 174
BRUNEI, 342
Bureau for International Youth Exchange, 211
BURMA, 341
Buro fur Studentenreisen (BfSt), 72
Bushwalking in Austria, 366

California State University, 96, 166, 367
California, University of, 96, 150, 166, 295, 312, 328, 334, 345, 367
CAMBODIA, 341
CAMEROON, 257–259
Camper's Companion to Northern Europe, 66
Camping, 66–67
Camping and Youth Hostels in Denmark, 82
Campus Accommodations, 365
CANADA, 16, 18, 19–20, 27, 377–385
Canada: A Travel Survival Kit, 382
Canadian Bureau for International Education (CBIE), 20
Canadian Bureau of Investigation (CBI), 382
Canadian Cycling Association, 380

INDEX

Canadian Rockies Bicycling Guide, 380
Caribbean Islands Handbook, 388
Carleton College, 99
Center For Global Education, 401
Center For Study in Israel, 239
Central Africa: A Travel Survival Kit, 257
Central University of Iowa, 75, 97, 115, 146, 160, 182, 413
Central Washington University, 99, 113, 161, 182, 413, 415
Charter flights, 44, 56
CHILE, 27, 436–438
CHINA, 22, 48, 305–316
China: A Travel Survival Kit, 310
China Books and Periodicals, 310
China Bound: A Guide to Academic Life and Work in the PRC, 310
China Guidebook, 310
Citizens Emergency Center (CEC), 6–7
Citizens Exchange Council, 216
College of Charleston, 96
COLOMBIA, 17, 22, 27, 439–443
Colorado State University, 182, 367, 414
Colorado, University of, 69, 98, 101, 114, 184, 187, 415
A Common Core: Thais and North Americans, 357
Communicating with China, 310
Community Service Volunteers, 179
Complete Guide to Bicycling in Canada, 380
Concordia, 95
Conflicts and Contradictions, 206
Connecticut, University of, 101
Continuing education, 40
Coodinating Committee for International Voluntary Service, 24
Coordinating Council for North American Affairs, 336
Copenhagen, University of, 84–85
COSTA RICA, 15, 22, 403–406
Council on International Educational Exchange (CIEE), 218–219
   Academic Programs, 97, 157, 160, 212, 312, 314, 328–330, 346, 394, 404, 406
   Council Charter, 44
   Council Travel, 44, 56–57
   International Student Identity Card (ISIC), 8–9, 43, 52
   International Teacher Identity Card (ITIC), 9, 43
   ISIC Scholarship Fund, 37
   International Voluntary Services, 20, 111, 128, 145, 153, 156, 202, 208, 217, 222, 249, 260
   Professional and Secondary School Programs (PSEP) 157, 466
   Student Travel Catalogue, 8–9
   Work Exchanges, 15–16, 93, 109, 176–177, 374, 396, 404–405
Courses for Foreign Students in France and Selected Programs in France–Summer, 96
Cultural Misunderstandings: The French-American Experience, 96
Culturgrams, 12
Cyclist's Britain, 175
CYPRUS, 17, 22, 27, 228–230
CZECHOSLOVAKIA, 19, 20, 198–203
Czechoslovak Travel Bureau (CEDOK), 202

Danish Cultural Institute, 84
Davidson College, 99, 113, 160, 296, 414

DENMARK, 19, 22, 27, 81–84
Destination Scandinavia: A Guide to Low-Cost Scandinavia, 81
Directory of Amerian Firms Operating in Foreign Countries, 26
Directory of Canadian Universities, 383
Directory of International Internships, 18
Directory of Low-Cost Vacations With a Difference, 53
Directory of Overseas Summer Jobs, 17
Directory of Work and Study in Developing Countries, 29
Disabled travelers, 13–14
DIS Travel, 82
Discover Young Ireland, 127
Distant Neighbors, 411
Dollarwise Traveler, 54
Drake University, 134, 137
Driving permit, 61
Dutch Language Courses for Foreign Students, 146

Earlham College, 327
East Africa: A Travel Survival Kit, 257
Eastern Europe on a Shoestring, 198
Eastern Michigan University, 67, 69, 200, 415
Economical Travel in Japan, 325
ECUADOR, 23, 443–446
Educator's Passport to International Jobs, 28
EGYPT, 223, 230–234
Egypt and the Sudan: A Travel Survival Kit, 257
Elderhostel Program, 41
Emplois d'Eté en France, 93
Employment abroad, 15–30
Employment Abroad: Facts and Fallacies, 29
Employment and Residency in Sweden, 165
Employment of Foreigners in Austria, 73
Encounter Ireland Program, 128
Encyclopedia of Associations, 25
England on $40 a day, 176
English Teaching Fellow Program, 28
Etudes et Chantiers, 95
Eurailpass, 58
Eurailpass Travel Guide, 59
Eurailtariff Manual, 58
Eurail Flexipass, 59
Eurail Guide, 49, 59
Eurail Saverpass, 59
Eurail Youthpass, 58
Eurocenters, 41
European Council of International Scholars (ECIS), 28
Europe: A Manual for Hitchikers, 62
Europe by Bike: 18 Tours Geared for Discovery, 61
Europe by Train, 59
Europe on $30 a Day, 67
Europe 101: History, Art and Culture for the Traveler, 67
Europe Through the Back Door, 67
Evansville, University of, 184
Experiment in International Living, 16, 96, 99, 103, 112, 121, 129, 134, 157, 161, 171, 182, 200, 208, 218, 244, 259, 265–266, 272, 286, 296, 300, 319, 346, 358, 368, 394, 413, 466

Falter, 72
Federation of International Youth Travel Organization (FIYTO), 9
Fellowships, 36–38

Fellowship Guide for Western Europe, 38
Fellowships, Scholarships and Related Opportunities in International Education, 38
Ffestiniog Railway Company, 178
Fielding's Budget Europe, 67
FIJI, 370–371
Fiji: A Travel Survival Kit, 371
Financial aid, 36–38
Financial Aid for Study Abroad, 37
Financial Resources for International Study, 38
FINLAND, 22, 58, 60, 85–89
Finland Camping and Youth Hostels, 86
Finnrailpass, 86
Finnish Student Travel Services (FSTS), 86
Fodor's Guides: *Australia, New Zealand and the South Pacific*, 362; *The Bahamas*, 391; *Canada*, 383; *Caribbean*, 388; *Central America*, 402; *Great Travel Values: Germany*, 99; *Great Travel Values: Japan*, 325; *Hungary*, 207; *Mexico*, 411; *North Africa*, 225; *People's Republic of China*, 310; *Southeast Asia*, 342; *South America*, 422
Ford's Travel Guide to Waterways of the World, 47
Foreign Policy Association, 11
Foreign Training for Veterans, Inservice Students and Eligible Dependents, 38
Foreign Visa Requirements, 6
Foundation for Field Research, 21
FRANCE, 17, 19, 22, 23, 41, 49, 56, 58, 63, 88–105
France Vacances, 90
Freighters Bulletin, 47
French Cultural Services, 92
French National Railroad, 90
French-Speaking Community in Belgium and its Universities, 80
Friends Overseas, 82, 86, 148
Friendship Force, 53
Friends World College, 67, 238, 266, 295, 313, 319, 406
Frommer's Guides: *Australia*, 366; *Austria and Hungary*, 207; *Canada*, 382; *Caribbean*, 388; *Eastern Europe on $25 a Day*, 198; *Egypt*, 232, *Germany*, 99; *Greece*, 121; *India on $25 a Day*, 294; *Ireland*, 128; *Israel on $30 and $35 a Day*, 237; *Mexico on $35 a Day*, 237; *New Zealand on $40 a Day*, 374; *Scandinavia on $60 a Day*, 165; *Scotland and Wales on $40 a Day*, 176; *South Pacific*, 362; *Spain and Morocco on $40 a day*, 156; *Switzerland and Liechtenstein*, 169; *Turkey on $25 a Day*, 249
Fulbright and Other Grants for Graduate Study Abroad, 37
Fulbright Teachers Exchange Branch, 27
Funding For Research, Study and Travel: Latin America and the Caribbean, 402

Georgetown University, 158
Georgia, University System of, 69, 98, 101, 103–104, 116–118, 139, 161, 186–189, 193, 201, 229, 313, 316, 330, 417
German Academic Exchange Service, 112
GERMAN DEMOCRATIC REPUBLIC, 203–206
GERMANY, FEDERAL REPUBLIC OF, 15–17, 19, 27, 41, 56–66, 106–119
Getting to Know Cuba, 388

GHANA, 22, 259–261
Goethe Institute-Language Courses, 112
Goshen College, 205, 311
Grants for Study and Research in Federal Republic of Germany, 112
Grants Register, 38
Great Canadian Bicycle Trail, 384
Great Decisions, 12
Great Expectations, 54
Great Lakes College Association, 183
Great Railway Bazaar, 49
GREECE, 17, 22, 60, 64, 120–122, 225
Greece on Foot: Mountain Treks, Island Trails, 120
GUATEMALA, 400–401
Guide to Careers in World Affairs, 29
Guide to Cruise Ship Jobs, 47
Guide to Trekking in Nepal, 299
Guilford College, 99, 113, 161, 185–188, 192, 200
Gustavus Adolphus College, 368

Health, 7–8
Health Information for International Travel, 7
Health Professionals, 26, 39
Hebrew University of Jerusalem, 240, 241
Heidelberg College, 133, 160
High School Programs, 40
Higher Education for Visiting Students, 166
Higher Education in the European Community: A Directory of Higher Education Institutions, 39
Hiram College, 115, 134, 137, 183, 186
Hitchkiking, 62
Holland Just For You, 145
Hollins College, 99, 183
Home Visit System, 324
HONDURAS, 22, 406–408
HONG KONG, 27, 208, 301, 303, 316–319
Hong Kong, Macau and Canton: A Travel Survival Kit, 318
Hope College, 76
Hotel and Culinary Exchange Program, 87, 95
House swapping, 66
How to Camp Europe By Train, 59
How to Read Study Abroad Literature, 35
How to Stay Well While Traveling in the Tropics, 7
HUNGARY, 19–20, 27, 58, 198, 206–209

Iberian Sun, 156
ICELAND, 22, 27, 64, 122–124
Iceland: The Visitor's Guide, 123
Illinois State University, 103, 117, 161
Illinois, University of, 180, 315, 368
Iowa, University of, 104, 413
INDIA, 48, 287, 289–294
India: A Travel Survival Kit, 294
India, Nepal and Sri Lanka, 290
Indian Wonderfare Pass, 292
Indiana University, 76, 99, 146, 158, 219, 240, 270, 313, 415
INDONESIA, 344–346
Indonesia Handbook, 345
Indonesia: A Travel Survival Kit, 345
Indrail Pass, 292
Inexpensive Accommodations in Copenhagen, 82
Information for Foreign Students Intending to Study at an Austrian Institute of Higher Learning, 73

INDEX

Insider's Guide to Poland, 211
Institute of International Education, 37, 39, 110
Instituto Allende Mexico, 41
Insurance, 8
Intercultural Communication: A Reader, 3
Intercultural Travel Program, 216
International Association for the Exchange of Students for Technical Experience (IAESTE), see Association for International Practical Training
International Association of Medical Assistance to Travelers (IAMAT), 7
International Association of Universities, 9
International Camping Carnet, 66
International Christian University, 329, 331
International Christian Youth Exchange (ICYE), 22, 73, 80, 83, 88, 96, 111, 124, 133, 150, 156, 165, 170, 179, 211, 260, 265, 268, 271, 276, 311, 327, 334, 367, 375, 405, 408, 412, 429, 433, 442
International Directory of Voluntary Work, 24
International Ecumenical Workcamp, 60
International Education Center, 329
International Educational Travel Planner, 39, 53
International Employment Hotline, 29
International Farm Camp, 178
International Liaison of Lay Volunteers, 22
International Meet-the-People Directory, 53
International Postal Reply Coupon, 10
International Research and Exchange Board (IREX), 199
International Scholarship Book, 38
International Schools Directory, 28
International Schools Service (ISS), 27
International Student Exchange Program (ISEP), 80, 88, 100, 113, 134, 143, 146, 158, 166, 183, 230, 272, 281–282, 284, 319, 335, 358, 368, 371, 383, 394, 406, 413
International Student Identity Card (ISIC), see CIEE
International Student Travel Confederation (ISTC), 8–9, 65
International Student Handbook, 383
International Teacher Identity Card, see CIEE
International Union of Students (IUS), 198
International Voluntary Services, see CIEE
International Workcamp Directory, 20
International Youth Hostel Handbook, 50, 198, 256, 287, 290, 303, 322, 323, 342, 381
Interrail Pass, 60
Introduction to Education in the People's Republic of China and U.S.-China Educational Work Exchanges, 311
Intourist, 217
IRELAND, 15, 19, 64, 124–130
ISRAEL, 49, 225
Israel: A Travel Survival Kit, 237
ITALY, 17, 27, 34, 56, 58, 60, 64, 130–140
Italy-General Information for Travelers, 132
Italian Educational System: A Brief Outline, 134
Italian State Railways, 132
Itinerary: The Magazine for Travelers with Physical Disabilities, 14
IVORY COAST, 255, 261–263

JAMAICA, 15, 23, 394–397
JAPAN, 17, 22, 48, 301, 303, 319–332
Japan: A Travel Survival Kit, 325
Japan: An Orientation for Travelers, 325
Japanese, The, 325

Japan Exchange and Teaching Program, 325
Japan Handbook, 325
Japan International Christian University Foundation, 457
Japan Railpass, 321
Japan Society, 325
Japan Solo, 325
Jeunesse et Reconstruction, 95
Job Opportunities Bulletin, 26
Jobs in Japan, 326
JORDAN, 17
Jordan and Syria: A Travel Survival Kit, 226
Jugendtourist, 205

Kalamazoo College, 100, 113, 160, 266, 268, 273, 276, 257
Kansas State University, 457
Kansas, University of, 461
Kashmir, Ladakh and Zanskar: A Travel Survival Kit, 294
Kathmandu and the Kingdom of Nepal, 299
Kent State University, 136, 171, 183, 218, 457
KENYA, 22, 264–267
Kibbutz Aliya, 238
Know Before You Go, 6
Know Colombia Visitor Ticket, 440
Korea: A Travel Survival Kit, 334
Kosciuszko Foundation, 212

Lake Erie College, 100, 113, 134, 158, 183, 189, 457
Language Courses at German Universities, 112
Language Institute of Japan, 327
Lancaster, University of, 461
LAOS, 342
LaSalle University, 457
Learn French in Canada, 383
Learning Vacations, 41
Let's Go guides, 51; *Britain and Ireland*, 127, 176; *Europe*, 66, 109, 123, 198, 227, 229, 232, 243, 246; *France*, 92; *Greece*, 120, 229, 249; *Israel and Egypt*, 232, 237; *Mexico*, 411; *Spain, Portugal and Morocco*, 152, 156, 243
Lewis & Clark College, 96, 113, 312, 334, 345, 367, 426, 457
LIBERIA, 22, 23, 267–268
Limits to Friendship: The United States and Mexico, 411
Lisle Fellowship, 295, 296, 346, 457
Live, 72
Living in Colombia, 441
Living in Holland: Practical Tips for Adjusting to Life Among the Dutch, 146
Loans, 36–38
Looking Back, Looking Forward, 14
Louisiana State University, 104, 138, 189, 397, 415, 457
Louisville, University of, 461
LUXEMBOURG, 27, 140–141

Macalester College, 68, 97, 183, 457
Madagascar and the Comoros: A Travel Survival Kit, 257
Maine, University of, 75, 461
Maison des Jeunes et de la Culture, 94
Making it Abroad: The International Job Hunting Guide, 29
MALAWI, 268–270

INDEX

Malaysia, Singapore and Brunei: A Travel Survival Kit, 349, 354
MALTA, 141-143
Management Study Abroad, 1989-1991, 40
A Manual for Integrating Persons With the Staffs and Volunteers of Service and Exchange Organizations, 14
Marquette University, 103, 457
Mary Baldwin College, 103, 138, 188-189, 191, 329, 457
Maryland, University of, 101, 117, 184, 434, 461
Massachusetts—Amherst, University of, 98, 162, 208, 212-213, 240-241, 313, 427, 461
Masterpiece Called Belgium, 79
Meet the Danes, 82
Meet the Swiss, 169
Mennonite Central Committee (MCC), 23
MEXICO, 17, 27, 41, 49, 400-402, 408-417
Mexico: A Travel Survival Kit, 411
Mexico: Neighbor in Transition, 411
Miami University, 457
Mi casa es su casa, 14
Michigan, University of, 461
Michigan State University, 69-70, 81, 97, 101, 103, 113, 116-117, 129, 136, 138, 146, 159, 161, 166, 171, 180, 183, 187, 193, 219, 240, 241, 286, 308, 314, 329-331, 338, 384, 389, 394, 457
Michelin Green Guides, 67, 92, 99, 132, 156, 169, 176
Middlebury College, 97, 115, 136, 160, 218, 457
Millersville University of Pennsylvania, 457
Minnesota University of, 76, 98, 159, 161, 180, 193, 212, 244, 265, 273-274, 294, 314, 394, 414, 441, 462
Mission Volunteers/International Program, 23
Mobility International USA (MIUSA), 13
Mona Winks: A Guide to Enjoying the Museums of Europe, 67
Monterey Institute of International Studies, 102, 457
MOROCCO, 223, 241-244
Morocco, Algeria and Tunisia: A Travel Survival Kit, 243, 246

National Association for Foreign Student Affairs (NAFSA), 35, 37, 457
National Association for Secondary School Principals, 457
NEPAL, 287-290, 297-300
Nepal Trekkers Handbook, 299
NETHERLANDS, 19, 27, 49, 56, 143-147, 301
Newfoundland by Bicycle, 380
New Hampshire, University of, 159, 184, 190, 219, 402
New York University, 63, 96-97, 100, 102, 104, 117, 137-139, 158, 161, 166, 187-188, 190-192, 215, 232, 305, 308, 329, 367, 415, 458
NEW ZEALAND, 2, 15, 360, 371-375
New Zealand: A Travel Survival Kit, 374
New Zealand Handbook, 374
NIGERIA, 17, 270-272
North Atlantic Treaty Organization (NATO), 78
North Carolina—Chapel Hill, University of, 98, 101, 103, 115, 117, 122, 135, 180, 185-186, 189, 240-241, 329, 414, 426, 434, 449, 462

North Carolina State University, 47, 90, 282, 314, 458
North-East Asia on a Shoestring, 303
Northeastern University, 68, 129, 458
North Texas, University of, 69, 185, 462
Northeastern University, 68, 129, 458
Northern Arizona University, 183, 312, 458
Northern Illinois University, 74, 76, 80, 97, 113, 158, 183, 413, 458
Northern Michigan University, 458
Northfield Mount Hermon School, 458, 466
NORWAY, 22, 27, 58, 60, 64, 147-151
Norwegian Foundation for Youth Exchange, 149
Norwegian Information Service, 150
Nothing to Declare: Memoirs of a Woman Traveling Alone, 411
Notre Dame, University of, 75, 98, 186, 240, 314, 328, 414, 462

Oberlin College, 458
Obirin University, 458
ODN Opportunities Catalog, 26
Oklahoma, University of, 462
Ohio State University, 102, 158, 162, 190-191, 312, 328, 458
Ohio University, 63-64, 75, 98, 137, 150, 187-188, 308, 401, 415, 458
Omnibus Passport, 123
On Being Foreign: Culture Shock in Short Fiction, 3
Open Door Student Exchange, 458, 466
Operation Crossroads Africa, 19
Opportunities Abroad For Educators, 27
Oregon University of, 101, 115-116, 136-138, 146-147, 159, 166, 185, 208, 240, 313, 328-330, 335, 367, 416, 462, 446
Overseas Demand for Dental Personnel and Materials: Directory of Programs, 26
Overseas Development Network (ODN), 26
Overseas List, 29

Pace University, 458
Pacific, University of, 312, 462
PAKISTAN, 28
Pakistan: A Travel Survival Kit, 289
Papua New Guinea: A Travel Survival Kit, 361
Paris à Pied, 91
Passports, 5-6
Patagonian Express, 49
Partnership for Service Learning, 23
Peace Corps, 25
Pennsylvania State University, 96, 328, 331, 367, 458
Pennsylvania, University of, 189, 462
People's Guide to Mexico, 411
PERU, 17, 439-446
Peru: A Travel Survival Kit, 448
PHILIPPINES, 23, 27, 349-351
Pittsburgh, University of, 68, 228, 304, 330, 423, 462
Pitzer College, 300, 458
Places of Interest by Public Transport, 318
Pocket Doctor, 7
POLAND, 19, 20, 22, 60, 197-198, 209-213
Pomona College, 458
Portland State University, 113, 116, 138, 158, 161, 315, 390, 413, 415, 448, 458
PORTUGAL, 19, 58, 151-153
Portuguese Youth Hostel Association, 152
Purdue University, 100, 114, 158, 458

Real Guides, 51
Real Guide to Morocco, 243
Reed College, 458
Reformed Church in America, 268, 327, 408, 458
R.E.M.P. ART, 95
RENFE, 155
Rent a Bicycle in Copenhagen, 82
Research in the Federal Republic of Germany, 112
Response, 22
Rhode Island School of Design, 134, 459
Rhode Island, University of, 96, 328, 461
Rollins College, 129, 161, 368, 415, 459
Rosary College, 100, 138, 183, 459
Rotary Foundation of Rotary International, 75
Rough Guide to Kenya, 264
Rutgers University, 100, 114, 134, 240, 413, 459

Saint John Fisher College, 459
Saint Lawrence University, 75, 158, 183, 266, 459
Saint Olaf College, 228, 290, 304, 358, 459
Saint Peter's College, 459
SAUDI ARABIA, 225
Scandinavia on $60 a day, 80, 85, 148
Scandinavian Seminar, 84, 88, 124, 150, 166, 459
Scholar's Guide to Sources of Support for Research in Russia and Soviet Studies, 217
Scholarships, 36, 38
Schools Abroad of Interest to Americans, 28
Schools for English Speaking Students in Italy, 133
See India Pass, 292
SENEGAL, 27, 273–274
Senior citizens, 41
SERVAS, 52–53
Service Civil International, 327
Service learning, 23
Servicio Voluntario International, 156
SIERRA LEONE, 22, 275–277
SINGAPORE, 339, 341, 353–355
Skidmore College, 104, 106, 159, 459
Sophia University (Japan), 32
SOUTH AFRICA, 27, 255, 277–279
South America Handbook, 402, 422
South America on a Shoestring, 427
South America on $35 a Day, 422
South America River Trips, 422
SOUTH KOREA, 22, 301, 333–335
South Korea Handbook, 334
South Carolina, University of, 462
Southeast Asia on a Shoestring, 342
Southern California, University of, 462
Southern Illinois University at Carbondale, 68, 69, 89, 122, 187, 250, 305, 330, 459
Southern Methodist University, 76, 100, 103, 137, 159, 190, 329, 459
Southwest Texas State University, 459
SPAIN, 17, 19, 22, 41, 56, 58, 64, 154–163
Spelman College, 459
Springfield College, 459
SPUTNIK, 198, 214, 216
SRI LANKA, 290
Sri Lanka: A Travel Survival Kit, 289
Stanford University, 134, 329, 330, 459
State University of New York (SUNY): Albany, 117, 146, 161, 184, 218, 314, 329, 354, 406, 434, 461; Brockport, 122, 434; Buffalo, 97, 134, 162, 329, 368, 460; Cortland, 112, 116, 129, 159, 184, 313, 460; Empire State College, 84, 240; Fredonia, 74; Oneonta, 76; Oswego, 98, 103, 114, 162, 415–416, 434, 460; Stony Brook, 98, 100, 103, 134, 138, 212
Stay With A British Family, 176
Staying Healthy in Africa, Asia and Latin America, 7
Stealing From A Deep Place, 198
Stephens College, 459
Stetson University, 98, 116, 161, 184, 460
Stichting Internationale Werkkampen, 145
Student and Youth Travel Service (SYTAG), Ghana, 260
Student Travel Catalog, 42–43
Study Abroad, 38
Study and Research Opportunities in the Middle East and North Africa, 227
Study by Correspondence, 180
Study in Australia, 368
Study in Britain, 179
Study in Scandinavia, 84
Studying at a University in Holland: Should You?, 146
Studying in Denmark, 84
Studying in Sweden, 166
Suggestions for U.S. Dentists Seeking Employment Abroad, 26
Summer Courses For Foreigners, 157
Summer Courses in Austria, 73
Summer Jobs in Britain, 177
Summer With a Purpose (SWAP), 319
Survival Kit for Overseas Living, 3
Sussex, University of, 462
SWEDEN, 17, 58, 60, 164–168
Swiss Pass Card, 168
SWITZERLAND, 22, 27, 49, 56–64, 167–172
Syracuse University, 68–69, 76, 100, 102, 134–136, 169, 184, 187, 189, 191–192, 240, 313, 331, 460, 467

Tahiti and French Polynesia: A Travel Survival Kit, 361
TAIWAN, 301, 335–337
Taiwan: A Travel Survival Kit, 337
Teaching Abroad, 28
Teaching in Austria, 73
Teaching in Britain, 177
Teaching in Taiwan, 337
Teaching of English as a Second or Other Language (TESOL), 28
Teaching Opportunities in the Middle East and North Africa, 227
Teaching Tactics For Japan's English Classrooms, 326
Teenager's Guide to Travel and Adventure Abroad, 3, 40, 216, 465
Tennessee, University of, 96, 215, 462
Texas, University of at Austin, 462
Texas A&M University, 460
Texas Tech University, 460
THAILAND, 289, 303, 355–358
Thailand: A Travel Survival Guide, 357
Time Out, 176
Tips for Americans Residing Abroad, 14
Tips for Travelers to Eastern Europe and Yugoslavia, 198
Tips for Travlers to the Middle East and North Africa, 225

INDEX

Tips for Travelers to the People's Republic of China, 207
Tips for Travelers to the USSR, 214
TOGO, 281–282
Toledo, University of, 172, 315, 462
Tramping in Europe: A Walking Guide, 62
Transalpino, 59
Transcultural Study Guide, 59
Transitions Abroad, 3
Trans-Siberian Railroad, 303
Travel Programs in Central America, 401
Travel Tips and Currency Guide, 10
Travel Warnings on Drugs Abroad, 13
Travelers checks, 10–11
Trekking in the Nepal Himalayas, 294, 299
TRINIDAD AND TOBAGO, 17
Trinity College, 135, 460
Trip Safe Insurance, 8
Tufts University, 114, 159, 184, 460
Tulane University, 460
TUNISIA, 17, 225, 244–247
TURKEY, 19, 223, 225, 247–250
Turkey: A Travel Survival Guide, 248

Union of Students in Ireland-Travel (USIT), 120, 126
UNITED KINGDOM, 15, 19, 22–23, 56, 60, 63, 172–193
United Nations Educational, Scientific and Cultural Organization (UNESCO), 24
U.S. Government: Agency for International Development, 25
  Department of Agriculture, 25
  Department of Commerce, 25
  Department of Defense, 27
  Department of Education, 36
  Department of State, 14, 24, 398
  Peace Corps, 25
  United States Information Agency, 27
UNION OF SOVIET SOCIALIST REPUBLICS, 60, 197, 213–220, 303
United Negro College Fund, 460
University Studies in Flanders, 80
University Study in Canada, 383
University Summer Schools for Overseas Students, 179
URUGUAY, 449–451
Utah, University of, 104, 118, 138, 162, 171, 190, 331, 415, 462

Vacation Study Abroad, 32, 38
Vademecum: A Consise Guide to Studying in the Netherlands for Foreign Students, 146
Valparaiso University, 96, 463
Values and Measures of the World, 10
VENEZUELA, 451–452
Vermont, University of, 462
Veterans, 38
VIETNAM, 341
Virginia, University of, 462
Visas, 6
Visit Argentina Air Pass, 424
Visit Bolivia Air Pass, 428
Visit Chile Air Pass, 437
Visit Peru Air Pass, 447
Visit South America Air Pass, 421
Voluntary Service Bulletin, 23

Voluntary Service, 19–25, 179, 257
Volunteer, 19, 22, 24
Volunteers for Mission, 22
Volunteers for Peace, 20
Volunteers in Asia, 463

Wake Forest University, 463
Walker's Britain, 175
Walker's Guide to Pokhara, 299
Walking in Austria's Alps, 71
Washington State University, 463
Washington, University of, 101, 115–116, 134, 136, 150, 185, 240, 243, 415
Waterloo, University of, 463
Wayne State University, 115, 463
Welcome to the U.S.S.R., 214
Wesleyan University, 463
West Africa: A Travel Survival Kit, 257
West Asia on a Shoestring, 291
Western Michigan University, 63, 65, 103, 190, 258, 463
Western Washington University, 101, 115, 136, 185, 415, 416, 463
Westminster College, 463
Wichita State University, 416, 463
Wilmington College, 75, 463
Windrose, 79
Wisconsin, University of: Madison, 209, 240, 297, 300, 435, 449, 463; Plattville, 463; River Falls, 463
Wish You Were Here, 92
Wittenberg University, 71, 463
Work Your Way Around the World, 17
Workcamp organizations, 24
Working Holidays, 17
World College West, 463
World Council of Churches, 20
World Directory of Engineering Schools, 40
World Directory of Medical Schools, 39
World Educational Encyclopedia, 39
World Health Organization (WHO), 39
World of Learning, 39
World of Options: A Guide to International Educational Exchange, Community Service and Travel for Persons With Disabilities, 14
WorldTeach, 265, 311, 358
Wyoming, University of, 185, 463

Yemen: A Travel Survival Kit, 226
Young Britain Guide, 176
Young Men's Christian Association, (YMCA), 17, 94, 111
YMCA World Service Workers Program, 23
Your Trip Abroad, 14
Youth For Understanding International Exchange (YFU), 464, 467
Youth hostels, 50
Youth Hostels in Japan, 325
Youth Hostels in Scandinavia and Hotels in Sweden, 165
YUGOSLAVIA, 19, 197–198, 220–222
Yugoslavia: A Climbing, Walking and Cultural Guide, 221

ZAMBIA, 283–284
ZIMBABWE, 280–281